Finding New Ground

Moving Beyond Conflict To Consensus

A Twenty-First Century Model For
Addressing Conflict, Building Consensus,
Fostering Civility,
Creating Community
through Collaboration
and Maintaining Individual Integrity

A Transformative Approach That Can Be Used By
Individuals, Family, Community,
Church, Education, Business And Government

One Tree Publishing Company
P.O. Box 235
Terrebonne, OR 97760

FINDING NEW GROUND Copyright © 2012 by Robert J. Chadwick. All rights reserved. Printed in the United States of America. No part of this book may be used or reproduced in any manner whatsoever without written permission except in the case of brief quotations embodied in critical articles or reviews. For information, address Consensus Associates, P.O. Box 235, Terrebonne, OR 97760.

Library Of Congress Cataloging In Publication Data:

1. Consensus. 2. Conflict resolution. 3. Circle. 4. Finding new ground. 5. Community. 6. Collaboration. 7. Relationships. 8. Facilitator. 9. Recorder 10. Listening with respect. 11. Communication. 12. Learning community. 13. Worst and best possible outcomes. 14. Triune brain. 15. Personal conflict. 16. Interpersonal conflict. 17. Intergroup conflict. 18. Empowerment. 19. Purpose.

Portions of this book are fictional, but based on real people and situations. Names and identifying characteristics of individuals described herein have been changed wherever appropriate.

Other Sources:

The author is grateful for permission to include excerpts from other material indicated below:

The American Heritage® Dictionary of the English Language, Fourth Edition
Copyright: 2000 by Houghton Mifflin Company. Published by Houghton Mifflin Company. All rights reserved.

Wikipedia, the free encyclopedia.

Drawn illustrations by Greg Cross: http//crossink.carbonmade.com/
ISBN: 1470175150
ISBN-13:978-1470175153

*To my mother and father
who gave me a life to live, love to live it with,
a purpose to fulfill, and the fortitude to fulfill it.
To my children,
who love me no matter what,
who gave me grandchildren, and great grandchildren,
and a reason to write this book.*

OTHER BOOKS BY ROBERT CHADWICK
TWO TREES

Contents

Preface	1
A Prologue	9
Introduction	22
Getting Acquainted With Conflict	33
Exploring Conflict	47
A Personal Experience of the Process	78
A Better Way—Seeking Consensus	82
An Intergroup Conflict	96
A Gathering of the Community	105
The Workshop Introduction	112
The Grounding Circle	121
Grounding Insights and Anecdotes	152
Listening with Respect	165
The Greeting Circle	175
Lifelong Learning	187
The Greeting Circle Insights	193
Lifelong Learning -An Insight	199
The Role of the Recorder in Building Consensus	212
The Role of the Facilitator in Building Consensus	222
Insights on the Role of the Facilitator	235
The Worst and Best Possible Outcomes	243
Our Best Possible Outcomes	261
Possibility Thinking Insights	268
Defining Conflict	280

The Worst Possible Outcomes of Conflict	308
A Relationship Process: An Insight	316
The Closure	333
Exploring Self-consciousness	342
Developing Collective Statements	354
A New Day and Collective Statements	370
The Best Possible Outcomes of Addressing and Resolving Conflict	410
Relationships	418
Fostering the Best Possible Outcomes	430
Exploring a Personal Conflict	446
The Situation	459
The Worst Possible Outcomes of the Situation	509
The Closure: Day Two	515
The Third Day: The Beginning	521
Nonverbal Communication	533
The Best Possible Outcomes of the Situation	544
It's Impossible—New Beliefs and Behaviors	549
Strategies and Actions	559
A Long-range Vision	587
Advice to the Leaders	599
Workshop Closure	615
Resolving Interpersonal Conflicts	630
But, Does It Work?	663
A Path to a Way of Being	682

Additional resources (tasks, insights, and anecdotes) for this process may be found at:

http://consensusinstitutes.com

http://www.findingnewground.com

NOTE: The website for Finding New Ground includes additional information for almost every chapter in the book. This information will add to the skills you have already developed.

~1~

Preface

Welcome to My World

"You will learn a process and skills that will change your life. You will never again see a conflict as unsolvable."

—M. A., workshop participant

Welcome to my world. A world where people like yourself acknowledge and resolve their conflicts with spouses, adversaries, friends and former friends, coworkers, business associates, church and community members.

It is a world where people listen with respect so they not only hear each other, but seek to understand and accept each other. Where people like yourself build environments of trust in the home, at work, and in the community; where it is always safe to be yourself, to speak your truth. A world where you can say, "We have a conflict and I want to resolve it with you," and it happens. Where others feel safe enough with you to speak their truth, and where all can feel acknowledged and accepted for who they are.

It is a world where people purposefully learn from each other, even those with opposing views, and build a more comprehensive view from their interlocking realities. A place where this knowledge is applied to create not just "common ground," but "new ground," where all can agree that their interests are taken care of and they *behave* the agreement, actually making it happen.

It is a world where individuals come together, each with their own beliefs, values, and behaviors, and collaboratively make decisions that meet all their needs, leaving the discussion with their individuality still intact. A world where resolving your conflicts builds your self-esteem, creating a future where you can become the best you can be.

It is with great excitement and pleasure that I invite you into this world through this book, *Finding New Ground*. This book is written in a way that you can experience this approach, learn about it, understand it, and then apply it in your conflicts with others in your life. You will create a way of being that sees conflict as a path for personal growth.

Creating consensus is the central theme of this book and of the work that I do. This requires addressing and resolving your conflicts that are personal (your internal conflicts), interpersonal (between yourself and another), and intergroup (between groups), finding new ground in all the arenas of your life.

This opportunity to learn about *Finding New Ground* is a gift given to you by the many people I have worked with who took the risk to address their conflicts and resolve them. Each of the fifteen hundred-plus conflict situations I have facilitated in the last forty years has taught me something about creating consensus and finding new ground. People like you have helped me continually create a new and richer understanding of this approach, a way of being that can be passed on to you and then on to others.

That is the purpose of *Finding New Ground;* to pass on to you this experience, learning, and knowledge. And you can take all the time you need to learn it, apply it, and make it yours. For it does take time to experience, learn, and apply the knowledge in this book.

While many thousands of people have been involved with me in some consensus-building activity, the contact has often been limited by time and the event. Normally, a complex intergroup consensus-building situation lasts three days. Some communities allow me to return and add to their experience and skills with another session. Most, however, are satisfied with resolving one conflict. With the pressure off, few have been willing to invest more of their time.

Knowing there is more they can learn and understand, I am often left wanting to help the group learn it all, yet recognizing the time is limited. So I feel unfulfilled, for them and me. This book can help to fill that void.

This book also allows you to do more by going beyond learning in the abstract to learning by doing, by experiencing. You will learn by focusing on your real issues, on those that are critical to your environment and your community.

This book is written in the hope that you will apply this approach first with yourself, then with others. My intent is to foster in you some new beliefs and behaviors, integrated with a process that will help you resolve conflicts and reach consensus in all aspects of your life: personal, family, work, church, and community.

> "This process works—it can give people the tools and necessary confidence to use it in their profession and personal lives."
>
> **—workshop participant**

The process itself is simple on the surface, but its impacts are complex. Just using the process is not enough. Understanding why it works is the ingredient for effectiveness and success, especially when working with others.

Experiencing *Finding New Ground* will help you learn how to move beyond the conflicts in your life to building consensus. As a result you will become a more adaptive person, addressing and resolving your everyday conflicts. You will become a model of adult behavior for the young people in your life, a model that will allow them to put aggression behind them and seek instead solutions for all, for consensus, and for community.

In this book you will experience a process as well as the beliefs, behaviors, strategies, insights, and art of effective and successful consensus seeking. You will create in yourself a willingness to risk addressing the conflicts in your environment and to then work toward a consensus agreement. You will know how to immediately foster civility and build community. You will see the benefits of doing this.

You will broaden your level of response to the rapid changes around you, which create increasing numbers and intensity of conflicts. Your eyes will be opened to managing the richness of the diversity that exists in people, races, generations, cultures, beliefs, and values. You will become more aware of power and how it affects relationships, and will be able to create environments of empowerment and equity among different people.

Where there is perceived scarcity, you will be able to tap that diversity to create environments of personal and professional richness, so you can do what needs to be done. You will be able to tap all the opportunities for learning and growth that conflict can bring us, in all times.

You will learn to create effective solutions out of controversy, conflict, and difference by bringing together those who are in disagreement and facilitating their progress toward a solution where all can win. You will be able to assist those who are competitive, adversarial, and polarized to become collaborative advocates for consensus solutions, fostering a willingness to agree to a community decision that values and protects the individual's beliefs, values, and integrity.

> *"How can you go wrong with such a peaceful approach? There is no conflict that cannot be resolved with an open mind, open ears, and a true understanding of all opinions presented in any issue."*
>
> **—workshop participant**

You will learn to go beyond the common approaches of avoidance, aggression, mediation, negotiation, arbitration and voting. You will move beyond compromise, developing skills and techniques that allow you and others to explore and discover consensus solutions. You will do it in a way that maintains your and others' individual integrity. In our culture, nothing is feared more than the loss of our individualism, our sense of independence and self-reliance. Everyday conflicts are filled with the fear that "I must win you over in order to keep my integrity and sense of who I am."

This process allows people to be who they are without judgment, to be listened to with respect. It allows them to listen to others with respect and to learn from them. It allows each person, if they choose, to adapt to new ways of perceiving, thinking, believing, and behaving. They can leave knowing they are still self-reliant and independent, while being part of the whole, and that it is always their choice to do so.

"This is a twenty-first century facilitation methodology. This teaches that the value of being heard is the key to moving off conflict and on to a purpose-driven process."

—**workshop participant**

This approach has been successfully applied by individuals, families, communities, churches, business, education, government, and diverse cultures. Because it has been developed by people in each of these environments, it works in these environments.

In each of these environments, the people have moved beyond finding common ground to finding **new ground**. The common expectation of conflict resolution is that we will reach some common area of agreement. The typical approach is to seek a compromise in which each group/person gives up something and gets most of what they want.

This results in negotiation approaches in which each group (or individual) asks for more than they expect, hoping they will get what they need in the final decision. Unfortunately, the other groups have the same expectations. The common ground then often means the "middle ground." We seek some place of balance where we all appear relatively happy, but equally feel like we betrayed ourselves.

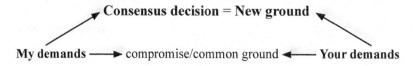

Consensus seeks to create a new ground that soon becomes a new common ground. A decision location that is hardly imagined in the beginning, new ground is some location that is not in the center, but off to the side, unacknowledged because of the focus on common ground, on compromise. It is a new belief, a new paradigm, a new approach, a place where all feel their needs are met: one solution that they can readily work together to accomplish in a new place where they can be authentic.

It is an approach that is transformative, changing the way we see the world, changing the way we see each other and ourselves. Once experienced, it is hard to let go of.

"But I just wanted to say to you that it was truly life transforming. There's no turning back!"

—workshop participant

Let There Be Conflict on Earth and Let It Begin with Me: An Anecdote

In the early '80s,' while living in Portland, Oregon, I was enjoying a "neighbor fair" on the banks of the Willamette River. It was a glorious summer-day experience. Tens of thousands of people were rubbing shoulders with each other in apparent peace and harmony. The young/old, rich/poor, Anglos, African Americans, American Indians, Asians, people with disabilities, city people, urbanites, rural people, homeless people had come together to have this annual communal experience.

Rotating bands provided music for all tastes. People sat on the grass, with picnic lunches, beer, and pop, listening to the music. Children ran around with balloons, careful to stay in the sight of their parents. People danced and sang to the music. Dogs ran around meeting one another or looking for food thrown away or carelessly left in the open, while the homeless people collected the discarded beer and pop cans.

Food booths ringed the crowd, their ethnic smells and tastes enticing the crowd to buy. Artisans hawked their wares in small booths alongside the inevitable advocacy booths selling ideas and pushing petitions for reform.

It was at an advocacy booth, "Oregonians against Nuclear War," that I saw the T-shirt. The shirt was light blue, with a white dove floating across the front. The words "LET THERE BE PEACE ON EARTH and LET IT BEGIN WITH ME" were imprinted above and below the bird.

I wanted it. I wanted not just the shirt, but the idea, the actuality of peace. Not just peace. I wanted to be rid of conflict: interpersonal conflict, mostly, but my internal conflict as well. I feared it, I hated it.

My environment seemed filled with unresolved conflicts. It took all my energy just to avoid them, to please the ones who were conflicting with me, to rescue those in need. The number of conflicts appeared to be building, out of control. My family, my job, my work, my community seemed filled with them.

Environmentalists were questioning the harvesting of trees in the forests I was managing, causing me to question my belief and value systems. My children were exploring alternative lifestyles in ways that challenged all my values. The world was playing the game of "Chicken" with nuclear warheads.

Why couldn't we just do away with conflict and live in harmony and peace? Then we could be like this group of sun and music worshipers. I bought not just a shirt that day, but the hope that I would purchase the peace I have been searching for all my life.

Conflict seemed fruitless, out of my control, and my desire was to run away from it, to avoid conflict. My childhood memories connected conflict to highly emotional states, to violence, to the possibility of death.

The emotional turbulence associated with conflict reminded me of the turmoil in a hot tub. As in a conflict, the energy bubbles and boils where opposing jets of water come together. My reaction is to put my hands over the nozzles to stop the jet streams, attempting to bring peace and calm to the tub. This is impossible, because the water jets out somewhere else. I use my feet, and still the water jets out.

I switch hands, trying frantically to control the energy, the turmoil, to stop all the jets of water. I don't have enough hands, feet, or energy to stop all the conflict. The result is I am exhausted, stressed out. I vow never to go back to the hot tub (conflict) again.

That was my response to conflict. I wanted to stop the turmoil, to avoid the conflict, to deny it existed with others. I wanted to please others rather than confront, to control the situations so conflict was overlooked. I wanted peace at any price.

I have since learned that conflict will always exist. It is a natural part of life. It can be postponed, avoided, run away from only at a high emotional and physical cost. It requires insincerity with those I am conflicting with. It requires that I subordinate my needs to others out of fear.

The only possible way we could do away with conflict would be to hold everything stable, to make everyone a clone of everyone else. We would need laws that ensure each person spoke the same language, belonged to the same religion, had the same beliefs and values, and were all the same age and experience.

That will never happen. We are continually changing and evolving beings, surrounded by other beings with different ages, values, beliefs, races, cultures, religion, and abilities. Our situations and experiences are continually shifting, responding to new perspectives from the local to the broader world. Each situation poses a challenge to us.

We can attempt to make others similar to us, to force them to believe in our beliefs. Or we can accept them as they are and seek a creative and consensus solution that meets all of our needs.

Conflict exists with purpose. It causes us to be aware, to be self-conscious. It establishes the opportunity for learning, for increased knowledge, for actualizing our being. Through our conflicts we create and refine our beliefs, values, and behaviors. It is through conflict that we form long-lasting relationships and evolve. As a member of one workshop commented, "Conflict is the irritant that creates the pearl."

Addressing the conflict requires an element of risk. I must confront the situation and be the catalyst for the emotional outburst that may be inherent. I must be ready to confront the violent consequences I fear.

When the moment of turmoil is past, there is the calm and the peace I seek. There is the possibility of new knowledge, of understanding, of the new beliefs and behaviors that will make me a more congruent and adaptive person.

I can sit in the hot tub, accepting the jet streams and turbulence as the essence of the tub. I can move through the fury and intensity, letting the energy massage my body and mind. I become relaxed and peaceful. My mind is open to new ideas. Accepting the turmoil brings the peace.

I know the peace won't last long. Conflict will rise because of my growth, my new beliefs and values. I must confront again. I can choose the times, places, and willingness to risk the confrontation.

Today I am willing to risk addressing my conflicts. I am still uneasy, uncertain, and anxious, but I want to grow, to learn from each person and conflict experience. This requires a willingness to be aware of when to risk. It requires being the one to start the conflict by addressing it.

I have a new idea for a T-shirt. I want a hostile goose, beak upraised in wicked threat, with the words "LET THERE BE CONFLICT ON EARTH AND LET

IT BEGIN WITH ME" on the front of the shirt. Let that be what you see first. Know that I am willing to engage openly in conflict.

On the back of the shirt, I want the dove with its peace symbol and the words "LET THERE BE PEACE ON EARTH AND LET IT BEGIN WITH ME," which is what you will see as you turn around in reaction.

Know that I will resolve that conflict and foster peace in my life and the lives of others I touch. This will provide the balance and possibilities for growth that I want in my life and in yours.

Welcome to my world.

~2~

A Prologue

Conclusions I Have Made that Will Help You Proceed

"This is a nonthreatening approach that frees people to dialogue openly."

—**workshop participant**

You are about to be introduced to a process developed over the past forty years, using real conflict situations as my applied research. The process has been employed in more than fifteen hundred conflict situations, many of them violent and regarded as impossible, directly involving more than thirty thousand people. It has been successfully applied with just two people in conflict and to groups of more than a thousand. And you can use it on your own personal conflicts—those you have with yourself internally.

The process has been used successfully with individuals and families, in the workplace and in the community. It has been applied with all levels of government, business, and education, and between different cultural groups. It has been applied in countries such as India, Thailand, Canada, Hong Kong, Belgium, and Russia.

Participants have included elected and appointed officials, public agency and private industry managers, big-business and small-business people, educators, law enforcement officers, those involved in union-management relationships, environmentalists, loggers, ranchers, housewives, attorneys, and others on contemporary issues. It has been applied with many cultures: American Indians, Hmong, Latino, African American, Thai, Indian. This approach has been applied with children from kindergarten age, to senior citizens in their nineties.

Based on my experiences in all these situations, I have come to these conclusions and beliefs:

1. All conflicts that confront any person and group today can be resolved—before they happen, as they are happening, or even after they have happened. There are no unsolvable issues.
2. A 100 percent consensus is possible in all situations and at any time, whether personal, interpersonal, or intergroup. Most feel this is impossible. It isn't. It happens every day.
3. The right time to resolve a conflict is always *now*: before it happens, as it is happening, or after it happened. Don't regret that it took twenty years to address the issue. Regrets about the timing of resolution weaken a person's ability to resolve a conflict. Just "do it now!"
4. Those involved in the conflict have the ability, knowledge, and intelligence to resolve it, if they do it together. They often already know the answer, but their fears prevent them from hearing that answer.
5. The key ingredient to resolution is the **willingness** of an individual or group **to risk addressing the conflict** in a consensus setting, with consensus expectations.
6. Conflicts are most effectively solved when the entire community of interest is involved in the resolution. This means including representation of all stakeholders, including those who are the most outspoken, the most polarized, the most cynical, the most disenfranchised; the powerless and the powerful; and those with closed minds.
7. Establishing an environment of **listening with respect** for all participants, whether two or a thousand-plus, will create a desired consensus setting that will nurture the development of a shared knowledge base sufficient to solve the problem.
8. When people develop healthy relationships, they are able to legitimately hear information that is important to solving conflicts. When information is shared in a consensus setting, it becomes common knowledge for the group, and this serves as a basis for wise and comprehensive decisions.
9. Each problem is a learning experience that helps us come together to learn as individuals and as a community. People involved in the conflict come to understand that they will learn and grow from the situation, become broader and more adaptive human beings. They learn that they *can* serve as facilitators for future conflicts in their communities.
10. Contrary to popular belief, people can change and *do* change, when provided the right environment: they are allowed to speak without

interruption, to be listened to with respect, to listen and learn from others. Then they can choose to change based on their experienced learning. It must be their choice and made freely.
11. For all conflicts, the ultimate desired result is the establishment of a sense of community or family in which each participant can be part of the solution as an individual and be respected for that.
12. The end feeling is always one of increased personal richness in relationships, recognition of the intelligence and creativity of their community members, and satisfaction at having successfully resolved the conflict.
13. There is an inherent wisdom in a group of people that transcends the individuals, an untapped store of knowledge and wisdom, a pool of creativity waiting to be used. Our last and most expansive frontiers lie in the creative potential of people willing to open their minds to uncertainty and committed to solving everyday problems.
14. People who have experienced this process learn from it and apply it in many facets of their life. They apply it with great success. They represent that old adage: *Don't provide me a fish that is only one meal. Teach me to fish and I will eat forever.*
15. Failure is rare. Success is the normal outcome.

"This workshop provides a clear and concise model for bringing people together. The process as a whole is a valuable asset, but each component of the process individually is a powerful and simple tool. These tools can be easily integrated into any community organization or project and after they progress, understanding and trust are almost certain outcomes. In short, conflict becomes an opportunity to collaborate instead of a roadblock to success."

—H. A., workshop participant

Our Best Years: A Personal and Interpersonal Anecdote

(Note: This anecdote is based on a number of similar situations.)
She walked up to me, held out her hand, and said, "Hi, I'm Mary. You probably don't remember me, but my husband, Mike, and I attended a workshop with you up at Coyote River Resort about twelve years ago. You were helpful to us in our marriage."

I looked at her, a stately, slender, and proud woman in her later years, and recalled Mary and her husband, Mike, and the incident that brought us together.

It was a year of drought in the West, a bad one; even the springs were drying up on the range. It was causing problems between ranchers, between those who had water and those who didn't. The feds and the state had declared a state of emergency.

I had been asked by the county commissioners to help a group of ranchers see if they could find a way to make it through the drought together. They all realized that meant confronting some of their traditional feelings regarding the use of their range allotments and water.

I agreed to help the group and scheduled a three-day workshop at a resort in the basin that was close to one of the ranches. Before the workshop, I interviewed most of the participants representing the different perceptions: ranchers, federal agencies, county commissioners, tribal folks, and others.

That is how I first met Mike, a tall, slender, and soft-spoken rancher who owned one of the ranches, one that had access to plenty of water. The interview went well, and Mike seemed positive about the workshop. He had only one concern. I had requested that the ranchers' spouses also attend the workshop. He, with some reluctance, told me that he and his wife were estranged. She lived and worked sixty miles away in another state, while he lived on the ranch. They had scarcely spoken or been with each other for quite a while.

"Should I invite her?" he asked.

"If she has ownership in the ranch, then she should be there," I replied.

"Waaahll," he drawled, "what if she won't come?"

"That is her choice, but you won't know unless you ask," I replied. "When you do ask her, let her know that during the workshop she will learn some skills that will help her in her work and in your relationship."

He thought a minute and then said, "Waaahll," drawling it out, "we haven't been together for a long time. I wonder what kind of arrangements I oughta make."

I looked at him, puzzled.

"I mean, should I get separate rooms or separate beds or one room and the same bed? I'm not sure what to do."

"Again, it seems to me that's a choice she ought to have. Let her know the options, and let her decide."

"Well, it's gonna seem sorta funny to even ask her." He had a reluctant look on his face.

"What is the worst possible outcome of asking her?" I asked.

He looked surprised at the question, hesitated, then answered without thinking. "That she would say no and not be there, and then no matter what we decide at the workshop, she will be stubborn about it."

"What will be the best possible outcomes of asking her?" I asked.

He thought a while. "She decides to come, and we stay together while we are there. And we can reach some agreement together on what to do," he answered thoughtfully, then paused. "About the water and about us."

"So, what can you do to encourage that to happen?" I asked.

Again he thought a bit. "I could be pleasant about it, I suppose, and let her know I really want her there. I can let her know what her choices are, and she can decide." For just a moment, something warm and moist flashed in his eyes.

"Try that then," I added. What I had just accomplished was to help Mike resolve a personal or internal conflict he had within himself.

I did not see Mike again until the morning of the workshop. He walked in with a woman following slightly behind, appearing somewhat reserved and anxious. He introduced me to Mary, and we shook hands. I welcomed her, expressed hope she would enjoy the workshop, and told her I would answer any questions she had during the workshop that might help her in her work. As she walked away, Mike squeezed my hand and said, "We got the same room." He lifted his eyebrow with a smile.

We went through two days before we talked again. At the end of the second day, there were signs that the participants were close to making some agreements. They had learned to listen with respect to each other, had developed an understanding of the issues, and had developed a common purpose that their solutions would have to meet.

Mike and Mary came up to me, standing closer to each other than they had the first day, and asked if I could help them. They wanted to talk to each other about their relationship but were not sure how to do it. They wanted me to facilitate their discussion.

I suggested they could do it themselves in the privacy of their room. They had spent two days at the workshop and already had experienced the process I would recommend. They had also learned how to facilitate. I said I would give them a process to use. As I was talking them through this, I wrote the process on some three-by-five index cards to make it easy for them to remember. It was the approach to managing interpersonal conflicts.

They asked me some questions for clarification, reviewed the notes I had given them, took a few cards, and then walked away with barely contained excitement, holding hands.

I saw them again the next morning, standing close together, holding hands, and talking to others. Mike looked over at me and gave me a thumbs-up with a happy, almost silly grin. The final day went quickly, agreements were made, final closing comments made, and the group broke up quickly, its members going their separate ways.

Mary came up to me and gave me a huge hug, thanking me for helping them. I shook Mike's hand and they were gone.

Now Mary was here twelve years later, talking about how that session had helped them. "Is Mike here?" I asked.

"No," she said sadly, her eyes getting moist right away. "He passed away about two years ago. He went so quickly."

I expressed my condolences, truly saddened.

"Don't be sad, Bob," she said. "Before Mike died he said that our ten years together were the best years of his life and our marriage. I agreed with him. Mike moved to town and we lived together, there and on the ranch. We were so happy," she said with tears flowing. "Oh, we still had some tough times, but you know, we used that process you taught us. Each time we just loved each other more," she said, laughing and tearing at the same time.

"I am so grateful for those years. Your help made it possible for us to be happy together. You were smart enough to make us do it ourselves. We could never thank you enough for letting us solve those issues together."

As she hugged me, I thought of all the individuals who had come up to me with similar requests, separate from the conflict that brought the groups together. In each instance, they took what they learned from the workshop and applied it to their own lives. In every instance, they appeared to be successful.

This group of forty-plus people met for three days and reached a consensus agreement. My role was to facilitate them; their role was to do the work. I helped them create the opportunities, they made the choices.

During this time, as the participants learned, many confronted personal and interpersonal issues that changed their lives in ways similar to that of Mike and Mary. This process is simple, yet complex. Interested in learning about it? Read on, the process I used follows.

The Process—Interpersonal

This is what I told them: "Start seated somewhere you can relax and be together. Be close enough to hold hands so you can keep contact, if you want. Then, beginning with you, Mary, tell Mike your view of your relationship, how it got to be that way, and how you feel about it. Mike, you listen, without interrupting, and when she finishes you tell her what you heard. You've seen this done and participated in it during the workshop. Don't take notes. Just listen, and then respond with what you heard, objectively, without judgment or comment."

"Then, Mike, you do the same thing, and, Mary, you listen and then tell him what you heard. If you want, each of you can then take one more turn adding some information; but make sure the listener always says what was heard, without comment or judgment. Again, you have experienced this in the workshop.

"Then, Mike, you tell Mary the worst possible outcomes you have for your relationship if you continue as you are and don't resolve your issues. Mary, you listen and tell him what you hear. Then you repeat what Mike did, and, Mike, you are the listener.

"Take a break here if you want," I said, "so you can both have a few minutes alone to think about what you learned. And...think about your answer to the next question: *What will be the best possible outcomes for both of you if you resolve your issues?*

"You might write your best outcomes down on a three-by-five card, if you want. Mary, when you get back together, you answer first; Mike you listen and repeat what you heard. This will keep you focused. Then, Mike, you do the same thing while Mary listens.

"These outcomes are what you want to make happen in your relationship. They are your purpose for being together. So take the time to think it through and talk about it.

"Then, start with you, Mike. Tell Mary what you are willing to do to make those outcomes happen. And...what you need from her to make the best possible outcomes happen. Mary, you repeat what you heard, and then you tell Mike the same thing.

"Finally, when you are done, each of you answers these two questions: *How do you feel about this discussion?* And, *what did you learn that will bring you both together?* Just listen to each other answer this question. Best outcomes to both of you!"

(Note: A simplified version of this process is ahead. You'll get to it. Hang in there and then try it for yourself.)

You can learn from this: What was my role? Who made the choices? How long did the learning last?

"These consensus workshops have changed my life and made me a more balanced human being."

—**R.S., workshop participant**

Try It Yourself on a Personal (Internal) Conflict

The anecdote "Our Best Years" included both the personal and interpersonal approach to resolving conflicts. I want you to experience the personal approach yourself. Personal conflicts are the ones you have in your own mind with yourself.

Try this approach, then read the book and learn why you are answering these questions. Along the way, as you read, begin applying this approach to your life.

Write the answers down, so you can see them, bring them to your consciousness. You don't have to write a book; be brief, using single words that acknowledge the conflict in your own mind.

Start with a situation in your life that you have been avoiding. It can be family, work, church, some organization, or community...just select one to start. Then, answer these questions:

1. **What is the situation?** Describe the situation in enough detail that you are conscious of it. Who is involved? Where? When did it start?
2. **How do you feel about this unresolved conflict?** Record any emotion or feeling that comes to your mind. Be conscious of it, acknowledge it.
3. **What are your worst possible outcomes of confronting this conflict?** Record the worst of the worst. This is for your eyes only, so be candid with yourself. Open up the bedroom closet door, look under the bed, and let all the monsters and fears come out.
4. **What are the best possible outcomes of resolving this conflict that would justify taking the risk of confronting it?** Record the best of the best—don't limit yourself. Who knows...it might happen!
5. **How will you feel when the best possible outcomes happen?** Come on...feel it! This is the payoff for resolution. Record it.
6. **What are all the reasons this is impossible?** You know this is what you are thinking right now. This is impossible. Well, tell yourself why you feel that way. List them all.
7. **What new beliefs will you need about yourself to make your best possible outcomes happen?** All your impossible statements are just

beliefs you have that will prevent you from resolving the issue. Set these demons aside; put them back in the closet and under the bed. Then consider: what beliefs do you have about yourself that will allow you to do the impossible?
8. **What specific first step can you take to move toward resolving this issue?** That's all you need right now—just one little step. The rest will follow without thinking about them.
9. **How do you feel about doing this?** This was an experiment. How did it feel to you?
10. **What did you learn from this that will make you successful?** This is an additional payoff. What did this experience teach you? Record it.

Jose and a Promise Made: An Anecdote

"When are you going to write that book?" he asked seriously, his dark brown eyes searching my face with that intense eagle-eyed stare.

"What book?" I asked, too quickly and defensively, my jaw settling into a stubborn line. A frown wrinkled my brow. I glared back at him, daring him to go further.

Jose Trujillo has been part of my life for over twenty years. He was a member of an early conflict-resolution group I worked with. He is like a brother to me, although we are of different cultures. He is Taos Pueblo and Hispanic. His graying black hair is clipped short and stands straight up like the porcupine quills on the roach of a fancy dancer at an Indian powwow.

I am of European descent. My long hair and full beard are gray. With my full beard, I am often mistaken for Kenny Rogers, Ernest Hemingway, or Santa Claus.

Jose leaned forward purposefully in his seat. We were in a booth at Jake's Restaurant in Fort Collins, Colorado. The remains of our dinner, a good meal, decorated the table between us. We had been reconnecting, talking about our respective experiences since we had last been together. Now we had come to the part of the evening where we explored our moves into the future, a pattern we had enjoyed for all these years.

He leaned closer to me, a look of sincere concern on his face. His brows furrowed into a ridge between his eyes, making him look even more like an eagle about to pounce on his prey. "You know what I mean. You are running yourself to death all over the country trying to help people, but you are not taking care of yourself. You are out of balance, my friend. You need to sit and rest, find some quiet time to think about what you are doing. Stay in place for a while. Write that book about what you do, about reaching consensus. Let others learn to do it for themselves."

He leaned back, his face more relaxed now, considering me and my response to his statement.

I responded vigorously, "You know that I have never wanted to write about this. I have said that before. That is not my purpose or responsibility. I want to do this work on real issues, focusing only on helping people confront their conflicts and solving them. They learn this 'way' by doing it, the real thing. I learn from them as I go. That is what I am doing. Why should I write about it?"

He smiled, then grinned broadly as I spoke. "You are arrogant, my friend. This has little to do with you. You have been given a great gift, the ability to bring people together over the conflicts that have kept them apart. You have used what you learned from The People, the American Indian, and what you know from your own culture. You put them together into a powerful tool, something that truly helps solve people's issues and creates a larger sense of community. This is a gift to you from the Creator. You have used this gift with respect and great skill. I know that you are grateful for what you received. I know that you honor this gift each time you use it.

"But now you need to express that in writing so the gift is passed on. I tell you, Bob, you have powerful tools to pass along to others. You know how it has helped me, how it has changed my life. You know you will never rest, retire, or stop and get the balance you need until you have written the book."

I rubbed my forehead and then my eyes. I was tired. I had been working three weeks out of the month, on the road for the last six months. There was too much to do, and I couldn't seem to say no!

How could I let go of this sense of responsibility I felt to the process, the people? Maybe Jose was right, maybe I needed to consider his viewpoint. After all, I am not important. What is important is the knowledge and understanding I have gained over these past twenty-three years. It is impossible to express it in all the sessions I do. There is just too much.

Then I felt it. There was a trickle at first, then a stream of thought that was the book. Damn! Stubbornly, I immediately closed it off.

"Writing a book, having it read, has never changed anything," I argued. "There are thousands of books out there, bestsellers, acclaimed by many, and they are passing fads. They do little good but entertain, divert people from their real need to learn." I said this with a wave of my hand, dismissing the idea.

"That's not for you to decide, Bob," Jose said, serious again. "You just need to write it. Then see what happens."

"Jose, maybe you are right about this," I said reluctantly. "You have been in the past. Maybe I am just being arrogant and stubborn. Maybe this is what I need to do to let go. But, I am not promising anything. I will consider the idea. That doesn't mean I will do it."

"I know," Jose said as he smiled with satisfaction. "I know you will give it proper thought and make the right decision." I could tell he meant that I would write the book.

"You sound the song, but you are only the drum. The Creator is the drummer and the singer."

— Al Smith, Klamath tribal elder

Jose...I Did It!

That incident occurred eleven years ago. Since then, countless workshop participants have asked me the same question: "When are you going to write a book about this for us?" I have answered "sometime."

I guess this is "sometime." Sometime has stretched out to be a long time, as I avoided writing in favor of working, doing what I really love to do: helping people address and resolve their conflicts, reaching a consensus, and while they do so, learning how to resolve their future issues by themselves.

Helping people reach consensus is my purpose in life. My purpose rises from a deeply held conviction that the most important skill we can have in this day of rapid change, scarcity, power struggles, diversity, incivility, and ideological battles is the ability and willingness to address and resolve our conflicts together in a way that meets the needs of all.

The process is simple to apply. The skills can be learned easily and are best learned in real time on a real conflict. Just as I learned as I worked with each conflict experience. The willingness to address the conflicts must be internally generated.

The fact is, this book has been developing for a long time. I have always written explanatory information in brief and focused text to help out an individual client or group. As a result of Jose's opening my mind to training others, I have hosted numerous Consensus Institutes, all at the request of my clients. These consist of four workshops, each four days in length, scattered over a year. For these it was necessary to develop "learning manuals" for the potential facilitators. Much of the material in this book was developed during that time.

And even with that, those who wanted to be practitioners kept saying it was not enough. Even though I presented much more during these institute workshops, they still wanted more.

So, here it is. This is "more." And you can find even more on the book website: http://www.findingnewground.com.

Just remember, I am still learning as I go. I hope you do, too.

THIS IS FOR REAL:

Everyone who reviewed this book before I finalized it said it was too long. They said I should use the approach of the "One Minute Manager," short and simple. This book would take too much time to read. As you can see I ignored the advice.

This suggestion is similar to the idea that I can resolve a difficult conflict in a 3 hour meeting when it would require a 3 day workshop. The results would be the same: Time spent with no visible results. This is followed by another meeting later for three hours with similar results.

You will learn that time is never the problem, the problem is the problem. When you solve the problem, you will have more time. If you invest your time wisely you will get the return you seek. Invest your time in this book and it will pay off for you.

I am not interested in starting a new fad, or in quick fixes. I am interested in real results. Learning and understanding this process takes time. There is no quick way to understand the process. I know it is best learned through experience.

This approach requires building the capacity of people in the conflict to be able to address and resolve it with a consensus, to find new ground. It requires understanding not only why the process works, but how to make it work. It requires knowing how and when to apply it in conflict situations that are personal, interpersonal and intergroup. It requires consciously choosing to change your relationship with conflict so it becomes a positive force in your life.

The process recommended in this book appears simple, yet it is complex in its impacts. I know how powerful this approach is, how successful it is. Thousands of people would validate that statement. They helped to create it. They know their time was invested wisely. It is a gift from them to you.

A Prologue

This book and process is about YOU! I am interested in something real happening, a real paradigm shift on your part. I am interested in helping you understand how addressing your conflicts can change your life, and you, in positive ways. I am interested in helping you to experience, know and understand this process so you can apply it.

When you finish this book I believe you will agree with my decision to include it all. You will be a different person, a more adaptive learning person, and others around you will be changed in powerful ways because of it. And you will have more ttime for other things.

In spite of all these words there are more. Additional information, insights, anecdotes and art can be found for almost any chapter in the website: http://www.findingnewground.com

~3~

Introduction

Our Purpose

"We can't keep doing business as usual. Look at what is going on in the world, and you don't believe it."

—Workshop participant

Unresolved conflict kills! It burdens the mind, starves the soul, creates spiritual and mental poverty, and eventually slays the body through unremitting stress. This is affirmed every day in the media and in our communities. The "post office syndrome," the killing of spouses, educators, judges, coworkers, and young children has intensified fear in many homes, workplaces, schoolhouses, and communities.

This is not a new situation!

> *"Kills a Professor, Ends His Own Life; University of South Carolina Grounds Superintendent Tries to Slay Two Others. Row over conflict in duty. Shooting in college building is culmination of a dispute over construction work."*
>
> —*The New York Times, May 7, 1922*

We have been taught as individuals and as a society, to avoid conflict. We put it off to avoid the pain involved in reaching resolution. We fear hurting other people, being hurt ourselves, or losing out. We fear physical pain or death. We seek coping solutions that distance us from the conflict, that put it off until some better time, and in so doing we inadvertently encourage and incite aggression from others and foster the very outcomes we fear.

> *"Two Die In Shootings: In the third shooting at a Michigan auto factory since September, an employee opened fire in a Ford*

Introduction

> *Motor CO. plant Saturday, wounding his estranged wife then killing her boyfriend and himself. (An employee) said, 'This is like family 12 hours a day and we never thought it would happen here.'"*
>
> **—Tom Coyne, Associated Press, January 8, 1995**

This avoidance behavior may have been appropriate in earlier times when there was more stability and civility, similar belief and values systems, a greater sense of community, and a perception of plenty. But confronted with rapid change, scarce resources, increasing diversity, expanding power struggles, incivility, ideological polarization, and the escalating need to regulate behavior, these unresolved conflicts can build up as outrage and become deadly.

> *"Many postal facilities consequently have toxic work environments, and they can be a catalyst or trigger for serious acts of workplace violence, including homicide and suicide."*
>
> **—Stephen D. Musacco, PhD, author of "Beyond Going Postal," Postal Employee Network Postal News, April 14, 2010**

By continually adding to the bed load of underlying, unresolved tensions in our families, at work, and in communities, we tend to intensify the conflicts in the larger scale: the community, the county, the state, the nation, the world.

> *"Nashville, TN: Facebook 'defriending' led to double murder, police say. A Tennessee couple who 'defriended' a woman on Facebook were murdered in their home by the jilted woman's father and another man, police said on Thursday."*
>
> **—Tim Ghianni, Reuters, February 9, 2012**

Addressing and resolving conflict changes all this. Resolution frees the mind, enriches the soul, creates spiritual richness, fosters healthy bodies, and releases energy that allows people to move to higher and higher levels of human functioning. Resolving conflicts in your own mind, with others, or with groups creates positive relationships and frees energy that is available to help solve conflicts at that larger scale.

> **OUR PURPOSE**
>
> a. We will do the impossible, resolving all our conflicts with 100% agreement.
> b. We will model this for our younger generations...
> c. Introducing You to a "A" Process...."
> d. Fostering new and adaptive behaviors...
> e. Applying the Art of consensus building...
> f. Sharing Insights and Underlying Concepts...
> g. Providing anecdotes and personal vignettes...
> h. Using the participants' actual words...
> i. Providing visual experiences that create internal emotional awareness and knowledge...
> j. Creating a Willingness to Take the Risk...
> k. Encouraging a State of Uncertainty and Wonder...
> l. Being open to intuition...
> m. And Being Changed by the Experience.

"Failure is unacceptable. Current practices are failing. We must find a new approach. This one works!"

—**Workshop participant**

A. We will do the impossible: I am a person who works with people in conflict, seeking to facilitate consensus solutions. I seek out those in the most difficult of conflicts to help them solve their issues and learn how to do it for themselves in the future. That is my personal mission. I do this with people from all walks of life, individuals and groups, all over this great country and in other countries around the world.

I do it because I believe that we can no longer avoid conflict as we have in the past. I want you and others to know how to reach consensus and, through this, to build a sense of community that will add immeasurable richness to your lives. When I say consensus, I mean 100 percent agreement of all.

Impossible you say? Most people say that, either verbally or nonverbally. They raise their eyebrows, roll their eyes, and look at each other with amused smiles on their faces. I admit to them: "I know it is impossible to reach consensus! That is why I do it, which is why we all must do it. Why would you settle for doing only the possible? That, to me, is settling for mediocrity. Anyone can do the possible."

You can choose to do what can't be done, to overcome your fears and outdated assumptions. It is possible that is the reason we were created or evolved as humans: to do what is thought to be impossible. I have seen the impossible happen with each community I work with. Why would you settle for less?

We can address the everyday conflicts that exist between people, the races, the generations, the political parties, and the special-interest groups. We can seek to resolve these everyday conflicts, reaching out for consensus, creating a new and revived sense of civility and community in all our relationships with friends, family, work organizations, this nation, and indeed this world. We can make it possible!

> *Believe in doing the impossible. Then do it!*

B. We will model this for our younger generations: Children learn by watching their elders. They must see adults addressing and resolving their conflicts and, better yet, reaching consensus solutions that meet all members' needs. We cannot teach our children this skill or encourage them to resolve their conflicts and then behave differently ourselves: *"Do as I say and not as I do."*

I believe the greatest gift we can give to our younger generations is the ability to confront and resolve their conflicts. We, the adults, can best provide this gift of conflict resolution to our children and grandchildren by modeling the skill for them.

We can give our children successful approaches that they can follow, in their own minds, in their homes, their relationships, their workplaces, their religious environments, and their communities. We can demonstrate how consensus building and community building can make democracy successful for all. If we don't, we will doom our children to a future increasingly burdened with unresolved conflicts and increasing regulation of behavior, resulting in spiritual poverty, ideological struggles, mental and physical pain, alienation from each other, and often violence.

C. Introducing you to "a" process: You will be introduced to *a* **process** that will help you address and resolve the conflicts in your life. It is a simple process, yet one that has complex and rich implications for you. It is on the edge, the cutting edge of managing relationships. It will help you change who you are and how you respond to life. You will be able to overcome your fear of addressing conflicts with others, and in doing so, you will change these others in positive ways.

The word *a* is highlighted because it is not the one and only approach to resolving conflicts and fostering consensus. This is not intended to be a new religion or business fad. It is simply *a* process that will foster in you some new understandings about yourself, your relationships, and how to manage them.

Once you experience the process and apply it, you will find yourself learning from it and adapting it to your needs. You will find yourself behaving in different and more appropriate ways that reflect the new beliefs and behaviors you have and, in that way, easily resolving conflicts. You will experience a positive and rewarding change in relationships with all those around you.

This approach is a way to get you started on a different path. If you choose, this will be an ever-evolving approach, leading to a life of change, creation, and fulfillment. With each group, I learn something that allows me to adapt the approach and myself. I expect the same will happen with you. It will always be a work in progress.

Everything in this process has purpose and meaning and is intended to move you to resolution, to personal growth. Not one moment you invest will be wasted. Each question, each activity has purpose, intending to move you effectively and efficiently to resolution. Each activity is designed to have multiple layers of impact.

"If you're not living on the edge, then you are taking up too much space!"—Gramma Ginny, 1997

D. Fostering new and adaptive beliefs and behaviors—paradigm shifts: Let there be no doubt about my intent. I want to impact your present beliefs and behaviors about conflict, about managing relationships with others. While the old beliefs and behaviors may still apply in many situations, they are inappropriate for those that are the result of the changes we have experienced since the late 1960s. They do not work in environments of rapid transformational change, perceived scarcity, power struggles, incivility, ideological battles, and complex diversity.

Introduction

For many of us, this new world requires **paradigm shifts**. By reading and experiencing this book, you will find yourself choosing new beliefs and behaviors, creating new paradigms that will continue to shift and adapt. I will not do it for you…the process will; you will. And, it will always be your choice.

Our present beliefs and behaviors are designed to either avoid conflict or to engage in aggressive ways that make the situation worse. These behaviors reflect the basic belief that conflict is harmful, that contrived peace and harmony based on power and control are good at any cost. They are based often on the need to please or to win, rather than the need to resolve.

The rules and admonitions of my generation won't hold today. We cannot go back to that simpler time of hard and fast rules, the tried and true of the past. It is possible that the rules may have been wrong at that time, anyway.

This book will provide you the opportunity to explore and develop new and adaptive beliefs and behaviors about conflict. It is intended to make you believe, think, feel, and behave differently. No matter your age or experience, this book is intended to impact your life, in a positive and powerful way.

The new rule is, *shift happens*. So, get ready for change!

> Shift Happens!!!!

E. Applying the art of consensus building: I will share with you *the art* of seeking consensus. In any science or technology, there is an associated art that makes the product shine. There are principles and methods employed in consensus seeking that foster success. There are tactics and tricks of the trade that facilitate consensus. Much of this art has not been researched; it is based on my personal observations and is continuously in development. Each method was learned during the actual experiences of consensus building and has been replicated, tested, and proven to be effective. This book is written in a way that makes the art of seeking consensus transparent.

F. Sharing insights and underlying concepts: As you are introduced to this process, I will disclose the *insights* I have gained while helping others confront their conflicts. These insights are intended to help you challenge your present beliefs, choose to shift your perceptions. They are intended to provide understanding of the process, of why it works.

Many of these insights have some basic underlying concepts I have gained through many experiences and subsequent extensive reading. I share these underlying concepts with you throughout the book.

These insights come in different shapes and sizes. There is the *factual:* what has been proven to be true. These have been extensively researched, such as knowledge of the brain. I caution myself to remember that this factual information may still be limited and often subject to change, and I remind participants of this. I have adapted some of the researched insights based on my personal experiences.

There is the *theoretical,* or what we think is true. These are normally processes, described in a linear way, that explain how we function as individuals or groups. They may not yet be the subject of mathematical interpretation, but are well documented by theoretical or subjective research. Theories such as Maslow's hierarchy of needs or the change process fit this category.

Other insights come from the participants themselves in the "collective statements" they develop during their workshops.

Most of these insights came after the fact. When I started, I literally did not know what I was doing. I only knew I had to do something. As I became conscious of these insights, as I understood what was happening, it allowed me to make the experience richer and more understandable for participants. All these insights are yours to use and share with others.

G. Providing anecdotes and personal vignettes: You will read anecdotes experienced while developing and applying this process. This anecdotal information is presented as what I have observed to be true. Most stories have come from my own observations of the impact of this process, my life experiences, or what I believe to be true. I have gained a wealth of experience and understanding about the behavior of people in conflict. Other stories are reported as anecdotal material from other sources.

Throughout this book I will share with you some personal vignettes, powerful life experiences that developed my relationship with conflict and provided impetus for the development of this process. They represent my own journey as it relates to conflict. In many instances I have asked and gained permission from others to use their personal anecdotes with their own vivid descriptions.

As you read the anecdotal material or personal vignettes, remember that these are my perceptions of what happened and reported as seen through my eyes, my senses, and my emotions. Others' perceptions may differ. I have checked many of these with my family, friends, and associates. I know they experienced some of these differently. I honor that difference but need to share how I experienced it.

The anecdotes and personal vignettes illustrate the points I am trying to make. They add humanity to the book. They are intended to show the impact that unresolved conflict has on the person, on subsequent generations, if not resolved. They are intended to show my progress toward finding a better way to confront and resolve these personal conflicts in my life.

For those anecdotes based on my personal experience, I have often changed the names, locations, timing, and so forth to protect people's privacy or prevent any embarrassment. I have often merged situations that are similar to add richness to the lesson implied. I apologize if I have misread any event or person or caused embarrassment to any person. It is not my intent.

In addition to the anecdotes and personal experiences, I have provided statements or paragraphs throughout the book to help you understand something specific about a particular topic. This knowledge came to me over time while working with groups all over the world and will help you apply wisdom that might otherwise take years to gain. This advice has been inserted into text boxes. Example:

> What I learned.

H. Using the participants' actual words: During the consensus workshops, the words and statements expressed by participants are often recorded exactly as expressed. These words portray better than I can the development of people as they move toward reaching consensus. They provide vivid descriptions of how people feel about conflict, how they feel as they move to consensus.

These words provide a sense of realness to this book. They are what people actually said, how they learned, how they changed, and how they resolved their issues. These statements are shown throughout the book as real words from actual workshops, woven into the text of the book, or as brief quotes inserted into the material as in the following example:

All words and statements that have come from real participants and facilitators, spoken in actual workshops, and used to present the process are displayed in this *different font.*

I. Providing visual experiences that create internal emotional awareness and knowledge: There are some times when words are not enough. They don't create the internal awareness and knowledge needed to move toward consensus. This has been a continuing challenge for me, so over the years, I have developed visual movements with people, small vignettes acted out by the participants themselves that help them understand a concept or idea. These are shortcuts to understanding, to reaching consensus, and are described in detail so you can use them if you choose. They are all powerful learning tools.

J. Creating a willingness to take the risk: When you realize you are on the "edge" of something big, you will have to decide to take the jump. I intend to foster in you a *willingness to take the risk* of addressing the conflicts in your life and deciding to resolve them, despite the perceived risks. This is the most important attribute I can foster in any person or group I work with. Without the willingness to take the risk, the new beliefs, process, insights, underlying concepts, and art are of little value. Part of the willingness to risk is to see benefits that will make the risk reasonable. You will experience and learn how to do that.

K. Encouraging a state of uncertainty and wonder: This process requires uncertainty. Not knowing. Without uncertainty, you will become fixed and immovable, untouched by the wonder that surrounds you. Uncertainty! Get used to the word and the feeling.

I was known as Mr. Certainty in my younger days. After one of my innumerable pronouncements about almost anything, people would ask me, "Is that right?" My stock answer was, "I'm sure!" End of discussion!

I was, and still can be, a famously addicted know-it-all. I got it from my family: we are Chadwick, don't tell us what to do, we already know it all, we are the one and only religion. In my profession: "If you want to manage the forests, go to school like I did!" I felt I was genetically predetermined to be certain and right!

This approach worked fine until the late 1960s and early 1970s. Then, certainty crashed in a major way. I was assailed from all directions: my family, my profession, my religion, and myself. Very little that I believed would hold true.

Everything came together to give me a perfect midlife crisis that was Oscar-award quality. A veil parted and I saw—at first with great fear, then great wonder—that the truth was a whole lot bigger and more complicated than I realized. Doubts assailed me, and no matter what I did, I could not erect that wall of certainty again.

Introduction

I am grateful that happened. It allowed me to look honestly at my relationship with others and, more specifically, with conflict. It allowed me to understand that the times had changed, were changing, and would continue to change. It allowed me to say, as I looked around me, "There has got to be a better way!"

I continuously remind myself that I don't know it all. Despite what I have experienced, read, researched, learned, there are still great possibilities that something else, other forces, are working in the process. I often refer to these forces as "the Universe" or sometimes as the "Coyote." It is enough to know that I don't know it all, because that leaves me open to possibility.

> "The only thing I am certain of is my uncertainty!"

L. Being open to intuition: When nothing else works, I must often trust my intuition. I make assumptions based on my sensing of what is going on. Knowing how to sense in ways that foster intuition is part of this process. When I work with my intuition, I will tell the individuals or groups what I am doing and why. Sometimes I will acknowledge that I don't know what I am doing, but that it feels "right." I keep it transparent so you can then tap your own intuition. When doing this, I always remind myself to: Trust myself! Trust the people!

> Trust Myself! Trust The People!

M. And being changed by the experience: After experiencing this process, you will be changed. You will apply it with success. You will improve relationships, creating safe environments for yourself and others. Your life and the lives of those who are impacted by you will change for the better.

A caveat: This approach has such a significant impact on those who experience it, that I worried about starting some new movement whose purpose was more focused on getting together because we believe the same things. With tens of thousands of satisfied participants, and thousands of practitioners, it has been difficult to not form a "Society of We-Know-It-All Consensus Builders." It has been difficult to avoid annual or quarterly meetings of those who "know." I have consciously avoided any attempts to allow that to happen.

My fear is that in writing down the process, I will limit it so it will cease developing and become inflexible. Or that people, not understanding, will use it in ways that are disrespectful.

But I realize that is a risk we all must take in life. Give me a bottle of aspirin, and I can use it sparingly to cure my headaches or all at once to kill myself. It is my choice.

It is my responsibility to write this book as well as I can, to make the process transparent to you, to foster new beliefs and behaviors that you choose for yourself, and to foster the continued ability to adapt. You then have the responsibility to decide whether to apply it, when to apply it, and how to apply it. I trust it will be done responsibly.

~4~

Getting Acquainted With Conflict

The Everyday Conflicts of Life

"I wanted oyster stuffing (in the turkey) and she wanted bread stuffing. Now she is stuffing it with my money."

—**Doc Severinsen** on *The Tonight Show Starring Johnny Carson*

This book is not about the big conflicts of life that are reported in the media. Iraq, the Middle East, North Korea, Iran are being taken care of by diplomats, Congress, the White House, and the United Nations, thank you. While the concepts and process you learn here are applicable in such global situations, it is beyond your personal scope to deal with them. I want you to engage *your* controversies, *your* strife.

This book is about addressing the everyday familiar conflicts that mar our personal lives at home, at work, and in the community. It is about the conflicts that affect you directly, that you have some control over. It is these everyday conflicts that we can learn to confront and resolve.

> **RECORD YOUR ANSWERS**
>
> Think about all the unresolved conflicts you have in your life at this moment.
>
> - What are the emotions they are creating that are repressed?
> - How much energy are they consuming?
> - How do they affect the quality of life, in your mind, at home, at work, in the community?

These are the everyday conflicts that will eat up your energy and focus if you don't resolve them. For example:

- You have teenagers and they want to drive before you are ready to let them. They want to date before you think they are ready. Your spouse disagrees with your decision. They are choosing the side that agrees with them. You stand alone.
- You are disagreeing with your spouse on the monthly expenses. You are at an impasse.
- The schools want to change the school boundaries, so your kids will go to another school. Or, they change the bus schedule, which will affect your going to work.
- You have employees who are not performing, and you have to tell them during their performance appraisal.
- Charlie and Jim are fighting at work and affecting everyone else at the office. They deny they have a problem. You don't know how to confront them or work the problem out, so you are thinking of reassigning them to jobs you can't afford to finance.
- The employees want to get rid of the new manager at the plant because he is bringing too much change. But you hired him to bring change. The employees will leave for another company if you don't fire him. If you don't resolve this issue, you know your business will fail.

Conflict is an integral part of life. We are faced with conflict in all facets of our lives and our minds are filled with them:

- *Should I work this weekend on that important project, or stay at home and play with the family? The boss wants me to work, but Jane and the kids will really be angry if I do.*
- *As union representative, I am here to tell you that we can't work these men overtime anymore. If you do, we will strike.*
- *I'm supposed to be in this cross-functional team and make team decisions, but my boss doesn't want me to sell out our department. I am torn by these loyalties.*

We will look at internal conflicts that you have with yourself, in your own mind. These are your personal conflicts. There are the interpersonal conflicts you have with your spouse or partner, children, coworkers, neighbors. There are the intergroup conflicts at the workplace, between departments, between and among professionals with differing viewpoints.

"Going through a remodel can push a couple to the edge," says Rachel Cox, a marriage and family therapist in Palo Alto, Calif. "Every tension they have gets magnified a hundredfold...In many cases, when the work is done, so is the marriage."

—**Karen Breslau, "Till Faucets Do Us Part,"** Newsweek**, January 30, 2006**

Before we proceed with this, let's look at what conflict is and isn't.

Conflict: A Definition and Insight

Creating consensus is the central theme of this book. This requires acknowledging, addressing, and resolving conflict. People like and are attracted to the notion of agreement, of consensus. They are repelled by the notion of having to confront conflict with others to reach agreement. I'll bet you are too. I know that I am.

What do you think of when you know that someone is in conflict with you? How do you feel? I have learned that being in conflict is probably the most feared, hated, and avoided experience in our society. We fear conflict because of all the past negative experiences and resulting feelings it has for us, personally and socially.

"My father was a kind person, quiet spoken. He was a likable person, because he would not speak ill of others. My mother, on the other hand, was a more confronting person, always at war with others, especially my dad. She frightened me, and I could not understand why she did what she did. As a result, I learned to avoid conflict, to be more like my dad. I chose his approach instead of my mother's."

—**Anita, workshop participant**

We avoid conflict because we don't understand it. Most people in conflict have never taken the time or energy to explore what conflict is, what it means to them, how it feels to them, and what the possible outcomes can be. The overwhelming majority of people I work with see conflict as negative, an experience to be avoided at any cost. They will even avoid talking or thinking about it.

"My father was an alcoholic, a drunk. When he was drunk he was abusive, so we children avoided him. We avoided talking about it. As a result, we learned to avoid conflict with others, and to not talk about it."

—**Brandy, workshop participant**

The definition of conflict is explicit; the noun—*conflict*—is associated with war. It is defined as:

> "A state of open, often prolonged fighting; a battle or war. A state of disharmony between incompatible or antithetical persons, ideas, or interests; a clash...denotes struggle between opposing forces for victory or supremacy...to show antagonism or irreconcilability."

That doesn't sound very inviting, does it?

Conflict applies both to open fighting between hostile groups and to a struggle, often an inner struggle, between antithetical forces. The archaic meaning of "conflict" as an intransitive verb is "to engage in warfare." This matches how most people feel about being in conflict.

> *Data gathered during workshops shows that over 90% in conflict fear it.... and avoid it!*

The only somewhat positive definition relates to drama: "Opposition between characters or forces in a work of drama or fiction, especially opposition that motivates or shapes the action of the plot." This definition hints at the need for conflict to create the plot, to establish the moment of learning. But it takes a leap of faith to see this.

These are the dictionary definitions. What are ordinary people's definitions of conflict?

Most of my understandings about conflict have been developed with people who meet to resolve conflicts using the consensus process. One of the first assignments I give these groups is to individually define conflict and describe how it makes them feel. These statements are then recorded exactly as they are expressed. They are developed into what I call "collective statements," which include all the statements, exactly as recorded. (This is explained later in the chapter on collective statements.)

Most of their definition statements about conflict are negative, often describing violent outcomes. This is important to know, because if people fear that confronting conflict will have violent outcomes, they are more likely to avoid them. When defining conflict in the abstract, there are normally three negative feeling statements for each positive one. What follows is a sample of what they say.

Conflict is a difference of opinion. This is the most common definition of conflict provided during the workshops by participants:

- *"Conflict is a difference of opinion, or a disagreement between two people or a group of people. This involves a difference of position, ideas, or concepts caused by each individual's own frame of reference."*
- *"Conflict is two very opposite opinions on any given subject. Conflict is two or more persons with different points of view and they don't know how to resolve them."*

This definition does not go far enough. We know we are all different; we even seek to minimize differences when we can. "Let's try to agree on what we have in common" is the usual suggestion. "We are really all saying the same thing" is another.

We seek agreement to put our differences aside. We want to avoid our differences because we recognize they are the combustible material for the flames of conflict. And an ingredient is still needed to trigger the fire.

Conflict: an experience with power. This added ingredient is "POWER." Power is the ability to influence others or things. Influencing can be done in an advocacy manner, stating a point of view, and hoping the other is moved to act on that information. Or it may be done in an aggressive or arrogant manner, forcing the other to agree to your point of view and to behave accordingly. This is the "flash point" for conflict. We now become *adversaries*, trying to impose our belief upon the other, rather than *advocates* trying to convince the other.

This is how participants in consensus workshops described the move to conflict:

- *"Conflict means against—opposing sides. Conflict is perceived power over truth. There is an imbalance of power which polarizes us into adversary roles, so that there are winners and losers."*
- *"Conflict elicits strong emotions and a determination to win at all costs. I'm not ambivalent, with no choice, I want to win!"*
- *"When there is a discomfort with differences in values, or when a struggle between contrasting value systems collide, we are at war."*

Implicit in all these perceptions is the notion of a "power struggle." When we get in this power struggle, the issue is reduced in importance, while the desire to win is increased. How does this happen?

The issue is reduced in importance; the desire to win is increased. Imagine you and me sitting in a meeting with our management team. We both want to impress our boss. You make an observation that I disagree with. I state my disagreement, trying to convince you, and the others, of the correctness of my view. You are somewhat taken aback with the intensity of my presentation. You are compelled to respond, to defend your point of view. Your viewpoint has suddenly attained an increased significance for you.

We have now entered the debate stage, each person advocating for a position. If we respect each other enough to hear the differing perceptions, it may be possible to hear information that convinces us to change our point of view. Or we may forge an agreement that represents both of our views.

If, however, I am committed to my point of view because it is connected to my ego, my sense of integrity, my need for recognition, my *self*, then I am compelled to win at any cost. This may require that I begin to respond more aggressively. I may laugh at or otherwise trivialize your point of view or your expertise in this matter or your level of intelligence. I may want to use my organizational position, my education, to force you to agree with me.

Now I am moving us into the world of conflict. What is important is no longer what the truth is. What is now important is who is going to win!

Conflict coping begins at this point. You may decide to use the "flight approach:" to conform, to deny there is a difference, to distance yourself from the issue. Or you may seek a third person to mediate the situation to a conclusion. Or you may become equally aggressive, equally disrespectful, setting up a no-win situation for both parties.

> "Competing interests create a we/they mentality. We are not getting along because we resist acceptance of the other's views. We are blocking their desires."
>
> —**Workshop participant**

Conflict: an emotional experience. As soon as it is apparent that conflict is looming, the impact on the emotions of the participants and the observers is apparent. As the competing parties argue, we become adrenalized, pitted in a confrontation that has attained significance beyond the issue. We may appear calm, cool, collected in our demeanor, but our voice tones are challenging, hard, quavery. Our faces are flushed, our muscles tense, our breathing is fast. We look to others for support.

> *"If not resolved, conflict can result in war, the opposite of peace, serenity, and calmness."*
>
> —**Workshop participant**

The observers are horrified. What was supposed to be a typically monotonous meeting has suddenly become a potential "killing field." Many take mental flight, glancing at the boss in the hope he will control the situation, or glancing at the clock to see if it is break time yet. Others seek to alleviate the tensions by attempting to change the subject or stating that the parties are "really saying the same thing." Some will make jokes to ease the tension. Others are anxious to join the fray, choosing sides with possible future rewards in mind. **All of these are coping mechanisms that do not resolve the conflict.**

Make no doubt about it: conflict is an emotional experience, not just an intellectual one. This is how workshop participants have described it:

- *"I feel self-conscious with a rush of adrenaline, headaches, stomachaches (it's Rolaids time) which produces a feeling that is overwhelming and exhausting. I have the 'fight or flight' syndrome."*
- *"Conflict is scary; you don't know the outcome of it. I don't like conflict; it's something that hurts you.*

When the body becomes adrenalized, it is motivated to either "fight" or "flight," and the perceptions of the people involved are altered. Survival needs rise to the fore, and worst possible outcomes magnify the significance of the situation. The world is divided into enemies and friends. Information gathered is intended to protect the person from harm. Defensive needs become paramount. All of these emotional responses serve to worsen the situation, to move it toward violence, rather than toward solution.

It is easy to see how such beliefs can match the dictionary definition of conflict described above. Conflict is seen as deadly! These are the feelings and beliefs that cause people to avoid confronting conflict.

"Conflict is when instead of a line in the sand there is a crater in the ground."

—Workshop participant

What Happens When We Talk about Actual Conflict in Our Environment?

During my work I often ask participants to "define conflict, and describe how it makes you feel."

Analysis of their feeling statements, as recorded by them, indicates 75 percent are negative, describing fear, avoidance, and denial that it exists. Their recorded statements are very descriptive, such as these actual statements from workshop participants:

- *"I hate conflict! I feel threatened. I run away from it. Avoid it at all costs."*
- *"I don't like it. I fear that I don't know what to do or can't do it."*
- *"Conflict is too painful, too scary, too out of control, and someone could get hurt."*

Defining conflict is abstract, less attached to reality. It is easier to express positive opportunities with the definition, or to see it as both bad and good.

I ask them another question to get at reality: "What is the evidence of unresolved conflict in your environment…and…how do you feel about it?"

Analysis of their feeling statements, as recorded by them, indicates 90 percent are negative, describing depression, stress, avoidance, hopelessness. Again, their own recorded statements are very descriptive:

- *"To me the evidence is the feeling in the room. It's uneasiness. I can feel the same thing in my stomach."*
- *"I want it to go away. I feel frustrated and cheated."*
- *"I get depressed, unmotivated to go to work, and I am physically drained."*

These answers are a raw and candid description of the evidence that conflict is real in their environment. It is a description of the hostile and toxic conditions they often work or live in. Why don't we do something about it?

The impacts on relationship. Unresolved conflict doesn't affect just you and me; it affects all of us. Our relationships are diminished. But why believe me? Let the workshop participants tell you in their own words:

- *"Conflict makes relationships hard, and it is difficult for people to work together at times."*
- *"There is gossip, fear, distrust, making jokes about the other sides."*
- *"Tempers flare, leading to fear and hostility."*
- *There is whispering where others suddenly stop talking and you wonder what is going on."*

Are you interested in living or working in that kind of environment? The great majority of us do. Consider the tens of thousands of people I have worked with who describe these environments and yet accept them as something they are helpless to change. Why don't they do something about it?

The impacts on productivity. If 90 percent of the people in our work environment fear and avoid the unresolved conflicts in their environment, what impact does this have on the quality of decisions made, or the productivity of the workers, or the impacts on their health? This is what workshop participants have said:

- *"I look around me at my colleagues and I feel we could be doing so much more if we had less unspoken and unresolved conflict."*
- *"I feel this really stifles creativity and collaboration."*
- *"Our unresolved conflict causes disappointment, eats up time and energy, and pulls us away from purpose."*
- *"I see people closing their minds to new ideas based on conflicts they perceive that are sometimes not really there."*

Bottom line: unresolved conflict is costly. I know this from my own experience as a manager. I know this from the many venues I have worked in. Get all the technology you want, come up with the newest fad for management, if members of your group are in conflict, it will all be for naught. If the employees have a conflict with the proposed change, they will resist it, often quietly, but they will resist until it disappears. In the end it all comes down to people who can get along, free of unresolved conflict.

In my view as a professional, as a former executive, as a business person, as a consultant, the untapped potential for productivity and creativity lies not just in new technology, but in creating relationships that are kept relatively free of unresolved conflict. Not free of *conflict*, because conflict is necessary for creating the new. It is *unresolved* conflict that is costly.

In order to change this, someone has to do something about it.

Conflict: "The irritant that creates the pearl." Each of us has had a different life experience with conflict. Most of us have learned, or been taught, to avoid conflict. We cope in many ways. We conform to the greater power, seeking to please or to get out of the line of fire. Or we deny the problem exists, insisting we are more in agreement than in disagreement. Or we may put distance between ourselves and the other.

Yet, in each of us is this understanding that our response is inappropriate. By avoiding the conflict, we somehow feel less—a loss of opportunity, a loss of self. This is how groups tend to move toward this realization:

- *"Conflict is stressful, but it can have positive outcomes. Conflict needs to come out and be talked about, but it's hard for me to get it out because I don't know the outcome."*
- *"I feel it's here to stay, and we must learn to deal with it in a kind, sincere, thoughtful way. I feel like if we could talk more about it, I'd feel good and hear both sides. It's all right and OK."*

There are intrinsic benefits to conflict; it is a natural process created by the infinite differences that are inherent in us as individuals or as groups in cultures and society. The people I have worked with recognize this; one in four people define their feelings about conflict this way:

- *"Conflict is not good or bad—but is just a normal, healthy part of our lives, like death and taxes. Conflict is an opportunity for growth, change, and leads to progress, which leads to better decision making."*
- *"I don't like conflict, but you need conflict to grow and move forward. Conflict is necessary; without conflict, there is no growth."*

We cannot escape the certainty of conflict in our life, nor can we escape the inevitable resolution of conflict. We can avoid it, deny it, foster it; but eventually, the situation must be resolved.

In each conflict is the opportunity for learning, the opportunity for the creation of new beliefs and values, an integration of differing views that allows us to grow, to move toward our ultimate potential as people and communities of people.

But some may not want new beliefs or behaviors. If we do not learn from the conflict, then we are sent back to do it over. We move from one marriage to another with the same consequences. We move from one job to the other with the same consequences. The conflict will recur over and over until we find resolution, until we learn what we are to learn.

The participants recognize at some level that there is a gift in each and every conflict, no matter how trivial. This gift is actualized only when the issue is resolved. And it provides a stimulus to life, an excitement that is the opposite of the fear we feel in its presence.

Some think it's exhilarating:

"I feel challenged by conflict. Sometimes I desire conflict when I'm ready for a good fight. It is an excellent way to manage life's juices."

—**Workshop participant**

Or, as one participant put it:

"Conflict is like the irritant in the oyster that creates the pearl."

Some Conflicts Don't Need to Be Resolved

"When you come from the Queens, a day without an argument is a wasted opportunity."

—**Mario Cuomo**

Some conflicts are not meant to be resolved. An associate talked about her husband's and her father's long-standing social argument about time zones. Each spring and fall when they travel to a cabin in the mountains together, they cross a time zone. Her husband, Bob, says they lose an hour, or gain an hour as they return. Her dad says they lose no time at all, that it is just a paper or mental gimmick. The time is the same in both places. They have never finished the argument, she said.

Of course not. This is a social argument, intended to foster male bonding, but doing it in a way that also manages to keep the power equal between the two people. The argument cannot be finished because if one of them won, the winner would be "one up" and the other would have to try to get even. This becomes a different game, one that is more serious and would drive a wedge between the two generations.

This is an argument that is not meant to be resolved. It is part of friendship bonding and the recognition that the friends are different, which can be a vehicle for excitement and fun in the relationship.

In like manner, there are many conflicts that, left alone, will resolve themselves in time.

Conflict—An Antidote to Boredom: An Anecdote

In my early years in the US Forest Service, I often lived in isolated ranger stations where the community consisted of those I worked with. We saw each other day after day, at work and outside of work. During the spring, summer, and fall months, we occupied ourselves with the hard work associated with our profession. We worked together and played together. We were bonded as a community.

In the winter, however, activities slowed down. The days were shorter, the nights darker and colder. The snow at the outlying stations was deep. Our activities were limited, but our contacts with each other were intensified. At first we kept busy with buttoning up the guard stations, bringing in the tools, completing reports, and talking about last year's fires. But this soon became repetitive and boring. The evenings spent with each other, away from the delights of real civilization, became boring.

It began slowly. Someone would criticize someone else. People would start rumors. People would take sides. This led to another disagreement between others on opposing sides. Friends chose different sides and became cool with each other. Additional rumors were started. Whose spouse was flirting with another's spouse? Wives stopped talking to each other. Men worked without speaking all day. Conversations around coffee were strained. People talked "about" each other instead of "to" each other.

Then any little thing became a major conflict. Angry words were spoken. Names were called. The District Ranger would try to soften the feelings by having poorly attended socials in the evenings or on weekends. People took their vacations to escape the feeling of gloom and doom that prevailed.

This is commonly known as "cabin fever," a set of behaviors associated with living together in small spaces without anything to create excitement. So the brain creates excitement out of the mundane. The brain just cannot stand boredom, or the sweet sickness of "harmony." The brain feels stifled, so it seeks excitement, moving to its lower levels and creating conflicts that need to be confronted.

We were a dysfunctional community.

Luckily there was an antidote for this. Each spring, as the grass began to grow, as more people came out into the forest, there was that first forest fire. A small one, a slow one. Nothing to get really excited about, but it motivated us to control it.

Fire was our common enemy; it brought us together. We were all engaged, connected, on the ground, in the office. All arguments were forgotten as we worked frantically, shoulder to shoulder, to overcome the fire and protect the forests. This is what we were meant to do. Hard feelings disappeared in the frantic environment that ensued.

When we returned to the station, our common mission accomplished, we had a new spirit of camaraderie. We relived the fire, talked about the coming field season, joked, and laughed. The spouses responded to this, starting a series of social events attended by all. We had something different to talk about. We became a community again. All those slights and rumors disappeared as if they never happened.

I often wondered...did the Ranger start that first fire?

Let's Just Get On with It!

> "All right, already, I get your point. I need to resolve my conflicts. Let's just get on with it!"

Is that what is going through your mind right now? Well, don't feel alone. This is the attitude people often have in their workshop, wondering when they are going to get to solve the problem. Everybody who comes to me with a conflict wants it solved—right now! They don't want a lot of background information, and they don't necessarily want to know how to do it; they just want the problem solved. Get on with it!

My response is always the same: why would you want me to do what you have always done and then end up with another failure? It is precisely that desire to have instant gratification that normally results in more and more unresolved conflict. You are looking for easy and fast solutions, not the right solution. Then you just have to do it over again and again and again.

My purpose is to help you "go slow to go fast." I want you to understand what conflict is, how it affects you and why it affects you the way it does. Then, and only then, can you begin to manage the conflicts in your life with a timely solution.

So, take a deep breath and relax yourself…you are exactly where you need to be. All of my clients have the same feeling at this point. They just hang in there until they finally get what they have always wanted: a solution to the conflict and a way of solving future conflicts. You will too.

~5~

Exploring Conflict

The Foundation of the Past

Conflicts like this surround us. They are everywhere: in our families, personal relationships, churches, communities, organizations, workplaces. They lurk beneath every relationship, a feral animal crouched, often caged in denial and avoidance, anticipating, waiting for the moment to strike.

Conflict Creates My Awareness

A Personal Vignette

My awareness of life began with that scream. I woke to its call with a start, propelling myself to a sitting position from a sound sleep. It launched me out of bed with its primal intensity and tone. It moved me rapidly to the door at the head of the stairs to behold my first remembered childhood scene of conflict, anger, pain, and violence.

I was two years old, to my reckoning. Did it actually happen as I remembered, or was it an early nightmare? In later years, answering this question became critically important to me. The nightmare haunted me in my sleep well into my thirties. I would wake at two thirty a.m. in a cold sweat, repeating that primal scream, disoriented and struggling for some control.

I remember the home we lived in. I know because I visited this place with my mother in my more mature years to get clarity on the event. My mother set my uncertainty to rest. It *was* real, all of it.

I looked down on a scene that appeared frozen in time. I am imprinted with it. My mother stood by the door, at the farthest end of my vision. My father was near the foot of the stairs, screaming words at her that I did not understand. Somehow, I understood the emotions. The tone of voice was obvious; there was meanness, rage, and pain in the words. My two older brothers were standing off to the side, emitting the screams that woke me. My own scream had risen from my throat to join theirs.

I felt catapulted to the scene, finding myself between my two older and screaming brothers. How did I get there? I don't know. There must have been some need to understand, to control, to prevent an event that appeared instinctively threatening to me personally.

I screamed because my brothers screamed and their screams were scaring me. I was a reactive visceral beast, calling out in pain for help from the two people who were unable to give it, who were the source of the pain. They paid no attention to us, riveted as they were on their own misery.

While I could not understand their words, I did clearly understand their tones of voice, the physical movements they made against each other, against us. My mother stood at the door, pulling a coat over her body. Rain beat heavily on the windowpane behind her, the skies weeping with us. Her body was leaned away from the force of Dad's verbal assault. He was casting her away with an outstretched arm, his forefinger a pointed stiletto. Their faces were set in grimaces of pain. They were hideous to view, to feel.

It was raining heavily outside; I could see through the window as it poured over the eaves in a torrent of water. It reminded me of the river that flowed by our backyard, swollen with the spring rains. I knew then that Mom was leaving to do some horrible thing, to JUMP INTO THE RIVER! I understood now! Dad was screaming at her to do so, to be gone from his life.

As she turned to leave, our presence caught her eyes. She looked at us with spiteful purpose, angry at us for our screaming, our presence. She screamed a message at us. My translation was one of blame: "If it weren't for you, if I hadn't had you, I wouldn't need to be here!"

I felt the judgment, the charge, the responsibility. I was shocked, my screams stopped; I was unable to comprehend what I had done. Was she looking only at me? My brothers had also stopped screaming. A silence enveloped the room. My mind whirled in its first truly self-conscious moment. What could I say, what could I do to redeem myself? What could I say to keep her from going?

She left. The door closed. The rain fell. The room became silent with emotional numbness. I remember nothing else about that night except a deep and abiding feeling of emptiness, loss, and disbelief.

I was awake, made aware and self-conscious. I knew the difference between "me" and "they." "They," the people I was dependent upon, were out of control, and somehow I was responsible for it. The moment was painful, fearful, triggering those personal survival instincts I would need throughout my life. It was the moment I began to create myself, to create my personal coping mechanisms out of fear.

Groundhog Day: The memory of that conflict event moves me deeply even now. It continues to affect and shape my life. I wonder if this happens to all of us as children. Exposure to some conflict event that frightens us deeply, startles us, creates our awareness of self, our sense of being separate. In its presence we feel helpless, powerless, caught in a web made by others. It connects us to fear, a sense of being unprotected from the unpredictability of others. It surely creates a personal desire for survival. It did for me.

The conflict drama above was repeated over and over, like the movie *Groundhog Day* but without a happy ending. Yet the reality was not as bad as the anticipation of knowing it would happen again. Waiting for the event made every moment anxiety ridden and potentially treacherous.

I suspect you experience some of these same feelings in the conflicts that surround you. And what do we do about it? For the most part, nothing. The people I have lived with and worked with are quite open about this. They do not like conflict; they fear it, avoid it, run away from it, act like it doesn't exist. They talk about it with others, but not to those they are in conflict with. If put to a vote, confronting conflict would lose every time.

The consequences of the childhood event might not be all bad. Without this moment of shock, we would be unaware, dependent on others. We would have no awareness to make decisions for our own safety, for our own survival…to cope.

If this moment of awareness is necessary, I wish there were an easier way to do it. Surely, as evolved as we are supposed to be, we could come up with something better. With all we know about humans, we adults could have solved this by now. If I had comprehended better, known how commonplace this frightening event would be, I would have gone upstairs, packed my meager belongings in a pillowcase, and left.

It is in our very nature to have conflict. It is part of who we are, part of our life experience. What follows is a description of some selected elements of our nature that foster conflict.

Duality: From One Was Created Two—and Conflict Was Born

You roll the toothpaste tube from the bottom up in an orderly way; she squeezes it out, creating a mess. You install the toilet paper so it rolls from the top down. She installs it so it rolls from the bottom up. You like to leave the lights on when you leave a room; she turns them off. You want the heat to be low, saving money; she wants it to be warm and comfortable and turns the heat up. Who is right? And the argument begins.

In any relationship you can be sure there will be these two oppositional forces. If he says yes, she says no. If she says let's go out, he says let's stay at home. He wants to watch football; she wants to watch ice-skating. If he is a Democrat, she is a Republican. "We cancel out each other's votes!" she says. And the argument begins.

Duality, our way of dividing our reality into opposing or contrasting views, underlies and provides the context for all conflicts. The world we inhabit is replete with dualities. The most common ones that come to mind are hate and love, wrong and right, young and old, conservative and liberal (right and left), rich and poor, for and against, defense and offense, good and evil, worst and best. The environmentalist believes man is part of nature. The industrialist believes man has dominion over nature. Who is right?

In America, cultural and political groups clash at the juncture of two opposing forces: a desire for freedom (the frontier) and for order (civilization). On one side is a belief in the law of the jungle, on the other side the law of civilization. In the law of the jungle is a belief in the survival of the fittest (an eye for an eye, a tooth for a tooth), an evolutionary force. On the other side is the possibility of survival for all (turn the other cheek), also an evolutionary force. Which is right?

It is possible they both are, and it depends on the situation. But if we become ideologically frozen at both extremes, the law of the jungle wins.

Who designed this anyway?

It's the Creator's fault?

We could blame the Creator, starting with the creation story. Anyone who has read Genesis from the Old Testament knows about the creation story. The Creator began by creating the heavens and the earth—a duality. "Let there be light, and the light separated from the darkness." These were called day and night, another duality. The waters were separated from each other, creating the land and seas. Two lights were set in the sky and named the sun and the moon.

Then the Garden of Eden was created, a place in which were planted all manner of fruit trees. One of these was the tree of life; another was the tree of knowledge about good and evil. The Creator created a man in his likeness, and from man, woman. All these are dualities, a division of reality into opposite forces.

"Don't eat of the fruit of the tree of knowledge about good and evil," the Creator commanded. For if they did, they would have knowledge and awareness…and they would die. Of course, we all know what the first humans did. They did what we always do when told not to do something: they disobeyed. They ate the fruit of the tree and in so doing, became aware of both good and evil. This is the duality that would provide context for the life of humans from that point on.

Fearful that they would also eat of the fruit of the tree of life and be able to live forever, the Creator banished the man and woman from the Garden of Eden. As a result, they were sentenced to live a life knowing they would eventually die. Life and death—the most important duality of all.

Whether you believe it or not, the creation story is a wondrous allegory, filled with all sorts of hidden meanings that can be discovered, created, and explored. Certainly duality is one of these. And with it came conflict, opposing views, each seeking to be right, hoping to make the other wrong. Then came making a judgment, for one must be "good," the other "evil"! In the end, it is about winning, about being the one having the power, about survival of the fittest.

These days we seem to be confronted by the basic dualities:

- Man has dominion over nature versus man is part of nature.
- Survival of the fittest versus survival of all.
- And eye for an eye versus turn the other cheek.
- Frontier versus civilization.
- The individual versus the community.
- Freedom versus regulation.
- Fundamentalism versus secularism.

All of these indicate a struggle based on "either/or thinking." It must be this way or that way. None consider the possibility of "and" logic. So how can we meet all the needs? How can we re-create "oneness?"

And the Two Became One: An Anecdote

"Why does the tree in the center have a fork at the top?"

I ask this of my elder, Al, who was one of the leaders of the Sundance. I had been invited to attend the Intertribal Sundance and was filled with curiosity about the entire ritual. I had watched as a group of tribal people dragged a cottonwood tree into the center of the dance floor, where a hole had been dug into the earth. They grunted as they stood the tree up, and it slid down into the hole with a thud. Now they were filling the dirt in around the base of the tree, packing it strongly so it could withstand the pull of those dancing in the coming days.

I was curious as to why the top of the tree had a fork in it. Why would they not just have a straight pole? I was to find that, like the creation story, this pole had many meanings.

"It is about the opposing forces in life," Al said.

"Huh?" I was confused, didn't understand.

Al laughed at the response. "Life is filled with opposing forces," he said. "For example, man and woman are opposing forces, surely you know about that?" And he laughed again.

"So that represents male and female?"

"That is one way of looking at it," he said. "It also represents coyote, who is a trickster and teacher, representing man and the Creator. It represents the earth and sky, the sun and the moon, the traditional ways and changing ways, doing it your way or doing it my way. It represents all of the ways that we get in opposition with each other. These opposing forces are many.

"The understanding of the man is different than the understanding of the woman," he said. "The understanding of the eagle is different than the understanding of the buffalo. The understanding of a flower is different than the understanding of the grass. Not better, just different."

"So," I asked, "what is the value of that?"

"You are only seeing the two sides of the fork, is that the whole picture?" he asked.

"Oh," I said, "you mean it comes together with the trunk of the tree?"

"So, what is the meaning of that?"

"Hmmm. You are trying to make me think, aren't you?" I continued without waiting for his answer. "Well, the easiest way to explain it is the fork became one. Oh!" I said, as it came together in my own mind. "So the symbol is that while we are two, our purpose is to make one from that."

"Is that the end of the story?" he said as his eyes crinkled with laughter.

I looked at the Sundance pole and imagined the dance that was to take place in the next four days. American Indian warriors dancing in the heat without food and water, some of them connected to the Sundance pole by rawhide ropes, suffering for the good of all. Suffering to give thanks for the gifts from the Creator—of life and death, sun and moon, of male and female, of the animals on the ground and the birds in the sky, of the food freely given and shared with all.

"By creating two," I answered, "the Creator gave us the gift of difference, and difference creates our awareness. With that awareness, we can either create conflict from those differences, or we can create a common understanding and from that, oneness with the Creator, as with the tree. Like coyote, the two branches try to trick us into believing there is a right and wrong. The teacher wants us to learn a lesson that will lead us to oneness. How's that for deep philosophical thinking?"

"That's a start," he said, nodding his head. "So are you ready to dance? I'll tie you to the tree. You could learn more."

That brought me back to earth. "Right now, I think I'll just learn from here."

Al laughed.

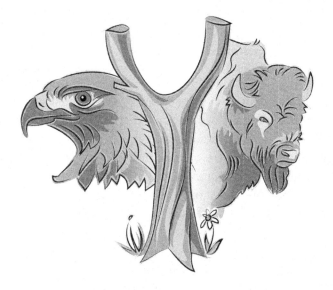

As a forester, I know this about trees: The food that is stored in the roots from the previous year rises to be distributed to the branches in the spring; it provides energy to grow the tree, to create the new branches and leaves (new dualities). Each leaf creates the food to grow the tree and to store later in the fall. In the fall, the food is accumulated as it is transferred down the stem, coming together in the roots to be stored for the next spring. But if I girdle the tree (remove the bark and underlying tissue in a ring around a tree trunk) and the forks do not allow that flow downward or upward, without that oneness, the tree will die.

As humans, our challenge is to create oneness from the duality.

"United We Stand, Divided we fall."

—**Patrick Henry**

Conflict and a Definition of Self

Underlying every conflict is our definition of self. We identify ourselves in many ways: our family of birth, our place of birth, our gender, our family traditions and culture, our religion, our racial makeup, the schools we went to, the number of higher degrees we have, the professions we are in, our sexual orientation, the job assignments we have. All of these we use to define our "persona."

> Persona: the aspect of a person's character that is presented to or perceived by others.

We are raised in our own unique family environments, encompassing place, religion, ethnicity, and occupation. Each of these qualities has its own cultural values and beliefs. The culture, beliefs, and values of a farmer are different from those of a mill worker, a military officer, a priest, or a politician. Each would raise a family with his or her unique outlook on life, steeped in his or her own social or religious beliefs.

We define ourselves by these qualities. They become our persona. They establish our character. They are not choices we made, we are born into them. For the most part, we accept them without question. I repeat that: They are not choices we made, we are born into them.

Ask people, "Who are you?" and these are the qualities they will use to describe themselves. "Hi! I'm Bob Chadwick, just came from New Hampshire to work as a forester here. Yep, I'm a graduate of the School of Forestry there in New Hampshire. Oh, us Yankees tend to be reserved, yet outspoken. Nope, not a Republican, but a Catholic Democrat. Married, have seven kids. Yeah, they're quite a bunch—they'll fill up your school."

Others also define us by their perception of our persona and their reaction to it. Others have stereotypes for each of the qualities we disclose. These are often wrong, often based on hearsay or past negative experiences they had with a representative of the group. They respond to us out of those unspoken stereotypes. Their description of our persona differs from ours: "Yeah, I just met Bob. He's one of those 'know it all' Easterners. An educated guy, one of those book learners. Probably never been on the ground. Should be fun training him, if he is trainable. Yeah, he does have a mouth on him. Doesn't know when to keep his opinions to himself. Just like all those other liberal do-gooders. Doesn't understand about birth control, trying to fill the world with Catholics."

Then, of course, the others have their persona, for which we have our stereotypes. Our responses to them are based on our negative descriptions or experiences.

If anyone attempts to challenge these persona qualities or threaten them, we feel duty-bound to defend them. It is a question of loyalty, not fact. We have loyalty to family values and beliefs, loyalty to our religious beliefs, our Bachelor of Science forestry beliefs. We define ourselves by these qualities; to question them is to question who we are. If someone imposes a stereotyped response to our persona, we are offended and feel misunderstood. We feel a direct challenge to our loyalties, our persona, and our sense of self.

Conflict, then, is often not a matter of personal survival, but of "persona" survival. If anyone threatens these qualities, our persona is threatened. Any threat to these is a threat to our "self." It creates conflict.

But let's face it, the persona hardly describes us. It is something we inherited, limited by the environment we grew up in and over which we had little say. We accept these personas as they are given to us, putting them on like jackets, covering our essential or authentic being. We develop a personality, a character based on these jackets. They are reinforced by those around us who love us and describe us. "Yes, he is a loving child, but so whiney," or, "He is so aggressive, just doesn't think of others."

In each stage of life, in each role you play, these expectations are imposed on you, until you are truly "jacketed." What others put on you, plus what you begin with, will all define you.

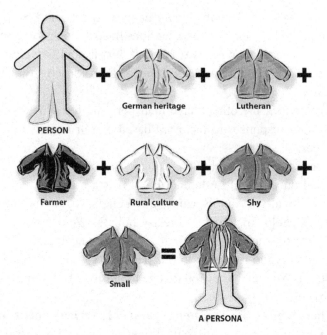

From person to persona.

There are two definitions of *character* that apply here: "The qualities distinctive to an individual" applies appropriately to our own unique, not-yet-realized character. The other, a "part played by an actor," properly defines the qualities of character we inherit as a result of birth. They are roles we are given and that we mostly accept.

In some instances we may rebel against these personas, not wanting to be described by outside forces. We reject them and choose an oppositional stance. We create **duality.** When we are in conflict with our parents, our culture, and others, we are doubling our jackets, with one role we reject but that is continually forced on us by others, and the oppositional one we chose as resistance. We have an interpersonal conflict with the external forces and a personal conflict as we try to internally resolve the difference between the imposed persona and our authentic self.

So, if my parents are strong Baptists and I become oppositional to that, I might choose to be a Buddhist just to establish myself as different from my parents. My parents and I then conflict over those decisions and views. And I am also conflicted internally about it.

A personal conflict between expectations.

Eventually we are faced with resolving these personal and interpersonal persona conflicts. There are three key times when we are afforded this opportunity: the terrible twos, the teen years, and our midlife crisis.

1. The terrible twos: This time is an opportunity for children to begin to express their will, to express who they are. It is also a time when parents hold their children to the boundaries required by their culture or their upbringing. It is necessary to protect inexperienced children in a dangerous world. The parents and their boundaries provide an environment of safety and security for children, a certainty and stability to grow with. They provide an environment of belonging to something, being accepted because they represent sameness, being loved because of that.

Children, however, want their autonomy, even though they are not prepared for it. They have choices: either accept and give in to the boundaries *(flight)* or rebel *(fight)*. If parents respond too harshly, this rebellion is just stuffed down into children, waiting to be free. Just waiting for the second chance: the teen years.

2. The teen years: As teenagers we are required, hardwired, chemically altered, to differentiate from our parents. This is an opportunity to decide who we are, separate from them and what they represent. It is a time of making our choices, learning about who we really are.

Unfortunately, this frightens the parents and other adults; they assume the child has "gone wrong." Their fear is twofold: without the boundaries, without their protection, the child will die; and "what will the others think of us?"

The need to increase control to bring the teenager "in line" leads to awful conflicts. It is a time of great fear and misunderstanding between adults and teenagers. The adults who have helped to acculturate the child feel they have failed in some great way. Few understand this is a natural process.

We all know that a teenager is changed physically and chemically, a preparation for adulthood. This stage in their development compels them to make choices that allow them to become the individual they really are, to become the masters of their own destiny. The psychiatrist Carl Jung named this goal of human development "individuation." It is a process of becoming fully aware of oneself through the different stages of our life, to become self realized.

Attempting to control the teenager prevents them from cutting the "apron strings" with the adult causing them to be tied to their parents, their family or clan for the rest of their life. They are still hindered by the values and expectations of others, never truly learning to think for themselves, never "stepping out of the box" they are in. They will fail to develop and become fully human, fully themselves. Managed by their fears they follow the crowd, never becoming a true individual.

Our purpose in life is to "individuate" to become an individual, compelled to be unique and different.

Teenagers will often choose an opposite persona to that of the parents or adults. From this vantage point, teenagers can, with understanding and support, decide for themselves which jackets fit and which don't. They can only do this by having life experiences. They must do it, understanding the fear it creates in those closest to them. Surprisingly, as teenagers move toward adulthood, they will choose many jackets from the original persona. But it is their choice, it is who they are…for the present. They are seeking to portray their *qualities distinctive to an individual.* They seek to be authentic. They have only a lifetime to do it in.

3. Midlife crisis: As teenagers grow through adulthood to their forties, another shift in perception occurs. Suddenly, they are aware of an emotional change. They are aware of mortality: a sense of impermanence, that time is short. They become aware of physical and mental challenges. They feel "over the hill." These birthdays are filled with black balloons and gallows humor.

At this stage we find ourselves assessing our life and how we are spending our precious and limited time. Most are disappointed with what life has given us. The personas we have lived with so well suddenly seem out of touch with who we really are. We want to finally find out who we really are. We want to individuate, to be unique and different, and to be accepted for that.

It is a difficult, confusing, and chaotic time, one of personal and interpersonal conflicts that are often not resolved, or if they are, often result in hurtful separation from those we love. We may change careers, change spouses, change our beliefs. Unfortunately, it often happens at the time our children are teenagers—who are also finding out who they are!

Who designed all this anyway?

This issue of self underlies all conflicts. Take twenty employees coming together to make a critical and difficult decision, each with his or her own persona well defined. As soon as their differences are expressed, this issue of self will underlie all the discussions. If I believe something to be true and you have an opposite belief, we are threatening to each other. If there is the imposition of power, everything changes.

It is not conflict if you disagree with me on how to accomplish the job I was assigned, as long as you let me do it my way. But if you require I do it your way and I believe that way to be wrong, it diminishes me; it is a direct assault on who I believe I am.

> *"We are interfering with our customs and lifestyle, our values. We question the need to learn about other beliefs and ways of doing things."*
>
> **—Workshop participant**

We are now in conflict—not over the issue, but over the underlying beliefs and values of each person. We tighten up and defend those jackets we are wearing. Loyalty and pride prevail. The issue fades into the background, serving merely as a focal point for the persona struggle.

"I want things my way and I don't want to argue about it."

—**Workshop participant**

Our persona is necessary in a dangerous world. Understand that the process of imposing personas on the child from the moment of birth is not wrong. It is necessary to protect the inexperienced child in a dangerous world. Boundaries provide an environment of safety and security for the child, a certainty and stability to grow with. They provide an environment of belonging to something, being accepted because they represent sameness, being loved because of that.

These personas provide a needed foundation of beliefs, behaviors, and values that people, as they age, can become aware of and assess and move beyond toward their authenticity.

Conflict provides the opportunities to become authentic. Most of the above is based on my many experiences and observations with thousands of people in dozens of cultures. Many books I have read validate the basics of this. But few refer to the impact of the persona on creating conflict. Few understand the value of conflict in helping people create who they really are.

Resolving your conflicts will cause you to remove those persona jackets that are not who you are authentically. You do not become less from this. Instead, you become aware of the infinite potential of your being, of the ability to set your own persona, respecting the impact on others.

I have tried to create a framework for understanding how our personas cause many personal and interpersonal conflicts. You will go beyond that to experience and learn how conflict creates an opportunity in which all our differences are exposed to the light of day, available to be reassessed in the present situation. It is a time of learning who you really are. It is a time of being able to make conscious choices.

I believe that any conflict resolution process must incorporate the impact of the persona and create an environment in which the jackets' value can be assessed and a choice made: "Is this really me?"

Don't Just Do Something, Stand There!

To sit back hoping that someday, someway, someone will make things right is to go on feeding the crocodile, hoping he will eat you last—but eat you he will."

—**Ronald Reagan**

A culture of avoidance: In my generation and my parents' generation, we were taught to avoid causing or confronting conflict. If we did, it was dealt with immediately—not to resolve it, but to put you in your place. It was a time of domination by men, subordination of women and children. It was a time of subjugation of minorities: poor people, immigrants, African Americans, Hispanics, Asians, and so forth. We knew our place.

These are some of the admonitions of my day:

"Children should be seen and not heard." The message was, "Don't do or say anything that will upset the adults." We were to be invisible. If we broke this admonition, punishment was quick and sometimes abusive. *"Don't rock the boat"* and *"Do what you're told."* This is the law of the industrial revolution. Questions were not encouraged; if you asked one, the answer was, *"Because I said so!"* We were expected to just follow orders. If we didn't follow orders, we didn't have a job!

"We have always done it this way." Any suggestion that an improvement could be made resulted in this answer. This is the law of an unchanging and static culture. We have done it this way in the past, and we will do it this way in the future. Everything was "tried and true." Therefore, conflict does not exist.

"Respect your elders." This meant that anyone older than you could tell you what to do, where to go, and how to get there, often in the meanest, nastiest ways possible. And you had to grin and bear it. They could tell you what to do and then do the opposite, and you had to accept it. This hypocrisy was confusing, and impatience with this attitude probably led to the cultural changes of the late 1960s.

"Don't be a tattletale (snitch)." If someone did something wrong or hurt you or treated you with disrespect, you couldn't say anything about it. You had to hold it in, grit your teeth; otherwise you were a snitch. This is still operative in schools and workplaces.

"If you can't say anything nice, don't say anything at all." I remember this being repeated in my home, in my presence, almost as if it were one of the

Ten Commandments. It required you to swallow your anger, your hurt; to act as if it didn't matter. You had to be insincere, fake.

"Know your place." This was often said to those who were subordinate, especially if you were female, poor, uneducated, or a minority with little social status. We were not allowed to speak, to take the spotlight, to be asking questions. We had to know our place.

A culture of confrontation: All of these relationships, rules, and admonitions changed during my children's school years in the 1970s. Their generation experienced the **countercultural revolution,** a young people's movement that swept this country in the '60s and early '70s. Although it occurred during the time of the Civil Rights Movement and the resistance to the Vietnam War, these were not the root causes of the rebellion.

Young, well-educated, and socially privileged children rebelled against the hypocrisy of the Victorian era and conservative social norms and values of earlier generations. They rebelled against white male dominance. They broke down barriers for women, minorities of all colors and races, the disabled, the poor, and immigrants. They rejected the hypocrisy of the adults' *"do as I say and not as I do."* They took a stand for equality. They took a stand for honesty and truth.

In doing this, they overturned all of the rules of the game:

- *"If you can't say anything nice, don't say anything at all"* became *"Tell it like it is!"*
- *"Children should be seen and not heard"* became *"I and my children, will be seen and heard."*
- *"Don't rock the boat"* and *"Know your place"* became *"Challenge authority!"* and *"Think outside the box."*
- *"Respect your elders"* became *"Don't trust anyone over thirty."*
- *"Do what you're told"* became *"If it feels good, do it!"* or *"Do your own thing!"*
- *"Don't be a tattletale"* became *"Become a whistle-blower."*
- *"If it ain't broke, don't fix it!"* became *"If it ain't broke, break it!"*

The most impactful changed value was: *"Do your own thing!"* These new, untested cultural values were about exploration, experimentation, and change. The boundaries and values imposed externally were rejected in favor of those experienced and developed from inside the person.

Social anthropologist Jentri Anders, based in California, has observed that a number of freedoms were endorsed within a countercultural community that she lived in and studied: "freedom to explore one's potential, freedom to create one's Self, freedom of personal expression, freedom from scheduling, freedom from rigidly defined roles and hierarchical statuses" (*Wikipedia's* "Counterculture" entry).

Nothing was sacred; everything would be challenged. And change happened as a result.

Except for conflict. It has become more intense. What this counterculture generation did was to set up lines of confrontation between those in power and those empowering themselves that still exist to this day. It was and is a generational culture war.

A culture of polarization—the culture wars: The movement toward more liberalism on the left created a countermovement toward fundamentalism on the right. Power in relationships will always be equalized in some manner. In situations where people are polarized like this, there can be no middle ground. You are for one side or the other. *"If you are not with us, then you are against us."* If you do choose a side, then loyalty to the cause is a prerequisite; truth is not.

It led to the "culture wars" we experience today. Ideologues—*"a person who follows an ideology in a dogmatic or uncompromising way"*—on both sides stand up for their righteous beliefs. Labeling people because of their beliefs continues and perhaps increases! Not exactly a good formula for resolution, collaboration, or consensus. Not exactly a good formula for what we call "democracy."

When the youth said, *"Challenge authority,"* and did it, they did not add the words *"and get their support."* When they cried, *"Tell it like it is,"* they did not add the words *"with respect for others."* When the cry was *"Do your own thing,"* they did not add *"and recognize how it impacts others."* Like the previous cultural norms, these were one-sided, without recognition of the impact on others. This is not intended as a criticism—it is my observation.

So how do we reconcile what is polarized and polarizing? How do we resolve the differences we have with others we have impacted? The answer is pretty much the same: we often don't. We don't know how, especially now that everything has changed. There has to be a way to overcome this.

When I describe my generational norms to my grandchildren, they look at me with a puzzled face. They wonder if I'm "off my meds." They were raised by my children, who challenged me during the '70s and changed my whole perspective on life. Yet this change only happened after I listened and tried to understand their point of view.

The lack of a process: I am not surprised that people have conflict in their work lives and personal lives. What surprises me is that they settle for it. The reason they do is simply expressed:

"I feel anger, frustration with the lack of a process to resolve the conflicts."

—**Workshop participant**

People feel they don't know how to do it. There is no process to deal with this—and so they tuck away the issues and emotions of these unresolved conflicts in their minds or in parts of their body as stress. If you can't resolve it, then act as if it is not there, even if you know it is. Makes them feel crazy at times.

It is not just about process, though. There are many processes presented in books, magazines, on TV, in education. Lots of consultants make their living writing about this. But people learn these processes in environments that are free of the conflict. It is abstract. Once they are back in that conflicting environment—

"Forget about it! No way am I going to be the one to take the risk!"

—**Workshop participant**

End of new process!

I've learned there are two main reasons people avoid taking the risk of confronting and resolving their conflicts:

1. *Fear!* People fear the possible negative consequences of confronting their unresolved conflicts, and there is currently no process that overcomes that fear.
2. The devil we know is safer than the devil we don't know. What we have may be bad, but the imagination makes everything else look worse. So we accept toxic living environments as natural.

There is a way. If you are one of those who resonate with the above statements, know that you are not alone. Lots of us are living in toxic environments of hostility and fear, filling our lives with stress. We are avoiding the conflict and settling for the stress. The question is: "Do you want to do something about it?"

I wish I'd had just a glimmer of hope when I was three or ten or twenty, forty, fifty...but I didn't. I knew there had to be a way, a better way. But it took me a lot of time to learn how. Because of thousands of people who took the risk and addressed and resolved their conflicts, I know now it is possible.

To be successful, the new process must be able to overcome or balance the fear with hope—enough hope to take the risk. It must result in environments that are safe, accepting, affirming, creative, joyous, stress free. To achieve that, you can't just talk about it, you have to do it, experience it! I have learned that people must experience the process in real time, on a real conflict, and learn the approach while doing so.

> It must be applicable to personal, interpersonal, and intergroup conflicts.

Do you want to create conflict-resolving, stress-reducing, joyous, creative, productive, loving, caring environments? Then continue reading. That is what we are about to do.

The Arenas of Conflict

Conflicts are diverse in nature and come in many forms, shapes, and sizes. Conflict within and among human beings occurs in three different arenas: *personal, interpersonal, and intergroup*. A person can get into conflict with other elements, such as the environment or other living or nonliving entities. This book is intended, however, to focus on the conflicts between human beings.

Whichever process is used to resolve and reach consensus, it must work in the three arenas.

Personal Conflicts

Personal conflicts are the disagreements you have internally, with yourself. You are confronting yourself with two or more opposing choices and can't decide what to do. Often, you are considering a choice that violates one of your own beliefs, values, traditions, or philosophies given to you as a child. At times the conflict is so intense it feels like you are warring with yourself. These conflicts are circular; you go round and round in your mind, continuously picking at them until it becomes a repeating loop you just want to get rid of.

Earlier I said, "We are all raised in our own unique family environments, encompassing place, religion, ethnicity, and occupation. Each of these has its own cultural values and beliefs. The beliefs and values of a farmer are different from those of a mill worker or a politician. Each would raise a family with unique beliefs and values."

Once you get out into the world, your values come in contact with the beliefs and values of others. They might be people who are important to you and yet who differ with you. They might be a friend, spouse, or coworker. They cause uncertainty and ambiguity in you through your debates with each other. The result is that you have to debate within yourself about what is right. Or you may have a decision to make that involves another, and you have a choice to do what is right for you or what is right for her. If you are a pleaser, you decide to meet her needs and then feel in conflict about what you have lost as a result. If you are a fighter, you will take care of your needs to the exclusion of hers and then feel somewhat guilty about having done so. These conflicts will continue in your mind until you have resolved them.

Perhaps you are tempting yourself to do something outside your values system, such as lying or cheating or stealing, committing adultery, missing church. All of these have a cultural penalty if you are caught. Yet the desire exists to put aside your best intentions and experience the temptation of the given moment. It feels easier. What do you do? Until you resolve this issue, it will remain as a personal conflict.

- *"Should I ask her to marry me or end the relationship?"*
- *"Should I buy the stove that costs more than I can afford but has all those do-dads, or do I get the one I can afford but can only do the basic cooking?"*

Personal conflicts often end up becoming interpersonal ones. While the debate about which way to go is going on in my mind, another person comes to me with a proposal to go in one of the directions. This often immediately causes me to choose the opposite direction, to create a duality. Now I have transferred the argument in my mind to another person. But it is still unresolved. I am now arguing with a surrogate. The following anecdote demonstrates this.

That Red Dodge Devil Saves Me from Myself: An Anecdote

You are the husband in the family room, watching your favorite team play football. During the commercial break, after you get a fresh brew, you see the commercial for the new red Dodge Ram pickup full cab with megabeam suspension, a double cab large enough for a small village, an acre of space in the bed, four-wheel drive, and a HEMI engine that can crawl up a tree or climb Mount Everest.

WOW! Your eyes bulge, your heart aches with wanting, your soul expands with new understandings about life. You feel HEMI envy, Ram envy, and your soul aching for the upward move in the "pecking order" this would give you with other males.

I should buy that, you think. *I deserve to buy that, to have that in my life.*

But, you say to yourself, *where would you ever get the money?*

Well...that is always the problem. Hmmm...there is the money Sally has been saving for our delayed honeymoon trip to Hawaii.

Yeah, but she would never agree to that. You know how long she has waited for this, and you did agree to the arrangement.

Well, yes, but everything needs to be reconsidered once in a while, doesn't it? Maybe we could go on a honeymoon in our new Dodge Ram HEMI pickup, like up into the wilderness, sleeping in the roomy cab.

Riiight! Like she would go along with that.

Hey! What's wrong with the idea? I mean, I'm the breadwinner, the one who works long hours to feed my family. It's my money she's saving. Why don't I get to decide what to do with it?

Well, you know how she feels about that. She gave up her career to marry you and have those two great kids. Her work is at home, she works hard in the kitchen, doing laundry, picking up your clothes, et cetera, et cetera, et cetera...

Yeah right! But that doesn't even begin to compare to my life at work with those dingbats who can't think for themselves. I need something that feels like a reward to me. **This is it!**

It may feel like it, but can you convince Sally of that?

Don't you worry...

Just then Sally comes in to the room.

"Hey, sweetheart, look at that commercial on the TV before it ends. Isn't that some kind of truck!? I mean, I know how you like a good rugged man, why not have a rugged truck to go along with him?"

"Are you serious?" Sally says. "What do we need a truck like that for?"

"Because we deserve it. Think of all the long hours we work to keep this family running. We could use it to go camping in the hills."

"But," Sally asks, somewhat shocked at the idea, "where would we get the money for such a thing?"

"We could use that money we have been saving. I'll bet we could almost pay it off."

"You mean the **honeymoon** money?!"

(Oh-oh, you thought you could handle this?) "Yeah, we are saving it for us, aren't we?"

"But I have waited so long to have that honeymoon! And you agreed to it!"

"Well, I have waited just as long or longer for this truck. Besides, it's my money we are saving."

"Your money! **Your money**? What happened to WE?! What happened to my giving up MY career to raise these kids of yours?"

"**My** kids! When did they become my kids? I thought we shared in this marriage. Why can't we share the money on this truck? The backseat could take two more kids than we have now."

Well, you get the idea. All you have done is transfer a side of the argument in your mind to your spouse. Now all you have to do is to defend one point of view, while the other—the wrong view—is your spouse's. And you lose control of the environment in which it is argued. You have just created an interpersonal conflict.

> Personal conflicts often end up becoming interpersonal ones.

I believe that most of my conflicts, probably 90 percent of them, are in my own mind. I am arguing with myself about some choices I need to make. The interesting thing about this arena is that I control the entire environment. If I can resolve these issues, it often reduces the interpersonal conflicts I will have. But I need a process to do that. The personal process you experienced earlier in the book is that process. You will experience this again later in the book.

Interpersonal Conflicts

Interpersonal conflicts occur with another person: a spouse, coworker, peer, clerk, and so on. These often occur as a result of an unresolved personal conflict. At times they occur unexpectedly, before you have had time to consider, resulting in you only reacting.

Maybe as a "flighter," you have always done what another person wanted. This keeps the other person happy, but the conflict about doing what you want is still unresolved in your mind.

Maybe you decide to change: you've had enough of being bossed around by the other person and you've decided to "stand your ground." This will surprise the other person, who will then feel it necessary to push back a little harder. When you push back at the other person, your power is being applied. The other person pushes back, with a power struggle ensuing. You are now in a linear relationship, an either/or relationship. There is only one right answer, and it must be decided with power. So you push, trying to win. This is how it's different from personal conflicts. In your personal dialogue, you are trying to decide for yourself. Once it is with another person, you are trying to win.

Interpersonal conflicts tie up your energy. Each time you see the person you are in a struggle with, your entire being is startled. Your whole being jumps; you are filled with adrenaline. You turn and walk away fast, not wanting to get into that struggle again. Or you move into it, confronting it, being adrenalized again.

Sometimes the other person has enough power that the decision or direction goes their way, and you are required to follow it. That does not mean the conflict is over. Often you will be rankled by the decision. Your commitment is shallow, your attention weak. You still argue with the person in your own mind, which means the other now has taken residence there.

Or you may get to an impasse because your power is equal. Neither of you can get the decision to go your way unless you can get others to support you. You have equal energy, so no movement is possible. When this happens, you seek support from others in the hope of overpowering your rival. Then you are moving toward creating an intergroup conflict.

> Interpersonal conflicts often transition into intergroup conflicts, especially if the pairs are at an impasse.

Intergroup Conflicts

Intergroup conflicts are those that occur between groups that have different approaches, beliefs, philosophies. They often begin with two individuals who are at an interpersonal-conflict impasse. Each person reaches out to friends for support, whining about how unfair the other person is, passing it off as a moral or legal imperative, wanting support from those friends.

Those who are approached must decide if they want to support their friend out of loyalty, common cause, morality, or legality. These decisions are often made hastily, without any thought. Once aboard, they are expected to become part of a "groupthink."

> Groupthink...is the mode of thinking that happens when the desire for harmony in a decision-making group overrides a realistic appraisal of alternatives. Group members try to minimize conflict and reach a consensus decision without critical evaluation of alternative ideas or viewpoints. *(Wikipedia)*

To keep their groupthink, they must meet often and long, repeating their rationalizations, checking for loyalty, brainwashing each other to make the same specific statements supporting their cause.

We now have two or more groups in conflict, pushing and shoving against each other to gain some advantage, to win.

When interviewing clients before a workshop, I often ask when their conflict began. Frequently, it was as long as twenty years ago. I ask how or who started the conflict. It was often two people who had differing opinions about a subject or activity. These are the people I can go to and get the original conflict information. Sometimes they are no longer there, having left for greener pastures. Yet, their conflict still lives on in those they leave behind.

In other circumstances, groups are already formed and primed to conflict over specific issues, such as the environment, zoning, land-use plans, and so on. These are different in that a special-interest group is prepared for the fight. They behave with the same "groupthink" rules described above.

In this book, you will be experiencing a three-day workshop where we are dealing with an intergroup conflict, one that also has many interpersonal conflicts.

The Generators of Conflict

After ten years or so of working with groups from all over the world, it became apparent that other causes than just our "persona" generate conflict. These are mostly the result of interacting with our environment and each other. We are often the major causal agents for these generators: rapid change, perceived scarcity, power struggles, increasing diversity, and incivility. Often all of these exist in some form in the situation I am working with. At other times, only one is present.

If these generators are present, but only as an underlying element of the conflict, the basic process described in this book is designed in the way that will resolve the conflict if the process is implemented appropriately.

If any of the generators are present in a form that requires a "transformational shift" or "paradigm shift," then the basic process is adapted to more specifically deal with that issue. This adaptation requires modified questions, tasks, different insights, and visual activities specific to that conflict generator. This book is not intended to deal with all the generators at that level. Each generator requires a book of its own. Hopefully, the success of this book will result in that happening.

I do want to provide a brief overview of these generators.

Rapid Change

"Certainty? In this world nothing is certain but death and taxes."

—Benjamin Franklin

In today's world, nothing is certain but death, taxes, *and* change. Paradoxical as it may sound, change is a constant in our environment. And change is changing. It occurs at ever-increasing rates. We are confronted with rapid change in almost every aspect of our life.

To illustrate this, I Googled the words "rapid change" and came up with 12,700,000 results. Areas cited are in architecture, computers (no surprise there), climate, politics, engineering, infectious diseases, maps, medicine, therapy, forest management, landscapes, capital markets...et cetera. Need I go further?

And...change has become transformative. It is no longer about modifying the situation, but about altering our basic worldviews, beliefs, and behaviors. It requires paradigm shifts.

Our natural response to change is to resist it. We are genetically driven to protect our existing patterns of thought and behavior. We justify our resistance by diminishing the proposed change: *"It is just change for change's sake."* We apply this belief even when the need for change is evident and obvious. But, for the part of our brain that resists change, *"The devil we know is safer than the devil we don't know."* So...resist the change.

The basic process presented in this book is modified slightly to help people move through the conflicts of change. Additional "right questions" are asked, and additional verbal or visual insights are provided. Participants experience the change process from both a logical and emotional framework. They create a common purpose for the change, new beliefs and behaviors, and then act to make the change meet those purposes.

It has always worked.

"When you're finished changing, you're finished."

—Benjamin Franklin

Perceived Scarcity

Perceived scarcity creates fear in the hearts of all those who experience it. The notion of scarcity puts people into a survival mode, a "survival of the fittest" mentality.

The automatic response to perceived scarcity is to "eliminate." Activities and resources are prioritized. Each of these reflects a diminishing mind-set. Those who must prioritize or eliminate are doing all they can to justify their own positions, their own projects, while denying the validity of others. It sets people in the community or organization or family against each other. It destroys community. It allows us to be manipulated by others.

There is another way of responding. All biological organisms will eventually replicate until they have filled their environmental space. Then they have the choice of reproducing less, eating their young, or adapting.

Adapting may not mean cutting back; it may mean growing, but in a different direction. As a rancher's wife told me when she learned that another person was coming to dinner, *"Well, I can't make my pie plate bigger, but I can make the pie deeper."* She just moved off into another dimension.

It is possible to agree to accomplish all the desired tasks even if the "funds" are not available. It is possible to move from "either/or" thinking to "and" logic, where the focus is on finding resources (human, emotional, and intellectual) not acknowledged before.

What allows this to happen is the development of a common purpose for all. A consensus. When people are focused on and committed to a common purpose, they find resources where they were not seen before. Each person recognizes they have an "essential" role in this. If we know that our purpose is to ensure that everyone survives, our perceptions of the environment around us change. We see resources that were unrecognized before. We see value in employees that were not recognized before.

Managing this focus introduces the participant to the skills, attitudes, and understanding needed to manage the behaviors and conflicts resulting from moving from an environment of plenty to one of scarcity. The participants learn to help others recognize and acknowledge the behaviors that result from scarcity and to create an awareness of the inherent richness in their environment that allows others to move from their worst fears to identifying and affirming the common best outcomes they want. It is this commitment to a common purpose that allows them to accomplish all the desired tasks.

"Our real scarcity is in the way we think!"

—Workshop participant

Power Struggles

Nothing makes people more uncomfortable than the management of the power struggles that exist in every environment. The subject is often too threatening and intimidating to even confront. It is more likely to be avoided. People don't even like the word. Yet this basic instinct to influence the environment in our own behalf lies behind many conflicts.

"Power is used a lot, I don't like this word."

—Workshop participant

In confronting conflicts of power, the participants must recognize their own needs—and others' needs—for power and control over each other and over their environments. The relationship between personal power and positional power must be understood and managed.

When managing the conflicts power struggles initiate, the basic process must be adapted. It requires additional and specific verbal and visual insights that help participants recognize the movement of power within their environment.

In the 1970s a major shift in power occurred with the empowerment of minorities, women, disabled people, gay people, American Indians, and so on. A movement from representative democracy to participative democracy occurred. The educated electorate would no longer allow the elected official to make the decision unless they were part of the decision-making process. The notion of shared, or participative, decision making was introduced.

Those who held the power are understandably reluctant to let go of it. An environment of scarcity aggravates the problem as special-interest groups vie for limited resources. Elected officials work best when they can distribute unlimited resources, putting them in a position of power. Their power is diminished when they must decide who gets a piece of a smaller pie.

The participants learn how to apply the consensus process so that participative decision making actually strengthens representative democracy and representative decision making. The participants learn how to apply this to the business climate, as well as to public interest situations.

Increasing Diversity

Difference (or diversity) exists in all areas of our environment and is a consistent, underlying generator of conflict. By our very nature, we are all "different." Differences exist not only in race, religion, sexual orientation, gender, age, mental and physical ability, but also in beliefs, values, and information base, as well as profession, organization, and role, and so on.

Difference is a basic underlying cause of all conflicts. If we did away magically with all persona conflicts and the other generators of conflict, difference would quickly reestablish conflict again. This is because we believe our perception of the world to be the right one.

"I want things my way and I don't want to argue about it."

—Workshop participant

In situations where the conflict revolves around diversity, I have participants explore sameness and difference:

- "What are the benefits of sameness?"
- "What are your concerns about difference?"

Their answers for sameness can be summarized in one word: *safety*.

> *"Sameness makes it comfortable. We are not afraid of meeting each other, there is a feeling of safety."*
>
> —**Workshop participant**

Their answers for difference can be summarized in one word: *fear!*

> *"Fear, because a core value is being challenged, that you may have to change, or have to question self. You may lose something that is a part of yourself."*
>
> —**Workshop participant**

By the very nature of being human, we are all different. We create different societies and cultures and religions. Each has different beliefs, behaviors, values. People tend to seek that which is like them, and avoid that which is different. When confronted with that difference, we are set up for conflict. And we don't always have a way to deal with it.

Our country is paradoxical. We say:

> *"Give me your tired, your poor, your huddled masses yearning to breathe free, The wretched refuse of your teeming shore. Send these, the homeless, tempest-tossed, to me: I lift my lamp beside the golden door."*—Emma Lazarus, "
>
> —**The New Colossus"**

We are a nation of immigrants. We are purposely creating a multicultural, multiethnic, multigender, multireligious society. But we want them to be part of the "melting pot" so we can be one people. We take all the diverse immigrants who come to us like varied ingredients for beef stew, put them in the "melting pot," and expect the outcome to be…potato soup, where everyone becomes the same. We want one culture, one language, one set of values, one religious view.

It's not gonna happen, because the '70s changed that expectation. We do want to be one people, but we also want to honor our birth culture and heritage. We want to be diverse, different, and accepted for that. We want to celebrate our different religious holidays, our different cultural and historical holidays. People of diversity are not satisfied with being tolerated. They want to be part of the stew.

They want acceptance! We all want acceptance for who we are.

In bringing a community of interest together, we ensure diversity by including a number of representatives from different cultural, professional, and interest groups. We purposely seek diversity of gender, sexual orientation, race, age, religion, and position. We seek to include the most disenfranchised, the most radical views, and the least understood people.

Each step in the process is intended to create acceptance of the strengths inherent in diversity. Each specific decision for "inclusion" expands the diversity and viewpoints of the group to get closer to the "truth." The experience helps others understand that it takes no more time to include "difference" in the discussion, that it adds richness to the knowledge base. It provides the basis for consensus solutions.

Incivility

"There is a lack of a common set of values today." "There is a breakdown of responsibility, with people thinking only of themselves." "There is no respect for others and self, as a result."

—Workshop participants

These statements are from a group exploring civility in the workplace. They express the loss of common values, standards of behavior, or civility in personal relationships, families, the community, and the workplace.

The loss of civility began with the introduction of "New Age" thinking in the late 1960s that openly condemned and shattered the then-current Victorian and conservative standards for civil behavior and did not provide new civil standards to replace them. Instead, the guiding principles were and are:

"Tell it like it is! Challenge authority! Do your own thing!"

No one added, *"with respect"*! None of these new directives indicated a need for respect, and they invited incivility into the discourse. Today, unbelievably, open rudeness is an admired quality. It is a staple of polarized politics, of discourse in the media, in the family, at work, in the community.

Our current polarization of views about our cultural values encourages incivility. When we see others in our conflicts as the "enemy" (adversary), it is easy to justify our disrespectful behavior toward them. This encourages hostile relationships in our environments.

Incivility is rampant in all areas of society. It seems we are competing to see how far we can push the boundaries of uncivil behavior. This leads to cries for more discipline in the home, community, workplace, and education system.

Incivility creates conflict. Conflict, in turn, creates an environment in which incivility can flourish. It is a vicious cycle. Civilization starts with the word "civil." I believe that everyone craves civility—not one that is imposed on them, but one they create for themselves, for their unique situation. (This is key!) And, paradoxically, when angry, they want an environment in which to be uncivil, with people who understand them and with an approach that will move them to becoming civil. Without this, civility becomes a false front.

This workshop module helps participants identify the standards of behavior that are valued by the affected community. The behaviors that represent these values are explored and agreed upon. But the final—and key—issue is creating the willingness of the community members to hold each other accountable for their behaviors.

~6~

A Personal Experience of the Process

Exploring Personal Conflict: A Learning Activity

The best way to learn the *finding new ground* process is to experience it in a situation that is personal to you. This chapter will help you do that. I am assuming, since you are reading this book, that you have an interest in, or a difficulty with, addressing and resolving conflicts. They probably cause you some continuing pain. You would like that pain to go away—without much effort, if possible. As you experience this book, you will get some idea of how to do that.

Thus it is best if you explore, with some awareness of your own life situation, how you can address a personal situation successfully. As you read further, you can connect the process to your own perceptions and emotions.

You may also be interested in facilitating others to resolve their personal conflicts. If so, this process can be used to do that. Experiencing it now for yourself will help you understand how and why it works.

In the following chapters, I will use an intergroup experience to help you understand the process of building consensus. This will be especially helpful to those choosing to facilitate conflict resolution. But right now we are going to focus on exploring the idea of conflict and the ramifications it has on your personal life.

The most important way to develop or build consensus is to ask the **RIGHT** questions. The consensus process has been designed to provide you with these *right* questions. Try it now.

Begin by finding a place you can be alone for a while. It helps to write this activity down, so bring some paper and a pencil with you. (I use three-by-five index cards.) This will help you capture your thoughts and feelings.

You will bring your unresolved conflicts into the open where you can see them. You will be amazed how much that will help you. By making them visible, you will be acknowledging to yourself that these conflicts really do exist so you can get over denying them.

This process will appear simple to you. It is—on the surface. But it is rich in its impacts, its underlying complexity. It is this complexity you will experience and understand by reading on.

The first purpose is to understand your personal relationship with conflict. So begin by answering these questions:

1. What is conflict, and how do you feel about it? This question is an exploration of your concept of conflict. In your own words, define what conflict is. Write as many definitions as you want. The more definitions, the richer your experience will be. Then write down how conflict makes you feel. Be thorough with this part of the question. Your feelings will generally disclose your old beliefs about conflict. As you answer, be aware of what you are learning about yourself.

2. What is the evidence of unresolved conflicts in your life, and how do you feel about them? The answer to this question describes the actual presence of conflict in your life: personal, work, and community. Be willing to disclose the answer to yourself. It is for your eyes only. This will create consciousness of the role that unresolved conflict is playing in your life. If you want, do these by arena: personal, work, community, and so on.

For each conflict, write the feelings you have as a result of the conflict; use complete sentences. When you finish, read through what you have written.

3. What are the worst possible outcomes of confronting these conflicts? This question helps you be conscious of the fears you have about confronting conflict. You can answer this in a general way because the statements will probably apply to more than one conflict. List as many worst outcomes as possible, and do not hesitate to write the worst of the worst. Don't hide anything from yourself. Nobody else will see this. The more you disclose to yourself, the more likely you will learn how to resolve the situation.

4. Pause: This is a good time to pause and rest. Read what you have written and then reflect for a while. As you read further in this book, you will understand why you were asked to explore your worst possible outcomes. For now, just reflect. Then, after five minutes or so, answer the next series of questions.

5. What will be the best possible outcomes of addressing and resolving your unresolved conflicts? How would you feel if you did that? These questions help you decide what you want to have happen from addressing these conflicts that are causing you pain.

The first question is one you probably never ask yourself; you are likely trying to determine *how* to resolve them, rather than first identifying your desired outcomes. This is referred to as *Ready—Fire.* You haven't aimed, and so it is likely you won't get what you want. Identifying *best possible outcomes* helps you determine the outcomes you want and the feelings associated with those outcomes. This is known as *Ready...Aim.* (We will do *Fire* in the next question.)

Write down all the best possible outcomes you desire. Answer generally or specifically, because best outcomes will also apply to more than one issue.

Next, read your best possible outcomes. Become aware that these are just as possible as the worst outcomes. Since you have not confronted the conflicts yet, your worst fears are future imagined events. The fears you have are merely possibilities. There is **no** assurance they will happen. Since any fear is a future event, it is just as possible that you can foster a best possible outcome. By writing the best possible outcomes, you have at least balanced yourself and added *hope* to the equation.

Next, record how you would feel if you were to be successful. Best possible outcomes produce entirely different feelings than worst possible outcomes.

Now let's explore how to make the best outcomes happen.

6. What are all the reasons this is impossible? You know this is what you are thinking right now. This is impossible. Well, tell yourself why you feel that way. List them all.

Remember that all of your impossible statements are just beliefs you have that prevent you from resolving the issues.

7. What new beliefs and behaviors will foster these best possible outcomes? If you have been avoiding conflicts in the past, there are reasons for it. Avoidance is probably based on some old belief systems. If you want to be successful with conflict resolution, you may need some new beliefs and behaviors. What would these new beliefs and behaviors be? Write them down.

Beliefs and behaviors are different than strategies and actions. In this book you will learn when to use each.

8. What resulting strategies and actions will foster your best outcomes? This question allows you to move beyond your new beliefs to putting them into action. You can establish specific strategies or actions for any of the unresolved conflicts you have described. You can also ask yourself to list the first steps you would take to move in the direction of resolving these conflicts.

9. How do you feel about this activity? What did you learn that will help you confront and resolve your conflicts? This last step will help you learn from the experience. It is closure for what you have done. Record your answers to both of these questions.

This is the basic process that you will read about in more detail in the following chapters. Applying it, however, is more complex and richer than this simple activity indicates. There are reasons for each of the questions. You will become aware of the reasons as you experience the process. As you gain this insight, you will become more willing to create the conditions needed to address your conflicts.

As you read ahead, keep your this information with you. Use it as a bookmark. There are chapters in this book corresponding to each of these questions. You can connect what you read to what you learned from this personal experience; it will add richness to reading what follows.

~7~

A Better Way—Seeking Consensus

My Personal Struggle for a Better Way

My personal struggle with conflict began as a young child in a dysfunctional and violent home, barely able to understand what was happening and why.

There Must Be a Better Way: An Anecdote

I lay in bed, my body clutched in my arms in a tight fetal position, muscles shaking as if with fever, yet feeling cold as death. I have rosary beads pressed between my fingers, and I pray with them to shut out the sound of violence and as an offering to God for peace.

They are in the adjoining room, the kitchen. The door is open so their angry voices can be heard. Their harsh words impact the room with their shock waves as they cut sharply through the air. They speak through clenched jaws. Their breathing is short, so their sentences are short, violent jabs. The atmosphere stinks of fear.

My heart beats rapidly as I imagine the worst. Will they kill each other this time? Will I be killed? I clench my teeth to hold back the sobs, the tears at the edge of my eyes.

It is another of a long and continuous string of arguments between Mom and Dad. The argument is the same. It is a replay of the initial remembered event. Dad came home drunk again, having spent much of his paycheck buying drinks for his friends, his need to be liked taking importance over his family. My mother is castigating him with her disappointment at his betrayal of the family. She is relentless and persistent in her scorn, her anger. He is just as relentless in his rebuttal, his justification. He seeks to echo the blame back to her; she seeks to deflect it back to him. They repeat phrases intended to provoke: "Put that in your pipe and smoke it!" Their voice tones clash against and over each other, intending to hurt, to ignite each other's pain and anger. It is a drama they know well.

The arguments start quietly enough. Dad is late. A sense of the inevitable hangs in the air. Mom sends all of us to bed, but she stays up waiting for Dad to arrive. Each of us eight children lie in our beds, unable to sleep, holding our breath if we hear some sound outside our rooms. We are anticipating the inevitable. Feelings of menace, fear, and anger are latent in the air.

Then the door slams. We are electrified with the shock of it. There is that one teasing moment of calm. Then Mom's voice starts with a quiet question. "Where have you been?" A simple enough question. Then the angry response, "What the hell business is it of yours?" The tone changes and the event is on.

I had not admitted to myself that there was violence until recently. It begins with a shove, then a slap. Bodies are shifted and we hear their struggle. There are bumps against the wall. Dishes are thrown, knives rattle on the floor. Who would wish to admit this about their parents? And who would blame me for not admitting it? Could I have done something to stop it?

God knows, I tried. I tried pleasing them during those times they were friendly, hoping to build a habit for peace. I tried changing the subject, talking about some other issue in the hope of diverting their attention. I would walk out into the kitchen, my eyes blinking in the bright light, asking for a drink of water or crying about a nightmare I was having. I built up gas pains in my stomach, my belly swelling, while I bent over in pain, screaming for their help. I was a momentary diversion. A gathering of anger, clouds of distrust and vindictiveness often burst forth before my failed diversion was over.

I prayed for intercession by the highest authorities I knew: God and the Blessed Virgin Mary. I retreated to the bedroom, to the string of rosary beads, praying for an end to it all. My fingers pressed the beads so hard they had dents in them. I promised to do a rosary each night if God and the Blessed Mary would only stop the arguing. My promises were greater than I could repay before the next argument. My prayer debt piled up like an unholy burden on me, unanswered prayers building a sense of hopelessness, responsibility, and guilt.

In these times I thought of death as an escape. I would die of some unknown malady, and they would hear me as I croaked my last words. They would be so sorry, so penitent, that they would both become loving and accepting of each other again. My sacrifice would be worth it.

Or I would kill one of them, probably my dad, because my mother was with me while he was gone. I thought of him dying just because I willed it so. He would choke, his eyes bulging out as he gasped for breath, his hands around his own neck choking him more, until finally he fell lifeless to the floor. I would stand back in contrived pain, satisfied that he was finally gone, and I would be alone with my mother and siblings.

Those were the feelings and thoughts of a seven-year-old child who watched as his parents failed in their relationship, failed to handle the differences between them. They had conflict, always; they never resolved it. It lay like a foggy mist in every evening, ready to rise and permeate the home with its terror.

I remember saying to myself, over and over, *"There must be a better way, there must be a better way."*

That was to be my mantra for the greater part of my life. It is how this book came into being.

A Personal Search Shows Results

My life has been a continuing search for better approaches to managing conflict. I asked myself, **"Isn't there a better way?"** I spent all of my youth and most of my adult life seeking the answer to that question.

I tried every approach. I avoided conflict. I pleased others, acquiesced, distanced myself from it, separated others from it, and often denied the existence of it. At times I became aggressive, winning at any cost. Other times I negotiated and agreed to compromises I later regretted. It was only after I acquired new beliefs that I was able to successfully engage conflict, resolve it, learn and grow from it, and move toward fulfilling my life potential.

This new understanding came to me as a district ranger in the US Forest Service. I was charged with the management of 135,000 acres of forest and rangeland for the good of the public. I did this during the most turbulent times for people involved with management of natural resources: it was the beginning of the environmental movement, and my work and profession were the focal point of the environmentalists' displeasure. I found that there was a simple equation:

If people disrespect each other, they will disrespect the land.

I could tell how people were relating to each other by simply walking across harvest areas and rangeland and observing how it looked. If the land was damaged, the people were damaging each other. If I observed people treating each other with disrespect, then I would observe the land being disrespected. In subsequent years I learned that when educators and communities treat each other with disrespect, the children will be disrespected and disrespectful. If management treats union workers disrespectfully, the product assembly line will be disrespectful and the product will be of lower quality.

In contrast, I also learned: *"If people respect each other, they will respect the land."*

When the land looks healthy and well treated, then the people are treating each other with respect. When the educators and the community treat each other with respect, the children are treated with respect and will be respectful. When management and labor treat each other with respect, the product assembly line will be respectful and the product will be of higher quality.

That was the beginning of my answer to "there must be a better way." I wondered, "How can I get people to respect each other?" I changed that to a purpose statement: "I can get people to respect each other. Starting now!" That is how this process began.

> I do not believe in the doctrine of the greatest good of the greatest number. It means, in its nakedness, that in order to achieve the supposed good of 51 percent, the interests of the 49 percent may be, or rather, should be sacrificed.
>
> It is a heartless doctrine and has done harm to humanity. The only real dignified human doctrine is the greatest good of all.
>
> –M. K. GHANDI

What Is Consensus?

"Just what is consensus, anyway?"
"What is your definition of consensus, Bob?"

These are two common questions as we start a conflict-resolution session. It normally happens after I state in my introduction that I believe consensus is impossible but that we, as humans, have the ability to do the impossible. People want my definition to see if it matches theirs. If I ask them to first give me their definition, they will normally answer "majority rules." Rarely will they state that "everyone agrees."

The definition found in the American Heritage dictionary is somewhat confusing and imprecise:

"An opinion or position reached by a group as a whole or by majority will: The voters' consensus was that the measure should be adopted."

So, the definition includes a range of support, from approval of the group as a whole (100 percent) to majority rules (51 percent).

In the US Senate, sixty votes, or a super majority, are needed to end a filibuster. In some states, 75 percent approval is needed for raising taxes. A landslide victory at the polls is considered to be 60 percent or higher. All of these would indicate some measure of *consensus* of the public will.

Or it might be defined by a family member this way:

> *"In my family," Bill said, "All that was needed for a consensus was 25%. If my mother said 'this is how it's gonna be,' then we three just all agreed and did it."*
>
> *"Dad told us boys," He continued, "that as men we should always have the last word in an argument with our wives. He said only two words were necessary.... Yes Dear!"*

There are many views or descriptions of consensus. A description I once found on *Wikipedia* is the closest description to my belief:

"Consensus decision-making is a group decision-making process that not only seeks the agreement of most participants, but also seeks to resolve or mitigate the objections of the minority to achieve the most agreeable decision. Consensus is usually defined as meaning both general agreement and the process of getting to such agreement. Consensus decision-making is thus concerned primarily with that process."

My answer is simple: a consensus is when all agree 100 percent to a decision, freely making that choice, being committed to act on it and then…acting on it! Each person has been able to advocate for their views, been listened to with respect, learned from others by listening to them, and can leave feeling their integrity is intact in supporting the decision. They feel whole, real, at peace with themselves.

An intact integrity. This notion of having an intact integrity is important to the process. We all come to the meeting as individuals, each with our perception of the truth. The gathering is a community of diverse views and interests. The question is, can I maintain who I am as an individual and still be part of that community decision? The common belief is that you cannot, that you will have to give something up, to compromise who you are, to compromise your beliefs, values, and persona.

However, reaching consensus requires reaching solutions I agree with, while still being who I am as an individual. That does not mean I am exactly the same as when I started the process. It *does* mean that whatever adaptations I make are my choice, they fit who I am, and I can still leave as an individual, secure in myself.

Finding New Ground. Most people want to seek common ground when they resolve their conflicts. While this is commendable and can often resolve an issue, I seek another level: *new ground,* solutions that have not yet been tried that better meet everyone's needs.

> In consensus building we seek "New Ground."

And the proof is in actually behaving in ways that successfully implement the decision and make their purposes happen.

But it's impossible, people say. I agree. We are asking a diverse, often ideologically opinionated group of stubborn humans to reach an agreement that is inclusive of all, while protecting their individual beliefs and values.

That certainly sounds impossible, especially in this day and age. Yet I know it **is** possible in all instances because I have experienced this in my work. Besides, we are always reaching out to accomplish the impossible: to get a man on the moon, to create an iPhone, to climb the highest mountain, to run faster than any other human, to present a speech that changes the world. And we are successful most of the time.

Consensus is a behavior. If you look carefully, you will see that we behave in a consensus all the time:

- Juries are expected to reach 100 percent agreement on some court cases, and they do this with regularity.
- We use our seat belts with very little disobedience.
- People say the Pledge of Allegiance, hands over their hearts, at countless meetings every day.
- Everyone stands, hand over their hearts, to sing the national anthem before every sports event.

- Religious people stand, kneel, pray, respond to prayers, and sing in humble consent to their religion.

There is the office consensus to meet around the water cooler at a specific time. There is the staff consensus that the place to express concerns and to whine is in the staff room. There is a consensus that we have coffee or some other beverage during our break in the morning and also about where we have it. In our country, cars drive on the right side of the road. In England, they drive on the left side of the road. We stop at red lights and go at the green. While it is true that laws regulate some of this behavior, it is also true that we follow these laws pretty much all the time.

All of these are behaviors. Behaviors are evidence of a consensus. The way to find the consensus of a group is to observe members' behaviors. If they state they believe in equality, yet their behavior is to discriminate openly, that is their consensus. They believe and behave with inequality. Their belief is: *"Do what I say, not what I do."*

If we operate with a consensus in such diverse behaviors every day, then it is certainly possible to create a consensus in any situation.

Fears about Consensus

Still, there are plenty of people who see consensus in a negative light. Others often quote to me famous people's negative responses about consensus. These are stated to convince me that consensus is not possible or desirable. This happens when I am interviewing people before a workshop or when listening to spouses or partners express their grievances.

> **PEJORATIVE QUOTES**
>
> *"Consensus is what many people say in chorus but do not believe as individuals."*—Abba Eban (b. 1915), Israeli politician, quoted in *The New Yorker*, April 23, 1990
>
> *"To me, consensus seems to be the process of abandoning all beliefs, principles, values, and policies. So it is something in which no one believes and to which no one objects."*—Margaret Thatcher (b. 1925), British Conservative politician, prime minister

Both of these quotes are just worst possible outcomes: a fear that in consensus we will give in or pander or allow ourselves to be co-opted for the common good. Or that we will seek a decision that represents the lowest common denominator rather than the highest. Or that it will take too much time, and no one will be committed anyway. And then we fail to follow through on the consensus.

These are the specific fears I hear from people in interviews before the workshops:

People will not change their views, but will try to bully others to change theirs. "What do you do if a group or person comes with the intent of stubbornly trying to get everyone to think as they do?" they will ask.

My response: "You mean they will do what you will also do: try to get them to change to your view?"

What everyone wants when they get together is to try to change others to agree with them. That is a given with a group when I start with them. It is *situation normal*. It is why they are in conflict. I do not require that anyone change this posture to get together to solve the issue. I *want* them to come with their deepest differences, their most stubborn behaviors. I want them to feel deeply. In fact, it is that very energy that makes it possible to reach consensus.

The purpose of any consensus process is to get people to freely choose to see the situation more fully and then choose to meet the needs of all. The consensus process must validate their views—all of them—and then move on to resolve the issue.

It is very common to have people shift their views to a better description of the truth after listening to others. Invariably, they will let go of their adversarial role as they get to know the others, as they learn from each other, as they begin to build a common knowledge base through listening with respect. They begin to openly advocate for their views in a safe listening environment.

It requires a safe environment of listening with respect where all speak, telling their truths and then listening respectfully to others, allowing them to choose to change if they wish.

There is a fear of being co-opted, of going along just for the good feeling that comes with everyone agreeing. This is a very real fear for most people in my sessions. Once everyone meets and begins to know others, there is a tendency to want to "go along to get along," to feel good about being in a community that feels safe. It is a matter of conforming, rather than norming. This can lead to agreeing to some decision they will later regret.

It is the facilitator's role to see that this doesn't happen. It is easy to sense when people are allowing themselves to be co-opted. It takes only an expression on my part:

"It is important for the group that you not allow yourselves to be co-opted just to feel good. The workshop is not about making people feel good, it is about making people feel real."

They will then get back to being real with each other.

There is a belief the process will take too much time. There is always this need to be efficient, to get together, identify the problem, and then get on with solutions quickly. The solutions rarely have a common purpose, nor are they reached in a way that commits people to their implementation. Rather, decisions are made to…just get on with it! They are normally based on worst possible outcomes. And nothing positive happens as a result of people's fears. Time wasted!

This is *going fast to go slow*! It means you will come back again and again to make the decision over and over. Little action is taken because of the lack of understanding, agreement, and commitment.

I believe in *going **slow** to go **fast!*** I help my clients acknowledge that time is never the problem. The problem is the problem. If you don't take the time to do it right, then the problem will eat up more time then you will ever spend in a consensus session.

Every conflict has a time commitment associated with it. It may take an hour, a day, or three days or ten days. If you do not take that time to resolve the issue with commitment, then it will continue to be unresolved. As a result, you will continue to spend that time over and over, making the decision over and over.

Consensus seeking is about going *slow* to go *fast*. Take the time to make the right decision; it will be implemented successfully. The time you save can then be used to address another issue.

> Time is rarely the problem! The problem is the problem. Solve it and you will have more time.

There is a fear that one person can scuttle the whole deal by being stubborn, purposefully refusing to reach resolution. This gives the individual tremendous power to subvert the will of the majority. It is in that person's interest to get attention by not *giving in.*

That is just a normal situation. Some people come with the intent of doing this. When this happens, it is an indication that the issue has not been fully vetted yet. The person who holds out is an indication of some unspoken, unresolved issue or fear of a worst possible outcome.

There are approaches that work to move the group as a whole to a consensus decision. It means focusing on listening to and understanding each person's needs. It means taking the time to go back and bring each person along, helping them to be in the same place you are. It sometimes means finally acknowledging the person is right!

Crossing the Finish Line Together: An Anecdote

"A candle loses nothing by lighting another candle."

—**Father James Keller**

I was sent the following story in one of those widely spread Internet e-mails. It is instructive because it expresses a tenet of consensus seeking: that we must help everyone to get to the finish line, the consensus; otherwise, no one really wins. This speaks for itself:

A few years ago, at the Seattle Special Olympics, nine contestants, all physically or mentally disabled, assembled at the starting line for the hundred-yard dash.

At the gun, they all started out, not exactly in a dash, but with a relish to run the race to the finish and win. All, that is, except one little boy who stumbled on the asphalt, tumbled over a couple of times, and began to cry. The other eight heard the boy cry.

They slowed down and looked back. Then they all turned around and went back...every one of them. One girl with Down's Syndrome bent down and kissed him and said, "This will make it better."

Then all nine linked arms and walked together to the finish line. Everyone in the stadium stood, and the cheering went on for several minutes.

People who were there are still telling the story. Why? Because deep down we know this one thing: What matters in this life is more than winning for ourselves. What matters in this life is helping others win, even if it means slowing down and changing our course.

On the other hand, there are supportive quotes.

> **SUPPORTIVE QUOTES**
>
> *"We must indeed all hang together, or, most assuredly, we shall all hang separately."*—Benjamin Franklin (1706–90), US statesman, writer. Comment at the signing of the Declaration of Independence, July 4, 1776, in reply to John Hancock's remark that the revolutionaries should be unanimous in their action.
>
> *"If you limit your choices only to what seems possible or reasonable, you disconnect yourself from what you truly want, and all that is left is a compromise."*—Robert Fritz
>
> *"A genuine leader is not a searcher for consensus but a molder of consensus."*—Martin Luther King, Jr.

What Consensus Is: An Insight

"The great pleasure in life is doing what people say you cannot do."

—Walter Bagehot

What follows are the attributes I believe must be present to reach consensus with a community in conflict.

Inclusive and balanced. The people who meet must represent all the perceptions and concerns in the community of interest. It must especially include those who are most outspoken, with the strongest, often most radical views, and at both ends of the spectrum. It must include men and women, young and old. It must include the old-timers ("townies" or "locals") and the newcomers ("newbies"). It must include those who are stubborn and ideological, as well as those who are respected as wise people. Where it is part of the equation, different cultural viewpoints must be included. It must include those who are deeply and emotionally involved, as well as those who have no interest at all.

If those involved express discomfort with attending or refuse to attend, then I ask them to designate a person to represent their views. I also tell them there will be a chair waiting for them if they choose to attend. They usually attend.

Participatory. The process must allow for complete participation by every person in the room. By participatory, I mean people speak, knowing they are listened to, and people hear, knowing it is important to do so. All people have their voices in the room for all tasks. Everyone's voice is heard in the creation of purpose; everyone's needs and desires are included.

Capacity building while exploring relationships and conflict. I learned early on that people need the capacity and beliefs to reach a consensus, and most of us do not have that capacity, which often means people must learn how to reach consensus while they are working on reaching that consensus. It is not enough to speak the word and it magically happens.

People must learn how to listen with respect; to learn from each other; to express their feelings; to create a safe environment; to see their information in a form that is inclusive of all; to be clear about how they can create a common knowledge base; and to understand the differences between problem, purpose, beliefs, behaviors, strategies, and actions.

Listening with respect. The most important behavior that fosters consensus is "listening with respect." If people can hear what others say without judging it or interrupting to deny it, then consensus is possible.

Learning from each other. Because all people see the world through their own personal perceptions, they must learn from each other before they can create purpose or reach a decision. They must be open to hearing and understanding each person's views.

Resolving individual and group conflicts. Often, the community of interest that participates in the workshop includes people or groups with a history of conflict between them. This is part of the capacity-building purpose: to provide people the understanding and skills and a process to resolve their other conflicts while working on the real issue.

This often happens individually off to the side, in a greeting circle or during a break. People who have been isolated from each other will approach, make contact, and begin to talk about their issue. Sometimes they will request my assistance.

Seek consensus to meet the needs of all. The group must know from the beginning that the purpose is to create a consensus, with 100 percent agreement, that it is understood this is impossible, yet we will still do it. It is OK if they don't believe it can be done; they can acknowledge this as a condition of their participation. But always they are reminded that we are there to reach a 100 percent consensus. Then they are provided the capacity to make it happen.

Taking time. Intergroup conflicts are the most difficult because they have a long history of adversarial relationships. These will require a two- to three-day conference, workshop, or work session—whatever people want to call it. The first day and a half is spent exploring conflict and building relationships and the capacity to solve their problem. The last day and a half is spent reaching consensus on the real issues.

It is OK if people believe this is too much time. It is OK if they say they will only devote a portion of a day to it. I will still schedule the three days knowing they will all come—they almost always do—and will all be there when it ends three days later. We will provide the time needed to resolve their issue so they can take the needed actions and be successful.

Reaching consensus on interpersonal conflicts normally takes one to three hours. The participants must be willing to invest this time. Personal conflicts can be addressed in fifteen to thirty minutes.

Purpose oriented. This process is purpose oriented. Not just any purpose, but a common purpose, one that has everyone's desires included in it. Without purpose, an expression of the community outcomes, there can be no success. As part of capacity building, the community is provided an explanation of the differences between purpose, belief, strategies, and actions.

Solution oriented. This process is oriented toward solutions that will result in the desired outcomes or purposes of the community.

A value-added approach. This approach, which I call consensus seeking, is value added over the more traditional approaches. Value added means we do not discard all our traditional approaches, but add new ones that may be appropriate for specific contemporary situations. There are times when the old approaches do work best.

Action oriented. No matter how good the process that created a decision, no matter how perfect the decision appears to be, it is of no value if action is not taken. This approach fosters action.

Continually seeking consensus. *Seeking* is a very specific word I use in this book. While the intent is always to reach 100 percent consensus, it may not be achievable because of time. Yet the intent is to keep seeking. This seeking may continue even after the decision has been made.

In a workshop I will often include an anecdote of a real conflict that represents these expectations. This is one of them:

Inclusive and Balanced: An Anecdote

Alex was the manager of a National Forest in the Northwest. During the environmental movement in the 1970's, following the original Earth Day, the Forest Service had been brought to a standstill by environmental appeals on timber sales. Most of these appeals were denied by the higher-ups, so the issue went to the courts. This resulted in a dramatic slowdown of timber harvest in the Northwest.

Alex had a timber sale that resulted from trees blown down during a severe storm. His sale was appealed because it was in a municipal watershed. The attorneys had recommended he come to me, since they did not feel they would win in court. At the time, I was working as an internal consultant on reaching consensus on just these kinds of issues.

When Alex asked me for help, I interviewed him, learning about the situation that brought him there. I explored how this relationship with the appellants happened so I could understand the relationships we were dealing with. I explored his worst possible outcomes for this situation. Then I asked him what his best possible outcomes were. Finally, I asked him who he felt should attend a consensus work session if we were to sponsor one.

He created a list of people, focusing especially on the timber industry side. I asked him to provide me more names of the environmentalists or people who opposed the sale. His list was still limited.

I asked him to provide me the names of people he did not want to be there, for whatever reason, from both sides. This second list was longer than the one we had so far. It included the most outspoken leaders of the movements on both sides, some considered radical, some considered troublemakers. He was understandably upset with all of them, had low regard for them, and did not consider them to be candidates for the workshop.

I gave him both lists and asked him to create a list of thirty to forty people, half of whom would come from each list. At first Alex balked; he truly believed only a moderate group could solve this problem. In the end, he acquiesced to my request.

I first interviewed the final balanced group, listening to them individually so I knew all of the perceptions about the situation. Then they met for three days, with a follow-up field trip to ensure the consensus decision fit the actual situation. The timber sale was approved by all, with some modifications, with their consensus agreement.

~8~

An Intergroup Conflict

A Context for Learning

From this point on YOU will get what you have been hoping for! ***Finally!***

Our purpose is to help you experience, learn, and understand a process for confronting and resolving conflicts and building consensus with 100 percent agreement. We will use an intergroup-conflict approach to serve as your context for learning.

This intergroup consensus-building workshop will take three days because of the complexity and emotional content of the issues.

For your experience, we will use the intergroup conflict setting with a three-day workshop because it provides the richest environment in which to present the process, the underlying concepts, insights, anecdotes, and art of the process. You will probably not use everything you read in this book, but it helps to understand everything if you are to be most successful in all arenas of conflict.

Intergroup sizes vary, but are usually from twelve people and up. The conflict and training groups vary from eight to fifty participants, averaging around thirty. The process is also successful with groups of three hundred to four hundred participants interested in creating, or accepting, a common mission. Groups as large as fifteen hundred people have successfully participated in this approach. While the emotional intensity may differ in these different circumstances, the beliefs, behaviors, process, and art of building consensus remains essentially the same. The group we'll work with in this book has thirty-three people in the community of interest.

Don't Just Stand There, Do Something!

YOU are there! Right from the beginning, I will introduce YOU as a co facilitator and full partner in managing a community of interest through the conflict. YOU have the choice of accepting this role to immerse yourself in helping this community through their conflicts, while experiencing and learning this process for yourself. This will happen as you read this book.

There are two dimensions to your assigned task, if you choose it. The first is the experience itself. As we take this community of interest through the process and you immerse yourself in it, be aware of how you feel; be aware of your resistance or your acceptance, your lack of understanding and your understanding, your frustration and impatience, and your patience. All these and more will be created by this experience.

The second dimension is the process itself. Our approach is really quite easy, but the dimensions of its impact are very deep and very complex. It is this ability to impact many different levels of human behavior and human development all at the same time that results in growing an individual, a trio, a group, a community that can reach 100 percent consensus.

Being conscious of both these dimensions, as well as being conscious of yourself, is a challenge you must meet. I assure YOU, it is worth it.

So…choose to take this journey with me as my primary cofacilitator. Anytime you see the word YOU, I am talking about YOU!

There Is Trouble in Coyote River Basin!

Coyote River Basin is on the west side of the Continental Divide, split by the Coyote River, which flows down its center to the mouth of the basin, into the foothills and beyond, until it reaches the Columbia River and flows into the Pacific Ocean. It is a high-country basin, with Coyote Mountain rising sharply from the Continental Divide. Coyote Mountain is a glacial, snow-covered mountain that provides a year-round stable flow of water—basic sustenance for all life in the basin.

Once an isolated basin accessible only by gravel and dirt roads, it was made much more accessible in the 1950s by a two-lane paved highway built from lower Metropolis, a major urban area. This road went through the three major communities in the basin: River City at the lower reaches of the basin is the seat of Coyote County, a community of thirty thousand people. Coyote Springs, population three thousand, lies at the center of the basin, surrounded by rich ranch and farmlands. This community is adjacent to the reservation for the Coyote Mountain Tribe. Chilly, a mining town located at the base of the mountain, holds three hundred hardy citizens who are used to being snowed in during the winter.

Coyote River Basin is a rich and diverse ecosystem, with high-country desert, open prairie, heavily forested slopes along the shoulders of the basin, and lower country meadows that are green most of the year and that form the basis for a ranching and farming economy.

The newly paved road brought with it an influx of new residents seeking employment with the timber and mining industries. River City grew the fastest, while additional small communities were developed throughout the basin. Thousands of two-acre lots were platted in hopes that the influx would continue and a stable economy would develop.

Once the timber industry and mining industry had become established, however, growth stabilized. In the late 1970s, an influx of environmentally oriented activists settled in the basin, focusing their concerns on restricting timber cutting and mining. These conflicts culminated in the 1990s—as they did in other parts of the country—with severely reduced timber harvesting and mining, ultimately resulting in closing down both industries. Without employment, many families moved downriver to Metropolis, seeking a more stable economy and diverse lifestyle.

During this time of change, the Coyote Mountain tribal rights for hunting, fishing, and gathering of native foods were acknowledged by the federal courts, Congress, and the state. The Tribal Council initiated programs to increase the return of salmon and other native fish and laid claim to the water needed to support these populations. In a move to improve the economic opportunities for its younger generations, the tribe was planning a large casino in the lower reaches of the basin. This would be located on former Bureau of Land Management (BLM) land that had been ceded to the tribe.

In the late 1990s, another influx, consisting of retired people and those with money to burn, entered the basin, seeking the beauty and isolation it offered. This resulted in additional subdivisions seeking to take advantage of rapidly rising prices. The retired people moved into both the older and newly platted subdivisions, while those with money purchased larger acreage and built small ranchettes.

This rapid and uncontrolled increase in growth disturbed many of the newer and older residents, which led them to form coalitions with the environmental activists seeking to create some form of growth control. Using their larger numbers, they were able to elect two new county commissioners, one an environmentalist and the other a growth-control advocate, changing the makeup of a previously conservative board. With this support, the activists forced the development of a new land-use plan for the county. Once it was approved, they moved ahead with the development of a zoning plan that would restrict growth within the county.

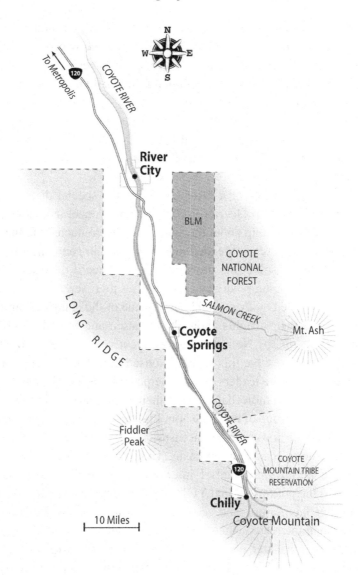

Objections to regulating a private owner's use of his land, raised by one conservative commissioner, resulted in a backlash. The backlash came mainly from the ranching and farming community, but also included real estate developers and the Chamber of Commerce. Small in number, but large in their response, they angrily resisted the proposed zoning ordinances, taking over meetings of the land-use planning committee and county commissioners. Their loudly expressed anger frightened many of the residents who had never before observed this kind of backlash.

Growth-control activists and environmentalists formed an advocacy group to counter the energy of the ranching and farming group. This resulted in confrontations between the two sides at every meeting held in the county. Law enforcement was often called upon to control the meetings, especially when the ranchers showed up armed.

The result was a polarization of the community. Letters to the editor in the local newspaper were filled with vitriol. Neighbors found themselves in opposition to each other. Anonymous threats and hate mail were sent from each side. It appeared everyone had to choose a side.

Donna, the director of a local government's special district known as the Rural Conservation District (RCD), became concerned enough that she decided to do something about the situation. She contacted the three county commissioners and recommended that they bring in someone from the outside to help them solve this problem. She had heard of a consultant who specialized in bringing polarized communities together.

I was contacted by Donna and later by one of the county commissioners. Both gave me their insights about the situation and how difficult it was. I was then contacted by Neil, the county executive, to explore how we could work together to resolve this issue. I advised him that I would first need to interview most of the leaders who participated in the confrontations, as well as those who were more balanced in their views. Following that, I would bring together a group of people whom I felt had the capacity to confront and resolve this issue and reach a consensus.

That is how I came to the basin. That is how I met YOU. YOU were one of the initial individuals I interviewed. While interviewing YOU, I entertained the possibility that YOU could help me cofacilitate the meeting, coach other facilitators, and serve as a resource for the basin after I left. YOU seemed interested when I broached the idea.

Three months later, a group of thirty-three basin residents met for three days in the Coyote Springs community hall. While many came reluctantly, all who were invited showed up.

This is where we will begin resolving this **intergroup** conflict.

You Might Have Some Questions

You may want to know if this is an actual incident. The answer is yes, but it is plural in its nature. I have taken as many as seventeen separate incidents and blended them together to create the information for this intergroup conflict. These incidents focused on the diversity of issues represented in the imaginary Coyote Basin: land use and zoning conflicts, mining and timber industry conflicts; conflicts between environmentalists and ranchers, between growth and no growth, between regulation and freedom; efforts to return salmon and other fish to rivers and streams; economic and social development of communities; and so on.

Each process segment of this intergroup conflict has its own information base for which I took selected actual statements from as many as seventeen separate workshops.

In most instances, the words and statements expressed by individuals in this scenario—*shown in this type font*—were actually expressed and recorded during these other workshops. In some instances, I blended statements together so they are more complete; the words, however, are the same. In a few instances, I paraphrased statements for purposes of protecting people who might have made them. Although they were altered by me, the original intent of these statements is the same. My own words as I present them in workshop, whether to the group as a whole or to the facilitators I am coaching (including YOU), are also shown in this type font (Calibri).

For the start of the meeting here—the **grounding** task—I developed the statements expressed by the thirty three participants. These are fictional people, fictional statements, but are based on my knowledge from many similar workshops of what each of the groups would say. There is a real basis for each of these people and the statements expressed.

YOU might also want to know if everything goes as easily as it appears to. The answer is yes. While I have reduced the amount of information normally provided for ease of your understanding and learning, the story and the statements expressed actually demonstrate the normal movement of people from severe conflict to consensus.

Contrary to most beliefs, highly polarized and angry situations move toward consensus rather quickly. The greater the energy, the easier it is to move people. The people who are stuck in these emotional situations do not want to be there and just don't know how to get out of them. When provided the opportunity, when they have learned to listen with respect, they move fairly rapidly to reaching an agreement that satisfies the needs of all present. It matters not how polarized they are—they will move.

> The greater the energy, the easier it is to move people to a consensus.

Contrary to most beliefs, people do not have to be ready to resolve. They often will resist the idea strongly. They come reluctant, interested in sabotaging the other groups. They may object strongly to everything when they first speak. What matters to me is that as long as they are in the room, whatever their emotional state, I trust they will reach consensus.

> As long as they are in the room, no matter their emotional state, they will reach consensus.

But, YOU might ask, how can a small group of people represent the whole? Great question! What I have learned when I use this process with a diverse and representative group from the larger community, one that represents the full continuum of polarized views, is that they will make a decision that would be replicated by another group from the community.

I was surprised to find this out. But it normally takes three days to reach that point. It requires listening with respect, honestly confronting the issues with each other, and then being open to the possibilities of outcomes to meet the needs of all while still retaining the integrity of the individuals.

Not all the words expressed in a three-day meeting are presented in this example. Each workshop would take a lengthy novel to do that. Instead I have used the recorded words of individuals that are normally summaries of their larger verbal expressions. In all other aspects, this scenario is a representative example of a sharply polarized community coming together and reaching a consensus of the whole. To me that means 100 percent.

The Convener

Every interpersonal and intergroup conflict needs a convener, a person who can bring the differing perceptions together. For my personal conflicts, I am the convener. I acknowledge the different views that I am expressing in my mind, bring them into my consciousness by using the process. Then I facilitate my own discussion, listening to all my internal views.

In all other conflicts, the convener is someone other than me. For an interpersonal conflict, it might be a person who wants to bring two of her associates together to resolve their interpersonal conflict in which they have been using her as a sounding board for their complaints about each other. It might be the board chairperson who brings two of the board members together and serves as their facilitator to help them resolve a difference of opinion. If I am asked to help, in either of the above examples, the convener would assist me in getting the parties together. They also can help me facilitate the parties to a resolution of their conflict.

For intergroup conflicts, the convener might be the client who asks me to come in and help the community. Or the client might know a person who is highly regarded by both sides in the conflict and to whom they would respond if invited to a workshop.

Sometimes the parties of the conflict will contact me and ask for help. If they all agree to act as conveners, I suggest they create a steering committee whose purpose is to invite those I select from my interviews. And they may decide to include others.

When interviewing, I may not know who the convener is. For some conflicts, I identify a convener during my interviews. I normally wait until all the interviews are completed to make that recommendation to my client. If my client is comfortable with this recommendation for a convener, then I establish a relationship with the person.

The convener's role is fairly straightforward. This person is responsible for inviting people to the workshop or meeting and then encouraging their attendance. I provide support in this effort if asked. While the convener may also make arrangements for the meeting, meals, transportation, and so on, this is normally provided by the client. For the workshop in this book, although the initial contact was made by a community member, the conveners are the county commissioners.

Selecting a Diverse Group

I stated this earlier: Consensus seeks to create a "new ground," which soon becomes a common ground. The new ground is a decision location that is hardly imagined in the beginning, some location that is not in the center, but off to the side, unacknowledged before because of the search for a compromise. It is a new belief, a new paradigm, a place where all feel their needs are met, one solution that they can readily work together to accomplish.

To do this, the community of interest must move beyond *groupthink* to *diverse think:* to seeking to understand all points of view and then asking, *How can we get all our needs met?* Breaking up groupthink is the first step to doing this. This is accomplished by ensuring that the community of interest invited to the workshop replicates the diversity in the broader community. I create an inclusive list of invitees shortly after the interviews are complete. The client or the convener may add additional people.

Sometimes members of the community who were not interviewed express an interest in attending. Normally these are added to the list. For our story, the final list results in thirty-three members of the community who are invited. They all show up, although one shows up on the second day.

I Work for the Entire Community

Potential participants in a consensus-building workshop are rightly concerned about my allegiance or loyalty to the broader group.

> *"How do we know that you won't just take the side of the client who is paying you big bucks?"*
>
> **—Workshop participant**

My answer to that is simple:

I work for the entire community. It does not matter to me who pays the bill or how much they pay me. It does not matter to me how important people are or how powerful they are. I don't care if they drive a Mercedes-Benz or a broken-down truck. It doesn't matter if people attempt to bribe me or offer me expensive gifts. I work for the entire community.

What I just stated are only words. But observe my behaviors. If I deviate from what I said, then confront me about it.

No one has ever had to confront me about it.

A reminder: I said earlier in the preface, "The process itself is simple, but its impacts are complex. Just using the process is not enough. Understanding why it works is the ingredient for effectiveness and success, especially when working with others."

This book is intended to help you understand the complexity of this simple process. When you get it, you will change your way of being. When you change, others will also be changed.

> If you change one, you will change them all.

~9~

A Gathering of the Community

Gathering at the Start

They enter the room cautiously, singly, in pairs or small groups. Some exclaim in a loud whisper, "Oh, no!" Each appears startled by the sight of a circle of chairs with no tables. They see four easels placed around the outer edge of the circle. They check the door anxiously to ensure they are in the right location. Some go back outside the room, and I wonder if they will return. They do—cautiously, like some wild deer entering a clearing from the forest.

Those who enter cluster together, seeking out people they know, even if recently. If in conflict, they avoid those in conflict with them, dividing the room into two or more groups of antagonists. The severity of the conflict determines the distance between them. They look around nervously, seeking out the instructor/facilitator.

I am busily hanging visual charts: simple statements written on easel paper for the session. In some ways I am just as nervous as they are, wondering: *How will this go? Why am I doing this? I could fail. Will I be adequate?* I sense and react to the nervousness, uncertainty, and apprehension that fills the room.

At the same time, I observe those who enter. I normally seek out one, preferably a woman (for balance), to help facilitate the group with the first activity. If it is a conflict group and I have interviewed the participants, then I have some idea whom I want. If I have not interviewed the participants or if it is a training group, I choose someone who looks likely.

In this case, I am looking for a specific person I interviewed: YOU! When YOU enter, I walk over to greet you, and we talk about the possibility of your facilitating with me.

While we are talking, the others head straight for the coffee bar, wanting something to do with their hands. They make chance acquaintances there, greeting each other, inquiring as to name, location, position. They look for name tags, but there are none.

One or two brave souls will enter the circle, choosing a chair that gives them a view out the window or that is near the door (maybe for a quick escape). They place their jackets on the backs of the chairs, their briefcases or purses under the chair. If they move to the coffee bar, they place other ownership artifacts on their chairs, signaling that this is their territory. Others roam around the circle, close but not too close.

In the minds of many are fears of a "touchy-feely session," of a "spill your guts" or "tell it all session." The circle of chairs may remind some of them of previous involvement in "encounter groups," a recollection from the 1960s and '70s.

When I signal a time to start, there is no rush. All appear to be waiting to see if anyone will move to the circle. When some do, others move in a herd fashion, following the leaders. Some wait until the last moment; they get another refill on coffee, letting the group decide which chair will be theirs.

The Community of Interest

There are two kinds of groups I work with. Most groups are in a conflict common to them all, seeking some resolution. They bring a diversity of viewpoints with them. The participants generally know each other, at least by hearsay or reputation. They have deep and strong emotional feelings about each other and the conflict event. They have grouped up and know who their enemies and friends are.

Other groups attend workshops to learn the skills for seeking consensus. Participants can come from around the country, strangers to all but a few in the room. They may have little emotional attachment to each other and are not aware of their common conflicts. They are often strangers, wondering who their friends or enemies are. My challenge is to create some emotional attachment to common issues so they can learn in a significant way.

I refer to each of these groups as a "community of interest." They may not live in the same physical area, but they are brought together by a common issue, need, or conflict. It is this conflict that creates their need to act as a community. They meet in a common location to confront and resolve their issues. This will be their communal "sense of place."

> A "community of interest" is brought together by a common issue, need, or conflict. Where they meet is their common sense of place.

This book focuses on a community of interest in an intergroup conflict. Each person in the community of interest will be affected by the resolution of the conflict. When the conflict is addressed and resolved and the lessons learned, they leave knowing their individual concerns have been met. They leave committed and ready to work together and carry out their decisions.

In this book I will refer to them as the *community* or the *community of interest.*

A reminder: The three-day workshop you are about to experience is for the purpose of experiencing and understanding the process and its underlying concepts. It is unlikely every reader will be hosting such a workshop. But understanding the process and underlying concepts makes it possible to effectively apply it to personal and interpersonal conflicts. It can be applied in staff meetings, team building, collaboration meetings, listening sessions, proposed changes in policies, and so on.

Sharing Power with You: An Insight

As the group enters the room, I search for a person who can help me facilitate the grounding. I normally seek someone who is not likely to be given this position of prominence. This may be a secretary, a minority female, a minority male, an outspoken person who is looked down upon, a custodian, a disabled person, or a disenfranchised person. The intent is to immediately and behaviorally send the message that we are all important and empowered in the circle, that we can all facilitate the process, that people are willing to risk the experience of doing this.

When YOU come in the door, I remember you from the interviews and decide you are the person to help me cofacilitate. After asking you to meet with me for a few minutes, I ask if you are willing to help with the beginning of the session. I hand you a three-by-five "cue" card to read. On the card are written these three questions:

> Introduce yourself. What is your relationship to our conflict in the basin?
> What are your expectations of this meeting?
> How do you feel about being here?

I tell you: Your task will be to explain that everyone is to do the grounding. This consists of answering three questions. You are to read all three questions and answer them yourself. Then read them out loud again so the participants are reminded what they are to do.

I further explain: Participants, in their apprehension, rarely hear the questions, even after being repeated twice. By answering the questions first, you are establishing a pattern that others can choose to follow. This is one of the few times a facilitator answers the questions first.

I caution you about passing the card around or continuing to repeat the three questions. The participants are here to listen and learn. If you pass the card, they lose their focus on themselves and the group. The card becomes important, rather than the group. And it makes them lazy; they don't have to recall what they heard.

After stating the questions and answering them, your role changes to a facilitator and listener. You will decide where to start, moving clockwise from your right or counterclockwise from your left. Then read the three questions again.

If they appear to forget the questions, ask them to answer what they remember. They will always answer the three questions. They are just being self-conscious and want to divert attention back to you.

You will foster each person speaking in turn just by listening intently to what they say. You do not have to say anything else. Don't acknowledge what they say or thank them or comment on it. Just listen. They will keep moving without your telling them to.

Do not demand that they answer all the questions. That is their choice. The importance is to establish a model for listening by assuring the speaker that at least one person in the group is listening and hearing.

When the circle is complete, you may choose to summarize the expectations and feelings you heard in the group. I'll remind you of that.

YOU are offered this opportunity five to ten minutes before the session starts. The time spent giving you instructions is less than three minutes. YOU will experience immediate self-consciousness. Only rarely does the person selected turn down this opportunity, even though their apprehension and anxiety is sometimes painfully obvious.

YOU will usually perform in an exemplary manner. Your voice may be a little shaky and you may express some embarrassment at being the leader. You are just being self-conscious. You may poke fun at yourself so as not to appear too powerful, or you may just lead right into the task professionally. All behaviors are acceptable to me because they are natural human behaviors.

By giving you this task, I provide YOU an opportunity to empower yourself. I provide the opportunity, but you make the choice. You carry out the task. You will now be seen by your community as being equal in power to the facilitator. This is a positive reflection on them, since you are one of them.

Empowerment—The Opportunity, the Choice: An Insight

I continue to coach you on the facilitator role.

This is a basic tenet of facilitating a consensus session:

> I, as facilitator, can provide the opportunity, but you must make the choice to take the opportunity and then do it.

The same holds true for asking questions of the group. The facilitator asks the question. **It is up to the individual to decide whether to answer.** Some people will describe the situation and not describe how they feel. Others will describe only how they feel. This is their choice.

Because I ask you how you feel, you will still feel. Whether you disclose that or not is your choice. I have no right to force you.

If you feel deep emotional reactions to the situation, but choose to express little emotion, it is your choice. You may feel all your emotions and write down only a portion of those you want to disclose to yourself. You then may express only a portion of what you wrote. That is all you choose to disclose at this time.

Mental View > Card View > Disclosed View > Each Is Smaller.

I have learned from observation that this approach actually fosters more disclosure. The participants immediately know that the decision to answer is in their hands. As others answer the thinking or feeling question, your self-censored disclosures will be expressed by someone else. You can then assess the consequences. If the consequences are nonthreatening, individuals are encouraged to disclose more in the next discussion. The intent is to create a safe environment in which you can disclose relevant, but sometimes threatening, information.

I respect your right to make these choices. If I try to force you to disclose more than you want to, you will become more closed, more restrained. This is a central difference between this approach and the typical group approaches. It is the responsibility of the facilitator to ask the right question and create a safe environment for disclosure. It is the responsibility of the individual to choose how to respond. It is up to the facilitator to accept whatever response an individual provides.

"Will We be Able to Shut Him Up?": An Anecdote

In one session between a support staff council (support staff includes custodians, secretaries, food staff, maintenance workers, transportation staff) and the administration of a school district, I was establishing a panel to speak to the administrators about the situation from their viewpoint.

I had a member on the panel from each of the groups the council represented. I selected a young man, a new member of the support staff council, to represent the custodians. He appeared to accept the assignment, but later returned and asked if he could decline. He expressed discomfort, a fear of being inadequate to represent the custodians, a fear of speaking to large groups. He didn't want to make a fool of himself.

I asked if there was someone else in the room that could represent the custodians. He felt not. I suggested some options. He could recommend someone to represent him on the panel, he could remain on the panel and speak only if he felt like it when it became his turn, or I could leave out the custodian point of view.

After talking to the other custodians, who were just as anxious and reluctant to speak as he was, he chose to remain on the panel with the option to speak.

When his turn came (I placed him near the end of the panel in order of speaking), he surprised himself and everyone else by very eloquently expressing the views of his group. He was somewhat nervous and stated this as he started, and then he clearly and succinctly expressed the custodian views. The silence when he ended was better than applause.

What was more interesting is the increase in the amount and quality of his conversation from that point on in the small groups. Some wondered if he might suddenly become overly verbal. "Will we be able to shut him up?" they asked to much laughter. When they asked me what happened to this shy and quiet custodian, I told them he was **in process.** He was empowering himself to change.

> Give them a choice to lead, to empower themselves.

Some may decide not to take the opportunity. I always honor that. Most are delighted and scared and accept the opportunity. Some become jittery, wanting to avoid it, yet wanting to do it. In any event, it is their choice.

In the past when you asked someone to do this task or a similar one and they demurred, you probably let it go. Those voices, that view, would then not be represented on the panel. In this process, the opposite behavior is encouraged. Give **them** the choice. Let **them** decide. They will normally take it.

~10~

The Workshop Introduction

The Introduction

I sit quietly and wait while the participants settle into their chosen places in the circle. They speak softly, laugh loudly, casting quick and covert glances around the group, making their initial assessments about importance, dress, makeup of the group, distancing, and relationship. They appear self-conscious, seeking some camaraderie or some anonymity with the group they are sitting with. Many try to make themselves comfortable, balancing briefcases and other meeting props on their laps. Others proceed to move their chair as far back to the edge of the circle as they can and still be in. I sit and wait until that last person is in the group.

I have learned, both from my own experience and from observing and talking with others, that meetings or workshops are very apprehensive affairs. People often do not want to be there. Many consider meetings a waste of time, while others may be thankful something is being done to bring the community together.

Perhaps they have been sent, or they came reluctantly because of the topic. This is especially true if the issue is one of deep conflict. They are sitting in the same room with people they disagree with or do not like and would prefer to be somewhere else. They are apprehensive, mistrustful about what will happen.

While most people arrive apprehensive, they become more so when seeing the circle of chairs. They often recoil in their apprehension. The arrangement—the circle—is different; they are not certain what will happen. These feelings are magnified even more when the session is about to begin.

I learned that participants will often not really hear or remember what I am saying in the introduction. They are not yet ready to listen. They are concerned about their own sense of safety and personal protection. My intent with the introduction is to help them get grounded, getting the sound of a safe voice in the room that they can focus on.

The Workshop Introduction

While I speak slowly and clearly, and they appear to be listening, I can sense they are distracted. At the coffee break, it is not unusual for participants to ask me where I live, even though I state this information clearly in the introduction. Their minds are often too full of fear and apprehension to listen and recall.

I speak slowly, glancing at each person, beginning to see who they are, measuring their responses to what I am saying, wondering myself what I am going to say next. I normally introduce myself, state that I live in Terrebonne, Oregon, and make some self-effacing joke about that tiny community. There is some polite, hesitant laughter. I then do a "grounding" (explained in the following chapter) expressing who I am, what I do, my expectations for the meeting, and my feelings about being there. I also explain how I became the facilitator for the group. Much of what I say is a summary of the introduction to this book.

Who I am: I am Bob Chadwick; I live in Terrebonne, Oregon, a small rural community in the center of the state. I have a home there on the edge of a rock bluff overlooking the Deschutes River, with views of eight major snow-covered Cascade peaks. A place of peace for me, a place I have difficulty leaving.

And...I do leave to do the work I do best: helping people address and resolve their conflicts. I have a business, Consensus Associates, and...you are looking at the whole business. I am the president, vice president, the entire board of directors, the custodian, the secretary, and the coffeemaker. I feed the office dog and cat and clean out the litter box. I have a good boss and good employees.

My life purpose is to help others to resolve their conflicts. I work with all kinds of groups, all over the country and in other countries. My guess is, any group you could name I have worked with. I am not a negotiator, a mediator, or arbitrator, but a facilitator.

I have two purposes: to help these groups address and resolve their conflict, and to learn how to do it themselves. It is like the concept, "Give a man a fish, and you feed him for a day. Teach a man to fish, and you feed him for life." I intend to help people learn how to resolve their conflicts for life, if they choose.

In reaching their decisions I require a consensus, a 100 percent agreement. I know many of you consider that an impossibility. (I can see heads nodding agreement). "How could you ever get 100 percent agreement?" Well, I do it all the time, because I believe in doing the impossible. I believe we are made as human beings to do the impossible.

Think of it. Why would you want to settle for doing only what is possible? To me, that is mediocrity. Anyone can do the possible. It is in doing the impossible that we become the beings we truly are. We have the capacity to expand and stretch our notion of what can be done, and then do it!

Who I work with: I have no business card, no brochure, no space in the Yellow Pages. People contact me based on word of mouth. They hear of me from satisfied clients and contact me to see if I can help them. I can work every day of the year if I choose. I must decide from all the offers where to invest my time, where I can have the most impact. When there is a choice, I will always choose to take on the worst of the worst conflicts.

My clients are in any venue or arena of society you can imagine. Whether elected officials at the local level, or state and federal levels, small and large businesses, boards of community organizations or business, or education at all levels. I work with all sorts of cultural and ethnic groups, between Indian and non-Indian, African American and white, Hispanic and Anglo, and within the cultures themselves. I work with family businesses and corporations. I have worked in corrections systems, medical systems, computer systems, educational systems.

In all of these, I work with people who seek to address and resolve difficult issues that have been around, often for a long time, tying up their energy, keeping them from being as successful or productive as they could be.

Creating my associates: And, those who participate learn how to help themselves in the future. They may use what they learn in their working or other living environments, or they may decide to become full-time practitioners. These are my associates. They work on their own, often contacting me for support or ideas, but always responsible for their own activities. I don't have to write their job descriptions or give them performance appraisals or create a budget for them. They are self-supporting, relying on their own success with satisfied clients.

*(**Note**: For some groups I will present the information here on the generators of conflict presented earlier, beginning on page 71.)*

Why I am here: I am here because I was asked to help this community confront your issues. The person who contacted me heard of me from an associate in her organization. In talking with her about your issue, I determined that my time would be well invested here. I agreed to work with your community, provided I could interview the key players involved with this issue. I have done that. I appreciate each of you who agreed to be interviewed, and others who are here to help with resolution of your issue.

I learned a lot from the interviews, feel I can help you meet your goals, to help you be a more productive and a healthier community.

I know that many of you would rather not be here. In the interviews you expressed your disbelief that anything good can come of this. And some of you are hard pressed at work and home to just keep up. So this is a major investment of your time.

I also know some of you are here just to test the waters. I appreciate your taking this risk. Just know you are welcome to stay for as long as this is of interest or value to you. I will try to make that happen for the entire session.

ACKNOWLEDGING CONCERNS

During interviews I will often hear of others' concerns about the workshop. They may run from "I am told to be here," to "We don't trust each other," to "This will be a waste of time and we all know it," to "we hate to come to work." I will acknowledge these concerns in the beginning of the meeting, putting them "on the table" so everyone knows I am aware of them. This tends to make people less anxious, more willing to be open.

Our purpose: In working with you, there are some things you need to know. I am your facilitator, not your idea person or decision maker. I will facilitate you to solve your own problems. As I do that, I will also make this process transparent so you know and understand what I am doing. Some of you will help facilitate this process. I will coach you so that these skills can remain with your organization or community after I am gone.

Our purpose is to resolve your conflicts. I have learned from the interviews they are based on some past and recent negative experiences that were never addressed and resolved, and they continue to bedevil you. They are causing relationships to be confrontational and demeaning. And they are affecting the quality of community environment you have. You describe it as being dysfunctional and toxic, divisive and nonproductive and unsafe. Many of you stated you "hate to come to meetings where people get together."

Our purpose is to resolve these conflicts, to establish relationships based on open and honest communications, to free you up to work together in creative and productive ways. We want to create an environment where you can look forward to coming together for the good of the community.

In doing this I will introduce you to new skills for facilitating ourselves. You will experience and learn a process that will help you keep your family, organization, or community free of conflicts, if you choose to use these skills.

*(**Note**: I may present at this point a brief description of the process described earlier, in the introduction on page 24.)*

Memory and recall: You probably notice there are no name tags. The reason you don't have them is because I feel you don't need them; they get in the way of really knowing each other. "But," you will protest, "I can't remember names." And in so doing, cause your brain to fulfill your belief and not provide you the names when you need them.

There are no name tags because I want you to learn the power of your memory and its ability to recall. You have no choice but to remember names or anything that happens in this workshop. You are a memory machine. Unless you are somehow brain impaired, you have billions of memory cells, just waiting to retain the information for you.

The issue you have is really not about memory. It is about recall. It is your belief, reinforced by that statement, "but I can't remember names," that is your undoing. First of all, it is not a true statement. You will remember them. Your brain is organized to remember. Those billions of memory cells can hardly wait to store a memory for you. It is "recalling" them that is the issue here.

If you want to recall each person in this circle—not just their names, but who they are—you must entertain the belief that you can recall what is said. Once you have done this, you will be able to "remember" what you remember. It is like downloading information from a computer's hard drive to the motherboard. The information is there just waiting for the right command. The right command is, "I want to recall..."

In like fashion, I suggest that you not take notes for this session. I see lots of serious and frantic writing going on as I speak. I know, for some of you, this is a stretch. You will also protest that you won't "remember what was said."

My answer to that is that words are only 7 percent of communication. (This is explained in-depth later in this book.) You will normally only record what you heard that you liked or agree with. You probably will avoid recording or reject what you disagree with.

And while you are writing brief notes about what you agree with, you will be missing what I am saying as you are writing. Since communication is only 7 percent in words, as you write, you will miss the other 93

The Workshop Introduction

percent—the tone of my voice and other nonverbal cues important to the message. You will miss the passion in my voice, the intensity in my eyes, the leaning forward as I speak—which are all part of the message. In short, you just won't get it all.

Finally, you will file these notes somewhere with all the other notes you have kept from other sessions. When you need the information at some meeting or at some conflict experience, those notes will be out of reach. Of what value are they then?

But your memory is always with you, and your ability to recall what you need is there to tap that memory.

If you want to recall what is said here, just keep yourself conscious of what is going on and trust yourself that you will recall it when you need the information. Many people I have worked with use what they learn here. They tell me that when they get in a situation where they need to use this process, they can actually hear me speaking to them, providing insights they need to help their group. Trust that that will happen.

In addition, I will create a report for you from this workshop that will be mostly in your own words. It will include all the tasks you work on, the reason for the task, and the insights that go with that task. This report and "learning manual" is yours to use as you continue to work together. It allows you to recall the workshop and its tasks and insights. It is copyright protected, but I allow you to share it with anyone in your organization or community.

If you really need to keep notes, I will not object. It is your choice.

> It is always your choice.

Drifting away: I will work you long and hard. Sometimes we will go beyond your normal work time. I will keep you focused on why you are here. It will be tiring. I know you may already be exhausted from your previous day, often working late at night, thinking about your work even when not at work. So you are already tired.

The result is you will feel as if you can't keep your eyes open or keep yourself focused on what is going on. Then you begin to lose eye focus, your mind wanders, your eyes close, your head nods, and you begin to sway in your seat. Those on either side of you worry about whiplash. Then, as you realize at some level what is happening, you will jerk awake, guilty, wondering if others noticed. You will startle those next to you. And soon repeat the activity again...and again...and again...et cetera.

My advice? Give yourself permission to just relax. Lean back, close your eyes, and drift off. I promise you that you will not snore—no one ever has. You will not fall off your chair; you will not speak in your sleep or embarrass yourself. I will not ask you a question because I see you napping.

This happens not just because you ate a lunch or you are tired or bored. It also happens because you are hearing information you cannot yet understand or agree with; you resist and try to protect what you know or believe. This is tiring, so drifting away is a way to escape.

This state of being lasts less than a minute normally. It won't bother me at all. Don't worry about missing anything, because I will keep talking and teach you subliminally. (There is much laughter at this.)

My caution is this: don't do this in meetings later with your boss. He will not be as understanding.

Meeting relicts: I notice that many of you have materials you brought with you: clothes, briefcases and books, and so on. Some of you have quite a pile. And, with no table to put them on, you have them heaped under your chairs or against them or on your lap. There are tables along the wall that you can pile this material on. I suggest you do that, because you will be moving yourselves into small groups later, and it gets tiresome carrying this stuff along with you. You won't need any of it; all you need is yourself. So relieve yourself of the burden during the break. Again, it is your choice.

Moving around: Once we begin a task—a talking circle, or an activity in a small group—we will continue with the task until it is completed. If you have a need for a break, do so quietly, one at a time. If you are done with the task while in small groups and are waiting for others to finish, stay with your group until everyone has finished. This is being respectful.

If your back hurts, or that other part of your anatomy, stand if needed. Again, be inconspicuous in this.

Asking questions: If you have questions, ask them. But do not be surprised if I don't answer them. If I believe you can answer the question yourself, I will have you do that first. Many times you can answer the question yourself later in the workshop, after you have learned more. Or I may ask the group to respond with an answer. Or if you ask the question during the break, I may suggest it be answered in the large group. And I will see that all your questions are answered before you leave.

The Workshop Introduction

> **Note**: Much of this introduction is intended to give people permission to just be themselves, to relax, let things flow as they happen. As a result, rarely do they have these old behaviors. Note-taking ends, often with sighs of relief. It is rare to see a person snooze or drop out. What I call relicts—their burdens they bring—are stored on the tables designated and not referred to or used. The relicts rarely show up on the second day. Often the questions people ask, they will immediately answer themselves.

My expectations: My expectations are to do the very best job of facilitating I can to help you resolve your conflict with a consensus agreement. I will keep the process transparent, so you always know what is going on and why. I will coach as many cofacilitators as time allows so that you can replicate this process in your home, work, and community environment. If the process needs to be adapted to meet your needs, I will do that. I will let you know when I do. Everything is focused on helping you. You are important, not myself.

My expectation is that, in addition to solving your problems, you will empower yourselves to experience and learn this process so you can use it in the future.

My feelings: Finally, I am grateful that you asked me to facilitate your issues. I chose to be here, believing I could help. For you to also be here, even if reluctantly, yet willing to work on this difficult issue, is gratifying to me.

I will do the best I can, knowing you will also.

The Community Circle: An Insight

I have learned from my experience that each conflict has its own "community of interest." This community includes all those influenced or impacted by the decision or conflict. That is what brings them together. They are the ones who are drawn to the conflict, who engage in the struggle. They are the ones who show up for this workshop.

They do not understand that they are a community, and they believe and behave as if they aren't. Yet the ultimate outcome of resolving their conflict will be to create a true sense of community.

It is this understanding of true community that is symbolized by the circle of chairs. The area encompassed by this circle is the community space; it symbolically represents community. If I keep people within this space, they will tend to move toward working together as a healthy community.

To establish this community space, I need to set boundaries. I distribute the easels I am using at equal intervals at the back of the chairs, a sort of exoskeleton. It establishes the edge of community, and all the small-group work will be done within that space.

This is different from most similar meetings. Typically, if the room is big enough, the small groups are scattered about the available area, as far from each other as they can be. A group will often meet behind the easel, somewhat hidden from view by the others. Or a group will take one of the easels and move it back into the corner and meet there, out of sight of the others.

In traditional large group meetings, the small groups are sent to "breakout rooms," where they immediately feel cut off from the others and wonder what they are doing there or what the purpose is. They will also wonder what the other groups are doing.

I have learned that this standard behavior is not practical when a conflict needs to be resolved. I have learned that the group needs to be in the same space or room and work within the area encompassed by the original large circle. All the small groups can see the other groups. The sounds of their voices intermingle in the room. They are connected, with the same task, visually and aurally available to each other. They are a community.

~11~

The Grounding Circle

The Grounding Circle: An Activity

The session begins, as it does each day, with a grounding, which follows my introduction. This activity begins to establish a code of conduct... ***listening with respect.*** It establishes relationships and gains initial information for the facilitator. It is a necessary activity for any meeting, whether the meeting length is for a few hours, a few days, or a week. I do this with one person or many. The reasons are described in an insight following this section.

After my introduction, I turn the workshop over to YOU. I first explain this to the community:

In this process we ask members of the community to assist with the facilitation, to develop people who can assist you in the future. I have asked YOU to perform this role in the next task, the grounding.

YOU must take control of the group by speaking. You may feel very self-conscious or anxious. All eyes are on you. They now see you as their facilitator. So, how does that make you feel, having thirty-two pairs of eyes on you? (Note: the thirty third person is added tomorrow.) How do you feel about being the center of attention, their representative as a facilitator?

The cue card helps YOU get started. You state the questions, repeating them a second time for clarity. You tell the person to your left (or the right, if you choose) that he will follow you. You then answer the questions yourself, first. You are aware you speak to thirty-two members of a community who are in conflict.

"Thanks Bob," you say, smiling as you do so, somewhat nervously.

You state to the group:

"My purpose is to get us all started in what Bob calls a grounding. I'm going to begin by reading off three questions and then answering them myself. Then I'm going to turn to my left and start with you, Tony, and we will go clockwise around the circle (motioning with your hand clockwise) and everyone will have a chance to answer the questions.

"Here are the questions:

"Introduce yourself; what is your relationship to our conflict in the basin?
"What are your expectations for this workshop?
"How do you feel about being here?"

YOU now answer the questions yourself.

> **CHOOSE TO BE YOU**
>
> Use your actual name here when you answer the questions. If you choose, you can develop your own statements in answer to the questions above. What would your answers be? Try it and see how it feels, to see what you can learn. Be my cofacilitator.

"My name is…YOU. I am a long-time resident of this basin. My parents lived here their whole life until the lumber mill closed in the '90s. We moved to Metropolis where my dad found work at another lumber mill. I left a job here to be with them.

"I had already decided to go to the university there, where I focused on the environmental sciences with a minor in the social sciences. I completed my master's degree. My thesis was on the impact of the changes that occurred in this basin when the mills were closed.

"I interviewed 120 people in the basin as part of my investigation, and that includes most of you in this room. While doing the interviews, I got homesick for the basin, so I relocated here and have been here now for five years. "After listening to the impacts of the mills and mine closing, I was very upset that I could do nothing about it or know who could help. Then I watched the zoning issue erupt into what I consider violent behaviors, and it scared me. I wondered if anything could be done about it, but I was clueless.

"I work as assistant manager at the grocery store, so I got all the gossip and news there about what was going on. When he interviewed me, I had asked Bob if it was possible to resolve these issues and bring the community back together. He said yes, and he asked if I was interested in learning how to do that. He decided then that I would help him cofacilitate this workshop. That's how I got here.

"My expectations are to learn how to facilitate a community to consensus. My other expectation is that you will all be able to listen to and learn from each other and reach a consensus for this basin that others will agree with and support.

"I feel both apprehensive and excited about doing this; I am very shy normally, so Bob has put me in a challenging position.

"I am going to repeat the questions and then start with you, Tony, and we will continue clockwise."

You now read off the questions from the three-by-five card for the second time:

"Introduce yourself, what is your relationship to our conflict in the basin?"
"What are your expectations for this workshop?"
"How do you feel about being here?"

"So, let's have Tony to my left begin to answer the question, and then we will go around the circle clockwise."

There is some self-consciousness again, normally, but the individual answers the questions, taking time to express his identity, his expectations, and his feelings. Once started, the person becomes less anxious.

The process continues clockwise around the circle, each person answering the questions in turn, their confidence gaining as the process continues. They are aware now that they will have their opportunity to speak; they will be listened to, unencumbered by the fear of interruption.

There is tension in some of the voices, and I often sense a person overcoming deep fears to speak out clearly for the first time in a group of strangers. Some actually preface their remarks with a statement like this:

"I don't normally speak in groups of people. I am basically shy (introverted) and anxious and prefer to speak one-on-one."

They then answer the questions to the whole group confidently, as if in making this declaration, they are free to ignore it.

I listen to the tone of voice as people speak. In a group of people fearful of conflict, the tone is soft, barely discernible, while in a group used to conflict (normally white males), the tone is loud and demanding or challenging. This helps me understand the character of the group.

As the grounding progresses, the attention people give to each speaker is unmistakable. They begin to lean in, to look intently at the speaker, to nod their heads. Those taking notes soon stop writing and listen intently. People begin to display the behavior I call *listening with respect.*

In having YOU facilitate, I send a number of nonverbal messages to the group:

- I am willing to share power with you and will trust you to facilitate yourselves.
- You have the ability to each facilitate yourselves.
- You can listen to each other and then represent what was said.

Let's listen to the people in the grounding.

Grounding Perspectives and Roles

(Note: The following are all fictional characters. Their comments are also fictional, created in my own mind for purposes of this book. However, I have worked with many people who match these descriptions and who expressed similar statements, so this group and what they express is representative of a real group.)

Tony Marshall (County Commissioner And Environmentalist):

"Good morning! I'm Tony Marshall, a relative newcomer to the Coyote Springs area. I came here a little over ten years ago when the basin development boom was just starting. I was fortunate enough to purchase forty acres from Jack, adjacent to his ranch. I have a ranchette there where I raise quarter horses and guide folks on horse trips into the Coyote National Forest.

"I retired here from California, where I had a number of sportsmen's stores. I was bought out by a large chain. I sought a place to retire where there weren't so many people and where people were friendly. I thought that's what I found here.

"I was talked into running for county commissioner six years ago by Lynn's group and was surprised to win. It's my first time in elected office, so I'm a little new at what I'm doing. My platform was around developing a new land-use plan for the basin with the intent of protecting this very unique area from overdevelopment. I know that sounds like I wanted to close the gate after I got into the valley, but frankly I realized quickly that the basin could be easily overdeveloped and lose its charm. I preferred that we become a destination-resort kind of place where people come to play and not to stay. That was also my platform.

"I'm hoping we're all here for the same reason and to bring our community back together. I am deeply disturbed that our decision to create some zoning regulations in the county would've created such turmoil and turn neighbor against neighbor. I know, Jack, you're pretty angry at me about my supporting the new zoning regulations. You've been able to be pretty blunt with me on your feelings about that. It feels like **OUCH**! And I never felt comfortable with you after you came to that last meeting with your rifle.

"Well, I don't want to be your enemy any more. I don't want to fear for my life anymore. I'd like to go back to being your neighbor. Our focus ought not to be on each other, but on what we can do to protect this beautiful place. I want people to come here to play and not to stay. I think that should be our purpose.

"So I'm feeling both apprehensive and hopeful about today. I'm apprehensive because this could be just another meeting that turns into a shouting match. Hopeful because I understand Bob has worked with other folks in the same kind of situation.

"I guess you're next, Jack."

Jack Trades (rancher):

"When I started out this morning, I never imagined I'd end up sitting between two of the people I am most upset with. But I guess that comes from being late and having only one chair left. But unlike the rest of you, I had work to do today, so it took a little time to get here.

"I'm Jack Trades, and I come from a family that has been in the basin longer than anybody else in the room, with the exception of Frank. I manage our family ranch, which is just outside of Coyote Springs. We own over fifteen thousand acres on the south side of the valley, adjacent to the river. We run our cattle there in the winter and early spring and on fifteen thousand acres of National Forest land in the summer.

"Being in the ranching business is not fun these days. There are higher prices for almost everything—for taxes, fertilizer, power, feed, gasoline, you name it. We don't have much of a margin of error, so we are always fighting to keep our ranch. Most of our family members have second jobs in order to support the place. Our biggest fear is we will have to sell the ranch and lose over one hundred years of heritage."

Jack stops speaking and puts his head down, waiting until he can control his emotions. Then he raises his head and looks around the group.

"I'll do almost anything to keep that from happening, including bringing my gun to that meeting," he says, looking directly at Tony. "It's my responsibility to protect my family—past, present, and future."

"I guess you all know that's why I'm here. I'm opposed to the zoning plan." (Jack has angry tones now.) "I'm opposed to all of you 'newbies' who came into the basin with your ideas about how to manage this area as if it was a city. Well, it ain't going to work!" (Raising his voice.) "We've been in this valley for over a hundred years, and we've taken good care of it. If you think it's beautiful and needs to be protected, it's because we had something to do with that."

Jack pauses, his head down. Then he looks up and continues.

"Now, I don't know what to expect here. I hear that Bob knows what he's doing, and I was impressed with him during the interview. I think this is just a hopeless cause. The best way to solve this problem is for all you newbies to go back to where you came from. It's beyond belief that we could ever solve this problem in three days. Now, with that happy news, I'll turn it over to you, Lynn."

Lynn Simmers (retiree/newbie):

"Thanks, Jack…I guess. I agree that this is the closest we have been in any meetings we've had in the past. Seems like we sat as far away from each other as possible. And I actually heard what you said—I believe for the first time—because you were not shouting. At least not much. So maybe this is a good sign.

"I'm Lynn Simmers, from Pittsburgh, Pennsylvania, originally, where my husband and I owned a hardware store. Like Tony, we were bought out by a chain, so we moved to the urban area outside Pittsburgh. It got so crowded around us that we began to look for an area that would not be developed, that was somewhat isolated and in the West. We did lots of looking, traveling by car, and on the Internet. We ended up settling here eight years ago.

"We have a small acreage on a subdivision not too far from Frank's ranch. In fact, I think it used to be part of his ranch. We became concerned about the amount of development that was going on around us and decided to look into it. It was like the nightmare we lived in Pittsburgh.

"When we found there was an outdated land-use plan, thousands of lots with no infrastructure and no zoning plan, we decided to get active and do something about it. It didn't take long for us to find that most of the people in the basin felt the same way we did. So we encouraged Tony and Marcia to run for commissioner because they have the same mind-set as we do.

"I am pleased that they were willing to be proactive in establishing a planning committee with a new county planner and develop a land-use plan that received overwhelming support. But the trouble really started when we pushed to have the zoning plan developed that would carry out the purpose of the land-use plan. That's when you-know-what hit the fan!

"My life has been filled with turmoil ever since. I never realized how angry people could get in a place where all I've met before were friendly people. I can't believe the horrible anonymous letters I am getting almost every week. I just don't understand what happened or why. I think my purpose is the same as yours, Jack, to keep this valley beautiful. But somehow we did something wrong.

"I guess that's what I'm here for. I want to do something right. I want to re-create that valley where everybody was getting along with each other, where everybody was kind. So, I hope we can leave this meeting setting a model for the rest of the community. I am willing to do anything to make that happen.

"I am so relieved that we are here. I'm so relieved that we're finally talking to each other. I know that three days is a lot of time, but we're dealing with the future of this valley and the future of our relationships with each other. So, I'll stick it out for a whole three days."

I look around the circle. All eyes are on the speakers. No one is distracted, leaned back, or disengaged. This will continue as the grounding proceeds. People are curious to hear what each person says.

Kathy Brewster (senior/retiree/townie):

"My name is Kathy Brewster. I guess I'd be called a 'townie' since I've lived here most of my life. I don't know where those names came from, but I think they are sort of cute. And they're being used in pretty mean ways. In all my years in this valley, I've never seen people be so mean to each other.

"I'm a senior citizen, a retiree, and I live in River City. I have worked in a number of places, including in the Forest Service, at the lumber mill for a while, and in the River City bookstore, which I later purchased and recently sold to Marcia. I even worked for a while with the Coyote Mountain Tribe. I guess it sounds like I couldn't keep a job, doesn't it?

"I read the news every day, so was interested when I heard about the move to develop a land-use plan. I believed we need an updated one, so I joined Lynn's group. I've been pretty active on it since. I was added to the county Planning Commission two years ago and helped to develop the zoning regulations.

"I don't believe any of us intended for the upset or mess that has happened. When it did happen, I became really frightened. I live alone, so I was very upset when I received some anonymous letters threatening me. And I didn't like seeing armed men at our meetings.

"I'm here because I want to bring this basin back together. We are all too intelligent to let this issue of zoning break us apart. I know that us folks that live in the valley hold grudges for a long time. But that's normally just been a few folks. This covers the entire basin.

"So let's get on with it. I feel like we have work to do here. I don't have that many more years left that I can afford to spend it in misery. I want to leave here happy. Let's get on with it."

Marcia Nelson (retiree/business owner/commissioner):

"My name is Marcia Nelson and I'm chairperson of the Coyote County Board of Commissioners. As Lynn said earlier, I was elected about six years ago, and I ran on the platform of doing something about managing growth here in the basin.

"I grew up in central Oregon, in the Bend area. My dad was in the logging industry so I witnessed the horrendous conflicts between the environmentalists and timber industry during the seventies. I was always torn about which side I was on. I agreed that there was too much timber being cut down with not enough care shown for the land, but also feared what would happen if the industry ever shut down.

"Of course you all know how the industry shut down in Oregon, just as well as it did here in the basin. It was a terrible thing to see. The timber-dependent communities dried up, families were broken up, and many were dislocated to other parts of the country. My dad lost his job, and he died shortly after from a heart attack. My mom followed him. When I came here, this basin was suffering the same consequences, with the mill closing and the mine closing.

"I was able to buy a bookstore in Bend and had a pretty good business for over thirty years. I left with my husband because I couldn't stand the influx of people into the area. People with lots of money were building big houses and changing the rural nature of the community. So we really escaped.

"We live in a subdivision between River City and Coyote Springs. When I and my husband got here, I was fortunate to meet Kathy, who was ready to sell her bookstore, so I bought it. I got to meet a lot of people from the basin and found them to be wonderfully friendly, open, and accepting of us. In the process I also heard about the concerns with unregulated growth in the basin. Having just escaped that, I understood the need for some controls.

"Lynn encouraged me to run for county commissioner, I did and won pretty easily. So I was one of those who supported hiring Kenney as county planner, getting in new people on the Planning Commission, and developing a land-use plan and zoning regulations.

"I guess I was listening to the wrong people, because I sure found out there were many people who disagreed with those decisions. Especially the ranchers. Frank and I got into a few shouting matches over the zoning plan, and I think all of you have seen Jack and I get into some shouting matches at the county commission meetings. We acted like fools.

"I'm not happy about what's going on here. I don't think people understand what could happen to this beautiful basin if we don't manage the growth. I know we need jobs here, especially since the mines and lumber mills have closed. But I believe we can bring people here to recreate, without having them stay. I'm not against growth itself, I just want it regulated, and I think most people in the basin agree with that.

"The controversies in this basin have affected my relationship with some of my customers and reduced my business. So this is personal to me. I just don't know why everybody has to be so angry about this zoning plan. So we better do something about it here.

"Donna invited me to coffee one day and told me about Bob. I talked to the other board members, and we agreed we should see if he would come and help us. He agreed to do that. So my expectation is just like I heard from Donna. We need a miracle from him.

"I'm glad to be here; my husband is taking care of the store for these three days. So I am ready to go to work."

Rayni Day (environmentalist/Audubon Society president):

"I'm Rayni Day, my dad and mom are Sonny and Liz Day who used to live right here in River City. I guess I got my name because it was raining the day I was born. My dad, of course, was born on a sunny day." (Laughter.) "I grew up in the basin, went to college in Berkeley, majored in environmental sciences.

"I came home just after the environmental movement began to appeal timber sales all over the country. I helped to form our basin environmental group with Alice. When we began to appeal timber sales on the National Forest land, people in the community got pretty darned mad at us. It caused some real problems between my dad and mom and I, because they worked in the lumber mill. As time went on, I decided to leave and go elsewhere because it caused too many problems within my family.

"So I spent eighteen years in the Northwest, working for the Sierra Club, writing timber-sale appeals. I came back here after the courts and Congress had pretty much shut down logging in National Forests. My dad and mom had moved to Metropolis to find work, and I'm renting their home from them here in the city.

"I am working for the Nature Conservancy and am president of the local Audubon Society. I am identifying areas in this basin that are unique enough that the Conservancy could buy them and manage them to their natural state.

"I joined a group that supported the land-use plan, was included on the Planning Commission the past two years as a member, and helped to develop the zoning proposals.

"I was not surprised by the response of the community, because people have been pretty much allowed to do whatever they want with their land. While people have rights to their land, water rights and heritage rights, they also have a responsibility to the land, the river, the fish, and also their children. We're not trying to take something away from you, we're just trying to help you use that right responsibly. If we learn to do what is responsible, then we won't have to worry about the courts or Congress coming in and making decisions for us.

"My expectation of this workshop is that somehow all of us can understand the responsibility we have and the opportunity we have to take control of our own destiny. I don't want to stop growth; I don't want to run the cows off the range; I don't even want to prevent timber cutting if it's appropriate. I just want us to do what is right for the land and the water and the people.

"I'm happy to be here. I like the circle. I feel at home here, with my friends and my neighbors and my community. Thanks to the commissioners for making this possible."

Johanna Shine (retired educator/member of the school board):

"Good morning! My name is Johanna Shine. I am a retired educator from Irvine, California, where I was a school superintendent. I came here with my family the same time as Lynn, and we bought a small lot in a subdivision just outside of River City.

"Like Lynn, we were also disturbed when we noticed lots all around us being developed at a fierce pace. They're being developed without the proper infrastructure. Roads are being built improperly or not graded and are muddy in the winter. Septic systems are faulty; we don't have access to city water, so we have to drill wells, and they are very expensive. We are out of range of the city fire department, so our insurance rates are high. If we had a forest fire, our homes would burn.

"I just feel we have a need to do some clear thinking about how we want to manage growth in this place. I don't want to close the gate behind me either, but I do want to make sure that when people come here, there is some order to how we develop the area. That's why I supported the land-use plan and continue to support the zoning plan. I don't want to see this area become like California.

"I feel like Kathy does—we have caused a lot of turmoil with our decisions on the zoning regulations. I think it should be just simple enough to listen to each other and determine what we can come up with that meets all of our needs. So I am happy to be here. Like Kathy said, let's get on with it!"

Kenney Couric (county planner):

"Hi. I'm Kenney Couric, county planner, responsible for all of the hullabaloo we see around the county. I was hired by the county commissioners about six years ago to help this county develop a land-use plan that would fit the twenty-first century. It was a hit, until we followed it with the zoning plan and ordinance.

"Like, wow! I have never seen animosity like this before in all my years of planning. The reason is, I suppose, I've always worked in cities or urban areas where people are used to being regulated. Oh, there might be some disagreements, but never to this extent with the amount of shouting and threats that we have here. I've never received threatening letters like I have here. My kids are even being harassed at school. I tell them it is just how democracy works sometimes.

"It is a real lesson for me. I realize now that in this culture, the concept of individual rights and property rights have real meaning. This is especially true with the agricultural community. So I do want all of you to know that I not only have a better understanding of the issue, but I believe there are some solutions that we can use to solve it. But we have to be together on it.

"This is not the only issue that faces the county that will affect agriculture. You all know that Metropolis is looking at buying water rights from this basin for their use. They have bought some in the past, but their needs could probably suck this basin dry. And the Coyote Mountain Tribe has asserted their rights to fish, which they can't do right now because the river flows and water quality are too low for spawning. Fisheries biologists at both the state and federal levels are pressuring us to do something about this immediately.

"You also know that we are in a pretty poor economic situation. With the lumber mills and the mines having closed, we just don't have enough work in the basin for those who need it. The only glimmer of hope on the horizon is the Coyote Mountain Tribe's proposal for a casino in the lower basin. This would bring many people in from Metropolis, and they would leave their money here and go home. This would fit Tony's declaration about 'coming to play and not coming to stay.'

"Each of these issues gets into the arena of personal or tribal rights. That means we need to learn how to solve these kinds of issues. If we can solve the one on zoning, then I believe we can solve the rest.

"So my expectation is we are here to solve the zoning problem so we can learn how to solve the others. I do believe there are solutions if we will just agree to work together. I am a person who believes we can do whatever we set our hearts and minds on. I'm hopeful you'll prove me right."

Laura Lincoln (county attorney):

"My name is Laura Lincoln. My husband and I moved here just a little over a year ago and opened a law office in Coyote Springs. I put in a bid a year ago to provide legal services for the county and was selected. This happened right in the middle of the zoning issue, so I have had a quick learning curve.

"I still don't understand all the complexities of zoning, nor do I completely understand the rationale for the highly emotional response. So I am still learning. I want to just listen, hopefully learning enough to be able to create some possible solutions.

"I really don't have a lot more to say. I am glad we're doing this. Like some of the previous people, I am very anxious about the threats that have been made. I just don't believe the basin community wants this. So, I'll just listen now."

Jon Efron (agriculture business consultant):

"My name is Jon Efron. I came to the basin from Calgary, Canada, with my family in the seventies, when business was booming. I have a graduate degree in agricultural engineering and provide consulting services to the agricultural businesses in the basin. I have business relations with the agricultural machine companies, the feed and fertilizer stores, the irrigation co-ops, and the individual ranchers and farmers.

"Agriculture is a big business in the basin and provides work for a lot of people. As you heard earlier, the economic situation is not very healthy for the ranchers and farmers. It is going to take a lot of ingenuity and community support to keep these businesses running.

"I have taken no stand on the zoning issue; I don't have enough knowledge to know what is right. I do know that it is affecting the ranchers in this room. The last thing they need is to put energy into this conflict rather than into their ranches. So my hope is that we can resolve this issue by the time the workshop is over.

"I feel three days is a lot of time to spend on this and hope we can maybe get it all done today. If this workshop is as unproductive as other meetings we've had, today is probably all I will spend.

Frank Sommers (rancher/commissioner):

"To start off, I'm madder than hell, like Jack. I shouldn't be here today; I should be at the ranch working on chores that need to be done. Most of you folks are getting paid today, but I'm not. I'm losing money every minute I sit here and doing nothing but talk.

"I'm Frank Sommers. I'm a rancher in the basin. Like Jack, my family has been here for over a hundred years. His family beat us here by less than a year. We own eighteen thousand acres of bottomland along the river and up into the forest, where we graze cattle. We also lease ten thousand acres from the Bureau of Land Management.

"I have two sons who help me manage the ranch and one daughter, Diane, who is just down from me a few chairs, who just finished college. Hopefully, she is smarter than the rest of us and will be able to help us through the tough economic times. I also have seven grandchildren who go to school in River City.

"We have a long heritage with ranching. We intend to see that continues with our children and grandchildren and great-grandchildren and hopefully longer. As Jack and Jon mentioned, these economic times make it difficult, but we have been through many difficult times before. We plan to be here a long time.

"But the last thing we need is for our own community, our own neighbors, to make it difficult to do this. We believe that the zoning plan is detrimental to our private property rights and our water rights. Now, I have been a county commissioner for over twelve years. I have been on the commission longer than anyone else. Originally I supported the land-use plan because I felt it was a way of looking at the future.

"I did not understand that a zoning plan or zoning regulation would be included that would be detrimental to the interests of the agricultural community. I voted against it, but was outnumbered. It was at my urging that the ranching and farming community and all the other businesses come together and oppose it. Hopefully, a little later, we will get a turn at telling you why we believe that. Not yelling...but telling.

"Kenney told us earlier that we will be faced with some similar issues in the near future. Every one of these is going to require that we make decisions together so that no one is left out. With our economic situation the way it is, we cannot afford to lose any of our existing businesses.

"I guess that describes what I am expecting to happen here...that we learn to work together and that we solve this issue together. If we do this, we can do the rest.

"Whether or not I feel good about this workshop will depend upon what happens today."

Donna Mason (RCD director):

"My name is Donna Mason. I am a newcomer to the basin, having arrived just three years ago. I came from northern California, where I worked as director of a local Soil and Water Conservation District. I was offered the position as manager of the local Rural Conservation District and accepted it because the area is very similar to the area I came from. I've spent most of my life in rural communities, with the exception of the time I went to college in Berkeley.

"The RCD is a special nonprofit district that works with both public and private individuals in the areas of land-use planning, soil and water conservation, wildlife habitat enhancement and restoration, and watershed restoration. Unfortunately, I came a little too late to help you with your land-use planning and zoning.

"Since both Jack and Frank are on my board, I ended up supporting the ranchers in their efforts to stop the zoning regulations from moving forward because of the negative impact they would have on agriculture in the basin.

"I am still a newcomer—I guess you call me a newbie—so I don't fully understand all of the history of this. I just know that what is being proposed would be disastrous for agriculture in this basin. I was concerned enough to contact Bob Chadwick, who I have worked with before on a similar issue, to see if he might be available to help us straighten this out. Marcia, I really appreciate that you followed up with a call to Bob and that the commissioners agreed to hire him to help us.

"My expectation is that we will take the time to listen to each other during these three days, to get some understanding of what is really going on. What I have noticed is that nobody is listening. I think if we just do that and get an understanding of the impact of zoning on agriculture, that would move us ahead as a community.

"So I'm happy to be here. I am paid to do this, as Frank said, so I'll do whatever I can to make this workshop a success. Bob, since I'm the one who recommended you, you better pull off a miracle here."

Todd Gimble (recreational resort owner):

"Good morning, everyone. My name is Todd Gimble, and I own the Chilly Mine Resort in the upper end of the basin. I have a special-use permit from the Forest Service, and we provide cabins throughout the year. Mostly our clients are people from outside the basin who come in for fishing and hunting, snowmobiling, and cross-country skiing. Business has been slow, and it would be much better if some of you local folks would come up and enjoy the services I provide. Thought I'd just throw in a little commercial there." (Laughter.)

"I've lived in this valley all my life. My dad and my granddad worked in the mine, and I worked there for a little bit too. But I could see that mining was a dead-end job, so I took my savings and bought the resort ten years ago. Like the ranchers, it's a marginal occupation, but it keeps me and my family up in the country that we love.

"I'm upset about the zoning regulations because I would be required to invest a lot of money in improvements to meet their standards. And I just don't have that kind of money. I don't see how you can begin to regulate people in a way that makes it more difficult to provide jobs in this valley. I am here because Donna twisted my arm and said I had to be here. Frankly, it's a waste of my time. But she's been a help to me, so I'm just paying back the favor.

"I am also worried about the condition of the Coyote River. When I was younger, about forty years ago, I used to fish for salmon with my dad, God rest his soul. I'll never forget those days; they were some of the happiest times of my life. But the mines have done some terrible things to this basin, to the river, and to the people. My dad died from lung disease at an early age. And the drainage of the mine tailings into the river has damaged the water quality to the point that the salmon can't return. This affects my business because a lot of people come here looking to fish. So I'm here to do whatever is necessary to clean the river up to get the fish back.

"I don't have any expectations, mainly because I think the people who want zoning are close minded. They have a city way of thinking that just doesn't fit up here. I'm not sure we could work together long enough to help the fish.

"I guess that's all I have to say."

Debbe Trujillo (National Resources Conservation Service project manager):

"I am Debbe Trujillo. I'm a project manager for the NRCS. I've lived in this basin my entire life. My dad, José Trujillo, has an eighty-acre truck farm just east of River City along the river, and we also run lots of different livestock there: cattle, goats, sheep, and llamas.

"The NRCS was formerly called the Soil Conservation Service, and my dad had lots of help and support from them over the years. I worked for them during the summers when I was a kid. The agency was changed to the NRCS some years ago. I have worked with the NRCS since I left high school and worked my way up to being a project manager for this basin.

"My dad never heard about the land-use plan until Donna talked to us about it. We also had no say in the zoning regulations. So I'm here to listen and learn, both for my agency and for the other farmers in the basin. We have lots of farms that raise wheat, alfalfa, mint, and even have some people exploring vineyards. I'm here to represent their views since they can't be here.

"The basin has a large number of Hispanic migrant families who work on the farms and ranches. Many of them used to work in the mills and mines. They are an invisible people in this basin. They need jobs, and they need low-income housing. So I am also here to see that they are represented.

"I want to thank Donna for inviting me here, and I want to thank the commissioners for having this workshop."

I continue to survey the group as the speakers continue. All are engaged. I notice that a few people are leaving for restroom breaks. They are quiet and respectful as they do so.

Dawn Marie Gade (county water master):

"I am Dawn Marie Gade. I have lived in the basin for three years now. The county commissioners hired me to take the place of the retired county water master. In addition to managing water rights in the basin, I have also been assigned the task of working with the tribal fish biologists and the National Marine Fisheries Service. As Kenney said earlier, we have been directed to develop a salmon recovery plan for Coyote River.

"I'm a single parent who raised three children who are grown up and on their own. Hopefully they're working on giving me some grandchildren soon. I graduated from Idaho State University with a master's degree in water management. So I am prepared to take on the task the commissioners have assigned me.

"We really don't have a water-quantity problem in the basin; we have a water-distribution problem. The water that is being diverted for irrigation purposes exceeds the water rights that have been filed in this basin. Part of the reason is that many of the residents in the subdivisions are diverting water from irrigation ditches for their use. They believe it's their stream.

"We also have large water losses with seepage from the unlined ditches. I am working with Donna at the RCD to see if we can get some grant money for piping some of these ditches so we can divert more water back into the river. I know this is a touchy subject for a lot of the agricultural interests in the valley. But I think we can work together and solve this problem.

"We also have a water-quality problem with the rivers and streams, mainly as a result of previous mining and logging roads. There's also some damage on riverbanks that is being done by the grazing of cattle.

"So I'm here to put in my two bits about the effect on the land-use plan and zoning regulations and to explore the possibility of setting up some sort of water-management group for the basin. Since I'm new here, I'm just going to listen and learn. I appreciate being invited."

Diane Sommers (college student/rancher's daughter):

"I'm Diane Sommers. I was introduced earlier by my dad, Frank Sommers. I lived in this basin all my life and just returned from college, where I majored in agricultural engineering. I've only been back for a year, but I have been surprised by the amount of animosity there is in the basin. Frankly, it's a little scary.

"I'm here to listen and learn and to provide advice where I can. My dad encouraged me to go to college because he knew that we were going to have to change our ways in managing the ranch if we wanted to keep it. After listening to everyone who was spoken so far, I have a better understanding of what he meant.

"My expectation is to learn as much as I can and help this group make the best decisions we can so that my family can continue to maintain our heritage in this valley.

"I'm a little nervous about being here; I believe I'm the youngest person in the room. I wish there were more people here my age, because it is their future we are talking about. I'm sure I'll have a lot more to say as I learn more."

Neil Gorman (county executive):

"My name is Neil Gorman. I am the county executive. I was hired about five years ago by the newly elected board. They hired me because they saw there were many issues in the basin that needed to be addressed, and they wanted someone to manage them. I went right to work with Kenney and the planning commission on the land-use plan and zoning regulations. We all did this with a sense of excitement and purpose and with a feeling that we were doing something that was proactive that would protect this basin from unregulated growth.

"Our purpose was not to prevent growth. It was really to determine how we could allow the basin to grow and yet maintain our rural culture. We tried to get as many people involved as possible, including all three communities, but the response was underwhelming at our meetings. So we made decisions with the people who agreed to participate.

"Obviously, the results were not very pleasant. We overlooked a lot of people because we weren't aggressive enough in getting people to all those planning meetings. It's been a real lesson for me and has brought a lot of us back down to earth.

"I really appreciate the county commissioners making a decision to bring everybody together. I have no doubt that we can solve this problem, and I believe we've been given enough time to do that in this workshop. That is my expectation.

"As I look around this room, I see a very diverse group of people, and I believe we have the right people here. So I'm feeling there are some possibilities for good outcomes from this workshop."

Susan Parkes (fisheries biologist):

"I'm Susan Parkes. I'm a fisheries biologist for the Coyote Mountain Tribe. I was hired to help the tribes develop a restoration plan for the Coyote River and its tributaries. I worked for the Forest Service before that, but got laid off. I've lived in the Coyote Springs community for eight years and love the people I have met. I have found that local people are highly interested in the idea of bringing the salmon back, especially the older people. They remember when they were young and they could fish in the river.

"I worked with the county Planning Commission and provided them information and advice that they could use in completing the land-use plan and then developing the zoning regulations. I was shocked at the response from the agricultural interests and other local people. Much of this has to do with protection of individual rights, property rights, and water rights.

"When I was first here, people described to me the battles between the environmentalists, the timber industry, and the mines. In the end, the courts and Congress made the final decision. I don't know if those were the right decisions or not, but it did take away the right for the community to make the decisions themselves.

"Our purpose, the Coyote Mountain Tribe, is to bring the salmon back. My responsibility is to improve the quality and quantity of water in the Coyote River and its tributaries. We are working with the ranchers on providing fish screens on the pumps in the river and on the water diversions. Cleaning up the river is going to affect everyone in this room. I would prefer to find the solutions right here in the basin.

"I am hoping that this is a good place to start that effort. I don't believe we can accept the present zoning if we are going to protect the resources in this basin. But I believe there is a zoning proposal that could do that. I'm here to support that kind of effort."

Jim San Luis (US Forest Service district ranger):

"I am Jim San Luis, I work with the Forest Service. I am district ranger for the Coyote Mountain Ranger District. I came three years ago from Colorado.

I live in River City with my family. We have three girls, and they are all in elementary school.

"I have been an observer when it comes to the land-use plan and zoning regulations because I am so focused on our downsizing. I have been pretty busy reducing the workforce in the district to reflect our new workload. We built up a large workforce during the heavy timber years, and now, with the mills closed and most of the district in roadless areas or wilderness, we need a much smaller workforce. So we have been laying people off the last three years as our budget declines. Not much fun, let me tell you.

"I know about the decisions related to the salmon, and we are directed to do what we can to rehabilitate the rivers and streams where they fall within our jurisdiction. That means we have refocused our work on closing logging roads and cleaning trash out of the streams.

"We are also focused on reducing fire hazards, especially in the areas surrounding those subdivisions. They are a fire hazard in themselves, with too many fuels on the ground and close to homes. They are a long way from fire protection. Someday a fire will wipe out one of these subdivisions, unless we do a better job of fire prevention.

"I am in support of new zoning regulations for the basin because the ones we have now are not appropriate for the conditions of today. But we need to be sure we don't overregulate and close out opportunities for economic development and reasonable growth in the future. It's going to be quite a balancing act.

"I would be willing to participate more in the further development of these zoning regulations, especially as they relate to fire control in the rural areas adjacent to or within the forest and a cleanup of the river.

"I agree with Debbe that we have many Hispanic people in the basin who are in poverty, without jobs, some without homes to live in. We need to create jobs and low-income housing for these people.

"This is my first real opportunity to meet most of you. I know most of the ranchers in the room, since we have worked together on their grazing leases. I hope to get to know the rest of you before the three days are over."

Crista Jackson (tribal economic development director):

"Bob, it is my turn to speak, but I would like to have my elder speak first. Is that possible?"

Yes, Crista, I say, you can speak when he is finished. And, I might add, I know this grounding is taking a long time. It is important to let the grounding continue without interruption until everyone in the circle has had their opportunity to speak and be listened to. I appreciate that you are taking care of your personal needs one at a time. We will take a break when the talking circle is completed.

> **ALWAYS FINISH THE GROUNDING**
>
> Sometimes the grounding takes a long time. When it does, continue until it is complete. Taking a break before the talking circle ends makes those who didn't talk feel left out, and it changes the entire conversation. Encourage people to take restroom breaks one at a time if they need them. I keep the circle moving.

Allen Smith (Coyote Mountain Tribal Council chairman; seated next to Crista):

Thank you, Crista. I am Allen Smith, chairman of the Coyote Mountain Tribe. I thank you all for inviting us here, for treating us with respect.

"I have lived in this basin all my life. My people have lived here since the beginning of time. Our elders tell us the story of how we were brought here by Coyote through the mouth of Coyote Mountain. We lived here in harmony with the land, getting our food from the rivers and plains. The fish, the antelope and deer, the buffalo fed us, and we lived happy lives.

"My grandfathers wintered in the lower reaches of the basin and moved to the mountain plains in the summer, camping by the mouth of the mountain, where the mine is now.

"We were a peaceful people. We welcomed the first white settlers over a hundred and twenty years ago, welcoming them to the basin and treating them as our friends. In return, they took the land away from us, digging into Mother Earth with their plows. They killed us with their diseases. Even though we were peaceful, they put us on a reservation and denied us the freedom to roam the land as we had always done.

"They killed the buffalo. They cut the forests that covered the mountains and mined the mouth of the mountain, desecrating our sacred site. Even though we fought in the world war, they denied us the right to our religion, the right to vote. They took our children away and denied them the right to speak their native tongue.

"Yet, we remained peaceful, trusting in the Creator. We have slowly learned how to get these rights back. The courts have acknowledged our rights to hunt and fish this land, our rights to the water, our rights to our religion and to vote. We have gone to the courts, and they have affirmed our rights to have salmon in the streams again and have directed all the federal and state agencies to make this possible.

"Alice encouraged us to be here. She has been a trustworthy friend of my people and has been an outspoken supporter in our fight to get our rights back. She invited us to help with the land-use plan and the zoning regulations. The tribe has supported the people who have been working on the land-use plan and who have developed the zoning regulations. We have done this because we see that will help us bring the resources of this basin back to my tribe.

"While we support their efforts, we have not been part of the loud arguments that are going on with the zoning regulations. That is not the way of my people. We prefer to do this in a more peaceful way.

"My hope is that we can all come together as a community of people who live and enjoy this beautiful land. My hope is that we can all speak our truth with respect and be willing to listen to each other. My hope is that we can bring back the native beauty of this land, that we can have enough clean water in the river to bring the salmon back so that my people can once again have the food that feeds our spirit and is the basis of our religion.

"I appreciate the invitation to be part of this group. I do not know many of you, but those I do know have good hearts. We will be here as long as it takes to bring peace back into the basin.

"That is all I have to say. I turn it back to you, Crista."

Crista Jackson (tribal economic development director):

"My name is Crista Jackson. I'm also a member of the Coyote Mountain Tribe. I've also lived here all my life except for the time I spent at college in Colorado. I came back here to work for my people, to see what I could do to make their life better. I am director of the tribe's economic development programs, including the proposed tribal casino.

"Our Tribal Council believes that the casino would be a creator of jobs, especially for our young people. But the council is also concerned that the casino will result in unregulated growth in the basin. It is important to our people that the land-use plan and the zoning regulations limit the growth until the basin resources have been allowed to replenish themselves. So we want that to happen before we move ahead with the casino. That is why we came today.

"I support the zoning proposals; they will make it possible to create economic development and still keep our basin beautiful. I know others in the room disagree with this, so I am willing to listen to your views.

"When I returned here from college, I married a non-Indian, and we purchased a small ranch adjacent to the reservation. We have four children, and our hope is that they will also go to college and return to help our people. We hope they will have jobs to come back to so they can stay. That is our hope for the casino, an opportunity for jobs for our people and other people in the basin.

"I am happy to be with all of you. We appreciate the invitation to participate in this. We are all part of this basin; we must work together peacefully.

"Wayne," she says, looking around, "you are next."

Wayne Lund (rancher):

"My name is Wayne Lund, and I've lived in the basin all my life. My family has a ranch in the upper end of the basin, at the junction of the three rivers that come off Coyote Mountain. We've been on that land for four generations now and hope that will continue to be in the family for many generations.

"Our ranch is on the opposite side of the river from the reservation, so a number of the tribal members work for me. I understand the concerns they have about the river and agree that something needs to be done about that.

"What Frank and Jack said about ranching and agriculture being marginal is correct. But I've been listening to Donna lately and doing lots of reading and believe there's a lot we can do about making our ranches much more productive. I think that is especially true about how we use our irrigation water.

"I also agree, however, that the zoning regulations that were proposed are not beneficial to the ranchers, farmers, or agriculture. They are much too restrictive. They might be fine in New York City, but they don't fit here. They limit the ability of the ranchers and farmers to sell parcels of land when the economy is bad. This provides them the financial resources to keep their ranches going for their younger generations. And there are concerns about your assumptions that you can manage our water rights, something that is very precious to our livelihood.

"I think we need to look at how we can rewrite those regulations so they actually help agriculture, rather than hurt it. And I have some ideas about that.

"That's what I hope happens here. We probably do need to update our zoning regulations so we can regulate how many people live up in this valley. I just think there is a middle ground between what we have now and what's been proposed.

"I'm happy to be here. I believe the decisions we make here are extremely important for the future of ranching in the basin. I'm happy I'll be part of making those decisions."

Mike Hatfield (rancher):

"My name is Mike Hatfield. I've lived in this area since my family moved here right after the Second World War. My dad purchased some ranchland downriver from River City, and we've been running cattle there ever since. We own twelve thousand acres of wheatgrass and sagebrush and lease out seven thousand acres from the BLM. When both my mom and dad passed on, I took over the ranch, and my intent is to pass it on to my two sons and hope they will continue to do the same.

"I agree with what Jack and Frank said earlier. So I won't repeat what they said. There aren't that many ranchers or farmers in this basin, probably less than 2 percent of the voting population. So that doesn't give us much of a say over what happens here if we decide by voting. But Donna tells me that we own over 15 percent of the land in the basin. Your proposal for zoning regulations would have a negative impact on the management of that land, taking away our water, limiting cattle access to the river, and limiting our ability to sell lands to keep our heads above water.

"So I'm here to be sure that my voice is heard. My expectation is that if you listen to us ranchers, you might change your mind about your zoning proposal. I hope that's the case. If not, then our time is wasted here. Then I guess we will just have to go to the courts.

"I'm not especially happy to be here today. I have a lot of work to do on the ranch. Thanks for listening."

Justin Scott (real estate agent, Coyote Springs City Council member):

"Hello, good morning. I am Justin Scott. I have a real estate business in River City. I grew up here, went to college in Michigan, and worked for six years in New York. I'm married with two children, and they are the reason that I'm here. I didn't want my children to grow up in a big city; I wanted them to grow up in a rural area, like I did.

"And their grandfather, Bud Scott, my father, has been pleading for me to come back for years. I worked in real estate in New York, so I opened up my own office here in the basin. I have been keeping my nose to the grindstone, so was really surprised when the conflict erupted around the zoning regulations.

"I read the zoning regulations and found them nowhere near as stringent as those I dealt with in New York. But they are a big change from what we have now. So I can understand why people are resisting this change.

"I'm here to represent the Chamber of Commerce and the Coyote Springs City Council, of which I am a member. Gil asked me to be here with him. I really have no specific expectations of this workshop, other than it is not wasted time.

"There are a lot of you here that I don't know, so I'm looking forward to meeting you. I guess that's all I have to say."

Cliff Ford (redeveloper/small-business consultant):

"I'm Cliff Ford. My wife and I own a real estate office in Coyote Springs, but I'll let her talk about that. I have a small business working as a small-business consultant. I often help Bud and the bank develop small businesses in River City and Coyote Springs.

"I am also a redeveloper. We purchase old homes, and I bring them back to their original condition. I am also active in the community as a member of the school board and am on the Coyote Springs Planning Commission.

"I don't like how the county developed their zoning regulations at all. We have our own city land-use plan and zoning regulations, and they are in conflict with the ones developed by the county. That's mainly because we were never asked to participate with the county planning effort.

"I really don't have any expectations of this meeting. I don't like meetings and I hate conflict and would not be here if Ann had not required me to be. (Laughter.)

"Three days is a lot of time to be away from my business. I just hope Bob can make this worth my while."

Marie Johnson (River City mayor, retired Hewlett-Packard employee):

"My name is Marie Johnson. I am the mayor of River City. I'm a former Hewlett-Packard employee, worked in Fort Collins, Colorado, for most of my career. My husband and I were looking for a place to retire and happened to spend some time at the Chilly Mine Resort, Todd's place in the upper basin. We both fell in love with the place, so when we retired, we purchased a home in River City. We purchased a beautiful home since the prices were right because the mills had closed and people were moving away. It happens to be one of the homes Cliff redeveloped.

"I got active politically in the community and was voted in as mayor two years ago. I believe that we need economic growth in the valley, but not the kind that will destroy its beauty. I believe that growth should be located around the edges of the existing communities so they can tap into our infrastructure. Also, I believe that we need some low-income houses so we can keep some of our younger families here.

"None of the elected officials from the city were involved in the county Planning Commission or in the decisions regarding land-use plan and zoning. I can tell you that all three communities agree that we should have been consulted more often, since zoning regulations will determine how our communities grow. We're a little upset that we were kept out of the loop.

"My expectation is that we will have a much clearer understanding of how the zoning regulations were developed and an understanding of how the final decision will be made. My expectation is that we will also be able to establish a communication link between the basin's communities and the county.

"I'm happy to be here representing the city. I'll do lots of listening and learning."

Bud Scott (River City Community Bank president):

"My name is Bud Scott, and I'm president of the local bank, the River City Community Bank. I've lived here all my life. My wife and I have raised three children, and they have given us six grandchildren. Two of my children live outside the basin, down in Metropolis and over in the Portland, Oregon, area. My son Justin lives here—you have already heard from him.

"When I was young, there were plenty of jobs in this area. The timber industry was going strong and the mining company was at its peak employment. If you graduated from high school, you could walk right into a good-paying job. Now our kids have to leave the basin because of the lack of jobs.

"I envy the older people in the basin who got to see their grandchildren grow up and stay here. I don't like having my children and grandchildren so far away.

"When I graduated from school, I got a part-time job at the bank and worked my way up to be president. I've seen a lot of changes in this basin and have encouraged and supported many of them. I've been a strong supporter of growth and economic development. The bank has invested in a lot of local small businesses since the mills and the mines closed.

"I was very supportive of the idea of the land-use plan, but I'm opposed to the proposed zoning regulations. I think it goes too far. It is especially damaging to the agricultural interests in the basin.

"My expectation is that we will come up with something here that is reasonable, that can allow us to grow at a reasonable pace, and that will create economic development in the basin. I support the Coyote Mountain Tribe's proposal for the casino because I think it will bring us lots of recreational jobs, even though they might not be high-paying ones.

"I should be working at the bank these three days because we're shorthanded this week. But I agreed to be here because it is important to our communities. I've not been involved in the details of all the controversy, so I'm willing to listen and learn here."

Gil Brothers (Chamber of Commerce president/developer/stockbroker):

"I am Gilbert Brothers. I'm president of the Coyote Basin Chamber of Commerce. I'm a land developer and also a stockbroker on the side. I grew up in the basin, went to college at the University of Southern California, where I got a business degree. After working with private industry, I came back here with my family to start my own businesses and have been successful in developing some of the subdivisions that people are complaining about.

"Frankly, I think the people who are opposed to growth are shortsighted in their thinking. I have four children, I would like them all to be able to go to college and come back here to find employment with reasonable wages. I would like my grandchildren to grow up in this basin. We need growth to get that.

"We can have the right kind of growth with reasonable changes in our present zoning regulations. I believe the proposed zoning regulations are designed to stop growth entirely. So I'm opposed to them.

"My expectations for this workshop are that we will find a way to develop zoning regulations that fit the needs of the basin. The present zoning proposal was developed by a small group of people who came from the outside and who are just trying to keep other people from coming in here.

"I agreed to be here to represent the business interest in the valley. I feel this will only be successful if what we do encourages economic development."

Alice Kimball (environmentalist):

"My name is Alice Kimball. I've been in this basin since I was born. I know all of the 'townies' in the basin and a good number of the 'newbies.' Like Kathy, I worked in a number of places in the basin, mostly in the school. I'm very concerned about our younger people, about their lack of opportunity for jobs in the basin since we lost the timber mills and the mines closed. But the only jobs they can get are working on the ranches or low-paying, temporary work during the summers. So our kids are all leaving and going other places where they can find better-paying jobs. I think it's a shame to see our young people leave.

"I am an avowed environmentalist, and all of you know it. I've never been shy about expressing my opinions about the clear-cuts in the National Forest, logging roads and all the damage that they have done. I've also been opposed to mining in the upper basin because of the damage the tailings have done to the river. And I believe that the ranchers and farmers are taking too much water out of the river for irrigation. Frank and I have tussled over this many times. The flows in the river are too low in the summer, temperatures are too high, and the water is dirty during the summer.

"We used to have so many salmon here that you could walk across the river on their backs. But the river is so fouled up now that they won't come back. I think it's a shame.

"I disagree with what Gil Brothers said about the proposed zoning regulations. He knows that I'm not opposed to reasonable growth. If we allow any more development on the subdivisions that are already platted and don't do anything about the inadequate septic systems, our rivers and streams will smell so bad we won't want to be near them. I would hate to see this valley lined with strip malls and fast-food places. That's what I'm afraid we're coming to."

Alice leans forward and speaks strongly.

"So I support the land-use plan, and I support the zoning. If you think it's too much, it's because we haven't had enough in the past. We have to do something to control growth.

"My hope is that we can leave here with some agreement about the land-use plan and the zoning regulations. I'd also like to leave here knowing we're going to do something about the kind of economic development that would protect this valley and provide jobs for our kids."

"I'm not exactly excited about being here, even though I know it's the right thing. I don't like getting threatened, and I don't like getting yelled at by people I grew up with. If that happens here, I'll leave."

George Hastings (resort owner):

"My name is George Hastings. I came here with that bunch of 'newbies' in the late nineties. I bought forty acres from Wayne, just above Coyote Springs. It's right along Coyote River. I built a lodge and some small cabins and hope to develop it further into a larger resort. It's going to be difficult to do that unless we clean the river up and get the salmon back. That's the major attraction here.

"I'm not opposed to growth here, but I am opposed to regulations that prevent reasonable growth. Some of the zoning regulations would restrict my development of the resort. I just think the regulations are more appropriate for a big city and not for a rural area like we have.

"So my expectation is that we will become more reasonable in what we hope for in this basin. We need economic growth here, we need places for our children to work when they graduate from high school. I don't see how we can do that unless we encourage reasonable growth.

"I support the tribe's proposal for a casino here in the basin. I think it would be a good thing and would have a low impact on the environment. And, it would bring me a lot of business." (Lots of laughter)

"I don't see how it's going to take three days to solve this little problem. So I'm reluctant to commit to that amount of time. I'll just see how it's going and decide day to day."

Ann Ford (real estate agency owner)

"I am Ann Ford. I live in Coyote Springs with my husband, Cliff. We moved here from Massachusetts twelve years ago when the area was beginning to grow. It was sort of a fluke; we happened to see a real estate agency was up for sale, so we bought it. We were pretty much city folks, so living in the basin is quite a frontier experience for us.

"People have always been friendly to us until this land-use plan and zoning regulations proposals. Now we feel like we're the evil villains who are encouraging unregulated growth. Some people in this room have been pretty nasty to us about it.

"We're just doing our job. If people want to buy a piece of land and build a house on it, that's their right. I don't know how you're going to have economic growth if you don't allow people to come up here to live. And you have to remember that increasing land values brings in more taxes to the county.

"Some of the lots that we sell have been here for over twenty years. It doesn't indicate to me there's a lot of growth going on. And the ranchers and farmers depend upon us to help them sell small pieces of land when they need the money to keep their places going. We're not out there twisting arms to put up land for sale.

"I'm here for the purpose of helping you folks see that we are not the enemy. We left Massachusetts because the regulations there had us all boxed in. I don't mind reasonable regulations, but the ones in the proposals have gone overboard. I hope we can help you see that.

"I was reluctant to come here, because I don't like being yelled at. If that happens, then I'm leaving with Alice."

Rob Painter (miner/bed and breakfast co-owner):

"I am Rob Painter; came down from Chilly this morning with Todd. I worked with the mine until it closed, just like my dad did. When they buttoned the mine up, they left a small crew behind to maintain machinery and stabilize the tailings. I manage what's left of the operation. I have crews up there now working on stabilizing and revegetating the tailings.

"My wife and dad and I are also partners in a bed and breakfast in Chilly. Eventually it will be our only source of income. So I'm interested in anything we can do to increase recreation business in the basin. I'm not opposed to growth up in Chilly, because the town is becoming a ghost town. Maybe we'll have to market it that way. Maybe Cliff you can come up there to redevelop some of our fallen-down houses.

"I agree with Todd about the fishing. A lot of our business comes from people looking to fish and hunt and so on. Anything we can do to clean up the river and bring the salmon back would sure be a help. We're doing our part by stabilizing those tailings, but it will be a while before they are fully stabilized.

"Like Todd, I'm here because Donna twisted our arms. She's been a great help to us so we're just paying back the favor. I'm not sure how I can help in this workshop so I don't have many expectations. I'll be here as long as it feels like we're doing something worthwhile."

Todd looks at YOU, sitting next to him, indicating he is done. YOU look at me and indicate nonverbally that you want me to take it from here.

It is time for an insight. But the group has taken a long time to complete the talking circle. So I say:

This grounding has taken a long time, so I am going to provide a seven-minute break so you can stretch your legs and take care of other needs. We will have a longer break after the next task.

I may also provide a longer fifteen-minute break at this time. It is my choice. In either case, I will provide an insight after the grounding.

> **TIMING FOR INSIGHTS: THE ART**
>
> Insights are provided *after* the task is completed, not before. This is different from the "normal approach," where the reason might be provided before the task; in a way this programs people to learn what you want them to learn, rather than acknowledging what they actually learned.
>
> By providing the insight afterward, participants will learn what they learn first, followed by an insight that is an addition to what they learned. They can then compare what I share with them with what they learned.
>
> In some cases, as with the greeting circle, the participants will actually be asked to express what they learned before I provide them an insight. This way, we can learn together.

~12~

Grounding Insights and Anecdotes

Grounding, a Here-and-Now Experience: An Insight

When the participants return from the break, I wait until they are all in the circle. This takes some time since they are already talking with each other in small groups around the room, coffee or tea in hand. I have to keep repeating, in a calm voice, We are ready to start; please return to your seat. Eventually they all begin to move toward their chairs.

The insight I provide is tailored to the group, its makeup, and its size. I may provide everything that follows or only those parts that relate to this group. In this instance, I am providing it all.

When all are in their chairs, I provide them an insight on grounding.

Thanks for getting back in the circle. I want to share some insights with you about the process you just experienced. As I said earlier, everything we do has purpose and meaning. You may have already learned some things from this activity that are in addition to what I will say or inclusive of what I have to say. Our purpose is always to learn from each other.

In presenting these insights, I will use the visual on the flip chart behind Johanna as a reminder to me of what I will say. It is also there to remind you about the purpose of grounding as we move through the workshop. This will be in the learning manual for this workshop.

I learned early on in the development of this process that everyone wants to get their voice in the room as you just did. The populace in our country are educated enough that they want to have their say. And they always have something to say. If you don't let them say it, then you cannot resolve your conflicts. The unspoken words act as a barrier to movement.

Grounding is one of the few descriptive words I use in this process. It is intended to refer to creating an awareness of being grounded in the present, the "here and now." Most people come to these workshops with a lot of anxieties on their mind. You are thinking of issues at home or the office, of work you could be doing, of how you otherwise could have used this time. You are thinking about the past.

You may be worrying about the workshop itself, that you might become ostracized or worse. There are implications for your relationships, work, family, church, and community. You are bringing your fears about the future.

With each of these concerns comes an array of feelings and emotions. Emotions can only be felt in the present, even if the event is in the future or the past. Expressing your feelings brings the community into the present.

This task allows you to express all of that, to become open about who you are right now. To be grounded.

THE GROUNDING

- It establishes that each person can speak, in turn, without interruption and be listened to.
- It establishes a "verbal territory" for each participant, a sense of potential equity.
- It introduces the talking circle and the notion of listening with respect to each other.
- It requires access to both the left and right brain, engaging the "whole brain."
- Left Brain: thinking
- Right Brain: feeling and emotion
- It allows apprehensions and hopes for the meeting to be expressed.
- It allows participants to express hidden agendas.
- It brings people into the "here and now."
- It provides initial information to the facilitator.

A Purposeful Activity: An Insight

There are many multilayered purposes for the grounding activity. It begins with each person answering the three questions:

- "Introduce yourself and what is your relationship to the issue?
- "What are your expectations for this meeting (workshop)?
- How do you feel about being here?

Once the talking circle starts, each of you speaks in turn. Each person speaks as long as you need to. There are no time limits. Each person can sense when you are (finally) being listened to.

By its very nature, the grounding has many positive outcomes:

It establishes that each person can speak, in turn, without interruption and be listened to. Once the questions have been asked and answered by the facilitator, the person to the left or right will speak. The conversation proceeds around the circle, clockwise or counterclockwise; it is a talking circle. The talking circle will automatically cause each person to take his or her turn, speaking his or her words in answer to the questions. No one will interrupt. This behavior is expressed and accepted immediately.

The sound of an unchallenged voice is a rare event for people, and this helps to allay the fears of those who are apprehensive. As each of you speaks, I can sense this awesome feeling:

> *"I speak and they listen, something I have never experienced before. Oh! The wondrous pleasure of being heard."*
>
> **—Workshop participant**

> *"Miracle? You say solving our problem is a miracle? I'll tell you what a miracle is: you listened to me when I spoke! Finally! Someone listened to me. No one has listened to me before, not my family or my coworkers. That's the miracle."*
>
> **—Workshop participant**

It establishes a "verbal territory" for each participant, a sense of potential equity (being treated fair and impartially). I have learned that to participate fully in a meeting, each of us needs to occupy the room with the sound of our voice, establishing a verbal territory, similar to a spatial territory. I refer to the right to express and represent myself in the beginning and at any time during the meeting. I want to speak long enough on issues of substance that are relevant and important to myself and the community so that my voice is heard and my presence established in the room.

In the grounding process, each person is provided the opportunity to speak at the beginning of the meeting to establish this verbal territory, this right to speak and be represented. Once your voice is in a room, it becomes easier to speak, especially if you know you will be listened to.

If I am never given an opportunity to speak in a meeting, then I have no "verbal territory" in that room. This verbal territory is captured instead by those who speak on and on and on, as if no one else has anything to say. If others speak and I can't, or if they attack me verbally when I speak, then I feel denied the opportunity to be represented. I can respond in either of two ways:

- If I am an aggressive person, a *fighter*, then I will begin to obstruct the communication flow by interrupting, trying to insert my voice in the room over the others. Or I will slam my fist on the table, shouting others down.
- If I am withdrawn, a *flighter*, then I will probably remain silent, allowing my mind to wander to other arenas of thought, doodling on the paper in front of me, idling away the time, hoping for the coffee breaks, waiting for the meeting to end so I can leave and ignore whatever agreement was reached. While a flighter is not aggressive openly, there is a passive aggression in withholding information important to the decision, in talking down or ignoring any decision that is made.

The three questions are designed to provide sufficient opportunity for each person to establish that verbal territory, while providing needed information for the group and the facilitator to work with.

People do not need much verbal territory to establish themselves. A group of eight people will take as long to go through a grounding as a group of twenty-four—about an hour. This allows each person three to eight minutes to make this first important venture into being represented. Beyond twenty-four people, the time needed is greater. The response to this is to create small groups, which will be demonstrated and discussed later.

It introduces the talking circle and the notion of listening with respect to each other. Establishing an environment of *listening with respect* ensures that the possibility of being heard is encouraged and fostered. As soon as the facilitator asks the three questions and you begin to answer them around the circle, the community automatically, without urging, begins to listen with respect.

People sense they are being heard. You can see it and feel it. People keep their eyes focused on the person speaking. Some move their heads forward to listen better. Others nod their heads. I suspect this happens because the questions provide a lot of information and we as humans are very curious about who people are, what people will say. These nonverbal messages of interest are picked up by those speaking and create a sense of acceptance.

"I can speak, knowing you will listen."

—**Workshop participant**

It is important that the facilitator listen fully to each person. Often the speaker focuses on the facilitator and, seeing the intensity of listening, feels encouraged to speak more openly.

Once listening with respect has been established in the room, it becomes a model thereafter.

It requires access to both the left and right brain, engaging the "whole brain." Research has shown that the left and right sides of the brain tend to function with different focuses. The left brain, in general, tends to be more logical, rational, sequential, and objective, and likes to break things into parts. The right brain appears to be more random and intuitive, looking at things as wholes, integrating disparate bits of information, and creating new insights.

There is a tendency to attribute left- and right-brain functions to the different sexes. Men are viewed as left-brained, women as right-brained. The male is characterized as more socialized toward being a thinking person, which causes men to be viewed as unemotional. Males do appear to have a preference for these attributes. The female is characterized as more socialized toward being an emotional person, to be more subjective. These are thought to be preferences for female attributes.

One sex appearing to be more emotional or more rational may be a function more of socialized roles than of potential. Up through the industrial era, the man was expected to work at the thinking tasks, while the woman was at home with the more emotional tasks. Yet, what male does not get emotional when a project is not finished on time? Which female does not have to use her intellect when confronted with the needs of teenagers?

The fact is that the brain is not really that specific in how it works; the attributes described can be expressed by both sides of the brain and by both genders. It is a whole organism, a part of us, just as we are the whole organism. But given that, the grounding questions will tend to access or engage both parts of the brain. This allows you to be a whole person.

When you introduced yourself, and spoke of your relationship to the issue, and provided your expectations, you accessed the left brain. It is the storage bin for your information. This information appears to be rational, analytical, sequential, and objective.

On the other hand, when you talked about how you felt, you accessed your right brain, which reports on how you feel in the *here and now*. This moment of here and now is important to consensus because it opens you up to your creativity and wisdom.

We are all whole-brained. One part of the brain, the corpus callosum, connects the right and left brains. The questions are intended to engage and tap the whole brain in the beginning of the meeting, to establish a connection between the two, to become whole. I want you to turn your whole brains on. This will help us resolve the conflict.

Thinking tends to bring us out of the present, into the past or the future. Thinking is based on our experienced perceptions and may represent a limited truth.

Feeling brings us an awareness of how we are now, internally, with our emotions. This information is both emotion and fact. We sense ourselves internally, and only we can express how we feel. This is our truth. No one else can tell us this information. We are the experts.

Sensing externally is another way of being in the present. Our sensing can make us aware of what is going on externally, here and now in the room. Unlike thinking, however, external sensing is more sensation than fact. I can sense if the group is tired. I can express that sense, but they must validate it to be truth.

Both feeling and sensing brings us into the here and now. Each "grounds" the person.

- *Thinking = Past or future. A limited truth.*
- *Feeling = Present, here and now, internally. Emotion and fact.*
- *Sensing = Present, here and now, externally. Sensation, a possible truth.*

Thinking/feeling/sensing are attributes you will use in seeking consensus.

As I speak, I look around and can see that I have the group's attention. Thirty-two pairs of eyeballs are staring at me. This is the result of an unspoken contract between the group and me. I listened to each of them during the one to two hours it took for the grounding. They will now listen to me for an equal amount of time. Since I will rarely take more than twenty minutes for the insight, I will have their attention for that amount of time.

If I sense I am losing that attention, I will adjust and focus on what is most important for that particular group. How do I know what to say? I just trust myself. I continue providing the insight.

It allows apprehensions and hopes for the meeting to be expressed. All of you come to meetings with some sense of apprehension or hope. These are normally hidden, not discussed openly, yet they affect the actions and behaviors of the members and their ability to participate or to listen. They are often referred to as hidden agendas. Their "sensed" presence in the community creates a concern about the intentions of members, which hinders open communication.

When talking about their expectations or feelings, people will often express their anxiety and apprehensions about the workshop. They can express misgivings, disbelief, anger, frustration, nonsupport, and so on. Rarely are these expressed at other meetings, so they remain as underlying pent-up energy that often gets in the way of communication.

Others will—often as a balance—express hopes for the workshop. They express their optimism, desires for togetherness, for community. They express positive possibilities and a willingness to explore with the group.

All these expressions are accepted as valid information. You are not judged. By feeling free to express yourself, the pent-up energy is released. The grounding process allows people to become calmer and more present. It allows you to hear what others are saying and to begin to accept information as it is. It allows people to understand each other, to begin to consider the possibility of views other than their own. You become "in process."

A CAUTION FOR THE FACILITATOR: THE ART

It is not unusual for negative statements or charges to be made directly to the facilitator during the grounding or in later talking circles.

> "I am concerned that Bob is just another manipulative facilitator, more concerned about the paycheck than about our basin."
>
> "I don't know why we trust Bob; he is paid by the people who got us into this mess to begin with. He'll just do what he is told."

> It is important when these negative charges or emotions are expressed that the facilitator does not take these on personally. They are not about the facilitator; they are about the person speaking. He or she has a desire to express the strongest negative feelings about being at the workshop; the facilitator is a symbol of that.
>
> We asked them to express their feelings. You do want them to be honest, don't you? So we must accept whatever they say, recognizing it is their moment of truth, not our moment of failure. I normally listen respectfully and allow the group to keep moving ahead. At the end of the task I will thank those who were honest and move on to the next activity.

It allows participants to express hidden agendas. People often come to the workshops with unfinished business on their minds. It might be a need to leave early, a wife who is sick, a flat tire they need to fix, a chore that needs to be done. They might have a hearing disability or be worried they are coming down with a cold and could infect others. They might have a scheduled phone conference.

These affect their participation, often causing them to appear withdrawn, preoccupied, worried. This nonverbal withdrawal is observed by and affects the other workshop participants.

In the grounding process, you will bring these out into the open:

- *"My kids are sick today, so if I seem preoccupied, it is because I am worried about them."*
- *"My son was arrested this morning and I can't do anything about it, so I may appear withdrawn."*
- *"I have an appointment this afternoon dealing with our budget. It is important I be there; I will return when the meeting is over."*

If stated, these can be responded to or may just become less important in the telling. Doing so allows the other participants to focus on the workshop, not on their concerns about others' nonverbal behaviors.

It brings people into the "here and now." Once people have answered these questions and feel listened to, they are open to hearing others speak. Their mind is clear. They may feel accepted; it relaxes them and releases their pent-up energy. They can now be here at the meeting, leaving their concerns in the background.

It provides initial information to the facilitator. I listen to everything you say, as well as how you say it. In doing so, I get a sense of the individuals in the group as well as of the whole group. I listen to the words you use when you describe the situation so that the questions I frame can use the same words.

By listening closely, I can sense the major issues in the group. I can detect the tensions between people. I can determine who can help me cofacilitate, who to put on panels. I can sense who is nervous, who feels responsible, who feels disenfranchised. This helps me decide who to empower.

I do not present all of these points at all meetings. Depending on the group and my knowledge of its members from interviews and the grounding, I may only focus on one or two of the points above. I will always focus more time on the issue of *listening with respect* because it is so basic to this process.

This is an e-mail I received after a workshop expressing one person's learning from the grounding:

HELLO BOB,

It just seems to me more and more that what I have learned from you is a combination of etiquette and treating people with respect. As a result, when I am at a meeting now and someone comes in late and is not greeted or acknowledged it just drives me nuts. When everyone has to fight for their right to speak (and some don't) I think it is a travesty.

At almost any gathering now that I am in charge of (and some I'm not) I request that everyone in the room just tell us how they're feeling, what they're thinking about. If I learn nothing else the rest of my life, I know that getting everyone's voice in a room is one of the most empowering, generous, respectful things one human being can do for another. I thank you for that... Jack

---

Where Did All the Shy, Uncommunicative People Go: An Insight

I am often asked by those who want to use this process how I deal with the shy person, the uncommunicative person who just won't speak. In my nearly forty years of working with this process, with more than fifteen hundred groups and thirty-five thousand-plus participants, I can recall only two people who felt constrained by their shyness or fear from participating in the grounding.

All the other individuals seized the opportunity to express themselves, to establish their right to speak, and to be acknowledged and listened to. Am I to assume that none of these was shy? Or is it possible that shy people are created by the environment they are in and the people they are with?

In my experience, there are few really uncommunicative people. Instead, there are many people who will not compete for verbal territory. They will not set themselves up to be interrupted as they speak. Rather than injecting themselves into a heated discussion where the issue is really who controls the verbal territory, they will just sit back, listen, and then ignore whatever decision is reached.

If my experience is true, then that says a lot for the normal meeting or problem-solving format. What is it that causes most of the participants in a meeting to be uncommunicative, judged as shy, inadequate, apathetic? Is it possible the meeting environment and the people they are with result in this behavior?

If we disagree and are not listening to each other, it is not long before the debate results in hostile nonverbal behaviors such as taut lips, gritted teeth, hard eyes, and raised verbal tones that alert us to the challenge, the possibility of violent conflict.

It is this enactment of the power struggle that possibly prevents most people from participating in the meeting.

The net result of people not participating is a loss of communication and a loss of information from those disenfranchised from the process. The listeners/observers have no commitment to carry out any decision made. The result is, there is no community with a common focus.

The first two activities, the grounding and greeting, are intended to move beyond these feelings, to create a new and safer environment to speak.

Creating the Environment for Listening—The Grounding Questions: An Insight

I continue to add insights for the group. One of the key concepts for this process is the development of the "right" questions. Right questions are those that move a group toward its development and its resolution. I introduce the participants to this by explaining the purpose of the questions asked in the grounding. This is a way of keeping the process transparent.

Asking the right questions is perhaps the most important skill I learned as this process was developed. These are questions that are appropriate in all situations, that cause movement toward resolution of the conflicts. It is normal to start the meeting or workshop with introductions. The leader of the event would ask us to state our names and agency or organization affiliation. What I observed was people, many feeling self-conscious or out of place, rapidly stating the information so that the introductions went at a dizzying pace through the room. In the end, few people knew anyone any better than when they started. You were lucky to retain more than one or two names and identities.

This always bothered me, because I knew instinctively that knowing each other would make us feel more comfortable and safer. And this would help us better solve the problem or learn.

For that reason, as this process developed, I sought an approach that felt more organic, that allowed people to speak long enough that we would know something about them, that we could approach the person during the breaks and have a basis to initiate conversations with them.

I tested different approaches, including what are known as warm-up exercises. But what worked in the end were the three questions.

I wanted people to have enough information about each other and their purpose for being at the meeting, even if—or especially if—it was negative, so that the initial conversations could start. I wanted them to initiate conversations from both the thinking and feeling sides of their brains. The questions are pretty much the same for all groups I work with. Each has a definite purpose.

"Introduce yourself and your relationship with the issue." This question allows people to express what they are used to expressing, but the addition of their relationship with the issue gives them a more specific identity. They still talk about their organization, maybe the number of years they have been affected by the situation, and then they express their connection with the issue.

This last piece of information helps people to place each other in relationship to the issue. They know who is for, against, and neutral. They have previously learned about the people in the room through hearsay, and now can know them as individuals. Often the difference between the hearsay and what they experience is quite different. When this happens, people shift their perceptions and become "in process."

As I explained earlier, this first question can be changed to fit any situation. For example:

- Introduce yourself and your relationship to the conflict.
- Introduce yourself and your relationship to the organization.
- Introduce yourself and your relationship to the situation we are confronting.
- Introduce yourself and your relationship to this bond issue.

When working with different groups, I use a question focused on that group.

"What are your expectations for this meeting?" All of us come to meetings with expectations. They are often different from the agenda of the meeting and are very important to us. Rarely do we get to express them. Often we try to piggyback our concern on a discussion unrelated to it. This is called a "hidden agenda."

I have found that people like expressing their expectations in advance. This provides me, the facilitator, information I need to design the meeting.

The purpose is to get everyone's expectations out so they know they are heard. Then we arrange for some way to deal with the expectation. If the expectation will be a focus of the meeting, I will acknowledge that at the end of the grounding talking circle. If it is not related to the meeting, then I arrange to have it covered in some forum off to the side. I often arrange this at the first break. This leaves people free to participate and focus on the issue we are there for.

"How do you feel about being here?" People come with feelings related to the meeting. Often these are feelings of anxiety, resistance, anger, often of hatred for another group in the room. Many don't want to be there. Many have delayed work they need to get done. They learn early on that these feelings can be expressed openly. No one will judge them.

Once expressed and listened to, these feelings lessen, often fade into the background, which allows people to settle themselves so they can be there in the present.

If, however, I were to criticize them for being negative or to disagree with their statements, then these feelings become hardened and increase their anxiety and resistance. Listening and accepting works best.

People mostly express satisfaction with being there. They are hopeful, willing to work on resolving the issue. They express their willingness to work with others.

It is sometime interesting that a group will start a talking circle being really negative in their expectations and feelings. As the conversation moves around the circle, at some point, halfway through or more, the conversation will begin to change to a positive note. Even people who were negative in the interviews, now speak positively.

I hazard a guess on this: When people at the start of the circle speak negatively, they say what others wanted to say. As this continues, those others feel their views are represented already and find themselves thinking more positively. The result is that they speak more positively than they originally intended to. This is the result of being "in process."

> **Being in Process**: When a person experiences something that feels positive to them, in communications or relationships, they begin to move toward that something. I call this "being in process." This movement is shared or experienced differently by each person in the room. This movement begins as soon as people walk into the room. It continues in the grounding as people feel heard, often for the first time.

~13~

Listening with Respect

There was a young owl,
Who sat in an oak.
The more he saw,
The less he spoke.
The less he spoke,
The more he heard,
And he grew up to be
a wise old bird.

(With thanks to Mother Goose)

The Circle—Listening with Respect: An Insight

"Oh the comfort, the inexpressible comfort of feeling safe with a person, having neither to weigh thoughts or measure words, but pouring them all right out, just as they are—chaff and grain together—certain that a faithful hand will take them and sift them, keep what is worth keeping, and with the breath of kindness blow the rest away."

—Dinah Mulock

The one insight I always focus on, the one I speak longest about, is the concept of *listening with respect*. This concept is the key to moving people toward consensus. Let's return to the group, where I am continuing insights about the grounding they just experienced.

Of all the insights I share with your group today, listening with respect, is the most important one. The concept is summarized on the flip chart behind Gil.

People focus on the flip chart for a moment until I continue to talk.

> *** THE CIRCLE**
>
> **IF YOU...**
>
> **LISTEN WITH RESPECT...**
>
> **UNDERSTANDING,**
>
> **TRUST,**
>
> **LEARNING,**
>
> **A NEW PERSPECTIVE,**
>
> **GROWING,**
>
> **RESOLVING**
>
> **ADAPTING**
>
> **WILL RESULT.**

Listening with respect means more than an apparent interest in what I am saying. It means focusing on my words, my tonal quality, and my body language, all at the same time. It means being aware of your own physical and mental responses so they do not get in the way of listening to me. It means being present with me, most of the time.

It means listening to what I am saying that you disagree with and dislike, as well as what I am saying that you agree with or like. It means stretching your listening during those times when you strongly disagree with me, without beginning to answer or debate with me in your mind.

There will be times when what I say will cause you to wander in your mind. I understand that. In a way it is an honor to me, because it indicates that I have influenced or affected you in some way. I know that you are affected by your needs, as I am by mine. But return soon to reconnect with me, listening to most of what I have to say. I will recognize when that happens through your nonverbal language and by my sensing. I will appreciate that.

Listening with respect means you will bend your ears around the sound of my speech or my dialect to interpret what I say. This is especially important if I am a person from another culture with an accent or unfamiliar dialect. It is easy to become impatient with my accents and avoid the energy it takes to listen to me. But today, people of other cultures are more numerous and evident in meetings. You cannot afford to miss my point of view because I am part of your community, part of the problem, part of the solution.

> The word "listen" can be converted to the word "silent."

Understanding: Listening with respect means you are trying to **understand me** and my point of view, as well as my needs and feelings. You don't have to agree with my point of view—just try to understand it. Many are afraid to try to understand because they might be accused of being brainwashed by the enemy by others on their side. That is the price of loyalty to what is called **groupthink**.

So, Jon might say, "I believe this is what Bob is trying to say."

Crista might respond, "You mean you agree with him?"

Jon: "No, that is not what I said. I just understand what he said. I happen to disagree with it, but I am trying to understand him."

Crista: "Well, just don't be agreeing with him, because if you do you are not part of our group!"

(**Note**: I am using actual people in the group to describe this possible conversation. This lets them know I can recall their names, and it keeps everyone focused on what I am saying.)

Agreement is not necessary in the beginning. Understanding is. If you understand, then agreement may happen later.

Understanding means you can express my point of view to others. Jon and Crista are now able to make decisions that take my interests into account. Before they listened to me, all they had were their views, their beliefs, and their concerns. By listening, you all now have my views and concerns in your memory. You can now ask, "What decision can I make that will meet my needs and Bob's needs?"

Trust: If you understand me or try to, then I will trust you. I do not trust people who do not try to understand me. They are only trying to meet their needs, and I am afraid they will get met at my expense. Therefore, I will mistrust them. I feel unsafe with them; I need to defend myself against them.

But if I sense that you are trying to understand me, then I will trust you; I will be more focused, more clear in my message. If you try to understand my point of view, then I will try to understand yours. I may not agree with it, but I will understand as best as I can. This will continue to build our trust.

Trust is important because it establishes a feeling of safety and security. If you are in an environment of mistrust, then you are in an unsafe environment. You must always be looking out for yourself. This is not the kind of environment one wants to return to. It is the kind of environment in which unresolved conflicts will continue to grow.

If I can't trust you, then I will not disclose information important to you and the situation. If I can trust you, then I will disclose what you need to hear.

Learn: And if we trust each other, then we will learn from each other. We will not learn from each other if we have no trust. In fact, if I do not trust you, then it matters not how important, educated, or intelligent you are, I will not trust your information. I will use my intelligence, education, and knowledge to dispute your information, to trivialize it, to prove you wrong.

I have seen this happen many times. It is one reason that conflicts become prolonged. While Lynn and Jack may have the information and the ability to solve the issue, they can't because of their inability to trust each other. Their information is not valid to each other. They have no credibility with each other. So their information is discounted, trivialized, or rarely heard or disclosed. The attack is focused on the person rather than the issue. If I can't trust you, then I won't try to understand you; instead I will pummel you with my truths.

This is especially detrimental to professionals who are asked to help educate those affected by the decisions being made. It makes no difference how much Donna knows about irrigation; if trust is not established first, all knowledge or advice is discounted. The investment in time, money, and intelligence is wasted.

This often means that professionals like Jon, Jim, and Donna may have to listen to their audience first, to understand their needs and concerns. By listening, they will establish sufficient trust so that their information is accepted when they present it. This also allows the professional to be more focused and meet the needs of the audience. And the person will be changed by what he listens to.

A new perspective: If we learn from each other, then we will develop a new perspective. This new perspective may not be the whole truth, but it will be closer to the truth than our individual views.

I develop an example of this with the community group that is seated in the circle and using what we see around us in our meeting room. I begin by designating YOU as the manager. What follows is a dialogue I create to make my point:

YOU are the manager here who wants to hang a picture in the room of a dearly loved person from the community, someone like Frank, perhaps. You ask the community members for advice.

When you ask George, sitting at the north side of the circle, to describe his view of the room, he will report on the large windows facing the parking lot and the cars in the lot.

Now Marcia, on the west side of the circle, expresses her surprise because she sees a window looking out on the putting green.

Debbe, on the south side of the circle, sees a solid oak wall with a large painting of a golf course on it, while Mike, on the east side of the circle, exclaims that the wall is a movable one, covered with a soft fabric, with no picture on it and no windows.

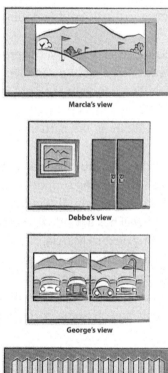

Individual views of the room.

George, at the north side of the circle, says, "You can't hang it on the wall because there are two picture windows there. There is no space."

Debbe, sitting opposite George, is confused. "I see a solid oak wall, but it already has a large picture on it, just left of the double doors. We would have to move the picture or remove it."

Marcia strongly disagrees. "I can see one picture window, but there is plenty of space to the left to hang the picture."

Mike observes quietly, with certainty: "Look, there is a folding wall and it can't hold the picture. Why talk about something we can't do? Unless, of course, you want to put the picture in the folds so it only shows when the wall is opened."

"A movable wall?" says Debbe. "Why, there is no movable wall and there is no window. There is an oak wall with a picture of a golf course on it. You could hang the picture to the left of the double doors if you took the other picture down."

"Double doors?" exclaims Marcia loudly. "There are no double doors and no oak wall. There are two large picture windows, which would prevent you from hanging anything. The windows look out on the golf course you are talking about, Debbe. It is real, not a picture."

There is laughter in the room as the participants begin to see what is happening.

"Well," says Mike, "I can see the movable wall quite clearly. Can't you?" he asks Kathy sitting beside him, seeking support.

"Yes, clearly, Mike," Kathy responds. "I wonder what the others have been drinking to believe the wall has a window or double doors in it."

"Well," says Wayne, sitting next to Marcia, "I can see the wall has a picture window with my twenty-twenty vision. That is more than you can say with your apparent bad vision since you both wear eyeglasses."

Kathy is angry at the remark. "You better clean off your eyeballs, because I can see clearly. Maybe you are on some sorta 'med' that is giving you hallucinations."

"You are hallucinating yourself. I can see the cars in the parking lot outside. You must have good nighttime vision and poor daytime vision," says Alice, sitting next to George.

"And I can see the double doors," says Dawn. "I believe," she says in an aside to Debbe, "these people are not telling the truth. They are just angry because you can see what I see, and they can't."

It is obvious to us that each person has a different perception of the room. It is obvious that they each have the correct perception from their view. It is also obvious they each feel they have the **ONE RIGHT PERCEPTION** to the exclusion of all others. They do not listen to, nor try to understand, their team members' perceptions.

And that is how conflicts start. Each of us has a different perception of the event or issue. Each of us has correctly described our view. This viewpoint is affected by our conviction about the situation, by our beliefs and values, our education, our ethnic background, our ages, our gender, and our relationships with the others.

We each do have a "correct" view. But we don't always have the **one and only correct view, because there are others who feel the same way.** In my attempt to convince you that I have the one right view, the truth, I stop listening to you. In this moment, I will try to change your version of the truth to match mine. Now the information becomes less important than the need to convince you of my rightness.

In time, if we disagree long enough, I will feel the need to convince you with power, with my need for control. I will raise my voice, I will trivialize or denigrate your information, and I will do anything to convince you to submit to my greater intelligence, my position of authority, or my rightness. I may refer to the BOOK, the BOSS, the SCIENCE, the LAW, or the BIBLE or any other authority figure that will validate my claims. In the end I will personalize the issue, focus on you and your faults. I am making you the issue, diverting attention away from the real issue. I will even describe you as having a mental illness or a screw loose, allowing me and others to discount anything you say.

Now we are moving from discussing the issue to seeing who is more powerful. If my adversary—because that is now what the other has become—is a FIGHTER, then her voice will also rise to match mine, and we will try to out-power each other.

If the person is a FLIGHT person, he will become quiet, withdraw, ignore me, or find some other way to disengage from the conflict, while retaining his disagreement. Often someone in the group will try to convince both parties that we are saying the same thing in different ways, in an attempt to create harmony, even if a false harmony.

At this point YOU, as the boss, may decide to make a decision. You see the same view that Debbe does from the south, so you decide to hang the pictures there, to the left of the double doors. But you also require that the others accept the view that you and Debbe see.

"George, there are no double windows; you are just trying to start trouble as you always do," you say. "Marcia, there are no putting greens that I can see, you are just dreaming about playing golf; but you are new here, so I can excuse your lack of vision. Mike, there is no movable wall; it is as immovable as you are in your views."

You are asking the others to accept yours and Debbe's view as the one and only RIGHT view. This requires the other three to be functionally insane, to accept a reality that does not match what they see. Often the only way to resolve this dilemma is for them to withdraw from the issue and say, "Let them go ahead and make the big mistake. Just don't expect my support or commitment."

Now we know this example is ridiculous. When we are in a room, we all know that there are four walls. But that is no more ridiculous than seeing a problem from one dimension, knowing that others see it differently. In both circumstances, the need to be right is paramount, and this excludes the other viewpoints.

Understanding others' perceptions is critical to resolving conflict. It is the recognition that we all see the room, or the situation, from our different perspectives. We each have a single-dimensional view that is right, but not necessarily the **only** right view. By listening with respect to what others describe as their view, we have the possibility of adding others' dimensions and creating the richness of our **collective** perception of the room/situation. **We move from a one-dimensional view to a three-dimensional view.**

It is the acceptance of the **possibility** of the truth of others' perceptions that allows us to develop the needed collective information base to resolve the issue.

- Listen to me with respect and you will understand me.
- If you understand me, then I will try to understand you.
- This will allow us to trust each other and learn from each other.
- We will then develop a new and richer perspective of the situation and ultimately a new and shared truth.

> **Consensus seeking is about inclusion, not exclusion.**

Inclusion of all views must occur. It is the willingness to accept the possibility of the rightness of another person's perception that will allow us to gather a complete view of the room/situation so we can make the right decision.

We grow. This new perception allows us to grow in our knowledge and in our being. We become different by understanding this richer perception. We can see other parts of our environment in a different way, through others' eyes, recognizing the possibility we still have a limited vision of the truth. It is the older, limited, single perception that prevented us from resolving the issue. The new, larger information base provides what is needed to solve it.

Consensus seeking depends on creating a common knowledge base within the group in conflict. If I know your point of view and have stored it in my memory, you are now part of my perception. I do not have to agree with your perception, just understand it. Now when we solve the problem, I am able to consider your needs. My information base is inclusive, as is yours.

We can now resolve the conflict that we confront, together. In the past, we tried to solve the issue with only our self-interests in mind, assuming they were paramount. To our surprise, we found that others are affected by the decisions we make, often adversely. We recognize that we must make a decision that is inclusive of others' views and needs.

We can now solve the issue in a way that meets all our needs, rather than the selfish needs of one or based only on the perception of the one. If I accept only my information as true, then I can answer only this question: "How can I solve this problem to meet my needs?"

This is based on "either/or" thinking. You can meet either your needs or my needs. This is an easier question to answer and requires a mediocre level of thinking and problem solving. But if you have excluded my views, your decision may turn out to be wrong because of it, or my support will not be available to you when you need it.

If I have included your information in my perceptions, then I can ask a different question: "How can I solve this problem and meet both of our needs?"

This is known as "and" thinking. I am willing to make a decision that takes your needs into account. This will require a higher level of thinking and decision making than the either/or approach. I must seek excellence, rather than mediocrity. It requires me to stretch my brain, to see other possibilities and other solutions that were hidden before.

> *"In that the wisdom of the few becomes available to the many, there is progress in human affairs; without it, the static routine of tradition continues."*
>
> **—Joseph Jastrow,** *The Story of Human Error*

Resolving issues does not mean we will run out of conflicts or problems. On the contrary, there will be new problems and conflicts that will be fostered by our new knowledge, our new actions, and our new behaviors. These new conflicts allow us to continue to learn and grow and see reality better.

The issue we confront is whether we want to spend all our time resolving the same conflict over and over, or to resolve this conflict and move on to new ones. It is a question of stagnant or stunted growth versus continual growth.

Adapting: This ability to resolve issues allows us to see the world more clearly, to choose to adapt to the new situation that is evident with the new perception, the new information. We are now different as a result of the experience. It is in choosing this adaptive behavior and perception that will allow us to continue to respond to the new problems that will arise in the future. It allows all of us to retain our individuality and integrity, because the decision is always inclusive of our needs.

The focus is on you: Be aware in this that the focus is on your **attitude of listening.** Attitudes cost no more money or time. This is a shift in the way you are willing to behave. Remember...shift happens! You have ears, two of them: an evolutionary signal to you. You are a listening entity. Use what you have worked for millennia to create, listening with respect so you will have whatever information you need to resolve your common problem.

With the end of this insight, I prepare the participants to meet each other in a more familiar and personal way. This next activity is called "the greeting circle."

~14~

The Greeting Circle

Selecting and Coaching Facilitators: The Art

When the group is larger than twenty-four, after the grounding insight I normally provide a break. It's about nine thirty in the morning. Before we break, I announce the names of four people who are going to facilitate small groups. These are people I identify at random during the grounding; I seek people who represent the larger group, choose people who are different in gender, ethnicity, role, physical ability, perception, and so on. I ask these people, including YOU, to come to the center while others are taking the break.

We are going to take a short break now, let's say seven minutes. Before you leave, I want Susan, George, Diane, and Cliff to come to the center of the circle. I also want Mike to come to the center of the circle. The rest of you can take a break and be back in seven minutes. We will have a longer break later.

I ask YOU to come to the center with me. Since you facilitated the grounding, you will help me cofacilitate additional activities. I am coaching you to take my place when I am gone. Since you are female, I will add a male to facilitate with us. YOU and I have determined that Mike and later Crista would be good cofacilitators at this time.

Both YOU and Mike will observe my instructions to the small-group facilitators. I am coaching you while coaching them. This is my purpose, to teach you to help yourselves. I will then demonstrate that with the facilitator group, talking it through with them as they experience it. In the center of the circle, with people milling about us on their way to coffee and other important destinations, I speak to the four facilitators and two cofacilitators:

Each of you has been selected to act as facilitator for small groups we will create after the break. If a group is smaller than twenty, I will often do the next activities in the large group. But in this instance, with thirty-two people, we need to create small and diverse groups, facilitated by you. If you accept, after the break I will have you first come to the center of the circle, where we will honor you for taking on that role.

You will then go to an easel that will be assigned to you so the others know where they are to go.

When you have your small group of eight people, including yourself, make sure the easel remains where it is and form a circle in front of it. Leave the easel outside your group circle.

I will ask you to have your group stand, and you will then lead them in a greeting circle. This is how you will do that:

You will be instructed to move inside the circle and greet the person to your left (or right), then continue inside the circle, greeting each person in turn. Those who have been greeted follow the person who greeted them last inside the circle. When the facilitator returns to his or her original location, those inside the circle will continue to greet them, a second time. This time, the person inside the circle is the greeter, not the greeted. This balances the power in the circle.

I then demonstrate the greeting circle with them.

After the greeting circle is done, I will ask you to have your group be seated. Be aware that I may stop the greeting circle before you are through both phases of greeter and greeted. Sometimes folks become so enamored with meeting each other that the circle slows and eventually stops. I will try to ensure that at least three people have been both greeter and greeted before I stop the groups. If you finish before the others, remain standing until I ask you to be seated.

When you are seated, you will be given two questions to ask your group members. YOU will ask these questions.

- *How do you feel about the greeting circle?*
- *What did you learn that will help us resolve the conflict we are here to confront?*

Ask the questions and then start to your right or left. Do not ask who wants to speak first; pick someone. If you let them choose, the person who always speaks first and tends to dominate the conversation will speak. Choose someone else to start the conversation. Be assertive as the facilitator.

After this activity, you will be asked to select another facilitator, and you will then become the recorder. Again, do not ask who wants to facilitate, but do the choosing yourself.

When you record, these are three directions I want you to act on:

- Turn yourself to face the flip chart, your back to the group, when recording. You will hear everything that is said. You do not have to look at people to hear them.
- Begin writing as soon as people speak. When you do this, you will hear and remember every word.
- Write what they say exactly as they say it. Do not worry about grammatical errors or how good your writing is. Your purpose is to serve the group as well as you can.

I will repeat all these directions as we move ahead. Are you willing to do this?

All nod and indicate they will take the assignment. I ask YOU to repeat the instructions.

Rarely does anyone turn down the opportunity to facilitate. It may be that a person has to leave before the activity, in which case I replace them with another person. I mention to them that they were selected for balance: male and female, administrator and worker, management and labor, for and against, and so on.

NUMBER OF EASELS AND FACILITATORS

The number of facilitators and the number of easels set up depends on the small-group size. I like to keep the small-group size between seven and twelve. Groups of eight to twelve will take the same amount of time to do a talking circle. More than twelve people doubles the time. I don't know why—it just happens that way.

I just divide the number of people by, let's say eight, and then select that number of facilitators. So, forty people equals five facilitators. In this case, thirty-two people are divided into four groups of eight.

The number of easels is determined in the same way. I add one easel for myself. So, forty people with eight people in each group equals five easels plus one for me, for a total of six.

(In training workshops I will create groups as small as five to increase the opportunities for facilitating and recording.)

The Greeting Circle—An Old Ritual with New Purpose: The Art

After the break the group slowly reconvenes in the large circle. If the group is twenty or fewer, I will normally lead the greeting circle with the entire community. In this situation we have thirty-two participants, so we will create four small, diverse groups facilitated by members of the community. The approach used with the large group is essentially the same as what follows for the small groups.

Honoring and assigning the facilitators. When the community has returned to their chairs, I inform them that we will be breaking into diverse small groups to do additional introductory activities:

For the next activity we will be creating small and diverse groups. I want all of you to stand so we can do this.

I would like people who have volunteered to be facilitators to come to the center of the circle.

I then honor the facilitators:

These six people have agreed to help facilitate the next activities. Their purpose is to repeat the task, then facilitate you through it. During the activities, these facilitators—Susan, George, Diane, Cliff—will ask the questions and see that each person speaks in turn, as we did earlier. The other two folks, Mike and YOU, are going to help me cofacilitate the whole group. Please honor these people for agreeing to serve you.

There is polite applause; people not quite understanding this approach.

Small group facilitators, I want you to number off to four.

Susan, "one"; George, "two"; Diane, "three"; Cliff, "four."

Return to the circle, remember your number.

Creating the small groups. I now direct the rest of the group: I want each of you to number off by four, beginning at my left and going clockwise. Remember your number, because that is the group you are assigned to. YOU and Mike will not count off, since you will be with me as cofacilitators.

When all have numbered off, I direct them to form their groups:

Take your chairs with you and form a circle in front of the easel of your numbered group. Close your circle so the easel is outside the group.

Flip Chart

The group immediately responds, moving to their groups, the facilitators helping them identify their locations. They form circles, loosely, now aware they are with people they really don't know. Many lean back on their chairs, appearing to want to flee.

When they are all settled in their groups, I get their attention. Standing at the edge of the circle, I explain to them that it is normal for people to sit with those they know or are similar to, seeking a comfort zone:

When you chose a place in the large circle earlier today, it was normal to select a seat next to someone you know, someone from your group. This creates a sense of safety. We call this "birds of a feather flocking together." It is normal to separate yourself from others different from you whom you don't know.

While this is a safe choice, it limits your information universe. You create what is called a "groupthink," which, while it is comfortable, limits your information universe to only those like you. Your interactions will be confined to a small and familiar group of people. It is likely you will see Frank, Wayne, and Mike together as a group of ranchers, but not Frank, Lynn, and Rob as a diverse group. The latter have no basis for a relationship.

We already know the people we feel comfortable with; there is little new to learn from them. We limit ourselves to superficial and ritualistic conversations. Information is slanted purposely to meet the group's needs or intents. Information that appears to disagree with the "groupthink" is wrong, disloyal. The group demands loyalty if you want to belong. "We have our mind made up."

What we just did is to create diverse groups in which you are with people who are unlike your groupthink. We created "diverse think," or better, "community think." Now you are with people you really don't know, but who have new and interesting information for you. So we see Frank, a rancher, and Lynn, a "newbie," and Jim, a district ranger, sitting together. It is a little uncomfortable, even apprehensive to be with those who are different or opposite. You are self-conscious and aware.

It is easy to create this diverse community. We just numbered off, because we knew this would redistribute those sitting together. You will experience a number of ways we create small groups in the time we have together. In a normal meeting of more than one day, you would rarely meet others than those you already know. In this workshop you will meet and interact with everyone. You will "know" them.

Remember that everything we do has purpose and meaning. This process is seductive, it will keep you focused; but in doing so, you may miss what you are doing and why. Be aware of what we are doing; you may want to use this in the future. I will keep reminding you of that.

> "Everything we do has purpose and meaning."

The Greeting Circle: Small-group Activity

I have the entire community stand in their small groups. I describe the greeting circle procedure:

You met each other through the grounding. Now you are going to meet each other in a more traditional way, by greeting each other. I want you all to stand.

All stand in their groups, looking curious, with some nervous laughter.

> **YOUR CHAIR—A SAFE HAVEN**
>
> People will tend to choose a chair location in the circle that is "safe," next to a friend or the door for a quick getaway. Once they sit in it and get their "bum warmth" on it, it becomes their symbol of territory and safety. If they leave their chair and someone else sits in it, when they return they will say:
>
> "THAT'S MY CHAIR!!!"
>
> When I move the participants to small groups they take their chairs. This is an anxious experience—leaving their friends behind, this is the only safety blanket they have.

Your facilitator is going to start greeting each of you by moving inside the circle, to their left or right. The first person they greet will in turn follow the facilitator inside the circle and greet each person. The people they greet will, in turn, follow them around inside the circle, continuing to greet people as the circle turns in on itself. Facilitator, tug the first person inside after you to get the movement started.

Eventually the facilitators will return to their original places. Those behind them in the inside circle will move to greet them again. You have previously been greeted by them, now you can be the greeter. This allows us to meet each other twice, being the greeter, then the greeted. This helps to balance power among you. Your facilitator will remind you to do this.

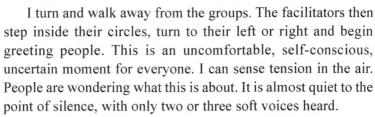

I turn and walk away from the groups. The facilitators then step inside their circles, turn to their left or right and begin greeting people. This is an uncomfortable, self-conscious, uncertain moment for everyone. I can sense tension in the air. People are wondering what this is about. It is almost quiet to the point of silence, with only two or three soft voices heard.

Then the sound begins to rise as more people get involved. Laugher may erupt, people slap each other's backs (males mostly), voices become higher and sharper, pitched with anxiety. Some are moving fairly quickly around the circle, while others are moving more slowly.

There are times when the group is quiet, their sound barely rippling the energy of the room. This may indicate the group is passive, needing more time to meet and know each other, to empower themselves to confront their conflict.

Then, as the groups become engaged in greeting, a sense of comfort seems to arise: the circle slows down; there is still laughter, but it seems softer. People are fully engaged in meeting each other now. Some groups slow as they get to the second round, switching greeters and greeted. People talk longer, look in each other's eyes. They have moved beyond the initial ritual of greeting to a more in-depth conversation. They are meeting real people in real time. They are *in process*.

Some groups finish quickly, hardly getting beyond the ritual greeting. They are left standing, looking at each other, self-conscious, not knowing what to do. They look at me for help. I am purposefully looking elsewhere or engaged in coaching YOU and Mike. They begin to talk to each other in the standing circle, taking turns, moving beyond the ritual, doing as the slower groups are doing, meeting real people. They cannot escape the purpose of the activity.

Moving on: In time, if I see that most groups are done and others have gone around most of the way, but are slowing down almost to a stop, I get their attention, talking loud enough to be heard and repeating myself:

Please finish with whomever you are greeting and return to your chairs. (Repeating continually in the same facilitative tone until they do this).

> **THE GREETING CIRCLE IS NOT A WARM-UP EXERCISE - THE ART**
>
> Many facilitators attempt to help a group connect with each other by using "warm-up exercises." I have done this myself, including during the development of this process. People who have experienced this approach attempt to apply some of their warm-up exercises to the greeting circle.
>
> An example of such an exercise would be to explain the greeting circle process, and then ask participants to introduce themselves and tell those they greet about "what I did last summer," or "my favorite aunt," or "a book I've been reading." In doing this, they are attempting to make the greeting circle less anxious, more controlled. The participants don't have to think about what to say; it has been determined for them.
>
> But can you imagine repeating the same information to thirty-two people? It just doesn't seem real. Structuring this task takes away the recognition that each person in the circle is different; therefore, each person deserves a different conversation. Trust people; you don't have to control everything for them. Stop being a control freak!
>
> All warm-up exercises work in some format, but not in the greeting circle. It is my intent to allow the participants themselves to choose what they want to say to each person, recognizing that each person is different. It is OK with me if they become anxious or self-conscious or fumble around about what they're going to say. This is real life. It is human beings meeting each other, *au naturel.*

A Large-group Greeting Circle: The Art

If I have a small group of people—eight or fewer—I may let the circle finish completely, each person being a greeter and greeted. If the group is larger, I wait until at least two-thirds of the group is inside the circle, so that one-third has been through the greeting twice. Then I ask the group to return to their chairs. While all may have been reluctant and uncomfortable about starting the circle, they are now more reluctant to stop. They are feeling the loss of not meeting the rest of the group.

I do this to allow different parts of the group to have different learning experiences. Some have greeted and been greeted, others have been greeters only, while others have just been greeted. Each is a different experience.

If I am leading the circle, I step inside the circle, turn to my left or right, and begin greeting people. This is an uncomfortable, self-conscious, uncertain moment. I am the only person with his voice in the room to begin with. It feels uncommonly loud, and I have to stifle the urge to whisper.

I am also cautious about hugging the first few people, even though I may know the person to my left well enough to hug, knowing it could establish an untimely and therefore inappropriate and disrespectful model for others.

I may give the group a break after the greeting circle, if they have not had one after the grounding, because of the emotional impact of the greeting circle. I will repeat the two questions before they take the break: How did you feel? and What did you learn?

This break allows those who want an opportunity to greet those they haven't yet met and an opportunity to think about what they felt and learned. After the break, when they are seated, I explain to them that it is common in our culture to be very verbal. That the circle will slow down and sometimes stop.

Coaching Facilitators: The Art

One of my purposes—in addition to helping the community resolve their conflicts—is to help them learn how to facilitate themselves. I do this by making the process transparent, explaining everything I am doing as we proceed, providing them activities and insights. I also provide them with a report and learning manual when we are done, so they have a written record of the process.

Another way to help them learn is to have them do most of the facilitating and recording themselves, so they learn by doing and experiencing. At this time, the community is working in small groups, performing the greeting circle, facilitated by members of the community. They are learning by doing.

As they work together in their small groups, I take this time to coach the two cofacilitators I have selected earlier, in this case, YOU and Mike.

I want you to notice that while we are working outside the circle, the groups are doing their work in the greeting circle. While they are engaged, we are off to the side, preparing for the next task. This is my time to coach the both of you for the next activities.

We stand far enough away from the circle to talk without interfering with the community at work. I use an easel or paper to draw a circle on it.

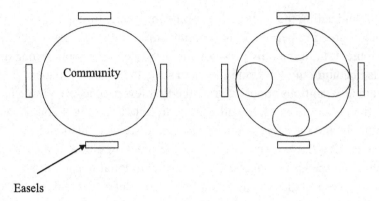

This represents the circle of chairs, I say to you and Mike. It has no structure to keep it in place, so I place the easels outside on the edge of the circle to define a boundary.

The circle symbolically represents community. I learned this mostly from experience. As I developed this process, I realized that people worked differently in a circle than in an auditorium style or organization style. This is especially true if they feel safe, if they feel they can speak without interruption or judgment.

This is a powerful symbol. People can sit anywhere they want in this circle. There is no head of the circle. All people are equal in this arrangement. They know they will be respected when they speak. People who would not otherwise participate will speak in the circle because they are part of a community.

When we create the small groups, as we just did, we ask them to form circles in front of their easel and to leave it in place. This allows the whole community, in their small groups, to meet inside the larger circle, inside the symbol of community.

As I am talking to the cofacilitators, I can hear the sound of the greeting circles; people are actively into it—loud sounds, some laughter. I continue:

This is important: if I let them, most people will move the easel outside the circle to a corner as far as they can from the others and meet behind it. This is called a breakout room, in typical workshop or conference style. This alienates people from each other and fosters groupthink. Each group becomes separate from the whole.

My observation is that when this happens, the groups become competitive instead of collaborative. Inside the circle they tend to be community oriented or collaborative.

I keep them inside the space occupied by the circle to foster community think. Even if the room is ten times the size of this one, I will keep them within this circle. If they move outside the circle, I ask them to move back and explain my reasoning to the whole group. This is a teachable moment.

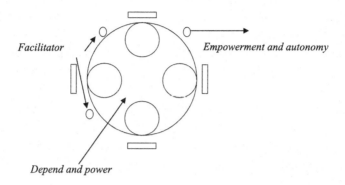

When I am inside the large group, as part of the circle, I will be seated, to remain at their level, to keep the power relationship equal. If I stand, I will take power from them because I am above them, looking down on them.

But when they are in small groups, I need to stand so they can all see me and hear me. Since it is important to keep my power as facilitator balanced with the group, I balance the power by where I stand. I will move to the edge of the circle and stand there for a moment, letting them sense I am there.

We are all naturally drawn to move ourselves to the center of the circle, because that is where the POWER is and we feel the groups DEPEND on us. This movement is not codependency, although it can be. It represents a belief that we are responsible for the group, they look up to us to lead them, so they depend on us to make sure they are doing it right. In order to do this, we must take away some of their power.

I have learned from experience to stand at the edge of the circle when providing the next activity or task. I stand and wait until they sense I am there. I may do a brief introductory statement for the activity, provide some task directions, and then state the questions for the facilitator. (I may repeat the question once.) I then turn and walk away, leaving them to their task.

When I turn to look at the circle, the facilitators have their groups already focused on the task. This fosters EMPOWERMENT and AUTONOMY. They are in charge of the task, each group performing it in a way that fits them. I do not have to explain anything in detail to them—they just go to work.

If I continue to stand at the edge of the circle, watching them, or begin to overexplain myself, eventually someone will ask me for a clarification, which is followed by questions from another group, or a statement of disagreement, and so on. Soon, I am the center of attention, engaged in a conversation that prevents them from focusing on their task. I am continuing to try to clarify what I want, they are continuing to create new "what ifs." Tires me out and stresses me just to think of it!

My advice is: ask the question, then walk away, turning your back to the group. They will take charge and resolve any issues they have within their circle. **Trust them**!

This allows us as cofacilitators to work together outside the circle, designing the next steps for the group, without affecting them.

I give YOU the three-by-five card with the next task written on it. (Or, sometimes I will state the task and have the cofacilitator write it on the card.)

This three-by-five card contains the next task. The questions on it are very precise, intended to help people balance themselves and learn. Please read the card so Mike can hear the questions.

> Close the circle, do not record. (Pause)
> Introduce yourself briefly.
> How do you feel about the greeting circle?
> What did you learn that will help us resolve our issues?

YOU read the questions, which is helpful to me because now I know you can read my writing. Then I continue coaching:

I will have the groups sit after the greeting circle, when all are done or when most of the group has experienced both the greeter and greeted roles. I will tell the group YOU will be facilitating them through the next task.

Then you will step to the edge of the circle and tell the facilitators to close their circles and not record the next task. Wait until they have stopped moving their chairs, and then read the questions. You may want to repeat them once. Then turn and walk away. When you get back to Mike and me, turn around and see what they are doing.

~15~

Lifelong Learning

Lifelong Learning Questions: An Activity

By now the group has completed the greeting circle, so I move to the edge of the circle and ask them to be seated.

Please finish with whomever you are greeting and return to your chairs.

I am repeating this continually in the same facilitative tone until they do this.

If you didn't finish the circle, it is OK. Our culture is very verbal. While the circle in the beginning felt strange and you felt self-conscious, as you met each other you became more comfortable. You realized the importance of meeting each other. You are curious about each other. The result is you begin to take more and more time with each person. The circle sometimes will slow down until it comes to a stop.

And this wasn't a race; you took whatever time you needed. You have met enough of your group to be able to talk about the value of what you did. That is the next task the facilitator will lead you in. You now have different experiences with the greeting circle. You can learn from them in this next task. My cofacilitator, YOU, will present your next task.

YOU walk to the edge of the circle and say:

"Facilitator, close your circle, do not record this next task. This will be a talking circle."

You wait until they are done moving. Then you read off the questions they will answer:

- *"Introduce yourself briefly.*
- *"How do you feel about the greeting circle?*
- *"What did you learn that will help us resolve our issues?"*

You walk away and when turning back, see that the group has immediately gone to work on the questions. *"WOW!"* you exclaim, *"that was really easy!"*

So, I say, you have experienced providing the task. How did you feel about it and what did you learn?

YOU reply: "I felt nervous, really nervous and self-conscious. I was glad I had the card to read. I've led groups before, but always felt that I needed to explain things to them in more detail. When I walked away, I felt like I should have said more.

"And when I looked at them and saw how they went right to work, it was amazing. It was so easy."

I provide an insight:

This happened because you walked away, sending a nonverbal behavioral message to them: "You are in charge now, we trust you to do the task."

Let's leave the coaching and listen in on Group 4.

Cliff Ford: "OK, let's get started," Cliff states in a very businesslike tone. "Since I'm the facilitator, I'll speak last. I'll start to my left and we can go this way," motioning clockwise with his hand.

"The questions are: how did we feel about the greeting circle, and what we have learned to help us solve the problems? Oh, and introduce yourself again. Let's start with you, Marcia."

Marcia Nelson: "OK, I'm Marcia, county commissioner. I have to admit that I was nervous about the idea of the greeting circle at first; I don't like touchy-feely stuff, so it felt uncomfortable. But as we went along, it felt better, and I especially enjoyed meeting those of you I haven't met before.

"So, Rob and Todd, you are new to me. I had never met you before either, Allen, so it was great to make this first contact. I knew you were on the planning commission, but we never officially met.

"I guess that is what I learned that will help us: just shaking hands and looking everyone in the eyes. It even felt new with you, Laura, although you and I have met before.

"So, you are next, Laura."

Laura Lincoln: "I'm Laura, the county attorney. Like you, Marcia, I was a little nervous about the greeting circle. It felt a little bit like being at the wedding reception last week. But I knew very few of the people in this group, so it really helped me. And I felt better as we went along. It seemed easier to talk.

"I was a little uncomfortable the second time through; I wondered why we did that. Then I realized that we talked more about personal things. The first time through, it was sort of, hello, how are you?

"I feel like I know all of you at least a little bit now, so it makes me feel more comfortable about being in this group. It is easier to talk. That is what I learned."

Laura looks at Allen seated next to her.

Allen Smith: "I am Allen Smith and I'm chairman of the Coyote Mountain Tribal Council. The circle feels good to me. We do something similar in our round dances. Only we don't talk quite so much.

"I'm happy to have met every one of you. I believe this will help us be more respectful to each other, because we have met each other as people. We needed to take this time to meet. I like that everyone speaks and there is no interrupting. We could have learned this sooner."

Rob Painter: "I'm Rob. This felt pretty weird to me. I'm not very comfortable about doing this kind of thing. I mean, we shake hands with each other individually, but not with a group like this. Made me nervous at first and uncomfortable, but I did enjoy it more as I went along.

"What I learned is we really don't know each other. We know surface things, but that's just about all. I was happy to meet you, Allen; I've heard a lot about you. I know your people were upset about what happened with the mine, but it's closed now and we are cleaning it up. So maybe we can work on a different relationship in the future.

"Also learned a little bit about Cliff's business, Restore and Renovate. I guess that's all. You're next, Todd."

Todd Gimble: "I'm Todd, from the town of Chilly. I felt all right about the greeting circle. Sometimes we do a similar thing at the resort when a group of people are up at the resort. Sort of a warm-up exercise, and it makes it easier for people to talk to each other.

"I'm sure it will help us here, just knowing each other. It makes it easier to listen to each other."

Neil Gorman: "I am Neil Gorman. I am the new county executive. I think the best thing about this circle is getting to shake hands and look everyone in the eyes. We got to know each other enough that it will help us as we move ahead.

"I agree it was uncomfortable. We went fast at first, but as we got more comfortable, we slowed down.

"I am learning some new ideas about how to work with groups. I wish we had done something like this when we started on the planning and zoning project. It might have helped. I think we listen better to each other if we take the time to do this."

Gil Brothers: "I'm Gil. I'm the Chamber of Commerce president and a developer/stockbroker. I'm not much for touchy-feely stuff, so I didn't enjoy the greeting circle at all. I'd rather meet people one at a time. I would rather be talking about the problems we have. Seems to me like this workshop may take a lot of time with nothing getting done.

"I don't mean to be negative. I do agree we know each other better right now, so this might be helpful. But I wish we could move faster."

Cliff Ford: "I'm Cliff, I own Restore and Renovate Development, and am a small-business consultant. Well, I didn't like it either. I hate warm-up exercises. They are probably necessary, but I get a little turned off by them. Just doesn't feel real.

"On the other hand, it felt sort of good, too. Feels like we know each other now, like we are a little community. And we are listening to each other, which is different. I just hope we can move a little faster.

"Anyone want to add anything?"

Rob: "Yeah. I'm wondering if you could come up to Chilly and look at all our old mining-town homes? You would find lots to restore up there. It's a shame to see those buildings fall into ruins, decomposing into the earth. And your wife might see some properties she could sell for vacation homes. I'd hate to see this community disappear."

Cliff: "You know, we might just do that. We have never been to Chilly; we are sort of homebodies when not working."

Gil: "The problem with Chilly is it is so cold there in the winter. Isn't it hard living up there?"

Todd: "Lots of people come up there in the winter. They like the feeling of deep snow, and a warm fireplace after a day of snowmobiling is something to look forward to. A hot drink, a hot fire, what more could you want?

"It is tough on the old-timers though. We have to make sure they have wood in the winter. They would freeze to death if the community didn't come together to do this."

Cliff: "They are trying to get our attention. Have we all spoken enough?"

Heads nod yes. Cliff signals they are done.

Note: At this time I may provide another short break or a regular fifteen-minute break.

Has Everyone Spoken at Least Once?—An Inclusive Question: An Insight

I am standing at the edge of the circle opposite YOU. Moving to different areas around the edge of the circle when speaking keeps a balance so that the focus is never in one place. All three days, we balance the location of power by continuing to move our locations for presenting the tasks, not allowing power to accrue in any one location.

I ask a question of the groups:

Has everyone spoken at least once?

I keep repeating the question until all groups indicate they have. Then I provide them an insight:

I want you to take note of the question I just asked, **"Has everyone spoken at least once?"** I didn't ask, "Are you done yet?" because that sends a different message. This question is an important one in building consensus and community.

In our culture we normally set a time limit and end an activity even if only half or slightly more of the group has completed the task. This is based on a competitive belief system. We believe in the survival of the fittest or the law of the jungle. This means that those who are faster should not be held back by those who are slower. A chain is only as strong as its weakest link, I have been told. Get rid of the weak links.

Somehow those who can't keep up must be excluded for this behavior. So we move ahead without them, or we say, "Let's move ahead, you slow ones can catch up later." Later never happens. This separates the group into the fast workers and the slow workers.

This approach tends to foster a difference between individuals and groups. As a result, the slower individuals do not get represented in the group situation. They become sensitive to this discrimination. They will begin to feel more apprehensive and drop out or become resentful and prolong their slow behavior. Either way, their information and ideas are lost to the group.

We have preconceived notions about this belief in the survival of the fittest. If you are taller, faster, more beautiful, slender, and outgoing, with the best grades, then it is assumed you are the top of the evolutionary heap. Not so, says Aesop, in his story of "The Tortoise and the Hare." As fast as the hare was, his arrogance got him, as he slept while the more persistent and humble turtle walked over the finish line.

The fact is, we don't know who the fittest will be. The tallest person may be the right one for the basketball team, but the shortest will be the best for traveling through space to the stars because it takes less energy to support him.

If we truly believed in the survival of the fittest, then why are we drawn to the smallest kitten in the litter? Why do we have a small-business loan program? Why did we save Chrysler during its downtimes? Why not let the others win?

The fact is, there is another survival and evolutionary mechanism. It is called "survival of all." How can we make sure all of us make it? This is the basis for consensus building.

I have learned that we all need to participate if we are going to resolve the conflict and reach a consensus. This requires that we allow all members to complete a task before moving ahead, even if it appears to take more time.

In all tasks, especially those that require writing or recording, I wait until each individual or group has completed the assignment. If a group finishes the task before the other groups, then they have time to dialogue informally. This is an uncertain moment at first. *"Who will speak? What will we talk about?"* Self-consciousness dominates the moment. This is their dilemma to resolve, their opportunity to seize the moment.

This means that the fast group has time to just sit and dialogue while the others are completing the task. Often, these discussions are more productive toward resolution of the issue than the assigned tasks. This is a good time, a balance for that group. Who knows what serendipitous material may be created as a result?

Before moving ahead, the facilitator asks the question: **Has everyone spoken at least once?** If the group facilitators signal they haven't, then the facilitator turns and walks away from the working groups. The message is clear: you are in charge. When the groups signal they have all spoken, then the facilitator moves the group to the next question or task.

When a conflict affects all of us, we must be concerned with the survival of all. This requires that we allow all to participate fully. The process must be inclusive, rather than exclusive. The process must allow for spare time to be experienced by some—just for balance, for serendipity.

When the process is inclusive, I have observed that the "slowness behavior" moves around among individuals or groups. The person or group that finishes fast this time is the last one the next time. The group that is slow now is faster later. This allows people to express a broader set of behaviors, to have a broader range of experiences.

~16~

The Greeting Circle Insights

The Greeting Circle—A Symbol for Oneness: An Insight

"The greeting is older than dirt!"

—B. C.

Everyone is listening to me as I present this insight. I can see them moving their chairs so they can both see and hear me, just as focused as they were in the small groups.

No ritual is older and none more anxiety ridden than that of greeting each other. We have greeted each other with some form of personal contact since we were tribes or clans making chance encounters in our travels during the Paleolithic and Neolithic ages.

Before we had verbal language, we had to communicate in some way. Often this was done with sign language, where the sound of the voice or movements and behavior sent the message. Clans would meet by chance in the glacial plains. Stare at each other. Then move forward with a palm held up or hand held forward, a sign of peaceful intent. A welcoming sound may be voiced. These were nonverbal behaviors, many of which are still with us to this day.

One of these is the handshake. We recognize the handshake as a greeting, a symbolic gesture of welcoming, of peaceful intent. It can be a hand clasp, the touching of the faces, kissing on the cheek, a hug, a gripping of the wrists, and any other gesture in which personal contact is made.

The intent is to convey that we are friendly, with peaceful intents. The contact acclaims that while we appear different on the surface, we are one people, connected, blood to blood. Many cultures, such as the American Indian, refer to themselves as "The People." For some of the Spanish-speaking cultures, they are *"La Raza."* There is an underlying universal recognition and acknowledgment that we are **one**.

For some cultures, other meanings have been assigned to the handshake. In Western culture, the handshake has evolved into a test of strength, a demonstration of trust. A contract can be sealed with a handshake. For others, a secret handshake, known only to those who belong, establishes the oneness of the group. Or it may symbolize success, joy—as evidenced by the "high fives" in sports. At weddings, the reception provides an opportunity to honor the newly wedded couple, but also to acknowledge the joining of two people, of two families, into one.

These applications are additions to and often eclipse the real purpose of the greeting: an acknowledgment of the peaceful intent of each other, affirming that we are one people. We want our contact to be safe. Even if we disagree, we intend to maintain security for the parties.

The fact that the handshake has been trivialized by its use at social and superficial gatherings does not reduce its impact in times of stress. It is a powerful symbolic action that affirms our need to respect and care for each other, for the good of the whole, as well as the good of the individual. It establishes an environment in which all people are equal, all are known, causing a hesitation in our strongly held stereotyped beliefs, a possibility of doubt that maybe this person, this group is different.

This deep symbolic meaning is attested to by the attention given recently to "global handshakes." The world held its collective breath when Yasser Arafat reached across President Clinton to shake the hand of Prime Minister Rabin.

These are the purposes of the greeting circle:

THE GREETING CIRCLE PURPOSE:
- Meeting friends and strangers
- Releasing anxiety
- Meeting the person and not the stereotype
- Reducing perceived intimidation
- Fostering open communication
- Fostering balance in relationships
- Initiating conflict resolution
- Allowing people to be self-conscious, to move through their discomfort and uncertainty
- Providing a learning experience that helps the group learn together

Meeting friends and strangers. The greeting circle establishes the opportunity for all participants to meet each other. We meet friends and strangers. It allows individuals to make a personal contact so needed before confronting the conflict. It allows us to experience our self-consciousness in a safe and accepted way. It creates a bond between the diverse people in the small group.

Releasing anxiety. The anxiety and apprehension of the individuals is confronted, encountered, and released. Energy, normally suppressed by the fear and anxiety of the unknown, releases into the room in the sound of high sharp voice tones, loud laughter, slaps on the back, hugs.

Meeting the person, not the stereotype. The greeting circle allows people to meet the person, rather than the role or stereotype. It is normal for people in conflict to never have met each other in person. They operate out of stereotyped perceptions gained from distant experiences or from others' perceptions. If the other is in conflict with us, they are often regarded as the enemy and are assigned the negative connotations that go with that role. Meeting the individual, in person, will dramatically alter these perceptions. The stereotypes become difficult to retain.

Reducing perceived intimidation. This activity reduces the intimidation that people tend to perceive with each other. You may be surprised that people are intimidated by you. Yet that is likely in conflict situations, and it affects communication.

Fostering open communication. The greeting circle provides a basis for knowing people. By reducing our stereotypical images and creating more personal ones, we open up communication, allowing each person to seek a common interest or topic. We enter the forming stage of developing a relationship. It establishes a beginning sense of community.

Fostering balance in relationships. By being both a greeter and a greeted person, the idea of balance is introduced. The first time I am greeted, the greeter is in power. When I am the greeter, I am in power. This balances our relationship.

This also allows the individuals to go beyond the ritualistic first greeting to finding a more real and common interest during the second contact. The first time around, we speak out of the ritual of meeting; the second time around, we must go deeper, to seek to understand each other.

Initiating conflict resolution. The greeting circle allows us to resolve some of the conflict nonverbally. It provides an opportunity for the first conflict resolution to happen.

People who are in conflict will often use distance as a coping strategy. We do this with actual space or by creating physical space: not seeing each other, averting our eyes, speaking superficially, and hiding our true information or feelings. We will stand at opposite ends of the room or sit in opposite parts of the circle. We are consciously aware of the presence of each other and maintain that distance.

I illustrate this on a flip chart. Then continue.

The distance between person "O" and person "X" seated in the circle represent their coping strategy. This distance is reduced by participating in the greeting circle.

```
SEPARATE/ALIENATED      O      X      (seated in the circle)
INTIMACY                       O X    (greeting circle)
```

The greeting circle provides an opportunity to reduce this distance. When they greet each other, only their personal space separates them. They must find some way for this to happen. They must somehow reduce the emotional distancing, in the same way that a couple will hug each other as a nonverbal way of resolving a dispute. This may be by joking about their distancing or reminding each other they were once friends, working together instead of apart.

Allowing people to move through their discomfort and uncertainty. It is uncomfortable, apprehensive, uncertain, and sometimes even feels fake. It fosters self-consciousness. Yet it is a necessary activity if the group is to have open and honest communications.

Providing a learning experience that helps the group. The activity is given new meaning when the two lifelong learning questions are asked and answered after the greeting. I always ask these two questions after the greeting circle. The questions allow the individuals to be grounded again and to learn from the experience

If there is time, I will share the following anecdote, because it is so powerful.

We Are One People—Blood to Blood: An Anecdote

We met in the longhouse, a place of community and religion for the tribe. There were thirty-six people, with half representing the non-Indian or white communities that lived off reservation and half representing the tribe. Elected representatives of the tribal council and city and county governments were present.

Members of the non-Indian community were anxious, having never been on the reservation before. This was the first time they had ever come together as two communities seeking to establish a new relationship, one of partnership. Few of the participants knew each other. After the grounding, I had them do a greeting circle in the large group, meeting members of both communities.

When the greeting was completed and all were seated, I asked them all to answer the questions: "How do you feel about the greeting circle?" and "What did you learn that will bring us together to help each other?" I did this in the large community, because this is how the tribal people would do it. They needed to hear all the community members speak. I honored their tradition.

> Whenever possible, honor the traditions of the different cultures.

When it was Keith's turn (the chairman of the county commission), he complained to the Indian people that their handshakes were "wishy-washy," weak like a "woman's" handshake. He said that if the Indian people wanted to be trusted, they needed a strong handshake, one that sent a message of strength and trust. "And some of you didn't look me in the eyes. That makes us distrust you." I felt a stir in both the tribal members and the women in the group.

When it came to John's turn, a tribal council member and elder, he stood and moved to the center of the circle and asked Keith to join him. Keith complied, acting somewhat self-conscious. All eyes were focused on them; everyone wondered what was to happen. I sat still, trusting in them.

As Keith came to the center of the circle, John held out his right hand. Keith reached out to clasp his. "Just let your hand relax," John said. They pressed palm to palm, firmly, but not strongly. "This is how we shake hands," said John. "Its purpose is not a test of strength; it is intended to remind us of who we are. We want to feel the warmth of each other's blood, to remind us that we are one people under the skin, 'blood to blood.' We are of 'the people'; we may disagree, but we need to do so without hurting each other. We are the people, we are all one. Let us find an agreement that meets the needs of all.

"We do not look you in the eyes because we feel it is disrespectful to do so. The eyes are the doorway to our soul, and to look into others' souls without their permission is to trespass on their being."

When they returned to their seats, I asked Keith to talk about how he felt and what he learned from being with John. He said he was a little nervous at first (laughter from the group) and suggested that the next time we did the greeting circle, we do it in the tribal way, with their handshake and not looking into others' eyes, so they could all learn while honoring the tribe. This was a simple sign of statesmanship, reaching out to the others.

The next morning we did a greeting circle with the tribal handshake. (Although I did not originally plan to do this, I adapted the process.) It was a powerful moment. A suspension of one culture's way to experiencing another culture. Later, during the following talking circle, John suggested that they experience each other's culture the next day by greeting each person with that person's cultural handshake.

Sunday morning, the greeting circle was one of experience and acceptance. People honoring each other's culture used the handshake of the person they greeted, creating a feeling of oneness, while still being different. It led to a talking circle that dramatically altered their relationship to one that was accepting of each other while using the strength of each other. It made their subsequent resolution possible.

ACCEPTING OTHERS AS FACILITATORS

It is not unusual for members of a group to act as facilitators by suggesting approaches that will move them ahead, as John and Keith did. It is important, as a facilitator of the large group, to be open to those ideas. They will normally help the group move forward. To do this requires the facilitator to trust the community members.

After the insight on the greeting circle, I will move to an insight on lifelong learning.

~17~

Lifelong Learning -An Insight

A Lifelong Learning Community:

People in conflict have to learn from each other if they are going to resolve their conflicts and reach consensus. If I have a group experience such as the greeting circle, I always, always, *always* follow that with the lifelong learning questions. Earlier today I said:

"When people develop healthy relationships, they are able to legitimately hear information that is important to solving conflicts. When information is shared in a consensus setting, it becomes common knowledge for the group, and this serves as a basis for wise and comprehensive decisions." This describes a learning community.

Our purpose is to learn. Being open to learning at all times is the best way to resolve conflicts. This is a major belief and concept of the consensus process. We must learn from each other if we are to resolve the problem, if we are to reach consensus. This concept is expressed by the Lifelong Learning Questions that are written on a flip chart behind Jon.

> **LIFELONG LEARNING QUESTIONS**
> What is the situation or experience?
> How do you FEEL about it?
> What did you LEARN that will help you be successful?

(**Note**: This is on a flip chart that all can see.)

Asking "How do you feel about the greeting circle?" allows the person to react out of the situation with their emotional content. It allows expressions of anger, apprehension, doubt, hurt, sadness, and also acceptance, excitement, hope, support. This engages two parts of your brain, the limbic system and the right brain, and keeps the experience in the "here and now."

Feelings are the reactive, the emotional material. Expressing them first facilitates and allows the learning to take place later. If the emotions are suppressed, they may serve as a block to understanding and learning. Or the learning is superficial and kept external to the person, or learning doesn't happen at all. The experience is unfinished.

Answering the "feeling" question after the greeting circle grounds the person in the moment, allowing people to feel real. It is OK to be angry, impatient, frustrated, or hopeful, caring, excited.

The next question, "What did you learn?" allows the person to be proactive, to use the intellect to create meaning from the experience. The question can be asked generally or made more specific if it is linked to the situation we are confronting. For example:

- What did you learn that will help you solve the problem?
- What did you learn that will help you successfully complete the mission?
- What did you learn that will create a sense of community?
- What did you learn that will make you a better person?

Asking this question allows the person to integrate the experience into the personal knowledge base, internal to the person. You know it experientially.

Accepting Their Answers

When asking the people "how they feel" and "what they learned" about the experience, the facilitator must be prepared to accept their answers. Often, the greeting circle, or any other exercise, doesn't feel good to those who experienced it. Don't feel apologetic or responsible if negative feelings are expressed. Don't feel smug if positive emotions are expressed. This has little to do with you as the facilitator. It's an expression of their truth in this moment about that experience. They are being honest. You do want them to be honest, don't you? If they are, then you are successful as a facilitator.

For some, the experience was frightening, embarrassing, and apprehensive. They might be afraid someone would hug them, be touchy-feely: "I was afraid Bob was going to hug me!" They would prefer not to repeat the experience. They will express this openly. They will speak their truth. That is what we want, isn't it?

For others it was exciting, affirming to them, and they want more: "I was hoping Bob would hug me, and he did!"

Any feeling is acceptable. Each feeling is real to the individual. Only she/he knows and can describe it. Being able to express it in a nonjudging environment will often allow the feeling to dissipate, thus making learning possible.

You as facilitator are not looking for support for the activity. It is not about you. You are looking for people to express themselves with openness and honesty. It helps people get to know each other. It humanizes everyone.

Sometimes participants will not express their feelings. For whatever reason, they do not feel they can disclose this information. This is their choice to make. They cannot make that choice, however, without feeling the emotion at some level. This may be enough to allow the learning to take place. At a later time, the individual may feel safe enough to disclose feelings. This activity is a step in that direction. They are "in process." In the meantime, the person will express what they learned.

In expressing your feelings, you may express my feeling. I vicariously experience the feeling and the release. If it is safe for you, then it will be safe for me when I express my feelings later. And by expressing your feeling, you open yourself up to learning.

The Vanna White Effect: An Insight

Asking the learning question sets into motion what I call the "Vanna White Effect."

There is a popular daytime TV show called *The Wheel of Fortune*. In it, contestants are shown a set of blank spaces representing words or phrases and given a clue as to what the blank spaces refer to.

The contestants spin the wheel, in turn, to find the value of their guesses. They are allowed to pick a letter that fits in the blank spaces until enough evidence is available to infer what the word or phrase is. Vanna White is the letter turner.

It does not take long for the contestants to guess the words. It is unusual for the entire word or phrase to be completely spelled before a correct guess is made.

This game works because of how our brains function. Our brains cannot stand to have an unfinished space. I must bring "closure" to the unanswered, the unresolved. I am compelled to go to great lengths to do so.

> The brain cannot stand to have an unfinished space. I must bring "closure" to the unanswered, the unresolved.

The second question, "What did you learn from the experience that will...?" taps the same brain function as *The Wheel of Fortune* does. We learn from the experience because we establish learning as our goal.

There are some experiences so painful that we learn from them immediately. A young child touching the hot stove does not have to repeat the experience.

There are other experiences we are slower to learn from. We find ourselves reliving an event even though the result may be painful or not what we intended. A person who continues to get speeding tickets is an example. For these events, we are doomed to repeat them until the lesson is learned.

It is not unusual for someone to fool or "con" a person, with disastrous results. The person exclaims, "Never again!" Then they are fooled again, because they are trusting or too greedy. Until the lesson is learned, they will continue to be taken advantage of.

Learning happens best when we consciously set out to make it happen. The consensus process purposefully creates learning experiences for people that cause them to feel and think. As an example, if I were to create the following incomplete task:

(I record these large letters on a flip chart that all can see:)

B__D

What would you do with it?

Many people in the groups are mouthing letters; some express them: "I put an "A" in there," Jon says. "I think "C" would fit," Rayni shouts.

It is normal for your brain to try to bring closure to this unfinished space. If we are working on a crossword puzzle and cannot get a word completed, we sleep on it, and in the morning it comes to us. If we are watching a mystery, we are duty-bound to try and figure out who the culprit is. Eventually, with enough clues, we get it!

What did you add when you saw this? Some possibilities for solving the space above are:

B<u>A</u>D   B<u>U</u>D   B<u>I</u>D   B<u>C</u>D   A<u>BCDE</u>   AB<u>E</u>D

There is no one right answer in this instance. It is interesting to me that most people select an "A" to fill in the space, creating the word BAD. I suppose there might be something Freudian about that. But, at the end of the day, they might add a *u* for BUD. Or an *e* for BED. There are many possibilities. The last two solutions above are creative in that they go beyond the bounds of the normal response. They add more possibilities.

Bringing closure to the unfinished space, the unanswered question, requires that the mind do the "leap of imagination" that taps the whole brain. I refer to this as the "Vanna White Effect."

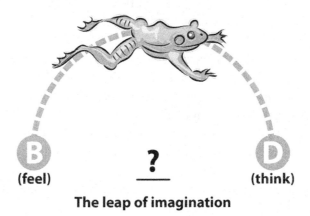

The leap of imagination

Here is another example. Read the mind trick below. Can you read the gibberish? Don't concentrate on this too much—just read it.

CAN YOU READ THIS?

I cdnuolt blveiee taht I cluod aulaclty uesdnatnrd waht I was rdanieg The phaonmneal pweor of the hmuan mnid, aoccdrnig to a rscheearch at Cmabrigde Uinervtisy, it deosn't mttaer in waht oredr the ltteers in a wrod are, the olny iprmoatnt tihng is taht the frist and lsat ltteer be in the rghit pclae.

The rset can be a taotl mses and you can sitll raed it wouthit a porbelm. Tihs is bcuseae the huamn mnid deos not raed ervey lteter by istlef, but the wrod as a wlohe.

Amzanig huh? ayah and I awlyas thought slpeling was ipmorantt.

Actually, because the brain cannot stand the unfinished space, it will automatically reorder the words to match the pattern of words in our brains. Pretty neat, eh? Imagine tapping this brain trait to resolve problems.

When I ask how you feel, I get an instant answer, because feelings are always at the surface. These feelings may get in the way of learning.

But, some ask, "What if a person doesn't want to tell you their feelings?" It matters not if you tell me your feelings; you will still become conscious of them. You will still feel.

After you have expressed your feelings or become conscious of them, then I can ask you what you learned or what you want to learn from the experience. This creates that opening, or gap, that fosters the leap of imagination. You must make sense out of the experience to close that gap.

Asking the right questions creates the possibility, the springboard, for leaps of imagination. Each time a person answers the feeling and learning questions in the circle, they introduce information that creates new possibilities for others. They are able to educate each other about their possible feelings and learning. They help each other make leaps of imagination. They have become a **learning community.**

This increased knowledge base creates the possibility of solutions for consensus. The purpose is to create possibilities, not just the one right answer.

I may tell the group the following anecdote to demonstrate this concept.

Beyond Impasse to Consensus: An Anecdote

It was after lunch, and I had a flight to catch in four hours. But the group had reached an impasse over some contract language on working conditions that affected the decisions on salary and benefits. The group had thought they had a consensus before lunch, but the management representatives had returned with a concern that some of the wording would prevent their executive board from agreeing to their decisions.

The union representatives were naturally upset, feeling misused and betrayed. They did not want to change the agreement they had made before lunch. They dug in their feet and moved from the issues to disparaging management, especially those not in the room. The management representatives felt mistrusted and unduly criticized and responded in kind. Resentments were stated and cross words were expressed. The room that had previously been full of agreement and harmony began to be full of recriminations. I listened for a while so I could understand what had happened, then got the group's attention.

"We appear to be at an impasse here as to whether or not to respond to management's need or to stay with the agreement made before lunch. The union members are understandably upset; they thought they had a consensus on the agreement. As I listen to you, I wonder if it is possible to actually create a better agreement that recognizes the executives' concerns and still meets the union's needs. I'd like to try doing that.

"I want each of you, beginning on my right and going counterclockwise, to answer these two questions:

"How do you feel about what has happened?

"What do we need to learn to create a better agreement that meets the needs of management and labor?"

The group had experienced these two questions before, so people were able to start answering them immediately. The first six people could only answer the feeling questions. Anger, bitterness, resentment, betrayal, feeling misunderstood, personally attacked, offended were the common themes. When it came to learning, each said some version of "I can't think about what we need to learn. I am too angry!" As these people spoke their emotions honestly and strongly, they represented the emotions of those who had not yet spoken. They helped the others move from emotion to thinking.

The next four to six people—management and union—began to acknowledge that they had lost control of their emotions and said things they did not really mean. They apologized to each other, acknowledged the respect they had for each other. They admitted they had solved bigger issues than this in previous sessions. And they began to express some beginning ideas. They recognized that the executives had real concerns; they were not just trying to wreck the negotiations. They recognized the union members' right to feel as they did.

As we continued around the talking circle, the speakers now only briefly touched on their feelings, having felt well represented in that regard by the earlier speakers. They suggested the executives were in their worst possible outcomes and that any solution had to be around best possible outcomes. They expressed their best possible outcomes and began to suggest some solutions, including wording they could use.

The final speakers began to develop specific statements that could meet the needs of both management and union. Few of them expressed feelings because theirs had been well represented, and they were ready to move on to resolution.

I asked the first six speakers, who only expressed emotions, to repeat the ideas they heard and supported, and to create a statement that would meet the needs of management and labor and be a better agreement. They did this easily, each speaking in turn, slowly and deliberately. Now that they had expressed their emotions and had them acknowledged by others, they were ready to reach resolution. They liked the ideas they had heard, and one by one, crafted a statement, improving it with each person so that it would meet everyone's needs.

In no more than an hour, this group moved from storming and anger to reaching a consensus agreement. At the final closure, all agreed it was a better decision. They felt proud they had moved through this crisis, with even more respect for each other.

Learning Environment

As you spoke in the grounding, I noted how many of you were anxious and uncertain about being here. Some of you are already impatient. On the flip chart behind Jon, you'll notice I have identified what a learning environment is. You can always tell when you're in a learning environment because you will feel anxious and apprehensive, frustrated, uncomfortable, uncertain, impatient, self-conscious, and other unsettling emotions.

But what that tells me is that you are ready to learn. Learning is not necessarily associated with feelings of calm and peace. If you are learning something, it means you have to add something to your base of knowledge. But doing that is not easy. It may disagree with knowledge you already have. Because it's different, you are not yet certain you agree with it.

This approach fosters a learning environment with all those emotions. It is intended to provide you the opportunity to learn if you so choose. In doing so, it means you will experience all of the emotions described on the flip chart.

A LEARNING ENVIRONMENT

If you are...
- Anxious,
- Confused,
- Apprehensive,
- Frustrated,
- Uncomfortable,
- Uncertain,
- Impatient,
- Self-conscious,

    Be aware!
    You are ready to learn!!!

When you feel that way, just remind yourself, "I am ready to learn."

For those of you who are impatient, I would like to share with you my definition of impatience:

"I just wish people would hurry up and move on and make a decision... **MY WAY!**"

That is how I always felt when people moved too slowly. I didn't want them to make the decision quickly; I wanted them to make it my way! I felt I already had the answer. So why waste time? That was before I realized the value of listening to others and their points of view to resolve very, very difficult decisions.

If you are impatient, it's OK. Just understand we are going to make decisions "our way!" When we do, the time you invest will result in the decision that everyone will be committed to and actually successfully implement.

Intimidation: An Insight

One of the most important purposes of the greeting circle is to reduce the sense of intimidation that naturally exists between people. Intimidation is a barrier to communication. Sometimes I talk about this after the greeting circle.

It is normal for people to act surprised when I discuss the idea of intimidation and point out that we all intimidate people. *"Who...me?"* they seem to imply with their expressions and their words. *"Yes...you!"*

We must understand that we each intimidate someone. The boss intimidates the employees, the employees intimidate the boss through their union; the board chairman intimidates the boss, the boss intimidates the board chairman; the male intimidates the female with his logic, the woman intimidates the male with her emotion; the parent intimidates the child with controlling actions, the child intimidates the parent with rebellion.

"Who? Me? But I'm a nice person!" you may claim, not understanding. But it is not you who decides whether you intimidate me. *I* am the one who makes that decision. *I* decide who intimidates me. You are the last one to know because I don't tell you.

We are intimidated by position, authority, elected officials, older people, younger people, people who are different from us, people who are taller, and people who are smaller. And those who intimidate us often don't know this.

More personally, I am intimidated by my wife at times. She is intimidated by me at times. I am intimidated by my older brother. He is intimidated by me. We know this by disclosing our feelings to each other. We know this by watching each other's behaviors.

You can tell by my behaviors if I am intimidated by you:

- Do I stand a long distance from you when we speak?
- Do I put an object, a chair, a desk, between you and me?
- Do I always bring others with me when meeting with you?
- Do I use a loud voice or a timid voice when speaking to you?
- Do I agree with you on anything you say?
- Do I write you a letter when it is easier to talk with you in person?
- Do I initiate rumors about you?

These are just some behaviors people use when feeling intimidated. They are a way of balancing power, of empowering the intimidated person. This is important to acknowledge, because intimidation dramatically impacts the communication process. If I am intimidated by you, I will keep you away from and deny you access to information I have that you may need. Or I may tell you what I believe you **want** to hear, rather than the truth, which may dismay you.

Either way, your information is incomplete. You cannot make the best decisions with incomplete information. When people have incomplete information, the parties in conflict assure me the great mass of people support them. When I interview the great mass of people, I find they are telling the parties what they want to hear because they fear disagreeing with them. The result is that the parties often are operating with information that is limited or incorrect. They make decisions that are later challenged in court or are disregarded and never get implemented. It is confusing to decision makers when this happens.

There are times when I share this anecdote to make this point:

A Small Group of Newcomers: An Anecdote

"There is only a small and radical group of newcomers who oppose the development of this new resort," the chairman of the county commission said emphatically. "A bunch of long-haired, unwashed, granola-eating, Birkenstock-wearing hippies!" The two others nodded in agreement. "They don't have the support of the locals, but the loudness of their voices keeps the reasonable people from supporting us. There is a silent majority out there. These radicals are outsiders and don't know our valley like we do."

I asked the county commissioners to provide me a list of people they thought were reasonable and who supported them. More than sixty people were on the list they created. I spent the next three days listening to these people, individually and in groups.

When I met with the commissioners again, I advised them of my findings. Almost 70 percent of the people I interviewed from their list opposed the resort. It was a threat to their way of life. They did not understand why the commissioners were supporting it.

The commissioners were dumbfounded. How could this be? These people had expressed their 100 percent support to them. I explained the "intimidation factor" to them. Being honest was risky. In some cases, long-term friendships were at stake; in others it was an issue of power. The commissioners had decision-making power that affected others' lives. So the "reasonable locals" told the commissioners what they felt they wanted to hear.

Their constituents did not necessarily lie, they just did not tell the complete truth. They may have said, "Well, I do think those outsiders are wrong, and I don't support them. But I never told the commissioners I supported the resort, either! We will lose our isolated communities."

Reducing the "intimidation factor" is necessary in seeking consensus decisions. Open and honest communication occurs in an environment where people feel secure, where intimidating feelings are minimal. It occurs in environments where people feel they can trust each other. This requires an environment of listening with respect. The grounding and the greeting circle are two ways to do this.

The shy and self-conscious person will meet his boss and learn that she is approachable, not to be feared. This alters the information that will be transferred between them.

It is not unusual for this to be discussed during the lifelong learning task. The boss finds out for the first time that the shy person was intimidated by her. She is surprised by it and compliments the employee for making her aware of it. This creates a truer reality for both individuals. It opens up the possibility of honest communications.

The greeting circle and the lifelong learning questions that follow help to reduce this intimidation factor.

We are now going to take a fifteen-minute break. During the break I want to speak to the facilitators of the small groups.

Coaching the Facilitators

Earlier, while the groups are answering the lifelong learning questions, I am coaching YOU and Mike for the next tasks. We stand in a corner away from the groups so we don't interfere with their work. I pass a three-by-five card to Mike and a similar one to YOU. On it are written two statements that you will use throughout the day.

> Has everyone spoken at least once?
>
> The facilitator will pick a new facilitator and become the recorder.

I explain: YOU will walk to the edge of the circle when you feel the group is almost done with a task. Wait at the edge for a moment so they can sense your presence, and then read off the first question, "Has everyone spoken at least once?" They may not hear you the first time, so repeat this until they have all responded in some way. If they indicate they are not done, then just walk away. Then YOU can check again later.

When they are ready, turn the group over to me.

After I have completed an insight on the greeting circle and the lifelong learning questions, I will give the group a break. After the break I will turn the group over to you, Mike. Walk to the edge of the circle and instruct them, "The facilitator will pick a new facilitator and become the recorder."

Wait until they have done this. You may, if you wish, instruct the recorder to stand at the easel, so you know they have done what you asked. Then read off this task. (I hand Mike a three-by-five card.)

> Record the answers to this question on the flip chart:
>
> *What is the role of a successful recorder in building consensus?*
>
> The recorder is to stand with your face to the flip chart and start recording as soon as someone speaks. Record exactly what they say.

We are now ready for the next task. YOU can see they appear to be ready. You walk to the edge of the circle and ask, "Has everyone spoken at least once?"

The groups are intently involved in and listening to each other. Since they do not hear you, you continue to repeat the question until they respond. The groups nod their heads or raise their hands to indicate they are done. You turn the group over to me.

When I have completed my insight on the greeting circle and the lifelong learning questions I give the group a 15 minute break.

> **TASK VERSUS EXERCISE**
>
> Words have meaning and have the ability to affect people's perception of what they are doing. Beginning facilitators will often refer to the next assignment as an "exercise." This word is often perceived as a practice or testing activity.
>
> In building consensus, everything has purpose and meaning. These are not exercises; this is about reality. The focus is always on working together on the conflict. For this reason, I refer to each assignment as a task, or an activity.

~18~

The Role of the Recorder in Building Consensus

Exploring the Recorder's Role in Building Consensus

We have all returned from the break. The participants are in their small groups. It is time to explore the roles of facilitator and recorder. The facilitator and the recorder roles are central to the consensus process, whether working with two people or a thousand. Seven facilitators—myself, two cofacilitators, and four small-group facilitators—have been models for the group. It is time for the groups to experience and learn to facilitate and record for themselves.

The participants are prepared for this. They have been together for three hours. They have experienced the grounding, demonstrated they know how to listen with respect. They have greeted each other and shared their answers to the lifelong learning questions in a talking circle. They have been facilitated by a member of their group. There is a sense of security and belonging. Now it is time to introduce this task.

The Role of the Recorder in Building Consensus: An Activity

Mike walks to the edge of the circle. He hesitates a minute before speaking. He is self-conscious, his hands shaking a bit as he speaks, getting the groups' attention. He reads the direction from the card:

"The facilitator will select a new facilitator and become the recorder. I'll know you have done that when the recorder is standing at the easel."

He waits as this is done, shifting his feet. When the recorders are standing at their flip charts, he tells the facilitators to have their group answer the question and record the answers directly to the flip charts:

The Role of the Recorder in Building Consensus

"What is the role of a successful recorder in building consensus?"

He reminds the recorders: "Recorders, turn to face the flip charts, your back to the group, and begin writing when the person starts to speak."

Mike turns and walks away from the groups *(detachment is explained later)* and lets them carry on the task. When he turns back to look at the groups, he can see they are all working. The circles have opened up, and the groups are focused on their recorders at the flip chart. There is some delay as the facilitator repeats the question and selects the person to start.

The facilitators are new at this, self-conscious, uncertain of this new position they have. Often, they have never done this before, so this is a powerful experience for them. Then as people speak, the recorder writes what is said on the flip chart. This is also "herky-jerky" as people get used to the idea of being recorded, and the recorder gets used to recording. This is all new to them; they are learning.

I rarely intervene in this task. There are some groups that violate all my beliefs about how to facilitate and record, but this is *their* learning experience. The groups will learn from each other as they progress. I trust them. I work with YOU and Mike during this time to plan our next steps.

As we are talking and coaching outside the circle, the groups are hard at work. In Group 1, the facilitator, Susan, selects her new facilitator.

*(**Note**: The statements in the dialogue below (and in subsequent small group dialogues) that are in italics are the statements that are recorded to the flip chart. This pattern will continue throughout the book. All of these are actual statements recorded in real situations, randomly selected from diverse workshops.)*

Susan: "Tony, could you facilitate the group now? I'll record."
Tony: "OK, I'll give it a try."
Tony asks the group: "What is the role of a successful recorder?"
Rayni responds: "Didn't he add 'in building consensus'?"
Tony: "Yes he did—forgot it. Susan, write the question on the board so we won't forget it."
As Susan is writing, Jon asks: "What is consensus?"
Marie: "Didn't he say 100 percent in the introduction?"
Tony realizes they are getting diverted by the discussion, so he raises his hand and gets my attention. "Bob, what is the definition of consensus you want us to use?"
I walk to the edge of the circle and speak to the entire group:

Group 1 has a question about the definition of consensus. My definition is: 100 percent agreement. But you can answer it with any definition you feel comfortable with.

I turn and walk away. The groups immediately go back to work.

Tony: "Well, it looks like we can use any definition that feels good to us all. Let's go ahead and start with you, Debbe."

Debbe: "I know what I want, Susan: *the recorder will write down exactly what the other person says.*"

As Susan writes, Tony tells the group the direction he wants to go in.

Tony: "Let's go clockwise, so Marie, you are next."

Marie: *"They will have an unbiased manner, unbiased by not being judgmental, and they will not decide what is important.* And, I have another one when you are done, Susan." (Pause.) *"She or he does not paraphrase, and to make sure they recorded what was actually said."*

There is a pause as they wait for Susan to finish recording. All eyes are turned toward the board.

Jon: *"A successful recorder will repeat what was said for clarification."*

When Susan is done recording Jon's statement, she reads it off to him. He gives her thumbs up.

Wayne: *"Provides a tangible record of everyone's thoughts."*

Susan again reads off what she wrote and gets a nod from Wayne.

Alice: *"The successful recorder is value neutral and maintains objectivity."*

Rayni: *"I think the recorder should be included, not excluded, from the group.* I can record for you when it is your turn, Susan."

Susan, while she is recording: "Thanks for that, Rayni; I wondered if I would get a chance to speak."

Tony: "I agree with that, too, Rayni. So, I want to state that *I think it's an accurate accumulation of data in chronological order that can be used later."* (Pauses while Susan records.) "So, Susan, it's your turn and Rayni can record for you."

Susan, sitting down: *"He/she will insure an accurate record of what was said and confirm the thought...they will not interpret what was said.*

I've been in groups where the recorder's words have been written instead. And it made me really mad. I didn't participate after that. Don't write that last part, Rayni."

Jon, raising his hand, gets a nod from Tony: *"To prevent manipulating, the recorder should be writing only what she hears."*

Wayne: "I want to add one that I learned during this task. Like Susan, I have been manipulated before—don't write this down yet, Rayni. I hate it when the recorder or facilitator decides to change what I said. Ticks me off. But this makes me feel like I want to participate. So, record this Rayni: *The recorder empowers the speaker, needs to be responsive, and crystallizes our thoughts.*"

Tony: "So, Mike wants to know if we are all done."

When it appears the groups are done, Mike moves to the edge of the circle. He can sense when they are complete if each person is represented with a statement on the flip chart. This means some groups will finish early and want to move on. They send us nonverbal signals indicating this. By now they know this won't make us respond, that all must speak before we will move on. They may then have informal conversations about the role of the recorder. Some groups go around a second time, recording more information.

Mike asks, "Has everyone spoken at least once?" The facilitators in two groups shake their heads no, so Mike walks away. Soon the facilitators indicate they are done, and Mike returns to the edge of the circle, appearing much more confident.

"The recorder will now read off the information recorded on the flip charts. We will start with group two and move clockwise around the circle."

We have the recorder read the statements because they can read their own writing. Having the facilitator read this material, stumbling over words he can't read, is an embarrassment to both people. The recorder deserves the honor of reading off the members' words.

When facilitating in the outer circle, it is important to allow the group to manage as much of the process as they can. So Mike will tell the groups to report and provide the direction he wants the reporting to go in: clockwise or counterclockwise. Then he steps back and allows the groups to manage themselves. He does not have to say anything when each group finishes—"thank you," "nice work," et cetera—because they don't need it. Just let them manage the process themselves. This keeps as much power as possible with the groups.

These statements are read off to the full community. This allows each person's statement to be heard by the larger community. Everyone now knows what all the groups came up with. In addition, all the groups can see how the other groups did their recording. Three groups recorded all the words in statements with some abbreviations. One group synthesized and wrote one- or two-word bulleted statements.

This is how the Group 1 flip chart looks:

GROUP 1: THE ROLE OF A SUCCESSFUL RECORDER IN REACHING CONSENSUS.

- *The recorder will write down exactly what the other person says.*
- *They will have an unbiased manner, unbiased by not being judgmental, and they will not decide what is important.*
- *She or he does not paraphrase, and to make sure they recorded what was actually said.*
- *A successful recorder will repeat what was said for clarification.*
- *Provides a tangible record of everyone's thoughts.*
- *The successful recorder is value neutral and maintains objectivity.*
- *I think the recorder should be included, not excluded, from the group.*
- *I think it's an accurate accumulation of data in chronological order that can be used later.*
- *He/she will insure an accurate record of what was said, and confirm the thought—they will not interpret what was said.*
- *To prevent manipulating, the recorder should be writing only what she hears.*
- *The recorder empowers the speaker, needs to be responsive and crystallizes our thoughts.*

Let's listen to Group 2's flip chart notes as the recorder reads them off:

GROUP 2: THE ROLE OF THE RECORDER.

- *The role of the successful recorder is to capture thoughts accurately and record exactly what the person says.*
- *The recorder focuses discussion. The recorder needs to keep us more focused to see where we've been and where we're going.*
- *The successful recorder has to remain impartial.*
- *The recorder needs to know how to use the board, they don't stand in front of the board or leave out words.*

> - *Some skills are: listening intently, double checking meaning, and writing carefully and legibly.*
> - *The recorder is writing for all to see, and uses multi;le colors. Spelling does not matter to be a successful recorder.*
> - *A successful recorder will check for clarification. If you don't do exact wording, check back to make sure you captured what was said.*
> - *A successful recorder is neutral and writes down comments word for word.*

When all groups have reported, Mike turns the session over to me for an insight. Normally, this activity takes about seven minutes to record and seven minutes to report to the larger group.

I agree with most of the roles the participants describe for the recorder. As you will find in my insight to them, there are some ways in which I have different views of the roles. I encourage them to use these new roles during this workshop, to see if they are helpful in resolving their conflict.

I walk to the edge of the circle and provide them my insight on the role of the recorder.

The Role of a Recorder: An Insight

This activity took about fifteen minutes to complete. During this time, thirty-two people have spoken and their words recorded. Notice the amount of information you have collected in this short time. (Normally thirty-two people will have fifty to sixty statements describing the role of the recorder.) While you were doing this task, you were also facilitating and recording your own process. Every person has spoken; every person's statements are recorded. Compare this experience with those you have in your day-to-day meetings.

The recorder determines the speed of the process. If you face the flip chart and begin writing as I speak, I will become focused. If, on the other hand, you are looking at me, fiddling with the marker, impatiently waiting for me to say something you feel like recording, I will dissemble, obfuscate, add chaff to the wheat to string out my message, hoping to find some words you will write on the flip chart.

If you convert my statements into shorter one- or two-word "bullets" that you feel conveys what I said, I will be offended. Who gave you the right to do that? If I am shy, I will let it pass when you ask me if what you wrote is what I said. And I will not speak again. And I will be resentful of you.

Or, if I am a fighter, I will confront you and say, "It is not what I said!" You will become defensive, protecting your actions from question. The result of this is a conflict between you and I that now prevents the other members from speaking and diverts attention away from the task. It eats up time, creates confusion, and belittles people.

I have learned to face the easel and start writing as soon as the person speaks. When I do that, I can remember whole paragraphs. If the speaker says more than I can record, I have that person repeat the part I missed. Sometimes I will abbreviate words or leave out "the" or "and" to get it all written. I may ask you if I got it all. If not, I will record what I missed.

I have had thousands of people answer this same question: **"Write it all or paraphrase?"** About 80 percent of all participants want the recorder to write down exactly what they said. They do not want you messing with their statements or changing their words! This is especially true of the public. Professionals may be willing to accept short statements with bullets, but the general public will not.

It does not matter if you can't spell or write well; all that matters is that you wrote down what I said. The word processor and spell checker will take care of the other. And since the recorder can normally read their own words, they can read off the information to the larger group. If you only allow those who write or spell well to record, you are denying others the opportunity to serve in this role.

Sometimes I might say that someone else already said what I wanted, so I don't need to repeat it. Ask me to speak anyway, because you want it in my words. When I make my statement, you will find my statement is different from any other on the board. I do this because I am self-conscious. I don't want to take up time. By encouraging me to speak, you allow me to empower and represent myself.

I encourage recorders to check with the speaker about the accuracy of the recorded statement. I also encourage you, the speaker, to let the recorder know if it is not what you said. It is your responsibility to ensure what was recorded is exact. Be your own advocate.

Because the recorder comes from your group and is serving you, it is important that person also has a chance to speak and have their thoughts recorded. You can have the recorder be seated and select another person to record, or the facilitator can play this role. Do not lose the information of this one person; they are a part of your community also.

You will learn in this workshop that every word you speak has purpose and meaning. We want the exact words, as much as possible. These words will be used this evening to create collective statements that are inclusive of all the views.

I know this is different from what many of you have been taught. In this process, I want the recorder to record every word as it is spoken. You will find it is easier than you imagine. You will capture a lot of information, and you will find it is faster. Your old way is still appropriate in many situations. But if it is not working for you, then you have this new approach available to you. This provides you a choice in approach.

The Historian:

The recorder role is as important in facilitating the process as is the facilitator's. For consensus seeking to be successful, each person must feel listened to and acknowledged. These two attributes allow a person to learn and grow. The recorder's actions facilitate this possibility.

When I come to a meeting with you, I have this need to be heard. I have something to offer. If this information is not presented or listened to, then I am left with that unfulfilled need, that unexpressed or unacknowledged information. This effectively stunts my growth. I cannot create a new perception until I have gotten rid of the old one.

The result will be that I will attempt to make my case at the next opportunity, even if it is an inappropriate time. If you reject me again, then I am left with that old information and that old need and a bunch of resentment over your rejection of me. Since I must have closure, I will seek to speak longer and louder at the next opportunity.

When I see you in the hall during a break, I capture you with my emotional feeling: "I keep trying to tell them about rinka rinka rinka dinka do, and no one listens to me. This is important to the group. **Why won't they listen to me?!**

You reply: "Well, I'm trying to get their attention on woofa woofa woofa win, and they dis me each time."

"You don't understand! I am trying to get you to hear me; I am not interested in woofa woofa woofa win!" I shout.

End of conversation. Neither of us heard the other.

If I am continuously rejected (my perception), then I must continue to seek to get heard. Otherwise I walk around with these statements and their attendant fears in my head. They are voices that impinge on every moment of my life. I walk around trying to avoid them, but the thoughts and fears won't go away. The result will eventually be that I become a nuisance in meetings, seeking to bring you back to meet my unfulfilled needs. I will speak long and loudly. I will bang the table. I will do anything to get your attention.

You will respond to this with the words: "I don't want to meet with Bob again; he always says the same thing."

This is not a reflection on me; it is a reflection on your unwillingness to acknowledge me. I want to be heard, to be acknowledged. I do not exist, at some level, unless I am responded to in some fashion. I need your reaction to know that I am there. Yell at me if you have to, just show me some attention! If I can only get that by disrupting the meeting, then I will do that.

The consensus-building process is designed to ensure that each person speaks. It provides the opportunity to be listened to with respect. It also provides a visual and permanent means for recording what I say, as I say it. This is the recorder's role.

When the recorder writes down my message, I can see visually that it is acknowledged. It becomes part of the message reported back to the larger group. It becomes part of the collective statement. It may eventually be included in the consensus statement.

Someone may refer to my statement and add to it. Someone may see it differently than I do, and this view is recorded on the same easel pad. I can accept this view, be influenced by it, as they may be by mine.

I exist! There is an acknowledgment of my existence on the flip chart. There is a history of my individual input, and it is made part of the group memory. This allows me to let go of the old information and resentments and move on to the new. I can now listen to new information flow into the space created by your acknowledgment of my old information. I can learn and grow, move toward my potential.

The recorder makes this miracle possible. The recorder facilitates the movement of these words, these ideas, to the easel pad so that I am released from them. The recorder writes as I speak so that I feel accepted and acknowledged. The recorder affirms my right to speak, to have a view, to be part of the history of the group's knowledge. If I happen to dislike the recorder, but he has just recorded my words exactly as I expressed them, this shifts my view of that person; maybe he is not as bad as I think.

Recording is the best way I know to increase your memory and recall power. You are focused on the person's information, serving that person, providing the sense of acknowledgment that will help that person grow. You will remember the person, recall what they said when you do the collective statements. You become a historian for the group as it proceeds toward consensus.

~19~

The Role of the Facilitator in Building Consensus

Coaching the Facilitators

While the small groups are working on the role of the recorder, YOU, Mike, and I talk through the next facilitator task. Because we're not worrying about "proximity" or directing the small groups, I can continue to coach and train while they are working. We can also begin designing how to meet the needs of this group based on what they are saying.

We are helping the group determine the roles of the most important positions in the group: the recorder and the facilitator. They are learning as they are doing. I continue to coach YOU and Mike:

After I have completed an insight on the role of the recorder, I will turn the group over to YOU. Walk to the edge of the circle and give them this direction first:

"The facilitator will pick a new facilitator and become the recorder."

This again moves the power on to others, allowing others to experience both of these roles. You wait until this has been done. You may, if you wish, have the recorder stand at the easel, so you know they have done what you asked. Then you provide them their task, reading the question and repeating it.

Then read off this task (I hand you a three-by-five card):

> Record the answers to this question to the flip chart:
>
> What is the role of a successful facilitator in building consensus?
>
> Remember that the recorder is to stand with your face to the flip chart and start recording as soon as someone speaks. Record exactly what they say.

Then instruct the new facilitator to reverse the sequence in the talking circle to bring balance to the circle. If they went clockwise the last time, then go counterclockwise this time. This ensures that the same people are not always speaking first or last.

Then turn and walk away. When you get back to us, turn and observe how they respond. Mike, I want you to repeat this to YOU.

Role of the Facilitator in Building Consensus: An Activity

When I am done with the recorder insight, I turn the group over to YOU. You walk to the edge of the circle and wait to get their attention. Then you give them the task:

"The facilitator will pick a new facilitator and become the recorder."

You wait until you see this is done and then read the questions on the three-by-five card, as described above. You remind them: "Remember that the recorder is to stand with your face to the flip chart and start recording as soon as someone speaks. Record exactly what they say.

"The new facilitator will reverse the sequence in the talking circle to bring balance to the circle. If you went clockwise the last time, then go counterclockwise this time. This ensures that the same people are not always speaking first or last."

You repeat the instructions and then walk away. When you turn around, you can see that they went right to work. People are listening to each other, intently observing how the recording is being done. The environment is calm; joyous laughter sometimes occurs. Remember, these are people who are in conflict with each other, some of whom hate each other. You never could tell it now. They have a common purpose around the question. They have accomplished tasks together. They are beginning to build relationships where they will listen to each other. They are establishing their standards of behavior for the recorder and facilitator.

Let's listen in on Group 3: Kenney, Diane, Ann, Kathy, Crista, Justin, Susan, and Donna.

Diane: "Kenney, I want you to take over as facilitator." (Diane stands and moves to the flip chart.)

Kenney: "I'll just do that. You've set a good example for me. My first task is to decide who speaks first. How about you Crista? You start, and then we will go to the left. Oh, almost forgot, this question is about the role of the successful facilitator in building consensus."

Crista "Hmmm, the role of a successful facilitator, let me think a bit...I know: *Make sure everyone gets a chance to speak.*"

Justin: *"A successful facilitator will allow enough time for everyone to think about their answer.* Like you just did with Crista, Kenney. And then I would add...*The role of the facilitator is to keep the group focused.* Got that, Diane?"

Diane nods her head while she writes fast.

Kathy *"A successful facilitator will give leadership and direction.* And I have another one, Di." (Pause while waiting for Diane to complete recording.) "And *the role of the facilitator is to make things easy for the group.*"

Kenney: "Hold on, Donna, let her finish that last statement." (A pause.)

Donna: *"I think the role of the facilitator is to keep the group focused. To do this, a successful facilitator will establish the ground rules."*

Diane: "Is that it? Did I get it all?"

Donna: "You did just fine."

Ann: *"The facilitator should model behavior expected of the group."*

Kenney: "I'll record for you, Diane." (Kenney and Diane change places.)

Diane: "This is what I learned just now: *he/she must keep the pace moving in order to keep information flowing, yet is able to give the recorder time to write things down.*"

When Kenney is finished recording, he and Diane change places again.

Kenney: *"The successful facilitator is to remain neutral or to retain neutrality. When everyone has had their chance to speak, the facilitator will have their own opinion,* just like I did now." (A pause while this is being recorded.)

Kenney: "Anyone else have another statement?"

Ann: "I don't have a statement, but I do have a question. Have you facilitated before, Kenney?"

Kenney: "Yes, but never like this. I normally take more of a controlling role. I see now that it is more limiting then what we are doing now. So, when we are done, I have a feeling I will be a better facilitator."

Diane: "Well, don't get a big head, but *you are a good one* already; at least I think so."

The Role of the Facilitator in Building Consensus

This is the flip chart for Group 3:

GROUP 3: THE ROLE OF A SUCCESSFUL FACILITATOR INCCONSENSUS

- *Make sure everyone gets a chance to speak.*
- *A successful facilitator will allow enough time for everyone to think about their answer.*
- *The role of the facilitator is to keep the group focused.*
- *A successful facilitator will give leadership and direction. The role of the facilitator is to make things easy for the group.*
- *I think the role of the facilitator is to keep the group focused.*
- *To do this a successful facilitator will establish the ground rules.*
- *The facilitator should model behavior expected of the group.*
- *He/she must keep the pace moving in order to keep information flowing, yet is able to give the recorder time to write things down.*
- *The successful facilitator is to remain neutral or to retain neutrality.*
- *When everyone has had their chance to speak, the facilitator will have their own opinion.*
- *Kenney is a good facilitator!*

When it appears this task is completed, YOU walk to the edge of the group, pause a few seconds so they can sense your presence, and then ask, "Has everyone spoken at least once?"

"**No!**" Group 1 shouts, waving you away. You turn and hasten back to Mike and me, a stricken look on your face.

What happened? I ask.

"Well, they obviously are not ready to stop yet," you say.

Why did they speak so loudly? I ask.

"My guess is they want to be sure everyone in their group gets to speak. And they don't want us to get in the way of that."

So they now feel they are in charge, that we serve them, instead of the opposite. As long as we meet their needs now, they will trust us to facilitate them the rest of the way. But you jumped when they shouted. How did you feel?

"Sort of resentful, I guess. Almost a little angry. They shocked me. I wanted to shout back." You smile as you make yourself aware of this.

"Exactly. When they shouted, they startled you, and you got a shot of adrenaline—the fight or flight chemical. As a facilitator you are trying to get them to take charge. When they do, it is often in an aggressive tone rather than assertive tone. This will startle you, but you have to be able to overcome that adrenaline rush when the moment happens. Relax yourself; this is a good event, not one to be resentful of.

They are advocating for the people who have not spoken yet. Imagine standing up for a person in the group that you may not have agreed with previously. It changes their relationship. By walking away, you send the message to the group that they are in charge. You honor the right for each person to speak. You have accomplished facilitating them into making this their workshop.

"I understand it now," you reply.

We spend more time preparing for the next tasks. I am coaching both of you so you can increase your understanding and skills. Most of this is done by letting you learn by observation and experience.

When YOU sense the group is ready (often the sound will rise in the room), you walk to the edge of the circle and wait until they know you are there. You have learned it is important to stand at the edge of the circle a while so they can become conscious of your presence before you speak.

> **A CALM APPROACH**
>
> Many people who are learning to facilitate in this manner will begin to speak as they are walking to the edge of the circle. Their movement and their words startle the participants. This is not what you want. Instead, move to the edge of the circle, wait a while until they are aware of your presence, then ask the question. Relax yourself!

YOU ask, "Has everyone spoken at least once?" You keep repeating this in calm tones, focusing on the groups farthest away, until all groups have acknowledged that everyone has spoken at least once.

You direct the recorders to read off their information to the larger group: "The recorder will now read off the information recorded on the flip charts. We will start with Group 4 and move counterclockwise around the circle."

Mike started with Group 1 and went clockwise. You start with Group 4 and reverse the direction to balance the power.

GROUP 4: THE ROLE OF A SUCCESSFUL FACILITATOR IN CONSENSUS

- *The successful facilitator will make sure that everyone has a chance to participate.*
- *A successful facilitator will create an atmosphere of inclusion.*
- *They keep the group focused on the topic, monitors the process, and knows what the purpose of the discussion is.*
- *The successful facilitator participates as an equal.*
- *The facilitator demonstrates patience and gives frequent breaks. To create a sense of order, a facilitator establishes ground rules and makes sure ground rules are respected.*
- *A facilitator is responsible for ensuring safety and equity in an atmosphere of freedom.*
- *A successful facilitator's role is to be seen and not really heard.*
- *The facilitator should be unbiased with no interest in the outcome and should not dominate or paraphrase.*
- *The role of the successful facilitator is to make groups feel like all ideas are welcome and to give ample opportunity for all to speak.*

There are substantially more recorded comments from this task. There are more complete statements and fewer bullets. (An analysis of seventeen groups showed a 26 percent increase in statements and a 41 percent increase in words over the recorder's role task.) This is a measure of both trust and productivity. Some groups continued after going around once, while others quietly conferred with each other. There are no more uncomfortable moments in the circles. They are engaged, so the amount of information and knowledge being shared increases.

When they are done reporting, you turn the session over to me for an insight. Normally, this activity takes about ten minutes to record and seven minutes to report to the larger group.

> **CONSENSUS BEHAVIORS**
>
> As the participants present and record their information, their behaviors begin to match their words. Everyone gets to speak, the facilitator is making it easy, and the recorder is writing it all down. These indicate a consensus attitude on the participants' part.

I am always amazed at how comprehensive the group's description for this role is. The roles match all that I have learned in more than thirty-plus years of facilitating groups. I agree with all these role statements.

Consider their reaction to creating these role statements themselves, rather than having me preach to or teach them about the roles. These statements came from their knowledge base and experience, not someone else's. And they did it in less than thirty minutes, while a training workshop on being a facilitator or recorder often takes days. They demonstrated they have the knowledge as a group to develop these roles themselves, using each of their different perceptions. I can then add role statements from my viewpoint, making the list more comprehensive.

After the recorders have read off the information on the flip charts, you turn the group over to me. I walk to the edge of the circle and provide insight on the art of facilitating.

The Art of Facilitating: An Insight

Your description of the role of the facilitator is almost exactly what I have learned in working with groups in conflict for over thirty years. And you created that role in less than thirty minutes. You were facilitating yourselves as you did this. You were tapping the power of the individual perceptions to create this information.

All of this recorded information will be used by you to develop collective statements this evening on the role of the recorder and facilitator. You will learn that:

> "Every word you say has purpose and meaning."

Every single statement or word on the flip charts will be used to develop these collective statements. In addition, here are some further insights on the art of facilitating that will add to your knowledge about this important role.

Right questions: It is the responsibility of the facilitator to ask the right questions that will lead you to resolution of the conflict. Most of these "right" questions are developed for you, and you will use them in this process. Other right questions will come from the group as you further explore your situation.

Your purpose is to see that each person in the group answers these questions without interruption. You do this by picking the first person to speak and providing the direction of the conversation, clockwise or counterclockwise, reversing directions from the previous talking circle. This provides balance so that "he who was first will be last, and she who was last will be first."

Interruptions: But sometimes, not often, someone in the excitement of the moment may interrupt a person who is speaking. When that happens, let the interrupting person finish. **Then remind the entire group that they are to take their turns without interrupting.** Don't scold the person or give them angry looks; after all, they have lived a lifetime of interrupting, and this is new to them. Let the whole group learn from the experience.

Then return to the person who was interrupted and let him finish what he was saying. Do not be surprised if the person interrupted cannot remember what he was saying. Interruptions create a startle response in people. They become adrenalized. They will often forget what they were saying, as a result.

If this happens, give the person time to think about what he or she was saying, or say you will come back to him or her when the talking circle is done. When you do this, people will usually finish the statement. Normally this experience is a lesson that everyone in the group will remember, and rarely will anyone interrupt again.

Can I pass? If people ask to pass during the talking circle, let them do so, but remind them you will return to them at the end of the talking circle. They will normally take their turn at the end.

People pass for a number of reasons: they are not ready to speak because they have been listening so intently; or they are afraid to speak, especially if someone has been interrupted; or they are worried that what they have to say will be laughed at, and so on. Some may do this to have the last say, a position of power. If they do, they will not do it again, because it is unnecessary.

Give them time to observe and experience the others speaking, and they will then speak at the end of the talking circle. If you forget to do this, your group will remind you. They want everyone to speak.

Speak last: When you are the facilitator of the small group, speak last. Your position is one of power, so what you say will become the focus of discussion. The rest of the group will divert what they were going to say to comment on your statements. Listen to them first, and be affected by what they say. Then speak last.

Speaking a long time: Some people will speak for a long time; it seems endless. Normally these are people who have not been listened to, who feel they have been rejected as not having anything to add to a discussion. Or what they say is not what people want to hear, so others "turn them off." A person can tell when they are "turned off." So they do not expect to be listened to. As a result they speak longer, saying the same thing in many different ways, hoping someone will hear them, let them "in."

Most people want the facilitator to confront and control this person. If you do, you send a message to everyone that you will decide who will speak and how long they will speak. This behavior then applies to everyone. Confronting the one gives you power over all.

Instead, I choose to listen to them deeply, attending to what they say with deep and respectful listening, nodding my head as I understand them, giving them attention and acknowledgment, accepting their views with a smile. When they become conscious of this, they will normally become more focused and shorten their message. As they see they are listened to in later activities, they become as focused as the rest of the group.

Sometimes, but very rarely, they will not end the behavior, no matter how much I listen to them. If they do this, I will speak to them off to the side during the break. I let them know that people are dropping out on them when they speak so long. They always acknowledge they know this, but don't know what to do about it. I offer to let them know with a nod or a movement of my hand that they are repeating themselves or that people are dropping out on them. Then I will let them speak again at the end of the talking circle to add additional thoughts to the group. They always agree. This helps them to learn to see for themselves when they have spoken too long. It helps them learn to focus, to choose to do so.

Whispering to others: You will also have people who whisper to each other when someone is speaking. It is disruptive to a group and to the speaker when this happens. When I observe this behavior, I will wait until the talking circle is done and then speak to the whole group:

"Sometimes people who are sitting together will whisper to each other while another person is speaking. This is disrespectful behavior. It affects the speaker, who feels disrespected, wondering if they are talking about her. It changes what a person will say. It also affects the rest of the group, creating a sense of discomfort. We know this is wrong and want to say something about it, but don't, and this makes us feel worse.

"If you have spoken and been listened to with respect, then it is incumbent on you to listen to everyone else. To whisper when others are speaking is disrespectful. We all know that. Keep focused on what people are saying. You will learn that everything people say has purpose and meaning. We cannot afford to miss one word.

"If someone next to you wants to whisper, and you participate knowing it is disrespectful, you are encouraging the behavior. Just shake your head and don't look at them; keep focused on the speaker. You help us all by doing this."

I provide an anecdote to reinforce this concept.

The Circle Whisperer: An Anecdote

Sometimes this first attempt doesn't work. I had an administrator, John, who always whispered in the beginning of negotiations between management and labor. I would make the statement above when this happened.

But John was persistent. He either did not hear or understand, or he felt he was not limited by what was said. So he would continue the behavior. I would then speak to him during the next break, off to the side. He always expressed surprise at my making him aware of his behavior, agreed it was disrespectful, and agreed to change his behavior.

He did try. It was more than he could stand. Eventually he would start whispering again, to people on both sides of him. In that instance, I would intervene after a person had finished speaking.

"I know you have all observed John whispering during this session. John and I have already had a talk about this, but the behavior is too ingrained in him, and he forgets. John does not want to be disrespectful. So I am asking those of you who sit on either side of him to not encourage this behavior. Help him. Just say no, and listen to the speaker."

I then check with John to see if he is OK with these instructions. He always apologized and agreed to the help.

John exhibited this behavior over the eight years I knew him. It took the same actions to get him to just listen. It never affected his participation or his decision making. He just needed that help.

I do this in three steps: (1) advise the whole group about the behavior; (2) talk to the person off to the side to make her aware of the behavior; and (3) make the whole group aware of the behavior and ask them to help her.

This three-step approach also helps when people are dismissive of others, laughing when they speak, or making snide comments, putdowns, et cetera. It always works and does not detract from your relationship with others because what you are doing is respectful, helping them to be respectful.

Then I continue to provide additional insights on the art of facilitating:

People who are emotional: It is not unusual for people in the talking circle to become emotional. It is normally a surprise to the person it happens to. The emotion just bubbles up as he or she begins to speak. A shaky voice, quivering lips, tears, sighs, crying can all happen. Your role as a facilitator is to sit tight and just listen to the person. Do not get up and walk over and console or hug the person. This will embarrass them more. It puts great pressure on them, singling them out. It causes them to stop speaking.

People who move to console the person do this because they become emotional themselves or feel self-conscious and embarrassed for the person. This is not about them. If people make to stand, signal them to remain seated. "Relax yourself. Just listen," I will say. Don't make a big deal about it. This is his or her private moment being shared with the rest of the group. (It is OK if someone passes the Kleenex box around.)

If people cannot speak, ask if they want to pass for now, and you will come back to them when they signal they are ready. Let it be their choice. They will always signal when they are ready. Your role is to listen and keep the group moving, allowing the emotions to just be part of the experience.

Providing insights: You will notice I provide you the insights *after* the task, not before. If I do this before, you will tend to try to have an experience that matches what I describe. If I do it before, I am "preprogramming" you to have *my* experience, not yours. By doing it after, you can decide if the experience you had matches my insight.

People often want to know if I give insights to every group for every task. It all depends: on the length of time I have with them, on the skills and knowledge of the group, or the severity of the issue. Sometimes I give only a few insights—the ones I deem will best influence the group's learning. Other times I will give them the whole load. What is important to me is to be sure the group knows what I am doing and why. I want to be as transparent as possible in this. This will reduce fears people have of being manipulated.

A Facilitator Must Be Assertive: An Insight

"The facilitator must be able to be assertive, but not dominating."

—Workshop participant

To do all the above, a facilitator must be assertive—that is, confident and forceful. A common misperception about the role of the facilitator is that the position should have little power and must remain passive. Rather, in managing a session, a facilitator must, at times, be very assertive.

During some of the tasks, the small-group facilitators are asked to select a new facilitator. This is often done by asking the question: "Who wants to be the facilitator?" Asking this question will confuse the group. They expect the facilitator to do this. It makes the group have the feeling of competitiveness, of people vying for the position or avoiding the position. These are standard fight-or-flight positions that the consensus process is trying to neutralize.

In addition, the person who normally takes this facilitator role, and the power it comes with, will volunteer. Nothing changes as a result. Those who never facilitate and experience the role can never do it. It is more appropriate for the facilitator to select a person, seeking someone who has not yet played the role. This avoids that moment of competition that is so unnecessary.

Be assertive and choose a person. By choosing the person, you are honoring them. Choose someone who would not normally facilitate, and let them experience and learn. They will surprise you with how well they do.

The same is true in choosing who speaks first. If you ask, "Who wants to start?" there will be an uncomfortable silence as each person wonders who will speak up. Finally someone will raise a hand and volunteer, and normally it will be the same person who always speaks first. Choose the person to start; choose the direction to go in. Be deliberate in who you choose. Let it be someone who normally is quiet or someone you disagree with.

"A successful facilitator will give leadership and direction."

—Workshop participant

"The role of the facilitator is to make things easy for the group."

—Workshop participant

As their facilitator, people want you to decide the questions, decide the process, choosing time for breaks, deciding who is on panels, ending the day, and selecting people to do the collective statements. They will answer the questions, learn from each other, move themselves to positive relationships, positive thinking and behaving, and make the final decisions. Your role is to make it easy. To do that you must be assertive.

~20~

Insights on the Role of the Facilitator

Taking a Break for Additional Insights

We are going to take a break from the story you are part of and learn some insights and read some anecdotes that will help you understand what is happening as you facilitate others.

You may skip this chapter if you want and continue with the story; you can return to this later. Or you can read this set of insights and then continue on with the story, which resumes in the next chapter.

A Guide on the Side: An Insight

Isoomituk: Inuit word for leader...the person who can create the environment to allow wisdom to reveal itself.

I have often wondered how to describe what I do when people ask me. I do not regard myself as a mediator, because I seek to have the parties mediate themselves. I am not a negotiator, because the parties negotiate themselves to a consensus. I am just a person who helps people resolve their own conflicts. The closest term I have found to describe my role is *facilitator*.

Normally a facilitator is perceived as someone who eases a process. But I know I do much more than that. There is no term yet that describes what I believe to be a new role in resolving conflicts. So I am willing to settle for facilitator.

The term is not as important as the beliefs and behaviors of what I do. I am willing to be called a negotiator, mediator, hired gun, or facilitator, as long as I get the opportunity to do what I do best: help people resolve their conflicts while learning to do it themselves.

Following are some of the beliefs and behaviors I consider necessary to facilitate people to a consensus:

- I must be willing to take the risk of failing in bringing people to consensus. I must be willing to risk confronting a worst outcome during a session and trust that I can help the participants work it through to a best outcome.
- I must be willing to learn, to accept my uncertainty as a condition for learning. If I am certain, I have no need to learn and thus limit my opportunities to gain the information needed to facilitate the group to a consensus.
- I must be willing to let go of control, the desire for power over others. I must be willing to serve the group to meet their needs and not mine.
- I must be willing to be powerful in the higher-brain sense, to be able to confront the group if they begin to conform to avoid an issue. I must be willing to confront the group when they violate one of their own standards for honesty.
- I must be willing to be open to and accepting of what the group needs are.
- I must be willing to let the community move the process in the direction that is right for them, giving up any predetermined direction of my own. I must be willing to let the group be apprehensive about their direction and still support their movement in that direction.
- I must be willing to let the individuals and group experience freedom: the freedom to speak, to question, to confront, to learn, to be who they are.
- I must be willing to let the group learn through experience, accepting behaviors or actions that are still immature as they learn. I must be willing to trust that their time together will create the maturity needed to resolve the conflict, to create consensus.
- I must be willing to stay in the background, allowing others to move forward, to represent, to learn, to facilitate, and to share the power.
- I carry out these behaviors by using this process, adapting it when necessary to respond to their organic needs.
- I will see that each person gets the opportunity to speak and is listened to with respect.
- I will see that each person has the opportunity to facilitate, to record, to be empowered in some way.
- I will ask the "right questions" based on my intuitive sense as the process progresses.

- I will remain on the outside, detached, observing for the group.
- I will provide insight to the group or individuals in the group to assist them in moving toward a consensus.
- I will push the group beyond the impasse, beyond their apprehensions and fears of the confrontation. I do this while being aware of and understanding of their uncertainty and fears.

The best description of my role was provided by a workshop participant: "You are not the sage on the stage, but the guide on the side."

Detachment—A Move to Autonomy

People in positions of authority have been taught, in word and deed, to take responsibility for the actions of those in their "care." The power (parent) figure is often seen looming over the shoulders of those given a task to do. They are there, of course, to provide guidance, to answer any questions, to immediately correct any deviation from the direction. There is even a name for it: proximity. This is known as *management control*. It is based on the subtle and never-expressed belief that those given directions must, like children, be guided by the parent figure.

As soon as participants sense that they are dependent on the power figure, they will begin to determine what they need to do to get acknowledgment and approval. This includes asking questions to clarify what the leader said—a ploy to get the leader's attention. Or asking how to do the task. The leader is prone to explain, then overexplain what is needed, often using tones that indicate the listeners are children or simple-minded.

Those who resent power will challenge the leader's information or task. This will lead to a power struggle until the leader asserts her authority. All this takes time and energy away from accomplishing the task, and focuses on the leader, rather than the participants, as the important person.

As the leader roams the room, looking and listening into each group, aloof yet in charge, members in the group will attempt to engage her in conversation. Or she may enter the group and end up in a debate over the task. The net result is to shift the attention to the leader, to allow the participants to behave as children, unable to cope with the simple task. This creates dependency behavior. The participants will continuously look to the leader, aware of her every movement, for signs of approval or displeasure. They look for nonverbal cues to determine what they need to do to satisfy the leader.

In the consensus process, this role is changed. The leader learns to detach from the group as soon as the task is given. Detachment means expressing the question or task and trusting them to work out what it means and answer it. When I turn the facilitation over to members of the group, I must trust the facilitator will do the task. Leaving the circle of participants while they are in small groups, after asking the task question, places the participants in control of doing the task.

If there are questions, the participants are told to use their own judgment. If they ask how to accomplish the task, they are told: "It is your decision. Whatever you decide to do is OK." If the facilitator is challenged about the task, the challenger is told to do what he or she feels is best. This leaves the power with the person, the group. They empower themselves to do the task.

If the group answers a question different from the one asked, the information is accepted as part of the knowledge or information base. Either the group must need to hear it, or the question answered was better than the one asked.

This is a different approach, because it means the leader becomes a facilitator, trusting in the individuals and the group, expecting them to respond in an adult way. Rarely will you be disappointed. Expect some laughter, some horsing around as the group becomes used to freedom. Stay with them, and they will eventually focus on the issues and the situation.

This leaves the facilitator time to think through the next task. When you return your focus to the group, they will be hard at work. By being emotionally detached, you will see the process at work, collecting information that will assist your intuition and insight for the next tasks.

Building Relationships and Skills: The Art

The recorder and facilitator tasks are important to do with a group whose members are in deep conflict with each other and who have not experienced consensus building before. They are not ready to confront each other in a respectful way, because they have not yet moved to the level of thinking and feeling that would facilitate this discussion.

These tasks, each of which normally lasts less than an hour, allow people to practice listening with respect, to establish calmer relationships with each other. They allow the group to focus on a common task and introduce them to facilitating and recording. They establish standards of behavior. They allow the group to experience a community-building activity together, while developing a community memory.

Each person gains the experience of being in small, diverse, and intimate groupings for three activities (greeting, recorder, facilitator). The facilitator and recorders are members of the group. They are behaving and experiencing these roles while they are exploring them. This is the most powerful form of learning.

Each person has spoken at least twice in each task, and their information is now in a group memory. Everyone has been listened to with respect, and the information has been recorded on the flip chart and shared with the entire group. These recorded notes will be used later to create collective statements.

Asking the Right Question: An Insight

It does not take long for the community to recognize the value of asking the right questions. They recognize it in the grounding as they answer the three questions and see how powerful they are. They recognize it when they develop the roles of the recorder and the facilitator.

The questions used in this process have been developed over thousands of workshops. They are very specific and will lead any group to resolution of their conflicts. They are designed to use the whole brain and to elicit learning and knowledge in the people. Each question can be modified to meet the needs of any specific group.

A question is powerful in that it creates a focus or arena of thought. If I ask you to look for the elephant, your mind will be occupied with the search for an elephant; everything else will tend to fade into the background. If I ask you what you did last summer, you immediately access that memory, including the description and feelings associated with it, to the exclusion of other memories.

Most of the questions in this process tend to be general. Asking "What is the situation?" provides a broader arena of thought than "How do you feel about the development proposal?" The answers to the first are much broader and bring in background elements of information important to the solution, while the latter question is too focused and leaves out important information.

Asking "What is the situation?" and "How do you feel about it?" brings emotion into the equation and engages the whole brain. It also grounds people in their emotions. They often are surprised at how strongly they feel about an issue when asked. It has not been part of their consciousness before.

Some questions can be modified. "What did you learn?" as a general question can be modified to focus on the present situation as "What did you learn that will help us resolve our conflict?" "What is the role of a facilitator?" will have a different answer than "What is the role of a successful facilitator in creating a consensus?" The words *successful* and *consensus* create different arenas of thought in the question.

Often a person in a group will ask a question during a small-group discussion. Rarely will the question be acknowledged or heard or answered. And yet it will often be the right question that will lead the group to an answer. Often community members will come to me with the right question, looking for an answer for themselves. They are surprised when I tell them it is a question that their entire group should answer.

Responding in this way requires the facilitator to be alert when questions are posed by members of the group. Often they are an opportunity to shortcut to a decision; in that situation, following the process because it is the thing to do is not appropriate.

Rhetorical questions also have great value. These are questions "asked for effect or to make a statement, rather than to obtain an answer." By asking such a question, I involve you vicariously in experiencing it.

The right questions are often phrased using the participants' words. If in the grounding the community talks about needing trust, then the learning question can be focused on that: "What did you learn today that will foster trust in your community?"

If during a talking circle near the end of a workshop, someone asks, "How can we make this happen, given all the problems we have had in the past?" I will have that person, at the end of the talking circle, ask the question, "What can we do to make this happen?" The community will answer the question either in the large or small groups. This creates the strategies and actions they will need to foster their best possible outcomes, their purpose.

The following anecdote will help you understand how this works in real life.

"What Can We Do to Make this Happen?": An Anecdote

They were a group of high school students, eighty in all, known as at-risk troubled kids. There were also twelve teachers/adults in the room. I had agreed to work with their alternative high school to help them lower the number of incidents of conflict in the building; physical fighting was endemic in their environment. At the end of the first day's activities, two students, Sherry and Dan, a female and male, both seniors, approached me and suggested we could role-play the next day.

"What do you have in mind?" I asked.

"We could set up a conversation where we play the roles of the students and the teachers or adults and have the (real) teachers just observe."

"Would you be willing to help me facilitate that?" I asked.

"Yes!" they said gladly. They left excited that I had responded as I did.

The next morning Sherry and Dan helped me design a role-playing task for the eight small groups. Four groups played the role of teachers or adults. Four others played the role of the students. Each group created a stereotype description for the other groups. The teachers/adults role groups developed stereotypes for the students. The student role groups did the same for

Insights on the Role of the Facilitator

the teachers and adults. They also created the stereotype description they knew the other group had of them. They answered these questions:

"What is your stereotype of the teachers (adults, students)?"

"What is the stereotype you know they have of you?"

Sherry facilitated the activity. Rather than have the teachers and adults just observe, Sherry directed them to record the information for the small groups. (There was one adult or teacher in each group.)

When the small groups were finished, they confronted each other with their stereotypes. They were all negative, horrendously so. They ended up shouting them at each other, anger in their voices. When all groups had spoken, an uneasy quiet settled over the group. They were all shocked at the anger and hurt that was represented in the room.

They realized all their stereotypes were negative, although we never asked them to focus on the negative. We just asked them to create stereotypes. They also realized they knew the negative stereotypes they had of each other. It was out in the open.

A young girl, a sophomore, a single mother who lived by herself with her child, raised her hand.

"Bob," she said with a catch in her voice, "this is all so terrible. How can we stop this? My mother was raised by my grandmother with this kind of abuse. I was raised by my mother with abuse. I am afraid I will raise my little girl with abuse. I may have already started. How can we stop this, it is so horrible?" She wept, as did others.

I suggested we take a break and think about her question. The students, teachers, and adults left the circle, all quiet and somewhat shocked. They gathered in small groups in the hall, spoke in low and serious tones.

I asked Kerry, the young woman, if she would help me facilitate the group later to answer the question she asked. She agreed to do so.

When the students returned, Dan, the student facilitator, had four of them pick a teacher or adult they could talk to. Each pair talked about how they would like to describe each other: student, teacher, or adult. The small groups then created new positive stereotypes for students, teachers, and adults in the building. This is the first time any of these students had considered that teachers, adults, and even they could have a positive stereotype.

"How would you like to describe each other: student, teacher, adult?"

When they were done with this task and read off the new descriptions they had of each other, there was a different feeling in the room. Now they had a description of what they wanted to create. This was their common purpose. And they wanted it!

I asked Kerry, the young mother, to give them the next task. With some coaching, she had developed the question she wanted them to answer.

She asked them: "What can we do to change the negative relationships we have with each other and with others in our life, and create positive relationships?"

She had the same role pairs of teachers and students work first on this question. Each member of the pair answered the question to the other, beginning to explore some solutions. The small groups then created new positive behaviors for students, teachers, and adults in the building. This was the first time any of these students had considered that teachers/adults would work with them to create a new learning environment. As for the teachers and adults, they were impressed with the students' willingness and ability to develop their own standards of behavior.

This discussion was facilitated by the students, with the teachers and adults being recorders but also participating in the answer. It was a deliberative and serious discussion. Each person took their turns. Everyone listened to the speakers in their groups, their heads leaning forward in the circles.

The result was a list of required behaviors for students, teachers, and other adults who came into the building. The most important one was "respect." For this behavior, they did an additional task: creating the evidence when people were disrespectful. Then they created the evidence that they were treating each other with respect. Each of these statements was a standard of behavior.

Those statements, written on flip charts in the students' words, were hung in the hall of the building. Anyone who violated the standards was taken to these charts and reminded of the required behaviors. New students were taken to the chart on their first day by the students and required to read the charts.

This alternative high school became known as the school where troubled, at-risk students who were in trouble at other schools could come, knowing they would never be in fights with others or abused by others. It became a school of choice for these students.

The design for the entire second day was based on questions or suggestions provided by the students. They facilitated the school community through these questions. It was their design, their workshop.

Let's go back to the Coyote River Basin!

~21~

The Worst and Best Possible Outcomes

One evening an old Cherokee told his grandson about a battle that goes on inside people. He said, "My son, the battle is between two wolves.

"One is Evil. It is anger, envy, sorrow, regret, greed, arrogance, self-pity, guilt, resentment, inferiority, lies, false pride, superiority, and ego.

"The other is Good. It is joy, peace, love, hope, serenity, humility, kindness, benevolence, empathy, generosity, truth, compassion, and faith."

The grandson thought about it for a minute and then asked his grandfather, "Which wolf wins?"

The old Cherokee simply replied, "The one you feed."

Worst/Best Possibility: An Activity

After the recorder and facilitator tasks, I can sense a difference in the room. People are feeling more comfortable and relaxed. They are learning and appear to like it. They know each other better. The room feels safe. There is a beginning sense of community, of belonging. They have a sense of confidence that they can be either facilitator or recorder and do the job well. They are aware that this is a different approach. They are waiting with interest for what comes next.

I have decided to facilitate this next task, while YOU and Mike work up a list of potential cofacilitators. I have asked both of you to select two people from each group who could potentially facilitate later in the workshop. I want people who do not normally facilitate, and I want a balance:

male/female, young/old, for/against, outspoken/shy, and so on. By selecting eight people, two from each group, we create a resource list of possible cofacilitators to be trained. We will select two that you and Mike will coach this afternoon.

I inform the group of the task that YOU and Mike have and repeat that this is done to share power in this process, to demonstrate that anyone in the community can facilitate. Always, always, I let the group know what I am doing and why.

> The process must be transparent to reduce the fears of manipulation.

While standing at the edge of the circle, I direct the facilitators in the small groups:

Please pass out the three-by-five cards that are at each easel.

Notice how focused and brief this direction is. No additional instructions, just a focused statement. They immediately respond. I wait until I see they all have cards. This pause is important; it allows them time to do the task before I introduce the question.

You have all agreed to be here for three days to work together and resolve your conflicts. This is a lot of time to spend together with people you don't necessarily like, and yet you have still chosen to be here. I know from the interviews and the grounding that you all have your doubts about spending this time. I want you to record the answer to this question to help get those doubts into the open:

"What are your worst possible outcomes of spending three days in this workshop?"

I turn and walk away, allowing people time to record. They are silent, immediately writing with great concentration on the cards. There is a sense of seriousness and importance in what they do. Some people finish early, and they remain silent, respectful of others. At times, some will talk quietly, trying not to interfere with others. Soon, I can sense people are done, although some are still writing. They might be just doodling, however. I need to know this. I walk to the edge of the circle. I speak softly in the silence:

The Worst and Best Possible Outcomes

When you are done recording, turn your card over.

I watch as most people turn their cards over. I can see that a few people are still recording, so I wait. When all are done, they look at me expectantly. The next question will move them to another perception of their expectations—the best possible outcomes. I say:

On the other side of the card, you are going to answer a different question. I do not "spend" my time with groups. My time is more important than that. I try to "invest" my time in situations where I know I will get a return.

Life is too short to just come to a meeting and not expect anything out of it but negative outcomes and then to feel "spent." I want my time invested so it is of value to you as a group and to me. So, when I choose who to work with, I ask myself, "Is it a good investment of my time?" In choosing to work with you, the answer is yes.

I want you to consider investing your time. Answer this question on the three-by-five card:

"Because you work together...what will be the best possible outcomes of investing three days in this workshop?"

I turn and walk away. Silence again descends on the room. People are thinking before they write. As a facilitator you wonder if they heard the question. When they start recording, it is with serious and deliberate intent. They stop, think, write some more. There will be much more said with this question than the other. This is often the first time they have ever considered that a workshop or meeting can have a best possible outcome. They will often write around the edges.

I again sense they are done, or nearly so. I wait a little longer, the silence unbroken. Then a few people start to talk. I hear some soft laughter in Group 3. This is a signal they are ready.

Has everyone recorded on both sides of the card?
People nod their heads.
Did you notice how silence was in the room while you were recording?
There is a nodding of heads as people become aware of this.
This is purposeful. We have all been talking since we started this morning: through the grounding, the greeting, the lifelong learning questions, the roles of the facilitator and the recorder. Your energy has been focused externally. I have learned if you do this too long, it becomes energy draining and is not good for you or the process.

The activity with the cards allows you to reverse that process, to balance yourself. You go internally, in touch with yourself, to think deliberatively about what you want to say. In doing so, we create silence, a moment of calm and renewal. It is a balance to talking externally, a time to talk internally. It takes only a short time to create that balance. It is healthy. It is purposeful.

I then direct the facilitator: The facilitator will pick a new facilitator and become the recorder.

I wait until I see this has been done. Sometimes I will ask the recorders to stand at the easel so I know they are ready.

For the new facilitator: have each person read off the information they have recorded on the card for the worst possible outcomes. Record the information to the flip chart. Once everyone, including the recorder, has done this, then turn the card over and reverse the direction of the talking circle. The person who spoke last will now speak first. Have each person read off their best possible outcomes and record them.

Changing directions introduces balance and equity. It manages the underlying power relationships in the group. If I always speak last, I will begin to resent it, because everyone may have already said what I wanted to. So, let me be first now and then.

Recorders will turn and face the flip chart and start writing as soon as a person speaks. You will be able to record everything that is said if you do this.

I turn and walk away to where YOU and Mike are standing. When I turn and look at the small groups, they are all hard at work.

I continue to coach my cofacilitators, YOU and Mike, outside the circle:

Note that there are four instructions for this task. I have learned to provide these with pauses after each instruction, allowing the groups to accomplish each one before I move to the next. If I give the instructions all at once, the members will get confused, missing one or doubting if they remember, resulting in questions to me, which results in more questions, and so on. A facilitator is supposed to make the process easy. I do this by giving each instruction separately with a pause.

People often get impatient and apprehensive with this task. They have recorded a lot of information on the cards. Their attention is focused on the flip chart rather than themselves.

Statements are slowly being recorded to the flip charts. The task is designed to slow people down, to provide the opportunity to say what they want to say without rushing, with the possibility of being heard, being acknowledged.

But many people will read fast, too fast to be recorded. They are self-conscious. The recorder will have to ask for repeats until the person becomes self-conscious and passes the card to the recorder. Or the person will edit what has been written, feeling embarrassed by the length of the statement. Sometimes the group will help this out with humorous, cutting remarks about the length of others' statements.

Some people will assert that their statement has already been recorded or that they feel represented by the others' statements. Some will become impatient with the group and say so before making a brief statement to be recorded as a sign of displeasure with the time it is taking.

All of these are normal reactions. This does not happen often, but if it does and seems to be affecting the group, I will get their attention, ask them to pause, and give them my insight on the situation.

We can see this is happening in Groups 2 and 3. YOU and Mike can see the confusion in the groups. So I'll address it now.

I walk to the edge of the circle, wait until they are aware of me, and get their attention.

I want to talk with all of you if you would pause for a few minutes. This task is designed purposefully to slow you down, to give you the opportunity to say what needs to be said, free of interference from others or of time constraints. In a regular meeting, because we are not used to getting our turn or are not listened to, we either speak fast or not at all. Only those who are more competitive will speak, and they surely know they are rarely listened to.

In this process, we will take the time to see that each person has their say. We will "go slow to go fast." You have time to read your statement slowly, so that all in the group can hear it, so the recorder can get it all recorded. This will feel different to you. You may feel self-conscious, because you don't normally get or take this much time to advocate for your view.

It is OK to have that feeling. This time is set aside to hear everyone's worst and best outcomes. It is a time to listen to each other, to learn of our fears and hopes. It is a time to begin recording what is said so we have a group memory.

Read your statement slowly and clearly to the entire group. Read it all, even if it is a duplicate of what someone else said. You honor the other person by affirming their thought. You will add to the richness of the information developed by the group.

For those of you who are listening, hear the best outcomes of others. You are learning what others in the community want from the workshop. Ask yourself if you can support their outcomes.

If you are used to doing the talking, are impatient, that is because you are now an equal member of the group. You can relax. You don't have to carry the entire load. Listen and hear what can be added to your knowledge base. More will be said in this time than in any equal time in your previous meetings, and it will be all recorded. Be patient and see if that is not so.

I step away from the group, and they return to the task. I can see they are more relaxed, taking the time to record everything on the cards. I continue to coach YOU and Mike:

Normally the group will become more centered and focused on the task with this information from me. I hesitate to do this, and do it only when it feels necessary to help the group be respectful to themselves. Sometimes I will do it after all have finished, as part of an insight. Normally this takes about two minutes to express.

When this task is completed, the thirty-two participants will have spoken at least twice, and their information is now recorded in 60–150 or more statements. It normally takes no longer than thirty minutes for this. We have a measure of their expectations from both a worst and a best standpoint. In addition, four more members of the community group have managed the process, while four others have established a model for recording.

It is not necessary to ask if all have spoken on this task. When they are done recording, the recorder will normally sit down. Sometimes the group will add additional thoughts not on their cards if they have time. This is easy to see.

Let's listen in on Group 2:

Jack: "Well, Frank, I guess that means you get to be a facilitator. I'll be your loyal recorder. Just tell me what to do and how to do it."

Frank: "Seems like I've been telling you what to do since you were a baby, and you mostly ignored my advice. Except of course when you married Sally. Now that was smart!" (Laughter at the banter.) "I guess I can do this. Let's start with you, George, then we'll go to the left, you being next, Jim."

George: *"This won't be worth the time or money invested."* (Pauses.) *"There is fighting worse than when we began."*

Jim: *"There will be no resolution so the citizens of the county get no benefit. You got it, Jack! Then…we don't get anything accomplished."*

Bud: "Well, you know I worry about our economic future, so…*Coyote River County becomes an undesirable place to our residents. We lose our agriculture community and our rural heritage in the county.* I'll turn it over to you, Johanna."

Johanna: "Did you know I grew up on a ranch in Montana?" She looks around at people shaking their heads no. They are surprised. "Well, I did. Left because there was no way to earn a living. I had hoped to stay here for a long time, but now I wonder. Anyway…Jack, write this down*: We don't break down our communication barriers."* She pauses as Jack records. Then speaks slowly: "And my biggest fear…*the ranchers sell out…and give up their generational heritage.…We lose the beauty of the agricultural lands…as well as the ranching heritage."*

Lynn: "Well, I'm new to the basin, so am surprised by the reaction to the zoning. My fear? *We will always have competing factions…and will approach…every basin issue as a polarized community."* (Waits while Jack records.) *"We never learn how to listen to each other and respect each other's perspective."*

Dawn: *"We have three wasted days where nothing happens and nothing changes."*

Frank: "OK, Jack, be seated, and Lynn will record for you."

Jack: *"We become abusive with each other and confrontational."*

Frank: "While you are up there, Lynn, might as well record mine: *This takes time away from the ranch, cattle work, so my wife and daughter have to work harder."* (Pauses.) *"I will still feel hostile and feel I have a reason to feel hostile."*

Lynn, sitting down: "Do you feel hostile toward me?"

Frank: "I feel hostile toward what your group has done to the ranching community, without giving any thought to us."

Lynn: "I hope we can talk about that while we are here."

Frank: "I hope so too, but not now—they are trying to get our attention."

These are their flip chart notes:

> **Group 2: Worst Possible Outcomes of the Workshop**
> - *This won't be worth the time or money invested.*
> - *There is fighting worse than when we began.*
> - *There will be no resolution so the citizens of the county get no benefit. We don't get anything accomplished.*
> - *Coyote River County becomes an undesirable place to our residents. We lose our agriculture community and our rural heritage in the county.*
> - *We don't break down our communication barriers.*
> - *The ranchers sell out and give up their generational heritage. We lose the beauty of the agricultural lands as well as the ranching heritage.*
> - *We will always have competing factions and will approach every basin issue as a polarized community.*
> - *We never learn how to listen to each other and respect each other's perspective.*
> - *We have three wasted days where nothing happens and nothing changes.*
> - *We become abusive with each other, and confrontational.*
> - *This takes time away from the ranch, cattle work, so my wife and daughter have to work harder.*
> - *I will still feel hostile and feel I have a reason to feel hostile.*

While the groups are recording, I ask YOU to facilitate reporting out the worst possible outcomes and to give your insight about this task. This is the first time you will speak an insight.

"What should I say?" YOU ask nervously when I tell you this.

Whatever comes to you as you listen that you believe will help the group move forward, I answer.

"That wasn't the answer I expected! I won't know what to say!"

That is one possibility. The other possibility is that you will know exactly what to say, and it will help the group. Trust yourself!

When YOU see they are ready, you walk to the edge of the circle and get their attention. Then you say: "You are going to read off the worst possible outcomes you have recorded on the flip charts. Let's start with Group 4. Read the statements on the flip chart, and then we will go in a clockwise direction with the rest."

You stand where you can see the flip charts without entering the circle. You listen to what is said and how it is said.

When all groups are done reporting, YOU look hopefully at me for some help on the insight. Then, resigned to just doing it, you speak to the group:

GROUP 4: WORST POSSIBLE OUTCOMES OF WORKSHOP

- *We never learn how to listen to each other and respect each other's perspective.*
- *This won't be worth the time or money invested.*
- *There is fighting worse than when we began.*
- *Participants come away feeling they have accomplished nothing.*
- *Time away from the ranch, cattle work.*
- *That we don't learn how to break down the camps and start open dialogue.*
- *We won't learn to really save salmon or do the impossible.*
- *My wife has time to rearrange the house again.*
- *The community remains fragmented.*
- *The tribe isn't successful. The Salmon don't recover.*
- *Increased anger and hurt feelings could result in a decrease in mutual understanding and respect.*

"Bob has asked me to give you my insight on the task and the statements. Both Mike and I noticed how quickly you did this task and how much information you gathered in such a short time. We also both noticed how gloomy the room got when you were recording the worst possible outcomes. We were working on another task Bob gave us, but we could feel it.

"It felt the same way just now when you read the worst outcomes statements. In fact, Jim, you made a comment that it felt like a 'wake' in here. I guess this means that our worst outcomes affect our feelings negatively.

"On the other hand, we noticed when you recorded the best possible outcomes on the three-by-five cards that the room really lightened up. People laughed a lot and looked happy. So, our worst and best outcomes affect our feelings differently. I can't wait to hear the best outcomes."

You turn and look at me with a satisfied grin and walk away as I walk to the edge of the circle. Normally, the worst possible outcomes are read off from the small groups, but I like to provide an insight between the worst and best, so I tell the group:

I want you to move back into the large community circle. We will read off the best possible outcomes after I talk about what you are doing and why.

There is some chaos as people move their chairs to the large circle. Some head for the coffee, others for a rest break. I am always patient with this. They are moving from one experience to another; this provides time for the transition. YOU observe that people are now sitting next to people who are different from them, many of whom would not do so previously. You point that out to me. This is an outcome of being distributed in the small groups. When everyone is back in the large community circle, I provide an insight on this task.

Worst/Best/Possibility: An Insight

"Why would you ask us to talk about our worst possible outcomes? I was taught by my mother to always think positive. Talking about the worst possible outcomes will only make things worse. I hate it when people get negative, they only make things worse."

—**Workshop participant.**

Why would I ask this question? Well, as you will experience in a moment, you will have a worst possible outcome for everything that happens in your life. You will have worst possible outcomes for the most simple and innocuous events. It is a natural human response, because your first responsibility to yourself is to survive.

In this task, we explored the fears and the hopes of the participants. It is important to explore the worst fears before the best hopes. Fears are uppermost in the minds of those who are in conflict, and they become apprehensive, uncertain, unwilling to confront the conflict as a result.

It is normal and right to immediately fear the worst possible outcomes of any event or moment. Consider these situations:

Alice...your boss calls you and asks you to come to her office. What goes through your mind? What are you imagining? How do you feel?

Kathy...you are picking up an airline ticket for your first ever cross-country flight. What are you thinking of? How do you feel? How does the takeoff impact you?

Kenney...you are driving down the freeway and are surprised to see a state trooper a mile behind you, coming fast, with lights flashing, siren screaming. How do you feel in that moment? What is the action you unconsciously take? What do you think will happen?

Cliff...you let your daughter use your new Jaguar for her first date. (Some laughter at this.) She was supposed to be home at eleven p.m. and it is now eleven thirty. She is not back yet. What is going through your mind? How are you feeling? What are you thinking?

Dawn...you are a middle school student. You answer your home phone, and your teacher asks to talk to your mother. What goes through your mind? How do you respond?

Wayne...you open up your mailbox and there is a letter from the IRS. What do you think, and how do you feel in that moment?

Your young toddler is chasing a ball toward the street. There are no cars coming. But how do you react? Even though there are no cars there, you experience the worst possible outcome—**THE CHILD BEING HIT BY THE CAR!** Not only that, you feel the emotion of that moment just as if it is happening right now!

You scream at him to stay away from the street, as you run as fast as you can, your heart beating, to grab his hand and drag him roughly from the road. You are scared, and this comes out as anger. You shake him and yell at him (creating great remorse for yourself later).

Consider how you would react to each of these situations.

In such a way, people fear the worst possible outcome of *any* situation and operate emotionally out of that fear, just as if it were really happening in the present. This is a major motivator for most conflicts and causes the behaviors and actions that continue to foster that conflict and prevents its resolution. It is instructive to consider how these people might react...(I am acting all of these parts.)

Alice might say, "When *my* boss asked me to come to his office, I immediately wondered: what have I done wrong? I begin to feel tense in the pit of my stomach. I can feel my jaw clench and my anxiety rise."

Kathy might say, "As I pick up the ticket, I am aware that I am putting my life at risk. The plane could crash and chances of survival are few."

Kenney might say, "I am sure I am over the speed limit, and this trooper is after me with a costly ticket in mind. My response to the state trooper is immediate. I take my foot off the accelerator and step slowly on the brake, assuming without looking that I am going too fast and that he is coming after me. I am working on angry denials in my mind."

Cliff might say, "My fear is that my daughter has wrecked my car or even worse. I am so betrayed and angry I will shout at her as soon as she comes through the door."

Dawn might say, "As a student, my first reaction is to tell the teacher that my mother isn't home. I am afraid she wants to tell my mother something negative about me."

Wayne might say, "I know the IRS is after big-money people, and I worry about an audit."

All of you are in your worst possible outcomes! You go there immediately, without conscious thought. You are hardwired to do that, because your first responsibility to yourself is survival.

Now—pay attention to this—none of these events we fear have happened yet. **They are all imaginings about the future!** They are mere possibilities. One of the blessings and curses of being human is our ability to imagine the future, and in imagining it, experience it as if it were happening right now!

Alice has not gone into her boss's office yet, but she is already experiencing a reprimand about something.

Kathy is nowhere near the plane yet, and she is experiencing her possible death.

The state trooper is a mile away from Kenney, who is already experiencing getting a ticket.

Cliff is experiencing the loss of a daughter and maybe a Jaguar. He is second-guessing himself about making that decision.

Dawn has no idea what the teacher wants, but she is afraid she is in trouble and decides to slip away to her friend's home without permission.

Wayne has not opened the letter yet, but he is already planning to defend himself from an audit.

By imagining a future based on worst possible outcomes, we experience it as if it is happening right now! But...these people will tell me they are justified, they have experienced such worst possible outcomes before.

Alice might say: "In the past whenever my boss asked me to come into his office, I was chastised or reprimanded."

Kathy might say: "I have a friend who died in a plane crash two years ago."

Kenney might say: "I already have twelve unpaid speeding tickets in my glove compartment. I don't need another one." (Laughter.)

Dawn might say: "I remember my brother getting in deep trouble when his teacher called last year."

Cliff might say: "I remember when I took my dad's car as a teenager; I wrecked it on him."

Wayne might say: "I was audited two years ago and it cost me five thousand dollars in back taxes. I'm still mad about it!"

(I look at and talk to each of these people as I go through this list. There are heads nodding, some laughter.)

So, worst possible outcomes are not only future imagined events experienced in the present, **but they have often been experienced in the past.** They have a powerful negative memory attached to them.

When you imagine these worst possible outcomes you are immediately attached to a feeling or emotion. All of these people feel some version of fear! Our emotions can only be felt in the *present*, even if they are for *future* events, and these emotions make the imagined events feel real now!

When this happens, you send a signal to the lower or reptilian brain. This is located at the top of your spinal column, about as big as my index finger. (I reach back to my neck and place a finger into the channel located there. Others do the same.)

This brain is called the reptilian brain because it behaves like a lizard's brain. Its primary responsibility is survival: survival of the species, survival of the young ones, of family, of clan. It is a nonconscious entity, reacting out of billions of years of programming. It (you) is hardwired for instant reaction...without conscious thought. We refer to these reactions as "knee-jerk responses!" All that counts is survival!

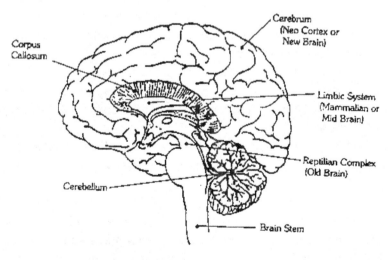

—From *Wikipedia*

This part of our brain provides the trigger for immediate physiological effects. We receive a jolt of adrenaline (also known as epinephrine), the natural "fight or flight" drug in our body. We are energized to take immediate action for survival. We overreact out of proportion with the event. Our emotions are magnified, our physical responses are magnified.

> **THE FIGHT-OR-FLIGHT RESPONSE**
> "Epinephrine (adrenaline) plays a central role in the short term stress reaction—physiological response to threatening, exciting, or environmental stressor conditions such as high noise levels or bright light.... When released into the bloodstream, epinephrine binds to multiple receptors and has numerous effects throughout the body. It increases heart rate and stroke volume, dilates the pupils, and constricts arterioles in the skin and gut while violating arterioles and leg muscles. It elevates the blood sugar level, by increasing hydrolysis glycogen to glucose in the liver, and at the same time begins to break down all the little bits in adipocytes. Epinephrine has a suppressive effect on the immune system._
> —From *Wikipedia*

Getting a shot of adrenaline has the same effect as putting gasoline on a campfire. The fire blazes up with intensified heat. In like manner, we are behaving as if we are faced with saber-toothed tigers in that office, rather than an imagined angry boss. This is because that is the only response the reptilian part of our brain knows. It is hardwired and not conscious in making the decision to respond. It responds instinctively in the same way it would have billions of years ago.

It is instructive to look at the dynamics of these situations. When *my* boss asked me to come to his office, I immediately wondered, what have I done wrong? I began to feel tense in the pit of my stomach. I can feel my jaw clench and my anxiety rise.

The event has not occurred yet. I am not in his office. Yet, I *am imagining a future feared outcome!* It is still only a possibility. Nothing has happened yet.

The ability to imagine the future is a human trait, but imagining that possible future also brings the image into the present. **This feared future outcome is based on some *past* experiences with bosses who asked me into their office only when they were upset with me.** Those were not pleasant experiences. I remember this unpleasantness, often magnify it in my fears.

I am imagining my worst fears, fearing a *future* outcome, based on *past* negative experiences, but I am feeling the emotions in the *present* moment. This causes biochemical and physical responses in my body that are more appropriate to life-threatening situations. I become adrenalized, my breathing speeds up, I feel anxious, tense. My strategies are defensive, based on preventing the worst outcome.

I rapidly search past events to determine potential mistakes I might have made. I mentally practice my defenses. My jaw clenches in anger at being confronted by such trivial situations. My chest is tight, my heart is beating rapidly, my voice is shaky. I am now in "fight or flight" mode. My family's livelihood is at stake, this is life or death. I will choose to fight!

Just imagine how I will look as I enter the office of my boss. I am adrenalized, tense, and this is apparent in my demeanor. I have a threatening, angry look on my face. My eyes bug out. My voice is strained. My mouth is dry. I slam the door open, shattering the glass window. I speak loudly, demanding to know, **"WHAT DO YOU WANT ME FOR?"** My hands are clenched in raised fists. I make excuses for the imagined event, not knowing that it is the wrong event. (I am, of course, really magnifying this image.)

My boss will not be pleased. His worst possible outcomes will come to the fore. His power is being challenged, and he will act in a defensive and controlling manner. He is the boss and he has the right to request my presence. He tells me so and sends me home with a reprimand. No matter the reason for the meeting, he will remember me with disapproving feelings. I am creating my own worst possible outcomes.

This is the way it works. The emotions are so strong that we behave as if the worst possible outcome was actually happening. What the research shows and what my experience with thousands of conflicts show is that we foster the negative outcomes we fear. They become self-fulfilling prophecies!

> **Worst Possible Outcomes:** These are imagined, feared, *future* outcomes, often based on *past* experience, with a *currently* experienced emotional, biochemical, and physical reaction. When people believe them, they affect their perceptions, beliefs, values, and strategies. They tend to become self-fulfilling prophecies when strongly held and acted upon.

Backwash: An Anecdote

Let me give you an everyday example of how this works. I was at my daughter's home, enjoying a day with my grandson Jeff, doing what we call "male bonding." We two, along with his dad, Mike, were watching a professional football game, each supporting a different team, debating their performance.

Jeff was thirsty. He wanted a soda, but his mother had told him, "Jeff, if you leave one more half-finished can of soda around this house, you will get grounded in your room for the day!" Well, he worried that this would happen, so he asked me if I would drink half the can of soda.

I agreed. After all, that is what grandfathers do for their grandchildren: we finish their glass of milk, eat the raisins they take out of their oatmeal, finish their crusts of bread. It is our heritage, our responsibility to support our grandchildren.

I finished my glass of soda and was enjoying the game. Jeff did not do so well. He still had some left and was worried about getting in trouble over it. So he poured the rest of his soda into my glass. Now, two things: I had agreed to drink half the soda, not two-thirds of it, and Jeff has a habit known as "backwash." He drinks in the soda, takes out the fizz, and spits the rest back into the glass. I am not going to drink his backwash. I'd just as soon drink from a spittoon.

So, I just turned and poured the soda back into his glass and turned back to the TV.

Jeff giggled a bit, waited until I appeared to be engaged, quietly poured the soda into my glass again, got up, and started to walk away.

I turned and clinked the glass as I poured the soda back into his glass.

Hearing that sound, Jeff returned and plopped down on the sofa. He waited a little longer, poured the soda into my glass again, and walked faster to get away, leaving me with the soda. I turned faster, clanked the glass, poured in the soda, and turned back to the game.

Now this was just part of our male bonding, a game of sorts. Jeff continued to try to pour soda into my glass without my knowing it, I poured it back. He tried all sorts of subterfuges. He couldn't move fast enough to get away.

He was ready to pour the soda into my glass for the twelfth time when his dad, Mike, sitting in the lounge chair across the room yells, "**Jeff, you are going to spill that on the rug**!"

Well...guess what Jeff did? He jumped at the sound of his dad's voice and spilled the soda all over the rug.

Pay attention to each of their outcomes. Jeff's worst outcome was that he would get grounded. He did. Mike's worst outcome was that the soda would be spilled on the floor. It was. Each fulfilled his worst outcome. When Mike spoke to Jeff, he used the fight-or-flight tone, normally reserved for life-or-death situations, and Jeff's body responded equally.

That is the way it works. The emotions are so strong that we behave as if the worst outcome were actually happening. The result may be that we foster that negative outcome.

It is right to imagine these worst possible outcomes. They ensure our survival. We focus on survival as our first priority. But survival is rarely the issue. The event is not life threatening. **It is just a life experience.** We are behaving in ways that may foster the very outcome we fear.

Creating Consciousness or Awareness: An Insight

The reptilian part of our brain is not conscious of its reactions because it is hardwired to respond without thinking. It believes a life experience is a life-or-death experience. When I say as the boss, "Alice, come to my office, I want to talk with you," her reptilian brain will hear," Alice come into my office, I want to *kill* you!" Her reptilian brain then will respond unconsciously with a fight-or-flight response.

This is the reason that consensus, or any other decision, cannot be reached through worst-possible-outcome beliefs, where the purpose is focused on individual survival, not community potential. The fears are individual; the reactions are defensive, aimed at protecting the individual and family/clan. People operating out of their individual and often competing worst fears are not interested in developing a win-win solution. They want to survive, even at the expense of the other. They are focused on survival of the fittest.

> Worst possible outcomes are focused on survival of the fittest.

Asking people the worst possible outcomes question allows them to become conscious of their fears so they can judge them with their neocortex, or the thinking brain. Recording the answer to this question allows them to become conscious of this fear, both visually and intellectually. Reading this statement and seeing it recorded brings the fear into everyone's consciousness. Reporting it out to all the groups reinforces this consciousness of the fear.

If you are conscious of your fears, you can manage them. Now that you know what your fears of the imagined future are, you can determine how to prevent them from happening or, if they do, how to respond to them consciously. This requires that we move to our thinking/feeling brains, which are a conscious instrument.

This is similar to the approach engineers use in designing buildings or roads or other developments. They do what is called a "failure analysis," an attempt to imagine potential failures before they happen so they can be designed out of the project.

> *"No passion so effectually robs the mind of all its powers of acting and reasoning as fear."*
>
> —**Edmund Burke**

~22~

Our Best Possible Outcomes

Our Best Possible Outcomes: An Insight

The insight on worst possible outcomes normally captures everyone's attention in the room. This insight is personal for all of them. They all experience the emotion of the rhetorical questions. Some come up to me later during a break and tell me how they actually lived through many of the examples I use.

Now it is time to shift the attention away from the worst possible outcomes, to balance the fears with hopes. I proceed:

Since the event has not happened yet, there is still the possibility of something much better happening—the best possible outcomes. We can imagine the outcome we want from being called to the boss's office differently. I can hope he has noticed the improvement in the quality of my work. I can hope he has noticed the extra effort I am making and wants to reward me in some way. I can hope the advice I gave in the last meeting had positive results.

This is a *future imagined* best outcome. I may have had such an outcome before. But given the normal situation, it may be highly unlikely I have experienced this in the past.

This is what makes the best possible outcomes different. **We may rarely have experienced the best possible outcomes, so how can we imagine them?** I worked effectively for many years without being recognized and rewarded. So how could I imagine being treated with positive recognition?

If I am a child who has always been abused by adults, how can I imagine a good adult/child relationship? If I have been divorced three times from bad marriages, how could I imagine a good one? If the teacher always makes me feel stupid or powerless as a student, how can I imagine being treated as an intelligent being, even after I am an adult? If I am a person of color, constantly hassled by white police officers, how can I trust law enforcement?

We are more focused on worst possible outcomes. They seem to occur more often because they are remembered more vividly. They are associated with our personal and group survival. We are constantly on our guard to protect ourselves. The good events may fade into the background.

When I was a child, my parents had an emotional and angry relationship. They fought bitterly, on the edge of violence (my worst fear), about Dad's alcohol abuse, money, the children, bills, house maintenance, relatives. I remember these arguments and the feelings associated with them. They are vividly imprinted in my childhood memory, with all the attendant fears and anxieties. I can get adrenalized when I focus on them. Nightmares triggered by these events used to wake me at two thirty in the morning, the time they normally happened. I woke fearful, with my heart beating fast, screams on my lips, adrenalized to flight.

From my childhood viewpoint, their relationship was a continual argument. Waiting in expectation of the event was often worse than the actual event. From my adult viewpoint, I realize they only occurred two or three times a month. The intervening times had some good, yet indistinct, memories. I have to work hard to recall them. They are overshadowed by the highly emotional and fearful events.

Many people have similar experiences. The result is they may find it difficult to imagine best possible outcomes. This is especially true when confronting conflicts. Can you remember a best outcome from a conflict?

It is possible to create a best-outcome memory. When I was sent to the Salvation Army summer camp, my relationships with adults there were positive and peaceful. I experienced adults working together in a positive manner. This is a memory I can tap. It was created for me by others. This is the function we can play in helping people confront conflict. We can create an experience that is positive and effective. This experience can balance our past worst possible experiences.

Best possible outcomes *are* possible. They are inherent in the situation. They are future outcomes imagined vividly in the present. They can be imagined just as vividly as worst possible outcomes. When we do this, with thought, verbally or visually on a card or flip chart, we are changed emotionally and biochemically. Positive feelings bubble to the surface; we are more hopeful, energized to make something positive happen.

When we imagine best possible outcomes, we must move to the neocortex, the upper part of our brain that can imagine, create, be conscious of what is happening, and respond in positive ways. In doing this, we change our state of being; we feel and act differently.

When we feel the emotional responses in the present, our bodies are changed as the limbic system sends a signal to pump in biochemicals called endorphins. These make us feel positive, calmer, and more hopeful. This changes our physical demeanor, softening our faces, creating happiness or smiles. Our bodies become more relaxed; we use our open hands to tell the story of what we want. We see the world through different eyes. We look different, we feel different, and we are different.

This change is evident in the features of people who attend the workshop. At the beginning grounding, faces were hard and stony, lips set, stern looks were everywhere, and voice tones were harsh. Now, faces are calmer, eyes are livelier, voice tones are normal.

Best possible outcomes have an emotional impact in the present moment, positively affecting the emotional, biochemical, and physical responses in the body. This creates new beliefs, new behaviors, new strategies, and actions that will tend to foster these outcomes.

The greatest gift you can give me is to listen to my worst possible outcomes, to acknowledge them, and then ask me, "What are your best possible outcomes?" Because I am immersed in my fears, I cannot consciously think of this question myself. Ask it and I will tell you my best possible outcomes and then be changed, empowered to make them happen.

> **Best Possible Outcomes:** These are imagined hopes for *future* desired outcomes, sometimes *not previously experienced*, but vividly imagined in the present, with *currently* experienced emotional, biochemical, and physical responses. When people believe them, they affect their perceptions, beliefs, values, and strategies. They tend to be self-fulfilling prophecies when strongly held and acted on.

Reporting Best Possible Outcomes: An Activity

"Each of the groups also recorded the best possible outcomes of the workshop. Let's start with Group 2 and read off the best possible outcomes, going counterclockwise."

> **GROUP 2: THE BEST POSSIBLE OUTCOMES OF THE WORKSHOP**
>
> *We begin to develop support for resolution of issues in the River City Basin.*
> *It moves us toward salmon recovery and agricultural and economic stability.*
> *Ranching and ranchers are supported, productive, profitable, and successful.*
> *People here and people we talk to will be comfortable calling each other up if there is something that needs to be talked about.*
> *Salmon are returning.*
> *Relationships are built and/or strengthened.*
> *There is an increased possibility of making progress toward mutual goals and building consensus.*
> *We provide for affordable housing that attracts a diverse community and provide commercial/business opportunities so they can make a living here.*
> *People take the time and effort to listen and value what others say, and we have agreed to a definition and state of the cause of disagreement in the basin.*
> *We identify individuals who are willing to lead and we empower them to do so, because we trust them to be fair, honest, and compassionate as they make decisions that affect all of us!*
> *The health of the whole River City Basin will become more sustainable.*

When all have reported out their recorded statements, I end this segment with a final short insight:

Worst possible outcomes tend to focus on "me," my survival or the survival of my family, my clan, my culture. It is focused on survival of the fittest. This makes it nearly impossible to make a communal decision, meeting the needs of others.

Consensus is possible with best possible outcomes, because they tend to be focused on "us," on relationships, on community, on survival of all.

> Best possible outcomes are focused on survival of all.

Best possible outcomes are "purpose statements." Each of these statements is a potential goal that this group wants to make happen. This is the direction you want your community to go in as a result of this workshop. This purpose statement will help the cofacilitators and me to design this workshop so that these outcomes happen.

We will put all these statements together later this afternoon and create a document that provides a collective view for the entire community. These are called **collective statements**. Every word you have recorded will be in those statements exactly as you stated them. To us, every word you express has purpose and meaning. Every word, every statement deserves to be included in the document.

There are times when I will share with the group a personal anecdote that positively changed my view of me and adults. I decide to do this with the large group.

A Son Just Like Robert: An Anecdote

When I was young, a victim of an abusive environment, I felt as if I was responsible for what happened. This resulted in the negative behaviors of a troubled youth. It took one person a small amount of time and attention to change my view of myself, to hope for a better future.

"Robert, could you please come to the front of the room?"

That was a request from my second-grade teacher, the most beautiful woman in the world. To me, she was Cinderella, Snow White, the Fairy Godmother, and Shirley Temple, all in one body. She was young, probably a new teacher. She graced our room with her happiness and her lightness of being. She was an image of health, beauty, and love to me.

She always began the day with her exercises, showing us how to have healthy bodies. I guess it was elementary PE in the forties. She didn't have the technological marvels we have today, so she used the doorway to set an example for us. She would push against the side of the door to strengthen her upper-body muscles. She did chin-ups with her hands holding to a bar she installed in the door. I'm sure she did others; these are what stand out in my mind from that day.

This one morning, after doing these exercises, she came to the head of the aisle between two rows of desks. I was in the last row of desks on the right side. She looked at me and said:

"Robert, could you please come to the front of the room?"

I remember the words as if they were just spoken. They still send shivers up my spine. I remember the shock, the fear that infused my body. I wanted to run and hide. The jig was up! This woman I secretly loved knew that I was a mean and evil child, responsible for all the trouble in my family. Of all the people I knew, she was the last person I wanted to know the truth about me. I was in deep, deep trouble.

I slid from my chair and reluctantly walked that long last mile to where she stood. My head hung down, I didn't dare look up. My Salvation Army shoes flapped. In those days the soles were sewn to the shoe. My soles had come loose as the thread had worn and broken at the front. So the soles flapped when I walked.

I remember the sound—flap, flap...flap, flap—as I walked that long aisle with my head down, my shoulders slumped, in despair. I was not just frightened; I was shamed in front of all the students. I wanted to die right there.

When I got to the teacher, she turned me around to face the class, put her hands on my shoulder, and said—to the entire class!—

"Someday I will be married, and when I am, I hope I have a child just like Robert."

I remember the words, nothing else about that event or the day. I can still feel her hands on my shoulders. They were light, soft, and smelled of Ivory soap, 99.9 percent pure. I remember the thrill of absolute love that infused my body, wiping away my fears, filling me with the most wonderful, inexpressible feeling of euphoria I have ever had, even to this day. I remember looking up and seeing the whole class looking at me, wishing they were where I was. I looked upward and saw her blue eyes looking at me with love. I must have died and gone to heaven.

I remember nothing else, only that moment. I don't remember the walk back to my desk. That moment is frozen. There were other times when she would greet me at the door in the winter, help me take off my coat and boots. She would hug me and say, "If you were chocolate cake, I would eat you right up." To this day, chocolate cake is my favorite.

In my adult years, I realized that she must have done this for other children, but I blocked it out. I am sure I was not the only one she graced with her love. It doesn't matter. She changed me that day. She did it in less than five minutes.

The difficult times in my life did not end because of that. I went home to the same turmoil. But I could never again think of myself in a negative way without remembering what she said. I was not always aware of it, but

I know that throughout my life, I always wanted to be a person who would make her proud.

I have been back to that classroom since, tried to research the teacher's location, with no success. I want to tell her: "You would have been proud of me if I was your child. And I thank you for making it possible."

It is such an event that makes us believe in the possibility of best possible outcomes.

~23~

Possibility Thinking Insights

Possibility Thinking—A Balance: An Insight

In the Coyote basin workshop, I continue with an insight about possibility thinking:

I am not suggesting **positive thinking**. I am suggesting **negative *and* positive thinking**. All events/issues have a potential worst or best outcome. Either is possible.

Typically, some of us choose to focus on either the worst or the best outcome. We are labeled as the pessimists or optimists. When these views become pitted against each other, we tend to see the worst outcome or the best outcome as the exclusive possibility. This results in a duality, a polarization of views and stereotyping of individuals as negative and positive. This pits us against each other. This is one of the major barriers to resolving conflicts.

The fact is this: all of us will have worst possible outcomes for any event. I know this because the thousands of people I have worked with have all expressed a worst possible outcome for their situation. Those for and those against had worst outcomes. Those who were positive had worst outcomes, as well as those who were negative.

The best outcome is often not acknowledged by people in conflict because they get hooked on talking about the worst possible outcomes. Rarely does anyone have their worst outcome acknowledged so they can move to the best outcome.

Sometimes people will deny the possibility of a worst outcome. These people explain that they have been taught only to think positively, to see negative as negative. Eventually these people realize how they are denying their own reality. While a worst outcome may be seen as a negative, it is right to have one. It ensures our survival. It comes with being human.

It is also right to have a best outcome. I know this because the thousands of people I have worked with have always expressed a best outcome for their situation. Those for and those against had best outcomes. Those who were negative had best outcomes, as well as those who were positive. It is highly unusual for someone to deny a best outcome. Everyone, even the naysayers, wants best outcomes.

In possibility thinking, you can acknowledge your worst possible outcomes. They are possible, and this will satisfy your survival needs. It honors the reptilian brain for ensuring your survival. Magnify these worst outcomes if needed to ensure they are well represented. Do it in a way that makes you conscious of them. Express them to another who can reflect them to you. Or write them so you can see them visually.

Then acknowledge the best possible outcomes; they are just as possible. They express the potential in any event or issue. Magnify them as you did the worst outcomes—they deserve to be affirmed. They provide a purpose, goal, and direction that all can agree to seek. They focus the positive efforts of people who are seeking the best.

It honors the role your neocortex can play. These positive outcomes will change your mental, emotional, physical, and biochemical makeup so you can imagine and implement the strategies to foster that outcome. You are now satisfying your needs for growth and for developing your potential.

It is like the electricity in our homes: we need both the negative and positive charges to make the light happen. In a similar way, acknowledging the worst possible outcomes and the best possible outcomes creates the energy needed to live a full and positive life.

Once your fears have been adequately expressed, when you are conscious of them, you can manage to minimize their possibility. Then your hopes seem more possible, easier to express and believe. This leaves the images, emotions, and words of the best hopes in the minds of all the participants. This will guide their thoughts and behaviors in resolving the conflicts.

Possibilities and Facts

To understand this concept, we need to look at the difference between **fact** and **possibility.** I believe we often get these two concepts mixed up. When we talk of the future, we are talking about possibilities, because neither the worst nor the best has happened yet. My experience is that we often treat possibilities as facts and then operate out of them as if they were facts.

"The sun will rise tomorrow."

This is a statement of fact. (Although a friend has informed me that the true fact is that the earth will turn and cause the sun to appear to rise. It is the earth that is moving, not the sun. Still, it is a fact.)

"You will see the sun tomorrow."

This is a statement of possibility. You may actually not see the sun because of clouds or rain, or you may be inside a building all day. So it is more correct to say:

"It is possible that you may see the sun tomorrow."

Another example of a fact might be a statement made to the workshop participants:

"You are here in this workshop."

This is a fact. I can see all the participants. There you are!

Another statement would move into the realm of possibility:

"You all want to be here in this workshop."

This is only a possibility because some of you may not want to be here or are here because you were told to be here. You may not know what the session is about and would just as soon be doing something else, especially after seeing the circle. It would be more correct to say:

"It is possible some of you don't want to be here, but I want you to decide it is a worthwhile investment of your time."

Often, potential members of a group will tell me as I interview them: "The parties just won't be able to find the time to deal with this conflict. Besides, we are all entrenched too much to allow any change." They are expressing their worst possible outcomes.

This statement will be made with an air of certainty, as if this statement is a fact. This is based on the fact that they've had past experiences with this outcome. Because the person believes this possibility to be a fact, no action will be taken to bring the group together, no time will be taken to confront the conflict, and people will become more entrenched in their positions. So, a possibility is treated as a fact, and it will then become a fact.

It hasn't happened yet, so how can it be a fact? It is also possible to state:

"The parties will take the time to confront this issue and will allow the changes in perspective needed to solve the conflict." (Best possible outcome.)

This possibility would result in searching for ways to bring the parties together, where they recognize it is in their interest to be there, and this opens the possibility of resolution.

Here are some statements of fact and possibility:

1. "The congressperson told me she would not attend under any conditions."
2. "We can get the congressperson to attend if she sees it is in her interest."
3. "We can still invite the congressperson and let her decide."
4. "The congressperson will attend if we go ahead with the meeting, because it is in her best interest."

Statements 1 and 3 are facts. The others are possibilities. Possibilities can become fact if they are acted upon. If we believe the congressperson will not attend and we don't invite him, then he will not be there. If we decide to invite the congressperson and establish that there are political benefits in his attending, he will be there or send an aide. The possibility determines the action we take.

That is why participants are asked to explore the worst and the best possible outcomes. The event has not happened yet, it is being imagined, so both outcomes are possible. Either will be fostered if we operate on them. If we want best possible outcomes to happen, we must know what that possibility is so we can focus on fostering the outcome. Otherwise, it will not be considered.

Here is a fact: "You are reading this book."

This is a possibility: "You are learning a lot by reading this book."

I hope that becomes a fact for you.

> **Possibility Thinking:** An acknowledgment that both worst and best outcomes are present and inherent in each situation up to, during, and often after the event. Either or both can be fostered when acted upon. This balanced view allows the movement toward desired outcomes.

The following anecdote reinforces what I have just said. I share this with the Coyote River Basin group because it is relevant to them.

"Will This Work?": An Anecdote
A Personal and Interpersonal Conflict

"Will this work for married people?"

He was a tall, slender young man, his hat pushed back on his head revealing a white forehead over a deeply tanned face. A rancher. He asked the question somewhat jokingly, but with a serious look on his face.

He had been in the workshop all day and had experienced being listened to by someone else in a deep manner. He had experienced the worst and best possible outcomes of the workshop. Now he wanted to know if it would work with his family.

"Tell me more before I answer the question," I said quietly.

"Well, I'm married, been married for a while, we got two kids. I own a ranch and have to keep finding ways to make money to keep the ranch. But every time I talk to my wife about ways to do that, like maybe buying or leasing additional land, she is always in her worst outcomes, she is so negative about everything."

"So what do you do when she is negative about everything?" I asked.

"I try to convince her it is not all bad, that there are some good things could happen, but that just makes her madder and more negative. Then we get in an argument. I hate it. It seems the more time we are together, the worse it gets."

"So, when your wife speaks negatively, you respond with your best outcomes, right?"

"Yeah, I guess," he said, looking at me, waiting for more.

"So she has worst possible outcomes. She is trying to tell you that bad things can happen, and you tell her the opposite: good things can happen?"

"Yeah. And it never seems to work."

"This is an insight for you. Your wife has fears you are not acknowledging. Instead you not only don't address those fears, you tell her that everything will be all right. This must drive her crazy!"

"Well, that's exactly what she tells me, that I make her feel crazy."

"Do you want to do something about that?" I asked.

"Sure, if I can. That is what I was hoping for. Maybe some ideas from you."

"The next time you and your wife are talking about something that makes her fearful, I want you to tell her what you heard. In other words, acknowledge her fears. You experienced this yourself in the workshop today. Then tell her *your* fears about that situation, because I know you have them. Now, what did I just say?"

"You want me to tell my wife what I heard her say when she is negative and then tell her I am scared also. But won't that make things just worse?"

"That is a worst possible outcome. So, you see, you can be negative too. It could make it worse, and it could also make it better. Make sure your wife repeats what your fears are."

"Yeah...I see...I think. It is a different way of thinking, for sure."

"Is this more than you expected from me?"

"Well, I really appreciate you're taking this time with me. I didn't expect this much, but don't stop. I'd really like to do something. Maybe even tonight."

"Then ask her what her best possible outcomes are, or phrase it as 'what do you want to happen instead?' After she answers, tell her what you heard, and then tell her your best possible outcomes. Ask her what she heard you say. 'What did I say?"

"You want me to have her tell me what she wants to have happen, instead of the negative. Then I tell her what I heard. Then she does the same thing when I tell her my best outcomes."

"OK. Now, ask her what she needs you to do to make those outcomes happen? How can you make her feel secure?"

"So, do you want me to tell her that?"

"No, she is going to tell you what you need to do to help her feel secure and to make your best outcomes happen."

"OK, I got it."

"And what are you going to do when she tells you that?"

"I'll tell her what I heard?"

"You got it. After you listen to her and tell her what you heard, then let her know what you would be willing to do to help her feel secure. Now, bring me up to date on what you heard."

"Well, I'm going to start by asking her what she wants me to do that would make her feel safe about the best outcomes. Then I'll tell her what I heard. And I'll tell her what I would be willing to do. Do those need to be the same?"

"No, you may be willing to do something totally different in addition to what she asks of you. That's up to you to decide in that moment. Trust yourself in this, you'll find yourself saying the right thing.

"When you're all done with this, then I want you to ask her how she feels about your discussion and what she learned that would help both of you create those best outcomes. She may have to take a while to think about this. Wait for her to answer. Then, what do you do?"

"Why, I'll just tell her what I heard, he said with a smile on his face. Then I suppose I should tell her the very same thing?"

"Yes, you tell her how you feel about the discussion and what you learned. That will end your conversation. But then, who knows what might come out of that?"

"How can I even remember all this?" he asked.

"If you want to stick around for a few minutes while I finish some business, then you and I will sit down and write the questions on three-by-five cards and put them in order so you know how to do this. That sound OK to you?"

"Yeah! Really, I appreciate you doing this, Bob."

When I was done with my task, we sat down and I went through the process again, while he recorded each question/task on a three-by-five card.

I showed up early the next morning, as usual, putting up collective statements, making sure the circle was a circle, moving flip charts around, beginning to think through how I want the day to go. Who was the first person to show up? You guessed it, the young rancher.

He walked in with a jaunty step, came right up to me, slapped me hard on the back, and said: "Well, it worked!"

"Careful there!" I said. "You darn near threw me across the room!" I said with a smile on my face. "So, it looks like you had an opportunity to listen to your wife last night?"

"Yep," he said with a twinkle in his eye, "and it went exactly as you said it would. I just had to get here early to tell you before you got busy."

He continued: "How could I have been so stupid all those years by making her feel crazy? She was so happy when I just listened to her talk about her fears. And then I told her what I heard. She was really surprised by that. Then I told her my concerns. She was surprised by that, too! She thought she was the only one that was worried. But I told her I felt pretty much the same as she did.

"Then we talked about what we wanted to happen if we were really able to do what I propose. She gave me her best outcomes, and you know what, Bob? They were exactly the same as mine. That we could make sure the ranch was big enough for both of our children to be able to inherit a piece of it. Just like her dad is planning to do with his children."

"So what did she ask you to do?" I asked.

"She just wanted me to talk to her dad before I moved ahead to buy or lease that additional land. He's done this quite a few times before, so she believes he can help me be smart about this."

"So how do you feel about that idea?"

"I'm more than OK with it! I would've done it anyways. He really is a smart man, and I believe he can help me make the best decision."

"How did you both feel about the conversation you had?"

"I guess I can sum it up by saying we both realize how much we loved each other, as a result of just listening to each other. We were working together for our future. It was really wonderful, and we expressed feelings we hadn't had for long time."

"So, now your question is answered. Does it or does it not work for people who are married?"

"You bet it does!"

This is an approach you can use for an interpersonal conflict, one between you and another person. It may start with your addressing the personal conflict you have in your own mind about the situation. It requires quite a bit of trust on the part of the other person to have you facilitate the process. If you just relax and recognize you have good intents, the other person will relax with you and participate.

This normally takes less than an hour. It can change a lifetime.

Creating a Best-outcome Environment

The *Finding New Ground* process is designed to foster the belief that best possible outcomes can happen. The following tasks and activities ensure that:

- Starting with the introduction and grounding, each person learns that he or she can speak and will be listened to with respect. They can have a safe environment in which people with different views can express them; they will not be interrupted, and they will be heard. It is not just talked about as a desirable thing—it is actual behavior!
- When greeting others in the circle, each person is recognized as a member of the community, even if there is disagreement between them. They are welcomed by those who disagree with them.
- In the lifelong learning questions, they all realize they can learn from each other, but it is their choice what they learn. It will not be imposed.

- The entire community will not move ahead until all have spoken either in the large or small groups. Members of the group will protect each person's right to speak when the facilitators check to see if all have spoken.
- The recorders will record exactly what participants say, without changing their words. These will be read to the larger group as recorded.
- When expressing their best possible outcomes, they are provided time to go internally, to think deliberatively about what they want and then record it on a card. The process will not move ahead until they are completed. The group will take whatever time is needed to get these statements recorded to the flip chart, no matter how long they are. Individuals know they can advocate for themselves.

Each of these ground rules creates organic responses, those that occur or develop gradually and naturally, without being forced or contrived. They create an environment in which people can believe in best possible outcomes. This is purposeful in the design of the process and creates the largest possibility that people can develop their best possible outcomes based on an experience.

Balance: An Insight

Balance is defined partially as *"a force that counteracts another, a bringing into proportion, establishing a pleasing harmony of various elements, creating a mental or emotional stability."*

Seeking consensus, whether among individuals or groups, requires careful attention to the notion of balance. By balance, I do not mean seeking a middle ground, a compromise. I refer to all the actions taken to ensure that each energy force, each point of view is counteracted upon by providing opposing points of view, seeing that all views are represented fairly or equally. This applies to beliefs, values, and behaviors, as well as thoughts and feelings.

Groups that have no balance, that are oriented around one emotion, one belief, one behavior, one view, one set of facts, will become a groupthink—ideologues—where there is little conscious thought and lots of loyalty to the agreed-upon group system of thought and resultant actions. While the environment appears to be peaceful and stable, it is subject to disaster if events occur that are outside the groupthink and that are detrimental to the group.

Consensus is focused on meeting the needs of the whole. That being the case, all views of the "whole" must be present, represented verbally and behaviorally, and listened to. It is important to have the aggressive and the peaceful in the same room. It is important to have the most polarized positions, for and against, represented in the room. It is important to have hate and love represented. It is important to have thinking and emotion represented. It is important to have sound *and* silence represented. These balancing attributes foster the potential of consensus and community.

During this process, a balance is created in many different ways, including the following:

- In the grounding, each person is allowed to speak with respect, knowing that others will not interrupt or question what is being said. Then each person must listen to the others with the same level of respect.
- In the greeting circle, a person experiences being the greeter and the greeted. Each is a different experience, a different position of power, providing a balance. The first time around the circle, the ritual of greeting dominates with a somewhat superficial dialogue. In the second round, the conversations are deeper and more authentic. This is a purposeful balance.
- When asking questions in the talking circle, the direction and sequencing of the participants is reversed, so that the last person is first and the first person is last. I can experience being first, last, and in-between. This gives me different experiences and different information and exposes different parts of my personality.
- For some tasks, individuals record their answers before expressing them and having them recorded to the group's flip chart. This brings silence to the room, balancing all the talking that preceded it. This allows people to go internal, as opposed to external. This allows people to write their thoughts in advance, to be proactive, rather than just emotional or reactive.

- Exploring worst and best outcomes provides a balance of emotions and information in responding to a situation. The entire brain—reptilian, older mammalian, and new mammalian—is recognized and engaged.
- Worst possible outcomes are mostly recorded directly to the flip chart. This is normally emotional and nonconscious material that is made conscious by being visually represented. It is at the "tip of the tongue." The best possible outcomes are the balanced view. They are recorded on a three-by-five card first because they are normally not explored. They must be imagined. This allows the mind to go internal to think deliberatively about what the individual wants.
- After a group has verbally explored an issue, they are asked to write on a three-by-five card what they heard or learned from others in the group discussion. Then they record on the other side of the card what they expressed in the talking circle. Both points of view are thereby honored and represented.
- Cofacilitators are male and female pairs. When establishing a panel, a diverse group of males and females is selected. I seek to pair up powerless and powerful, old and young, blue collar and white collar, for and against, emotional and intellectual, racial and ethnic. The grounding is facilitated by a female and the closing by a male. This provides balance in representation.
- There is a balance between the experience and learning from the experience. This is done with the lifelong learning questions after an event. It is also done with the grounding and the closure at the end of the day.
- We ask questions that require thinking and feeling answers. This not only taps the right and left lobes of the brain, but seeks to express the whole self. It fosters balance in ourselves.
- A person may start as a member of a panel and then become the facilitator of a small group. He selects a new facilitator and becomes the recorder. When the next facilitator is selected, he is seated as part of the group. Each of these is a different and balancing experience.

Many might question if all this is necessary. In my experience, it is not just necessary, but critical.

If the underlying tensions that exist between male and female are not acknowledged and represented, they will piggyback onto the emotions related to the conflict. The focus will eventually become male versus female, rather than on the real issue.

If a meeting is focused on worst possible outcomes, nonconscious emotional fears, then the meeting will foster those outcomes. Expressing both worst and best possible outcomes allows focus on the possible failure events as well as the desired successful outcomes.

Many might scoff that reversing the direction of the dialogue is not important. I can tell you from experience, it makes a difference—enough to foster consensus where none was possible.

~24~

Defining Conflict

Being Moved Deliberately, Safely - An Insight

It is about now that the group will break for their first lunch together. Sometimes lunch will occur after the recorder and facilitator roles. Either way, the process remains the same. I will suggest that the members of the small groups have lunch together to get better acquainted with each other. They will often do this. I have learned to take advantage of every opportunity to help people change their relationships.

Before they break, Mike announces the names of six people who will meet with YOU and me in the center of the circle. These are people we selected for a panel after lunch and as cofacilitators to be coached.

We have been with this group of thirty-two people for four hours now. They have spent their time becoming acquainted with each other, delaying their focus on the conflict issue they came to resolve. They are being moved deliberatively toward considering their conflict, but we are first establishing an environment that feels safe, forming the relationships between people that will foster open communications. They were distributed into small and diverse groups to do this. In this time, the community has moved from being strangers to each other to being acquainted with each other.

In the grounding, they experienced getting their voices in the room, being listened to with respect. They have greeted each other in an experience they can learn from. Each person shared how they felt about the greeting experience and what they learned, and in the process, disclosed important information to each other.

They moved from being facilitated to facilitating their own process in the small groups. The group has now recorded four pieces of information: the roles of the facilitator and recorder and the worst and best outcomes of the workshop. These are their first visible products. These recorded statements will be used to develop the collective statements that are described later in this book.

All of this has happened in only the first four to five hours of the three-day session. Each person has spoken at least seven times, which is equal to 224 people speaking in that time (32 times 7). This will happen only if a process has provided for each person to speak uninterrupted in a safe environment where he or she will be listened to with respect. The result is that everyone is fully engaged.

At this point, I may decide to move right into the issue at question. This is especially true if I have worked with the group before and participants are prepared to confront the issue. But more frequently, the group is not yet ready—the relationships are not yet fully formed, and people are still uncertain about their ability to resolve the issue.

After lunch, I want the group to look at the notion of conflict—before they confront their real conflict. This allows me to help them further develop their relationships and the knowledge base necessary to address their conflict in a real way, with a confidence that they will resolve the issue.

There are two ways I approach this. The first is to be abstract, exploring the concept of conflict. This allows the group to deal with it more as a concept and less personal attachment. The second approach explores the reality of conflict in their environment. This allows the group to explore the specific reality of conflict in a more emotional context. I can use both approaches at the same time by assigning the two questions to different groups.

As I am considering my options, George, the owner of a small resort, approaches me with a question:

"Isn't it taking a long time to get to our problem? I wonder how this process of yours helps people if it takes this much time. I know some people are getting antsy."

I respond not to the question but to the statement he is making.

It sounds like the amount of time we are taking is concerning you. You want to get right to solving the problem.

"Right! We should be able to solve this in a few hours, don't you think?"

Since you said others are concerned about the amount of time we are taking, let me respond to the whole group, I say. Are you OK with that?

"Yeah, I know they would appreciate it."

Creating a Panel: The Art

Just before the last activity before lunch, I asked YOU and Mike to select two people from each group who could potentially be on a panel or help cofacilitate later in the workshop. While the small groups are working on their worst and best possible outcomes, we go over this list, selecting one person from each group to be on a panel: Kenney, Marie, Johanna, Todd. We also select Laura and Wayne to help facilitate this afternoon.

These people represent the diversity in the room with balance: male/female, young/old, for/against, outspoken/shy, and so forth. I like to make sure that a shy person is on the panel, as well as an outspoken person.

Mike will facilitate this panel. I hand him a three-by-five card with the questions on it and explain the process.

> What is your definition of conflict, and how do you feel about it? (2 groups)
>
> What is the evidence of unresolved conflict in your environment, and how do you feel about it? (2 groups)
>
> Record directly to the flip chart.

Mike, we will meet with our panel members just before lunch to give them their assignment. Kenney and Marie will answer the first question about the definition of conflict. Johanna and Todd will answer the second question about unresolved conflict. They will be seated wherever they wish in the large circle.

After lunch I will get the group's attention. They will be in the large community group. I will summarize what we have done so far and then tell them they will be exploring conflict this afternoon. Not the real conflict, but the notion of it. I also will describe how we selected the members of the panel.

YOU will take Laura and Wayne aside during and after lunch and begin coaching them in the art of facilitating outside the groups with us. I want you to explain the circle, where they are to stand, how to present the questions and the reasons for this. *(See the section "Coaching Facilitators, the Art," on page 183.)* We will have them each facilitate at least one task this afternoon. Then Mike will be retired to join the large group. I am going to retain YOU to help me coach for the rest of the workshop.

As the groups break for lunch, we get the selected panel members and cofacilitators together in the center of the circle. I explain to the panel members what their role is:

You have been selected to introduce the notion of conflict, to create a context and an arena of thought in the minds of the rest of the group, focusing them on their personal relationship with conflict. Mike will read the questions you will answer.

Mike reads the questions off the three-by-five card. He explains the assignment.

"We are assigning the first question to Kenney and Marie and the second to Johanna and Todd."

Kenney has a question. "Where do you want us to sit as a panel? Do you want us to sit together?"

Good question, Kenney, I respond. This normally comes up when I am establishing the first panel.

In the traditional way, panel members would sit up at the front of the room or in some other area designated as the focal point for the group. In this process, you can sit anywhere in the circle that you want. You're just another member of the group, equal to them. When we start with the panel, Mike will pick one of you to begin with and then direct you to move in either a clockwise or counterclockwise direction. He will repeat the question for each of you to make it easier to remember.

> Panel members sit wherever they want to sit in the circle, just another member of the group, equal with all.

After you have all spoken, you will be asked to go to the center of the circle. You will be honored there and then asked to return to your small circle. You will serve as facilitator for your group, selecting a recorder for the activity.

Mike will repeat the two questions and remind you of the selection of a recorder for the group. Your groups will answer the same question you did for the panel and record the answers directly to the flip chart.

I have Johanna and Kenney repeat what I said, then release them to lunch.

After lunch, when the group returns slowly to the large circle, I note how the room feels. Normally, there is a sense of excitement, but sometimes a sense of uncertainty. The group has learned a lot about each other and about the process, but they're beginning to wonder where they are headed. They are sometimes slow to return, engaged in animated conversations with each other.

I have learned to let them come back in their own time. I keep reminding them that we are ready to start. Sometimes I will begin to talk or sing a song to keep them moving. Anything to remind them we are ready to start. I prefer not to use the loud whistle, since it startles and adrenalizes people.

When they are all back, I begin by answering the question George asked.

Going Slow to Go Fast

> *"Anything worth doing is worth doing slowly."*
>
> —Mae West

Welcome back to the circle. From the sound in the room, you not only had good food but good conversation also. Normally during the first day, someone makes a statement or asks a question about how slow the process is going:

"I don't see how you can get anything done with this process. We just don't have the time to do this," or "Are we using our time effectively? I thought we were here to solve the problem, but it doesn't seem we're going anywhere. I think this is going too slow."

A number of you have spoken to me about how slow we are going. I suppose to at least some of you, it must seem like it takes an interminable amount of time.

I can see heads nodding in agreement.

"There is never enough time." That is the complaint and the excuse of most people when asked to consider addressing conflict. As a result, they set aside a one-hour meeting that fails because time for creating the appropriate environment and processes were not provided for. This traditional approach comes from the belief that there is truly one right answer for an issue and that if only the right person can provide this answer to the protagonists, they will agree with the logic of it and move on quickly.

This just doesn't happen. A conflict is based on a power struggle. It is based on deeply held beliefs that are associated with strongly felt emotions. Unless these are dealt with by the parties, these beliefs and emotions will continue to get in the way of productive relationships. No one person can find a resolution. All the parties must fully participate. The hour does not allow that to happen.

This results in another meeting in which you make a decision, again. And nothing is done.

"We make all these plans and then they just get put on the shelf and nobody uses them. Then we start all over again on another set of plans."

—**Workshop participant**

There is a common saying in our culture:

> "We never have time to do things right, but we do have time to do them over, and over, and over, and..."

In my introduction, I told you I would slow you down, provide an environment in which you could speak to each other and know that you will be listened to with respect. I would help you create an environment in which you could speak honestly with each other and develop the kind of relationships needed to resolve the conflict. Along the way, I would introduce you to skills that would help you facilitate your own process and resolve the conflict. That's what we've been doing.

Outside this room it seems like we are always on the move, in a rush. And the pace is increasing every day. As a result, we get into conflict with each other and never take the time to resolve it. We then make decisions quickly, with little support from those who must carry them out, so very little gets done.

I have learned that each problem has an allotted time needed to solve it. You can take a shortcut and assume you have saved time, only to have to confront the problem over and over and over. This is not only unproductive, it is exceedingly frustrating, leaving those in charge feeling out of control, often betrayed. It does no good to demand we get along. We cannot move until the conflict is resolved.

It is for this reason that I take the time to get the conflict resolved. Deeply held issues take at least three days of intense discussion and deliberation before they are resolved. Other issues can take one or two days. Personal conflicts can be resolved in twenty minutes. But rarely can you resolve a major issue for the long term with a two-hour meeting.

In order to build consensus, you must go **slow** to go **fast.** You solve the problem, and then it takes little time to move through it with success. To take this stance, you must recognize the following truth:

> Time is not the problem; the problem is the problem.

People tend to get confused on what their real issue is. Is the purpose of the meeting the resolution of the conflict, or is it to save time? These tend to become either/or approaches, resulting normally in saving time at the expense of not solving the problem. We tend to make short-term solutions that don't work in the long term, sometimes lasting no longer than the end of the meeting. Then the conflict breaks out once again and takes more of our time. It feels like the movie *Groundhog Day*.

The time it takes to make the decision over again is time that could have been used to do something else. Instead, "something else" is delayed. Or a short meeting is set up to make a quick decision about that "something else" with the result that nothing happens. This builds a continuing burden of unresolved issues.

Time is not the issue. The unresolved conflict or the problem is the issue. If the conflict is unresolved, it will take time and energy that should otherwise be focused on the work or relationship. The consensus approach has a different belief:

> We take the time to do things right, and then we have time to do something else.

Any problem or conflict that is resolved will release energy into the relationship: the family, organization, or community that has been tied up in managing or coping with the conflict. This energy is available then to focus on something else.

What we have done so far is an investment in time, which results in the relationships you need to resolve the conflict. It helps you understand each other, to gain knowledge about each other's perceptions, so that each of you has enough information to make decisions that will meet the needs of all. When you get to the decision-making time, then you will go fast.

> When seeking consensus, you learn to go SLOW to go FAST!

Going slow does not mean wasting time, hoping the more time you spend, the better chance you have of solving the issue. Going slow means taking time to build relationships and a safe environment and to create the shared knowledge base needed to resolve the issue. The time must be carefully invested, resulting in an outcome that saves time in the long run.

> **A CHOICE**
>
> We never have time to do things right, but we do have time to do them over, and over, and over...
> So
> We go **fast** to go **slow**
>
> Or:
> We do things right the first time and spend our extra time on other issues.
> So...
>
> Consensus seeking requires that we...
>
> Go *Slow* to Go *Fast*

On a flip chart.

By the end of our time together, you will understand how to apply the consensus process on major issues that might take three days or minor issues that might take one day, on interpersonal issues that can take one to three hours, and on personal issues that take less than twenty minutes.

I understand your impatience in going slow. But going fast does not work for you. That is what got you here. Why would you want me to do what has already failed for you? So take a deep breath and relax. You are about to have a different experience. Learn from it. In the end it will save time for you.

But, will people come back if they feel it is too slow? That is always the concern. The answer is yes. It is very rare for a person to drop out of a consensus workshop. Just because a person feels the session is too slow and expresses that concern, does not mean they will not come back. In my experience they will return, especially if they are allowed to express that concern, to have it validated before the whole group, and if they learn from it.

> Albert Einstein reportedly defined insanity as doing the same thing over and over and expecting different results.

The Panel Speaks

I move ahead, providing an overview of the morning and introducing the next task:

When we started this morning, many of us did not really know each other. We knew we were all engaged in the same conflict, but we were not truly aware of each other. Now you have all had a chance to be grounded, to get your voice in the room, to be listened to with respect. You were separated into small groups that are diverse. You greeted each other and then experienced how to learn from this task. You took over the role of the facilitator and recorder while you were describing the roles and recording the information. Then we had you develop your worst and best possible outcomes of the workshop. All the information you have recorded will be used this afternoon to develop what I call collective statements.

Now we want to help you explore conflict. We are not directly going to confront the real conflict, but explore what it means to you, both in the abstract and in reality.

Mike and YOU helped me create a panel of four people to get us started. You will also note that we have asked two other people, Wayne and Laura, to assist us this afternoon. We are coaching and training others from your community to help support you after the workshop.

Mike will now facilitate our panel.

Mike reads off the names of the people on the panel. He states that they will answer the questions when they are ready and in their turn.

"Kenney and Marie, please answer this question: What is your definition of conflict, and how do you feel about it?"

Marie looks at Kenney, who nods. She leans forward as she answers:

"Well, conflict to me is when two people can't agree on something, and they don't know what to do with it other than argue. It happens all the time at work and slows us down. I really don't like it, mostly because it remains unresolved, and I don't know what to do about it. I try to avoid it if I can."

Mike waits until Marie is done and then repeats the questions for Kenney. Kenney pauses as he thinks. Then he answers:

"I agree somewhat with Marie. *But conflict is when people just have different views about something that they believe in deeply. They see things from opposite views. I don't mind conflict and like to start it myself sometimes. I have strong beliefs and can normally win my case.*

"That's at work, but at home it is different. I just don't like conflict at home, and with three teenagers, there is lots of it." (Laughter.) *"I avoid it if*

I can and let my wife make the decisions with the kids. But I rarely like what she decides. I don't say anything about it, though."

Recognizing Kenney is finished, Mike reads the second question to Johanna and Todd:

"Johanna and Todd, what is the evidence of unresolved conflict in your environment, and how do you feel about it?"

Johanna answers right away:

"By how stressed out I am. The more stressed out I am, the more conflict there is. What stresses me out are people who won't listen, won't talk, and won't acknowledge the other side. I just wish it would go away."

Todd follows with his answer:

"I can see our hostile behavior. There are real threats from people representing different points of view if it's not working in their favor. The result is people don't want to communicate so they can avoid conflict. I hate what we have but don't know how to change it."

Mike pauses a bit, trying to remember what to do next. He looks at me. I tell the group:

Please all stand. Mike will honor the panel. This is part of building relationships and consensus.

Mike realizes that was his next task, so he says, "Panel members, please come to the center of the circle."

The four panel members come to the center, looking self-conscious, with uncertain smiles. Laura and Todd shake hands. This is the first time they have met. Mike honors them all:

"We want to honor you for the role you have just played in defining conflict and the evidence of conflict. You have spoken from the heart, and that will encourage the rest of us to do the same."

Mike leads the applause. After the applause is finished, Mike says:

"The panel members will now go to their small circles, and the rest of you will do the same. You are in the same group you were in this morning."

Honoring—Nutrition for the Soul: An Insight

When they come to the center of the circle, the panel members are obviously uncomfortable and self-conscious. They look around nervously as the honoring words are expressed, and then they look even more self-conscious as the applause begins. Marie begins to walk back to the larger circle and the others quickly follow, all before the applause ends.

When the applause has stopped, I ask everyone to remain standing. I ask the panel members to return to the center, and I walk out with them. I provide them an insight on honoring from the center, all eyes on me:

Probably the easiest thing in the world to do is to trash other people, to speak badly about each other. It rises instinctively within us. We seem to expect it to happen. But...who said we must speak badly about others? Who told us to do this? I often wonder if we have a prebirth workshop in trashing, because it is so automatic and so easy to do. Or...maybe we just learn as children watching adults do this to each other and decide it is the cool, the right thing, to do.

So we are all surprised when others want to honor us. We are surprised to find ourselves honoring others, especially those we disagree with.

We have this belief, often expressed to others, that we are never appreciated for what we do. You will complain to your spouses, your friends about how unfair life is, how unfair the family, the organization, or the community are, to not appreciate and respect you for what you do.

Yet, when someone expresses appreciation to you for a job well done, you will deflect the words, diminish them with statements such as, "Oh, I really could not have done it without help," or "It was just blind luck," or "It was easy; anyone could have done it," or...et cetera, et cetera, et cetera. Or you will walk away from it, as the panel members just did.

Why do we do that? It's as if we are Teflon-coated and bounce whatever appreciation we do get away from us. We must not realize we do this, because we will again complain that no one appreciates us. The truth is, we are unprepared or unwilling to accept appreciation from others. We are not sure we deserve it. It makes us self-conscious! And self-consciousness makes us walk from the center as fast as we can, lest those honoring us see us for who we **really** are!

Some would say we have been taught to not be vain, to be humble instead. Well, if others choose to honor you, it is not your vanity that caused it. If someone honors you, you can still accept the gift with humility. You don't need to walk around with a blinking neon sign that says you were appreciated...finally. What you need to do is simple: accept it!

Here is a truth. Trashing others is not good for our souls. Being trashed by others is not good for our souls. Appreciation is nutrition for the soul; it nourishes those who appreciate and those who are appreciated. Isn't that what we already know?

The problem is we don't know how to do it. We don't know how to accept it.

Here is another truth. None of us will ever get the appreciation we deserve, not from our family, our organization, or our communities or...ourselves! We are all doing things that are small or magnificent in their impact. But the world is not prepared to honor all of us. So we have to learn to honor ourselves, as we just did.

I suggest that in this community, we learn to honor each other. When that happens, those of you who are being honored have to stand in the center of the circle and take it! You cannot accept the gift unless you are self-conscious, aware of the honor and accepting it.

I want you be like vacuum cleaners and suck it all in and feel how nutritious it is. Let this nutrition feed your soul, because we will need that to resolve this conflict. Experience how this feels and see if it isn't a healthy thing to do.

I step back to the edge of the community and lead the applause, which is much more real, which seems heartfelt. The panelists stand in the center, grinning, almost in disbelief that they like it, turning around to see the people honor them. They will often reach out to each other, shaking hands or hugging. When the applause is over, the panel moves to the edge of the circle, and we move on to the next activity.

But, is it real? Now, that is a fair question. Often, especially at the start of the workshop, those in the outer circle may not feel like appreciating those in the center. They may differ with them, be angry with them, think badly of them. They may have been actively trashing a person in the center. Now they are expected to honor them? It won't feel real.

So they applaud weakly or not at all or have a look of disbelief on their faces: *What in the world am I doing?*

When this question is asked of me—*"But is it real?"*—or if I observe that the community is having a difficult time with being able to honor someone, I just bring it up with the group:

Because we are so used to trashing each other, we find it difficult, almost unbelievable that we would honor a person, especially if we don't like the person. We feel strange, uncomfortable, and perhaps fake. This is to be expected in a group that is in deep conflict.

Yet each person who has attended the workshop to confront the conflict has shown courage in choosing to do so. Each person who speaks their truth in the small groups has taken a risk in doing so. Each person who recorded the words of another, even though they might disagree with them, has shown integrity in doing so. Each person who speaks on a panel provides us some important piece of information that will lead us to resolve the conflict. Just because we might feel negative toward a person does not mean they do not have good traits. They can still be of service to all of us by sharing their views honestly.

This is the basis for people honoring each other. You are meeting people who have more depth than what has been demonstrated in the conflict. You already know this from your experiences this morning.

Yet it will still feel strange. It is like buying a new pair of shoes or a suit. They will feel strange, stiff, and not yet comfortable to wear. That doesn't mean you won't wear them. It takes time and experience to get them to fit just right. That is the same with honoring. You have to choose to experience this until it fits.

It may feel strange at first, but as the workshop moves on, the honoring will become more authentic. It will focus you on other attributes of members here than those connected to the conflict.

If I don't help the participants experience honoring, they will never have a choice. All they will have is *trashing*. This approach provides another choice, one that is healthy.

HONORING: THE ART

I honor people who are facilitators, cofacilitators, recorders, panel members who speak their truth, people who confront others for the good of the group, people who hold the group to a high standard, invited guests, special speakers, those who speak their truth, even if they are alone in it. I will honor the person who is the most disenfranchised, who others avoid, when he speaks his truth. Each of these is serving the larger community.

The approach is simple:

I have everyone stand. A standing applause has symbolic meaning in our culture.

I have the person or persons being honored come to the center of the circle. They will become self-conscious, which is necessary to accept the honoring.

I select someone to express words of appreciation for those being honored.

> I may do the first honoring to demonstrate the concept. Then I will have a cofacilitator do the honoring. Then we choose people from the group to do the honoring.
>
> In time, participants will come up to me and ask to honor someone in the group. At the beginning of the next activity, I let the person do this. Often they will honor someone they previously disagreed with.
>
> That is healthy, isn't it?

After my insight, Mike instructs the members to go to their small groups. "The panel members will now go to their small circles, and the rest of you will do the same. You are in the same group you were in this morning."

When all are in their small groups (again, this seems to take a long time, but it is just a few minutes), Mike walks to the edge of the circle and repeats the questions:

"Marie and Kenney, your groups will answer this question: what is your definition of conflict, and how do you feel about it? Johanna and Todd, your groups will answer this question: what is the evidence of conflict in your environment, and how do you feel about it?

"You are each facilitators for your group. You are going to record this directly to the flip chart, so each of you select a recorder."

Mike turns and walks away, and three of the groups go to work immediately. Group 4, however, has a question. The facilitator, Todd, has raised his hand. I step to the edge of the circle and get the entire group's attention.

Sorry to interrupt, but one of the groups has a question. I'd like you all to hear the answer. Todd, what is your question?

"What do you mean by our environment? Are you asking us about work or family or what?"

I respond, "Answer the question in any way you decide. Each person can determine their environment."

I walk away and turn to see how the groups are doing. They are back at work.

"Whatever You Decide"—Empowering Others: An Insight on Coaching

As the small groups work, I coach the facilitators:

Members of groups will seek out the "higher authority" when there is uncertainty or some disagreement within the group on the task. If the facilitator walks over and works only with that group, the rest of the groups are watching the nonverbal behavior and wondering what it is about. It distracts all the groups. It also introduces "power plays."

In facilitator parlance, there is a concept known as "proximity." When working with groups (or pairs, trios, etc.), the facilitator travels between them, checking to be sure they are on task or if they have questions. The result is that someone in each group will ask at least one question, managing to obtain the attention of a facilitator.

Often this is just an attention-getting opportunity. It has little to do with the task. If I answer the question with that small group, then someone else in the group will ask another question. If I'm not careful, they will invite me into the group, and I will soon become the only person speaking.

In the meantime, everyone else is observing my behavior. This is a matter of perceived power. If we have captured you in our group, then we are "one up" on the rest of the groups. So, someone in another group will raise another issue with the intent of getting my attention. I will then move to that group, then to the next group, then to the next group. Sometimes, I only get to one group before the time is up. Those that are "left out" feel that way.

Not every group will try for that attention. Some will view it for what it is, just getting my attention. They feel they can do the task without my help. Still, they are affected by what I do with the other groups.

My experience is that "proximity" is disturbing to the group process. It results in power being transferred to the facilitator rather than to the individuals in the groups.

My intent when I give the question on the edge of the circle is to immediately turn responsibility for the task to the groups themselves. The facilitators have the task. The facilitators know their role is to see that each person speaks. It is now the responsibility of the facilitator in the group to carry that task out. When I turn and walk away from the edge of the circle, they will immediately go into action. When I turn around, I can see groups hard at work.

If the question is a valid one that is based on a misunderstanding, then I will answer it for the whole group while standing on the edge of the circle. I first get their attention, then state the concern, and finally provide clearer directions. Then I turn and leave.

> Questions asked by individuals or groups are answered with the entire community hearing the answer. This allows all to feel treated equally.

Sometimes I will be approached during the break by a person with a question about the process, about the previous activity, or about application of the process. If it is just for that person's clarification, I will answer. If, however, I believe that the answer would be applicable to everyone in the room, I will tell the person that I will answer the question for the entire group.

When the group is back together, I will repeat the question I was asked and then provide the answer to everyone. That way everyone gets equal attention.

My role as a facilitator is to make everything as easy as possible. It is also to transfer whatever "position power" people give me back to the members of the circle. I do this by providing them choice. If I am asked a question I believe they can handle themselves, I will say to them, "Whatever you decide."

This always seems to satisfy. I have never had anybody question me further. I suspect they are looking for affirmation for some point of view that has been raised in the group and are seeking my "wisdom." I just return it to them and let them use their own "wisdom."

Defining Conflict: An Activity

When Mike returns to our cofacilitator group outside the circle, we observe the participants at work. They have immediately focused on their task, with recorders at the flip charts and group members already expressing their statements. In the meantime, YOU have been coaching Laura and Wayne on how to cofacilitate.

Let's listen in on Group 4, Allen, Laura, Rob, Cliff, Gil, Marcia, Todd, and Neil:

Todd: "Well, I guess I better select a recorder first, so...Marcia, could you do that?"

Marcia: "Are you sure? I don't write very well, but...I noticed you didn't either, so I will try." (Laughter from the others.)

Todd: "OK, Marcia, but you noticed I got better as I did it. Let's start with you, Allen, and then go counterclockwise, with Rob next. The question is: what is conflict and how do you feel about it?"

Allen: "Let me see...*I think conflict is when you don't agree with someone.*" (Pause) "*I don't like conflict. It scares me because I feel powerless to do anything about it. I just don't like it, and I am uncomfortable with it.* Do you want me to repeat that, Marcia?"

Marcia: "Just the last sentence; I got the rest." (Recording as she speaks.)

Allen: "Well, your writing is just fine. I said...I just don't like it, and I am uncomfortable with it."

Rob (pausing while Marcia finishes): "I think *conflict can bring out the best in us. It's a learning mechanism. I am not good with it because my feeling is that we don't communicate with each other very well.* At least I don't... you don't have to write that last statement, Marcia."

Cliff: "*Conflict may be disagreement between two or more people, each one thinking their way is the right way.*" (Pauses.) "*I have a desire to avoid conflict, because I see it as a threat. I can get angry and lose control, so I try to avoid conflict.* Especially with my wife, Ann....Good job, Marcia. You're doing better than I could. Leave out the part about Ann."

Todd: "Well, you'll get your turn, Cliff." (Laughter.) "Sorry, Gil, you're next."

Gil: "I think *conflict is necessary and good and can be destructive or creative. It is inevitable, and it is present to have a true democracy. I don't mind conflict.*" (Pauses.) "*It's what produces growth, and it all depends on what you do with it. I deal with it every day as a manager, and that's OK with me.*"

Todd (speaking to Mike who asked, "Has everyone spoken at least once?"): "No, we have a few more people to record. Go on, Neil. They are just checking on us."

Neil: "It is *people who do not accept a difference of opinion or the ideas of other people. It is difficult to deal with when I am personally involved, but I hate unresolved conflict. I don't like it, but I have a big need to deal with it and resolve it respectfully.*"

Neil repeats his statements to help Marcia with recording them.

Todd: "I'll speak now and then we can finish with you, Marcia. OK?" (Marcia nods.) "I think *conflict is differing viewpoints that starts with a feeling that moves to a look and then leads to a blowup.*" (Pauses.) "*There are power struggles, mistrust, and anger which is going head to head.*" (Pauses.)

"I am very uncomfortable about conflict." (Pauses) *"I don't like it personally and with coworkers, even though their opinion is just as important as mine."*

Todd (pausing until Marcia has finished recording): "OK, Marcia, why don't you be seated, and Cliff will record for you."

Cliff: "You'll be sorry." (Cliff stands, moves to the flip chart, and picks up a marker.) "Go ahead, Marcia."

Marcia: "To me *conflict is a difference of opinion by opposing forces. I want to get away from it because I feel angry. I feel threatened, scared, and I don't like it. I shut down.*" (Pauses.) "You write well, Cliff. I guess you learn fast."

Cliff: "Wait until you try to read it!"

Rob (raising his hand, then speaking when Todd nods to him): "Marcia, I just want to thank you for writing everything I said. I have never felt listened to like that before, by you or others. So I thank you."

Marcia: "Being the recorder makes us really listen. Hopefully, you will do the same for me."

Todd signals to Mike that the group is done. Mike walks to the edge of the circle. He asks the recorders of the first two groups to read off the information from each flip chart on the definition of conflict and how they feel about it. Group 4 starts and the recorder reads the statements.

GROUP 4: DEFINITION OF CONFLICT/FEELINGS

- *I think conflict is when you don't agree with someone. Don't like conflict. Scares me because I feel powerless to do anything about it. I just don't like it & am uncomfortable with it.*
- *Conflict can bring the best out in us. Learning mechanism. I am not good with it because my feeling is that we don't communicate with each other very well.*
- *Conflict may be disagreement between two or more people, each one thinking their way is the right way. A desire to avoid conflict, b/I see it as a threat. Can get angry and lose control, so I try to avoid conflict.*
- *Conflict is necessary and good, can be destructive or creative. Inevitable and it is present to have a true democracy. I don't mind conflict. It produces growth...all depends on what you do with it. Deal with it every day as a manager/that's OK with me.*

> - *People who do not accept a difference of opinion or ideas of other people. Difficult to deal with when personally involved, but I hate unresolved conflict. Don't like it but I have a big need to deal with it and resolve it respectfully.*
> - *Conflict is differing viewpoints that starts w/feeling, moves to a look, then leads to a blowup. Power struggles, mistrust, and anger which is going head to head. I am very uncomfortable about conflict. I don't like it personally and with coworkers, even though their opinion is just as important as mine.*
> - *Conflict is a difference of opinion by opposing forces. I want to get away from it b/I feel angry. Feel threatened, scared/ don't like it. I shut down.*

Once the conflict definition groups have read their information, I provide an insight on the task while standing at the edge of the circle.

Defining Conflict: Insight on the Task

This task has allowed some of you to explore the notion of conflict in the abstract—what is its definition, and how do you feel about it? And you have shared that definition and those feelings with the rest of the community. The questions allow you to represent both the logical and emotional context, to engage your whole brain. Most of you have never considered what your definition of conflict is, so it is a way of making you conscious of that. You are now aware that everyone has a different definition and feeling, and these have been recorded on the flip charts.

I want to visually demonstrate to you what conflict isn't and what it is. I will ask some of you to help me demonstrate this.

I move to the center of the circle to demonstrate how conflict is more than difference.

Conflict Is More than Difference: A Visual Experience

Most people initially define conflict as a difference of opinion, values, or beliefs. Or they may state it is a disagreement between two or more people. **But a difference of opinion has no action attached to it!** I want you to understand that conflict is more than disagreement, that something is added to that difference to cause the conflict. Unless energy is imposed to make one opinion-holder succumb to the opinion of the other, there is no conflict. To do this, I will use a visual activity that physically involves some members of the group and mentally and emotionally involves all of you.

I ask two members of the group to help me do this—normally two males, although I have used female and male pairs. Sometimes I use the cofacilitators and have them practice this while the groups are working. Other times I will use two people who represent the different sides of the conflict. I may have them practice the visual while on a break.

Jon and Jim, please join me in the center of the group. The rest of you can move your chairs so you can see this activity.

A Demonstration of Difference or Disagreement:

I want you two to face each other, a few yards apart.

Jon, I want you to tell Jim that you want to walk forward in your direction. Jim, I want you to do the same, telling Jon you want to walk in that opposite direction.

Jon: "I want to go that way" (pointing ahead).

Jim: "I want to go that way" (pointing ahead and in the opposite direction).

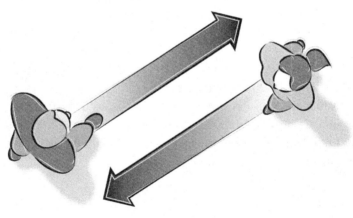

Differing views.

They each walk in the direction indicated and turn to face each other again.

This is a visual example of what difference **or disagreement** is. They each want to do something different than the other. But this is not conflict.

Take a look around you, and see all the differences that are represented. People look differently than you do: their features, race, age, sex, height, shape, and form. People dress differently than you do. People talk with different inflections than you do. People eat different cereals than you do. This is attested to by the large number of choices that sit on the shelves at the grocery store. People drive different cars than you do, representing different tastes and different income levels. People buy and live in different homes, decorate them differently, pay different mortgage rates.

Difference, by itself, is not conflict. Each person has made an individual choice, and no one is threatened by it. So, what is the additional ingredient for conflict?

An Added Ingredient...Power:

I have the two men repeat their statements, but this time, Jon tells Jim that he wants him to go his direction:

Jon: "I want to go this way" (pointing ahead).

Jim: "I want to go this other way" (pointing ahead and in the opposite direction).

Jon: "No, I want you to go this way with me."

Jim: "I want to go this way, not your way" (starting to walk ahead).

Jon: "Well, I want you to go my way" (standing in front of Jim and blocking him).

Jim: "You can't tell me what to do; I want to go this way" (trying to step around Jon).

Jon: "I want you to go this way" (steps in front of Jim and pushes him back with his hands on Jim's shoulders).

Jim (pushing back on Jon's shoulders): "I want to go my way, not yours."

Both men are now pushing against each other, straining to gain ground. Suddenly I tell them to **freeze**! They stop shoving, but lean heavily on each other, straining their muscles, at an impasse.

Defining Conflict

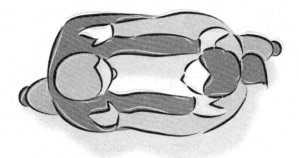

Power is added. An interpersonal conflict.

What has happened to their energy? I ask the group rhetorically. How much of this energy is available for the community focus?

Frank responds quickly. "They are both pushing against each other, so their energy is tied up in the conflict. They are not going anywhere; they are stuck. That's what we're doing in this community!"

Thank you for that insight, Frank. I say, you are right! Conflict is difference or disagreement with power attached to it, and it ties up your energy. The focus is now not on the work you will do, but on who will win. Each of these people feels his or her way is the right way...the one right way."

An Interpersonal Conflict Becomes an Intergroup Conflict:

These two have created an interpersonal conflict between them over which direction to go, over who should decide. Their struggle and the loss of energy is plain to see by everyone in the organization or community. This struggle concerns those who watch it—in the workshop and in real-life situations. It diverts your attention away from the original focus.

Jim, you are at an impasse, you need help. I want you to get some help from someone in the group.

Jim looks back over his shoulder and cries for help: "Frank, come help me." (Frank does this and moves to push against Jim's back.)

Jon (responding in kind, looking over his shoulder): "Jack, come help me." (Jack does this, pushing against Jon's back.)

These people respond, pushing in the direction of their friend. A representation of *I have your back!* As the two continue to ask for help, others join in the pushing and shoving, until there are two groups of four people pushing in opposite directions, two groups of struggling individuals. There is much fun and laughter in doing this.

Finding New Ground

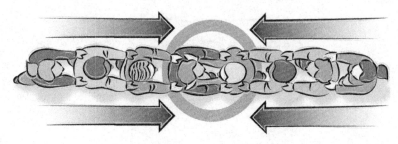

An intergroup conflict.

Frank looks across the line of people and sees Jack.

"Jack!" he exclaims, "What the hell are you doing over there? Why aren't you on my side?"

Jack replies: "Because this is the right side. Why are you over there?"

Then I suddenly ask them all to **freeze!**

What has happened to all the energy of these people? I ask rhetorically. Why did they join this conflict? How much of their energy is now available for their work?"

People joined this fray out of loyalty to their friends. They may not even know what the argument is about. But they have chosen a side now, and in so doing have created an intergroup conflict. Some friends will realize they have chosen opposite sides of the argument. This negatively alters their relationships. This refocuses the energy of the group on the conflict, instead of their work.

Tapping the energy of the conflict:

The two groups are still leaning against each other, their energy tied up. I point to the two principals:

Jim and Jon are the people who have the conflict. It is strong enough that they are willing to push against each other to see who can be right. It is strong enough that they will ask for help from their friends.

Jon and Jim are important to the group because they make you understand there is a conflict, that it needs attention. This is their role for the larger group or community. Instead of joining them, their friends need to understand this is not their conflict, but they can help to resolve the conflict.

So, why join them? Instead, form a group of interested friends and help them to solve the conflict.

I move the pushers from the backs of their friends until the entire group stands in a circle around their friends. We now have a full circle.

Defining Conflict

Reframing to a circle.

So now you can form a circle to listen to these two explain what the issue is and why they are expending such energy on it. (What is the situation, and how do you feel?) Your purpose is then to tell them what you heard and what your perception is of the situation. This moves the energy from the two protagonists to the larger group. It allows the two protagonists to hear what they said from others, reducing their emotions so they can move to their rational brain.

This is just the start of the process for becoming aware of, understanding, and then confronting an issue. And you need these two to make you aware of the conflict, to help you understand the differing views and then confront the issue. We will actually do this tomorrow.

I want you to all stand and honor these folks for doing this for the whole group.

The entire group stands and honors those who participated in this learning exercise. They have helped them see that conflict is more than difference; it includes power. When one person decides that the other must do what he wants, then energy must be exerted to make that happen. If the other resists, then there is conflict. This is interpersonal at this stage. But if others are asked to join and do so out of loyalty, then an intergroup conflict results. It takes power to make that happen.

And they have seen themselves in the center, knowing they have their energy tied up in their conflict, which diverts their attention from the real issues. They know they can play a different role, tapping the energy of the two to become aware of and confront an issue.

Now, let's look at the consequences of that unresolved conflict in your environments.

The Evidence of Unresolved Conflict

I want the community to understand the impact of that unresolved conflict between Jim and Jon in their environment, whether at home, at work, or in the community. I turn the session over to Mike, and he has the group recorders who answered the question "What is the evidence that unresolved conflict is present in your environments, and how do you feel about it?" read off their statements.

Mike: "Let's start with Group 1 and then Group 2. Have your recorders read off what is on the flip chart. Be aware that these statements describe in words the outcomes of the pushing and shoving you just saw."

GROUP 1: THE EVIDENCE OF UNRESOLVED CONFLICT IN OUR ENVIRONMENTS

- *People are frustrated, and can be seen grumbling when someone leaves the room.*
- *Some people totally avoid one another.*
- *There is a reluctance to share specific incidents and outward statements. "I don't want to get involved."*
- *We are not effective. The lack of communication hampers people from getting projects completed or studies done.*
- *There is back biting and gossiping—a divided staff.*

> - *People take small problems and make them into large conflicts, because they don't resolve small issues.*
> - *There is a tension like a rubber band ready to snap.*
> - *We see bad attitudes, low morale, and negative talk.*
> - *It is exhausting our energy with grievances.*
> - *How We Feel*
> - *I feel very uncomfortable and I want to fix it.*
> - *Feelings that occur as a result of this are sadness, anger.*
> - *Some of us are challenged. I always thought it was good to disagree as long as you understand why you disagree.*
> - *It is uncomfortable, with a feeling of hopelessness, like nothing can be done about it.*
> - *I feel reluctantly responsible. It feels like it's my problem.*
> - *I feel this really stifles creativity and collaboration.*
> - *I think there are opportunities that are being missed.*
> - *I am exhausted and tired of caring. I just feel I want to get the work done.*
> - *Conflicts are natural because of our diversity...but we have to get them resolved.*
> - *It feels that people are discussing the same things for four to five years, and nothing gets resolved.*

The recorders for Groups 1 and 2 stand and read off the recorded information in turn. Note that Group 1 separated their definition and feelings statements.

After the recorded information has been presented, I move to the edge of the circle and get the group's attention by just standing there. Then I provide them an insight into what we did.

The Reality of Conflict: An Insight

> *"Conflict is when instead of a line in the sand there is a crater in the ground."*

> **—Workshop participant**

Describing "the evidence of unresolved conflict in your environment" provides a description of the reality of conflict in your life. It identifies the indicators that you have unresolved conflicts. It is a description of the environment you have created as a result of these unresolved conflicts where people are struggling against each other. As the visual activity demonstrated, this is how your energy is tied up.

It is not unusual for clients to tell me during interviews that they have no conflicts and cannot understand why I have been brought in to help them. They do not feel they need help and are offended by my being there. During the grounding in the workshop, this is often expressed.

"Why are we here? We don't have any conflicts that I know of."

It makes me feel crazy...wondering, have I been brought here for no reason at all?

Then, when they answer this task question during the workshop, they will fill the flip charts up with numerous examples of the evidence of unresolved conflict, as you just did. What is going on here?

You are typically not fully conscious of this environment. You become so used to the consequences of the unresolved conflicts, so used to the toxic environment created, that it seems natural to you, an expected and accepted condition. You are operating from your reptilian brain.

Oh, you will complain about it. It makes good fodder for group discussions in the lunch room or over coffee or out in the parking lot. But you will take no actions to correct it. If you did, what would you talk about? In fact, your actions will tend to solidify the situation.

By asking this question, I am making you conscious of the impact that unresolved conflicts have in your environments—in the community, in the home, and at work. Once you become conscious of this, of how it eats up your energy, then you may want to do something about it.

The evidence you just described is the consequence of adding power to difference. In the visual activity, you were able to see and feel how your energy becomes bound up by the constant power struggle, taking your focus and energy away from your real purposes.

Why don't you resolve these issues? Because you have such a negative sense about conflict, it is difficult to do this. When defining conflict, 75 percent of the participants have negative feelings. Only one in four (25 percent) contribute positive feelings about the conflict definition. This is heavy weighting toward avoidance.

But it gets worse when exploring "the evidence of unresolved conflict in their environment." When confronted with the reality of unresolved conflict, in groups I have worked with, 90 percent of the participants had negative feelings about the situation, while only 10 percent had positive feelings.

This does not bode well for confronting and resolving the conflicts. It results in avoidance, in the acceptance of a toxic relationship environment as normal. Many will not confront the conflict because of an old saying: "The devil you know is safer than the devil you don't know."

People feel more positive about the abstract notion of conflict, but more negative when confronted with the reality of its existence. In our next activity, you are going to explore and understand why people feel so negative about conflict and unresolved conflict.

The reports from all the groups are later developed into collective statements. You will read about and experience this process later in the book. Simply put, all the words recorded on the flip charts are organized so they provide a collective view of the situation in the community.

~25~

The Worst Possible Outcomes of Conflict

Break and Coaching the Cofacilitators

Normally, this is a good time for the group to take a three p.m. break. YOU step to the edge of the circle when I have completed my insights and say:

"We will all take a ten minute break. Please return when it is three fifteen."

The group heads for the coffee and soda bar, pairing off or talking in trios. It is always interesting at this time to note that people talking with each other are from the different perspectives. This is an indication that *groupthink* is beginning to shatter, and new relationships are forming among the groups.

While the small groups were exploring conflict, YOU and Mike have been coaching Laura and Wayne in the art of cofacilitating. Laura and Wayne observed Mike as he facilitated the group, and they later give feedback to Mike.

I review the approach we will use after the break with the four cofacilitators:

After the break, Laura will facilitate the next activity. This is the card she will use.

I pass the card to Laura and have her read off the questions.

What are the worst possible outcomes of...

    Confronting (2 groups)
    Not confronting (2 groups)

...unresolved conflict in your environment?

The facilitator picks a new facilitator and becomes the recorder.

Laura, there are two questions. The groups have just listened to the evidence of unresolved conflict in their environment; now I want them to look at their worst possible outcomes of confronting and not confronting these unresolved conflicts.

The first question will be assigned to Groups 1 and 2: "What are the worst possible outcomes of confronting the unresolved conflicts in your environment?" The second question will be assigned to Groups 3 and 4: "What are the worst possible outcomes of **not** confronting the unresolved conflict in your environment?"

After you assign the questions, direct the facilitator of each group to select another facilitator and become the recorder. Mike, you will observe Laura and coach her when she is done.

I have Laura repeat her assignment. Then we all take a well-deserved break.

The Worst Possible Outcomes of Unresolved Conflict: An Activity

After the break, I call participants together, reminding them to return to their small groups. They are always a little slow to do this. They are talking with each other, deep into conversations they are reluctant to end. I just keep repeating the statement in calm tones:

Please return to your groups. We are ready to start.

> ### GETTING THE GROUP'S ATTENTION: THE ART
>
> As participants become better acquainted with each other, begin to trust and learn from each other, it becomes increasingly difficult to get their attention to return to the circle. This is an automatic outcome of the process. They are reluctant to end their conversations.
>
> It does little good to yell at them, because they will often not hear it, or if they do, it adrenalizes them—not exactly the outcome you want. Sometimes members themselves will shout or whistle loudly to get others' attention. It startles them and moves them, but too abruptly!
>
> I find it easier to just repeat the statement in a facilitative tone, "Please return to your groups. We are ready to start." I will continue to repeat this until there is movement. Then I will start with the introduction to the next activity.
>
> If they are still in conversation, I will have a member of the group act as my herder, slowly moving them toward the circle: "Jim! Start moving those people into the circle for me, would you please?" Or, "Sam, clean out the hallways or outdoors for me."

When they are together in their small groups, I do a brief introduction:

Mike and YOU have been coaching Laura and Wayne in the art of cofacilitating. So you will begin to see them facilitate this afternoon.

Unresolved conflict in your environment occurs because people fear conflict, and they have no way of moving through that fear. This next activity will help you understand what is behind that fear and those negative feelings you have just recorded. Laura will facilitate this activity.

Laura steps up to the edge of the circle. Her self-consciousness is plain to see and feel. She shifts her feet, then settles down and reads from the card, obviously nervous:

"These are the questions you will answer: What are the worst possible outcomes of confronting or *not* confronting the unresolved conflict in your environment? Before you do that, I want the facilitator to pick another facilitator and become the recorder."

She pauses and waits while the groups do that. Then she continues with more confidence:

"I want Groups 1 and 2 to answer this question: What are the worst possible outcomes of *not* confronting unresolved conflicts in your environment?"

She pauses, looks at Groups 3 and 4, and says:

"I want Groups 3 and 4 to answer this question: What are the worst possible outcomes of *not* confronting unresolved conflicts in your environment?"

Laura reads the directions off a second time, then turns and walks away. Mike steps to her side and begins to talk about how she facilitated, giving his advice. YOU and Wayne walk over to be included in the conversation. They are now working as a team of facilitators, helping to coach each other, learning as they go. Often they will ask me to join them, to add additional insights. They often have questions of application to their family, work, or community.

The small groups are quickly at work, answering the questions and recording the answers. This is always an easy task. Worst possible outcomes are at the tip of their tongues, so the statements are quickly expressed in brief, often bulleted form. They know their fears, especially with the awareness created by the evidence of unresolved conflict in their environment. While they know their fears, rarely have they been able to express them as they are doing now. They are making themselves conscious of their fears.

Let's listen in on Group 1: Tony, Marie, Debbe, Jon, Alice, Susan, and Rayni:

Jon: "OK, who wants to be the facilitator...oops! I forgot, Bob said not to do that. Debbe, I want you to be the facilitator, and I'll record."

Debbe: "So much for having a choice! I've never done anything like this before, but I'll give it a try. Let me see, I guess we're supposed to talk about our worst possible outcomes for confronting conflict. Write that on the flip chart, Jon."

Jon: "OK, boss. You're catching on real quick." (Group laughter as he records the question on the flip chart.)

Debbe: "Alice, why don't you begin?"

Alice: "I love seeing a man record." (Laughter.) "Don't record that though. Let's see...*if we confront... We are not working it out and not coming to agreement. So...nothing will change.*"

Tony (pausing until Jon is done writing): *"They will 'shoot the messenger.'"*

Marie: *"The conflict begins to trickle down into your personal life, and the conflict goes home every night with you. I hate when that happens!"*

Susan: *"We will escalate the conflict so that it involves others who don't want to be involved or are not there."*

Rayni: "This is depressing! I have all those reasons and more...OK, Jon: *I hate conflict, so my personal inability to deal with conflict could end up by me being caught in the middle.*" (Pause.) "Jon, put the word **personal** before inability. Yes, now you got it."

Debbe: "Jon, you're next, so sit down, and I'll record for you."

Jon: *"Everyone involved never talks to each other again. I've had that happen to me before."*

Jon returns to the board when Debbe is done recording.

Debbe: *"If at first you don't succeed, you will never try again. I could get labeled as someone who causes problems."* (Pauses as Jon records.) *"There may be retribution that comes afterwards."*

Rayni (as Jon is recording): "Debbe, I had that happen to me, where I was labeled as a troublemaker because I tried to help solve a problem. I sure learned a lesson there—I won't do that again."

Debbe: "Laura wants to get our attention. Jon, you read off what we have when it is time."

This is Group 1's information on their flip chart:

Laura walks to the edge of the circle and asks the question: "Has everyone spoken at least once?"

> **GROUP 1: WORST OUTCOMES OF CONFRONTING**
> - *If we confront...We are not working it out and not coming to agreement. So...nothing will change.*
> - *They will shoot the messenger.*
> - *The conflict begins to trickle down into your personal life and the conflict goes home every night with you. I hate when that happens!*
> - *We will escalate the conflict so that it involves others who don't want to be involved or are not there.*
> - *This is depressing! I have all those reasons and more...I hate conflict, so my personal inability to deal with conflict could show by me being caught in the middle.*
> - *Everyone involved never talks to each other again. I've had that happen to me before.*
> - *If at first you don't succeed, you will never try again.*
> - *I could get labeled as someone who causes problems. There may be retribution that comes afterwards.*

She repeats the question until she has everyone's attention. All groups are ready, so she directs the recorders from Groups 1 and 2 to read off the information on their flip charts.

"Now, let's have Group 3 and 4 report out their worst possible outcomes of not confronting."

She steps back and Justin stands to read off the flip chart for "not confronting conflict." This is Group 3's recorded information:

> **GROUP 3: THE WORST POSSIBLE OUTCOMES OF NOT CONFRONTING**
> - *Problems remain unsolved and resurface. Never go away.*
> - *Conflicts do not get resolved/do not get fixed.*
> - *Problem may escalate, power struggles become greater/ this sometimes results in violence.*
> - *The conflict becomes institutionalized and becomes a way of life. It becomes an accepted mode of behavior, which leads to the preventing of reaching our goals within the community."*

The Worst Possible Outcomes of Conflict

> - *You get caught up in bad feelings and can't concentrate on what you have to do.*
> - *Frustration leads to hostility —> violence.*
> - *Like a cancer, if you don't work with it/check it, it will grow and grow.*
> - *Family/friends split often for generations, long after the issue is forgotten.*
> - *Will become depressed, disillusioned, become deceptive/turn to drugs.*
> - *People will feel isolated and alone.*
> - *Groups in conflict will alienate each other.*
> - *Conflicts take a tremendous amount of energy, therefore, we have tired people all of the time.*
> - *Causes irritability, pent up emotions, and uneasiness.*

As we listen to the information recorded for both questions, two things become apparent:

- The room becomes deadly silent, with a cloak of doom and gloom.
- The statements recorded for both questions appear to be almost the same.

When all the information has been shared, I make those points at the edge of the circle:

How many of you felt the mood of this room as you read off these statements? To me, it felt heavy. Feels depressing, doesn't it?

(People nod their heads.)

This is a result of being in your worst possible outcomes; you change your mood when you are there. Your brain is encompassed by fear of survival, even though nothing has happened yet. That's why the words "violence" and "hostility" are there. This is a possible overreaction to this situation.

How can you get together to solve your problem if you are feeling this way? You will just be working in an environment of dread! It is difficult at best to solve a problem this way.

And if you paid attention, you will notice that the statements to both questions are essentially the same. Both talk about nothing happening or changing. Both talk about the conflict getting worse. Both talk about possible violence.

Violence! When you use that word, you shift to your lower brain, and all your responses are now autonomic or automatic reflexes, without conscious thought. You now have only two choices: fight or flight. Most people take flight because of their worst possible outcomes. They avoid the conflict. When they do so, they enable the toxic working or living environment you described in the evidence of unresolved conflict.

Yet, listening to that description, who wants to live in that kind of environment? Unfortunately, many of us do and we accept it.

Others decide to fight, doing so out of their worst possible outcomes, and end up creating these outcomes because they don't know any other way. The result is as stated by a participant in Group 3:

> "The conflict becomes institutionalized and becomes a way of life. It becomes an accepted mode of behavior, which leads to the preventing of reaching our goals within the organization."

Creating Consciousness

Recording the worst possible outcomes is important in bringing them to your consciousness. Because worst possible outcomes center in the reptilian brain, they are autonomic, nonconscious material. You are not totally aware of how and why you are behaving as you do.

It is not unusual for a member of a community to stand up and rage before the elected officials, saying things that are ugly and abusive. He will later deny he said them. He is not lying, he is just not conscious of what he said.

Or, to say something, knowing it is wrong to say it, yet you do it. It is the lower brain managing you.

> *"Courage is not the absence of fear, but rather the judgment that something else is more important than fear."*
>
> —**Workshop participant**

Recording your worst possible outcomes allows you to be visually conscious of them. This allows you to decide if that is what you truly believe or want. It allows you to plan how to prevent them from happening.

Tomorrow will be a day for focusing on relationships and how you can build relationships of trust. I have an insight for you before we finish for the day that will help you with that.

~26~

A Relationship Process: An Insight

A Relationship Process

Of all the influences we have in our lives, relationships with others are perhaps the most important. We exist within relationships. We communicate through relationships; we have conflicts because of relationships; we demonstrate our power in relationships.

During the sixties and seventies, and earlier, many studies were done with groups, trying to understand the way in which relationships are formed. A series of developmental stages were identified that apply equally well to one-on-one relationships. These have been described in many ways, using different scientific terms, but I have found the following description the easiest to remember because it rhymes—referred to as a "mnemonic...a pattern of letters or words formulated as an aid to memory."

Forming...Storming...Norming...Performing.

Remember, though, that this process is a like a road map. It appears linear because it is described in stages, each following the other. In actual experience, we each go about this in very different ways. Some of us go through the stages fast, others slow. Some of us may skip a stage or go through it quickly, while some stages may be repeated. Be aware of this as I explain it to you, or as you explain it to others.

The following insight is an anecdote from my life that I share with you to explain the process for developing relationships. This anecdote is partly based on fact, with lots of fantasy and fun thrown in to keep your attention. It is intended to attach the process to a reality you can relate to vicariously.

Stage 1: Forming

We first meet as strangers, seeking something that will bind us. Our initial conversation is a search: "Where do you live, who do you know, what do you do? Do you know...? Have you ever been to...?" Each of these seeks some commonality that we can talk about, begin to develop a relationship around.

This is the time when similarities are important. We develop a relationship at a level that is safe. We like to be with people who are the same as us. This is the most nonthreatening stage of a relationship. There are some who seek difference, who purposefully seek out that which is different from them. Those they find are also seeking difference. This is their similarity as a basis for the relationship.

Some relationships we do not experience this stage in. A person who has been defined by yourself or others as the "enemy" is stereotyped. This person has little chance of "forming" a relationship with you, because others have already formed your perception. You start this relationship with the second stage: "Storming!"

Forming: An Anecdote

I almost bumped into her as I walked into the civil rights office to see my friend Sam. We were both startled and stepped back. I chuckled and stuck my hand out, introducing myself. She accepted and stated her name was Rosy. Rosy was evidently of American Indian descent. Since I had been on a National Forest created from the former Klamath Indian Reservation, I had heard of her position in the regional office from some of the Klamath tribal members.

"Stop in and see her," they said. "Both of you have an interest in helping the people in their relationship with the U.S. Forest Service and the lands they manage."

Since I was single at the time, it appeared they also had other plans for me.

So, after introducing myself, I invited her to coffee the next day, if she had the time. It took a few days before we had the opportunity to do this. We shared coffee-break time and talked about our mutual interests. We decided to partner in creating better relationships between the tribes and the National Forest managers. In the next five years, we had many opportunities to do this.

As we worked together professionally, we began to develop a personal relationship. We both came from large families and enjoyed the tradition of the holidays that brought our families together. As a result, we often shared our holiday traditions with each other, enjoying the stories we told of our family experiences.

A Relationship Process:

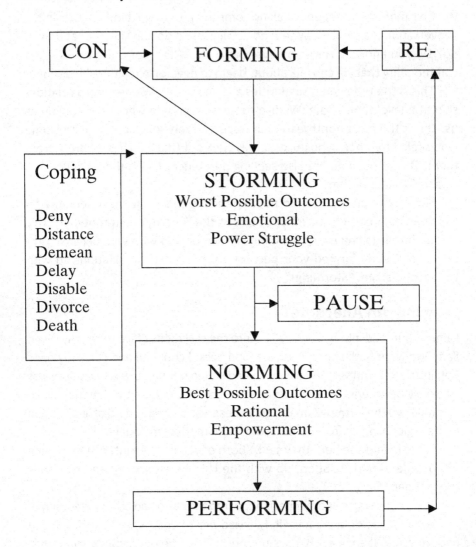

We also attended tribal conferences together, which provided us an opportunity to have meals together, as well as attend social events. In time, six years later, we developed a close friendship. In time, it developed beyond that.

One day we looked at each other, and everything seemed to change.

"How long have we known each other?" I asked.

"Six years," she answered, a smile on her face.

"Long enough to go beyond friends, don't you think?" I asked.

"I wondered when you would notice," she answered.

That began our time of courting each other. During that time we got to know each other on a more intimate and personal level. We talked about all the things we liked, about all the things we could do if we brought our two families together, since we were both interested in managing diversity. We saw the merging of our two families as an opportunity for each to learn.

The result was that we married in the moment, in Las Vegas. The week after we returned, Rosy moved into my apartment and immediately began to distribute her belongings.

"Where will I put my picture?" she asked.

"Well," I said, "the walls are already pretty well filled with my pictures, so...maybe we could store them. Or maybe put them up in the garage?"

Neither of these suggestions fit, so the pictures remained in boxes for a long while. Both of us felt a little strange about that, but the newness of our relationship and the happiness we shared allowed us to put it aside.

This is the forming stage, a time more relaxed, getting to know each other. Now we are ready for the storming stage.

I point to the flip chart with the process on it.

Stage 2: Storming

This stage begins when we are confronted with our differences. Because we are curious creatures, we are normally unwilling to be satisfied with the boredom of sameness. We begin to test the boundaries of our relationship. We begin to try to mold the other person to meet our needs and expectations.

In some way, we are all different from each other. We differ in our ages, our cultures, our experiences growing up. We want the other person to look like us, act like us, believe like us. In truth, to just be a mirror image of us so we can feel safe.

Shortly after Rosy and I were married, we realized Christmas was close.

"Well," I said, "I can't wait until we go into the forest and select a beautiful white fir tree for our Christmas tree. You will just enjoy this experience so much!"

"Why go out in the forest?" she asked, a shocked look on her face. "I'm not going to tramp in the snow in the forest to get a Christmas tree! The snow will be over my head! Why don't we just go down to the supermarket and buy one of those spruce trees they have?"

"A spruce tree? You have got to be kidding? Why would we get one of those old and dried-out trees when we can get a beautiful, fresh-smelling white fir? Besides, spruce needles are sharp and hard to work with."

"White fir trees don't smell good at all!" she stated emphatically. "They don't call them 'piss firs' for nothing! You know they stink!"

"Well, that may be true, but you don't notice the smell after a while; it just disappears. You forget about it and enjoy the view. Especially when you get the tree decorated. You will like it with my white Christmas bulbs."

"White bulbs? I don't like those at all—they are boring. I like the colored sparkly lights that go on and off."

"Oh, man! You have just described the worst thing for me. Whenever I walk into the room with those blinking bulbs, they make me anxious. I get nervous twitches in my shoulder. My nerves keep jumping up and down with the bulbs. Besides, when you throw the tinsel on the tree, it just slides down the tree in a very natural way, it covers the white bulbs, and they glow through the tinsel. It is beautiful to see."

"Throw the tinsel on the tree?" She frowned and glared with her deep brown eyes. "You just throw the tinsel on the tree?"

"Well, no, I don't just throw it! There is an art to it! You have to know how to do it so that it gets a proper fit."

"Well, I'll pass on that. I like to put tinsel on one piece at a time," she said.

"One piece at a time? Oh my God, that will take days. That's almost four thousand pieces of tinsel. It is much easier to just throw the tinsel on the tree, believe me."

Thus began our first real argument. We had common beliefs about the ritual of Christmas, but we differed strongly in the traditional ways that carried them out. We were now *storming*!

Con-forming: I look at the participants with a serious stubborn face.

In my English culture, the male is the final authority. I will get to decide! I expect my wife to comply, to go back to the "forming stage" and "conform" to my desires (there is an ominous stir among the women, followed by laughter) This is the approach I was taught to use in my culture. It is the normal approach we all use: just conform to my wishes. Go back to being like me.

I learned to conform to authority, to what was expected. In fact, my generation was known as the "age of conformity." We wore the same clothes, worked an eight-to-five shift, had "standard" job descriptions, worked to "keep up with the Joneses." They wrote books about us. (*The Age of Conformity*, Alan Valentine, 1954.)

My wife, however, was younger, a feminist, coming from the age of rebellion, the sixties. She was also American Indian, which is often a matriarchy, and decisions such as this are left up to the woman. If she decided she would not conform, she had every right to have a say in this issue.

Now we were entering the stage of storming. We had different approaches to the Christmas tree that had to be resolved. Normally they are resolved by you conforming to my needs, so that you continue to "look like me." That is the safest, most stable relationship to have. (It is also the most boring, uninteresting relationship to have.)

"Not to worry, Rosy," I intoned in my deepest alpha-male voice. "In my culture, the English culture, a man makes these decisions. Come on, Rosy, you will enjoy the white fir tree. Especially when it is decorated with my bulbs and tinsel."

"Well, I am worried," she said. "When my family sees that, it will be offensive to them. They want to see their tradition. And besides, in my culture, it is the woman who makes these decisions. So, prepare yourself to enjoy a spruce tree with blinking bulbs. And, I am hoping you will help me put tinsel on…one…piece…at a….time," she said slowly and pointedly.

Needless to say, both of us being very stubborn, both of us being very loyal to our own cultures and traditions, we got into a contentious argument over who was going to have their way. The result is we both stomped off mad—Rosy to our bedroom, I to the basement workshop.

There I took my hammer and banged on everything within reach to release my frustration. When I'm in that mood, with hammer in hand, anything appears to me to be a nail.

What is going on here is demonstrated on the flip chart. Each of us wants the other person to conform their views to our tradition. Conformity means that when we look at each other, we see no difference. It is just a mirror image.

What if you look in the mirror and see difference? What do you do if you have a spouse who is stubborn and will not conform?

You cope!

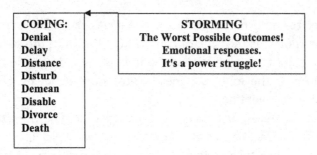

Storming Behaviors

What if you don't conform? What if you stand up for your views? Then I must "force" you, and that is the beginning of the "power struggle," the beginning of real conflict. If I am a flight person, I will appear to comply and move the storming to the nonverbal arena, by resisting quietly, with passive aggression.

If I am a fight person, I will pit my power against yours. We are in a power struggle; a real storm is occurring. We are now reactive, emotional, motivated by worst outcomes. This results in the underlying responses that affect our words and behaviors.

The Worst Possible Outcomes: As soon as the differences are exposed and confronted, the parties immediately respond from their worst possible outcomes. These are numerous, but certainly include:

- "Yikes, this could destroy our relationship! We won't know how to solve this. I could lose something important to me."
- "I'll lose her respect and love if I can't solve this."
- "This could escalate and affect the other members of my family."
- "OMG! We could get violent like my parents did!"

Emotional: Our emotions are immediately engaged, all based on fear.

- "I am soooo uncomfortable, defensive, I can feel my blood pressure rise."

- "It's scary, threatening, intimidating...I want to stay and I want to run away."
- "I am worried about controlling my anger and myself."
- "This is so stupid, such wasted energy, just go along with me!"

A Power Struggle: We are now pitted against one another, struggling to win for the sake of our family traditions, for protection of our personal egos, unwilling to give in.

- "If she wins she will have all the power in the relationship. I'll never get my say in the future."
- "What if the guys hear about this? I could lose my alpha-male status!"

Coping Strategies:

There are an infinite number of possible approaches for coping with conflicts. We use these every day without being conscious of them. While the approaches are many, there are some common ones you will recognize.

Denial: *"We really don't have a problem. I think we are saying the same thing, and I know we both want to enjoy Christmas. So I know we will get it done (my way!)"*

This is the easiest approach. Just deny at a superficial level that a problem exists, and hope it resolves itself in your favor.

But it doesn't go away. And at some level, you are aware of this.

Distance: *Rosy heads for the bedroom; I head for the basement.* We distance ourselves, getting as far away from each other as we can. If you are good at reading nonverbal behavior, you can tell when my spouse and I are not getting along. Just look at the distance between us when we stand in the room. If we are really in sync, we will be touching. If we are really angry, she'll be in one room, I will be in the other.

If we happen to meet each other in the hallway, we back up against the opposite walls, trying not to come in contact. If we happen to come into the kitchen for a cup of coffee at the same time, we don't look at each other. Our eyes focus on the ceiling, on the floor, off to the side, on the TV, anywhere but on our spouse. This is distancing—the use of space to reduce the tension between the adversaries.

Organizations use this approach when they have two employees who just can't seem to get along. It is labeled a "personality problem." They solve the problem by moving the employees to separate buildings, or separate departments, attempting to keep them apart. They don't solve the problem; it still exists. Eventually, the problem will just raise its head again in those new locations.

Delay: *"Let's solve this later, when the time is better."* We delay dealing with the issue, waiting until after the family dinner, or until after Thanksgiving, or until the last minute, when the decision must be made. A delay gives us a space in which we hope that somehow some magical solution will happen. Unfortunately, new excuses are found to avoid the issue: "I'm tired, we'll do it later." "Can't we wait until the..."

Demean: We talk mean about each other. We demean each other with other people. *"Yes, he is articulate, but he never stops talking." "If I've heard that story once, I've heard it a thousand times."* We take attributes that used to be charming or something to be proud of and reverse our feeling about them. This is a way of getting even, but the conflict is not resolved.

Disable: We get in each other's way. I am watching the football game on TV, trying to calm my feelings, when Rosy decides she's going to vacuum the living room. She starts in front of the TV, of course! Just as the last play of the game occurs! I miss the sight and sound of the play. This results in an angry dialogue between the two of us.

Not to worry, I think. When her parents show up this afternoon for dinner, I'll decide to work on the garbage disposal in the kitchen while she's cooking. We'll just get in each other's way, trying to get even.

Or worse, we physically disable each other, resorting to physical violence.

Divorce: *"If I can't have it my way, then it's the highway!"* If the problem persists and our coping strategies don't work, and we have no other out, then what we do is end the relationship. But when we leave the relationship, we bring the unresolved conflict with us. When we enter any new relationship, that unresolved conflict is perching on our shoulders, like a vulture, waiting to jump. *"Wherever I go, there I am!"*

The employee who keeps getting moved because of "personality problems" says, *"I'm quitting! I have been moved to fifteen departments now, trying to solve conflicts. I always end up being the responsible one. I don't want to be moved anymore. I'll move myself. I quit!"*

> **WHEREVER YOU GO, THERE YOU ARE**
>
> Avoiding the conflict rarely solves anything. Unless you are one of the lucky few who learn, you will carry the unresolved conflict with you, it is a part of you. It is you.
>
> Without consciously knowing it, you will seek out people and situations that will bring the conflict to the surface again—at least until you learn the lesson of the conflict and change who you are.

Death: Increasingly today, unresolved conflict leads to death: the "post-office syndrome," "automobile-factory-worker syndrome," "student-killing-student syndrome." These are all a result of years of unresolved conflicts piling one upon the other until the burden is too great for one person. People who live under relentless, unremitting conflict will eventually break.

The way they solve the problem then is: "I shoot you, I shoot our boss, I shoot me." Problem solved!

The Cost of Coping—The Startle Response

All of these are just coping approaches. None of them solves the conflict. In each there is a hope that somehow the conflict will resolve itself, just melt away. It doesn't. This is especially true if you're stubborn people.

If I am angry at you at work, I may not even let you know. But I go home and stew about it. I kick the dog, I get angry at my wife, I shout at the kids; but the issue that underlies these behaviors is the conflict with you that I am avoiding.

When I see you drive into the parking lot next to me, I am startled. My whole being is jolted, like an electric shock. I keep my head down, I avoid recognizing you. I don't want to acknowledge or talk with you. My heart beats fast. I'm reminded of my anger. I curse. My day is ruined. I have a hard time focusing, unable to clearly think because of my anger.

During the day, when I walk into the staff room, I open the door and see you there. Alarmed, I close the door, turn, and quickly walk away, ashamed of my cowardly response. That "startle" response jumps inside me, a reminder that we have this unresolved conflict between us.

I am reminded of my unresolved anger each day, each week, and each month that I see you. The unresolved conflict finds a place in my body, and each time I think of it, I add additional layers of alarm over my anger. It's like earning interest on money in a bank.

I may clench my jaw when awake and then when sleeping. I may tense my muscles and begin to get cramps in them. The weight of the anger gets bigger and heavier, so I add weight to my body. I may become depressed, my immune system is weakened, and I begin to get sick more often.

I talk to other people about it and infect them with the conflict. I ask other people to take my side and create an intergroup conflict. During all this time, I have avoided you. You may not even be aware that you are in a conflict with me.

Trying to force people to conform just does not work today. It worked when I was a child because we paid attention to authorities. They were more powerful than us, they had more education, and they were bigger than us, so we were used to conforming, accepting our lot.

But the conformity approach went out the window in the seventies. People want their individuality, they want to advocate for who they are. People are more empowered, educated, and economically secure, so they will not be forced into conformity. They resist instead. The only option left is to go through the storming and find the way to the next stage: norming.

How can we do that? Well, I found it helps to have a pause.

Stage 2a: The Pause that Refreshes

> **PAUSE**

I don't know if this stage is referred to in the behavioral literature, but I have observed it is necessary. Once the confrontation occurs, a pause is instrumental in facilitating the norming. The pause is similar to "distancing" in that it allows some time to consider, to adapt.

In a consensus session, I will provide a break after a group has described the situation and explored their worst possible outcomes of the situation. This leads them through the storming and prepares them for the norming. A break allows the mind to reconsider the situation, to reassess the severity of the worst outcomes.

After the pause, exploring the best possible outcomes can develop the basis for the norming. Developing beliefs and behaviors that foster the best possible outcomes are part of norming.

After confronting each other, often in a reactive way, Rosy and I will separate, go to different rooms, or I may go for a walk. This allows us to think about what was said, to reassess our emotional reaction, to become more proactive. We can decide how much we overstated our case. We can decide how much of our connection to the way we do it is "loyalty" to the past or to family traditions. We can reconsider the points of the other party.

If during the "pause" you become aware of your worst possible outcomes, aware of the consequence of behaving out of them, you will naturally begin to consider the best possible outcomes. It is this awareness that makes it happen.

Do I really want to be down here in the basement mad for the rest of our relationship? Do I want to lose what I have? NO! I overreacted out of my worst fears. It is not what I want. I want to behave out of my best possible outcomes, to strengthen our relationship, not weaken it. I need to sit down with Rosy with a more sober outlook and see if we can create a solution for this.

Now we are ready for "norming."

Stage 3: Norming

> **NORMING**
> **Best Possible Outcomes**
> **Rational**
> **Empowerment**

In this stage, the participants recognize that these differences must somehow be dealt with in a mature and grown-up way. A decision must be made that the relationship is too important to end. The participants must first affirm that the differences exist. They seek to understand why they are present. This means learning to understand the other person better. Then the question is asked:

How can we have these differences and still remain in the relationship?

For Rosy and I, the answer was obvious. The relationship was too important to be the cause of dissension.

I had worn out my anger in the basement. I had lots of time to reconsider. I walked up the stairs and into the kitchen to get a cup of coffee. I saw Rosy in the living room, picking up clothes. They looked like mine. I thought about how much I love her. I poured a cup of coffee for her and brought it into the living room.

"Let's have a cup of coffee and just talk for a while."

She accepted the coffee, and we sat together on the couch.

"Boy, I just can't believe how angry we got over this whole issue of the Christmas tree."

"I know," she said sadly. "It scared me. On the one hand, I'm worried about what my family will think if we don't have a tree like we're used to, and on the other hand, I'm afraid you will be so angry about this that you will leave me."

"Well, I don't think that's going to happen. I committed myself to you for the rest of our lives. I am worried, too, that when my kids come over and see your tree, they will feel offended, like I've been disloyal to them. And I worry that it would become an issue we never resolve, never talk about again, so that we just don't have a good relationship."

"Well," said Rosy, "thinking about it, I want us to have a Christmas that blends what we both have. We have a blended family, so let's have a blended Christmas. Our families will adjust."

"I agree. Let's have your spruce from the supermarket."

"And you can have your white bulbs," Rosy said. "Then you won't be walking around twitching all the time."

"And I am OK if you put the tinsel on the tree one piece at a time, just as long as I don't have to do it," I said jokingly.

And so we had a pretty good Christmas that year, though each of the families were unsettled by how we had blended our traditions. But they saw enough of their traditions that they accepted it.

I do have to admit it was difficult to watch Rosy put the tinsel on a piece at a time. She even picked up the tinsel that fell on the rug and replaced it on the tree. My way? Just kick it under the tree apron. It took a lot of patience, and I admired her for it, but...too much patience for me.

For the next Christmas, Rosy showed me a large box of potpourri she had purchased.

"I want you to have your white fir this year," she said, "so I have this potpourri to cover the smell in the room. It will smell like orange spice, and that feels like a real Christmas."

"Well, then let's use your blinking light bulbs this year, and I'll just stay out of the living room when they're on."

"And," she said with a twinkle in her eye, "you can show me how to put the tinsel on the tree by throwing it."

Wow, I couldn't believe it! She actually was willing to let me show her how I threw the tinsel on the tree. It was exciting.

Once the Christmas tree was up and I had put the blinky bulbs on it (but didn't turn them on), I prepared the room for the tinsel.

"You'll have to stay in one place," I told Rosy. "Don't move. The slightest movement of air will throw my toss off. Disconnect the phone so you won't have to answer it if it rings. Lock the front door so nobody can come in. Turn the heat down so there is no movement of air. Shut off the ceiling fan."

I then took out a package of tinsel and, with my hands, began to spread it into a fan, in that instinctive way I had developed over years and years of experience. Finally, when it was separated enough, I was ready. I slowly turned to the left and, in a smooth clockwise move, threw the tinsel toward the treetop. It hit the tree and slid down the branches, distributing the tinsel in a flow. It was a glorious toss. One of my best!

It was so stunning that Rosy drew in her breath in awe; she couldn't help it. It was so flawless. Of course, that movement of air affected the way the tinsel landed on the tree. It had a little hitch in it. Well, I couldn't blame her, it was so beautiful to see.

I gave her a packet of tinsel, helped her take out the tinsel, helped her as she spread it out, and then stood aside as she prepared for her throw. She leaned to the right because she was right-handed and threw the tinsel in the air, aiming at the top of the tree. Well, I was so concerned that she do it right that I sort of moved as if I were throwing it myself. Of course, that affected the way the tinsel landed on the tree. It slid down, covering up the other in an irregular pattern.

It was not a perfect throw, for sure. But then, it was her first time. And you know what? Despite myself, I have to admit the way the tinsel lay created the most beautiful tree I had ever seen. Somehow it just seemed more natural, perfect...because it was imperfect. We looked at each other and laughed. What a hoot!

We had a great Christmas that year—although her family did comment on the twitch I had in my shoulder whenever I came into the room when the blinkety bulbs were on. Rosy assured them it was temporary.

We had begun to seriously norm, adapting slowly so we were able to accept and appreciate each other's differences. We were proactive, thinking our relationship through, fostering best outcomes.

The Best Possible Outcomes: Moving to best possible outcomes requires a conscious hope for a future positive outcome whose value is greater than always being "right!" It needs to be something that brings us closer together. We want to help our own families to learn to accept difference. And we want to create a tradition that is ours:

"*I committed myself to you for the rest of our lives.*"

"*I want us to have a Christmas that blends what we both have.*"

Rational or Logical Responses: Once we begin norming, we move from the emotional state to the logical state. We move from our lower brain to the mammalian brain, allowing us to see possible approaches that will foster these outcomes.

"*We have a blended family, so let's have a blended Christmas. Our families will adjust.*"

"*I agree. Let's have your spruce from the supermarket.*"

"*And you can have your white bulbs.*"

"*And I am OK if you put the tinsel on the tree one piece at a time, just as long as I don't have to do it.*"

Empowerment: This allows us to be empowered, to take actions that are for the good of both and the families. We are not stuck in fear, anger, coping with unresolved conflict. We are working our way to a solution that fits us at this time.

Stage 4: Performing

From this point on, once the norming is established, the relationship can perform at peak levels. There is still difference, but it adds to the richness of the relationship experience because it is understood, accepted, appreciated. The relationship flows in a natural way, saving time because there is a common focus and an understood approach.

The following year, we bought the prettiest tree we had ever seen. We both liked it, a noble fir. We also bought some new bulbs. And, believe it or not, I found the patience to decorate the tree with her, a strand of tinsel at a time. We enjoyed the experience together. Each time I glanced at her, I felt this sense of love and pride. It was truly a magnificent evening. And our families enjoyed the new tree and decorations.

PERFORMING

Now we are performing. We are experiencing each Christmas differently. One Christmas we even had a large larch tree, which loses its needles in the fall. It looked like the skeleton of a tree. We called it our Charlie Brown tree. When it was decorated, it was beautiful.

Stage 5: Storming–Reforming

But wait, are you worried that we won't have any more conflict? Are you worried that we will become bored? Not to worry.

Rarely will a relationship remain for long in the performing stage. The journey through the storming to the norming stage will cause movement and growth in each person. This changes the nature of our perceptions and our information base. These changes, in turn, affect our beliefs and behaviors. We will become different people.

> **RE-FORMING**

In time, a new issue will arise between the parties. One party will want to do something new and different, as a result of personal growth. The result is a movement to storming and, as resistance builds, a desire for conforming or reforming again. The other party resists, wanting to keep things in the new and accepted way, wanting the other to conform to this new way.

That following Easter, Rosy said we were again invited to her mother's for dinner.

But I said: "Hey, how about we go to my mother's place this year? You haven't met her yet, and we can enjoy the family in the east."

"Oh, I can't do that," Rosy said. "I have to be here for Easter."

"Why is it so important for you to be here for Easter?" I was trying to understand.

"I have to be there because I'm the one who cooks the ham."

"Why?" I responded. "Your sister Bonnie knows how to cook a ham."

"She makes the salad," Rosy said crossly.

"Well, why can't she make the ham too?," I said impatiently.

"She just can't, that's all. This is the tradition we have in our family."

"But that means I will never get to have Easter with you at my mother's home. Then I'm not going to dinner!" We just moved to Re-Forming!

We both realized we had just entered into another conflict. We looked at each other and smiled. "I know," I said. "Think this through."

This will require the relationship to repeat the process for forming, storming, and norming in order to return to performing.

The cycle is continuous, to be repeated as each person continues to grow and seek to reach his or her potential. Yet the desire will continue to be to seek stability, to have conformity, to make the other persona a replica of yourself. That approach is easier, on the surface, and the reactive and emotional storming stage can be avoided. But not for long!

~27~

The Closure

The Closure: An Activity

The last task of the day is the closure. While the small groups are working, I meet with the four cofacilitators to assign that next task.

Wayne, you are going to facilitate the last question of the day. This activity is called the closure. It allows people to look back at their day and assess it. We ask two questions that we want them to answer:

> Close your circle, do not record, the last facilitator is the facilitator.
>
> *How do you feel about today?*
>
> *What did you learn that will help you resolve the conflicts in your environment?*

Before you read these questions, ask the groups to close their circles. Tell them not to record; this is a talking circle. And the last facilitator will facilitate this task.

When all groups have reported on their worst possible outcomes, I speak to them about the implications of that task. Then I turn the group over to Wayne. He walks to the edge of the large circle and asks them to close their small groups' circles. Wayne is a large, bearded man, so when he walks to the edge of the circle, he is noticed right away. The group gives him their attention. They do this with a scraping of chairs and much laughter.

"You will not record this task. It is a talking circle. The facilitator for the last task will facilitate this. Please answer the following questions:

"How do you feel about today?

"What did you learn that will help us resolve the conflicts in our environment?"

He turns and walks away, a smile on his face.

"Wow, that was really easy. They just went right to work. I didn't have to hardly do anything."

You are learning this by doing, I say. Now, Mike, Laura, and Wayne, I want you to join your groups, or a group, to experience this closure. I will do the final insights for the day after the closure.

The groups are highly engaged. Even though they had worked all day, they still take their assignment seriously. Their heads are leaning in as they listen to each other. There are bursts of healthy laughter.

I am always amazed at how seriously people will take each of the tasks. The closure at the end of the day is an example. These people have been with each other for nine hours now. Most of that time, they have been talking with each other, facilitating their own process, recording their own information. They are now exchanging personal information about each other as they talk.

I know they are tired. So my expectation is that they will answer the two questions quickly, knowing they will be able to leave soon. Surely they must be thinking, "What a relief that will be!"

The opposite happens. What could take less than ten minutes often takes thirty to sixty minutes. There are no signs now of tiredness or resistance. They are seriously engaged with each other, sharing information and ideas, listening to each other, nodding heads in agreement. It is a significant time for them.

I Have a Plane to Catch: An Anecdote for the Reader

They were a school district leadership team in the last day of a three-day session. They were brought together to address and resolve the conflicts between the leadership in the central office and in the separate buildings. Substantial progress had been made. Issues had been identified, and purpose developed around those issues. Confrontations over different views had gone well, and the group had a sense of togetherness, of community, as a result. Today they would develop a set of strategies that would move them forward toward their purpose.

Before we started in the morning, five members of the group advised me that they had planes to catch later in the afternoon, so they might have to leave before it was all over. They assured me that they were reluctant to leave but had these previous commitments.

I suggested we start the final closure after an early lunch, and I would allow them to start first. Then they could leave at an appropriate time for their flights. They agreed to this.

After the early lunch, the group of forty-seven people sat in the large talking circle to do the closure for the workshop. They were asked to answer the following question on a three-by-five card:

"If you are to be successful, what is the next step that needs to be taken?"

They recorded their answers in silence. When they were done, they were asked to answer the closure questions—"How do you feel about this three days?" and "What did you learn that will make us successful?"—and then read off their answers from their three-by-five card to the question "If you are to be successful, what is the next step that needs to be taken?"

The group had been successful earlier in developing a set of strategies and actions that they committed to. The closure began just shortly after noon. I started with those who needed to leave early, as I had promised. All stayed in the circle since they still had some time before they needed to leave. There were more than forty additional people who still had to speak.

Two hours later they were still in the talking circle, which had gone only halfway around. The closure was taking much longer than I anticipated, despite the fact that they had spent two and a half days together already. I also noticed that none of those who needed to leave early had left yet.

At about two thirty p.m., I noticed that some of those who had spoken to me were leaving, but their possessions were still by their chairs. Each of them returned a little bit later. I assumed and later confirmed that they had made arrangements to reschedule their flights. Only one of the five who spoke to me left before the end of the meeting.

Why would they do this? Well, they had spoken and been listened to by the others. It felt disrespectful to leave. They also became deeply engaged in listening with respect to a discussion that had become very substantive. What was intended to be a very brief closure became a very rich discussion on how this leadership team could move forward more rapidly.

The talking circle ended at about four in the afternoon. Unbelievable! They all should have been dog tired, but most stayed after the closure to talk in small groups until past five p.m.

This is a common behavior, both at the end of the day and at the end of a workshop. People stick together talking for an hour or more before they leave, no matter how tired they say they are. It is a sense of community that holds them together.

The Coyote River Basin group is evidencing the same behavior, in deep and deliberative discussions. Oh, there is some laughter, but all heads are leaning in, listening intently.

Let's listen in on Group 1:

Debbe: "Well, let's pull our chairs in so we can hear each other." (Chairs are pulled in close.) "I'll start with you, Marie, and we will go counterclockwise, so you are next, Tony. The questions are: How do you feel about today? and, What did you learn that will help us resolve the conflicts in our environment?"

Marie: "This is tiring. I have never done so much talking and listening. It is hard to listen! I keep wanting to interrupt. That is part of what I learned. If I listen I learn a lot about each of us. If we did this at work, there would be some changes. But I don't think I could get anyone at work to do this."

Tony: "I'm tired, too, but mostly of sitting in this chair. I am used to being active, so this got tiring today. I also am wondering where we are headed. It doesn't seem that much of this is getting us closer to dealing with the conflict. Frankly, I think we could have solved it all if we focused on it today.

"I have to admit I liked learning about the worst and best outcomes. We are all in worst outcomes on our issue. And that story that Bob told about the Christmas tree describes my wife and I.

Rayni: "I loved today, and I really feel energized. Tony, I didn't realize how much I was intimidated by you before we started. Now I find you are really a nice guy, just with different views than me. That is why we need to take this time, I think. Until we know each other better, how can we solve this problem?"

Susan: "I agree with you, Rayni. This has been really a unique experience for me. Normally I don't even speak in groups. I've always felt too shy. But today I find myself speaking up way more than I ever thought I would when I was invited here. I'm excited by it!

"If we could do this in the meetings that we have around our issue, I agree with you, Tony, that we could get this over with in a short time. But we don't know how to do this, and I guess we're going to have to learn first and then solve our conflict.

"I, too, loved the idea of the best and worst outcomes. I think one of the reasons that I'm so shy is that I am always in my worst outcomes. I always worry that people will laugh at what I say, that they'll think I'm stupid. But I didn't feel any of that here. If all of us can feel that way, like we are listened to, then maybe tomorrow we can solve our conflict."

Alice: "Well, I'm with Tony. I'm just used to getting things done and getting it done fast. And I felt frustrated all day.

The Closure

"But I have to say that I learned a lot, in spite of that. I have really never thought of conflict in the way that we looked at it today. And I was really disgusted when I heard that other group's description of unresolved conflict. Pretty much describes my work environment. Like Bob said, why do we put up with that?

"I do wish we could get to the issue right away. But we already tried to do that, and we failed. What I learned today is that we just need to listen to each other. I mean really listen. My head is worn out from listening. But I see every one of you so differently than I did at the beginning of the day. I just hope that in the end it's all worthwhile. I guess my worst outcome is, it won't be. But, like Bob said, I guess I need a best outcome, and it would be that it is all worthwhile."

Debbe (waving to Bob): **"NO! WE HAVE THREE MORE PEOPLE TO SPEAK!"** (To her group): "Bob is just checking to see if all of us have spoken at least once. Go ahead, Wayne."

Wayne: "I had an interesting day. I had an opportunity to cofacilitate with Bob and the other three. So I have seen this group from the outside, and it is really interesting. You would be amazed at how hard everyone is working. I have never seen this group work together this way before. It is just amazing. And I learned an awful lot that I don't want to share with you right now, because I don't want to hold everything up. But I can tell you that I think we have to learn how to solve this problem before we can solve it."

Jon: "Yeah, I feel the same way as Tony. I am still doubtful that we will be able to leave here with everything solved. But I am not as doubtful as I was this morning. I hate to be in group sessions. So I have not been very comfortable today, and I think it's going too slow.

"So I'm going to have to reassess and see if it is worthwhile to be here tomorrow. I have a lot to get done at work, and coming here just to learn some of this touchy-feely stuff may not be my priority.

"But, on the other hand, I might decide to come back. I mean, I have had fun with all of you today, and I don't want to say I didn't learn anything, because I did. I'm just not sure that it will have much value in solving the problem.

"I was a little uncertain about recording all our information. I would've just used bullets. It would have been faster and easier. I found it hard when I was recording to get it all down. I just wonder if it's necessary. I did like it when my words were recorded, though."

Debbe (holding up her hand and waving at Bob, then indicating one person): "I have never been a facilitator before. I have never been a recorder before. So these are all new experiences for me. I would never have had them if I wasn't here. So I guess that is a plus. I am tired, but it seems like a good tired.

"I'll be back tomorrow, because I learned quite a bit today. I was really struck by the worst and best possible outcomes. I think I spend a lot of my time in the reptilian brain." (Laughter.) "I think it's creating all those worst outcomes that I'm worried about. So I'm looking ahead to tomorrow, because frankly I'm tired of living in a negative, toxic world. Whatever time it takes to make things positive, I'll spend it." (Waves at Bob indicating the group is done.)

The Closure: An Insight

When I hear lots of laughter and notice the groups are talking across the circle, it is evident they have completed their task. I walk to the edge of the circle and ask the question: "Has everyone spoken at least once?" It takes some time, repeating the question, and I get lots of pushback from the groups. And soon all groups are ready.

I provide a final insight for the day:

I have often found the closure to be the most important task of the day. You have been together for a day now, and this provides time to make sense of what you did and what you learned. Your relationships allow you to be more open and honest, so your words are impactful. Your listening is intense, you are learning from each other. You are assessing your own actions in this day.

When you are instructed to close your circle, you do so, reducing the distance between yourselves, making it easy to hear. Nonverbally you are stating, "We feel closer now."

The feeling question allows you to say you did not like the day or that you did. Either answer is right. But most facilitators feel uncomfortable when their clients say they don't like what they did. I know I want only glowing reports about how wonderful the day was.

But at this stage, people are honest and will say what their truth is. It does no good if you as the facilitator become upset about it. After all, you did ask them the question; you do want them to be honest, don't you?

So relax, this is about them, not about you as the facilitator. They are doing what you hoped. You are all sharing your honest feelings with each other. This can only help when you confront the real conflict tomorrow.

When you express what you learned, everyone can learn from that. Since each of us experiences the day through our own filters, our information will be different from others'. And it may help the others learn what they had not yet learned.

This is called a learning community. A group of people who have had the same experience and now share their different learning with each other. The group learning is richer as a result.

"No! We Have Three More People to Speak": An Insight for the Facilitator

I provide an insight to YOU about Debbe's loud response to me when I checked on the small group's progress. At the beginning of the day, I explained to the small groups that we would ask them on occasion if everyone had spoken at least once. This is to ensure that the process is inclusive. When we start to do this, the facilitators are hesitant to speak up. When they do, their tones are submissive, indicating they might be worried about going too slow.

I explain to YOU why the more assertive response from the groups now is what we have been encouraging:

When we asked the group if everyone had spoken this morning, who did they feel had the power?

"I know," YOU say. "They felt we had the power when we asked them that question. They always looked a little bit intimidated, like they were supposed to be done."

So who has the power now, from their viewpoint?

"They do!" exclaims Laura. "I mean, they just yelled at you!"

What happens during the day is that as it becomes evident we trust them to manage their own process, they will begin to empower themselves, to take responsibility for ensuring that each person speaks and is listened to. When we intervene with our question, they want us to know that they are in charge and will let us know when they are done. They don't want to be rushed. They will make sure each person speaks and is listened to this is what we want to have happen. We want them to empower themselves, to feel responsible for managing their group. But when they feel empowered, their voices will be on the edge of the "fight or flight" tone. As a facilitator, you have to be careful that you don't respond out of your reptilian brain. You have to be conscious when it impacts you and make a choice to recognize that we have fostered that sense of empowerment.

We are managing nonverbal communication when we do this. Watch when I check on them again.

I walk to the edge of the circle and ask: Has everyone spoken at least once?

I get nods from the groups, but Debbe's group indicates one person is left. I turn and walk away from the circle. I ask YOU: What was my nonverbal communication on that?

"When you walked away, you were saying they were in charge until everyone is done speaking," YOU say.

Much of this process is based on using nonverbal communication. It is easier to communicate that way.

Debbe is signaling their group is done, so I walk to the edge of the circle to provide instructions on developing collective statements. However, Rayni raises her hand and asks a question:

"Earlier you talked about being self-conscious and said you might have us do an activity about that. Is that possible tomorrow?"

Well, I respond, let's take the time to do that now. Is there any disagreement with taking a few minutes to explore self-consciousness?

Looks like you are willing. I'd like YOU to pass cards out to everyone.

I wait for this to happen. (This is continued in the following chapter on self-consciousness.)

While they are passing out the cards, I may tell them a story about a group that empowered themselves to make the workshop their choice.

"Let's Go!...No, Let's Stay!": An Anecdote

It was at the end of the first day, a long day for the thirty-six people in the workshop. Ranchers, agency people, Paiute tribe members, county commissioners, environmentalists, and others had spent a day talking with each other about their drought situation on the range. I asked them to do the closure, to answer two questions: How do you feel about today? What did you learn that will help resolve this issue?

Starting with the first person, they focused mostly on their feelings, which were all negative. They did not like the slowness, the "touchy-feely stuff," "all that talk and no action," a feeling of wasting time doing all this learning and no deciding, and so on. Some did talk about what they learned but it had the same negative message. "I learned to not come to these workshops again."

When the circle finally got to me (this was a long and unpleasant experience for me), I realized they were saying they did not want to continue. So

I affirmed that for them. "I get the feeling you would just as soon end this workshop right now rather than continue what you feel is an unpleasant experience. So you have two choices. You can either pack up tonight and go home, or stay the night and enjoy the resort facilities and leave in the morning."

There was silence. Then Ann, one of the rancher's spouses, blurted out, "Wait a minute! We might just be cutting off our noses to spite our faces. I think we are just frustrated by not jumping in and making decisions right away without being prepared to do so. Bob has helped us to listen to each other. We do understand each other better, and we are getting to the issue tomorrow morning. I think we better stay and finish what we started."

I suggested they continue around the circle and respond to what Ann proposed. They did that, talking about the positive aspects of what they had learned and the possibility that today had provided a foundation for resolving the issues, even if it was slow. And they had agreed to three days, so they knew this was going to take some time.

When the circle came to me again, I affirmed that they decided to continue with the workshop. "But I know you have a night to think this over and might change your mind. So I will start the meeting tomorrow morning, and if you all show up, we will move on to resolve this issue."

The next morning they all showed up ready to work. And two additional participants showed up to increase the group's size. Two days later they reached a consensus.

Remember it is their choice. It is not about YOU. Your job is to provide them that choice. Then trust them!

~28~

Exploring Self-consciousness

Being Self-conscious

Touchy-feely! That is an expression I have heard since developing this approach to building consensus. "I don't want to go if there is any of that touchy-feely stuff," they will say with a grouchy, repugnant look. When I ask what they meant, they could not answer other than to make a dismissive motion with their hands or head. They didn't appear to want to talk about it or describe it.

It normally comes up during the interviews or when being invited to participate in the workshop. *Touchy-feely!* What in the world does it mean? That is what I continued to ask myself over the years.

Many would believe it is just a male response to being in groups. But I have also heard this from many women. I suspect it is partly a generational thing; many in my generation and my parents' generation were not very demonstrative in public. I suspected the response was also the result of the encounter groups many people participated in or heard about during the late 1960s and into the '70s—which could certainly be considered when they see the circle of chairs.

There are two components to touchy-feely. The first relates to touch, or *"Don't touch me!"* The second refers to feelings, or "Don't ask me how I feel! (And don't expect me to answer!)" These appear to relate to the notion of intruding into a person's personal or emotional space without his or her permission.

A similar expression is often made in jest during the grounding: "Maybe we'll hold hands and all sing 'Kumbaya'!" I suspect this also expresses an underlying fear that people would end up "giving in" for the sake of being a soft, mushy, touchy-feely group, that they would lose their individual identities.

I was also confused because I observed many circumstances in our culture where touching and feeling were very acceptable. Especially for men in sports. In a football game, it is common to see players slap each other's butts or touch each other and express emotional feelings toward each other. Or to see soldiers in warfare hugging each other. These are our heroes. And they are being touchy-feely, and it appears to be acceptable.

I really do not allow these expressions to affect my moving ahead, because people who express them still participate in the sessions. It does, however, test one of my values or beliefs, which is that:

> *I'm not interested in intruding into others' personal space or emotional being.*

I want to provide an environment where people have choices that allow them to protect themselves or to personally choose to open up. *It's about their choices.*

In time, I observed behaviors that went along with the words. I remember an executive of a large company who would stammer and stutter when trying to express his point of view to a group of people. Or another participant whose face became red, blushing deeply before he spoke. Or people who passed when it was their turn or waved attention away from them. There were people who told jokes completely incongruent with the discussion at the table.

In time I realized that *self-consciousness* was the actual experience that people fear. Having their physical space invaded made people feel self-conscious. Having to express their personal feelings caused them to feel self-conscious. Putting them "on the spot" caused them to feel self-conscious. Asking them to speak in a large group caused them to feel self-conscious. They felt "exposed" before they were ready for it.

In short, the experiences of being in a meeting, being in a conflict, managing relationships with others caused people to feel self-conscious. And I knew from my own experience that self-consciousness is a frightening, anxiety-ridden experience.

It was this insight that allowed me to help people learn how to better manage their own experiences in consensus-building workshops. It was very simple: I just made them conscious of being self-conscious. I helped them to understand that being self-conscious was a natural component of being human, that while it was an anxiety-ridden experience, it was also an expression of being fully human. I helped them become conscious of the behaviors they use to cope with being self-conscious. I provided a simple approach that could help them cope in a positive way.

Self-consciousness—A Painful Experience: An Insight for the Reader

You are asked to speak. You didn't expect this, and you are not prepared. You are suddenly aware of yourself, of a feeling of expectations of others, or of your sense of inadequacy. You are aware that others are looking at you, waiting for a response. You feel exposed. Your heart begins to beat rapidly, and your face flushes. You try to speak and find that you can't. Your mouth gets dry. You breathe deeply and make some self-deprecating remark, causing laughter, hoping the tension will release a little. You pass and hope they don't come back to you.

You are experiencing self-consciousness: an awareness of self, a being that is separate from everything and everyone else. This condition happens with the focused attention of others, especially when you least want it or expect it. Self-consciousness is one of the most common and most avoided experiences in life, at least equal to addressing conflict.

I see it during groundings, when participants speak for the first time. They are often nervous, flushed, anxious, their voices shaky: self-conscious. This is often the first time these individuals have spoken their truth before this group, and they are painfully aware of the sound of their voice being present in the room. Often they will precede their statement with a qualifier—"I don't often speak in groups"—as an excuse for their nervousness. Or they may tell a joke to take the pressure off as others laugh. They may ask for the questions again to gain some breathing and thinking time. These are all behaviors of the self-conscious person.

I believe that all humans are basically shy creatures. We cover up that shyness with many subterfuges. We cope without being conscious of it. We use "deception," a lower or reptilian brain response, to protect ourselves. We become like chameleons, changing to fit the situation.

I find it interesting that the one trait that supposedly separates us from the animals and makes us "God-like" should be so feared. Self-consciousness is nothing more than consciousness of self, an awareness that I exist as a separate entity. *"I am."*

It is a gift, a birthright. Yet we avoid it for the comfort of being "nonconscious," operating on autopilot, unaware and therefore comfortable and safe.

The definition of self-conscious implies this sense of fear and pain:

> *"(Being) aware of oneself as an individual or of one's own being, actions or thoughts. (Being) socially ill at ease: a self-conscious*

teenager. (Being) excessively conscious of one's appearance or manner: a young, self-conscious executive. Showing the effects of self-consciousness; stilted: self-conscious prose."

In the creation story of Adam and Eve, when they ate of the fruit of the Tree of Knowledge and became aware of good and evil, they immediately became aware, self-conscious, especially of their nakedness, and they were ashamed. So they covered their nakedness with fig leaves.

Until then they did not know awareness, consciousness, shame, nakedness, or the judgment of nakedness. They did not know self as a separate entity. They were happy, comfortable, and unaware. Then God told Eve to stay away from that one tree. Now, how smart was that? Surely he/she must have known that this was an invitation and not a limitation to a human. So we ate fruit from the tree of knowledge and became self-conscious. We became aware of good and evil. What was one now became two, a duality.

I have learned from my own life experience and from watching and listening to others that self-consciousness is a painful experience. Once you are aware, there is truth, and truth is often frightening. Once you are aware, there is judgment of right and wrong, a judgment that you and others will make.

You become aware of your own negative character traits and fear that others will see what you have kept hidden in your shadow. Or you realize you must do something about these hidden traits. This is a painful decision because it requires you to be uncomfortable, open to judgment and thus to shame.

Yet we cannot be truly human until we are aware, self-conscious. The neocortex of the brain provides us that self-consciousness. Without it, how can we truly tap the potential of that part of our brain?

It intrigues me that everyone wants themselves and their children to have self-esteem, to be highly functioning people. To do that, they must first acknowledge they are a self. To have a self, they must be self-conscious.

If they seek comfort, they will seek to avoid consciousness, to not know, not be aware. Watching television as a spectator sport fosters nonconsciousness. This makes life easy, comfortable, as you become nonconscious, nonself. The result is you have no experience of self-esteem. You are protected from being self-conscious.

The danger is that you can be easily manipulated, letting others make decisions that affect your life, that are not in your best interest. This nonconsciousness often gives rise to groupthink or mob rule.

I intend, in my sessions, to avoid comfort, to purposefully foster self-consciousness. Addressing a conflict to resolve it requires self-consciousness. This begins with the grounding, which allows each person the opportunity to speak. Each person must make the choice and decide what to say. In the greeting, participants meet one another, including strangers and adversaries. This is a highly self-conscious experience.

When I assign a person the role of facilitator, recorder, or panel member, they are often surprised, then anxious, concerned about their ability to respond and be adequate. This is an experience in self-consciousness.

I purposefully do this because I know that conflict can only be resolved in a consensual manner if the participants involved are self-conscious, aware, willing to work with truth.

> *We can learn to be comfortable with being uncomfortable.*

Exploring Self-consciousness: An Activity

When I observe that the self-consciousness of individuals in a group is a detriment to moving ahead, I will have the group explore and learn about it. I pass out three-by-five cards at the end of the first day, or maybe after the grounding. I introduce the topic with a brief expression of the information and insight above and then have them answer two questions.

Although Rayni is the one who asked about self-consciousness, I noticed throughout the day how often many of you felt self-conscious about expressing yourself in this group. This is a very natural and normal behavior. Self-consciousness is an attribute that makes us human. Unlike the animals, we are aware that we exist. We are also aware that others exist. And we fear that those others are judging us. This creates a state of anxiety. You want to avoid it.

One of the best ways to accept the notion of being self-conscious is to explore it. That is what I want you to do. I am passing out three-by-five cards for your use in recording the answer to two questions. I'll give you those questions when you each have one of these cards.

Before we start, know that since this is a personal experience for you, we will not be reading these cards off in the large group. I will, if you allow me, pick up these cards and develop the information into a collective statement and report that back to the group tomorrow morning. This will allow you to see how the group experiences self-consciousness and how the group responds to it.

You also do not need to write the answers on the three-by-five card. I would encourage you to do so, because it helps make you conscious of how you feel about self-consciousness and how you respond. But you can choose to just think this through in your mind and listen to yourself answer the questions.

(This provides the participants a choice.)

On one side of the card, record the answer to this question:

"How do you feel about being self-conscious?"

I wait until all have completed their recording.

Turn your cards over when you have completed writing. (I pause.) Record the answer to this question on the other side of the card:

"How do you respond to self-consciousness?"

Note that the questions are nonjudgmental and invite either negative or positive descriptors. Participants do not read this information off, since I regard it as personal. I ask for the cards, if they choose to provide them. I use the cards to develop a collective statement for the whole group.

This is how one person described her self-conscious experience to me:

One Person's Account

How do you feel when you are self-conscious?
My first reaction to this question was: embarrassed and as you say... exposed. I am very uncomfortable. I question my authenticity, my ability and what I know to be true. 'What am I doing here?' 'Get me somewhere safe!'"

How do you respond to being self-conscious?
"My face turns red, my heart beats faster, I cross my arms and legs and try to become small and protected. Sometimes I talk too much, sometimes I shut up completely. I'm thinking nervous talking is more common for me. I will do anything to avoid the situation again and shift the focus."
—Kris

On the following pages are participants' descriptions of their experience with the self-conscious state and how they respond to it. These are from a number of different sessions with a diversity of participants.

Self-Conscious Feelings: A Collective Statement

This is an accumulation of feeling answers to the questions on exploring self-consciousness from a sample of workshops. Feeling anxious, scared, intimidated, embarrassed, and adrenalized are the most common behaviors. The numbers in parentheses identify the number of times the descriptor was used.

Feelings of Avoidance—I want to avoid the situation:

I feel vulnerable (3), exposed, and apprehensive. I am anxious (4), scared, and nervous (11). I feel rigid. I feel uncertain (2), somewhat uncomfortable (11).

I am intimidated. I feel uneasy (2), the situation is disturbing, intimidating. I am scared, fearful, afraid.

I am embarrassed. I blush, feel "red" and hot. I feel awkward (3). It makes me feel like everyone is looking at me, and I want to hide.

I am uneasy, fluttery, and feel my heart beat all over. I am adrenalized (2), with an adrenaline rush, then the fight-or-flight syndrome (2). I flight.

I feel disconnected in some ways from the group, separate, strange, and isolated. Sometimes it is like being outside of yourself—that others are looking at you like "who are you?"

It makes me feel like everyone is looking at me and I want to hide. I want to hide behind my hands or anything else I can put in front of myself. I feel lonely, alone.

I stop focusing on what I am doing and get bound up with myself. I become egocentric, selfish; why am I so consumed with myself?

I feel clumsy, insecure (4), and scared. I am unsure of myself. I am unsure, afraid of not measuring up to others' expectations. The need to please is greater than my need to keep my integrity.

I feel observed, looked down on, not meeting the others' perception. I feel inadequate, like critical eyes are on me, I am the focus of someone's attention.

I feel perhaps unprepared and incompetent. I feel sometimes that I am not up to the task. I am unsure, I feel that I may not measure up, but at the same time (I am) wanting to be accepted.

Feelings of Acceptance

These are appropriate feelings when feeling self-conscious, describing the state of accepting being human; "I am willing to be me":

I am feeling "self-conscious," a good feeling, more focused, more aware, more honest and relieved. I am aware (8), very aware of myself. If self-aware, I feel pleased.

There is a need to be alert (3), hypersensitive. I am in touch with my feelings and physically aware of my senses. It is exciting and a little bit risky, my pulse quickens. I am excited (5).

Self-Conscious Responses: Coping with Self-Consciousness

This is how people say they respond to their feelings about self consciousness. The numbers in parentheses identify the number of times the descriptor was used. Talking, joking, and withdrawing are the most common behaviors.

Cover-up Behaviors
How I try to appear to be in control:

I talk (17) and act out, talk more, talk excessively, acting "erudite." I talk too much, too loud, and too fast to cover any pauses or gaps. I talk quickly, and then talk even faster.

I joke (11) around and use humor (5) in starting conversations. I laugh (4) with a nervous laugh. I use self-deprecating comments or act silly. I try to say something funny.

I withdraw (6). I try to make myself inconspicuous, avoiding and dropping eye contact (4). I become silent and quiet (2) or get away from the crowd. I flee, imagine that I am someplace else.

I look down, not looking people in the eye. I avoid eye contact, look down or away, hide. I just don't look at people. I look off into space. I flee, imagine that I am someplace else.

I have great intensity, flipping out of and into, emotions. I stammer. I struggle with words. I fidget and speak louder, twirl my hands. I turn red. I will be overly cheerful or withdrawn, depending on the degree of my discomfiture.

I talk and try to engage in a conversation with someone in the group. I search out others I may know to get back the feeling of security. I focus on the other person.

I cover up. I stop thinking clearly and fill up the space with meaningless words. I say things I think people want to hear rather than what I truly believe and feel.

I try to avoid the situation that I think will cause self-consciousness. I abbreviate what I have to say so I can get out of the moment. I will pass leadership to another person.

Responsive Behaviors

These are appropriate responses to being self-conscious, describing the state of accepting being human; how I acknowledge my situation and adapt:

I become a focus to myself, using the word "I." I admit it…"I am uncomfortable with this." I tell myself that I have something to share, do some self-talk.

I just sometimes plow ahead with confidence. I forge ahead with the task. I tell myself to get past it and move on with the task at hand. I will be more concise and direct with the task.

I want to acknowledge it. I go on, just like the guy in the example. I pace myself, I breathe deeply to relax, and I smile.

These are the statements made by people who are men and women, rich and poor, managers and workers, college students and high school students, who wear three-piece suits and blue jeans. There is no distinction between them when it comes to being self-conscious.

When managing self-consciousness, it is important to acknowledge the moment, to recognize that it is natural to have this feeling as a human being. By doing so, you will learn to feel comfortable with being uncomfortable.

I Thought I Was Crazy! An Anecdote

> *"What is necessary to change a person is to change his awareness of himself."*
>
> —Abraham H. Maslow

When I asked Gayle to facilitate with me, she refused. She looked shocked. I asked her to think about it and make a decision by the afternoon. Not surprisingly, she came to me at the next break and reluctantly agreed to try. "But I'll be real nervous," she said.

By the afternoon of the following day, Gayle had facilitated two activities, and I was coaching her for a third.

Exploring Self-consciousness

"After the small groups have recorded their information, then you will have them report to the large group as you did earlier. When they have finished, I want you to provide them an insight on what you learned from that activity that will help the group understand this process."

"Oh, I could not possibly do that!" Gayle exclaimed. She had a shocked look on her face.

"Because?" I asked.

"I just couldn't do it; it would be too much. I don't mind reading off the three-by-five cards, but to speak in the moment? *No!* I think my mind would just stop when it came time to speak."

"It would make you feel self-conscious?" I asked.

"Yes, definitely!" she answered.

"Well, let me give you an insight about that. You are a human being. One attribute—and an important one—that separates us from other beings is that we are self-conscious. That is, we know that we exist. And we also know that others exist. And those others have the capacity to be able to judge us.

"Now, if you are not self-conscious, that means that you are nonconscious, not aware of what is going on. It also means that you lose an important attribute of being human. Knowing you, I just don't believe you would be willing to accept that. So this is your choice: I am going to provide you something you can say that will allow you to be self-conscious and still feel confident.

"This is what I want you to do. When you go to the edge of the circle, pause for a bit and say this to yourself: *I am self-conscious and it is OK. I will trust myself.*

"Then it is your choice. If you want to speak with an insight, do that. If not, then turn the group over to me. So, what am I suggesting?"

"You want me to tell myself that I am self-conscious and that it is OK. Then tell myself to trust myself?"

"You got it. Remember, it is your choice."

When the group had completed the task, Gayle had them read the information from the flip charts. When they were done, there was a pause. She looked at me, then turned back and took a deep breath. Everyone was waiting. She then proceeded to provide an insight that absolutely blew me and everyone in the group away. Her wisdom shifted the group's perception of the situation they were in. Then she just stopped. I saw her get a frightened look on her face. The whole group waited while she decided what to do.

"I am self-conscious," she told them. "And it just scares the hell out of me to do this!" Everyone in the group laughed.

"But Bob assures me that it's OK to be this way. So I'm going to trust myself and move ahead and finish this if you will be patient with me."

She then proceeded to complete her insight, sometimes stumbling, but persisting. When she was done, the entire group stood and applauded. They had experienced this moment with her because each of them knew what it meant to be self-conscious.

That evening, before the closure, I had the group answer the two questions on the three-by-five cards: *How do you feel when you are self-conscious?* and *How do you respond?*

I later put together a collective statement for both questions. The next morning, after a brief introduction, I selected two members of the group to read the self-conscious responses I had recorded on the flip charts. When these two were done, I asked the group, starting with the person to my right and going counterclockwise, to answer two questions:

"How do you feel about the statements about self-consciousness, what did you learn?"

The participants proceeded to do that. When it was Gayle's turn, she could not speak. She had tears in her eyes. "I can't do it right now. I just can't do it."

We proceeded around the circle until everyone had spoken. I turned to Gayle and asked if she would like another opportunity to speak. She nodded.

"I'm sorry," she said, "I just couldn't talk after hearing all of those descriptions on the flip charts." She paused, then looked at everyone around the circle as she spoke. "Every one of those statements described me!" she said with emphasis. "I thought I was the only one who felt that way! I actually thought that I might be crazy at times. I never realized that the rest of you felt as I did before. Oh my God, what a relief!"

I asked the group, "How many of you in this group felt as Gayle did, that you were alone in this and you actually might be crazy at times?"

At least a third of the group members raised their hands.

"All of you are self-conscious beings. All of you will feel the fear that comes with this state of being. All of you will develop coping responses to protect yourselves from the judgment of others and from yourself. You will cover up, not be authentic.

"I suggest you learn to embrace self-consciousness, learn to be comfortable with being uncomfortable. Acknowledge that everyone else feels the same way. Acknowledge: *I am self-conscious and it's OK. Trust myself.*

"It is difficult for anyone to develop consensus around an issue if you are all in nonconscious states and are coping to protect yourselves. It takes energy to do this; it prevents you from being authentic. It changes the conversation so the information comes from a worst possible outcome state, and you cannot reach agreement with that kind of information.

"If you are comfortable with being self-conscious, with being uncomfortable, then you can develop approaches authentically, and these you can reach consensus on."

~29~

Developing Collective Statements

Developing Collective Statements

At the end of the day, after the small groups have completed their closure and recorded their information on self-consciousness, I assign the task of developing collective statements. I leave participants in the small groups and begin by asking the facilitator to stand at the flip chart, then give them directions:

Turn back to the first page on the easel, "The Role of the Recorder."

I wait until they do this. There is often some confusion; I relax, wait until it is worked out. I take this one step at a time.

Now the facilitator can be seated. I want the person who recorded the role of the recorder to stand by the flip chart.

Again, there is some confusion as the groups try to remember who recorded the task. I just wait until I see recorders at the flip charts; sometimes I will repeat the task. Then I give the recorders a direction:

I want the recorder to tear off the pages that have the recorded words for the role of the recorder.

When the recorders have done this, I go to a visual I have on a flip chart or on a wall where all can see it and explain the process.

I want you to work in pairs (or trios). The recorders for Groups 1 and 2 will work together and develop one collective statement for your two groups. So, Susan and George, you will do this by first categorizing all your statements into like groups. Some statements may be one word or an incomplete sentence. But adding another similar statement will make it a complete one. Link them together (with connectors such as the, and, etc.) so they keep the original intent.

Then, put these like statements into paragraphs that express similar ideas. Each category can be one or more paragraphs. Keep paragraphs from being too long. Link no more than three to five sentences into a paragraph.

Use **all** words and statements. You will find some statements that appear to be the same and want to just record one of them. Record them all, even if they say exactly the same thing. This allows the speaker to see that others had the same ideas. So, if there are four people who say "boring," then express that as "boring, boring, boring, boring." Makes much more impact that way. Later, when building consensus, the people who made the statement can choose to change it.

When you add words as bridge words, like *the*, *and*, et cetera, which you will need to do in some instances, they must not change the intent of the statements. These added words can be put in parentheses, in script or underlined, or in a different color. This is your choice. We want those who spoke the statements to know these words were added.

DEVELOPING COLLECTIVE STATEMENTS

1. Categorize the individual recorded statements into like groups using numbers, colors, categories, etc.
2. Link like statements together where they express a complete idea, adding bridge words (the, and, or, etc.) if needed.
3. Put like statements into paragraphs (categories). Each category can be one or more paragraphs.
4. If some statements appear repetitive, record them. Use all statements and words; do not summarize, synthesize, interpret, or otherwise change any statement.
5. If you add words, put them in (parentheses), underline them, or in *italics*, or in a different color.
6. Record the results on a flip chart. Put the paragraphs in some order. You will observe that a story is being told by the group when you do this.

When you have completed the task, record the results on the flip chart. You will be presenting this in the morning to the entire community group.

So, recorders for Groups 3 and 4, Diane and Cliff, you are paired to do the same thing. You will develop a collective statement for the role of the recorder using your notes.

Now, I want the person in each group who recorded the role of the facilitator to stand at the flip chart.

The recorders for that task stand, and I have them rip off the pages they recorded. I assign them in pairs (Groups 1 and 3, and 2 and 4) to develop the collective statement for that activity. If there were six groups, I would assign this to trios of recorders.

I do the same for the worst possible outcomes, the best possible outcomes, the definition of conflict, the evidence of unresolved conflict in their environment, and the worst possible outcomes of confronting and not confronting unresolved conflict in their environment. As I do this, participants become aware of how much work they have done this day, how much information has been recorded. This engages twenty-four of the thirty-two participants.

This presentation is as brief as reading through the procedures. I intend for the pairs to develop their own unique approaches to preparing this statement.

Even though the group members were tired at the end of the day, they accept their tasks (they always do) and begin to work together. Some use scissors to cut individual statements in strips and then put the similar statements together. Some number the similar categories; others use colors to identify the categories. Each has their own approach; all approaches are right.

Members of the groups who are not assigned to the collective statement task tend to cluster and talk together, even though they can leave. They are normally tired and subdued because they have worked hard all day—talking, listening, facilitating, and recording. Many have newly found doubts. The people they have met are not as bad as imagined, many better than imagined. Many have newfound hopes. They have heard and learned new information that is challenging their information and beliefs about others. Others are speaking to friends separated by the conflict

I will pick one or two of these remaining participants and ask them to observe what is going on with the process of developing the statements. They walk around doing this. Then, they come back to me. These statements are typical of what I hear.

"Well, I noticed that they have gone to work right away, as tired as I know they are. Each is doing it differently, but they seem to each have reached decisions on how to do that. They seem to be working well together."

"I noticed the same as she did, but also how informal and relaxed they are. They are on the floor, on their knees, and busily doing the task. Can I ask a question?"

Sure!

"Do you purposely pick people who don't get along and put them together? I noticed that is the case with some of the pairs."

On occasion I do. I had a manager and a union leader, male and female, who did not get along at all. They barely spoke to each other, and when they did, it was not with kind words. I decided they could work together on a collective statement because, in the end, their relationship would influence how their members responded the next day.

So, I brought them together and explained what I was doing and why. I told them I was aware of their distanced relationship and wanted to provide them an opportunity to work together for the good of the entire group. I explained the collective statement tasks and asked them if they were willing to do this. They both agreed.

My observation was they worked well together in developing the statement. There was laughter at times, but mostly they were serious about the task. They stayed long after they had completed their statement and talked.

The next morning, when it was their turn to read off their collective statement, I asked them to tell the group how the activity went. Both agreed it was fun, that it changed their relationship, and that would certainly help as we moved ahead. They read off their statement, taking turns with each paragraph. I then had them honored for taking that risk.

The importance of this was that their members saw these two leaders working together for the common good, a visual symbol of what was possible.

So I will do this on occasion, but mostly I just rely on the "universe" to put the right people together when I select them, as I did this afternoon. The recorders wrote the words, so it is easier for them to read them. So, the pairing of people who don't get along is fairly random.

Someone invariably asks:

"Do we have to use every single word?"

Yes, I answer, every single word. When you report tomorrow morning, the participants must see and hear their individual statements when you read the collective statement.

"Well what if there are duplicates or almost duplicates? Can we drop those out?"

I answer: Use all the words, use all the statements. If there are statements that are actual duplicates, then use all the statements as written. As I said earlier, if three people say "boring," then repeat it: "boring, boring, boring," because it reinforces the feeling; it reinforces the statement.

Input and Impact: An Insight for the Reader

> "I'm sick of having input! I want IMPACT!"
>
> —Workshop participant

In the early 1970s, a movement began that fostered more public participation in community and government decisions. The public was invited to attend public "input" and "public involvement" sessions. In these meetings the public was provided an opportunity to express their view on the topic under discussion and to recommend decisions.

The public showed up for these meetings. They had their say. Then something went wrong. Despite having their say—often in opposition to the proposal—the decision was made in opposition to their input. This had two impacts. The public just decided not to attend additional meetings, so the numbers of people at these input sessions declined. Or, more likely, the public became aroused, angry that they had been invited to speak their minds and then ignored. This caused the development and coalescing of interest groups intent on making their point and getting their way.

"They already had their minds made up!" was the response. "Why do they ask for our input if they are not going to use it?"

"They took notes on what I said, but when the notes came out; my words were not in there. They wrote it in bureaucratese."

In two workshops, in totally opposite parts of the country—Oregon and Georgia—I heard two people say the same thing: *"I am tired of input; I want impact!"* No longer would the public be seduced into thinking that they were participating in decision making. They want proof today that they are being heard and that their words have an impact on the decision made.

This consensus process is designed to ensure that participants feel they are having input *and* impact. Each person gets a chance to speak. Visually seeing and verbally hearing that each statement is part of the collective statement is a reinforcement of this. Each person's statements are recorded to ensure that the message is affirmed, acknowledged, and available for the development of the collective statement. Each statement is expressed by the recorder to the larger group.

These statements are linked together into collective statements, each affirmed and acknowledged by those who develop the statement. The collective statement is then read to the entire group. Finally, the statement may be developed into a consensus statement by the whole group. Each of these activities affirms and acknowledges the individual's input and impact. The words are there in the group's memory, the collective statement.

Collective Statements: An Insight for the Reader

"Every word spoken has meaning." This is a basic tenet in seeking consensus. There is no such thing as "throwaway words," spoken in jest or added as inappropriate afterthoughts. Every word spoken has meaning. Every word and statement must be listened to and placed in its context in the story of the community.

> Every word spoken has meaning.

Collective statements are based on the belief that each of us perceives the world from a distinct and limited viewpoint. This point of view is developed as we experience life. It is structured by our genetics; our culture of birth; our sex, childhood, religion, astrological sign, education; our generational experience, age, status, geographical location, profession, Myers-Briggs type; our position in the family, organization, or community. There are an infinite number of variables that will determine our point of view. Another way of saying this is:

"We, as individuals, are limited in our perceptions; as a community we are infinite in our perceptions."

—**Workshop participant**

What a powerful perception to have in an environment of conflict,to know there is an unlimited resource available to us in our differences.

But each view, while being true for the individual, is limited by what is filtered out by all those cultural and values variables. Each of us perceives the same reality differently. Our individual views are like pieces of a puzzle. Each piece (view) is a true representation of our perception, but a limited one. It is when we fit all the community pieces of the puzzle together that we get the full picture.

Collective thinking assumes we can all learn something from each other.

"If we listen with respect, then we will understand, then trust, then learn something from each other, developing a new and richer perception of the situation."

—**Workshop participant**

Developing an Actual Collective Statement: The Art

To illustrate this process, we will use original recorded statements of Groups 3 and 4 on the role of the facilitator:

Stage 1: Recording the Statements as Expressed

(**Note**: the original statements in Groups 3 and 4 are **not** numbered as shown. This is done below so the reader can follow the process. Also, to differentiate them, Group 3's statements (1-11) are presented in regular font, while Group 4's statements (12-20) are in *italics*.)

1. Make sure everyone gets a chance to speak.
2. A successful facilitator will allow enough time for everyone to think about their answer.
3. The role of the facilitator is to keep the group focused.
4. A successful facilitator will give leadership and direction. The role of the facilitator is to make things easy for the group.
3. The role of the facilitator is to keep the group focused.
5. I think the role of the facilitator is to keep the group focused.
6. To do this a successful facilitator will establish the ground rules.
7. The facilitator should model behavior expected of the group.
8. He/she must keep the pace moving in order to keep information flowing, yet is able to give the recorder time to write things down.
9. The successful facilitator is to remain neutral or to retain neutrality.
10. When everyone has had their chance to speak, the facilitator will have their own opinion.
11. Kenney is a good facilitator!
12. *The successful facilitator will make sure that everyone has a chance to participate.*
13. *A successful facilitator will create an atmosphere of inclusion.*
14. *They keep the group focused on the topic, monitor the process, and know what the purpose of the discussion is.*
15. *The successful facilitator participates as an equal.*

16. *The facilitator demonstrates patience and gives frequent breaks. To create a sense of order, a facilitator establishes ground rules and makes sure ground rules are respected.*
17. *A facilitator is responsible for ensuring safety and equity in an atmosphere of freedom.*
18. *A successful facilitator's role is to be seen and not really heard.*
19. *The facilitator should be unbiased with no interest in the outcome and should not dominate or paraphrase.*
20. *The role of the successful facilitator is to make groups feel like all ideas are welcome and to give ample opportunity for all to speak.*

Stage 2: Categorizing

The statements are categorized into like groups with similar intent. In this example, the following categorization occurs:

First Category:

1. Make sure everyone gets a chance to speak.
2. A successful facilitator will allow enough time for everyone to think about their answer.
8. He/she must keep the pace moving in order to keep information flowing, yet is able to give the recorder time to write things down.
12. *The successful facilitator will make sure that everyone has a chance to participate.*
13. *A successful facilitator will create an atmosphere of inclusion.*
17. *A facilitator is responsible for ensuring safety and equity in an atmosphere of freedom.*
20. *The role of the successful facilitator is to make groups feel like all ideas are welcome and to give ample opportunity for all to speak.*

Second Category:

3. The role of the facilitator is to keep the group focused.
5. I think the role of the facilitator is to keep the group focused.
14. *They keep the group focused on the topic, monitor the process, and know what the purpose of the discussion is.*
4. A successful facilitator will give leadership and direction. The role of the facilitator is to make things easy for the group.
6. To do this a successful facilitator will establish the ground rules.

16. The facilitator demonstrates patience and gives frequent breaks. To create a sense of order, a facilitator establishes ground rules and makes sure ground rules are respected.

Third Category:

9. The successful facilitator is to remain neutral or to retain neutrality.
18. A successful facilitator's role is to be seen and not really heard.
19. The facilitator should be unbiased with no interest in the outcome and should not dominate or paraphrase.

Fourth Category:

10. When everyone has had their chance to speak, the facilitator will have their own opinion.
15. The successful facilitator participates as an equal.

Stage 3: Linking

Next, the statements are put together, words added where absolutely necessary, keeping the original intent as much as possible to form the final draft collective statement. Words that are added in the process are shown here in parentheses:

- The successful facilitator is to remain neutral or to retain neutrality. *The facilitator should be unbiased with no interest in the outcome and should not dominate or paraphrase. A successful facilitator's role is to be seen and not really heard.*
- (A successful facilitator will) make sure everyone gets a chance to speak. *The successful facilitator will make sure that everyone has a chance to participate. The role of the successful facilitator is to make groups feel like all ideas are welcome and to give ample opportunity for all to speak.*
- A facilitator is responsible for ensuring safety and equity in an atmosphere of freedom. *A successful facilitator will create an atmosphere of inclusion. A successful facilitator will allow enough time for everyone to think about their answer. He/she must keep the pace moving in order to keep information flowing, yet is able to give the recorder time to write things down.*
- The role of the facilitator is to keep the group focused. I think the role of the facilitator is to keep the group focused. *They*

keep the group focused on the topic, monitor the process, and know what the purpose of the discussion is.
- A successful facilitator will give leadership and direction. The role of the facilitator is to make things easy for the group. To do this a successful facilitator will establish the ground rules. *To create a sense of order, a facilitator establishes ground rules and makes sure ground rules are respected. The facilitator demonstrates patience and gives frequent breaks.*
- When everyone has had their chance to speak, the facilitator will have their own opinion. *The successful facilitator participates as an equal.*
- The facilitator should model behavior expected of the group. Kenney is a good facilitator!

Stage 4: Final Statement

The final product is created by removing the parentheses, highlighting the first paragraph sentence in **bold**, and cleaning up obvious grammatical and tense errors while retaining the original words and intent:

"The Role of the Successful Facilitator"

The successful facilitator is to remain neutral or to retain neutrality. The facilitator should be unbiased with no interest in the outcome and should not dominate or paraphrase. A successful facilitator's role is to be seen and not really heard.

A successful facilitator will make sure everyone gets a chance to speak. The successful facilitator will make sure that everyone has a chance to participate. The role of the successful facilitator is to make groups feel like all ideas are welcome and to give ample opportunity for all to speak.

A successful facilitator will create an atmosphere of inclusion. A facilitator is responsible for ensuring safety and equity in an atmosphere of freedom. A successful facilitator will allow enough time for everyone to think about their answer. He/she must keep the pace moving in order to keep information flowing, yet is able to give the recorder time to write things down.

The role of the facilitator is to keep the group focused. I think the role of the facilitator is to keep the group focused. They keep the group focused on the topic, monitors the process, and knows what the purpose of the discussion is.

A successful facilitator will give leadership and direction. The role of the facilitator is to make things easy for the group. To do this a successful facilitator will establish the ground rules. To create a sense of order, a facilitator establishes ground rules and makes sure ground rules are respected. The facilitator demonstrates patience and gives frequent breaks.

The successful facilitator participates as an equal. When everyone has had their chance to speak, the facilitator will have their own opinion.

The facilitator should model behavior expected of the group. Kenney is a good facilitator!

Stage 5: A Summary

A summary can be developed by using the first, or **bolded,** statements. This provides a more focused view of the role of the facilitator:

"The Role of the Successful Facilitator"
A Summary

- **The successful facilitator is to remain neutral or to retain neutrality.**
- **A successful facilitator will make sure everyone gets a chance to speak. A successful facilitator will create an atmosphere of inclusion.**
- **The role of the facilitator is to keep the group focused. A successful facilitator will give leadership and direction.**
- **The successful facilitator participates as an equal. The facilitator should model behavior expected of the group.**

Selecting Pairs or Trios: The Art

In most instances, the members of a workshop group will develop the collective statements themselves. There are many good reasons for this, stated below. There are times when I will develop or help develop collective statements or have the cofacilitators help others do this. I often like to do the "Best Possible Outcomes" collective statement myself because it gives me a good insight on their purposes.

These are some approaches I use:

- I will assign the task to the recorders for each task. They recorded the words and have the group memory to understand what the words mean. This is my preferred approach.

- I normally select pairs or trios to do the collective statements. That depends on how many groups there are. Four people working on a collective statement results in one person not participating. Trios work better, involving more people and providing an opportunity to develop more relationships conducive to consensus building.
- I will, on occasion, put people together who have a need to work with each other. They may have a history of being in conflict or being at opposite poles of an argument. If I choose people for the purpose of having them work together, I tell them this openly:
  You have indicated to me that you have not worked well together in the past, so this is an opportunity for a different experience. I have chosen the two (three) of you to work on this collective statement for the group. I would like you to use this task to demonstrate your ability to work together, to yourselves and to the group.
- I have never had a pair (trio) turn down this assignment. They often seem intrigued by the opportunity to do this. In the morning, they will proudly report to the group how well they worked together.
- Sometimes I let nature take its course, selecting pairs or trios at random or as they arrive in the morning, and assign them a task at random. At these times I am often struck by how the "universe" will randomly put people together who have a need to work together.

I always attempt to obtain balance, to have men and women work together; different generations work together; different cultures, races, and professions work together. Selecting people in pairs or trios provides the opportunity for this balance and gives participants an experience that helps them later in resolving their conflict.

"Do I Really Have to Use All the Statements?": An Anecdote

"Do I really have to use all the statements?" Sam was a tall man, six feet four inches, and as broad as a barn door. He towered over me, glaring down at me, willing me to tell him that he did not have to use all statements.

"What's the problem?" I asked.

"Just look at these—none of them make any sense!" He read some of the statements that had offended him so much.

Sam was working on some recorded flip chart notes from that afternoon. He, along with five other facilitators, had recorded for six small groups, or a total of sixty people. I had asked them to help me develop the collective statements for the work done that day. I had assigned Sam one of the collective statements related to the situation that we were there to confront. Sam had not recorded the information, so he was not connected to the people who made the statements. He was offended by most of the statements because they disagreed with his views.

Sam was adamant that he would not be able to include statements he obviously felt were wrong.

"Let's try this, Sam. Why don't you create a collective statement that will satisfy your needs? Then let me know when you're done with that."

About fifteen minutes later, Sam came to me with his collective statement. I read it, and it certainly was a greatly reduced amount of information.

"Ron, could you come here?" Ron was one of the other facilitators, and he had just completed the collective statement I had assigned him. "Would you take the flip chart notes from this group and put them together in a collective statement as you just did for your group?"

"Sure," Ron said. "I'd be glad to."

In about fifteen minutes, Ron came back to me with a collective statement that included all statements. I asked the rest of the facilitators to gather around while we read off all their collective statements. I wanted them to see the results of their work and to sense the impact it would have on the group the next morning. When we got to the group that Sam developed the collective statement for, I had him read his version to the group. Then I had Ron read off his version.

"I'd like to go around the circle and give each of you a chance to comment on these two different collective statements."

There was a large amount of laughter and friendly kidding as the facilitators expressed their views. Essentially, they told Sam that what he had done was to eliminate everybody else's ideas except those he agreed with. They advised him that the statement Ron had developed was more inclusive of the group and better expressed what they had heard during the situation discussion that morning.

Sam reluctantly admitted that he had done exactly what they said. He also agreed that Ron's statement was much more complete and did not offend him quite as much as the individual statements did.

Our tendency is to want to limit the views of other people. This is because we believe we have the one right perception. Any other perceptions that appear to differ from ours are a threat to what we believe. Our tendency then is to exclude this information.

A separate but similar incident for that same group occurred. When the report for the three-day session was sent to the participants, one member, Dawn, sent me an e-mail. She stated that she did not agree with the description of the situation in the report. I e-mailed her back and suggested that she rewrite the statement the way she felt it should be expressed. I also suggested that she read that off as a separate statement at the meeting so the group would be allowed to compare the two.

At the meeting of almost sixty people, when it was her turn, Dawn read off her version of the situation statement. I then had another member of the group read off the version that was in the report. I asked the group to respond to how they felt about the two versions and what they could learn from them. Their judgment could be expressed in the same two statements: Dawn had removed every statement that disagreed with her point of view. This offended them. They felt excluded, because their words were not in there. They learned that the inclusion of everyone's point of view provided a more comprehensive description of the situation than the version that Dawn developed. And it was more acceptable to them because of that.

I asked Dawn how she felt about the two statements and what she learned from the discussion.

"I feel embarrassed to see what I did. I have accused the agency people of doing that same thing, and now I did it, so that is what I learned. It is easy to want everything to be your way.

"I guess I learned that I need to listen to everyone's point of view, then take my own advice I have given to the agencies."

"I Matter": An Anecdote for the Reader

"I didn't think I mattered...until today."

Those words were spoken by a junior in high school, a young blond-haired teenager. She was speaking to the students and adults at the end of the day as they were doing the closure. All eyes and all attention were immediately upon her.

She spoke these words carefully and deliberately. Her head was up and her eyes focused on the group. She was looking at fifty-five other students from her high school, a multicolored, multiethnic group. These would have been considered the at-risk children in the school, children with learning problems that were physical, emotional, intellectual. They would be considered problem children by most of us.

To their teachers who were present and their principal, who sponsored this day, they were an opportunity. The group of sixty adults and difficult high school students was brought together for two days to explore the learning environment they had created in their school. Their purpose was to explore and establish a movement to create the kind of learning environment that would motivate them to learn and become capable, caring, growing human beings.

The students had engaged themselves in this exploration with great focus and intensity, surprising all the adults with their interest in creating a learning environment that was healthy and functional. They knew what the situation was and why it was, and they knew what they wanted and how to get there.

At the end of the day, after listening to the collective statements for the best possible outcomes and the learning environment they would create, the whole group sat in a circle, and each adult and student answered the closure questions:

"How do you feel about this session today?"

"What did you learn that will help us create that learning environment that you want?"

When it was her turn to speak, the young woman thought for a moment before speaking, her head down slightly. A pause. Then, speaking softly, but purposefully, she said:

"Before today, I didn't really think that I mattered. I didn't think I mattered to my family, to my classmates or teachers or to anyone else. No one even knew who I was or cared to know. I often thought that it would make no difference to anyone or anything if I was even here."

She paused.

"I knew I didn't matter. I often thought of not being here [meaning alive], and if that happened, that nobody would even notice that I was gone."

The shocking nature of her statement was felt by the entire group. My hair stood on end, and a shiver ran up my back. At this moment the entire attention of the group was focused on this young woman, expressing herself truthfully, authentically. At this moment, she mattered to them, and it was obvious.

"Today has changed all that," she said as she continued.

She spoke these words carefully and deliberately. Her head was up and her eyes focused on the group. Her eyes were misted with tears now, as were the eyes of many in the group.

"I realized today that I did make a difference, that what I had to say in this workshop was important, because it was different than what others

Developing Collective Statements

had to say. And I was listened to when I said it. Then I heard the statement [collective statements] that we read at the end of the day, and I could see what I said was in there. And it made a difference...I made a difference.

"That is what I learned," she said softly but clearly, her voice catching somewhat, "that I make a difference, that I matter. After today I will never forget that. That is what I learned."

There was a pause, silence for a moment, then a few sounds of applause, and then more, people stood until all were applauding and standing. As they did this, I sensed they were not only applauding this young person and what she said, what she learned. They were applauding the impact of the statement on them, adults and students. They realized they mattered, they made a difference, and she had expressed this for all of them.

That is what recording my words exactly as I say them and including them in the community statement can do for people. No matter how much time it takes, it is worth it.

> "You are a child of the universe, no less than the trees and the stars; you have a right to be here."
> —*Desiderata,* Max Ehrman

"

~30~

A New Day and Collective Statements

A New Day: Preparation

I start the second day with a low level of anxiety. I always wonder, "Will they come back?" I imagine myself sitting there all alone at break time, wondering, "What happened? Where is everyone?" Many of my associates report the same feelings when they start the second day of their workshops. These are just worst possible outcomes. When the first participant walks through the door, those anxieties are relieved.

Normally, I and the cofacilitators are busy hanging the collective statements developed the previous evening on flip charts and the walls. I like to put them in order so we can read them around the circle.

People who enter the room head for coffee and the continental breakfast at the table in the rear of the room. Most are still grouping up, talking with people like them. But some have stepped across the group boundaries; I can see a businessperson, Bud, talking to the local environmentalist, Alice. They are from the same generation and have both lived in the community for a long time. They used to be friends, but the conflict has caused a rift in their relationship.

I also note a new person in the group (the 33rd member). A number of people come up to tell me that.

I bring the four cofacilitators—YOU, Mike, Wayne, and Laura—together with me, and we go over our tasks for the morning. I tell them:

I will begin the day with an introduction of a new person who is in the room. I want you to observe the process, because I will be asking you to do this for the next new person who arrives. After that, I will take the group through the collective statements, task by task. During that time I will demonstrate with a visual activity how the collective-statement process works. Again, observe how I do that, because you can replicate it with your community at some future time. It will be described in your report and learning manual.

When we are done with the collective statements, I will review the direction we will be taking during this day. Mike, I will be honoring you for your role as facilitator yesterday. You will then return to your small group.

I look at YOU.

YOU are going to be honored, but you are going to continue to help me facilitate and coach people.

I want to establish new groups this morning. We will do this by honoring the different groups represented in the room. I will ask the individual groups to come to the center of the circle. I will then honor the first group, and when this is done, we will have them count off to four.

Again, pay attention to how I do this, because I may have you do this tomorrow. I will have you honor the remaining groups and then start having the community members do the honoring.

Once all the groups have been numbered off, I will ask them to go to the flip chart designated for their group. Then, Laura, I want you to give them their first task. When you can see they are done with their task, you will ask them if everyone has spoken at least once. We will take a break after that.

This is the three-by-five card I handed Laura:

> Close your circle, do not record.
>
> How do you feel about the collective statements?
>
> What did you learn that will help you resolve the conflicts you have in your community?

I provide both Laura and Wayne with a three-by-five card with the two statements that will help them move the groups during the day:

> Has everyone spoken at least once?
>
> The facilitator will pick a new facilitator and become the recorder.

When everyone has spoken, then turn the group over to me. I will provide them an insight on the development of relationships. When I've completed that, we will take a break.

After the break, Wayne, you will present the next task. This is a little different, in that three-by-five cards will be used to record their answers before recording to the flip charts.

I pass the card with the question on it to Wayne and have him read the instructions:

> Pass out 3 x 5 cards.
>
> Working together...
> What will be the best possible outcomes of addressing and resolving the conflicts in your environment?

When you tell them to pass out the three-by-five cards, step back and wait while they do it. Remember that the task of a facilitator is to ease the process, so give them the task a step at a time, rather than all at once. Otherwise, they will always be asking you to repeat the instructions.

Then instruct them: "Record your answer to this question: Working together, what will be the best possible outcomes of addressing and resolving the conflicts in your environment?" Again, step back and let them do this.

When you sense they are done recording on the card, step back to the edge of the circle and ask the facilitator to select another facilitator and become the recorder. Ask them to record their statements to the flip charts.

I ask Wayne and Laura to repeat their tasks to me. Then we get the community together.

Day Two Introduction

With a signal from me—

We are ready to start. Please come to the circle.

—the community begins to drift into the circle. Some people go for that last cup of coffee and another cinnamon roll or a plate of fruit. Others are reluctant to stop their conversation with each other. But eventually they hear my oft-repeated "We are ready to start." They are all there as I begin to speak.

Welcome to all of you. I feel a great sense of relief now that you're all in the circle. I always have a fear that no one will show up for the second day. But here you are. You all worked really hard yesterday. Each activity brought you closer to being able to confront and resolve your conflict. I want to start today with a review of what you did.

Our first order of business is to introduce a new member into the group. Then we will listen to the collective statements that were developed last evening. After that we're going to create some new small groups. I will demonstrate to you an additional way of doing that.

We will then continue with an exploration of conflict. If you remember, we ended it with the worst possible outcomes of confronting or not confronting conflict. Today we'll take a visual look at a relationship process and see how it is impacted by conflict. Then we are going to identify the best possible outcomes if you are able to both address and resolve the issues you have.

Before the morning is over, I would like you to understand why you need to resolve the conflicts in your environment and in your community. You will see a visual expression of the impact that conflict has on your relationships. Then I would like you to explore the kinds of beliefs, behaviors, strategies, and actions that will foster those outcomes.

I want you to have an opportunity today to apply the approach you have experienced on a personal conflict you have in your life. By later this afternoon, you will be focused on the issues that brought you together. You will apply this basic process to your conflict. You will learn how to listen to each other in a way that creates a common knowledge base.

By tomorrow morning, we should be able to have a common purpose for this community and be developing strategies and actions for resolving your conflict.

So this is where we are headed. Let's start with bringing our new member into the group.

Welcoming New Participants: The Art

There will always be new people who show up for a workshop. They will be late for many reasons:

- "I didn't want to come yesterday, but after listening to those who were here, I decided to do so today."
- "I had a previous engagement yesterday, and Bob assured me I could come today even if I was late."

- "I wasn't sure it would be safe to express my opinions, so I stayed away. But I heard from my friends who were here that you could do this. So I am taking a chance that they were right. But I won't hesitate to leave if this is just another shouting match; I have had enough of those."

When new people join a group, their sudden presence will affect the participants. This happens especially if the person is one they don't know or is one of the most radical protagonists. The tendency will be for participants to censor what they are saying until they know who the person is and what side they are on. A community cannot afford to lose this information.

New people, meanwhile, feel like intruders. They don't know what has happened or will happen and what their role is, so they are fearful. They want to make themselves as small as possible, their entry as quiet as possible. They will be afraid to speak because they don't know what is going on. Or they will speak out of turn or interrupt someone and immediately feel from the nonverbal messages that they were out of line.

As a facilitator, it is critical to welcome the new person and make them part of the group as soon as possible. If they come in the middle of an activity, I will wait until that activity or task is finished. Then I use this simple process:

I start by talking directly to the new person in the circle. (Sometimes if I know there is a new person before the circle starts, I will pull him or her aside and explain this process, providing the questions in advance.)

Hi, I am Bob Chadwick, the facilitator for the group. My purpose is to help this group resolve their conflicts and also help them learn how to manage future conflicts. I am sure you are wondering what has happened so far, so I will help you gain that information.

I will ask you to answer the same three questions that the members of the group answered yesterday:

- Introduce yourself and your relationship to the issue.
- What are your expectations of this meeting?
- How do you feel about being here?

When you are done, I will have three people respond to you. Alice, Bud, and Justin, I want you to answer these three questions. I'll repeat them when it is your turn to speak.

- Introduce yourself, and what is your relationship to the issue.
- How do you feel about yesterday?

- What did you learn that will help this community resolve their issues?

Turning to the new person, I say:
So, Mark, answer the three questions:

- Introduce yourself, and what is your relationship to the issue?
- What are your expectations of this meeting?
- How do you feel about being here?

The new person responds, normally self-consciously:
"I am Mark Hanson. I am a relative newcomer to the community and came here for the peace and quiet of a rural community. I come from Los Angeles, California, bought a home here to retire with my wife. I did not expect to find myself in the middle of a community conflict, but I did because of my support for the new land-use rules.

"I did not expect the anger and bitter relationships that would result. Where I used to live, this was an easier thing to do because we are used to regulations. So, I did not come yesterday because I did not want to be the focus of a shouting match. I have done enough of that already. It is tiring to be the focal point of all that anger. It makes me wonder if I chose the right community to live in.

"I heard that the meeting yesterday was really a respectful conversation and that everyone listened to each other. I came here to see if that was true. I feel a little bit anxious because I was not here yesterday and feel like I am behind the curve. And I feel anxious because I don't want to be the cause of more anger here. I appreciate you letting me join this group, even though I am late."

SELECTING LISTENERS AND RESPONDERS:

I am often asked how I select people who are listeners and responders. There are three key elements for me:

1. I want people who are representative of the balance in the group: young/old, male/female, for/against, old-timer/newcomer, rancher/environmentalist, etc.
2. I want to make sure that everyone, at some time, is a listener and responder.
3. I trust myself. I trust my instinct and the value of randomness, so try not to be too deliberate about it. I just randomly look around the group and select people who are diverse.

When Mark is finished, I remind the three members of the group, Alice, Bud, and Justin, that they are to answer the three questions:

- Introduce yourself, and what is your relationship to the issue?
- How do you feel about yesterday?
- What did you learn that will help this community resolve their issues?

Let's begin with Justin.

"I am Justin S. I grew up in this town. I own a real estate business in the community that I started after college. I came here because the conflict has affected our business. With all the strife, people are reluctant to come to the community.

"I feel pretty good about yesterday, especially after thinking about it last night. We at least got together and talked and listened to each other. I am a little cynical still that we can accomplish what we need, but what we have been doing and how we are doing it is not working either. And I am a little anxious about the time it is taking.

"But I learned one major thing yesterday and that is about the best and worst outcomes. I hope you get a chance to learn about it too. We are all in our worst fears and in our reptilian brains over this conflict. We've been through worse events in our community and solved them together, but this one is different. I hope we can get this done today and get back to what we normally do."

Justin looks over at Alice.

"I am Alice. Well, I am the dreaded 'environmentalist' in this town. I have lived here all my life and have not liked how the community has been developed willy-nilly without looking at the consequences. I hate all the turmoil, too. It has affected my life in a lot of negative ways. Some of the people in this room used to be my friends.

"I feel pretty good about yesterday. I have been to similar workshops before, but this one is different. We are the ones who are doing the work, not Bob, although he is facilitating us nicely. I actually feel safer than I have for years in the community.

"What I learned is we have to go slow to go fast. Bob talked about that. We can't listen very well to each other if we are talking over each other all the time. And trying to make the decisions in a short time frame causes us to not listen.

"I'm hopeful for today. I didn't sleep very well last night, going over what happened here. I am hopeful we can prove the cynics wrong.

"Bud, you are next!"

"I'm Bud S. I'm the banker in the town. I have lived here all my life, started with the bank when they first opened. We have always seen ourselves as being supportive of development so that we can keep the kids here after college. So the increased development has our support. But we won't get any business to come here with all this uncertainty about our land development.

"I feel like yesterday was really long. I am used to sitting in chairs at work, but I can get up and move more than I did yesterday. I was tired at the end of the day. I went home and just tried not to think about the day.

"I don't like conflict and what it does to the community. Alice and I used to be friends and often met for coffee. We realized yesterday that this conflict has come between us. What a shame this is.

"I learned that we can only solve this problem if we do it together. The new folks have to listen to us old-timers, and we need to listen to them. They are going to be part of our community from now on, unless we close the door and run the ones we have out of town. I don't think any of us want that to happen. So, let's get this thing solved.

"Welcome to our community, Mark. I hope you can stay."

I spoke to the group when Bud was finished:

What we just did is welcome the new person and prepare him for being part of this workshop. He had an opportunity to introduce himself to the community, and then three members of this group introduced themselves and provided him some insight on what happened yesterday. As all these people spoke, I noticed you were all focused on listening. No one I observed was distracted. You were curious to hear from the new person and to hear the others' insight on the workshop so far. Now the group knows who he is, and he has some idea of who is in the group and what has happened. But it is the actual welcoming of the new person that makes the change, that fosters a sense of safety.

This also works for those who leave in the middle of the day and then return the following day. I change the questions to:

- Introduce yourself.
- How do you feel about what happened after you left yesterday?
- What did you learn or experience that will help this community resolve their issues?

This allows the person to reenter the group. They always have interesting experiences when they leave, because they reenter a world totally different from the one they experienced the day before. Often they will talk about how chaotic the meeting was that they attended, about how few people spoke, about how boring it was, talking in circles, and how little was accomplished.

I may then share this anecdote with them.

"Save Me, I Am Going in Circles": An Anecdote

Dave, the executive director of the Chamber of Commerce, was not present when we started the grounding. Sixty-six members of the community in southern Minnesota were waiting to get started. They included businessmen, elected officials, educators, students, community members, fundamentalist Christians, Hmong immigrants, African American community members, medical professionals, law-enforcement personnel, and a homeless person. It was a real vegetable stew of people.

Before going into the circle, the mayor of the community approached and asked if Dave would be there. My response was: "He was invited and I had hoped he would be here, but I know he was reluctant to come. My guess is, if you want him here, you will have to go get him."

The mayor turned on his heels and said, "I'll be right back."

I waited for a while and then, with the help of my cofacilitator Kathryn, began to gently move the group into the circle. I started my introduction and was close to turning the group over to Kathryn, when the mayor and Dave walked into the room. It was obvious Dave was coming reluctantly and was frustrated by it. They both had to find a chair to slip into the circle. So there was a lot of movement as I continued talking.

Kathryn then introduced herself and started the grounding. When it was Dave's turn to speak, he expressed his displeasure with having to spend the time in the workshop.

"I am Dave B. I am the executive director of the local Chamber of Commerce. I came to this community about three years ago and was provided direction by my board of directors to find ways to make this the best community in the nation. That is a tall order. So you can understand why I might be a little frustrated by having to spend time with this group. I can see a number of the board members here, and I really feel they can represent me in this workshop.

"But when the mayor comes to get you, how can you refuse? So I am here, but I feel like I've been kidnapped. I am not sure I can spend the whole day; in fact, I might actually be a hindrance to the process if I did. I just have a lot to do."

Dave did leave a little early, but it was at the beginning of the closure at the end of the day. I scheduled him to speak first, because he had urgent business to take care of for an evening meeting.

The next morning Dave arrived a little late again, walking real fast, slipping into the circle as quietly as he could. I asked Dave to introduce himself, tell us how he felt about leaving the meeting, and what he learned last evening that would help his community.

"My name is Dave and I'm with the Chamber of Commerce." He paused. "I'm here to beg for your help. I'm afraid I've been infected with 'circle mania.' I had a meeting last night with a bunch of different agencies and groups, that I talked to Bob about. That's why he let me speak first at the end of the day.

"I sat around the table with about twenty people and listened while the meeting droned on and on and on. There were really only four or five people who spoke, and I'll bet you can guess who they were. They always take over our meetings. When anyone else tries to speak, they just interrupt them. I had never really seen or realized this before.

I was so frustrated, that before I knew it, I was asking them to help me get rid of the table. And then I had them set the chairs up in a circle. And then I had each person in the group take turns and talk about one of the issues that we had. I can't believe it! They did what I asked them to do. And the meeting went much smoother as a result, and we actually made some decisions.

"I need your help! I'm afraid I've been brainwashed. Am I doomed to sit in circles for the rest of my life?"

There was a lot of laughter as he finished.

Dave continued to show up at the meetings, resistant up until the end. He continued to be a latecomer, sometimes leaving the meeting to take care of business, but he always returned.

People who show up late or who show up unannounced or who are in and out of the meeting are often sources of important information that the community can use to help resolve their issues. This only happens if you make certain they are welcomed into the group, or back into the group, and if they are asked to share what they learned with the group.

Honoring the Facilitators

Before the groups start the day, I have the two original cofacilitators express their learning to the entire community group. This allows them to bring closure to their experience, to share the learning with their community members, and to reinforce the belief that the community members can facilitate their own process. Each answers the questions that were in the closure:

- *How do you feel about the facilitating experience yesterday?*
- *What did you learn that will help resolve the conflicts in your environment?*

YOU and Mike, I want you to introduce yourself and answer these questions so the group can learn from your experience. I'll start with YOU and then go to Mike. Everyone, please stand.

The circle of thirty-three people stands with much noise, scraping of chairs, mumbles. YOU begin to speak:

"I am YOU. When Bob asked me to cofacilitate, my first reaction was one of fear. I didn't know how to facilitate or why he chose me over the rest of you. But he told me just to trust him, and I did. And I'm glad I did. You probably noticed us talking with each other while you were working in your group. Bob takes a lot of time not only helping us understand what we are to do, but why we are doing it.

"This is what I learned after I stopped being so anxious about facilitating. I don't have to give you complete instructions on how to do your tasks. Just ask the question, and you just went right ahead and did the task. It was easy in one sense, but in another sense, I had to give up overexplaining to you what you had to do. I learned to just trust you. Mike?"

"I am Mike. I agree with what YOU said. I never imagined I would be asked to facilitate a group. It was really strange to do the things Bob asked us to do. It was opposite to all that I have been taught. I felt like I really wanted to be part of a small group. I missed the interaction that you had with each other.

"I am amazed at how well you all listened to each other. I just wish we could do that in the meetings we have had around our conflict. It seems we spend most of our time interrupting each other. I am probably the worst one at doing that.

"I'm interested in being with one of the small groups today and seeing what actually goes on. I really appreciate having the opportunity to work with Bob."

When YOU and Mike have spoken, I ask you both to come to the center of the circle. I then ask one of the members of the community, George, to honor them. George looks surprised then thinks a minute and speaks:

"I want to thank both of you for showing us that we can facilitate our own meetings. I was really impressed by how well you did it. I kept wondering how I would do if it was me. And then I wondered if I would be too uncomfortable doing it. So I know you took a risk for all of us. I want to honor you for doing that."

The entire community applauds the two people in the center. Both of you become somewhat self-conscious, Mike turning red in the face, YOU looking down. Then you shake each other's hands and do a sideways hug. You do not leave until the applause is done.

Reviewing the Collective Statements

Once the new person has been welcomed into the group, we can move into a review of the previous day's work, using the collective statements. This allows Mark and the participants to gain an understanding of what happened yesterday and the process we used.

I want to start with a review of yesterday, using the collective statements that were developed from your recorded statements on the flip charts.

REPETITION

Much of the following is a repetition of what I discussed earlier with the cofacilitators, then with the larger group, with the small groups, and finally repeat today before reading the collective statements. This is purposeful. I am asking this community of people to do what they have never done before. They will often not hear or understand the task the first time through.

I am also coaching people—not only the facilitators, but everyone in the group—in the process of developing consensus. I am trusting that this replication will allow them to recall both the task and the process at some later date.

It is like Lebron James shooting baskets from the foul line—thousands of them—to ensure when the time comes he can put the ball in the basket. He can count on it.

When facilitating a conflict I want these people to be able to count on knowing what to do, to be able to recall the tasks and the process when they need it.

We started yesterday with what I call the "grounding." In this activity, all of you answered three questions related to an introduction, your expectations for the workshop, and how you felt about being here. We just did that in introducing and welcoming Mark. These questions are very specific in that they not only provide important information to the group, but they enable you to turn on your "whole brain."

In the grounding, every person spoke, without interruption, experiencing what I call "listening with respect." This is a rare occurrence in our culture today, because we have all been taught that it is OK to interrupt each other. This is disrespectful behavior. It is what gets in the way of being able to resolve the conflicts in your community. Listening with respect allows you to hear the information that is needed so that you can learn from each other and develop new perceptions and resolve your conflict.

After the grounding, we developed small groups by counting off. Because we tend to sit next to the people who are like us, who we are comfortable with, this results in separating those relationships and creates diversity in the small groups. This is purposeful.

The greeting circle: Once you were in the small groups, your facilitator had you stand. You then experienced a "greeting circle." This allowed you to meet friends and strangers, to get to know each other personally, reducing the sense of intimidation in the group. It fostered the beginning of a sense of community.

I always use the greeting circle at the beginning of a workshop because it helps people get over being self-conscious, and it creates the kind of relationships that will help us move ahead.

And I always follow the greeting circle with two lifelong learning questions:

- How did you feel about the greeting circle?
- What did you learn that will help us resolve the conflicts in our community?

This allowed each of you to express the feelings you have, and in so doing, it helped us to learn a little bit about who you are. Talking about what you learned turns the greeting circle into a learning experience.

A member of your community facilitated both of these small-group activities. You also had two members of your community helping me facilitate the entire group. You are all learning facilitating and recording skills by experiencing them, and in the process you are developing new relationships. These will serve you long after this workshop is successfully completed.

That activity was followed by an exploration of the roles of the recorder and the facilitator. The facilitator was asked to select a new facilitator and then become the recorder. You were now facilitating and recording your own process.

Your first recorded task was to answer the question: "What is the role of a successful recorder in building consensus?" While you were answering this question individually, you were also learning how to record. When you completed that task, the recorder read off the information on the flip chart to the larger group.

This information was used to develop the collective statement. The recorders worked in pairs last evening to develop these statements. They followed the instructions on that flip chart (turning to point it out).

I want those who developed the collective statement for the role of the recorder to please go to the flip charts with that statement. I want you to take turns reading off those statements.

Susan and George walk to their flip chart and read off the collective statements on the role of the successful recorder. When they are completed, I have the group honor them for developing that statement.

THE SUCCESSFUL RECORDER'S ROLE IN BUILDING CONSENSUS
Groups 1 and 2

The role of the successful recorder is to capture thoughts accurately and record exactly what the person says. *The recorder will write down exactly what the other person says.* A successful recorder is neutral and writes down comments word for word. *To prevent manipulating, the recorder should be writing only what she hears.* He/she will insure an accurate record of what was said, and confirm the thought...they will not interpret what was said.

The successful recorder has to remain impartial. *The successful recorder is value neutral and maintains objectivity.* They will have an unbiased manner, unbiased by not being judgmental, and they will not decide what is important. *I've been in groups where the recorder's words have been written instead.*

She or he does not paraphrase, and to make sure they recorded what was actually said. If you don't do exact wording, check back to make sure you captured what was said. A successful recorder will check for clarification. *A successful recorder will repeat what was said for clarification.*

The recorder focuses discussion. The recorder needs to keep us more focused to see where we've been and where we're going. The recorder needs to know how to use the board; they don't stand in front of the board or leave out words.

The recorder provides a tangible record of everyone's thoughts. *The recorder empowers the speaker, needs to be responsive and crystallizes our thoughts.* I think it's an accurate accumulation of data in chronological order that can be used later.

Some skills are: listening intently, double checking meaning, and writing carefully and legibly. The recorder is writing for all to see, and uses multiple colors. Spelling does not matter to be a successful recorder.

I think the recorder should be included, not excluded, from the group.

(**Note**: Group 2's statements are in *italics*)

This is a collective statement, not a consensus statement. It represents all the views that were stated about the role of the recorder yesterday.

As these statements were read off, how did you feel about seeing your statement in this collective view? That is the way people feel when they experience seeing that they had input and impact. Their words are in the statement as they expressed them, and they are part of the story developed by the whole group.

If you don't see your words there, how does that make you feel? Normally, people who don't see their words included will say so. I then ask them to express what they said and have the recorder include that in the statement.

I want Diane and Cliff to read off your statements regarding the role of the recorder.

Cliff and Diane walk to their flip chart and read their statements off. When they are completed, I have the group honor them for developing that statement, applauding from their chairs.

Remember, I said the recorder determines the speed of the process. If, as the recorder, you stand with the marker in your hand looking at the speaker and not recording, then the speaker will just talk on and on, waiting for you to record something. If you turn to the chart and record as soon as the speaker expresses his or her view, the speaker will become more focused. You determine how wordy they are by your response.

As your collective statements indicated, people want the recorder to record exactly what they said, without changing it. This is what most people want. If you summarize or "bullet" what was said, reducing or changing their statement, expect them to respond negatively.

Your facilitator was asked to select a new facilitator and then become the recorder. This new task answered the question:

"What is the role of a successful facilitator in building consensus?"

While answering that question, you were facilitating your own process, just as you had for the two previous activities. For these two activities, you were experiencing the roles while you were developing them. This is one of the most powerful ways to learn.

After changing facilitators, you developed the role of the facilitator. I want those who developed the collective statements to read them off.

Marie and Frank go to their easel and read off their collective statement on the role of the facilitator. Then Donna and Allen read off their collective statement. As each pair finishes, the community honors them for the work they did, applauding from their chairs.

The facilitator role is not only to be neutral, but to also see that each person speaks in turn without being interrupted. They are to ensure that the recorder heard and recorded what was said. The facilitator ensures that the recorder has an opportunity to speak after everyone else has done so.

Moving the role of the facilitator and recorder ensures that each person in the community plays these roles. It is a way of sharing power, of empowering ourselves. It helps you feel confident in facilitating your own process in future conflicts. It also allows others to see us in these different roles, thereby changing the limiting stereotypes we have of each other right now.

"THE ROLE OF THE SUCCESSFUL FACILITATOR"

Groups 3 and 4

The successful facilitator is to remain neutral or to retain neutrality. The facilitator should be unbiased with no interest in the outcome and should not dominate or paraphrase. A successful facilitator's role is to be seen and not really heard.

A successful facilitator will make sure everyone gets a chance to speak. The successful facilitator will make sure that everyone has a chance to participate. The role of the successful facilitator is to make groups feel like all ideas are welcome and to give ample opportunity for all to speak.

A successful facilitator will create an atmosphere of inclusion. A facilitator is responsible for ensuring safety and equity in an atmosphere of freedom. A successful facilitator will allow enough time for everyone to think about their answer. He/she must keep the pace moving in order to keep information flowing, yet is able to give the recorder time to write things down.

The role of the facilitator is to keep the group focused. I think the role of the facilitator is to keep the group focused. They keep the group focused on the topic, monitors the process and knows what the purpose of the discussion is.

A successful facilitator will give leadership and direction. The role of the facilitator is to make things easy for the group. To do this a successful facilitator will establish the ground rules. To create a sense of order, a facilitator establishes ground rules and makes sure ground rules are respected. The facilitator demonstrates patience and gives frequent breaks.

The successful facilitator participates as an equal. When everyone has had their chance to speak, the facilitator will have their own opinion.

The facilitator should model behavior expected of the group. Kenney is a good facilitator!

Worst and Best Possible Workshop Outcomes: Collective Statements

The next task was recorded on three-by-five cards. You first recorded the answer to the question, "What are the worst possible outcomes of spending three days in this workshop?" You turned your card over when done and answered the question, "What are the best possible outcomes of investing three days in this workshop?"

While recording, the room became silent. This was purposeful. You had all been speaking externally, your energy moving externally, all morning. This task allowed you to go internally, to deliberatively determine the answer to these questions.

THE WORST POSSIBLE OUTCOMES OF THE WORKSHOP

Groups 2 and 4

We have 3 wasted days, where nothing happens and nothing changes. Participants come away feeling they have accomplished nothing. We don't get anything accomplished.

This won't be worth the time or money invested. The community remains fragmented. There will be no resolution so the citizens of the county get no benefit.

There is fighting worse than when we began. I will still feel hostile and feel I have a reason to feel hostile. We will always have competing factions and will approach every Basin issue as a polarized community.

Coyote County becomes an undesirable place to our residents. We become abusive with each other and confrontational. Increased anger and hurt feelings could result in a decrease in mutual understanding and respect.

We lose our agriculture community and our rural heritage in the county. The ranchers sell out and give up their generational heritage. We lose the beauty of the agricultural lands as well as the ranching heritage.

We don't break down our communication barriers. We never learn how to listen to each other and respect each other's perspective. That we don't learn how to break down the camps and start open dialogue.

We won't learn to really save salmon or do the impossible. The tribe isn't successful. The Salmon don't recover.

This takes time away from the ranch, cattle work, so my wife and daughter have to work harder. Time away from the ranch, cattle work. Being away from my family, not home when they need me.

My wife has time to rearrange the house again.

When all had written their answers, the facilitator was asked to select another facilitator and become the recorder. This continued to move the power of that role on to other members of the group. Let's listen to the collective statements for both of these tasks.

Those of you who developed the worst possible outcome statement, please go to your flip chart and read it off.

The pairs who developed these (Debbe/Jim and Kathy/Rob) go to their flip charts and read their collective statements for the worst possible outcomes of the workshop.

These are a product of the reptilian brain. They result in actions that are not consciously determined. By asking this question and recording the answers to the flip chart, we are making these emotions and beliefs conscious so we can do something about them.

You will have these worst possible outcomes automatically, without conscious thought. They will in fact become the underlying purpose of the conflict you are in. If you listen to these worst possible outcomes closely, you can determine whether these are the outcomes you are creating from the conflict you currently have.

> **Worst possible outcomes:** These are imagined, feared, *future* outcomes, often based on *past* experience, with a *currently* experienced emotional, biochemical, and physical reaction. When people believe them, they affect their perceptions, beliefs, values, and strategies. They tend to become self-fulfilling prophecies when strongly held and acted upon.

The Community Is Telling a Story: A Visual Insight

For years I sought for a way to help people understand at an integrative, or organic, level the value of the collective statements and all the activities that lead up to it. It was the storytelling approach of a Native American elder that helped me see how to do this.

Everyone Is Telling a Story

I ask six to eight people who are seated together in the circle to stand and move one step into the circle. I walk out into the center of the circle and act as the director of this story. These are the participants, standing in a straight line:

        Rob Kathy Laura Jon Debbe Dawn Crista

I have learned that every conflict has a community of interest, that it brings together those who are influenced or impacted by the decision. I am asking these people to represent a "community of interest."

I have also learned that each conflict has a community story to tell, but the individual members do not understand that. They each come to the gathering believing that **they have the entire story in themselves,** and they are there to convince the others of the "truth" of what they know.

To demonstrate this, I am going to ask this group to tell a story. They are going to do this in a kindergarten manner, where the teacher asked us to each tell a part of the story. We begin with Rob, who will repeat the first sentence I give him. This is the beginning of the story. Then Kathy will add her sentence to the story, followed by Laura adding a sentence, and so on, until Crista, the last person in the line, will create an ending for the story. Crista, I want a Pulitzer Prize ending. (Laughter from all.)

I state for Rob the first sentence for the story: ***A porcupine walked into the meadow.***

Rob: "A porcupine walked into the meadow."

Kathy: (thinking first): "It was a warm and sunny day."

Laura: "He saw another animal in the meadow."

Jon (pausing to think what he will say): "It was a bear, an angry bear just waking up from a winter nap."

Debbe: "The bear growled at the porcupine when he approached."

Dawn: "This frightened the porcupine, so he climbed a tree to get away from the bear."

Crista (after long pause): "There he met a female porcupine who became his mate for life."

With the ending of this story, the large group will normally laugh and applaud. The members of the story group are often self-conscious about speaking and trying to come up with the "right" sentence that makes sense.

I repeat the learning I have had about communities of interest:

I have learned that every conflict has a community of interest, and that community that is drawn together has a community story to tell. But they don't know that. They each think they have the full story.

Everyone Thinks They Have the Whole Story

I have Rob and Crista step out in front of the storytellers, turning to face each other. I encourage them to repeat their sentence to each other, to let the other know what the "true" story is.

<pre>
        Kathy Laura Jon Debbe Dawn
              Rob ->   <- Crista
</pre>

Rob: "The porcupine walked into the meadow."

Crista: "There he met a female porcupine who became his mate for life."

They both look at me, and I encourage them:

The other person hasn't got it yet. Keep repeating it until he gets it.

Rob repeats to Crista: "The porcupine walked into the meadow."

Crista repeats: "There he met a female porcupine who became his mate for life," with an impatient tone of voice.

Rob repeats with more vigor: "The porcupine walked into the meadow."

Crista, her hands on her hips, leans forward and repeats firmly: "There he met a female porcupine who became his mate for life!"

Rob: "*No!* The porcupine walked into the meadow!" He speaks with steely confidence: this is the truth!

Crista, before he is done, loudly, with emphasis and pointing her finger into his chest: "There he met a female porcupine who became his mate for life."

Rob, leaning forward now, with more emphasis and a loud voice: **"The porcupine walked into the meadow...and that is all there is to it!"**

Crista, now leaning nose to nose with him and just as loudly: **"There he met a female porcupine who became his mate for life."**

The group laughs, often applauds; they recognize themselves; they have seen this in many meetings. I ask them, rhetorically, Have you ever experienced this kind of argument before? They all nod their heads.

Everyone Wants the Group to Repeat Their Story Line

I have Rob and Crista return to the storyteller group. I turn to the others:

What Rob and Crista both want is to win this argument and have everybody else repeat their sentence as the entire story line.

I ask Rob to repeat his sentence and for the others to repeat it exactly as he said it.

Rob: "A porcupine walked into the meadow."

Kathy: "A porcupine walked into the meadow."

Laura: "A porcupine walked into the meadow."

Jon: "A porcupine walked into the meadow."

Debbe: "A porcupine walked into the meadow."

Dawn: "A porcupine walked into the meadow."

Crista (resisting): "*No way!* There he met a female porcupine who became his mate for life."

Again, the community laughs. They understand the implications of this activity. Now, they know, Crista wants everyone to repeat her sentence, because *she* has the truth.

The Story Is All Mixed Up

In addition to everyone wanting to be right with their "story line," when the group meets, they are seated out of order. I move the standing participants around, mixing their order:

Debbe Laura Rob Dawn Kathy Crista Jon

Then I ask them to repeat their sentence.

Debbe: "The bear growled at the porcupine when he approached."

Laura: "He saw another animal in the meadow."

Rob: "A porcupine walked into the meadow."

Dawn: "This frightened the porcupine, so he climbed a tree to get away from the bear."

Kathy: "It was a warm and sunny day."

Crista: "There he met a female porcupine who became his mate for life."

Jon: "It was a bear, an angry bear just waking up from a winter nap."

Now, this discussion doesn't seem to make any sense, especially if you are the manager who needs to make the decision about the meadow. These people all appear to be in conflict with what they are saying. There is no similarity. Who should you believe? What can you base your decision on?

In the consensus process, we encourage each person to express his or her view, and we record as it is being expressed. These are the different perceptions of the entire community. Then we take that information from this group and any other group and write a collective statement. When we do that, it sounds like this:

I move the storytellers to their original position and have them repeat their sentences.

Rob: "A porcupine walked into the meadow."

Kathy: "It was a warm and sunny day."

Laura: "He saw another animal in the meadow."

Jon: "It was a bear, an angry bear just waking up from a winter nap."

Debbe: "The bear growled at the porcupine when he approached."

Dawn: "This frightened the porcupine, so he climbed a tree to get away from the bear."

Crista: "There he met a female porcupine who became his mate for life."

This collective statement tells the "whole story" and is inclusive of everyone's views. Now that you know the whole story as a manager, you can begin to take action to do something about what is happening in the meadow:

"It sounds to me like we have an angry bear up in the meadow. We better tell other humans about this to keep them away. Or better yet, have the bear removed to a safer place, so the porcupines can climb down the tree and return to their home."

If We Exclude Others, We Don't Get the Whole Story

I then remove four members of the group. This is who is left:

                      Kathy   Laura   Crista

Rob is excluded because he looks like a hippie, and we certainly don't want to give him any recognition. Jon is always looking for the negative in things, so leave him out. Then Deb is a member of the public—what does she know about these things? Finally, don't include Dawn; she is part of that rabid environmentalist group. So we are left with this story:

Kathy: "It was a warm and sunny day."

Laura: "He saw another animal in the meadow."

Crista: "There he met a female porcupine who became his mate for life."

Now, is that the same story? It is certainly a warm and positive story, but it is incomplete and leaves out important information. If you made a decision to send a group of people up to this meadow, would they have all the information they need? Will they know about the angry bear?

Coalitions Form and a Battle Begins

The four people who were excluded find they have a common purpose. They were not included, acknowledged, or their information listened to. They form a coalition to get the attention of those who make the decision. They form a line facing the "included group" and begin shouting their sentences at the same time to the others, wanting attention and acknowledgment of their views.

                      Kathy   Laura   Crista
                   Rob   Jon   Debbe   Dawn

All spoken at the same time:

Rob: "A porcupine walked into the meadow."

Jon: "It was a bear, an angry bear just waking up from a winter nap."

Dawn: "This frightened the porcupine, so he climbed a tree to get away from the bear."

Debbe: "The bear growled at the porcupine when he approached."

This causes the "included" group to come together as a block, expressing their point of view just as loudly and at the same time. No one listens; if they did it would just sound garbled.

All spoken at the same time:

Kathy: "It was a warm and sunny day."

Laura: "He saw another animal in the meadow."

Crista: "There he met a female porcupine who became his mate for life."

Again, the message is visually and intellectually clear to the larger group. If you exclude people, do not hear or acknowledge their information, they will form coalitions and oppose you, and do it loudly. In doing so, while all the needed information is expressed, little of it is actually heard. The result is lots of loud noises and chaos.

The manager might exclaim: "But they are not saying the same thing!"

Good observation. It is not their view that brings them together, it is their common experience of being excluded. And the people are providing the right information; it is just not being heard.

Including Everyone, Hearing the Whole Story Results in Community

I bring back the excluded members, and they are integrated into the whole story. I remind them that the collective statement includes all words expressed by the individuals in the group. The purpose of the collective-statement writer is to write the story.

"A porcupine walked into the meadow. It was a warm and sunny day. He saw another animal in the meadow. It was a bear, an angry bear just waking up from a winter nap.

"The bear growled at the porcupine when he approached. This frightened the porcupine, so he climbed a tree to get away from the bear. There he met a female porcupine who became his mate for life."

When this is done, Kathy sees her statement is in the story. It is between Rob's and Laura's statements. (I have Kathy hold Rob's hand and Laura's hand). She is part of the story connected with them. In like manner, Laura is connected by the story to Jon and Jon to Debbe, et cetera. Soon, all the storytellers are connected. (All are holding hands.)

This is community. Everyone has had their say, been listened to, and acknowledged. And what they have said has been put into a collective statement, linking them together. Each has had their impact on the story. Now they can decide what to do about this story they have created.

I ask the members of the group to honor these people for helping them learn. They all stand and applaud. I ask those in the story to take a bow, still holding their hands, making a curtain call.

This visual activity can be used in your community to help people understand the purpose of collective statements. The instructions will be included, step by step, in your learning manual developed from this session.

So, let's listen to the best possible outcomes for the workshop.

The cofacilitators (Wayne, Mike, Crista, Laura) were assigned to develop this statement. They go to their flip chart and read their collective statement.

The Best Possible Outcomes of the Workshop

Note: This statement is inclusive of all four groups. The statements are actual statements from real workshops, in the participants' actual words. Statements in *italics* are those previously shown on the flip charts for development of this task.

A community vision will be created that allows everyone to work together to create a future with healthy families, healthy community, and healthy environment. *We begin to develop support for resolution of issues in the River City Basin. We are finding common ground.*

We develop a general agreement on focus and direction for the River City Basin. *There is an increased possibility of making progress toward mutual goals and building consensus. We can come up with a positive plan agreeable to the majority and can move forward with it.* The county will get direction again with the renewal of a land use plan that we will all have a mutual understanding of.

We agree on a process that is inclusive of a wide range of views and that is effective. *It moves us toward salmon recovery and agricultural and economic stability.* We plant the seeds that lead to a River City Basin Plan which resolves our problems on a mutually beneficial approach the entire county can take heart on.

We have a healthy community and watershed. We create sustainable communities for our families, the folks we work with, the people who depend on us, and our land the people depend on. *The health of the whole River City Basin will become more sustainable.* That twenty years from now, as the basin moves toward a healthy, sustainable and productive system, these days will be viewed as a critical step. *Agricultural and ranching communities will have certainty and predictability.* The river is restored. *Salmon are returning.* Return of the salmon.

From this point on the community is whole. We will form a sound foundation of people who trust in each other, and we are able to resolve our current and future concerns. Everyone trusts one another and listens with respect to each other. *People here and people we talk to will be comfortable calling each other up if there is something that needs to be talked about.*

We create a renewed sense of community, working together to preserve our basin heritage, while respecting each other. The community works together as one, helping each other meet their needs, resolving differences, saving our heritage and way of life. Our newcomers are seen as bringing new ideas and energy to the county, and will also appreciate and respect the heritage of the basin.

We learn skills to help defuse conflicts in the community. *That we will find ways to move forward to solve the problems of land and resource stewardship that we all must deal with while ensuring that we have a viable and successful rancher, business, tribal, and salmon community.* It has been demonstrated that the process works and that what we learned will not stop here!

Our ability to communicate with each other will greatly improve, and through communication in this activity we will be able to resolve differences for the benefit of our community. *People take the time and effort to listen and value what others say, and we have agreed to a definition and state of the cause of disagreement in the basin. We need to learn to listen better and this is a good opportunity.* We will personally feel more relaxed because we have the tools to help make other, less vocal views heard.

There will be civility among and between groups, including respect. We also heal some of the divisions among the community. We can understand the issues and have a collective understanding that disagreement is OK and often generates new solutions.

I understand how I can contribute to progress toward solutions. *I have an opportunity to speak my truths.* That two people who feared each other will connect in a positive and constructive way. We are getting to like "strangers."

There is an emergence of new leadership. *We identify individuals who are willing to lead and we empower them to do so, because we trust them to be fair, honest, and compassionate as they make decisions that affect all of us!* That our leaders will develop networks so that when a crisis happens, rather than involve the same old contacts, they will pick up the phone and call the network.

The River County Rural Conservation District will understand the issues that the newcomers, the landowners, and the ranchers have. A clear idea about what my organization can do to help all basin residents accomplish their vision. This will allow the River County Rural Conservation District to better represent stakeholders when dealing with the county and other agencies. *Ranchers receive enough information to feel secure.*

We move beyond either/or's to find ways to retain and develop land, lifestyles, and improve water quality and quantity. River City Basin becomes a model for a sustainable healthy watershed that other areas dealing with issues of agriculture, growth, and urbanization can look to. *We provide for affordable housing that attracts a diverse community and provide commercial/business opportunities so they can make a living here.* It is a place you want to stay.

Our plan allows land to be developed responsibly so as to protect the beauty of the our basin. *County Land Use controls that will regulate River County development will have basin support.* We maintain our ranches, controlling planned growth so we protect our heritage and beauty of the basin, with the evolution of a community stewardship consciousness. *Ranching and ranchers are supported, productive, profitable, and successful.* Development be controlled, our aesthetics managed, and all necessary social services will be available.

We leave with a sense of empowerment and become a catalyst for change. We each leave determined to increase trust and civility in the district and influence others to do the same. *We establish closure of bad feelings.*

I provide additional insights, referring to the visual on best possible outcomes.

> **BEST POSSIBLE OUTCOMES**
>
> Best possible outcomes are also future imagined events or outcomes, but these are positive, and they have currently experienced emotional, biochemical, and physical responses, which tend to foster the desired outcomes.

These best possible outcomes create a purpose statement for the workshop. As your facilitators we will be designing the session so that these best possible outcomes are accomplished.

Conflict Collective Statements

After the best possible outcomes of the workshop, we began to explore the notion or concept of conflict. Rarely do we have an opportunity to do this, despite the fact that conflict is a major event in our lives.

We began with a panel of four people. Two of these, Kenney and Marie, answered the questions regarding a definition of conflict and how they feel about it. Johanna and Todd answered the questions regarding the evidence of unresolved conflict in their environment and how they felt about it. They were then assigned the roles as facilitators of their groups.

> **THE PURPOSE OF THE PANEL**
>
> To create an arena of thought in everyone's mind by answering the question to the whole group, so the small groups can continue the effort.

Their first action was to select a recorder for their group. Let's begin with these recorders, Alice and Justin, reading off their collective statements on the definition of conflict and how you felt about it.

> **A DEFINITION OF CONFLICT**
>
> **Groups 3 and 4**
> **Conflict is an expression of different points of view.** It is opposing viewpoints or attitudes. Conflict is a difference of opinion by opposing forces. Conflict is differing viewpoints that starts w/feeling, moves to a look, then leads to a blowup. Power struggles, mistrust, and anger which is going head to head. Differences of opinions sometimes to an extreme.

> **Conflict is a struggle for control**…it can be huge between countries, or small between family members. Conflict is the result of a struggle for control over either ideas or material resources. Perceived competition: an either/or situation.
>
> **Conflict is just a disagreement.** I think conflict is when you don't agree with someone. People who do not accept a difference of opinion or ideas of other people. It is a disagreement which is difficult to recognize and resolve.
>
> **Conflict may be disagreement between two or more people; each one thinking their way is the right way.** It can be a disagreement either between yourself or other individuals. Conflict can be some sort of struggle either within two groups, between two people, or within a person
>
> **Conflict is necessary and good can be destructive or creative.** It is inevitable and it is present to have a true democracy. Conflict can bring the best out in us. It is a learning mechanism. It produces growth. It all depends on what you do with it.

> **HOW I FEEL ABOUT CONFLICT**
> ### Groups 3 and 4
> **I don't like conflict.** It scares me because I feel powerless to do anything about it. I just don't like it and am uncomfortable with it.
>
> **I have a desire to avoid conflict, because I see it as a threat.** I can get angry and lose control, so I try to avoid conflict. I hate it. I want to get away from it because I feel angry. Feel threatened, scared/don't like it. I shut down.
>
> **There is the fear of not getting your way.** The fear of losing something. You don't know what could be worse.
>
> **I am very uncomfortable about conflict.** I don't like it personally and with co-workers, even I try to avoid conflict. I am tired of it…leave me alone, though their opinion is just as important as mine. I am not good with it because my feeling is that we don't communicate with each other very well.
>
> **My own inner conflict is extremely hard to deal with.** It is difficult to deal with when personally involved, but I hate unresolved conflict. The questioning of my own beliefs and thoughts is stressful. It serves to point out my personal viewpoint and its limitations.
>
> **I don't mind conflict.** I deal with it every day as a manager/ and that's okay with me. Don't like it but I have a big need to deal with it and resolve it respectfully.

When they finish reading their collective statements and are honored for the work they did, I remind the group that in a large sample of workshops, 75 percent of those who expressed a definition of conflict had negative feelings about it. I note that many people feel that conflict is just a difference of opinion. Then I say:

I demonstrated to you visually why conflict is more than a difference of opinion. Conflict is difference of opinion with power added to it. If two people have a disagreement and each begins to force the other person to believe the way he or she does, then the disagreement becomes a conflict. It is an interpersonal conflict. If they are equal in power and reach an impasse, then they will ask other people to join them in the struggle. The conflict now is an intergroup conflict.

The struggle that you saw in that visual experience is represented by the evidence of unresolved conflict in your environments. I want Dawn and Gil to read off their collective statement for the evidence of unresolved conflict. As they do this, ask yourself if you are satisfied with working or living in that environment.

The Evidence of Unresolved Conflict in Our Environment.

The lack of communication hampers people from getting projects completed or studies done. We are not effective. (There is) no communication or poor communication. Work is halted right now, we are not going anywhere. There is a reluctance to share specific incidents and outward statements. "I don't want to get involved."

People are frustrated, and can be seen grumbling when someone leaves the room. Some people totally avoid one another. (There are) hard feelings.

We see bad attitudes, low morale, and negative talk. Evidence is blaming, taking sides, power struggles, heckling, making jokes about the other sides. There is back biting and gossiping—a divided community. (There is) obstructionism—disagreeing with little things for the sake of disagreeing.

People take small problems and make them into large conflicts, because they don't resolve small issues. It is exhausting our energy with grievances. The more stressed out I am, the more conflict there is.

There is a tension like a rubber band ready to snap. Often there's no evidence of conflict because there's agreement, but there's insidious, underlying conflict which could erupt eventually.

It can get very stressful and dangerous so that someone can want to shoot someone. Stress levels are high to the point of violence, even to self, often resulting in suicide, alcoholism, drug use, prison.

It's time to change and use other processes because eliminating the person leads to eliminating another, which leads to eliminating another, which results in the same.

When Dawn and Gil finish, I speak to the group again:

I noted earlier that 75 percent of those who defined conflict had negative feelings about it. But when confronted with the reality of *unresolved* conflict, 90 percent had negative feelings about the situation, while only 10 percent had positive feelings. This just indicates that in the abstract, we are more willing to consider the possibility of positive outcomes from conflict. When faced with the reality of conflict, we have a higher percentage of negative feelings. These negative feelings are what get in the way of confronting and resolving our conflicts. These are the feelings and beliefs that create the negative environment you experience.

The evidence of unresolved conflict in your environment measures the consequences of not confronting and resolving the conflict. Why do you accept this situation? It is because of your worst possible outcomes. The next task allows you to explore the worst possible outcomes of confronting and not confronting the unresolved conflicts in your environment.

Marie and Johanna will read off their worst possible outcomes of confronting conflict.

The Worst Possible Outcomes of Confronting Unresolved Conflict in Our Environment

There is no resolution, no real solution to the problem. If we confront, we are not working it out and not coming to agreement. So nothing will change. We don't know how to do it.

It escalates the problem, and it gets worse. The initial conflict becomes greater. We will escalate the conflict so that it involves others who don't want to be involved or are not there.

The entire workplace becomes infected. We begin to involve more people. It will grow into other areas and parts of the group. The conflict now begins to trickle down into your personal life and the conflict goes home every night with you.

Those who are trying to resolve the conflict get blamed. I could be labeled as someone who causes problems. They will "shoot the messenger"! We lose the respect of others and lose trust.

Things won't go my way and individuals will attack me personally. When one takes a stand and find out they are alone or wrong, there is a fear of failure and a loss of prestige and power.

The situation causes people to be angry, to say things they didn't intend—and then they can't take back those comments. We would not say what we really want to say, or think.

> **This would make it more difficult to work with people we are required to work with.** Relationships are hindered. Losing a friend, not getting along with a family member, and because of the confrontation, administrators could be brought in, and things could really mushroom.
> **The job is not getting done.** Because production stops, there is a stalemate, and a loss of staff. We would feel performance anxiety. As a result, non-productiveness reigns and "I quit."
> **We are missing out on strategic opportunity because of unclear direction.** We feel split between what we believe we should be doing and what we got caught up in.
> **People become more withdrawn or more confrontational.** We will turn a candle light into an inferno. The result could be physical violence, and maybe even result in death by a shooting. A big old fight or riot could result in a confrontation that can escalate into violence.
> **Division in communities and counties cause hatred and war.** Fear of death and killing. People quit or possibly commit suicide; shoot co-workers (initiate bodily harm). They kill you. WAR!
> **If at first you don't succeed, you never try again.**

If you don't confront the conflicts, then what are the consequences? Todd and Kenney will read off their collective statements.

> **The Worst Possible Outcomes of Not Confronting Unresolved Conflict in Our Environment**
>
> **The conflict stays as it is, unresolved.** Problems do not get resolved, (so) they do not get fixed. Unresolved conflict continues, and the atmosphere remains the same.
> **The conflict or issue will escalate, it will grow to become larger and/or worse.** Not confronting the issue makes it worse. Problems may escalate, power struggles become greater. Other issues are brought in and people lose sight of the original issues.
> **The problems still exist and they begin to mutate into something else.** The problem may escalate, power struggles become greater, and this sometimes results in violence. It creates a balloon effect that gets bigger and pops, when power becomes the concern, not working.
> **If you don't confront it, it will always be there.** If not resolved, it will continue to be brought up in the future. Problems remain unsolved and resurface.
> **The conflict becomes institutionalized and becomes a way of life.** It becomes an accepted mode of behavior, which leads to the preventing of reaching our goals within the organization.
> **There is an acceleration of negative energy or feelings.** There is no more harmony in the people environment. Unresolved conflict causes irritability, pent up emotions, and uneasiness.

> **People get their needs met in unbalanced and unhealthy ways.** The negative impact is one that is physical and emotional. We will become depressed, disillusioned, become deceptive, or turn to drugs.
>
> **There will be displaced anger that confuses people and causes a loss of esteem, deterioration of relationships, and a bad use of energy.** People will continue to become more isolated and will trust fewer colleagues.
>
> **Unresolved conflict stops productivity.** Agency wise there will be a loss of productivity. Production slows, resulting in poor productivity. Energy is usurped within the conflict and unavailable for productive efforts.
>
> **The conflict absorbs energy that we need to have to fulfill our mission.** With a dysfunctional staff, we lose focus on why we're here. Work effectiveness continues to decrease, and the effective scope becomes smaller and smaller.
>
> **You cannot reach positive results as long as conflict is unresolved.** Conflicts take a tremendous amount of energy, therefore, we have tired people all of the time. You get caught up in bad feelings and can't concentrate on what you have to do.
>
> **Frustration leads to hostility leads to violence.** They become frustrated and start up violent behavior. This may result in rumbling, physical violence, litigation, interpersonal antagonism, a loss of money, or suicide. Somebody is apt to be seriously hurt or possibly killed.

You will note that the outcomes are essentially the same: the conflict will remain or get worse, it becomes accepted as part of the work environment, it affects productivity, it damages relationships, it eventually results in violence, maybe even death. Those latter statements are the response of the reptilian brain. Underlying all these statements is the fear of death. This fear is the motivation for all your actions and words responding to the conflict. These responses will then tend to foster the outcomes you fear.

We ended the day with a closure. This is done at the end of each day or the end of a meeting. It is a way of assessing what we did, of learning from it. Answering the two lifelong learning questions allows you to close your circle, to speak to each other about how you felt about the day, what you learned that will help you to resolve your conflict. From my vantage point, you were all deeply engaged in this discussion. You heads were leaning in, raptly listening to each other. Heads were nodding in agreement at times. You were learning about each other and from each other.

While it was the end of a long day, one in which you were focused on each other for over eight hours, you took your time with the closure. You listened to and learned from each other.

That is the result of the time we spent yesterday. Notice how much information you created. Notice how it all makes sense, how inclusive it is.

Creating New Small Groups: The Art

Once the review of the collective statements is done, the group can move forward to complete their exploration of conflict. I begin by demonstrating a different approach to creating new small and diverse groups.

We will do one task with new small groups to get you grounded and then take a break. In creating small groups today, I want to use a new approach. We will be honoring each of the representative groups in the center of the circle. Then we will number them off to create the diverse small groups.

Remember that we stand to honor people. (I stand and the others follow.) I want the elected officials to come to the center of the circle.

Bob, Frank, and Marcia, all county commissioners, come to the center, followed by Jack, the mayor of the community. Allen steps out and then hesitates. He is the tribal chairman. The other officials wave him in, so he saunters out to join them, a shy smile on his face.

I honor these elected officials for serving you, some for no pay. I honor you for taking the time to be here at this attempt to resolve your conflicts, at your willingness to take the risk to sponsor this session, hoping that some resolution will come from it. Help me honor these people.

The standing community honors these people with great applause. There is much more sincerity this time because they know each other better, having a common experience yesterday. The officials look down, a little sheepish at the positive attention. Frank attempts to leave the center quickly, but returns when I give him a "look." I smile and shake my head, motioning him back to the center.

When the applause is over, I ask the officials to number off.

We are going to create four small groups. You commissioners will be the first facilitators for the groups. I want you to number off to four, starting with Frank and going clockwise.

They do this, with Frank one, Tony two, Marcia three, Allen four, and Jack one. Then they return to the circle. As the officials return to the circle, I remind the group:

Remember, honoring is a self-conscious experience. You can't accept the gift unless you stand there and take it. You have walked away in the past. Now try staying there. You deserve it, so stay in the center.

I want the tribal members to come to the center. Tony, county commissioner, I want you to honor these representatives.

The tribal members walk out to the center, and Tony steps forward a few paces to face them. I made the assumption he would know what to do with this honoring. He does not let me down.

"Allen and Crista, I really appreciate you representing the tribes at this meeting this week. You are, after all, the original people of this land. I know you have a concern about the water and about the fish. When we came here, the land was in its natural conditions. I'm afraid we haven't done the best job of keeping it that way. This land-use plan is intended to do something about it, but again, we haven't done the best job in producing a plan that everybody agrees to. So, I'm looking forward to you helping us with some of your wisdom. We want some of your ideas for keeping the land and taking care of it as best we can."

He steps back into the larger circle and states, "I would like all of us to honor these people." The applause is instant and heartfelt.

Allen, I state, you already have a number, so Crista, you are in group two. Allen and Crista return to their places in the circle.

I want those who are ranchers to come to the center. I want Laura to honor these folks.

The ranchers walk to the center. Tony, the commissioner is also a rancher, so he asks, "Do I go out there again?"

Yes, do this for any role; just don't number off again and keep your original group number.

Wayne, Mike, Jack, Diane, Tony, and Frank are now in the center. Laura honors them.

"I want to honor you ranchers for all you do and have done for this community. You are often overlooked when we make county decisions because you are such a small number in the county, and yet your lands are a major part of the county. And you are always there when we need you in an emergency. It was your concerns over land use that caused us to come together.

"I know you really cannot afford this time away from your ranches, and yet you are here. We thank you for being here."

The applause is again heartfelt. The ranchers stand self-consciously, with red faces and nervous movements. They look askance at each other. They are not used to being honored this way.

Laura directs them to number off:

"We are going to start with you, Diane. You are number three, and then number counter-clockwise around the circle."

The ranchers number off: Diane is three, Mike four, Jack and Tony already have a number, while Wayne is working as a cofacilitator. They stumble through this, but work it all out themselves with some humor thrown in.

I want the businesspeople to come to the center now.

Marie, Jon, and Bud come to the center.

Justin, a real estate broker, asks, "Do we come to the center at this time?"

I think a bit.

No, let's do the real estate and developers separate. But let's include the resorts and mines in this group.

Marie, Jon, Bud, Todd, George, Rob all walk into the center.

Frank, I want you to honor these businesspeople.

Frank hesitates and then speaks: "Waaalll, I know you folks because I do business with you all the time, especially Bud, our banker. I know you are like us, finding it hard to take three days of your time to work out this conflict. It has an effect on profits. But you are here, and you were very interesting to listen to yesterday. We appreciate it because us ranchers don't often get this much time. Thanks for being so civic minded and taking the time."

Applause is instant and heartfelt. These people are well-known and respected in the community. They stay in the center and appear pleasantly surprised by the response. When the applause dies down, Laura proceeds to have the businesspeople number off.

She asks Bud to begin with one. Bud counts one, Marie two, John three, Todd four, George one, and Rob two. Since Frank already has a number, he just returns to the circle. They all return to the larger circle.

I want the environmentalists to come to the center, and Mike (rancher), I want you to honor them.

Alice and Rayni walk to the center. Mike, finding himself in the uncomfortable position of having to honor one of his adversaries, has to think a minute. Then he says:

"You know, my family has been in this country for over five generations. And we believe that we've done a fairly good job of taking care of the land. So it is easy to get mad at newcomers who see things entirely different than we do. I don't agree with much of what you say, but I do agree that change is here. And we need to start doing things differently. I already learned yesterday, just by listening to both of you, that you're decent people, and you have some pretty good ideas. I don't like how we got here, but I'm glad we are here together. So help me honor these folks."

This is probably the first time these two people, members of the community, have been acknowledged in a positive light. They both smile and acknowledge him with a nod of their heads. He could have easily just turned this into a rant.

Alice, as stated, you are in Group 3, and Crista you are in Group 4.

Both return to their places in the circle.

Don't forget to remember your group number, I remind them.

We have a few more groups to honor and number off. I want the retirees and senior citizens to come to the center.

Mark, Lynn, Johanna, and Kathy walk to the center.

Crista, I would like you to honor these folks.

"Thanks Bob," Crista says, delighted that she is able to do this.

"Well...most of you are new to this community. So you are learning how to be a member of the community. As leaders of the drive to get the new land-use plan, you sure caused a great fuss. But I know your hearts are in the right place; I know you never intended to do harm to any of us. Your presence here indicates your willingness to help us do this differently. I'd like to honor you for that."

The applause is light, but feels sincere.

Mark, start at one and then go clockwise.

Mark numbers off one, Lynn two, Johanna three, and Kathy four.

The retirees move back to the circle.

We continue with the remaining groups. The real estate developer group comes to the center and is honored by Joanna, the retired educator. Then they number off. The county and city employees come to the center and are honored by Diane, a college student and rancher. They then number off.

When all have been honored and have a group number, we direct them to the flip charts numbered for their group.

I want you to each take your chair and go to the flip chart designated for your group and form a closed circle in front of it.

The group does this with much humor and noise. Some go quickly to their group and then sneak off to the coffeepot or to a rest break. It takes a little doing to get them together and seated, but that's just a matter of continuing to ask them:

Go to your groups, form a closed circle, and then we'll move ahead to the next task. When this task is over, then we'll take a break.

Sometimes I will provide them a break at the time, if they ask for it.

When they have all settled down, I remind them that they now are in a small group that is still diverse and made up of different perspectives, different from the previous day.

So the next task is for you to meet each other and to learn from the collective statement experience of this morning. I have asked the county commissioners, Frank, Bob, and Marcia, and Allen, the tribal chairperson, to be the facilitators for this first activity. Laura will give you your task.

Collective Statement Grounding

Laura steps up to the circle and asks them to close their circle. "This is not a recorded task," she advises them. "These are the questions you are to answer:"

> Close your circle, do not record.
>
> Introduce yourself.
>
> How do you feel about the collective statements?
>
> What did you learn that will help you resolve the conflicts you have in your community?

When Laura turns and walks away, the groups go to work immediately. There is a quiet hum in the room. It all sounds like a bubbling brook to me. The community is grounding itself.

Let's listen in on Group 1, Frank, Dawn, Bud, George, Debbe, Jack, and Mark:

Frank: "I'm Frank, a longtime rancher in the valley. I'm more used to the comfort of a saddle than I am this chair. No use complaining—you all have the same chairs. So, I'm supposed to speak last. Let's begin with you, Mark, being as how you are new."

Mark: "And what is the question?"

Frank: "Gosh darn it, I forgot the most important part! The question is how we feel about the statements and what we learned that will help us with our conflicts. Then we all take a turn at answering, so Jack will be next after you."

Mark: "OK. Well, this is new to me. I am impressed with all the work you did yesterday and somewhat overcome by the statements and what Bob talked about. I guess it will all make sense to me if I stay today. It is evident you all did some real listening. And everyone seems to have played a part in this. So, I'll just listen now and hopefully become part of what is happening."

Jack: "Welcome, Mark. I'm glad you decided to come. I am also impressed with what we did yesterday, and the day seemed to move pretty fast. I like the way Bob described the collective statements. I also like the idea of listening to everyone's views and creating those statements. Seems to me that if the county had included everyone initially, and really listened, and made decisions that took all views into account, we wouldn't be here today. It's hard to be here, but I really want to stay, because I am beginning to think we might have something here."

Debbe: "Thanks for being here, Mark. Like Jack, I am impressed with what we did. I liked seeing my words in all those statements, makes me feel like I make a difference. We are learning a process one step at a time, and it is different than anything else I have been part of. I still don't know what to make of it all, but I am willing to invest another day in this. I like the collective statements; it is the way it seems to me to resolve our zoning issue. I also feel like we are on the edge of something pretty great. That's all I have to say."

George: "Well, I returned in spite of myself. Things are slow at the resort, and I learned a few things yesterday that I can use in my business. So, after thinking on it, I decided to spend another day. I like the collective statements, especially the best and worst outcomes. They are a new idea to me, especially learning we all have fears about the zoning, even those who sponsored it. And I like those best outcomes, although they seem too good to be true. But who knows? Maybe this will work."

Bud: "I am still weary from yesterday. I didn't sleep well last night; lots of thoughts crossed my mind. My business in banking is pretty stodgy, we do the same things today we have done for years, so to experience what we did yesterday is really stretching me. I am used to stability, this is flexibility. So I am trying to get used to it. I like what happened to us yesterday. We actually met each other, listened to each other. If that isn't community, I don't know what is. Those collective statements seem to have been made by different people than us. Yet they are our words. I am here to learn, hoping this is the answer we have been seeking."

Dawn: "I woke up early also, my mind full of what I learned yesterday. There is no doubt that when we talk about water use and water rights that we all go immediately into our reptilian brains. And I now know that if we stay there, we will make those worst possible outcomes happen. The only way we will solve our water and salmon problem is if we work on it together, as we did yesterday. The collective statements provide a great way of including everyone's voice in the problem and solution. How could we disagree with our best outcomes for the workshop? That is the best community statement I have heard since I have been here. It includes everybody. It still seems impossible to me, but I am ready to learn and make that outcome happen."

Frank: "Well, I don't know if I can follow that. I am a little more cynical, I guess. I liked that statement, too, but it means people have to change their views a little bit. Probably including me. I thought this was going to be a waste of time, still believe in the end that will be the outcome. But I do like the idea of making that best outcome happen. Just don't expect me to sell out my heritage to make that happen. Until I know the ranchers and agriculture are protected and supported in the community, I'll keep my cynicism."

Mark: "Can I speak again?"

Frank: "Yes, but Laura is wondering if we are done. Maybe you can speak and I'll let her know we have one person left."

Mark: "Thanks. I am really amazed at this conversation. No one interrupted, everyone listened, and everything you said was very instructive. And you are all being so honest! I find this so different to our previous conversations in the community, I can hardly believe it. As a new member of the group, I want you to know I support what is going on here. I feel very safe, very much a part of this group. Thanks for letting me belong."

Frank: "Thanks, Mark. OK, Laura, we are ready."

Coaching the Facilitators: The Art

While the groups are working, I continue coaching the cofacilitators. I tell YOU, Wayne, and Laura:

When this task is done, we are going to take a break. After the break, Wayne, you will present the next task. Why don't you review what you are going to do with Laura and me?

Wayne considers this for a moment, then states that he plans to walk up to the edge of the circle. "When I get there, I'll wait just a minute, while they are settling down. And I'm going ask them to pass out the three-by-five cards that they have at the flip charts." He pauses.

"I remember now that you want me to step back and wait while they did that, don't you?"

I nod my head. He continues:

"When they all have their cards, I'll read this question to them: what will be the best possible outcomes of confronting and resolving conflicts in your environment? I'll tell them to record the answer on their three-by-five card and then turn and walk away."

So why did you do that, Wayne? I ask.

"Well, if I just stand there, they will wonder if I have more to say, and of course I don't. So, by walking away, it's a signal to them, nonverbally, to answer the question."

So what's next? I ask.

"When I see they are done writing, then I walk back up to the circle and have the facilitator pick a new facilitator and become the recorder. Right?"

What do you think Laura? I ask.

"I think you got a winner!" Laura says.

"But wait, there's more," Wayne says. "I'll wait until I see everybody is done writing on the flip chart, and then I'll walk up to the circle and ask the recorders to read off what they have recorded. I'll start with Group 1, and then move clockwise around the circle and have them report out their information. Then I'll turn the group over to you."

Nicely done, I say. What I also want you to do when they have completed reporting, is to give them your insight about the best possible outcomes. Just listen to them and see if you can come up with some information that will be helpful to them in moving forward.

"OK," Wayne says with a smile.

Laura has observed that the groups are finished with the grounding. She walks to the edge of the circle and asks: "Has everyone spoken at least once?"

The groups are so intent on talking and listening to each other that they do not hear her. She repeats the question and then adds the statement that we are ready to take a break. That is the magic word. She receives confirmation from each group that they are done.

"We will take a break now for fifteen minutes, and then return to your small groups."

Laura turns and walks away as the groups slowly disband. One group continues to talk very intensely, everyone's head leaning forward, listening to one member of the group speak. In a short time, the group breaks up and takes their break.

~31~

The Best Possible Outcomes of Addressing and Resolving Conflict

Best Possible Outcomes of Resolving Conflict: An Activity

When participants return from the break to their small groups, I get their attention by starting to speak about the activities we will doing this morning. I start by talking about the worst possible outcomes of conflict:

We ended this morning with the collective statement of the worst possible outcomes. Remember that you will imagine these worst possible outcomes for almost every event in your life. You will do it without conscious thought, instantaneously, and begin to behave in a way that fosters those very outcomes. This is especially true when it comes to conflict. Your description of the worst possible outcomes probably describes what is already occurring in your community. They have become self-fulfilling prophecies.

It is natural to have these worst possible outcomes. They ensure your survival. But the issues that confront you are not life-or-death issues. They are life experiences that can be managed. To do that, you will have to focus on the *best* possible outcomes. Your reptilian brain is not capable of answering this question; it is hardwired, so its ability to think is limited. Developing these best possible outcomes moves your thinking to the upper part of your brain, the conscious part of you. This is the task that Wayne will give you next.

Wayne walks to the edge of the circle as I walk away. He provides direction to the groups: "Each group has three-by-five cards at the flip chart. Please pass one to each member of the group."

He steps back from the circle and waits while they do that. Then he steps forward and asks them to record the answer to the question: "Working

The Best Possible Outcomes of Addressing and Resolving Conflict

together, what are the best possible outcomes of confronting and resolving conflicts in your environment?"

He steps away from the circle and waits. When he observes that the group has completed writing, he steps up to the circle and asks the facilitators to select a new facilitator and to become the recorder. He steps back while that is done. Then he steps forward again and directs the facilitators to have their group members read off their best possible outcomes in turn and have the recorder put those on the flip chart. "Take your time," he encourages them, "this is an important task."

Let's listen in on Group 2:

Rob: "So, Lynn, you are the recorder. We are recording our best possible outcomes of conflict. I'll start with you, Susan, and then we will go to the left."

Susan: "This is what I have been waiting for, positive stuff. I'm sick of going over all our worst outcomes. So, record this, Lynn: *We utilize creative cooperative solutions to the benefit of everyone....Our community energy is concentrated on solutions rather than dissipated arguing over who is right.*"

Tony: *"Because of what we have learned here, the situation gets better and people get along....We can move forward and get on with life and work."*

Kenney: *"The issue of conflict will get resolved with more listening. We will create a cohesive community with a clear and shared vision."*

Marie: *"I'll wait until you are done with Kenney, Lynn....We begin to laugh together instead of talking about each other."*

Crista (speaking slowly with pauses): *"The Coyote Mountain tribe will have profitable growth and protection of their resources, especially water and salmon, which results in healthier people and the earth is healed."*

Ann: *"Coyote Basin ranches and farms are expanding and able to hold on to their land. We will feel relieved that it is taken care of, that tensions disappear and we can do our job without taking special precautions."*

Rob: "I'll give mine, Lynn, then Susan can record yours. OK? *We will resolve issues and after successfully resolving one conflict, people will approach succeeding conflicts with confidence.*"

Lynn and Susan change places when Rob's statement is recorded.

Lynn: *"We see better relationships, and develop skills, tools, and techniques to help solve other problems. There is a sense of community among the residents of the county."*

Rob: "I see Wayne is at the edge of the circle, so it must be time to report. Lynn, you will do the reporting."

Wayne is at the edge of the circle. He can see the groups are done. He directs the recorders to read off their information beginning with group 2 and going clockwise.

> **Group 2: The Best Possible Outcomes of Resolving Our Conflicts**
> - *We utilize creative cooperative solutions to the benefit of everyone.*
> - *Our community energy is concentrated on solutions rather than dissipated arguing over who is right.*
> - *Because of what we have learned here, the situation gets better and people get along.*
> - *We can move forward and get on with life and work.*
> - *The issue of conflict will get resolved with more listening.*
> - *We will create a cohesive community with a clear and shared vision.*
> - *We begin to laugh together instead of talking about each other.*
> - *The Coyote River tribe will have profitable growth and protection of their resources, which results in healthier people and land.*
> - *Coyote Basin ranches and farms are expanding and able to hold on to their land.*
> - *We will feel relieved that it is taken care of, that tensions disappear and we can do our job without taking special precautions.*
> - *We will resolve issues and after successfully resolving one conflict, people will approach succeeding conflicts with confidence.*
> - *We see better relationships, and develop skills, tools, and techniques to help solve other problems.*
> - *There is a sense of community among the residents of the county.*

When all of the groups have completed reporting out, Wayne steps forward a little bit and says:

"It is interesting to see how much information you recorded in such a short time. Your new groups went to work as if you had been together for a whole day. I also noticed how much laughter there was in the group. Developing the best outcomes is apparently a much more pleasant task than doing the worst possible outcomes.

"My best possible outcome of resolving our conflict is that **we would be able to work in our community in diverse groups.** Just as we have here. I am very impressed."

Wayne turns and signals to me. I walk toward the edge of the circle and provide an insight:

Best possible outcomes are future imagined events, just as worst possible outcomes are. The difference is you have to move to your neocortex (human brain) in order to answer the question. While these are future imagined events, because the emotions you experience are in the present, Wayne could sense these emotions as you developed a statement. The room is happier; it has a sense of possibility and hope.

Group 1: The Best Possible Outcomes of Resolving Our Conflicts

- *We are able to define our problems and we work together as a community to reach consensus.*
- *It will be a relief being able to speak openly about everything and there will be no repercussions.*
- *There is a new norm and expectation for community interaction and dialog.*
- *We will be open and honest with each other, creating a safe environment.*
- *The feelings created through consensus building include a loving, caring, supportive relationships.*
- *This will help to cut tension and build trust.*
- *Future conflicts may be resolved quicker and effectively.*
- *People feel good in their hearts about the land.*
- *There is preservation of our agricultural lands with regulated growth that provides for all segments of our community and cultures.*
- *We will be more willing to try new things.*
- *There are less appeals and litigation and more community support for decisions.*

Your best possible outcomes are your purpose: *The reason for which something is done or for which something exists*. This is your intention. We often get confused over what a purpose is and what a strategy or action is.

The purpose is the reason for which something is done. A strategy is a way to make it happen.

> **Purpose:** The reason for which something is done or for which something exists

When you express your worst possible outcomes and they are recorded where you can see them, you are becoming self-conscious of material that is normally not conscious. You are expressing a hidden purpose. Strategies and actions that are developed from the worst possible outcomes will, in the end, foster those worst outcomes. By recording the worst possible outcomes earlier, you make yourself conscious of these negative purposes.

By asking you the opposite question, the best possible outcomes, I am helping you develop your positive purpose for the conflicts you have. Not just this conflict, but any conflict. Once you are clear about your purpose, then you can develop strategies that will foster those outcomes. But, you have to know what a purpose is.

Ready, Fire—or—Ready, Aim, Fire: An Insight

Most of us when we have a problem want to immediately move to a solution. (I write the following on the flip chart.)

PROBLEM ⟶ SOLUTION!

Often we will do this without adequately describing the situation (problem). It is natural to do so. But that is like a command for...

"READY ⟶ FIRE!"

without aiming for the target. It is a problem without a conscious purpose. The result is that often the solution does not fit the problem, so the problem remains unresolved.

One result of this approach is that the solution, or strategy ends up becoming the "purpose." That would be like saying that the process we are using here is the purpose. It isn't; it is the process. It is a "how-to," a tool, a way of getting something done. It is not the "something." That something is "the purpose."

The purpose of this process is to help you confront and resolve your conflicts with a consensus agreement. The process helps you get there.

> **Process** is defined as: a series of actions, changes, or functions bringing about the intended result.

If you have a problem or conflict, the normal approach is to try to find a solution, without creating a purpose. This is "READY—FIRE!" There is no "AIMING" in this approach. What tends to happen is that the solution is based on nonconscious worst possible outcomes. These, then, become the unstated purpose.

PROBLEM ---- (WORST POSSIBLE OUTCOMES) ---- SOLUTION

The purpose of the approach we are using today is to resolve your conflict by understanding your purpose for resolving the conflict, both as individuals and as a community.

When we explored conflict and unresolved conflict and how you feel about it, we were becoming "READY!" This is a description of the situation or the "problem." When we explored the worst possible outcomes of confronting or not confronting a conflict, we were exposing to our consciousness those fears that are nonconscious and will affect our behaviors, attitudes, strategies, and actions in resolving the issue. This exposes the negative "purpose."

We then determined the best possible outcomes of confronting and resolving this conflict. These are the positive results you want from any actions you will take. This is your "AIM!" This is your purpose.

PROBLEM-----BEST POSSIBLE OUTCOMES (PURPOSE) ----SOLUTION
READY---------AIM--FIRE

What we will do next is develop the beliefs, behaviors, strategies, and actions that will result in the purpose you have developed, both as individuals and as a community. This is the basis for the solutions, or taking the action to "FIRE!"

What you will have then is a problem, purpose, and a set of approaches to foster the purpose.

It is important to know the difference between a purpose and a strategy in this workshop. Your purpose is to resolve the conflicts you have in your community. Your strategy is to bring the community together for three days to resolve it.

Later today or tomorrow, we will develop the best possible outcomes or the purpose that you wish to create for the actual conflict you have in your community. We can then develop the strategies that will foster those outcomes that meet the needs of every person in the room.

You Can Reach Consensus with a Sense of Community: An Insight

When expressing our worst possible outcomes, it is common to focus on our individual needs or what our group thinks it needs. We are concerned about me, my family, my clan, my profession, my work assignment, my organization. This results in "exclusive thinking." Because of this, it is nearly impossible to reach consensus, much less compromise.

In the best possible outcomes, the word *community* is most commonly referred to three times more often than in the worst possible outcomes. This results in "inclusive thinking." It is much easier to reach consensus with the individuals involved by developing their best possible outcomes.

The process you are experiencing is a strategy or approach that will foster the purpose, or the best possible outcomes that you developed for this workshop and that we listened to this morning when reading the collective statements. My associates will often say, "Trust the process." But if the process does not appear to be fostering the purpose that the group has developed for their workshop, then I will adapt the process so that it does. We are here to serve the people, not the process. I trust the people. I trust you.

> TRUST THE PEOPLE

Once we have developed the purpose of conflict, then we can look at developing approaches that will foster this purpose. We will take your intention and develop means to accomplish that intention. To do this, you have to understand the difference between beliefs and behaviors and strategies and actions.

"When we are motivated by goals that have deep meaning, by dreams that need completion, by pure love that needs expressing, then we truly live life."

—Greg Anderson

BEST/WORST OR WORST/BEST?

I have noticed how people will describe the process as the best and worst. They end with the word "worst." It happens all the time. I was rereading a recent learning manual from one of the groups used for this book and realized that the task's lead-in was described as best and worst possible outcomes. I did that!

Often people will tell me about helping people explore the best and worst possible outcomes. Or, in describing their workshop to a new member, they will describe how yesterday, they learned about best and worst outcomes.

It may seem a little thing, but the lower brain seems to have the upper hand in all of this. The concern for saving our life is its main paramount concern. So it will always leave you with the worst in your mind.

It takes effort to remember to say worst–best. It is an effort that is worth it. Always leave with the best in your mind.

~32~

Relationships

The Ties that Bind: A Visual Activity

"I try to take one day at a time, but lately several days have attacked me at once."

—**Anonymous**

When the insights are completed on the best possible outcomes, I provide an insight that will help the group to be more willing to confront their conflicts.

We are going to demonstrate the relationship process visually. You are going to help me do that by representing people and their relationships in the center of the circle. Remember that this experience is for descriptive purposes and so the situations may be generalized. If I use a specific example from this group, be aware that I am presenting my perception of the relationship, and this could be overstated or misrepresented. I will rely on you to tell me if this is so.

What is a relationship? The dictionary says it's "the way in which two or more people or things are connected or the state of being connected. The way in which two or more people or groups regard and behave toward each other."

1. Two People, Two Relationships:

I ask two people, Susan and Mike, to help me in the center of the circle. I have forty-plus pieces of yarn in my hands, each about forty inches long. I refer to them as relationship strings, the "tie that binds."

Let's start with Mike and Susan coming to the center with me. I hand each a piece of the yarn. These strings represent your relationships with each other. You are going to connect these with each other as I tell this story.

Relationships

Susan and Mike are friends. They have known each other since high school. She tells her friends:

"Mike is the man for me. He takes me everywhere—to the movies, the football games, we watch Monday night football at the tavern together. I even play pool with his friends. I beat them once. He was really proud of me. He tells me his deepest hopes and fears. I know he is going to ask me to marry him some day."

That describes her relationship perception. I connect Susan's string (⟶) with Mike.

$$\text{Susan} \longrightarrow \text{Mike}$$

Mike tells his friends: "Susan is a wonderful friend. She is just like one of the guys. She goes to the football games with me and we watch Monday night football at the tavern together. She even plays pool with my friends. I was really proud of her when she beat them once. She is always available when I want to see a movie. I sure like to tell her these crazy ideas I have about life. I hope that when I meet the right woman, she will let me keep Susan for a friend."

That is his perception of the relationship.

$$\text{Susan} \longleftarrow \text{Mike}$$

In each relationship there are two relationship strings. Obviously, each person has a different perception of their relationship. Yet, they believe and behave as if their perception is the same.

It is only when Susan wants Mike to go to a wedding with her on a Saturday, when she finds that Mike has a date with the guys to watch the football game that he won't change, that their differing needs and wants become obvious. Her disappointment and his confusion are a measure of their differing perceptions.

Susan has a closer relationship than Mike did. (I move her hand down her relationship string so it is closer to Mike.) Mike, on the other hand, does not feel his relationship is as close.

$$\text{Susan} \rightleftarrows \text{Mike}$$

2. The Multiplier Effect:

Let's suppose, though, that Susan is right. They do get married. In a fit of Super Bowl passion, Mike asks Susan if he can be the quarterback of her life. She responds positively, provided she gets to choose some of the plays in the game.

They decide to have a family. Soon, in the appropriate amount of time, they have a bouncing baby boy born to them. (I signal to Wayne that I want him to join Susan and Mike.)

Cute little Wayne arrives with a relationship string for Mom and a relationship string for Dad. They each also each have a relationship string for him.

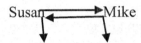

When Wayne comes to the center of the circle to be Baby Wayne, I have each of them connect their strings, a clumsy and uncertain process, just as the establishment of relationships is.

This is how the relationship strings look now.

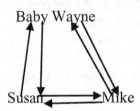

I ask the group how many relationship strings are in the family now. Someone calls out "six."

Be aware of the number of relationships strings as we proceed. So, while they have introduced one new member to the family, they have increased their relationship strings to six, a *threefold increase*. Each person added to the family has a multiplier effect.

Baby Wayne thinks, "If I cry, Mom will drop everything to feed me." Mom's response is, "I can't leave this stove while the food is cooking, so he will have to wait." They have two relationships, each based on different perceptions.

Dad buys his son a baseball mitt for Christmas. He wants him to play ball professionally. Wayne is sad because he wanted a guitar. He wants to make music, to sing. Each is disappointed by this misperception. They have two relationship strings, each based on a different perception. But they both believe they are the same.

Suppose they have a second child, a beautiful, intelligent girl, Ann. (I ask Ann to come into the circle). Ann has three relationship strings, one each for Mom, for Dad, and for Wayne. They each have one for her.

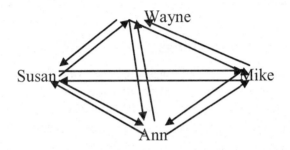

How many strings are there? I ask rhetorically. While they are trying to puzzle it out, I have the family members connect their relationship strings. It is an awkward process, each person trying to get theirs connected first. Jon says there are twelve relationship strings now.

Jon is correct! This is six times the original two relationship perceptions! This indicates that it will take six times the amount of energy to manage this family. Those who are married with children know how much additional energy it takes to manage this new situation.

Ann loves her brother; he is her hero and she wants to be anywhere he is. Wayne is embarrassed by his younger sister tagging along. He teases her and sends her home crying. Each person has a different perception of the relationship.

In this workshop group, there are thirty-four people. We are managing 1,122 (34 x 33) relationships. This is a lot to manage. That is why I have you meet in the small groups. In your groups of eight, you are managing fifty-six relationships. By using small groups, we reduce the amount of energy it takes to manage the process. (If in a group of nine, it would be seventy-two relationship strings, a 30 percent increase.)

> **RELATIONSHIP FORMULA**
>
> The number increases as more people are added to the relationship circle. The formula is: number of persons times the number of persons minus one: N x (N – 1). Ten people have ninety relationships (10 x 9). Twenty people have 380 relationships to manage (20 x 19).
>
> A manager making a change presentation to an audience of one hundred doubting publics is managing 9,900 relationships (100 x 99). This is why it is important in these situations to use a small-group process. Each group of ten is then managing only ninety relationships.

3. Relationships with Things:

We also have relationships with things. You have a relationship with your car, and it has one with you. You depend on the car to start, until one morning it decides to let you down. It is not as dependable as you perceived.

Or you may have a relationship with alcohol. You believe you can stop drinking any time you want. The alcohol knows you can't and is able to tempt you to continue.

This relationship with a thing may affect the entire family, just as a person does. I can tell if it does by listening to family members. If Mom complains to her husband about him drinking all the time, she is connected to the alcohol. If the daughter is embarrassed by her Dad's drunken behavior at a ball game, *she* has a relationship with the alcohol. If our family above has an alcoholic father and this affects their relationship, the diagram looks like this:

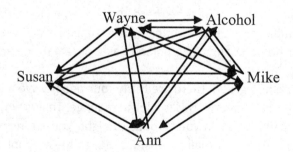

When Mike comes home drunk after Monday night football, he affects all the members of the family. Susan argues with Mike over the drinking.

Wayne and Ann may choose sides, one of them defending their father, the other the mother. This affects their relationship with their mother and each other. Since the issue of alcohol is connected to all of them it becomes part of the relationship system in the family. It impacts energy, as an additional member of the family with its own relationships would. They are now managing twenty relationship strings (5 x 4). This increases the energy it takes to manage their family by 67 percent (from twelve to twenty, a 67 percent increase.)

A caveat is needed here. This string visual is only representative of the relationships situation. The amount of energy stated is also relative to the situation. They are not actual measurable facts, but a way of demonstrating the relative impacts, helping you understand the nature of relationships and how they are affected by conflicts. The intent is to help you understand how important it is to resolve them.

4. Relationships with Organizations:

We can have a relationship with an impersonal thing, such as an organization. Mike believes that the computer business he works for is like a family. He has no concerns about his job, because they will take care of him. Then the organization sells out to a larger firm that replaces Mike. Mike feels betrayed because he thought the organization had the same belief he has. There are two different perceptions of the relationship. Rarely are these differences ever brought to awareness and talked about so they are understood.

If Mike just works normal hours and doesn't take his work home with him, then the organization relationship is only with Mike. But if Mike works late at nights and is unavailable for his family because he is always in deep thought about his work, then the organization relationship is connected with the family.

Susan will complain to him about his always being at work. Wayne is mad because Dad can't attend his soccer game. Ann is miffed because he missed her birthday party.

Because of the organizational impact, they may now have thirty relationships to manage (6 x 5), an increase of 50 percent from the previous situation and a 250 percent increase from the original family of four with twelve relationships.

If Susan has a relationship with the church that keeps her away from the family, this, too, affects them all. It increases Mike's reliance on alcohol. The children act out to get their mother's attention. They now have forty-two relationships to manage (7 x 6).

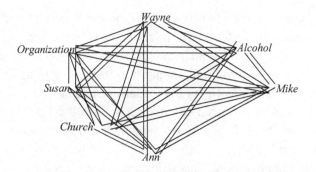

5. Relationships Become Interrelated:

Each unresolved conflict becomes intertwined with the other unresolved conflicts. Susan complains that Mike is never home because of the organization, and when he is, he's normally drunk. He tells her he wouldn't drink if she were home more often instead of always being at the church.

As long as they remain unresolved, these conflicts become more fodder for the argument.

6. Relationship with Values:

Arguments often rise over values. Mike was raised in a family that was very strict and used punishments to keep the kids in line. Susan was raised in a family that was more permissive, allowing the children to experience the consequences of their actions. Rarely is an issue such as discipline talked about either before or after the child is born.

The outcome is arguments over how to discipline Wayne or Ann if they get poor grades or don't do their chores. How will they discipline for disobedience? These become constant sources of irritation and stress in the family. This is especially true when the children become teenagers and begin to assert themselves against their parents' control.

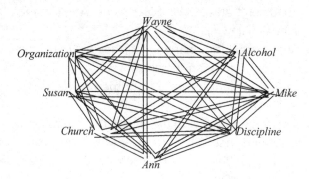

They now have fifty-six relationships in the family (8 x 7).

7. Relationship with Traditions:

Differences in family traditions have a way of becoming part of the relationships in a family. If Dad and Mom have an argument over where to spend their holidays or the kind of Christmas tree they want for Christmas, this eventually affects them all. The children roll their eyes when they argue over this and escape to a friend's home. The parents argue about how they should discipline the kids because they left without permission. Again, they may take sides. Mike just works more, drinks more, using the holiday as an excuse. Mom spends more time with the church.

(Note: The graphic below includes both the tradition issue and the change issue.)

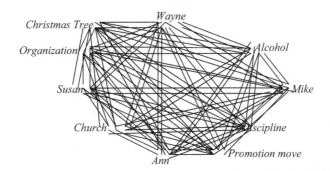

8. Relationship with Change:

Mike wants to move to a new location where he can get a promotion. He can't understand why Susan won't move. Maybe they could start over in their relationship and leave the old one behind. Besides, he rationalizes, her clothes would all be new to people in a new location. It would save the family money.

Susan doesn't want to leave the security of her work with the church. She doesn't want to leave the friends she has developed over the years. The children don't want to leave their school and their friends. She is upset he would equate moving with her clothes. With the addition of the holidays and the possible change, this family is now managing ninety relationships (10 x 9). This takes forty-five times the energy to manage the situation than when it was only Wayne and Ann, or eight times the energy with the whole family.

9. Relationship with Loss—A Doubling of Energy:

If Susan gives in and agrees with a move, this creates more stress. For each member of the family, there is a process of "letting go" and "taking hold" that must happen. Mike must let go of the old position and take hold of the new one. Susan has to do the same with the church, the children with their friends and school. This is a representation of Susan letting go of her old church and taking hold of the new:

Old Church (Letting go)　　Susan　　　　New church (Taking Hold)

Susan must work through the loss of the old church relationship, clearing the way to take hold of the new church.

But what if she resents the loss of the old church and takes those unfinished feelings with her? Then the number of relationships with church will double.

Old church　　　　Susan　　　　New church

This means she will have doubled the relationships with church (from two to four). The feelings about the loss of the old church are a resentment she may hide.

But what if she applies the resentment to the new church, trying to get the congregation to accept her old church ways in their services? She wants to retain the old church feelings in the new church. If church members disagree and push back, then she has created a relationship problem between the old church and the new church.

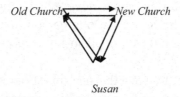

Old Church　　　　New Church

Susan

Now Susan is managing six relationship strings, or three times the energy than with the old church.

Unless the family resolves its emotional feelings about leaving the old situation for the new, they face a doubling or tripling of the energy needed to maintain their family in the new situation.

But if they accept the move, it will still affect their schools, friends, church, and organizational relationships.

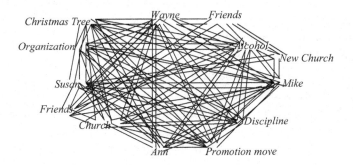

With the proposal to move, this family is trying to manage 156 relationship strings (13 x 12). No wonder they feel stressed out when they get together. No wonder they don't get together very often. Susan is at church, Mike at the bar, the children with their friends.

These unresolved relationship perceptions take energy to manage. Each unresolved conflict and change event "piggybacks" energy on the other. When Mike and Susan argue over alcohol, their instruments of war become the church, the tree, the promotion, the school, and friends.

10. Relationship with Stress:

Continuing to build up unresolved issues or conflicts eventually results in high levels of stress. These continuing high levels impact the mood of the individuals, the family, damaging their relationships, often causing family members to seek unhealthy ways to reduce their stress.

The high level of stress affects the immune system and often results in severe health problems. Each health problem—heart ailments, cancer, continuous colds, or flu—adds additional relationship strings and increases the energy it takes to manage the family system.

11. Releasing Energy by Resolving Conflicts:

The purpose of the relationship-string visual is to help you see how unresolved conflicts affect the energy in your lives. It also provides a measure of the energy releases you can gain by resolving your conflicts.

To reduce the stress resulting from managing all these unresolved relationship perceptions, this family must confront and resolve their conflicts regarding the organization, alcohol, their holidays, the church, discipline, and the changes they are going through.

What you will learn is that if you resolve just one unresolved conflict in your organization, in your family, or in your personal relationships, you will release the maximum amount of energy into that situation.

Susan and Mike, who love each other dearly, decide they must get counseling to save their marriage and the family. At their second session, they decide to postpone any change in location for Mike's job. By setting just this one this issue aside, with mutual agreement, and having reduced their concerns about change, they have reduced the relationship strings they are managing from 156 (13 x 12) to 132 (12 x 11). This reduces the energy needed to manage the family by 15 percent. This is an energy increase of 15 percent that is available to focus on how they can further improve their situation.

The sense of relief and hope allows this family to decide what is really important to them. It also releases the stress related to leaving their friends. That reduces the strings to ninety (10 x 9). This results in a further increase of energy, reducing the stress by an additional 27 percent. The decision to stay allows Susan to refocus on her existing church and reduces the need to worry about connecting to a new church. This reduces the stress to managing seventy-two strings (9 x 8).

At their fourth counseling session and with the encouragement and support of the computer organization, Mike agrees to outpatient treatment for his alcohol abuse. His willingness to do this delights all members of the family and improves his standing as a father and husband. As he controls his use of alcohol, the family is now managing fifty-six relationship strings (8 x 7), a total reduction of a hundred strings, resulting in a total of 64 percent energy release into the family.

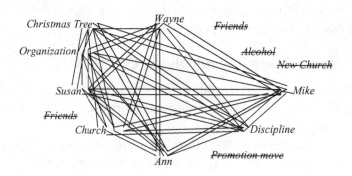

This energy release is now available to continue to make this family healthy.

At their fifth and sixth counseling sessions, Mike and Susan agree to limit the amount of time they spend with their respective organizations. They agreed to be home every evening and to set time aside for communicating with their family. These two changes reduce the number of strings they're managing to forty-two, a total of 73 percent increase in energy.

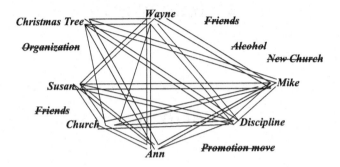

Every unresolved conflict you resolve releases energy into your family, your community, your organization, and your personal relationships. You do not have to resolve every conflict; just resolve one or two so that you release the energy necessary to manage the others. Eventually, if you have a positive attitude toward the resolution of conflict, you will resolve conflicts as they are created and continually release energy into your situation.

Remember, this is only a *representation* of how your energy can be tied up with conflict. We have the capacity to manage a lot of strings. Continually increasing the strings, however, eventually causes stress and reduces your ability to manage the situation. But solve one, and the energy increase will be measurable.

~33~

Fostering the Best Possible Outcomes

Beliefs, Behaviors, Strategies, Actions: An Activity

When I finish relationship visual insight, I move the group to the next task.

Now that we have developed the best possible outcomes, or our purpose, we can take "aim" on specific approaches that will make them happen. Fostering the purpose will require looking at beliefs, behaviors, strategies, and actions. Each of these is a different focus.

On the flip chart behind Laura, I have symbolized your person as a set of concentric circles. In the center are your beliefs. From your beliefs rise your behaviors and attitudes. These are in the next concentric ring. This ring is larger, because many behaviors or attitudes can rise from a single belief. In the next ring are your strategies, or your overarching approaches to whatever actions are needed. There are many potential strategies for any situation. In the next ring are your actions, the specific steps you will take to resolve your conflict. These are almost infinite in their possibilities, but are appropriate only if they represent the beliefs in the center.

Beliefs: Beliefs are convictions or opinions, firmly held and often based on widely held opinions learned from your upbringing in your family and in the environment you grew up in. They are also the result of your life experiences, from which you draw conclusions and then hold them as firm beliefs. Our beliefs underlie all of our behaviors and attitudes.

Behaviors: These are the manners and attitudes created by our basic individual beliefs. They describe the deportment or demeanor we have toward others. It is the way we operate based on our beliefs.

Behaviors that are incongruent with a person's openly expressed beliefs may often be expressed. If I state that I believe that women are equal to men and then treat women in a subservient or discriminatory way, my behavior indicates the opposite of my expressed belief. Or I may say I am "fine" when my nonverbal signals say I'm not. This often confuses people because they read the nonverbal behavior as reality.

Beliefs and behaviors are inextricably intertwined. It is difficult to separate the two. I do not try to separate them. It is not unusual for a small group to get into an argument over which is which. When they bring the concern to me, I just advise them to record whatever the person says as either belief or behavior. It is that person's choice. This resolves the issue and allows the group to move ahead. A behavior description can easily be reworded to become a belief and vice versa.

Strategies: A strategy is a plan that is intended to carry out a purpose, vision, or mission. It is an overarching statement that encompasses a whole series of specific actions. Strategies must be able to accomplish the belief or purpose of a person or group to be successful.

Actions: These are specific deeds or acts that carry out the intent of the strategy. Actions must be able to accomplish the belief or purpose of a person or group to be successful.

We are used to focusing only on strategic plans or action plans. Only rarely do we focus on the beliefs and behaviors when trying to resolve an issue.

I explain the need for a paradigm shift in confronting their conflicts:

Managing a paradigm shift: Focusing on strategies and actions is appropriate only if the conflict requires a modification of the way we work together. It does not affect your basic beliefs. If, however, our basic beliefs are in opposition and prevent us from addressing and resolving a new situation, it is necessary to revisit them. Creating new beliefs and behaviors is known as a paradigm shift (remember...shift happens!).

A paradigm is a pattern, a mental map we use to recognize our world. This pattern is based on our cultural mores, basic or core beliefs, the experiences we have had, the determinations we have made from these experiences, our professional beliefs, religious beliefs, et cetera. This pattern has worked for us before, but it may not be working for us now. This requires that we look at these basic or core beliefs and behaviors to determine if they need to be changed.

Because you indicated your belief that conflict can, for the most part, only result in worst possible outcomes, and you want to create best possible outcomes, then it is appropriate to look at making a paradigm shift. Otherwise, your present beliefs will get in the way of resolving your conflict. In this instance, new and adaptive beliefs must be developed.

That is the activity you will do next. As you do this activity, be aware that I am providing you the opportunity to reprogram yourself when it comes to conflict, to establish some new potential beliefs and behaviors that will allow you to resolve the conflicts in your life. Not just the conflict that brings us together today, but any conflict. I want to remind you that it is your choice. All of your answers are the right answers.

I have asked Laura to facilitate this task. (I had coached Laura while the small groups were doing the best outcomes task.)

> Pass out the 3 x 5 cards. (Pause)
>
> What new and adaptive beliefs/behaviors will foster the best possible outcomes?
>
> Change facilitators.

Laura walks to the edge of the circle and provides them direction for the task:

"Please pass out the three-by-five cards that you have at your flip chart."

Laura turns and walks away while they do this task. When they are done, she returns to the circle and says:

"I want you to record the answer to this question on your three-by-five card: *What new and adaptive beliefs or behaviors will foster the best possible outcomes of your conflicts?*"

Laura turns and walks away while they do this task. Once again there is silence in the room as the participants deliberatively think about and then record the new and adaptive beliefs or behaviors they will need to foster the purpose (best possible outcomes) of their conflicts.

As Laura observes that only a few people are still writing, she moves to the edge of the circle, waiting until they have all completed their recording. She provides the next direction:

"The facilitator will pick a new facilitator and become the recorder."

She steps back and allows groups to make that decision. She steps forward and provides instructions for the completion of the task:

"When you have selected your new facilitator, each of you will read your new beliefs and behaviors, so they can be recorded on the flip chart. Take your time with this; make certain all that is written on your card is recorded on the flip chart. It is OK if some statements are repetitive."

The small groups immediately focus on recording their information to the flip charts. There is an easy feeling in the room. A sense of community. As participants read off their new beliefs and behaviors, others in their group nod their heads. Some record on their own three-by-five cards what they heard from others.

Laura turns and walks away to join YOU and Wayne and me. While the small groups were recording their information, I review the next steps in the process.

Next Steps: Coaching the Facilitators

Wayne, you will facilitate the next task. Now that they have identified the beliefs and behaviors that will help them resolve the conflict, we want them to develop strategies and actions that will rise from those beliefs and behaviors and foster the best possible outcomes.

I give Wayne a 3 by 5 card with the task questions. When we have reviewed this, I began to update Wayne and Laura on the process for this afternoon.

> Pass out the 3 x 5 cards.
>
> What strategies or actions will foster the best possible outcomes?
>
> The facilitator picks a new facilitator and becomes the recorder.

Arenas of conflict: When we have completed the actions activity, I will bring the groups back to the large community. Laura, I will want you to pass out three-by-five cards to everyone. I will then review with them the basic consensus-building process they have just experienced. I want them to understand that there are three arenas of conflict: personal, interpersonal, and intergroup. I will then provide them an opportunity to explore a personal issue using this basic process. This allows them to apply what they have learned to the conflict they have in their personal arena.

Advocacy panel with listeners: When that has been accomplished, we will begin to help this group address the conflict that confronts the community. We will start with three to five pairs of people representing the strongest opposing views. These pairs will be allowed to express their strongly held views about the conflict at hand. While they do this, they will have listeners, who will ensure the person spoken to hears the message. We will do this to bring the issue into the circle.

Small-group advocacy: When the pair encounters are done, we will honor them and move them back into the small groups. The pairs will act as facilitators and recorders for their groups. This will be a talking circle with no recording. Each person in the small group will have the opportunity to express their strongly held views about the conflict.

Recording: When everyone has spoken, we will ask them to record the views they heard from others, as well as the views that they expressed, on a three-by-five card. This information will then be recorded to the flip charts. This activity normally takes an hour or more, so it may be the last activity we do for the day.

If there is time left over, we will have the group develop the worst possible outcomes of resolving or not resolving the issue in the community.

Finally, we will end the day with closure as we did yesterday. We will then assign collective statements to the people who recorded them.

Selecting panel members: Wayne, I want you and Laura to do two things for me during the next task. I first need you to select a male and female pair who can replace you tomorrow as facilitators. You will begin to coach them this afternoon.

I also want you to select four pairs of participants, preferably two people from each group, who can represent opposing viewpoints about the issue that brought us together. I want this to be a balanced group, with gender balance, new people and longtime people, young and old, and representing the different perceptions in the room. Take time doing this, because these are the people who will be raising the issue with their strongly held views and placing it in the circle.

Back to the Community

While we were working on the process for the rest of the afternoon, the rest of the groups were busy at their task. Let's listen in on Group 2 as they record their information to the flip charts:

Bud: "OK, let's get started. Ann will record as you read off your statements. Let's start with you, Bob, and then we will go clockwise. We will finish with Ann."

George: "These are the ideas I wrote...*A belief in openness, open-mindedness, willingness to be honest about our own feelings and issues.*" (Pausing as Ann records.) "Yeah, you got it! Then...*Listen with respect.* OK..." (Slowly, waiting for Ann to catch up.) "*Really pay attention to the speaker with the intention to understand and accept that every opinion is part of the solution.*"

Marie: "I like those, George. Don't record that, Ann. This is my first: *Conflict can be good and result in positive change.*" (Pauses.) "Next... *We can* (underline that Ann) *if we think we can.*"

Kenney: "*Each person is right in their own mind. We are all equal. We are not alone. People need to become involved.* Do you want me to repeat those?" (Repeats more slowly.)

Ann: "Thanks for slowing down there, Kenney. I'm getting a cramp in my hand."

Rob: "*We believe people need to feel that the process will be safe and their opinions valued and equally respected.*" (Pauses.) "*Listen better to value beliefs that are different from ours. Make sure everyone's voice is recorded accurately.* Especially mine!" (Laughter.) "Don't record that last part, Ann."

Lynn: "My thoughts are based on what we did today. I'll read these slowly, Ann. *Respect is fundamental.*" (Pauses.) *"Value everyone's thoughts and feelings, it is important for the acknowledgment of others."*

Susan (speaking slowly): *"Be aware of, and understand, the reptilian brain syndrome. As we involve others in resolving conflict, we gain. Use the power of imagining the best outcome."*

Crista: *"Truly believe that diversity is good; make an effort to be inclusive of differing viewpoints. Everyone is valuable and has something to contribute, each in their own unique way."*

Bud: "OK, I guess it is my turn, then we will do yours, Ann. My first belief...*Listening to everyone's input should be our goal.* Second...*Trust people more by understanding.* Third...*We need to believe in achieving the impossible, that going slow to go fast makes good sense.*

"OK, Ann, be seated and...Susan, could you please record for Ann?"

Susan, getting up to the easel: "I am ready, Ann."

Ann: "My statements are based on what I have learned so far. This is the first one...*People have the ability to resolve their own conflicts.*" (Pauses.) *"Even if negative feelings occur, we still can have best outcomes.* And this final one is something we need to do...*We will celebrate our accomplishments.*"

Bud: "Does anyone have anything to add?"

Kenney: "I am really amazed at how easy this is today. Yesterday it felt like driving in deep mud, but today everything just flows."

Lynn: "I am sort of amazed at how close we all are in our statements. We really have a lot in common."

Bud: "We better pay attention right now; Laura wants to know if we have all spoken. I guess we have?" Bud nods to Laura that the group is done.

Group 2: Beliefs and Behaviors

- *A belief in openness, open-mindedness, willingness to be honest about our own feelings and issues.*
- *Listen with respect.*
- *Really pay attention to the speaker with the intention to understand and accept that every opinion is part of the solution.*
- *Conflict can be good and result in positive change.*
- *We <u>can</u> if we think we can.*

Fostering the Best Possible Outcomes

> - *Each person is right in their own mind.*
> - *We are all equal.*
> - *We are not alone.*
> - *People need to become involved.*
> - *We believe people need to feel that the process will be safe and their opinions valued and equally respected.*
> - *Listen better to value beliefs that are different from ours.*
> - *Make sure everyone's voice is recorded accurately.*
> - *Respect is fundamental.*
> - *Value everyone's thoughts and feelings, it is important for the acknowledgment of others.*
> - *Be aware of, and understand, the reptilian brain syndrome.*
> - *As we involve others in resolving conflict, we gain.*
> - *Use the power of imagining the best outcome.*
> - *Truly believe that diversity is good; make an effort to be inclusive of differing viewpoints.*
> - *Everyone is valuable and has something to contribute, each in their own unique way.*
> - *Listening to everyone's input should be our goal.*
> - *Trust people more by understanding.*
> - *We need to believe in achieving the impossible that going slow to go fast makes good sense.*
> - *People have the ability to resolve their own conflicts.*
> - *Even if negative feelings occur, we still can have best outcomes.*
> - *We will celebrate our accomplishments.*

By this time, all the small groups have completed their task. They are busily engaged in conversations that are important enough that each person's head is leaning in toward the center. There is a lot of good, healthy laughter.

Laura walks to the edge of the circle and asks: "Has everyone spoken at least once?"

She has to repeat this four times before she has everyone's attention. They all signal they are done.

Speaking from the edge of the circle, Laura asks the recorders to read off their recorded statements. "Let's start with Group 1, then we will go clockwise."

> **Group 1: Beliefs and Behaviors**
> - *There is a belief that you or I are not above the rest.*
> - *I believe that everyone has unique talents to enhance the group.*
> - *Acknowledge the worst and focus on the best.*
> - *People must believe in themselves and know what they say is important.*
> - *Learn how to link the ideas of others without synthesizing words.*
> - *Relationships are everything and taking time to develop them to solve problems is powerful.*
> - *To encourage people to speak their minds and to treat them with respect.*
> - *Look at the situation from another person's viewpoint.*
> - *Others truly are interested in conflict resolution.*
> - *You don't have to agree or own to listen to others.*
> - *We will treat each other with compassion, trust, and integrity and will consider the effects of our beliefs on others' lives.*
> - *Slow down and create a listening environment.*
> - *Everyone should be allowed to be heard.*
> - *Understand that voicing an opinion or concern does not equate to demanding an agreement.*
> - *People are basically good.*
> - *Listen and trust what you hear.*
> - *Release anger and fear so that I can listen with an open mind.*
> - *Each participant truly wishes for a change.*
> - *Everyone has a right to their own opinion and will be listened to with respect.*

When all have reported on their work, I walk to the edge of the circle to present an insight.

Congruent Behaviors: An Insight

"Don't do as I do, do as I say."

There is a saying on the street that "if you're going to talk the talk, you've got to walk the walk." This is the same as saying, "Your actions speak louder than words" or "Practice what you preach."

I can tell when a group is prepared to confront their conflict by watching their behaviors with this task. You are behaving the beliefs you have described in your groups. For example, "Listening to everyone's input should be our goal." Or "Value everyone's thoughts and feelings, it is important for the acknowledgment of others." Or "Make sure everyone's voice is recorded accurately."

I observed that each of these statements is being behaved in your groups. This makes your beliefs congruent with your behaviors. This establishes integrity. It means you are now prepared to confront and resolve your conflicts.

Wayne will present your next activity.

> **CONGRUENT BEHAVIORS**
>
> When the individuals' behavior in the groups matches the words being recorded, I know they are ready to resolve their conflict.

Strategies and Actions: An Activity

Wayne walks to the edge of the circle and presents the task: "Pass out the three-by-five cards."

When all have cards, he continues: "Answer this question: *What strategies or actions will foster the best possible outcomes?*"

He steps back and waits while the participants record in silence. When they all appear to be done (normally the silence is broken by people talking and laughing), he steps to the edge of the circle and presents the final step:

"The facilitator picks a new facilitator and becomes the recorder. Record your information to the flip chart. Reverse the direction from the previous activity."

The groups go to work immediately. Their voice tones are low, like a bubbling brook. There are thirty- people in the small groups, yet the sound level is about that of two people speaking in normal tones. Their voice tones now facilitate listening with respect.

> **OPTIONS: BELIEFS/BEHAVIORS/STRATEGIES/ACTIONS - THE ART**
>
> I don't normally do both the beliefs/behaviors and strategies/actions tasks. If it appears there is a paradigm shift, I will focus on beliefs/behaviors only. Then the strategies and actions are developed on the real issue.
>
> Sometimes I will have half the groups focus on the beliefs/behaviors and the other half on strategies/actions.

Let's be a fly on the wall with Group 4:

Gil: "OK, has everyone finished their recording?" He looks around the group. Rayni is still writing. "When Rayni is done, let's start with you, Allen, then go counterclockwise. We will finish with Rayni."

Mike: "Should we be identifying strategies and actions separately?"

Gil: "Bob said earlier to let the person speaking decide that on the beliefs and behaviors. I imagine he means the same here."

Rayni: "I'm done, Gil."

Mike: "OK, I just thought I would check."

Gil: "Glad you did, Mike. Rayni, are you ready to record for us?"

Rayni (getting up to record): "Yes, just speak slowly for me. I am not a fast writer."

Allen (speaking slowly): *"We will include diverse populations and make sure all participants, including the Tribal and Hispanic population, are being brought in."* (Pauses.) *"Allowing everyone to be heard."*

Wayne: *"I have four statements; I'll read them slowly, Rayni."* (He pauses between each statement, watching Rayni as she records.) *"Acknowledge the fears of the worst possible outcomes...Bring all people to a room and arrange so that they are facing each other... Resolve the conflicts at the early stage...All resources and the public should be heard. Thanks, Rayni."*

Rayni: "Did I get them all right? I'll read them off from now on, OK?"

Everyone nods yes.

Todd: *"Making collective statements and identifying a mission statement by listing our beliefs about the conflict is key. Using a step-by-step process and structure can make people listen to and build a foundation for communication and trust."*

Jim: "I agree with Todd. *We need a concept of the future...how far are we managing? Then...Not waiting for someone else to improve their behavior before you improve yours. Finally...We will have no hidden agendas.*"

Mike (speaking slowly, looking up as Rayni records): *"We are to listen respectfully to everyone's views and not react too soon. Think first, be assertive, and speak your truth. We will involve community members in decision making, because consensus is needed for strategies and actions."*

Gil: "I just have two, Rayni. I'll go slow so you can go fast." (Laughter from the group.) *"This process is put in place to confront issues and to practice skills we have been learning. We will be taking time, and not placing time constraints on meetings."* (Waits until the last words are recorded.) "Rayni, I'll record yours for you."

Rayni (sitting down as Gil goes to the flip chart): "Mine is long. *Change existing behaviors...to ensure that small problems or conflicts are dealt with directly...rather than have them left as a cancer inside of somebody...or to be discussed without that person present. We must not use positional power to solve problems.*"

Gil (sitting down as Rayni returns to the easel): "Is that it, or do you have another?"

Mike: "I thought of one as you were writing. *Have no side conversations and delegate facilitating to the unexpecting person.*" (The group laughs loudly.) "OOOPS! I wasn't referring to you, Gil. I just meant we need to include everyone in the facilitating."

Gil: "I got the idea, Mike. I'll add this statement, Rayni. *A feeling of inclusiveness will result.* Finish that, Wayne wants us to move on."

Wayne has walked to the edge of the circle and asked if all have spoken at least once. When Group 4 acknowledges they are done, he asks the recorders to read off their information.

"Lets begin with group 3 group 4 and go counterclockwise."

GROUP 4: STRATEGIES AND ACTIONS TO FOSTER THE BEST POSSIBLE OUTCOMES

- *We will include diverse populations and make sure all participants, including the Tribal and Hispanic population, are being brought in.*
- *Allowing everyone to be heard.*
- *Acknowledge the fears of the worst possible outcomes.*
- *Bring all people to a room and arrange so that they are facing each other.*
- *Resolve the conflicts at the early stage.*
- *All resources and the public should be heard.*
- *Making collective statements and identifying a mission statement by listing our beliefs about the conflict is key.*
- *Using a step-by-step process and structure can make people listen to and build a foundation for communication and trust.*
- *I agree with Todd…We need a concept of the future…how far are we managing?*
- *Not waiting for someone else to improve their behavior before you improve yours.*
- *We will have no hidden agendas.*
- *We are to listen respectfully to everyone's views and not react too soon.*
- *Think first, be assertive and speak your truth.*
- *We will involve community members in decision making, because consensus is needed for strategies and actions.*
- *This process is put in place to confront issues and to practice skills we have been learning.*
- *We will be taking time, and not placing time constraints on meetings.*
- *Change existing behaviors to ensure that small problems or conflicts are dealt with directly rather than have them left as a cancer inside of somebody or to be discussed without that person present.*
- *We must not use positional power to solve problems.*
- *Have no side conversations and delegate facilitating to the unexpecting person.*
- *A feeling of inclusiveness will result.*

When all the information has been presented, Wayne turns the groups over to me for an insight on this task.

Once again your behaviors indicate that you are being congruent with your statements in all groups. Listen to these statements you recorded. (I read these from the flip charts at random.)

"We will also not impose our will on others. Acknowledge the validity of other's concerns. Through respectful listening we will be looking and listening to one another. We will include diverse populations and make sure all participants, including the Tribal and Hispanic population, are being brought in. Have no side conversations and delegate facilitating to the unexpected person. We will be taking time and not placing time constraints on meetings."

These indicate you are congruent in your behaviors and words.

Now I want you to form the large community circle.

The small groups move their chairs and merge with the other groups into the large circle. When I get their attention, I talk about the afternoon.

We are going to take a break for lunch. After lunch we will be in the large circle, where I will go over the basic consensus process you have experienced. I will also introduce you to a quick way to resolve your internal personal conflicts—that is, those conflicts you have with yourself in your mind.

Then we are going to focus on your real conflict this afternoon. We will begin with pairs of community members speaking and listening to each other in the large circle. They will begin the discussion of the existing situation and how it came to be that way. That will probably take the rest of the afternoon.

Before we break, there are six people I want to talk with in the center of the room. I want Jack and Lynn, Bud and Alice, Mike and Allen.

Being with Real People: An Insight for the Reader

I stand back and observe the group eating their lunch. This is a decidedly different group than the one that I started with a day and a half ago. There is very little tension or anxiety in the room. The people sitting together at the round tables are totally different from those at yesterday's lunch.

Yesterday the groups eating together were people of like mind. Today the groups eating together are diverse, often including those who were the most alienated or angry at each other. It does not feel like there are any adversaries in this room.

The reason is that all these people now know each other. They have listened with respect to each other for a day and a half. In doing so, they are gaining an understanding of each person and through this, developing a sense of trust that will help them resolve the conflict.

But they have not only listened to each other, they have also recorded each other's words on the flip charts for all to see. Just imagine how this simple act can change the relationship between two people who are adversaries, who have stereotyped each other as "the enemy."

People who are seen as adversaries are stereotyped in negative terms. They might be described as stubborn, interested only in their selfish needs. They will be seen as greedy, self-serving. They are hardheaded, narrow-minded, and could care less about your concerns. They are conservative, radical, idealistic, unrealistic, liberals, tree-hugging hippies, and hypocrites. They are too educated and out of touch or ignorant and disillusioned. They might be spineless "wackos" who are slow to change, who hate to communicate because they are too comfortable with their beliefs. They tell us what we want to hear and then do something else that is detrimental to our needs.

All of these negative stereotypes can result from two people, who each believes has the right perception, forcefully arguing with each other. If they cannot convince the other person of the rightness of their position, then they will begin to personalize the issue by demeaning the other person. They do this through negative stereotyping.

The impact of this: if a person is your enemy, then anything he or she says is of no value to you, even if it would help you solve the conflict. You don't hear what that person has to say because your intent is to deny or diminish whatever the person says. You are in a defensive mode, protecting the rightness of your view.

In a community meeting, such adversaries can use up all the verbal territory of every single person in the room as they challenge each other, debate each other, verbally jousting back and forth. No matter how many people are in the room, very little of what is spoken is listened to or retained. The result is garbage in, garbage out. People leave these meetings with their positions hardened and their stereotypes of "them" also hardened. A lot of time is spent in such meetings with no gain. It is a waste of people's time. But these people eating lunch together have listened to each other; they have heard each other.

If you and I have been adversaries for quite a while and have negatively stereotyped each other, normally when you speak, I won't listen, but I will interrupt. But we are now in a small group together. When you speak, I listen without interruption. When it is my turn, I speak and you listen without interruption. Think about how that will affect our relationship. Think about how it will affect the view we have of each other.

But more importantly, be aware that you are now hearing what I am saying. I am hearing what you are saying. For the first time, we move beyond personalizing the issue to hearing information about the issue. This is a shift in our relationship, a paradigm shift.

We have not only listened to each other, but have also recorded each of those words on the flip charts for all to see. When you speak, I record all your words, pretty much as you stated them. Then I later read these words off to the larger group. Consider how that must improve our relationship.

The net result is that we move beyond the stereotypes and the personalizing of the issue to describing and learning about the actual issue. And we create relationships based on a new perception of "real people."

~34~

Exploring a Personal Conflict

Applying the Process: An Activity

At the end of the strategy and action task, we reform the large community circle and take a lunch break. When everyone has returned to the large circle after lunch, Bob, the county commissioner, raises his hand to ask a question.

"When we started yesterday, you said that time is not our problem, the problem is. But we don't often have the time to spend three days on a simple conflict? Can you help us out with that?"

Yes. I also said we would use this three-day workshop to build your capacity to resolve other conflicts that are simpler, that involve fewer people. For instance, I am going to have you now learn about the consensus-building process by exploring the resolution of a personal conflict.

But first, let me introduce you to the arenas of conflict.

With that introduction, I proceed to describe the three arenas of conflict (*see arenas of conflict on page 65*). In that segment of the book, I state that whichever process is used to resolve and reach consensus must work in the three arenas. (This is on a flip chart visible to all.)

> **THE ARENAS OF CONFLICT**
> Personal
> Interpersonal
> Intergroup

I describe the three arenas of conflict:

Personal conflicts are the disagreements you have internally, with yourself. You are confronting yourself with two or more opposing choices and can't decide what to do. Often you are considering a choice that violates one of your own beliefs, values, traditions, or philosophies that you were given as a child. At times the conflict is so tense it feels like you are warring with yourself.

Interpersonal conflicts occur with another person: a spouse, coworker, peer, clerk, and so on. These are often a result of an unresolved personal conflict. At times, they occur unexpectedly, before you have had time to consider and can only react.

A difference between these conflicts is that in a personal conflict, you are trying to decide for yourself. Once the conflict is with another person, you are trying to win!

Intergroup conflicts are those that occur between groups that have different approaches, beliefs, philosophies. There are two or more groups in conflict, pushing and shoving against each other to gain some advantage, to win. This is the situation you find yourselves in.

We will now explore a personal conflict you have. This can be done in as few as fifteen minutes. Applying the process to yourself is important, because your interpersonal and intergroup conflicts normally arise from not resolving your personal conflicts.

It is my belief, not substantiated by any research, but a personal opinion, that 90 percent or more of our conflicts are personal conflicts. Something happens that conflicts me, and I spend an inordinate amount of time arguing with myself about whether to confront the issues or not. If I can resolve my personal conflict about a situation, it often won't require any other action.

Let's do that now with the process you have learned. You experience it, and then you decide how your personal conflicts affect you.

You each had a three-by-five card on your seat when you returned to the circle. You will use these to record your responses as you apply the consensus process to a personal conflict. You will not be sharing this information with others. It is for your personal use, unless you choose otherwise.

You may also choose to not use the card, but instead just imagine the answers or visualize the situations in your own mind, your private space. The advantage of using the card is that you will be able to consciously see the information.

> Remember this: Consensus is built when people are provided choices that they can freely make.

People stand and leave the circle in search of writing instruments. I wait until they return. I point to a flip chart.

The process we will use is on the flip chart behind me. This summarizes the approach we used in exploring conflict.

A CONSENSUS-BUILDING PROCESS

What is the situation or experience and how do you feel about it?

What are the worst possible outcomes of the situation?

What are the best possible outcomes of the situation?

What new beliefs/behaviors or strategies/actions will foster the best possible outcomes of the situation?

Personal conflicts are those we have with ourselves, arguing in our own mind about what to do and never reaching resolution. The result is we spend a lot of energy in a continuous cycle of mental arguing. It keeps us from being centered and present, because we are always in our minds. Resolution of this conflict begins with a deliberate expression of the situation and how you feel about it.

I want you to begin by thinking of a personal conflict you have and that you wish you could get solved. Then, write a brief statement about that conflict—some description that summarizes it for you. What it is, who is involved, how long has it been going on, et cetera.

I wait in silence as the community goes to work. Most are writing on the cards; a few are imagining it in their minds. When I see they are done, I give another instruction:

How does this conflict make you feel? Record a feeling or emotion that comes to mind when you think of the conflict.

I pause while they write.

And where does this feeling reside in your body?

I pause again.

The room is silent as everyone is diligently and deliberatively recording their information or imagining it. Everyone is intensely involved. This obviously has meaning to them. Their behavior tells me they all have personal conflicts they want to explore. I provide them an insight so they can understand the purpose of the emotion question.

Every conflict has an emotion attached to it. If it is not resolved, that emotion is stored in the body somewhere. My son often gets a painful back pain when he avoids his conflicts. For him, if the problem is really bad, then his cars won't start. Sounds funny, but there it is—it happens.

I am going to tell you a story of an event that actually happened, with names and conditions changed. I am telling it from what I remember. I will use this as a context for you to continue to explore your conflict.

This is an approach to addressing your personal conflicts. The process is simple. It is intended to help you experience the consensus-building process. Then you can try it on yourself or with someone else. This is the story and the process to use in these kind of situations.

Resolving a Personal Conflict: An Anecdote

It began with a phone call from Sarah. I could tell something was not quite right from the tone of her voice. She had a raspy throat, a sign she was in conflict, holding back her emotions. "Come on over," I suggested. "We'll have some coffee and talk a while." She agreed.

When Sarah arrived I poured a couple cups of coffee, and we talked small stuff for a while. Then I asked her, "What's going on with you and Tom? How are you feeling about it?"

What is the situation and how do you feel about it? This is the question you already answered on your cards.

Sarah had agreed to be the breadwinner, working as a legal aid while her husband, Tom, started his own cabinet business. While they worked well together raising their family of four, it was natural that Sarah take on the homemaking tasks. After four years of this, she was tired. "I'm burned out," she said as I listened, tears in her eyes, her throat husky.

"I am just tired of doing it all. I want some time for myself; I want to have time to develop some adult friends. Now all I do is spend time with lawyers and children. I want to have time to volunteer, to work in the hospital or in the schools with other adults. I can't do it with the pressure I have on me now. I feel like I am **losing** myself.

"But...I am afraid to talk to Tom about it. So, I've been going over and over it in my mind. It is just wearing me out, trying to act like there is nothing going on."

That is her description of the situation. I want to move her on to the next step. So I ask her, "**What are your worst possible outcomes of the situation, of talking with Tom?**"

"When Tom comes home late at night, he is so tired. Sometimes he is really grouchy, and I tell the kids to give him space so he can relax. And we are so busy on the weekends with the kids or working on the house. I just know if I talk with him about this, we will get in an argument. He will feel like I am questioning his ability to make a go of the business. This will upset the kids; they are always concerned that we will get a divorce like many of their friends' parents have. They worry they will have to make a choice between us.

"And I worry I will botch it up, not being clear and crying before I have hardly started. I know he is sensitive about the business. He always worries about not making it, I know he does, and I worry that if I talk about this, it will affect his confidence and—" She talked more hurriedly now, tears running down her face, speeding up as she went. "—*he will fail* because of me, and this will affect our relationship and we could *really* get divorced!"

I repeated what I heard her say, so she knew I had heard her. Then I got up to freshen our coffee, providing a break before the next question. This pause is helpful, especially if the situation is very emotional and much is at stake.

So those were her worst possible outcomes of the situation. She didn't have to think about it; the answers just flew out of her mouth. This is the burden she carries, the fear that prevents her from confronting the issue. So, answer the same question she did:

What are your worst possible outcomes of your situation?

When you answer this, be sure to report the worst of the worst fears to yourself. You are the only one who will see this. Get them all out. Empty yourself so they are all where you can see them, so you can be conscious of this normally nonconscious information.

The group members bend to their work again. When they are done, I continue:

After we had a few sips of coffee, just chatting, I asked Sarah to answer the next question: "**What are your best possible outcomes of the situation, of talking with Tom?**"

She didn't hesitate to answer. "I would find a time when we can sit down, and I can talk about this calmly. We talk about it and Tom understands I am not criticizing him or that I have stopped believing in him, because I do believe in him, but that I just need to let him know how I feel. If I can do that, it might even be enough, at least for a while, and he would know what my needs are. I'll have to find a time when the kids have something to do while I talk with him.

"I know if we talk that we will work it out, we both love one another. He is so supportive of what I do, and I know he is working hard to make things work. I want him to be successful, and if having this talk would help make that happen, it will bind us even closer together.

"And the kids will see their parents talking about this in a calm way; they will see how they can handle these kinds of conflicts when they are married.

"And, eventually I will get the support I need financially from Tom so I can work less and have time to do some things I long to do. I get to work at the hospital and see if I am still interested in physical therapy, or work in the schools with special education kids and see if I am interested in that. And I will make some good adult friends.

"And...we are together for the rest of our lives. I get to live with this man that I really love and admire."

That is the question I want you to answer now:

What are your best possible outcomes of your situation?

As you do this, record the best of the best possible outcomes, as you did with the worst. Imagine the greatest best possible outcomes you can.

Silence descends on the room as the members record their answers. As I see they are finishing, I add another question:

And...how will this make you feel when you do this?

Again I pause for a while, and then I add another question:

And where will you feel this in your body?

I pause again before adding some additional insight:

The feelings you have with your best possible outcomes and their location in the body will normally be different for each conflict. Record this in your memory, so when you have worst fears, you can go to that hopeful place and remind yourself of how it will feel to have hope.

Sarah was not hesitant to express her best possible outcomes; she is a hopeful person. She also has been through this a number of times with me. And to make these happen, she has to have some new beliefs and behaviors. So I asked her: **"What do you believe about yourself and Tom that will make those outcomes possible?"**

She answered right away: "I know that we love each other, and I believe we will always be together; we have weathered other issues as bad as this. I think we can do it better than we have in the past. I believe Tom wants me to have time to do what I want and will support me as soon as he can. I know he wants to be the breadwinner, and I know he will make it.

"And I know I can present this in a way that he will hear me and help out. And I know just talking about it will help. And...I know we will always be husband and wife."

Sarah blossomed as she expressed her beliefs; they came easy to her. I could sense a change in her mood and her emotions, just as I sense it here in the room. Now, what are the new beliefs you will need? Answer this question: **What do you believe about yourself and any others involved that will make those outcomes possible?**

Your current beliefs are preventing you from resolving your conflict. **So, again, what new beliefs or behaviors will you need if you are going to foster your best possible outcomes?** Record them on your card or imagine them.

The members immediately record on their cards, or close their eyes and imagine the new beliefs. I wait in the silence. When they are done, I continue with the story:

"Sarah, if you are going to make this happen, then what is one strategy or action you can take that will start the process of resolving to happen?"

"Well, as I was talking, I realized there is a way to quiet ourselves down while we talk about this. You know that Tom likes to relax with a good glass of wine, and we have a bottle of good wine that was a Christmas gift that we haven't touched. What I can do is set it and two glasses on the dining room table and invite him to share a glass or two with me, before dinner or after dinner. And when we are relaxed I can bring the topic up with him.

"And I can pick a night when the kids are watching TV in their rooms. I'll tell them we are having a parent talk and would like some privacy.

"I can also ask Tom how the shop is doing and let him know how much I support what he is doing.

"And then I can just start talking and hope the tears won't start before I am finished."

I speak to the community:

You are now at a moment where you can decide what to do if you make a choice to address your conflict. Answer the question Sarah did:

What is one or more strategies or actions that will make your best possible outcomes happen?

On this question, some of the members immediately record, while many others think for a while before writing. Then they, too, bend to the task of recording on their cards. I wait until I see they are done writing.

The closure.

One final set of questions; record the answers on the card. If you need another card, you can get one from YOU.

A few people ask for a card, and YOU pass them out to them.

How do you feel about this exploration of your conflict?

What did you learn that will help you take the risk to resolve it?

Most people are thinking about the questions, then writing, taking quite a bit of time. When they are done, I complete the insight:

I know that you will ask me anyway, so I will tell you the end of the story. Hopefully you will be able to see similar ends to your story.

A few days later...how it went. Sarah called to check in with me. I asked how she was; she knew immediately what I was asking for.

"I'll come over if you have coffee."

"I'll put the pot on right now."

When she got there, we filled the cups with that black liquid, talked a few minutes, and then she got right into it.

"It was so easy and actually funny. When Tom came home and saw the wine and glasses on the table, he said, 'Oh! A serious talk, eh?' I just laughed and said yes, but I wanted to relax with him first. So we sat there and talked about our day, really sort of connecting again. We both mentioned how busy we were and how this was sort of nice to take this time. I asked him how the business was going. I do this other times, but in a hurried way. This time I really listened.

"Then, after a while, he reached over and took my hand and wanted to know what was going on. He had a worried look on his face, so I decided to tell him about my feelings and desires. Oh, he listened so good, not talking, just held my hand. In a way, I almost felt bad talking about this, he was so attentive. And, of course, after a while, tears came into my eyes.

"He said, 'Look, Sarah, I understand what you're trying to say. I have wanted to talk with you about this too, but you know how we are so busy, and I keep forgetting to take the time. I am doing well in the business, better than I thought I would be at this time. My equipment is being paid off, the truck is almost paid off, and in a few months I will be able to help you with the house and some of the other payments we have.

"'What I have been thinking is that both of us need some time together to talk about this. Why don't you and I go to the coast, leave the kids with friends, and spend a long weekend together. We really deserve one, and we can work this out.'

"That really got me, and I had such tears and smiles and I just hugged him. I am so glad I did this the way I did."

The end of the story: Well, what I know is that Sarah did reduce her hours of work, volunteer at the hospital, and work with special education students in the school. And Tom is a successful businessman. And after a while, Sarah, her desires fulfilled, went back to her original work schedule. She was satisfied.

It is not difficult to use this process. The questions on the flip chart are simple and lead you into making the situation visible, conscious. Then you can do something about it. Try it on another personal conflict. Use three-by-five cards and just write shortened statements. But do it so you can see or imagine the words, and bring the situation to your consciousness. Then, end it with these two questions:

- How do I feel about this exploration?
- What did I learn that will help me resolve this conflict?

And finish it off with two words: TRUST MYSELF!

Finally, realize you can do this in ten to fifteen minutes. You can resolve any of your personal conflicts, because you control the entire environment. You are all of the voices in your mind; make them work for you. Then if your conflict involves another and won't go away unless you talk with that other, foster the willingness to take that next step. This is an anecdote of a person who did that with a successful outcome.

An "Aha" Moment: An Anecdote

Brenda was an older, heavyset woman, well-known in the community for her boisterous manner; a fearsome biting tongue; and outspoken, stubborn views. She had come up to me earlier in the day, having had an epiphany.

"I wanted you to know I had an 'aha!' just a while ago in my group. I was giving my opinion, and I realized I was in my reptilian brain. I was adrenalized and almost yelling, and was shocking the others by the looks on their faces. I guess I looked pretty fierce. I stopped what I was saying and then apologized to them. I told them I was in my reptilian brain.

"We all laughed and then talked about it, and they said I did that quite often in community meetings. Apparently I have quite a reputation in the community. They agreed to let me know when that happened again. I know I do it with my husband, too. I want to be aware of that so I can stop doing it."

She approached me again after the close of the workshop, just after we did the personal conflict task.

"Well, it happened again," she said.

"Did you get adrenalized again?"

"No," she said, "I had another 'aha!' on my personal conflict. And I did something about it. You know that Andrea and I have competed for years, running against each other for office. She beat me the last three times running for Mayor. I have been pretty hard on her, disagreeing in public about her proposals and votes. We normally can hardly stand being in the same room."

I responded, "I didn't know that, Brenda."

Brenda continued. "I used that as my personal conflict and realized how stressful that was in my life. It affects me every time I see her or hear someone talk about her. I get very stressed, and my reptilian brain goes into overdrive. I get stressed just talking about it now.

"So I decided to take my first step with that. I just went up to her and told her I was tired of avoiding her just because she beat me. I also told her I believe she is doing a wonderful job and I think she is a good Mayor. I am proud of her. And I said I would not run against her again. I meant it, too!"

"*Wow*," I said, really impressed, "that was awesome! What did she say?"

"You know, she got tears in her eyes and hugged me. Imagine that! She hugged me. And thanked me. I feel so good and so relieved. I feel lighter. This is a load off my shoulders."

We talked a while about the energy release that comes from resolving a conflict. Then we moved to the dining room. We had organized a meal for all the participants and their spouses. There was a hosted bar, and people began to slowly move in there as the spouses arrived. I did my "meet and greet" with spouses and children as they arrived. I always enjoy the young people, so I spent time talking and listening to them when I could.

The meal was informal, no special agendas, just a time for people to meet and for the spouses to hear about what they were learning. I left before the evening was over, needing time to think through the next day.

The next morning, Brenda was one of the first to arrive. I was hanging flip chart papers as usual when she came over to me, obviously excited.

"Did you see what happened last night at dinner?"

"Tell me and then I'll answer the question."

"Andrea and her husband Alex came to the table where my husband and I sat and had dinner with us. We had such a long talk and it was so pleasant. I feel like I have made a friend. She even asked my advice on some issues she has. People are already asking me what is going on with Andrea and I. They can tell things are better between us."

"I did not see that! That's exciting, isn't it?"

"Yes," she said. "You know, I belong to a lot of groups in this community. I've probably created a lot of conflicts with my reptilian brain. I know that I can take what I learned and be a better community member. People are going to have to change their view of me."

Not every person tells me of their experience with the personal conflict activity. Some do—normally because it was successful. I have no idea if all have similar experiences to Brenda's. I regard this as a personal activity, so I do not ask people to share it, with me or others.

I do know that people who know Brenda and Andrea will have to change their conversations about those two people. These people, in turn, will be changed in some fashion. Think of the energy release that causes in the community. That is the power of resolving conflicts. "Change one, and you change them all."

The Potluck Theory for Consensus: An Insight For The Reader

Reaching consensus is a lot like holding a series of successful potlucks. Potlucks are a traditional way of preparing a meal for community gatherings in the West. Because the ranchers lived so far apart, they would often get together in some central location for a meeting and/or a dance or other social event. The women would bring some of their favorite foods that were then shared by all at lunch or dinner. The various foods were displayed at a table, and the guests could select the foods they wanted on their plates.

In the same way, people come to meetings differing widely with their favorite perceptions, beliefs, and ideas about the issue at hand. They expect that they will have the opportunity to express these ideas, to "put them on the table," and be listened to with respect. They expect those who listen to consider their point of view, maybe even add it to their plate. They can also learn and put on their plate what they choose to learn from others.

No one idea takes central stage to the exclusion of others, just as no one food is presented at the table with the others held back until that one food is gone. We don't eat just one salad while the others are held secretly in the back room. The women would not accept that. They want them all spread out on the table so we can make a choice.

It is sometimes true that a spouse, sweetheart, or friend may convince someone to eat some of their particular food. And if it is not good, the diner can compliment it and never eat it again.

In the same manner, to listen only to one person's ideas for a whole meeting and let the others be held back is not respectful or effective or mentally nutritious. Everyone's ideas and beliefs must be presented and laid out on the table.

And while some may have agreed to support an idea out of loyalty to a friend or spouse, seeing the whole table of ideas often allows them to sample these and decide for themselves what is mentally nutritious for them.

That is what happens in the talking circles. Each person's ideas are expressed, laid on the table, and listened to, considered with respect. That allows us to choose which of the ideas, or statements we heard that we want to consider, those ideas that seem to intrigue us at this time. We add these to our plate!

> **Choice is important for building a meal at a potluck, and...**
> **equally important in building consensus!**

In the same way, we look at all the foods at the table and choose the ones that fit our appetite at this time. Not choosing a food doesn't mean that it is bad or rejected. We may just not be ready for that food at this time.

We have the same response to information or ideas we may not be ready to accept yet, while the possibility exists that we may be ready to consider them later.

Sometimes we take too much on our plate, and some of the food is not eaten, is discarded. Or we may not have enough on our plate, so we go back for seconds.

In the same way, we may become overloaded with the information we have received in a discussion, so we discard that which is excessive. Or, we may ask someone during a break to give us additional information, because we have room for more.

We then digest this food—just as we digest the ideas we were given. This serves to provide us physical or mental nourishment. As a result of this food and idea nourishment, we become different people. We may now go back to the table, listen to new ideas, put another meal together that is different than the first. We are changed by the first discussion, the first meal. We are ready to try some new foods, some new ideas.

No one's idea is rejected, just as no food is rejected. It may not be selected now, but at some future time it may be on our plates because we are ready to make that choice.

After a number of potlucks, or talking circles, most of us will have eaten and digested most of the foods presented, or most of the ideas listened to. This has created a common connection and knowledge base among the community of people. Now we can make the decisions we need to make out of this common connection and knowledge and experience.

This may also result in the creation of new menus, resulting in new meals, or creation of new ideas that create new ground.

This is the potluck theory about consensus. Implicit in this theory is the **presentation of all the ideas** (foods) so that we can then **choose** which to put on our plate (mind) to digest (consider). This leaves us open to other food, or other ideas. And it is always our choice.

They Were Real: An Anecdote for the Reader

They stood in a circle, in the dim light of twilight through the windows. It was a late evening; the lights had gone off because of an electrical problem.

The group of sixty people had reached a consensus. It required setting aside a management/labor contract that had been worked out over twenty years of difficult negotiating between management and labor in a school district. But there had been a change of political parties at the state level, which had resulted in major reductions in their funding. Without public support they were faced with declining programs and an inability to pay their employees.

They spoke with grief in their voices, tears in their eyes. This was a difficult consensus decision they had made. But they stood tall, they expressed their commitment to change their situation through working together in their new relationship, building support within the district, within the community, and within the state. It would take time, but they would create that support for the good of the people they served: the students, the parents, and the community. They would bring the programs and the compensation back.

And, they did!

~35~

The Situation

The Real Issue

It is time to begin discussing the "real issue" for the Coyote River Basin community. Everything we have done up to this time has been preparation for this moment. These people know each other now and treat each other with respect. They have beliefs that are congruent with their behaviors. They trust each other enough to be open and honest.

This activity normally happens sometime after lunch on the second day. Sometimes the upcoming personal-conflict task extends into the afternoon. If so, when completed, we take a short break and then bring the community group together to begin to discuss the real issue.

Before the lunch or during the break, I ask the following people to come to the center:

- Lynn, a newcomer, a retiree from Pennsylvania, an activist who led the effort to convince the county commissioners to upgrade their land-use plan.
- Jack, a rancher leader who instigated the rebellion against the land-use decisions.
- Allen, the tribal chairperson of the local Indian nation and a member of the planning commission who supported the land-use decisions.
- Mike, a rancher who is a member of the group that started the rebellion against the land-use issue.
- Alice, a senior citizen who is also an environmentalist, a longtime member of the community, and a supporter of upgrading the land-use provisions.
- Bud, the manager of the local bank, a senior citizen and longtime member of the community, who opposed the land-use changes.

Each of these people was selected while the small groups were working on their last task. I did this with the help of my cofacilitators. I wanted to have a panel of six key members of the community who were deeply involved in the confrontation over the issue of the land-use plan. I wanted the strongest opposing views.

Before lunch, I ask the six people and my cofacilitators to come to the center. The group stands around me in a circle, a curious look on their faces. I speak to them about the task they will have after lunch:

You have been selected to be on a panel after lunch. You will each be able to present your views, as strongly as you desire, on the issue that brings us here. Jack, I am going to begin with you, as you led the effort to prevent the land-use and zoning plan from being accepted. In my interviews, I also felt you had the strongest views as the leader of the rebellion group. You are going to be speaking to Lynn.

Lynn, you are going to be listening to Jack. After he has spoken, you will give your point of view as a newcomer to the community and someone who led the movement to get the land-use plan and zoning requirements upgraded to protect the values of this basin.

Allen, I am asking you to represent the Coyote Mountain Indian Nation in this discussion. You are going to be talking to Mike, who manages his father's ranch in the lower end of the basin. Mike, you will speak first, presenting your views of the situation to Allen. Then, Allen, you will have an opportunity to express your concerns about the issues to Mike.

The last pair will consist of you, Bud and Alice. Both of you are longtime residents of this community, once friends and yet you find yourselves on opposite sides of this issue. I want you to listen to the previous two pairs as they present their perceptions of the issue. I would then like you to speak to each other about what you heard and what your views are of the situation.

To ensure that what you say is being heard, I am asking each of you to select a listener, someone you trust, who can convey to you the message that was presented by the other member of your pair. These listeners must be very objective and able to convey messages without judgment.

One important condition, however, is that all of you must select a listener of the opposite gender. So as an example, Alice, you must select a male listener. Bud, you must select a female listener.

The reason for this is that the listener provides a balance for each of you. If I have a male speaker with a male listener and a female speaker with a female listener, the issue slowly converts into a gender struggle, rather than a focus on the real issue. So these listeners are intended to provide a balance, to make sure we keep focused on the issue.

> **CREATING AUTHENTICITY: THE ART**
>
> When establishing a panel, I will purposefully delay giving them the instructions for their task until sometime immediately before they are to make the presentation. I also do this with specialists or speakers who come in to provide information, providing them a shorter time frame than they normally expect.
>
> The reason for this is to give them the least amount of time to prepare themselves to speak. If they have too much time to prepare, they begin to question themselves and what they were going to say. They will begin to censor, try to be more pleasing, or maybe make jokes or want to get off the topic.
>
> I want them to be authentic, to be speaking in the moment. I want them to be listening to what the other panel members are saying, instead of worrying about what they're going to say.
>
> The same is true of any speaker who makes a presentation in the workshops. Normally, speakers are allowed way too much time to present the material they are there for. They can normally present their sixty-minute speech in five to ten minutes. I may even give them less time. I want them to take out all the filler material, jokes, unnecessary explanations, and side comments, and focus on what they were asked to present.
>
> We are not here to be entertained! We have work to do!

In addition, since you, Bud, will be listening to Alice, your listener—a female—will be presenting you with what she heard. The opposite is true then for Alice. Her listener is a male.

During lunch I want you all to select your listeners. After lunch I will bring you together and go through this again.

I repeat these instructions again so that they understand their task. I ask two of them to convey what they heard me say. When I am satisfied that they have the task down, I release them for lunch.

The Situation: An Activity

After lunch and before the group starts, I invite my panel and the listeners they chose (Wayne, Donna, Kathy, Laura, Rayni, Kenney) during lunch to the center of the circle.

I want each of you to pair up so the speaker and listener are standing together.

I wait until the pairs are standing next to each other before I continue with the task.

So here is how this will work. Jack, you will speak first. Your questions will be:

- *What is the situation that brings us together?*
- *How did it get to be that way?*
- *How do you feel about it?*

You will express the answers to those questions directly to Lynn. That is important. Speak to Lynn, not to the group. The group will still hear you, but you are conveying your concerns about this issue to one person.

When you have finished, Wayne, as Lynn's listener, will tell Lynn what he heard you say. While you do not have to have the exact words, Wayne, it is important that you convey as much of what you heard as you can without judgments or editorializing.

Do not attempt to take notes because you will miss part of what is said. Trust yourself to recall what is said. Do not summarize—recall what you can. I will provide you a backup listener during this first activity.

After you have heard Wayne convey Jack's message, Lynn, you will express your answers to the same questions.

Donna, as Jack's listener, when Lynn is finished, you will convey the information you heard to Jack. Again, it is important to present as much of the information as you can recall. For you, I will also provide a backup listener.

I repeat this for each of the pairs and then ask if they have any concerns or questions.

I speak further to the pairs:

When you speak, it is OK if you are angry or emotional. Be who you are in that moment. While it is possible the person you are speaking to may be affected by your emotions, her listener will see to it that the information you have expressed is conveyed to her without the emotion.

As members of the panel, your purpose is to establish a level of openness and honesty, of candor, that the remaining members of this community can model when they get together and talk about or answer the same questions.

> **IT IS OK TO BE EMOTIONAL: THE ART**
>
> When a community moves to the stage where people with different views confront each other, with listeners, I will often give them permission to be emotional— angry, sad, frustrated, anxious—whatever emotion they might wish to be.
>
> There is a reason for this. I have learned that people who are angry in an environment that they feel is unsafe tend to speak louder, more aggressively, and longer than if I give them permission to be angry. When I tell them that it is safe to speak in the room, they take me at my word because I have helped them to be safe until this point.
>
> What this means is that an angry person can still be angry and yet speak clearly, without magnifying their information. This allows others to hear what is said, separate from the emotions. This allows the person to speak with different verbal tones, with different physical nonverbal messages. The description of the issue is less magnified, more reasonable. This graphic uses font size to visually describe the difference:
>
> ANGER IN AN UNSAFE ENVIRONMENT.
>
> Anger in a safe environment.
>
> People can hear everything well, as a result.

Finally, when you have all spoken, I will bring you to the center of the room and have a member of the community honor you for the work you have done. You will then return to the groups we created this morning. As members of the panel, you will act as a facilitator for that group. If there is more than one panel member in a group, you need to work out between you who will play that role. Your task will be to facilitate your group in answering the same three questions that you did. What is the situation as you see it? How did it get to be that way? And how do you feel about it?

You will not be recording this information to begin with. I will ask you to close your circle and select a starting point. Then go either clockwise or counterclockwise, allowing each person, in turn, to answer the questions. This is a talking circle.

I will repeat all of this before we start this activity and before you get back in your groups. We are now ready to deal with the real issue.

As we sit in the large circle, I recognize that I am with a different group of people than the one I started with. All of these people know each other. They have listened with respect to each other for over twelve hours. They have facilitated one another, recorded for one another. They have worked together to develop collective statements for the entire group. They have shared their views about conflict with each other, they have explored their fears about confronting conflict, and they have developed a purpose statement for the conflict around the best possible outcomes. In each of these activities, they have learned about each other. These are no longer people who have been stereotyped. They are known individually, based on dozens of conversations focused on the tasks.

The sense of anxiety that permeated the room on the first morning is gone. These people know that this is an environment where it is safe to speak the truth. They know it because they have done it for a day and a half.

These people are willing to learn from each other, they have experienced disagreement and created an agreement during the consensus process. Most importantly, they know they can disagree with each other. They know they can speak the truth and will be listened to with respect.

Before we start this afternoon, I want you all to stand so we can honor the people who have helped me as cofacilitators. I want Wayne and Laura to come to the center.

I select someone from the community to honor Wayne and Laura for their participation as cofacilitators. I then introduce the new cofacilitator, Diane. I reaffirm that YOU are helping me to coach the new facilitators and to also facilitate.

This afternoon, we are going to be focusing on your community conflict regarding the land-use plan and the zoning plan. I've asked six members to be part of a panel. Their purpose is to answer three questions: What is the situation that brings us together? How did it get to be this way? How do you feel about it? Each of these people has selected a person to listen for them. When a panel member speaks to another panel member, the listener for the second panel member will convey to them what he or she heard, as accurately and nonjudgmentally as possible. That panel member will then have an opportunity to speak to the other panel member. The listener for that person will convey what he or she heard to that person.

The panel consists of three pairs. Jack will be speaking to Lynn. Lynn's listener, Wayne, will then convey what he heard to Lynn as completely as he can recall. Lynn will then speak to Jack. Donna, his listener, will convey what she heard from Lynn as accurately as she can recall.

This will be repeated for the remaining two pairs. Mike will be talking to Allen, and their listeners are Laura and Kathy. We will finish up with Bud speaking to Alice, and their listeners are Kenney and Rayni.

Your purpose is to listen and learn as they speak. Their purpose is to help you begin to think about your perception of the situation, your view about how it happened, and how you feel about it. When the panel is finished, you will return to your small groups. Your group will be facilitated by one of the panel members. You will then have the opportunity to answer the same three questions as they did. I'll repeat these directions before you start the small-group work.

> **ASKING THE RIGHT QUESTION**
>
> You have probably noticed that my questions tend to be more general than specific. "How do you feel about the land-use plan?" is more specific than "What is the situation?" The purpose of general questions is to create the broadest arena of thought and discussion possible, to be as inclusive as possible about the situation.

With that, I turn to Jack.

Jack, I want you to speak to Lynn. Answer these three questions: What is the situation that brings us together? How did this happen? And how do you feel about it?

Wayne will be your listener, and Laura, I want you to be a backup listener for Wayne.

Jack looks across the circle at Lynn and then begins to speak:

"Well, I guess I'll have to start with how I feel a little bit first. *I feel pretty damn mad!* You folks who are newcomers are lucky that we locals know how to control our tempers. But, it sure wasn't easy." (Appreciative laughter in the group.) "You stretched me to the limit, and I didn't appreciate it at all!

"My family has been in the basin for five generations now. We are a century ranch with over one hundred years of ranching. We settled on seven thousand acres on the eastern side of the basin, and we grazed on an additional twenty thousand acres of National Forest.

"We have done that ever since my great-grandfather settled in the area over a hundred and twenty years ago. He was one of the first settlers here. He had to work hard to create this ranch for all of his succeeding generations. Allen..."

He turns to Allen from the Coyote Mountain Tribe.

"Allen, your great-great-grandfather was probably one of those who welcomed my great-grandfather into this valley. It probably felt like an invasion to them when we showed up, but we were few and they were many. And somehow they worked out an arrangement whereby my great-grandfather was able to establish the ranch that remains in our family today. We probably couldn't have done it without your tribe's generosity and understanding."

Allen nods his head with a slight smile on his face. Jack turns to face Lynn as he continues.

"So we've been here a long time, and you newcomers haven't even been here for a generation. I heard Lynn say yesterday that she has just been here for seven years. Well, that makes her a newcomer who really doesn't know what the hell is going on in this valley."

Jack looks down, obviously angry and emotional. He pauses for a while. During this pause I remind him:

When you speak to Lynn and use the words *her* or *she*, it sounds like she is not in the room. It sounds like you are talking *about* her rather than *to* her. Speak directly to her.

Jack acknowledges my comment with a nod of his head.

"Now, I don't mean to say that I don't welcome you, Lynn, but to you it appears that way. You have every right to come here, to buy land and settle in. You have every right to protect your rights to your land. But what you don't have the right to do is take away my rights.

"My family depends upon this ranch. Agriculture today is a pretty marginal business to be in; it always has been. In order to keep the ranch running, my sons Jeff and John both have second jobs here in this community. My wife and daughter-in-law work in the school district. If we did not have that income, it would be pretty difficult to hold onto the ranch.

"In the hard times—and there have been many of these—we may have to sell off a piece of our ranch in order to get the finances to keep our heads above water. We have been able to do that for every one of the generations since my great-grandfather settled here. We hate to do it, but our purpose is to protect the heritage that we have, to protect our way of life, to keep our freedom. To see that my grandkids and great-grandkids will have an opportunity, if they wish, to work on this ranch, maybe even to own it.

"So, I don't understand how you did it in Pittsburgh. I don't understand how other newcomers can come into this basin and decide that I can't sell my land. I believe that is my right. I don't see how you can decide that I have to keep my land green so you can have open space. What you're talking about is my ranch, and that's not open space. It's working land!

"We run cattle on the ranch, eight hundred of them this year, and they are pretty much our main source of income. So, are you going to tell me that my cattle can't eat the grass that is within your sight from the main road? Of course you are—that is exactly what you're trying to do. Are you going to tell me that I have to turn all my irrigation water back into the river so that the sportsmen can have more fish? Of course you are, because you don't understand why that water is needed on the land. And did you folks come up and become acquainted with what we are doing so you could understand the impact that would have on our ranch? Of course you didn't! You just decided to take away our rights, without even considering that we exist.

"What you have to know is that in this basin over fifty percent of the land is owned by the federal government. Another fifteen percent of that land is in ranching. But the number of people who own or manage that land is less than three percent of the voters in this basin. So that means that we don't have much power when it comes to making decisions about how our land is going to be used under this zoning plan.

"That's part of our problem. Even though there are other folks who feel the same way we do, we are outnumbered by those of you who can decide that we need to keep the land natural. You want to be able to come here and build your retirement home and then make rules and regulations to keep everybody else out.

"Well, we wanted to do that too. We wanted to keep you out! But we respect your right to come in and purchase a piece of land if you want to do so. But, by God, you need to respect our right to keep and manage our land for our family!"

Jack draws a deep breath and then sits back relaxed.

"Well, I probably could say more, but I know Mike is going to speak in a few moments, so I'll leave some for him to say. Give me a chance to cool off a bit. I do want to say, Lynn, that I appreciate you are listening to me. I don't mean to offend you, but Bob asked us to be honest. This is the first time anybody has listened to my views, although I have spouted off a number of times. So I'm interested in hearing what you have to say."

When Jack finishes speaking I turn to Wayne and ask him to convey to Lynn what he heard Jack say: Wayne, tell Lynn what you heard Jack say.

Wayne speaks to Lynn.

"Well, first of all, what I heard is his family has been here for a lot of years, sounds like at least five generations, and they're here because it sounds like the tribes had a very lax immigration policy." (Laughter from all, including Jack.) "I think you can tell that he feels deeply about the land-use plan and of course, most importantly, how he wants to pass his land on to his children and grandchildren and even his great-grandchildren.

"But he feels like the land-use and zoning plan would make that impossible. Since ranching is a marginal business, his family has to have more than one job to have enough money to keep their ranch going. And in these really tough times, he and others like him often will sell a small piece of their ranch in order to get enough money to keep the ranch going.

"He believes that the new land-use plan would prevent them from doing that. In addition, he is really concerned that you don't understand what his ranch and his land is about. What you see is green space with a pretty view on land that he works, that he runs cattle on to provide most of the income for his family. He calls it 'working land.' He wonders how you can make a decision that takes away his right to manage that land for that use when he's been doing it for generations.

"He's also worried about you taking away his right to use the water because of that plan. He is fearful you just want to take that water away and put it in the river so you can help some recreationists.

"He is pretty darn mad about you taking away his land rights when he had really no say in the matter. He said that ranching and ranchers are a very small percentage of what goes on in the county. I heard that means that if this new land-use plan comes up for a vote and it's not in their best interest, they don't have enough support to be able to prevent you from taking away his rights, his land, and his heritage."

Wayne turns to Laura. "Laura, is there anything that you would add that I might have missed?"

Laura responds: Well, I heard him say, Lynn, that you want to have the right to come into this valley and buy a piece of land and build a home on the land and be protected from other people living alongside of you, but you don't want to provide him the same right to keep his land and to manage it the way he wants to.

"He also said that you want to live in this valley because it's so beautiful, but once you get here, you want to keep everyone else from coming in. He indicated that if he felt that way, the same as you do, why he would've kept you from coming into the valley. But he is willing to support your right to buy land here and to do with it as you want.

"He also acknowledged that his family would not be in this basin if the tribes had not agreed to their being here."

I look at Jack and ask, Do you feel heard?

He nods his head. "For the very first time," he says emphatically.

I address the community: Before we move ahead, I want to underscore the importance of the listener. The listener's purpose is to convey the message that he or she heard from the speaker to their client. They must do this objectively, without making a judgment about what was said. They are able to convey the intent of the message, which might have been missed because of the speaker's emotional feelings. The anger would get in the way of the client's understanding or hearing what was said, which is what happens in most discussions like this. If both people are angry, what they say is never heard. Only the emotion is heard.

"Now it is Lynn's turn to speak to Jack, to express her view of what the situation is, how it got to be that way, and how she feels about it. Donna will be the listener. Wayne, I want you to be a backup listener for Donna. Lynn, speak to Jack."

Lynn leans forward to speak to Jack, looking directly at him.

"What I also heard you say, Jack, is that you were pretty damn mad about what happened in the land-zoning issue. Well, when I first heard you at the planning commission meeting, that was my impression of you, that you were pretty damn mad." (Laughter from the group.) "As a result, as Bob said, I don't think I heard a single word you said. I just thought you were more than mad, that you might have even been irrational. I'll have to admit that you scared me. So, I guess I made a judgment about you before I even really knew you.

"You are the first rancher I have ever met in my life. When we greeted each other yesterday, I told you that I was really moved by what you said in the grounding. I meant that. I'll have to admit that I really did not understand the views of you and the other ranchers. I realize now I have a very incomplete understanding of the issues the ranchers have to face, even after spending two days listening to you. I have learned how much misinformation or worst-case assumptions are affecting how we relate to each other.

"I'll also have to admit that I didn't really try to understand. I just felt you were a bunch of local people who wanted to keep the status quo. I felt you didn't understand the danger to the community of having unlimited and unregulated growth.

"That may tell you a little bit about me. I have been an activist all my life, supporting causes that I felt were important. Many of these causes were around land use and the need for regulation. I did this because of my self-interest. I lived in Pennsylvania for most of my life. I became tired of being surrounded by so many people with so many unsolvable problems. So my husband and I moved outside the suburbs. We bought a piece of land in the country. It was so beautiful. But in less than a year, other people bought the lots around us with the same idea. It did not take long before we were surrounded by homes and roads, businesses, fast-food places, and the once-beautiful view was gone. I found myself feeling almost the same way I did when I lived in the downtown city.

"So when Tom and I retired, we decided to move west, to get as far away as we could from the growth. We looked for a long time and found this beautiful basin that was away from everything else. When we came here the first time, we thought we had found heaven. It was beautiful. We were surrounded by pine trees; we had two acres of land, which, to us, felt as big as a ranch does to you. We felt like we had unlimited space, unlimited views. When we built our home, we did so with careful thought for the impact it would have on the environment that surrounded us. We were happy there for three years.

"Then other people began to buy the tracts around us. At some level, we knew that we were in a subdivision that had a number of lots on it. We did not know how large this number of lots was. We were focused on the one that we purchased. As soon as these people began to move in adjacent to us, I checked the subdivision maps for our area. We found that there were a hundred lots in the little valley that we have selected. And we found that hundreds more were being planned.

"As isolated as the space is, it is not far from the metropolitan areas or many of those large cities that are out of control with growth. What we learned was that this basin was also being subdivided in the hope that people would purchase these lots as second homes or vacation homes. What we saw was a repetition of what we had escaped in Pennsylvania. I think Bob would call that our worst possible outcome. And, of course, that is what propelled us into action.

"Well, I guess I wasn't ready to be retired, because my activist instincts took over. Driving up the basin I noticed that much of what we call a green space was also being subdivided, with upscale homes being built on it. The beautiful views in this valley were about to be destroyed by this ungoverned growth.

"As more and more homes were being built around us, I decided to do something about it. I felt there wasn't a way to control growth, to have a more regulated zoning for the basin. When I checked with the county commissioners and their planning people, I found that we were still operating under the zoning pattern that had been developed forty years ago. While the land-use plan had been updated, the zoning that was intended to go along with it had not even been started. So, I decided to be a reason to get it started.

"I gathered around me a number of people who were of like mind. Alice, who was a longtime member of this community, has been very helpful to me in doing that. The first thing we did was to run people for the commissioner positions who agreed with our point of view. And then we began to attend the planning commission meetings and push for a new land-use plan and zoning plan. We also got some people with our views added to the planning commission.

"I'll have to admit that we were pretty narrow-minded about it. We knew what we wanted, and we decided to get it. And I'll admit we weren't much interested in other people's views about this, either. We understood the danger of unregulated growth. We were going to do the best we could to save this basin.

"When you came to some of those early planning commission meetings, I made no attempt to understand what your point of view was. I just thought you wanted to keep things the way they were. I just thought you wanted to be able to sell your land to the highest bidder and make as much money as you could. So I did not listen to or understand your views.

"I guess that's where we went wrong. I do not understand ranching. I see the land is fenced out in some places, and I assume that land belongs to somebody. I see the cattle out there: but in the fall, after they had grazed the land down and it appears dry and dusty, I get upset about the impact that has on this view of this beautiful basin.

"So I guess I and many in my group made no attempt to understand the impact we would have on you and your families. And for that I can tell you I am truly sorry.

"I've been in small groups with you. I have listened to your point of view. I have found you to be a very decent person who was just trying to save his family's heritage. I want you to know I would do the very same thing if I were in your shoes.

"So I hope our discussion today is the start of something different. I certainly don't want you to lose your ranches. I want your children to be able to inherit the land and keep them on the land.

"But, I have to tell you I am still concerned about the impact that unplanned and unregulated growth will have on the basin. I'm concerned about the thousands of small lots that are scattered throughout this basin without any plans for roads, utilities, or other needed services. I am concerned that people with lots of money, who can afford to build large houses, will increase the land values to the point that people like Tom and I won't be able to afford to keep our homes here. And you will be pressured to sell your land because of the high values.

"I wish I had met you earlier, Jack, and had a chance to listen to you and understand your point of view. If I had, with others who are supportive of what I'm doing, I believe things would be different. So I'll admit it. I feel sad that didn't happen. I did not respect you or your rights or your family's rights. I think I can do better now, even if I still don't understand it all."

Lynn sits back and waits for Donna to convey her message to Jack.

Donna, I say, tell Jack, what you heard Lynn just say.

"Well, Jack, I hope I can do this. Lynn said an awful lot. So I'm going to try to recall as Bob advised. She started by saying that she heard you say that you were damn mad about what happened. She remembers you from the meetings you attended. It gave her a feeling you were just trying to keep everything the same; the result is she didn't hear anything you or the rest of your group said. She was a little afraid of you.

"Then she said she'd never met a rancher before. And she later said she didn't even know what ranching meant. She said that when she first met you yesterday, she was impressed by what you said in the grounding, and I could tell that she was impressed on meeting you in the greeting circle later. I could tell she was impressed listening to what you had to say in the small group. So I think I could say that she was being educated by you.

"But I think she also felt that you didn't understand what she was trying to say. So she tried to tell you who she was and how she got here. She came from Pennsylvania. She spent a good part of her life as an activist. She and her husband, Tom, didn't like living in the city with people so close to them, who had so many problems. So they moved out to the countryside. It sounds like they found a beautiful lot and they felt they were the only ones there.

"Eventually, however, other people began to build around them, and the once-beautiful view they had eventually disappeared. It made her feel like she was living back in the city. There was a beautiful view, but too many people. And too many fast-food places.

"So when she and Tom retired and came here, they felt that they had found heaven in our basin. There are not many people here and they found a lot that was surrounded by pine trees and they were the only people there. But it didn't take long before they were again surrounded by people who built on other lots that surround them.

"When Lynn checked on our land-use plan, she found that there were lots of subdivisions throughout the basin. Not all of them were developed yet, but I think she got scared by what could possibly happen. I guess she and Tom felt that it would be the same all over again.

"So, being an activist, she decided to do something about it. She found that the county had needed a new land-use plan, and they didn't have a current zoning law. And the old zoning would not prevent the land from being built on that would keep the community from having unlimited and unregulated growth.

"So with Alice's help, she formed a group whose purpose was to put limits on growth. Her group supported the election of two of the county commissioners who currently sit on the board. And then her group put pressure on the planning commission to do something about updating the land-use plan and the zoning that would support it. The result was the land-use zoning proposal that we have before us and that the ranchers and others have rebelled against.

"I think she is sorry that she did it the way she did. She feels that if the both of you had a chance to have this discussion earlier under different circumstances, that everything would be different. While she didn't specifically say it, I believe she wants it to be different."

Donna looks at me to signal that she is done.

I turn Wayne. Do you have anything to add?

Wayne nods his head and speaks. "Only one thing. Lynn said that she felt that what she did was to protect the basin from unregulated growth. Her intent was good, but the process left people out."

Jack, would you like to respond to what Lynn said? Wayne, you will be the listener, and Donna, you will be his backup.

Jack leans forward, places his elbows on his knees, and looks directly at Lynn.

"I'm not very happy about all of the subdivisions that are going on in this basin either. I heard we had something like six thousand different lots scattered all over the county. But some of them have been there for at least twenty years and have not been sold or developed. So I'm not sure that the number of subdivisions and lots we have is any indication that we're going to all of a sudden be like Metropolis. I am concerned with the development we have so far, because the county is taking on budget responsibilities for maintaining the roads, providing law enforcement, and making sure they're not taking water that's scarce or digging wells and tapping irrigation ditches. Doing that takes money, and that means increased taxes.

"Now I can understand that you might see this more clearly than I, because in my lifetime I have seen very little change in this basin. The biggest change came when the lumber mills shut down ten years ago. That took away our strongest economic opportunity in this community. Both of my sons worked in the woods until the timber industry was shut down. The jobs they have now don't bring in anywhere near the income that the timber industry jobs did. So that makes it more likely that we will have to take another piece of our land and sell it in order to get the money we need to keep a ranch going. You can blame all that on the environmentalists.

"But, under that land-use zoning proposal, we won't be able to do that. You have too many restrictions there. So I'm not very happy about that. I'm not necessarily opposed to some zoning to bring some order for growth in the basin. But I don't think it should take away the rights of people to do what they want with their land as long as it doesn't impact anybody else.

"I also think with all the new folks that have come into the basin that we need to make them aware of the importance that agriculture has to our communities. We're the ones who provide that open green spaces that you call so beautiful. That view is pretty much the same as when my great-grandfather came to the place.

"And there needs to be a better understanding of the impact of decisions that are made on the people who earn their living from the land and who keep it looking as green as it is.

"Maybe what I need to do is get you up to my ranch and put you on a horse and introduce you to what a rancher is and what ranching is. I suppose I'd have to make sure my insurance is paid up just in case you might fall off on your head." (Laughter.)

He sits up straight, leans back, and crosses his arms and long legs.

Wayne, I say, would you tell Lynn what you heard Jack say?

"Lynn, Jack said that he's aware of how many subdivision and lots there are in the basin, but he's not sure they will ever be developed. Some of them have been there for a long time. While he's concerned that we not become another Metropolis, he doesn't feel there's much chance of that happening.

"And he does agree that there is a need to be concerned about all of these subdivisions and lots.

"He hasn't seen a lot of change in the basin during his lifetime. The biggest change was when the lumber mills shut down about ten years ago and took away some high-paying jobs. This made it more difficult for his family members to support the ranch.

"He understands, now, the importance of helping newcomers, like yourself, become aware of the importance that ranching has to the community. If you want to protect the green spaces, which are the ranches in the valley, then you also need to understand the impact that your actions might have on the people who earn their living from the land.

"So he's suggested maybe what needs to happen is for you to visit him on the ranch, and he could take you around and help you understand what it takes to manage that ranch. He's even willing to take the risk of putting you on a horse."

Wayne pauses and then looks at me.

Donna, did you hear anything that Wayne might have missed?

"Yes, Jack said that because of the economic decline in the valley due to the loss of the timber industry, it makes it even more important to have the option of being able to sell off a piece of his land to keep the ranch going. If the county continues with the present proposal, it would prevent him from doing this. The restrictions are too great. He's not opposed to zoning, he just wants to be sure it allows him to keep the option of being able to sell some of his land if he has to."

Thanks, Donna. Lynn, would you like to respond to Jack? Donna will be the listener. Wayne, you will be the backup.

Lynn also leans forward, looking directly at Jack.

"Jack, my intent with the zoning is just to attempt to guide our growth so we can make intelligent decisions about how to keep the basin as beautiful as it is. I have a feeling that we went too far because we didn't understand or consider the needs of agriculture in the basin. I know that growth has been slow here in the basin in the past, but with the pressures I see all around us and adjacent counties and basins, it appears to me that it will eventually get to this area. I may have overreacted to that, but I just believe we should be prepared for it.

"I also agree with you that we need to find ways to keep ranching viable and make sure it's possible for you and your community to survive. That means we need to slow down and maybe even take a step back and see how we can make that happen.

"And I agree that those of us who are newcomers and who don't understand agriculture maybe need to have a quick course in that. Maybe we could have a community barbecue out at your ranch, Jack, so I and other people like me could get acquainted with agriculture and ranching. And I appreciate your willingness to invite me to saddle up with you to look over your ranch. I've ridden horses most of my earlier years, so I believe I can hang on and minimize your risk with your insurance."

There is general laughter at this, and Lynn looks at me to signal that she's done.

Donna, would you convey to Jack what you heard Lynn say?

"Jack, I heard Lynn say that while her intent was to protect the valley, she now understands after listening to you that they might have gone too far. So she is willing to consider the possibility of taking a step back and working closely with the ranchers to see if they can find a way to make sure that the agricultural community can survive.

"She also agrees that the newcomers like herself need to be educated about agriculture and ranching. She suggested the idea of a barbecue out at your ranch in which all of the newcomers could participate and get to know the ranchers. Then she said she'd be willing to saddle up with you and take a look at your ranch. She assured you that she knows how to ride a horse."

I speak to the larger community, looking around the circle as I do so, gaining their attention:

Both of these people have had an opportunity to state their view of the situation, how it came to be this way, and how they feel about it. Each of them had a listener who was able to convey what they heard. This was done to be sure that listening and understanding was happening.

While this was going on, each of you has also been listening to these two people and in the process gaining a better understanding of each of their points of view. As I observed you during this discussion, everyone was focused on this conversation. Many of you were leaning forward, many of you nodding your heads in agreement.

Now, what these two people have done is to serve the community. They have taken the risk of speaking honestly and openly with each other. So what I'd like to do is to have everyone stand.

Jack and Lynn, I would like you to come to the center of the circle.

Jack and Lynn walk to the center of the circle as the larger community stands. They stand close, not touching, eyes averted.

Wayne, I would like you to honor these two people for the discussion they just had.

After a moment of thought Wayne says; "Jack and Lynn, I would like to honor you for what you just did, because I truly think it's going to be helpful for this entire community. As you talked I got a much better understanding of how we got to be here today. I actually had a feeling of hope, as I understood that you were truly being honest and truly listening to one another. I have to tell you, it was not easy to remember or recall what you said, but as I repeated it to you, I got a better understanding myself of what was said.

"So, I want to honor you two for having spoken so candidly to each other, for letting us listen to this conversation. I think you have really helped this community by doing so."

The applause is deafening. Jack and Lynn reach out to shake each other's hand and after doing so, reach out and hug each other. The applause gets even louder as the larger community see the two adversaries reaching out to each other, accepting that hug. It is symbolic of the old-timers and the newcomers coming together.

It doesn't mean that they have solved the problem yet. It doesn't necessarily mean they agree with each other. It just means they are willing to accept the fact that they both exist in the community, they have a right to be here, and that by listening to each other, they can perhaps make decisions that are inclusive of their needs and views.

When the applause is over, Jack and Lynn walk back to the circle.

REACHING OUT TO EACH OTHER

One of the values of honoring people in the center of the circle is it puts them in proximity to each other. It allows them, if they choose, to reach out to each other, to shake hands. Or put a hand around a shoulder of another, or sometimes even hug.

This visual is seen by all members of the community: two members who are often adversaries reaching out to each other in peace. It affects everyone, changes their view of the situation and of each other.

And it is always their choice.

Donna and Wayne, I'd like you to come to the center of the circle.

Donna and Wayne walk to the center of the circle.

Lynn, I would like you to honor your listeners.

Lynn steps forward a little bit, then stops.

"Donna and Wayne, I am so appreciative of you doing such a good job of listening to what we had to say. I was amazed at how much information you were able to retain. I don't believe I could have ever remembered that much. It really helped me because I didn't hear everything that was said. So, Wayne, when you repeated it to me, I got an even better understanding of what Jack said. Donna, I know you did the same for me when you spoke to Jack. I want to thank you from the bottom of my heart for taking the risk of listening to us."

The community applauds, Donna and Wayne shake hands and then hug each other.

When the applause dies down, they return to their places in the circle. I continue:

We are going to continue with the panel. We'll use the same approach. We will start with Mike speaking to Allen. Kathy, you will be Allen's listener.

I turn to YOU. You are going to facilitate this conversation in the same manner as I did and as I coached you.

"Thanks Bob," YOU say. "Mike, I want you to speak to Allen, answering the same three questions: What is the situation that brings us together? How did this happen? And how do you feel about it? Kathy, you are the listener, and Wayne, you are the backup."

Mike thinks a while with his head down. Then he speaks:

"Allen, I have to tell you that I agree very much with what Jack said earlier. We were really caught unawares by this zoning proposal. So it is understandable that we got pretty upset about what was happening and about how it happened. Like Jack, I'm still upset about it. It seems to me that everybody acted as if we didn't exist in the valley, when we have the largest amount of land outside of the federal government. That our lands are being called 'open space.' People treated us as if we didn't even exist.

"Normally we're pretty quiet people, sort of like a blowfish in the ocean. Not bothering anybody. But it seemed to me that when we were left out of this, that we talked up really loud and our spines came out. So we are all blown up with these spines. But all we were doing was just protecting our interests. It felt like survival to us. We didn't want to be very easy to be with.

"The agricultural community is already highly stressed and on the brink of collapse, so additional rules, regulations, and expenses would be the final straw to break our back. You folks have to understand it's pretty difficult to make a living ranching these days. This is because of the high cost of electricity for pumping water and power machinery and fertilizer, and the price that we get for our product is pretty low. So it's a marginal living at best. But we do it because it's a lifestyle that we like to live, and we're willing to make the additional sacrifices and have a second job to keep the ranch going.

"I'll tell you this, the economics is driving people off agricultural lands, and they're losing the ability to choose this lifestyle. So it is important to us that we keep agriculture viable in this basin. Otherwise all this land will be subdivided.

"It's not like we aren't taking actions ourselves to make agriculture viable. With the help of Donna at the Rural Conservation District, we're looking at new ways of ranching so we can increase productivity and get a better return for what we're doing. I don't think we can do it alone. We have to have the support of the community. And we definitely can't have the community taking away some of our options.

"We want to be sure that we can pass our land off to our future generations, just like our dads and granddads and our great-granddads did. To do that, we feel we need to find ways to preserve our property rights. We have to balance the desire to keep the valley green with the desire to maintain our property rights.

"We also want to protect our freedom to do what we want with our lands. I mean, our family has spent generations protecting this land, creating the open space that you want to save. But you can't save it if we can't keep ourselves profitable.

"If we fail, then all of this land will be purchased and subdivided. Those upscale homes that bother you will cover our working lands. Then you won't have anything of what you want. So we have to maintain the value of our ranch lands. We have to protect other farming and agricultural land.

"My view is, if you want us to preserve the ranches as open space, then you have to pay us not to develop. If you're not willing to do that, then you have to leave us the option of being able to sell some land to keep the ranch viable.

"I have to tell you we get pretty upset when you call our ranches open space. It indicates that you have some rights to the land. Which you don't. It's only open space because we have kept it that way. This is ranchland, it is working land. Because of that, you have the ability to see that open space that you're trying so hard to protect.

"One of our other problems has to do with solving the water issues we have. I think you know everybody is trying to get the water rights that we have for irrigating our lands. Those green areas wouldn't be near as green if it weren't for the water that we divert to irrigate. They would be browner and dusty earlier in the summer, not exactly the scenery that you want.

"But there are many people who don't want us to have that water. I know that your tribe, Allen, is concerned about getting more water into the river for the fish. Well, those big communities we have over the other side of the mountains are also after our water. They got some pretty thirsty people in those cities. And they're willing to pay almost any amount of money to get it.

"And then we got problems with the number of people on these lots that are drilling wells up in the hills. There's indications that the water table is being reduced and affecting the flow in the streams that we divert for our irrigation.

"We need to be able to keep this water on the land. We have to protect these water rights; otherwise that green area is going to turn brown. It's bad enough that we've had to make it through three years of drought. To reduce our water supply anymore would be disastrous.

"We can't afford to be divided on this, because if we are, we will lose what makes this basin so beautiful. The agricultural land will be gone, bought up, subdivided, with houses built all over the place. Lynn, that is what you don't want.

"I guess that's all I got to say, Allen."

"Kathy," YOU say, "tell Allen what you heard. Wayne, I want you to be her backup."

Kathy turns to Allen and speaks to him:

"Allen, I heard Mike talk about how upset he and the other ranchers were that they weren't even considered when the zoning plan was developed. He said that makes them feel like they didn't even exist. He said that they normally are pretty quiet people and don't like to speak up or make a fuss, but when they were surprised by the zoning plan, they puffed up like a blowfish and became pretty prickly.

"I get the feeling he'd like to go back to just being a shy blowfish. In order to do that, he feels that we need to understand that ranching is not that easy these days. The high costs of managing their ranch make it difficult to make a living. Yet his family will do it because it's their lifestyle. They accept that they are not going to make an awful lot of money.

"He indicated that Donna and the Rural Conservation District are helping the ranchers figure out some ways of managing their ranches so they can get a better return on it. They're willing to do this because they want to be sure they can pass their ranches on to their kids. Just like the previous generations have.

"He said that ranchers get pretty upset when we call those ranches open space or green space. He said it's only that way because they've been able to keep their ranches going. He said if the ranches fail, then all we will see up there will be subdivisions, and then there won't be more green space anymore.

"He also talked about water rights. He feels that everybody wants the water that they use to irrigate their lands. He talked about the communities over on the other side of the mountains that are willing to pay almost anything to get the water we have. He also told Allen he understands that his tribe is concerned about putting more water in the river for the fish.

"Then he spoke about how the subdivisions are drilling wells and drawing down the water table, and this is affecting the amount of water that's in the streams. So he wants us to be sure we keep our water in this basin.

"I think that's about all I remember. Can you help me, Wayne?"

"Yeah. I also heard you say if the community wants you to preserve these ranches, then the community maybe needs to pay you not to develop the land. And if we don't do that, then you need to have the option left open to sell some of that land so you can keep the ranch.

"I also heard you say to Allen that the tribe wants more water in the river for the fish. This is just another demand for your water. And I also heard you say that you want to protect your freedom to do what you want with your lands. And you feel that it's because you've protected these lands and managed them right that it's protected the kind of open space and green space that the community wants to look at."

Wayne indicates that he is done. YOU look at Mike, and he nods to indicate he is satisfied.

YOU say: "Thank you, Kathy and Wayne, for being good listeners. Now, Allen, I would like you to speak to Mike about the situation as you and your tribe see it, how did it happen, and how you feel about it. Laura, you are the listener, and Kathy will be the backup."

Allen looks over at Jack and begins to speak:

"Jack, when my grandfathers welcomed your grandfather to this basin, I'm sure they had no idea of the consequences of their generosity. And while we were generous and welcoming, those who followed your grandfather did not return the favor." He looks around the circle. "My people have had a long history of broken promises and lies. These broken promises have led to a broken trust.

"When I was younger, I was much more radical and outspoken about this. I think you can remember that time, Jack. But then, you were a little rowdy yourself, I remember." (Laughter from the group; Jack nods his head and smiles.) "With age, I had to take on a different perspective. My elders taught me to do more listening than I did talking. They taught me that no matter what has happened in the past, we in this basin are stuck with each other. That is the reason that I ran for the position of chairman of our tribal council. I want to do something about that.

"Our grandfathers lived in harmony with the land. The river produced our food with enough fish for all of our communities. The forests and the plains provided us the four-legged animals that were our food. These were gifts from the creator, and they were plentiful. And we treated them with respect.

"Now that river, which once provided our food, can no longer do so. Water is removed for irrigation, it is diverted to communities downstream and outside the basin, and what is left over can hardly sustain fish. For us, the fish are more than a food; they are our religion. Because they are no longer available to us, our people are sick, physically and spiritually. The plains that provided us the buffalo, the deer, and antelope are now overhunted. My people eat foods that are not native to us. What we eat now is packaged food and canned food from the grocery store.

"I am afraid of what will happen to this basin in the future. This basin can hardly take care of the people who are here now. When the lumber mills shut down, many of my people lost jobs. Poverty on the reservation has increased as a result. How can we bring more people into this basin, unless we can find more opportunities for work? I think we need to focus on economic development instead of encouraging people to move here.

"I know, Mike, that the ranchers need water to irrigate your lands. But I also know that the fish need the water in the river. It's not just a matter of the amount of water, but also the quality of the water. When your cattle graze the riverbanks and get water from the river, it reduces the quality of the water. From my people's perspective, we need to do something about that.

"Running water in open ditches is no longer the best way to irrigate your land. We know that a lot of that water leaks back into the ground. We believe that water should be in the river. So we think ranchers need to be looking at more efficient uses of transporting water to the land, by piping it.

"To us water is sacred. It exists to provide life for all the creatures in the basin. It provides for the fish, for the winged ones, and for the four-legged animals, and for all of us humans. We need water in order to have life. We treat it as if it is an unlimited resource when it isn't. Like you said, Mike, many people from outside the basin want our water. We cannot afford to let it leave the basin. If we want to keep our way of life—all of us—then we have to come together, like we are doing here, and find a solution.

The Situation

"It is for this reason that I supported Lynn and her committee on limiting growth. I'm not sure that the zoning plan is the right way to do it, but it seemed to me like it was a start. More importantly, Lynn's committee was willing to include us and listen to our point of view, even though we make up less than one percent of the people in the basin. It's the first time we've really been listened to in this basin. Before, we were invisible, just like you feel now.

"We want the salmon to come back. We want the wild animals to come back. Like you, we want to continue our heritage as a tribe and as a nation. We can understand why you want to keep your heritage. The question is, are we willing to work together to make it happen for all of us?

"In order to do that, we have to have trust. My people have to overcome their distrust of your culture. In order to do that, you have to include us in solving this problem. If you help us meet our needs, we will help you meet your needs.

"I have said what I need to say."

YOU look at Laura and say, "Laura, please tell Mike, what you heard."

"Mike," says Laura, "Allen first said that when he was younger, he wished his tribe had a better immigration policy." (Laughter.) "He said that while his grandfathers treated your family with generosity, those who came after did not return the favor. He reminded us of how the Indian people have been treated poorly, with promises that were not kept. So his people do not trust us as a result.

"He talked about how he was more rebellious when he was young, but as he has matured and with the help of his elders, he sees things differently. He also reminded us of how rowdy you were at the time. He feels we are stuck with one another, so we might as well work together. He became chairman of its tribal council so he could do that.

"He said that the river was a source of food for his tribe. But it is not any longer that. Water is being removed by the ranchers for irrigation, and it's diverted to communities downstream and outside our basin, and there are many communities who would like to purchase this water from us.

"So the fish are no longer sustained by the river and are no longer available to his people. This has resulted in his people becoming sick, he said, both physically and spiritually. To his people, the salmon are a part of their religion. He said that the foods his people eat are no longer native foods, and they come in plastic packages from the grocery store.

"He knows that the ranchers need water to irrigate their lands, but he also knows that same water is needed by the fish, and he's concerned about the impact that grazing and the cattle have on the quality of water. He feels there are better ways of irrigating the ranches, that the ditches leak water into the land, so it's not the most efficient way of getting the water to the land.

"To the tribe, the water is very sacred and it exists for all life. He said we need water in order to have life. We treat it as if it is unlimited, but in fact is very scarce, and he said that if we want to keep our way of life, we've got to get together to find a solution.

"That's the reason that he supported Lynn's committee. He also said that it was the first time his tribe has been listened to, even though they make up a small percentage of the basin.

"He wants the salmon to come back. He wants to do this so his people can maintain their heritage in the same manner that you want to maintain your heritage. But he said we have to work together to make that happen. He ended up by saying we have to trust each other for doing this. And they have to be included in coming up with the solution."

Laura stops and looks at Kathy. "I know he said more than that, Kathy. Can you help me?"

"Yes," says Kathy, "Allen pointed out that his grandfathers lived in harmony with the land, because it provided their food. They saw these as gifts from their creator. But now the river and the land can't provide the food because of how they have been treated.

"He also stated that he was afraid about what would happen in this basin in the future if we continue to bring people here. There are hardly enough jobs for people now, especially since the mills have shut down. So he would like to see more focus on economic development. This would be for all of us.

"I think it is commendable that he and his people have realized that even though we have broken promises in the past, we all have to work together in order to solve this problem. To him, it is an issue of trust."

I can see that Kathy is done and looking around to see what to do next. I say, Thanks to YOU for facilitating so well. And, thank you, Kathy and Laura. Our final pair is Bud and Alice. Bud you're going to speak first to Alice.

Alice, I'm going to change the rules a little bit. I'm going to ask you to be the listener and tell Bud what you heard him say. Kenney, you were going to be her backup listener. After that Alice, you will tell Bud about your view of the situation. Then Bud you'll going to tell Alice what you heard her say. Rayni, you will be Bud's backup listener.

I have moved the primary listening responsibilities to each member of the pair. The listeners have demonstrated that they can hear and recall quite well. Now I want to move that ability to the speakers.

Bud draws in a deep breath before he speaks. "I haven't been here as long as Jack and the other ranchers' families. But I did grow up here. I've spent my whole life here. And it's been a pretty wonderful life, but things have changed.

"It used to be when the lumber mills operated and the mines operated that we had work for everyone who wanted it. When our kids graduated from high school, they could go directly to work in the woods or in the mines. Neither of those choices is available today.

"That is the biggest change I see in our community. We just don't have enough jobs for all of our people. Those jobs we do have don't provide wages sufficient to support a family. So today when our kids graduate from high school, they have to look for jobs elsewhere. That's not a good sign, because it means our community will get older and older as our young people leave.

"As Allen said, it's especially hard for the Coyote Mountain Tribe. They relied on these jobs to feed their families on the reservation. For them, it's pretty hard to leave their homes and their people. I know, Allen, that your tribe is considering the possibility of a casino in this basin, which could help us with that. I also know we could be of great help in supporting you in that if we could come together as a community.

"Alice, I remember you from grade school. We went through high school together, and over the years, we became very good friends." (Alice nods her head.) "But this issue of a zoning plan has caused a big separation between us because we appear to be on opposite sides of this issue. So this issue has caused me to lose a friend. And I'm pretty sad about that.

"I've been a banker all my professional career, and I provide the money for many of the small businesses that exist in this community that have since closed their doors because of the shutdown of the mills. So we need new businesses to come in here, big ones and small ones.

"But I can tell you that businesses won't come to a community that is split right down the middle. It won't come to a community that doesn't have a good education system and doesn't have housing for its employees or doesn't have the employees it needs for its business. We don't have an awful lot to offer right now.

"I know how hard it is for the ranchers to make a living, because my bank provides them the money they need to keep going. It's just getting tougher and tougher for them. But it's just as tough for the small businesses, out here on Main Street. Unless we find a way to bring people in those stores, we're going to continue to decline as a community.

"I'm upset about the new zoning plan, because any kind of regulation now appears to limit people's freedom to do what they need to do. It is going to prevent us from growing economically.

"It's not that I disagree with you, Alice; it just seems to me to be bad timing. Like Jack, I don't see many of those lots that you're concerned about being developed, because they've been around for over twenty years. I admit that our basin will become a draw in time, and people will flock here like they have to the other places that surround us.

"But for now, I think our biggest issue is trying to find a way to create an economic base that keeps the people here who have been here, who have been a part of our community for many years. I think we need to find a way to keep our kids here. I think we need to find some low-income housing that can help those who can only find low-paying jobs.

"I don't think the real-estate developers are the problem. They are trying to make a living just like the rest of us. If it weren't for them, ranchers wouldn't have the ability to sell land when they need to get the money to support their ranches.

"I think the biggest problems we have are the divisions that exist in this community. Not just the ones between growth and status quo. We have divisions over the kind of economic development we want, over how to manage our water, over providing low-income housing, over supporting the schools in the county, and competition between the cities in the county. If we don't resolve these issues, I don't see how we can create the kind of economic support that we need.

"We seem to be real good at coming up with issues that pit one against the other, but we fail when it comes to making decisions to take care of all of us. I'm aware that we've been together for the last two days with people who have disagreed with each other, sometimes pretty violently over the past few years. And yet look at us! We are sitting here listening to one another for the first time in my memory. Somehow it seems much easier than I thought it would be.

"We need a way of helping these communities come together to understand each other's issues. We need to understand the tribe's issues, the rancher's issues, environmentalist's issues, the real estate issues, small business owner's issues, the Hispanic issues, and especially the issues of our young people. Unless we do that, we're just going to sit still and let those outside influences come in here and pick our pockets.

The Situation

"If we are going to be able to make decisions as a community, then we have to be able to continue to talk openly and honestly, long and hard, and listen like Bob is teaching us, to hear each other. I don't think anybody is wrong here; we just all see things from our different perspectives. And I think all of us want what's good for the broader community. We just don't know how to get there. Maybe what we're doing this week is good start.

"Alice, you know I love this community. And I know you love this community. Even though we disagree on some things, we are doing it for the good of the community. So I want to start by telling you I want our friendship back. I want to listen to your point of view, and you should be able to listen to mine, and then I want to be able to work with you to see if we can find a way to solve our differences to benefit everybody here in this room.

"I want you to know that while I disagree with the present zoning plan, I do think we need something that sets boundaries on where we're going to allow development to take place and the kinds of development were going to allow here. I also believe that those who develop in these areas need to provide the entire infrastructure that's needed for that: roads, water, sewers, and support for education.

"To do otherwise would put a heavy burden on our locals, who are finding it difficult to just make it from one day to the next. So I believe that is a basis for our getting together and figuring out how to do this. How to prevent growth from being too fast, but also allowing the kind of growth that would help us build community. That is sound, socially and economically. And I'm willing to start doing that with you.

"That is all I have to say, Bob."

Alice, would you tell Bud what you heard him say.

Alice looks at Bud.

"The most important thing I heard, Bud, is that you want my friendship back. You've got it, you've always had it, and it's just that this zoning issue kept us apart. So I want you to know that we're friends, and no matter how much we disagree in the future, I want to keep the friendship.

"You first started by saying how long you have lived in this community and how it's been a pretty darn good life. That was when the mills were running and the mine was operating. Things were pretty good for all of our families, because we made enough money and we knew our kids would stay home when they graduated from high school.

"You said that this all changed when the mills closed. Those good-paying jobs were gone, it was more difficult to support our families, and our kids have been leaving when they graduated from school.

"You pointed out that it has been especially hard on the members of the tribe. Because they can't leave, it means they can't support their families very well.

"As you said, we were pretty good friends when we went to grade school. And all the way up to high school. And we kept that friendship even though we've been disagreeing with each other. But we never really got disagreeable." (Bud nods his head.)

"You stated that you have been a banker all your professional life and have been able to support our local businesses from that position. That is, up until the mills closed. Since then, lots of these small businesses have closed, and you are finding it difficult to encourage other new businesses to start.

"But it's difficult to get new business to come to this area because of the unrest that we have in the community. If we are always arguing with each other, that's not a good climate to bring a business. If we don't have the employees who can do the work, or we don't have the education system we need, then people are not going to come here with their businesses.

"You're upset with the new zoning plan because you see it as limiting people's freedom to do what is needed to do in order to grow with the community. You don't necessarily disagree with me on that, you just see it as bad timing. It appears to you to be a barrier to improving our economic base.

"So you see our biggest barrier as being all these divisions in the community. And if we don't find a way to bring people together, then you don't see how we can get the kind of economic development we need. You'd like to see us find a way that we can solve this problem. We can bring the community together like we're doing here. We would try to understand each other's issues and try to solve problems to meet our needs.

"You stated how you love this community. And you know how I love this community. You're willing to agree to find some kind of boundaries in how we're going to allow development to take place. And you're willing to support the developers providing the infrastructure that we need so that the county residents aren't paying for it.

"And you're ready to start doing that with me.

"Did I get it all, Kenney?"

Kenney pauses before speaking. He seems surprised by Alice's request.

"I was so moved by what both of you said that I almost forgot to listen. I'll try to fill in the spaces. He said quite a bit, so I probably won't get it all either. He said that because of his position in the bank he knows how difficult it is for families or small businesses or the ranchers to earn a living.

"He also mentioned that the Coyote Mountain Tribe is looking into putting a casino in the basin. And he believes we need to provide them support for that, because it would be seen as economic development.

"He also said that the subdivided lots in our county will probably not be developed in the immediate future. They have been around for quite a while. And he feels that the real-estate developers are not the real problem. He feels that the one big issue is trying to improve our economy. If we do that, it will keep our community together.

"That's all I remember, Bob."

I respond. Thanks, Kenney and Alice. So now we will allow Alice to speak to Bud, and Bud, you will be the listener and Rayni will be your backup.

As I say this I notice that Lynn is motioning to speak. Lynn, did you want to say something?

"Yes, I wanted to say that I also heard Bud say that we seem to be good at coming up with problems that pit us against each other, but we can't make decisions together. He also said that in the time that we've been together, we've been listening to one another for the first time. And that it somehow seems much easier than he thought. I happen to agree with him on that. I noticed the same thing."

Thank you, Lynn. I always appreciate it when people from the group help us remember what was said. It means listening is now a community responsibility. OK, Alice, it is your turn to speak.

"Bud, you know I always have been oriented toward environmental causes and, like Lynn, have been an activist in that area. I worked for the Coyote National Forest after I graduated from high school, in their administrative office. So I have their view of the management of resources, and my husband, Tom, worked in the lumber mill. I understand the need to use our resources for creating jobs.

"But I could never get used to the notion of clear-cutting areas in the National Forest. I could see the damage that was done with the runoff over those bare soils. And I could see the specific impacts in the river that runs through our basin. And, of course, all those roads they built weren't maintained well. Many of them caused erosion into the streams.

"I've always been worried about the river. I didn't like seeing how the water was diverted from the river, both for our use here in the basin or for uses outside by those other communities. I felt always the water belonged in the river where the fish could make use of it. Even though Tom and I have a small ranch and raise cattle, I never liked seeing the cattle feeding on the stream banks or watering in the river. It just didn't seem right to me.

"I never said much about this because you know it's difficult to speak about environmental issues in this community. The responses make you feel like you're not welcome. So I tended to keep my opinions to myself.

"When the mills closed, Tom lost his job, and we had to rely solely on what the ranch provided us and on my Forest Service pay. I was later laid off by the Forest Service because they didn't have the budget to keep me on. So both Tom and I had to look for different ways of earning a living, in addition to the ranch. We've had to tighten our belts quite a bit. Funny thing about it is, I'm glad that my children were able to graduate from school and go on to college and find jobs outside the basin. But I would sure like it if we had the jobs here that would bring them back.

"The basin that we live in is beautiful. We are surrounded by magnificent mountains covered with the most beautiful pine forests. All the streams that run into the river that goes down through the heart of our basin provide the opportunity for the salmon to grow and reproduce. All of the land along both sides of the river is a beautiful rangeland. Most of this is native grasses. And we've been grazing these rangelands ever since Jack's grandparents first came into this valley over a hundred years ago. It is still a beautiful place; it's a place I want to live for the rest of my life.

"But, like Lynn, I'm really concerned about the possibility that we could be invaded by people from outside the basin, looking for a cheap piece of land so they can have a second home or so they can retire here. As mentioned briefly previously, there are thousands of undeveloped lots. What would happen if people came in and began buying it and building on it? I think the impact on the resources in our basin, on our soils and our water, would be terrible. I'm not opposed to people coming here; I just think we need to manage the growth.

"And we need to have growth that will improve our economy. We need to spend as much time looking for new businesses to come into this place as we try to get people to come in and buy those lots. Otherwise all the jobs that we have will just be low-paying jobs. They also need to be businesses that are sustainable and that protect the resources of the basin.

"So I felt that we could control what happened in the future by having a good zoning plan. We could develop this while we still have green space. We would allow businesses if they protected our basin; we would allow people to build their homes while making arrangements for their providing the necessary roads, utilities, and controls in the subdivisions.

"And we need a comprehensive water plan as the first step for future collaboration with the community as a whole and with the state, in order to best protect our water.

"Also, I know I have been part of creating the problem that brought us here today. I make no apologies for it, because I do believe something has to be done. If we didn't do the job well this time because we didn't listen to everybody, then it won't take that long to do this over again and do it right. At least we now have everyone's attention, and that includes you ranchers.

"I believe, like Allen and his people, that there is an interconnectedness of all things. Whatever actions I take will impact the entire basin. And they will have long-term effects. So I have to make certain that whatever we do on our ranch considers that interconnectedness.

"In these two days, I have learned that we are really all very similar, but we lack a sense of trust and connectedness between the ranchers and tribe, the fishermen, loggers, the agencies, and the communities. We all feel interconnectedness with the land, and yet we have no understanding of the interrelatedness between the different groups in the basin. Until we create that connection, we can't do what is best for our homeland.

"I believe that we all have a sincere love for our land and for our ecosystem. We all want to pass on our land and our heritage to the next generations. Our ties to the land go far deeper than just using it for economic gains.

"And yet, we need to make economic gain if we are going to survive as communities in this basin. I believe the tribe's casino proposal could have economic benefits for this community. But it could also be the draw that would result in uncontrolled growth in the basin. So we need a zoning plan first.

"We need to change things *now*! Or...the ecosystem could be converted to houses.

"Now, it's your turn, Bud. Didja hear me?"

Bud laughs then leans forward to speak to Alice.

"You reminded me of your environmental interests, which I know you demonstrated early in high school. You pointed out how being an environmentalist in this community is not an easy thing. So you have tended to keep your opinions to yourself. I have to admit I don't ever remember you doing that." (Alice laughs with Bud, and others join in.)

"When you graduated, you went to work for the Coyote National Forest. And when you married Tom, he was working in the lumber mill, earning enough money to keep his ranch going.

"You both lost your jobs when the mills closed, and so you had to depend upon your ranch for a living. And we both know that's not an easy thing to do. You had to tighten your belts, while being pretty happy that your children graduated from high school here and went on to college and have found good jobs outside the basin. You sure wish they could come back, however.

"You talked about how beautiful Coyote River Basin is. Your description reminded me why Lynn and others wanted to move here. We have beautiful mountains, with the forests, streams, and rivers that provide the opportunity for fishing.

"You pointed out that the ranches are a part of that beauty, although you would prefer that they not graze their cattle along the edge of the rivers. You stated that even though the ranches have been here for over a hundred years, there are still native grasses in our rangelands.

"You are very concerned about uncontrolled growth, with people moving here because the land is cheap, and there are many undeveloped lots available to them."

Bud stops and thinks for a while. Then he looks at Rayni and says, "I know I missed a lot, can you help me?"

"Yes," Rayni says. "I heard you say, Alice, that you have been an environmentalist all your life, and it hasn't been easy living in this community. You also worked for the Forest Service and disagreed with some of their timber-cutting practices.

"You are fearful, like Lynn is, about us being invaded by people looking for cheap land for a second home, and you feel this would be terrible for the basin resources. Not that you are opposed to growth; you just want to have it controlled.

"You agree with Bud that we do need economic growth for the valley, but they need to fit the basin, to be sustainable and protect our natural resources and beauty. This is why you supported a zoning plan—it would control the growth. It would make people responsible for the roads and utilities in their subdivisions.

"I heard you say that we need to collaborate on a comprehensive water plan as a first step. That would have the aim of protecting our water, keeping it in the basin."

Bud speaks up as Rayni pauses.

"You have been part of creating the zoning plan problem, but you make no apologies, because you felt it was needed. So you may not have done it right, but at least it got everyone's attention. Now, you suggest we can do it right.

"You also feel we are the same in our love for this basin and the land. We know we are connected to this land and the water and the mountains. But our problem is we are not connected to each other. We don't understand each other. You feel this is what we need to do, is create that connection with each other.

"And you want to change things now, before it is too late.

"While you have not been happy about the clear-cutting areas in the National Forest or some of the damage that you have seen in the rivers, you still feel this is a beautiful place and you want to live the rest of your life here."

The room is quiet after Bud finishes repeating what he heard from Alice.

I want all of you to please stand.

Everybody stands.

I want Mike, Allen, Bud, and Alice to come to the center of the circle.

They all move hesitantly to the center.

Donna, I would like you to honor these four people for being part of the panel.

"Thanks, Bob." Donna pauses and looks at the four in the center before speaking. "I want to honor all of you for being so willing to express your personal feelings about what is going on in this basin. While each of you had your own views, what is common among you is your commitment to and passion for the basin that we call home. I don't think any one of you held anything back when you spoke. I think what you have done will make it easier to move on now to find a way to solve our problem. I thank you for that."

The applause is deafening and long, with a few yells and whistles. During the applause, the four people in the center shake hands with each other. Some end up hugging each other, and then finally they connect arms and stand facing each other in a small circle together.

OK, I say, you can return to the edge of the circle. They do this. Now I would like the listeners Kathy, Laura, Rayni, and Kenney to come to the center. Allen, I would like you to honor your listeners.

Allen steps forward into the circle and stops.

"I personally appreciate how well you listened for us during the panel. I found myself being glad that I didn't have to be one of the listeners. It was a difficult job. And yet you are able to recall what we said, almost completely. When you did so, I found I had missed a lot of what Mike had said to me. So it was important to me to get that additional information.

"I'm beginning to understand that I don't listen very well, and this means that I might not understand what you're saying at all. How can that help us? So I appreciate all of you making it possible for us to hear the whole message. And I appreciate that it was not an easy task. But you all did well."

He steps back to the edge of the circle.

Again, the applause is loud and keeps on for quite a while. During this time, the listeners shake hands as the others did and end up hugging each other.

We're going to take a fifteen-minute break, I say. During the break, I want to talk to the six panel members and their listeners in the center of the circle.

Coaching the Small-group Facilitators

The circle empties slowly, with people stopping to talk to each other or to go over to the panel members and thank them for their presentations. It makes it a little difficult to get the panel members and the listeners together, so I have to wait patiently, reminding everyone that I want to speak to them.

When I have the six panel members and their six listeners together, I turn the task over to YOU. I have already coached YOU to talk to them about how they are going to manage the small groups through the next task. This is what you say:

"Each group has at least one panel member who just spoke. I want one of the speakers to facilitate each small group for the next task. This will be a talking circle, where people speak and are listened to; you will not have to record the information at this time.

"If you were a listener for the panel, you may become the recorder when it's time. If there is not a listener in your group, the facilitator will select another person as a recorder.

"Facilitators, when you are in your small group, have them close the circle. Repeat the questions that they will answer. These are the same questions as you answered.

- "What is the situation that brings us together?
- "How did it get to be that way?
- "How do you feel about it?

"Diane will give you this task. Start with a person who has not spoken yet or been a listener. That means that the panel members will speak last. You have already had your say. Now it is time for those who were listening to you to have their say.

"Remember, you will not be recording at this time. This is a talking circle, an opportunity for each member of your group to speak, answering the three questions and being listened to with respect.

"When everyone has spoken, including the listeners, and ending with panel members, we will have you pass out the three-by-five cards. At that time, we will give you two questions to answer, one on each side of the card.

"You are going to experience how you can gather information around an issue like this, where there are lots of statements and words to be said, and focus it down to key statements developed by the members themselves. These are the questions I will ask:

Pass out the 3 x 5 cards.

What are at least two statements or issues that you heard from others? (on one side of the card)

What is at least one statement or issue that you expressed? (On the other side of the card)

"This activity makes the members responsible to create a common knowledge base beyond their individual views. It begins to develop an understanding beyond the individual statement. It provides affirmation that people are listening to each other. It subtly changes people's relationships, as each person hears others express what they heard and support. It introduces silence, balancing each person's energy internally.

"When everyone has recorded their statements, you will then select the listener or another group member to act as recorder for the group. Record all of the information on both sides of the card, reversing direction as you do so.

"Mike, can you tell me what you heard? And Lynn, you can be his backup."

Mike repeats what YOU said, and Lynn fills in information he might have missed.

"Remember," YOU say, "I will repeat all of this information before you start so that everyone can hear it. This is just preparing you for the activity."

Exploring the Situation: Small Groups

During the break, the community members have come together in small groups, trios, or pairs. They are both talking and listening to each other. Most of these groups are very diverse. For me, reading the nonverbal communication, it means this group is coming together as a community, ready to meet the needs of all the different views.

I have coached YOU earlier through the activities of the day. You are going to play a major part in facilitating today. When the break is over, I have you get people's attention and encourage their movement to the circle. You get their attention by simply stating from the edge of the circle:

"We are ready to begin the next task, which will allow each of you to speak about your view of the situation and how it got to be that way."

You repeat this statement until they are all seated in the large circle. People continue to talk while they're moving. The energy in the room is excited and positive. They continue to talk with each other when they are seated in the circle.

You ask the panel members and their listeners to come to the center of the circle. This gets everyone's attention. You begin to speak, and there is a respectful quiet in the room.

"Each of these panel members or listeners was selected from the four groups that we had earlier today. They will now become facilitators and recorders for your groups. Since there are at least two panel members or listeners from each group, they will determine who will be the first facilitator. I want all of you to take your chairs and form your small circles in front of your flip charts. When you have done that, I will describe your next task. Diane will then give you your task."

When the groups have reformed themselves, you step to the edge of the circle to speak.

"We are going to start with a small-group talking circle. You are not going to record to begin with. Your facilitator, who was a panel member, will ask you to answer the same three questions they did. The facilitators will then choose a person to speak and move around the circle either clockwise or counterclockwise, with each person taking their turn to talk.

"We want those who were not on the panel to speak first. The panel members will speak last since they have already spoken.

"It is important for this task that you should not interrupt each other. It is important that you listen with respect. I encourage you to be just as candid, open, and honest as the panel was. If you are angry, be angry; it is OK here.

The Situation

"When everyone has spoken at least once, Diane will ask the facilitator to pass out three-by-five cards that are at the flip chart. You will then record information on the three-by-five cards that will later be recorded to the flip chart. We will give you those tasks when you complete this one.

"Diane will now give you your task.

YOU have coached Diane for her role as cofacilitator. I have provided her a three-by-five card with the task and questions on it. YOU and I are now operating in tandem, coaching and facilitating.

Diane steps to the edge of the circle and reads from her three-by-five card. She reminds everyone to first close their circle. She waits for this to be done. There is a scraping of chairs and much movement as the groups close their circle, leaving the flip chart out of it. Members of the small groups are now facing each other, as they are when we have them in the large circle.

She reminds them, "This is a talking circle. Do not record, but listen with respect, and take your turn speaking." She then reads off the three questions.

Close your circle, do not record, take your turn, listen with respect.

What is the situation that you want to address and resolve?
How did it get to be that way?
How do you feel about it?

Diane steps away from the circle, turns around, and walks toward me. I have her turn around again so she can see how quickly the groups have bent to the task. Then YOU take Diane to the side and continue to coach her through the remaining tasks for today.

This task normally takes one to two hours. Each small group is focused on listening to whoever is speaking. Their heads are leaning in. It is rare to see anyone leaning back or with their chairs pushed away from the circle. Everyone is engaged either in talking or listening.

There are many nonverbal movements: nodding of heads, smiles, expressions of amazement, sadness, empathy, sometimes laughter—all reflecting a group of people who are committed to listening to each other and who are being impacted by the words that are expressed. This community can listen, understand, and develop a statement describing the situation that brought them together.

I walk over to YOU and Diane. Diane, I say, when the group appears to be done, you should walk to the edge of the circle and ask them, "Has everyone spoken at least once?" You have seen the facilitators do this earlier. The purpose is to find out if everyone has had a chance to speak. Then we know if they are ready to move ahead. If they state that they are not ready, then you just turn and walk away from the circle. You can then try again later.

Diane nods her head and states, "YOU already took me through this before you honored them."

Oops, I say, I guess I need to just trust that you already know what needs to be done. She smiles and nods her head.

YOU, when they are done, I'm going to have Diane also manage the next task. I pass out a three-by-five card with questions written on both sides.

Diane, when you have provided the task, standing at the edge of the circle, step back and wait while they do that. They will probably stand up and go searching for their pen or pencil. Relax yourself while they do that. This is a normal behavior. Then wait until you believe they are, for the most part, done recording. If they are not done, they will let you know if you try to move ahead.

Then step back to the circle and ask them to turn the card over when they are done recording. You will do the same for the next task.

Pass out the 3 x 5 cards.

What are two descriptions of the situation that you heard from others?

(Turn your card over when done.)

(Opposite side of the card)

What is one description of the situation that you expressed?

When you observe that everyone has turned their cards over, provide them the question on the back of the card.

When they are done recording, return to the edge of the circle and have the facilitator pick someone to be a new facilitator, while they become the recorder. When you can see they have done this, then give them the task:

Record the information on the first side of a three-by-five card, and then reverse directions of the circle and record the other side.

Then turn and come back to me.

I have Diane repeat this to YOU to make sure we are clear. This is always an interesting time for me as a facilitator. It will take from one to two hours for groups to do this task. As they are talking, you and I are coaching the cofacilitators. And we still have time left over to just relax and observe the groups in action.

It is forty minutes later that Diane can see that the groups have finished. She walks to the edge of the circle and asks, "Has everyone spoken at least once?" She repeats this three times before she has everyone's attention. (YOU have done a great job of coaching. I am so proud.)

Diane says: "It appears that you have all spoken at least once, so now you are going to record this information. Pass out the three-by-five cards."

Diane steps back to allow this to happen. She returns to the edge of the circle.

"On one side of the card please answer this question: What are at least two descriptions you heard from others about the situation and how it got to be that way?"

Diane steps back and allows this to happen in silence. Some members stand up and go searching for their pen or pencil and return quickly and quietly. When Diane determines that people are done recording, she steps forward.

"Please turn your card over when you are done." (Pauses)

"On the other side of the card answer this question: What is at least one description you expressed about the situation during the talking circle?"

Diane steps back and waits for them to complete this task. During this activity, silence is introduced into the room, allowing participants to think deeply and deliberatively about their answers. When they are done recording, Diane steps to the edge of the circle and provides directions for recording to the flip chart:

"The facilitator will assign the panel listener or another member of the group to become the recorder. Facilitator, start with the first side of the three-by-five card and have everyone provide their information for the flip chart. When this information is recorded, reverse the direction and have the information on the other side of the card recorded."

When she is done, Diane steps back, turns, and walks toward us. When she turns around, she can see the group immediately went to work. While they work, YOU continued to coach her for the next tasks.

Following are some sample cards from the group. (These are actual recorded statements taken from real workshops.)

What I heard	What I said
The ranchers and farmers are very upset that they were not considered in developing the plan. *We don't understand the newcomers, and they don't understand us. We have to find some way to understand each other.*	*While the basin does not experience much growth now, in the future the pressure could be much greater.*

Gil's card, side 1   Gil's card, side 2

What I heard	What I said
The real estate people can help us develop the zoning that would provide for the infrastructure on each of the subdivisions. *People who move here believe that they have found heaven. But they soon find out other people are looking for the same location.*	*If we didn't have water on the land, it would not be as green as it is.* *We need to decide how to manage the water so we can keep it in the basin.*

Todd's card, side 1   Todd's card, side 2

What I heard	What I said
We're good at getting into arguments with each other, but not so good at making decisions that we can all agree to. *It may be that the new zoning plan came too soon. It was bad timing. Being in a ranching business is difficult, because of high costs, and that means they have to have more than one job.*	*We've been meeting for two days now, and have not had one argument. We are able to speak and listen to each other.* *We need to find a way to bring the community together to work out on these broader issues.*

Mark's card, side 1   Mark's card, side 2

Because this task is recorded on the three-by-five cards, it is not necessary to ask if everyone has spoken at least once. Normally, you can tell the task is completed, because everyone will be seated. There are times, however, that the recorder will remain standing at their flip chart, so it is difficult to say if they are done. In that instance, the following question can be asked by Diane:

"Has everyone had their information recorded?"

When this is confirmed, Diane asks the recorder from Group 4 to report out and then continuing in a clockwise direction with the remaining groups. This allows each group to hear the information gathered.

GROUP 4: WHAT WE HEARD

- *Some of the ranchers have been here for over a hundred years and want to continue with their heritage.*
- *The ranchers are willing to welcome newcomers, just as long as they don't take away their rights.*
- *There is great community concern about the irrigation water being diverted from the river.*
- *The tribe feels like they were included in the planning, and this was the first time that has happened.*
- *Because we are listening to each other with respect, we are each getting a different slant on the situation. We are getting much more understanding of our interconnectedness.*
- *Doing the zoning plan over would not take very much time if we all work together.*
- *If we don't protect this land, it will be purchased and subdivided.*
- *Everyone agrees we need to keep the water in the basin so that we can manage it more effectively and maybe return some of it to the river.*
- *We need to make the new folks who come here more aware of the importance that agriculture has to our communities.*
- *Those who worked on the zoning plan feel they might have gone too far, because they did not consider all the agricultural groups.*
- *The ranchers are trying to find what new ways to ranch so they can be more profitable.*
- *There is great support here for the tribe's proposal to have a casino. While the jobs would be low-paying jobs, it would still attract new businesses to the basin.*

> **GROUP 4: WHAT WE SAID**
> - *Water is sacred to the tribe. They believe that it exists to provide life for all of us.*
> - *We learned that Allen and Jack were pretty rowdy when they were younger.*
> - *Everyone would like to keep their kids here in the basin, but we need economic growth to do that.*
> - *We all love this community, but we disagree on how to protect it.*
> - *There is great concern that we could be invaded by people from outside the basin.*
> - *People are not opposed to growth, they just want to have control.*
> - *The ranchers want the option of selling some of the land so they can subsidize their operations.*
> - *When the lumber mills operated and the mines operated, we had work for everyone.*

When all of the groups' information has been presented, I step to the edge of the circle and provide an insight on the process.

Exploring the Situation: An Insight

The first question you answered, "What is the situation you want to address and resolve?" allows each person to give their perception of the conflict you want to resolve.

The second question, "How did it get to be that way?" is often necessary to help the community understand what events created the conflict. It is not unusual to find that some conflicts were created a decade or more in the past, when two members of the community who could not agree invited people loyal to them to join in the argument, thereby creating an intergroup conflict. It is not unusual to find out that those two people have since left the community. And yet the conflict continues.

Answering this question also helps many of those who have joined in a conflict, and chosen sides, to understand what events led up to the conflict. This enlightenment is very instructive in helping people understand the conflict. It facilitates movement toward a solution.

For the reader: The following is the entire collective statement based on the three-by-five cards, including "what we heard from others" and "what we said." This includes all the perceptions of the group. This is normally developed at the end of the day's session and read to the large group the next morning. It is included here so you can see the results of this discussion and relate it to what follows.

The Situation that Confronts Us: What We Heard and Said
The Collective Statement

The ranchers and farmers were caught unawares by the zoning proposal. The ranchers and farmers are very upset that they were not considered in developing the plan.

The ranchers feel outnumbered and not considered. People engaged in agricultural activities are only a small number of voters in the basin. Most of this land in the basin is owned by the federal government, while about 15 percent is in ranching and farming. They don't have enough power to protect themselves from the majority. The ranchers are willing to welcome newcomers, just as long as they don't take away their rights.

Being in a ranching business is difficult because of high costs, and that means they have to have more than one job. Since ranching is a marginal business, their families have to have more than one job to keep the ranch going. The ranchers want the option of selling some of the land so they can subsidize their operations.

Everyone wants to find a way to pass on their heritage to their succeeding generations. Some of the ranchers have been here for over a hundred years and want to continue with their heritage.

The tribe has the same concerns as the ranchers, trying to preserve their heritage and religion into the future.

The ranchers provide the open green spaces that we call so beautiful. The ranchers consider the open space as working land. They are offended when it is called open space. The open spaces are only green because they are irrigated with the rancher's water rights. The ranchers believe that if you want to keep their land as open land, then perhaps you should pay them to not develop the land.

For the tribe the fish are more than a food, they are their religion. If they lose their religion, then they will lose their culture. The tribes need the salmon to return so they can keep their culture and religion alive. We (the tribe) need to find ways to help our culture be more viable.

The tribes were very generous and welcoming to us, just as we are generous and welcoming to newcomers today. If the tribes had a more strict immigration policy, we would not be here.

We need to make the new folks who come here more aware of the importance that agriculture has to our communities. Many of the newcomers have never met a rancher, nor do they understand what ranchers do.

Probably we should provide more support to the Rural Conservation District. The ranchers are trying to find what new ways to ranch so they can be more profitable.

While the basin does not experience much growth now, in the future the pressure could be much greater. People who move here believe that they have found heaven. But they soon find out other people are looking for the same location. There is great concern that we could be invaded by people from outside the basin. If we don't protect this land, it will be purchased and subdivided.

There are a lot of subdivisions scattered throughout the basin with many lots. Many have been here for over twenty years and have not been sold or developed. While there are many subdivisions with many lots in the basin, they've been here for a good number of years. Many people doubt they will ever be developed.

The real estate people are not responsible for the situation. They respond to the need, they don't create the demand. The real estate developers are helping the ranchers to sell land when they need to get money for their ranches. The real estate people can help us develop the zoning that would provide for the infrastructure on each of the subdivisions.

People are not opposed to growth; they just want to have control. Those who are activists are fearful that the present land-use plan will allow unregulated growth. The intent of those who supported zoning was purely to attempt to guide growth in the basin. The zoning is intended to make intelligent decisions about protecting the basin.

There is agreement on the need for a zoning plan, but it needs to include everybody, and it needs to protect the agricultural lands. Those who worked on the zoning plan feel they might have gone too far, because they did not consider all the agricultural groups. Doing the zoning plan over would not take very much time if we all work together.

Those who supported the zoning plan wish they had spent more time listening to the ranchers and farmers and others affected by the zoning.

The Situation

The people who supported the zoning approach had no idea of the impact it would have on ranching and their families. The people who supported the land-zoning plan admit that they did not pay attention to what the ranchers had to say.

It may be that the new zoning plan came too soon. It was bad timing. While a zoning plan created a divide between us, at least we now are focused together on the issue.

There is great community concern about the irrigation water being diverted from the river. It makes it difficult to bring the salmon back. People are concerned about the impact that grazing along the stream banks has on water quality. The ranchers are fearful that people want to take their water away in violation of their rights.

Everyone agrees we need to keep the water in the basin so that we can manage it more effectively and maybe return some of it to the river. There is a fear that the metropolitan area will try to take our water away from us. The fear is that the courts will make the decision unless we get there first.

A comprehensive water plan would be a first step for future collaboration with the community. People who are drilling wells and subdivisions appear to be drawing down the water table. We need to manage this.

The loss of the lumber mills and the mines caused great economic losses to people in the basin. Jobs are lost or have become low-paying jobs. The loss of the mining and timber industries has had a bad impact on the tribe and their people. While the people who lost jobs could leave to another area and find other jobs, the tribal people want to stay. This makes it more difficult for them.

When the lumber mills operated and the mines operated, we had work for everyone. Everyone would like to keep their kids here in the basin, but we need economic growth to do that. Our children used to have jobs here after high school, and now they have to leave.

The tribe's casino proposal could have economic benefits for this community. There is great support here for the tribe's proposal to have a casino. While the jobs would be low-paying jobs, it would still attract new businesses to the basin. We need a zoning plan before we can move ahead with that.

We need to recognize that recreation is a commodity that we can provide to the public. Bringing the salmon back to the basin would provide economic benefits that might be larger than those we lost on the closed industries.

Businesses won't come to this community if we have divisiveness. It is difficult to get new business because of our unrest in the community.

The divisions in the community are probably our biggest problem. We're good at getting into arguments with each other, but not so good at making decisions that we can all agree to. We are all working in all of our worst possible outcomes, the ranchers, the supporters of the zoning, and the rest of us. All love this community, but we disagree on how to protect it.

We don't understand the newcomers, and they don't understand us. We have to find some way to understand each other. Because we are listening to each other with respect, we are each getting a different slant on the situation. We are getting much more understanding of our interconnectedness. If you help me meet my needs, I will help you meet your needs.

We need to find a way to bring the community together to work out these broader issues. In order to work together, we have to have trust. In order to have trust, we would have to include everyone in the solution to this problem. The tribe trusts us because they are involved and we are listening to their views. The tribe feels like they were included in the planning, and this was the first time that has happened.

We've been meeting for two days now and have not had one argument. We are able to speak and listen to each other.

We learned that Allen and Jack were pretty rowdy when they were younger.

This description of the situation and its history is created by the people, using their words. There are ninety two statements recorded in an hour or less. It is a description of the problem representing all sides of the situation. It goes beyond describing the situation to beginning to suggest approaches for resolving it. It represents all the perceptions, it is the community view.

Uncapping the Well—Releasing the Flow: An Insight for the Reader

I'll bet you're wondering if people actually listen as well as indicated by this discussion. The answer is: yes, they do! When assigned as a listener, they are asked to not take notes, but just to listen deeply with the intent to recall what they heard. They are to repeat it, being objective, without making judgments and without making editorial comments.

The great majority of people, probably over 90 percent, are fearful of being a listener. They will say, "I can never do this!" The only way to get them to overcome that fear is to give them the choice of doing it. Despite their verbal protestations, they will always choose to accept the assignment.

When we assign this, we always provide a backup listener. The first time you may not recall 100 percent—maybe only 50 percent. The backup may get the next 40–50 percent. But the second time you listen, you will find that you get pretty close to 80 percent of what a person says. Eventually you will get it all, to the surprise of everyone, including yourself. This only happens if you are provided the opportunity, if you choose, and if you know what the boundaries are.

What I know, based on years of experience in numerous and diverse situations, is that we do not listen to, or hear, most of what other people say, especially if we are emotional. The words the panelists expressed during the panel discussion have been stated before in the meetings where they discussed the zoning plan. But because they were angry or emotional, because there was no directive to listen, what they said was never heard. Often it was shouted down or deliberately ignored.

If I come to a meeting with a deep concern, one that has triggered my worst possible outcomes, I need to be able to express this concern in a safe environment where I know I am heard. When I sense I am not listened to, then I must find some way to repeat myself so that you can hear it. So I may speak louder, longer, with more aggressive behaviors. If you still don't hear, then I must find a way to get your attention by speaking longer, louder, or through some nonverbal behavior, such as banging my fists on the table. (In one situation a member took his shoes off and threw them into the center of the circle!) Or I may bring a rifle to a meeting to get your attention!

If I cannot get you to hear me, I am left with the unacknowledged information, repeating it to myself in my mind as a personal conflict, going around and around with it. When I cannot get rid of it, it becomes like sludge, inhibiting my normal flow of energy.

This prevents me from having new thoughts or developing new information. All interactions are seen through this filter of sludge. It's like capping an artesian well and letting the water at the top become stale and stinky sludge after a while. I am sick of carrying it around. I am sick of this dominating my thoughts. And yet, who will listen to me?

In this process when you speak, you are listened to with respect. You may have a listener who demonstrates he/she heard you. That person tells you what he/she heard without judging or making personal comments. Once you have been heard, you don't have to repeat it. It is like taking the cap off the artesian well, releasing that sludge, then letting fresh water overflow—that sweet taste of new ideas and thoughts. Freedom at last!

Just imagine the feeling of that fresh energy flowing through your being. This is what happens when you empty your mind. New information, new insights, new emotions fill in that space. Now instead of repeating yourself over and over again, you can continue to say something new. It is precisely that release that allows the consensus approach to work.

~36~

The Worst Possible Outcomes of the Situation

The Worst Possible Outcomes

Sometimes, this is the last activity at the end of the second day. There are times when this task occurs on the third morning. We still have time to do an additional task before the closure. It is preceded by a short break after the task on the situation. People need a release from the intensity of their talking circle.

While they are working on the situation task, I coach you and Diane on where we are going next:

This group has consistently talked about working together as a community to solve the conflict. Having just described the situation and how it happened, we can now move ahead and explore the worst possible outcomes of changing or not changing the situation. But the question is asked in a way that it includes the notion of working as a community.

- What are the worst possible outcomes of *not working* as a community to solve the situation?
- What are the worst possible outcomes of *working* together as a community to solve the situation?

These questions include worst possible outcomes of not only solving problems, but of not working together as a community.

During the break, YOU will coach Diane on facilitating the worst possible outcomes, providing her with a three-by-five card with the questions and process. I want YOU to introduce the task, then turn it over to Diane. After the task, provide an insight that will help the group.

> *What are the worst possible outcomes of...*
>
> *-not working as a community to solve the situation? (Groups 1 and 2)*
>
> *-working together as a community to solve the situation? (Groups 3 and 4)*

Reassembling the group is difficult. Everyone is deeply engaged in conversation, often with people whom they have disagreed with strongly. I just keep announcing time and time again:

I want you to return to your small groups. We have one more task to record, and then we're going to do a closure for the day. So the quicker you get back, the better. (A pause, then repeat, with variations, etc.)

I don't mind repeating the statements at all. Watching these people having sincere dialogues with each other is gratifying. The time they are spending together now is definitely part of the process of reaching a decision tomorrow.

It may take about five minutes, but eventually everyone is seated in the small circles. They are still talking with each other, so it is difficult to get their attention. When I do, standing at the edge of the circle, I give them a short insight:

The activity we did previously describing the situation is what you have been talking about for the past year. It's just that you haven't listened to or heard each other. So what we have done is given you an opportunity to each express your views in an environment where you are listened to with respect. That is what is different. It is a paradigm shift. Now you have developed a description of the problem where you can see all sides of the situation. That is what allows us to move ahead.

YOU will now move the community ahead with the last task before the closure.

Worst Possible Outcomes of Working/Not Working as a Community: An Activity

YOU walk to the edge of the circle and introduce the next task based on our discussions earlier:

The Worst Possible Outcomes of the Situation

"Deciding to move ahead will immediately cause people to fall into their worst possible outcomes. It is necessary to expose those fears in order to be able to move ahead. But the question must be focused around statements that you made earlier during these panel discussions. Many of you talked about the need to act together as a community in solving this conflict. We will attach those words to the worst possible outcomes question.

"Diane will give you your task."

YOU step back as Diane walks forward and stands on the opposite side of the circle from you. Then she says:

"First I would like the facilitator to pick another facilitator and become the recorder. When you are standing at the flip chart, I will know that you have done this."

Diane pauses and waits while the groups perform this task. "You are going to record immediately as you answer this question. We are going to look at the worst possible outcomes from two perspectives. The first is not working together as a community; the second is working together as a community.

"Groups 1 and 2, you are going to answer this question: What are the worst possible outcomes of not working as a community to resolve the situation?"

"Groups 3 and 4, you are going to answer this question: What are the worst possible outcomes of working together as a community to resolve the situation?"

After repeating the instructions, Diane turns and walks away from the circle. The groups immediately go to work. The statements being recorded are rich in detail and impact.

While the groups are working, YOU coach Diane through the purpose and process for the remainder of the day. When the groups began to speak louder, we know they are done. Diane walks to the edge of the circle and asks the question, "Has everyone spoken at least once?" All groups respond yes nonverbally—raising hands, nodding, and so on.

"Now, Groups 1 and 2 will read off their flip charts, which are focused on the worst possible outcomes of *not* working together as a community to resolve this situation. We will start with Group 2."

> **GROUP 2: THE WORST POSSIBLE OUTCOMES OF NOT WORKING AS A COMMUNITY TO SOLVE THE SITUATION**
>
> - *The tribes stand to lose their identity, their way of life...such as songs, ceremonies, traditions, and an important cultural, spiritual symbol, the salmon.*
> - *We will continue to develop a crisis situation and won't be able to deal with it effectively.*
> - *Taxpayers will be pissed off at us for not doing something.*
> - *We will have less choice the further we go, so if we deal with it now, we can choose better.*
> - *There are fewer opportunities for jobs in our communities.*
> - *Our young people are graduating and leaving because they are unable to afford to live here.*
> - *The situation will get a whole lot worse. Things will remain the same.*
> - *We'll never know what we could have done, and things will continue to be the same and grow worse.*
> - *We will have wasted an opportunity, resulting in lifelong regrets for not having made the efforts to change the way we work with opposing groups.*
> - *Coyote River Basin will become filled with 1–10-acre ranchettes.*
> - *The community is going to suffer and will get locked in.*
> - *The ranchers throw in the towel and sell off their land for subdivisions.*
> - *There will be less water, not just poorer quality, but less water.*
> - *Being unable to sell some marginal property may be the final straw.*
> - *People at large start operating from their reptilian brain.*

Group 2 is followed by Group 1. We move on to the other two groups, which had a different question.

"Now, Groups 3 and 4 will read off their flip charts, which are focused on the worst possible outcomes of working together as a community to resolve this situation. We will start with Group 4 and move to Group 3.

GROUP 4: THE WORST POSSIBLE OUTCOMES OF WORKING AS A COMMUNITY TO SOLVE THE SITUATION

- *A sincere effort ends up with a negative result. It will be a waste of time.*
- *What I believe to be fact and truth will be proven wrong, or worse yet...I will change my belief!*
- *Coyote Basin becomes a playground for the rich.*
- *Water quality and fish will be negatively impacted by development.*
- *Our young families will not be able to afford living here.*
- *There will be disorderly unplanned growth with no regulations to set boundaries on development.*
- *The ranchers throw in the towel and sell off their land for subdivisions.*
- *I have to do what everyone tells me, even if I don't want to (or don't think it will work).*
- *I'll lose my land, and my grandchildren will have nowhere to come visit, no home.*
- *There will be lawsuits leading to court mandated in-streams.*
- *With total desecration of rivers and streams, the salmon will go extinct.*
- *Also, there will be more damage to wildlife because of subdivisions and fencing the creeks off so the livestock can't get to them.*
- *There will be no jobs. No young families are prospering.*
- *Fish are gone from the Coyote River and the salmon numbers dwindle to zero.*
- *There will be no open space and no agriculture, so we sell the place.*
- *We are still a divided community.*
- *It will be the end of the way of life as we know it.*
- *The community is dysfunctional.*

As the groups listen to their worst possible outcomes, the room becomes gloomy and some exclaim, "This is depressing!"

YOU go to the edge of the circle and speak:

"This is really depressing material, isn't it? But I think it reflects how we have been feeling in this community about what is going on. I have heard many people say it is depressing to read the newspapers, to read about all the fighting we have been involved in the basin on this zoning plan. But I watched as you went to work on this activity, and there was no hesitation! You all worked together as a community! And it took only about fifteen minutes! Thirty-three people spoke and their statements were recorded. Fascinating, isn't it? It gives me hope.

You turn and walk away with a satisfied grin on your face. "I never imagined I would do that." she said. "I hardly knew what I was going to say until I heard that comment on "depressing."

I walk to the edge of the circle and speak:

These are your worst possible outcomes of working together. If you paid attention, many of these are already happening. They are becoming self-fulfilling prophecies.

Remember that worst possible outcomes are natural responses in a changing situation. They are your reptilian brain's attempt to make sure you survive. But they are only possibilities. Many of these have not happened yet; you can still make another future happen.

We will explore that future tomorrow morning. For tonight, you have worked hard enough. We will do a closure for the day. Diane will give you the task.

~37~

The Closure: Day Two

The Second Day Closure: An Activity

YOU have previously provided Diane a three-by-five card with the task on it and coached her.

> Close your circle, do not record, the last facilitator is the facilitator.
>
> How do you feel about today?
>
> What did you learn that will help you create a consensus for this community that will allow you to move ahead together?

She walks to the edge of the circle and reads the task. Then she turns and walks away from the group as they go right to work. The room buzzes with a low murmur; people are talking, taking turns. The rest of them are leaning in, fully engaged in the conversation.

This activity could be done in less than ten minutes. These people have worked for a full eight hours today. We have kept them focused on their tasks, facilitating, recording, speaking, listening. Surely they would go through this activity quickly.

Not a chance! It is forty minutes before we are able to move the group ahead. They are deeply engaged with each other now. They have spoken honestly with each other, expressed their issues with each other, doing the storming in a healthy way. Now they can move ahead together to solve their issues.

Assigning Collective Statements

When the groups are done, I assign the collective statement tasks for the different activities. Pairs of recorders work together on the four activities from the flip charts: best possible outcomes of conflict, new beliefs and behaviors, the situation in the basin, and the worst possible outcomes of working and not working together to resolve the situation.

This engages sixteen of the group's members. The remaining members linger for at least another thirty minutes, talking with each other, sharing ideas, slowly leaving. Some agree to eat together or go to the bar together—groups of people who previously avoided each other.

When they complete their collective statements, this is how they look. Note that the statements for Groups 2 and 3 are shown in *italics*.

The Worst Possible Outcomes of Not Working as a Community to Solve the Situation - A Collective Statement

(Note: All of these are actual statements from real workshops.)

Unchecked development will happen, all of our scenic and quality of life reasons people enjoy living here will be gone. *The ranches and other private lands in the basin become small developed parcels; the scenic quality of the basin is degraded.* Local residents will leave to go to places where this hasn't happened yet. *Coyote River Basin will become filled with 1–10-acre ranchettes.* We'll have brown 2-acre plots with trailers and tacky homes up and down this valley, driving all of the wildlife away.

There will be continued and increasing isolation in the basin if we don't change our ability to communicate and listen respectfully. Neighbors won't help neighbors. *I pass my neighbors in the store and they don't greet me. The community is going to suffer and will get locked in.* It also hurts the local economy.

The tribes stand to lose their identity, their way of life...such as songs, ceremonies, traditions, and an important cultural, spiritual symbol, the salmon. Both fish and tribal people are impacted and lose, which in turn means the loss of other species supported by salmon and nutrients in the streams. Our grandchildren and your grandchildren will never have the opportunity to see a salmon return.

Ranchers that stay lose their water rights (2). Loss of water will cause the loss of sustainable agriculture in River County, which will cause the loss of our pristine area—which will never again be replaced. We end up losing water for stream flow.

Without community support, the ranches and ranching families fall on hard times. They will disappear, and the small communities and towns that rely on them dry up too. *Being unable to sell some marginal property may* be the final straw. The ranchers throw in the towel and sell off their land for subdivisions.

We will see the drying up of rivers, streams. *There will be less water, not just poorer quality, but less water.* The ground water is polluted and being depleted. If some ranches are lost, their water will be sold for interests outside the basin.

We will do many things poorly because we do not have a clear vision of what we can do. *We will continue to develop a crisis situation and won't be able to deal with it effectively.* We'll make changes based on what people want, it won't help and we'll get blamed. *Taxpayers will be pissed off at us for not doing something.*

We limit our choices in decision making about how we address the zoning issue. *We will have less choice the further we go, so if we deal with it now, we can choose better.*

There are fewer opportunities for jobs in our communities. Our local businesses continue to fail, so we have boarded-up storefronts. We have higher crime rates, reduced agriculture, and a community that is divided.

Our young people are graduating and leaving because they are unable to afford to live here. Our community schools are not able to provide the levels of education that we desire. Young people are leaving, thus there are no service workers and essentials like teachers, professional people, cops, firemen, etc.

People who are the most vulnerable will take the biggest hit. There are dire consequences to the most vulnerable citizens due to limited personal resources and cuts to programs essential to them even though they are a low priority.

The situation will get a whole lot worse. Things will remain the same. People at large start operating from their reptilian brain. We can't fix the problem because we fail to trust each other, and all the efforts of the agriculture agencies fail to help the ranchers survive.

We'll never know what we could have done, and things will continue to be the same and grow worse. We will have wasted an opportunity, resulting in lifelong regrets for not having made the efforts to change the way we work with opposing groups. By not working together, we lose a lot of time, energy, and work. We are a divided county.

The Worst Possible Outcomes of Working as a Community to Solve the Situation

Nothing will change. *A sincere effort ends up with a negative result.* Coyote County continues to be divided on many issues. *We are still a divided community.*

It will be a waste of time. An extended time investment will yield no results. It will lead to the lowest common denominator approach to planning and zoning.

The community is dysfunctional. There will be a lack of effective communication—real, honest, filled with integrity. *What I believe to be fact and truth will be proven wrong, or worse yet...I will change my belief!*

It will be the end of the way of life as we know it. A sense of loss and frustration would drive good people both in the county, the agencies, and the agriculture community into giving up and allowing political agendas to direct our future.

There will be disorderly unplanned growth with no regulations to set boundaries on development. We see houses everywhere. The basin is covered with tacky houses and trailers on tiny lots. *There are strip malls, fast-food restaurants, and gas stations strung out along the highways.* The community becomes a Metro area. *Coyote River Basin becomes a playground for the rich.*

No ranches or ranchers remain. *There will be no open space and no agriculture, so we sell the place.* The community will lose open space.

The ranchers throw in the towel and sell off their land for subdivisions. I have to do what everyone tells me, even if I don't want to (or don't think it will work). I'll have to sell off my fifth-generation prized bull, and I'll have to sell my cattle to a stinky feedlot.

The survival of agriculture will be on the line from here on out. *I'll lose my land, and my grandchildren will have nowhere to come visit, no home.* I'll lose my land, and my grandparents are buried there.

There will be gridlock, and decisions will be influenced by small but powerful entities. Everything will change due to the most assertive people winning. I won't get what I want if they get what they want.

Water quality and fish will be negatively impacted by development. We will lose all our water. Ranchers are essentially giving up some water.

In the end, a judge settles everything. *There will be lawsuits leading to court mandated in-streams.* The courts take over, and in frustration the landowners abandon all efforts and leave the land.

With total desecration of rivers and streams, the salmon will go extinct. Because they lose their religion, the tribe will go extinct. Fish are gone from the Coyote River, and the salmon numbers dwindle to zero. Also, there will be more damage to wildlife because of subdivisions and fencing the creeks off so the livestock can't get to them.

We will have total business dislocation. *There will be no jobs. No young families are prospering. Our young families will not be able to afford living here.* A poverty mentality is created as everyone fends for survival at the cost to the greater good. The Coyote Tribe Casino will be voted down.

Creatures from the Closet: An Insight for the Reader

For myself, I begin to feel the second-day blues. This group has had the most difficult discussion today, and they came through it well. But they have been here before; the only difference is they didn't listen to or hear each other, so they eddied in the same pool, going round and round until the whirlpool drew them into the center without moving ahead. This afternoon they moved back into the current, moving ahead. They know their fears have kept them from being a community, from working together.

But I wonder if I have done enough. I worry I may not have asked the right questions. I may have spoken too often. There might not be time tomorrow to do all that needs to be done.

All of these concerns, of course, are just my worst possible outcomes for the work remaining. But even though I know that, I am still influenced by them. They settle on my shoulders like vultures on a tree branch looking down on their prey. When I return to my hotel room that night, I am, as always on the second night, in a state of anxiety. I want so much for this group to be successful, but I cannot do it for them; I can only help them do it. I doubt my ability to do that. I mope and moan, eat only a bite, can't watch TV because I am too distracted. It is like waiting for one of my children to be born.

I go to bed, unable to sleep, tossing and turning, those vultures getting close and closer.

I finally fall asleep from sheer exhaustion. But it doesn't last long. At two thirty a.m., the witching hour begins. I wake with that fear on the edge of my mind, and it seems much bigger in the dark. Now I really am in my worst possible outcomes. All those fears in the closet and ghouls under the bed come out. I could fail. I made so many mistakes today. I spoke too much, using precious time. I put too many people on the panel. I should have pushed them harder. They are going to be angry tomorrow, will not want to work together. They will feel like they have been duped. And it goes on and on, ad nauseam.

Finally the moment comes when I have had enough.

Enough! I say. Back into the closet!

And I mentally put all these fears, those vultures, into my fear closet. They have been acknowledged, now…*step aside!*

I begin to remind myself of my best hopes, my purposes. I know these are all possible, I know this is risky, but that is what I do in my work—take risks. And I have always been successful; the groups have always been successful. I did my best today; I will do even better tomorrow.

This group will resolve their issue and move ahead and make their best possible outcomes happen. I will be their guide, trusting them to find their own solutions. So they will be successful. I believe that. I will trust myself!

With that I go to sleep. When I wake in the morning, somewhat groggy, I am ready for the day. Ideas flow to me; the right questions become obvious. I am ready.

Why do I share this with you? Not for pity or empathy. Because every person who has been trained in this process and who practices it, reports to me that they experience the same thing. It is just part of the process. Before I can help my group, I must experience these worst possible outcomes, open that closet and let them all come out. Let them come into me and raise my fear levels. I can then acknowledge all of them. When I do, I can send them back to the closet. I know they are there; they know I know. Now…I can focus on my best possibilities. I can remind me to: Trust myself. Trust the people.

In a sense I am merely acknowledging my reptilian brain, acknowledging that a worst outcome could happen, and I am conscious of that.

And I can activate my neocortex by acknowledging the best possible outcomes. I can "trust myself, trust the people."

~38~

The Third Day: The Beginning

Preparing for the Third Day

I always arrive before the group convenes. I have time, with YOUR help, to move the collective statements around on different flip charts, putting them in an order that will flow around the circle. I get brief glimpses of the statements, am impressed with how well the people have done.

The night's anxieties return, but I relax myself, acknowledge my purposes for the day, and trust myself to achieve them.

As I do this, I run through with YOU the possible schedule and timing of events this day, focusing on how we can get them to their end point, their best possible outcomes for the workshop (pages 393-395). You and I go to where their best possible outcomes statement is hung on the wall. We look at the leading statements in each paragraph, which reminds me of what the group is expecting. These are our purposes today, to help them reach these outcomes:

- We will move past the impasse and can put our energy back toward our purpose. Constructive energy is focused toward common goals.
- Perceived impossible issues are worked through, and sustainable solutions are implemented that help to build strong communities to help improve our natural resources.
- We implement a plan that succeeds in bringing back salmon while still allowing people, ranchers, and communities to prosper.
- We have world-class agriculture and a world-class fishery.
- Our way of life continues and thrives.

Some have already been met:

- We will be open and honest with each other, creating a safe environment.

- Relationship building through improved communication will enable everyone's voice to be heard.
- People will feel empowered and successful because they have used and learned a process that worked well. We have a healthier, happier environment with less tension, and as a result we get more accomplished.
- Everyone has more of an open mind and understands each other from a different perspective.

We have asked Diane to help us again and paired her with Neil, the county executive, from Group 3. She is over by the coffee, coaching him on his responsibilities. We will have developed three pairs of facilitators to leave with the community. While Diane is coaching Neil, YOU and I are going through the schedule for the day.

People begin to drift in. Some stop by to ask me questions, normally about applying what they have learned in their work or family environment. People gather around as I listen and then provide an insight.

As our free time grows short, we meet with Diane and Neil, our cofacilitators for the day. YOU brief them on our schedule for the morning:

"We will begin today with Bob making a brief introduction and then move into reviewing the process so far and presenting the collective statements from yesterday. Once that is done, we will create more new groups to work together today. We will do this as we did yesterday, by bringing the different groups to the center, honoring them, and then numbering them off to create the new groups.

"Neil, when we are done, I want you to round up Debbe, Dawn, Kenney, and Jon, and bring them here. They will be the facilitators for the small groups this morning. We will honor them first and have them number off, assigning them to a group. Diane, I am going to ask you to facilitate the honoring process this morning. You and I will agree on the order in which groups will be honored and over the process for honoring."

YOU pause to think, to recall, and then continue:

"Once the groups have been formed, Neil, I will introduce them to the non-verbal greeting circle. They will experience the power of non-verbal communication. When they are done I will provide them an insight on non-verbal communication.

Then you will facilitate the grounding process for the small groups. In the previous mornings, we have used the question *what have you learned?* Today we are going to change that somewhat to: *What do you need to learn?*

The Third Day: The Beginning

"The reason for the change is that previously we have helped them to assess what they have learned in the past activities. Today we want them to shift their thinking and feeling to learning for the future."

You provide Neil with a three-by-five card with the information for the process and the questions.

> Close your circle, do not record.
>
> How do you feel about the non-verbal greeting circle?
>
> What do you need to learn so you can work as a community to resolve the situation?

"While the groups are working on the grounding, we will talk about where we're headed next. What I want you to do now is to find Debbe, Dawn, Kenney, and Jon, and bring them here."

When Diane and Neil bring the four facilitators, YOU inform them of the role we are asking them to play as facilitator:

"Bob will be doing an introduction this morning and reviewing the collective statements from yesterday. Once that is done, we will create four new small groups for working today. I would like each of you to be the facilitator for a group. Each of you has already played this role, so you're prepared for it. We will be asking you to facilitate the group through a non-verbal greeting circle. This will be followed by a grounding focused on the future. Neil will read the task to you."

Neil reads off the task on the card.

"It is up to you to facilitate your group for these two questions. I want you to number off to four now to select the group you were going to facilitate."

Now that we have four facilitators, I'm ready to get started with the introduction. I ask the cofacilitators and the small-group facilitators to help me round people up and move them toward the circle. I begin to notify the participants:

We are ready to start, move toward the circle. We have a busy day ahead of us, lots to do if we are going to solve your problem today. So start drifting here toward the circle.

I continue to repeat this until everyone is seated in a circle. I do it in a normal, calm, facilitative tone of voice. Then I start the introduction.

Introduction: Welcome back to the third day of this community workshop focused on creating a new movement toward your community working together to develop a consensus around the planning and zoning regulations. Many of you are probably thinking, "This is the end of the workshop." In my view, this is really the beginning of your work.

When you have completed your work today and reached a consensus, then you'll begin to make it happen. I believe you will get there by the end of the day. You will leave here today with the capacity to be successful, with new skills and new understandings of the situation and of each other. Your success, however, is measured through actually acting on your proposed strategies to create your desired purposes.

Beginning today, you will start to apply those new skills and new understandings toward developing a community working together to successfully accomplish your purpose. We have developed three pairs of community facilitators in the last two days who can help you succeed in carrying out your plans.

I'm wondering if any of you had a fitful sleep last night, as I did. (I notice many heads nodding.) The second night of the workshop is always the time when I get the "heebie-jeebies." All my fears burst out of the closet, crawl out from under the bed, and attack me all at once. I am besieged by doubts about what I have done, and then believe that I won't know what to do to get you to a consensus.

I know that these are just worst possible outcomes and that my subconscious is setting them free at two thirty in the morning. These doubts are magnified sometimes beyond reason. It is my special "witching hour."

It is possible that many of you had a similar occurrence last night. It is just part of this process. As you get closer to reaching your consensus, you worst possible outcomes will rise naturally. They may even overcome you.

I open up to these worst possible outcomes, knowing I have to deal with them anyway. While I hate it, hate the feelings that are associated with it, I just know it is part of the process. Once all of my fears have been acknowledged, I just put them back in the closet, sweep them under the bed. They've been acknowledged, and it's now time to move ahead.

So, I just reaffirm my best possible outcomes for this group. That is: you have the capacity now to create a consensus that will enable your community to create the best possible outcomes. That is my purpose for today.

We're going to review what we have done to date. Then we are going to read off the collective statements that were prepared from yesterday's activities. When that is done, we are going to form four new small groups, and you're going to have an opportunity to do a grounding. You'll be introducing yourselves again, since you will have new members in your group. We will then have you focus on what you need to learn in order to be successful today.

From that point on, we will be developing your purpose for working together as a community. You will then identify the beliefs and behaviors you will need to accomplish your purpose. Then you'll develop strategies and actions that will help you get this done. Finally, you will decide if you are committed to making those best possible outcomes happen.

So that is the order of the day.

Let's start today with the best possible outcomes of working together as a community to resolve your situation. I would like the people who developed the best possible outcomes of conflict to come to the flip chart and read that off. (Note: just Groups 1 and 2 are reported in this book.)

Best possible outcomes are future imagined events. They have not happened yet. They are possibilities. When you develop best possible outcomes, you move your brain from the reptilian brain to the neocortex. You will have an emotion associated with these best possible outcomes, normally one of happiness, which triggers a biochemical response, putting endorphins into your system. These endorphins allow you to see your world in an entirely different way. The result allows you to see the information and people available to help you make the best possible outcome happen.

(**Note:** All collective statements include recorded statements from actual workshops and real participants.)

GROUPS 1 AND 2: THE BEST POSSIBLE OUTCOMES OF RESOLVING CONFLICT

Our community energy is concentrated on solutions rather than arguing over who is right. We utilize creative cooperative solutions to the benefit of everyone. There are less appeals and litigation and more community support for decisions.

Because of what we have learned here, the situation gets better and people get along. We can move forward and get on with life and work. We begin to laugh together instead of talking about each other.

We see better relationships, and develop skills, tools, and techniques to help solve other problems. We will be more willing to try new things. The feelings created through consensus include loving, caring, supportive relationships.There is a new norm and expectation for community interaction and dialog. We will be open and honest with each other, creating a safe environment. It will be a relief being able to speak openly about everything, and there will be no repercussions.

> The issue of conflict will get resolved with more listening. We will feel relieved that it is taken care of, that tensions disappear, and we can do our job without taking special precautions. This will help to cut tension and build trust.
>
> We are able to define our problems, and we work together as a community to reach consensus. We will resolve issues, and after successfully resolving one conflict, people will approach succeeding conflicts with confidence. Future conflicts may be resolved quicker and effectively.
>
> There is a sense of community among the residents of the county. We will create a cohesive community with a clear and shared vision. People feel good in their hearts about the land.
>
> The Coyote Mountain Tribe will have profitable growth and protection of their resources, which results in healthier people and land.
>
> There is preservation of our agricultural lands with regulated growth that provides for all segments of our community and cultures. Coyote Basin ranches and farms are expanding and able to hold on to their land.

These best possible outcomes are also purpose statements; they are the "aim" in "Ready, aim, fire!"

Once you developed your purpose statements, we had two groups explore the new beliefs or behaviors that will foster those outcomes. The remaining two groups explored strategies and actions that will foster those outcomes. I would like those of you who developed those collective statements to read them off.

You have avoided conflict before due to the beliefs that convinced you it was dangerous, risky, and would be unsuccessful. What we wanted you to do was transform those into new beliefs. These beliefs have the purpose of fostering those best possible outcomes. I would like you to read the beliefs from the flip charts. Let's start with the statements from Groups 1 and 2, and then go to Groups 3 and 4.

GROUPS 1 AND 2: BELIEFS AND BEHAVIORS

Conflict can be good and result in positive change.
- – I will accept that conflict is natural.
- – People have the ability to resolve their own conflicts

A belief in openness, open-mindedness, willingness to be honest about our own feelings and issues.
- – We will treat each other with compassion, trust, and integrity, and will consider the effects of our beliefs on other's lives.
- – Really pay attention to the speaker with the intention to understand and accept that every opinion is part of the solution.

We can if we think we can.
- – We need to believe in achieving the impossible, that going slow to go fast makes good sense.

Everyone is valuable and has something to contribute, each in their unique way.
- – Everyone should be allowed to be heard.
- – Truly believe that diversity is good; make an effort to be inclusive of differing viewpoints.

Everyone has a right to their own opinion and will be listened to with respect.
- – Look at the situation from another person's viewpoint.
- – Slow down and create a listening environment.

Listen with respect. Listening to everyone's input should be our goal.
- – Listen better to value beliefs that are different from ours. Listen and trust what you hear.

- – Value everyone's thoughts and feelings; it is important for the acknowledgment of others.

There is a belief that you or I are not above the rest. We are all equal.
- – I believe that everyone has unique talents to enhance the group.

We can use the power of imagining the best outcome.
- – Acknowledge the worst and focus on the best.
- – Release anger and fear so that I can listen with an open mind.
- – Even if negative feelings occur, we still can have best outcomes.

We believe people need to feel that the process will be safe and their opinions valued and equally respected.
- – People must believe in themselves and know what they say is important.

> - To encourage people to speak their minds and to treat them with respect.
> - Understand that voicing an opinion or concern does not equate to demanding an agreement.
>
> People are basically good.
> - Each person is right in their own mind.
> - Others truly are interested in conflict resolution.
> - Each participant truly wishes for a change.
>
> We will celebrate our accomplishments.

Groups 3 and 4 then read off their new beliefs and behaviors.

Now let's hear the strategies and actions that would rise from those beliefs and expressed through behaviors. The pairs that developed the collective statements will read these off to the group. Let's start with the collective statements for Groups 3 and 4.

> **GROUPS 3 AND 4: STRATEGIES AND ACTIONS**
>
> We need a common vision/goal.
> - We need a concept of the future...how far are we managing?
>
> All viewpoints and opinions have a right to be heard or listened to.
> All resources and the public should be heard.
> - We will make special consideration to involve diverse people in the process, i.e., gender, ethnicity, or age.
> - We will include diverse populations and make sure all participants, including the Tribal and Hispanic population, are being brought in.
>
> Through respectful listening we will be looking and listening to one another.
> - Become an active listener with a curious and creative attitude.
> - We are to listen respectfully to everyone's views and not react too soon.
>
> We will speak honestly and with diplomacy.
> - Think first, be assertive and speak your truth.
> - We will have no hidden agendas.

> Acknowledge the validity of other's concerns.
>   – We will look for the possibilities within what other people have to say.
>
> Treat others as you would have them treat you!
>   – Not waiting for someone else to improve their behavior before you improve yours.
>   – Expecting yourself to change as much as you expect others to change.
>
> We will be more proactive in confronting conflicts.
>   – Resolve the conflicts at the early stage. Don't be afraid to recognize and resolve conflict when it arises.
>
> Using a step by step process and structure can make people listen to and build a foundation for communication and trust.
>   – This process is put in place to confront issues and to practice skills we have been learning.
>   – Acknowledge the fears of the worst possible outcomes. Identifying worst and best outcomes.
>   – Making collective statements and identifying a mission statement by listing our beliefs about the conflict is key.

Beliefs/Behaviors/Strategies/Actions Collective Statements: An Insight

When all collective statements have been read, I provide a brief insight:

What you have, then, is a purpose statement for your conflicts, a new set of adaptive beliefs and behaviors, and some specific strategies or actions. As you developed these three activities, I observed that you were behaving in a manner that you were describing on the flip chart. Your words and your actions were congruent. That assures me that you are ready to focus on and reach a consensus on your issues.

You then had an experience of resolving a personal conflict using the basic process. This allowed you to look at some unresolved conflict in your life. I took you step-by-step through the four basic questions. My experience is that a large portion of my conflicts are personal. That is, they are struggles in my own mind. Knowing that I can use this basic approach to resolve my conflicts frees me from an impasse so I can move ahead. It keeps me from getting mentally stuck.

In addition, personal conflicts, if unresolved, eventually become interpersonal conflicts. In turn, if an interpersonal conflict reaches an impasse, that results in an intergroup conflict.

So there is power in knowing how to resolve the conflicts you have in your own mind. The process that you experienced will be in your learning manual you will get at the end of the day. I urge you to use this personal process whenever you can. If you going to give a speech, then explore for yourself: what is the situation, your worst possible outcomes for that speech, your best possible outcomes, and then specific strategies and actions that will help you make that happen. It will allow you to present your speech in an entirely different manner, and, you will find yourself being successful as a result.

It was time to begin to look at the real issue. We selected six members of this community to be on a panel. They were paired up to speak to one another. Jack spoke to Lynn. Each of them had a listener who conveyed what the speaker said. They focused on the questions:

- What is the situation that brings us here?
- How did it get to be that way?
- How do you feel about it?

Once all six panelists had spoken, we honored them and assigned them the task of facilitating and recording for the small groups we created earlier. You then returned to your small groups with the task of answering the same three questions. When all had spoken, we had you pass out three-by-five cards and answer two questions, one on each side of the card. "What are two descriptions of the situation that you heard from others?" This question allowed you to honor the other members of the group by acknowledging that you heard what they said. "What is at least one description you expressed about the situation?" This allowed you to record at least one statement or more of your insights on the situation.

This information was then put together into a collective statement. I want those of you who developed the collective statement to read it off. (This statement is on page 503-506, so it is not repeated here.)

Finally, we ended the day by having you explore the worst possible outcomes of not working together as a community to resolve your issues or the worst possible outcomes of working together as a community to resolve your issue. I would like the people who developed these collective statements to please read them off the flip charts. (These statements are on pages 511-512, so they are not repeated here.)

When the statements are read, I continue my insights summary:

Worst possible outcomes are feared future imagined events, often based on past negative experiences, with currently experienced emotional, biochemical, and physical responses, which tend to foster the outcomes we fear.

It is like a dog chasing its own tail. Whatever you fear, if you respond out of that imagined fear, you will end up getting it. It is known as the self-fulfilling prophecy. As I listened to these worst possible outcomes, it is evident that some of these are already happening.

We are not just talking about "positive thinking." Proponents of positive thinking do not consider the impact of the immediate "negative thinking" that occurs around any event. In an environment in which everything feels positive and the sense is that there are more than enough resources to go around, positive thinking will work.

If the environment is one with a perception of scarcity, a fear of survival, positive thinking will be run over by the negative thoughts and emotions that are associated with the worst possible outcomes. You can have all the positive thoughts you want, but if you hide your fears, the lower brain, whose job it is to ensure your survival, will take over.

This approach acknowledges both negative thinking and positive thinking. It is your primary responsibility to survive. In order to do that, you have to acknowledge the fears of your lower brain. It doesn't matter if it's just a day-to-day issue. If you have moved to the worst possible outcomes, the reptilian brain will take over, and its billions of years of programming will override rational thought. The purpose is to ensure your survival; everything else is put off to the side.

By acknowledging you worst possible outcomes, your deepest fears, you are also acknowledging that part of yourself that is intent on ensuring your survival. When you do this, you bring the fears to your consciousness, especially if you record them so you can see them visually. Being conscious of the fears, you can do something about them.

Once you have acknowledged your fears, then you need to balance yourself. You are, after all, dealing with possibilities, not facts. By identifying your best possible outcomes, you will move to the neocortex, which differentiates us from most of the other living beings. This is a conscious instrument. While aware of the possibility of potential failure events, you can balance the situation by looking at what would make you be successful. Your purpose, your best possible outcomes, provide you that balanced view.

With that introduction, we will begin later this morning to look at the best possible outcomes of working together as a community and develop your short-term purpose statement. To do that, we need to create four small groups. To help me with that, I would like Debbe, Dawn, Kenney, and Jon to come to the center of the circle. The rest of you can take a fifteen-minute break. Come back when the big hand is on the three.

The Best Possible Outcomes and Coaching

During the break, the tone of the group this morning is one of excitement. I see people talking animatedly in small, diverse groups. There is a lot of laughter; people are at ease with one another. Some find an opportunity to ask me questions, some of which I answer, some of which I may present to the group first.

YOU review the process again with Debbe, Dawn, Kenney, and Jon, the four small-group facilitators. After the break, with the help of the facilitators, we bring everyone back to the large circle. YOU then provide the introduction to the next task:

"In order to be successful at work today, we need to have four new groups. This will allow you an increased opportunity to spend quality time with members of the community you have not met yet. We are going to begin by creating four small groups.

"I would like Debbe, Dawn, Kenney, and Jon to come to the center of the room: These four people have agreed to act as your facilitators to get us started today. I would like you to honor these people for taking on the task."

You then turn the task of honoring the different groups and distributing them to the small groups to Diane. She follows the process of honoring the groups and counting off that we used the previous day.

When the groups have been formed and all are in their small circles, I introduce the community to the schedule for the day:

We are going to begin with a nonverbal activity, followed by a grounding. Neil is going to facilitate you through the grounding. We will then move into developing the purpose that you would like to foster as a result of working together as a community. This will be followed with the development of strategies and actions to carry out your purpose. We will end the day with an opportunity to commit to carrying out your proposed actions.

~39~

Nonverbal Communication

A Nonverbal Greeting Circle

I begin the day by introducing the concept of non-verbal communication.

During the last two days, I have observed a number of instances where you read each other's nonverbal behaviors, and I believe you read them wrong. It is not unusual to mistake a person's passion for anger; the tones of voice are almost the same. And if you respond to the possibility of anger, you can create a conflict based on misinformation.

I want you to experience a nonverbal activity and then learn from it. You remember that we did a greeting circle on the first day. That was a verbal greeting. Today I want you to experience a nonverbal greeting circle. Please stand.

The entire community stands in their small groups.

I want the facilitator to lead the greeting circle. You will turn to your left or right and greet that person, then continue greeting inside the circle. The person you greeted will follow you, and the person she greets will follow her, so the circle turns in on itself.

Remember, when the facilitator returns to his/her original place, you will continue to greet each other, so that you are both greeted and greeters.

And I want you to do this nonverbally, without words or sounds. I want the room silent. I want you to meet and see your community members who have volunteered this time, who will create a consensus today on how to resolve the situation you described yesterday. I want you to look at and acknowledge the people who have volunteered this time to help your community. I want you to be aware of how you see these people differently than on the first morning.

Be cautious about greeting people with a hug. Do this only if you get a nonverbal message that it is OK.

I want YOU, Diane, and Neil to join one of the groups to experience this.

I step back and watch as the greeting circles begin. At first people are quiet, moving slowly, taking time to look at each person. Soon there are sounds of people patting backs, high fives, and then some laughter. It is almost impossible for the group to be quiet. There is an air of excitement and acceptance in the room, a feeling of community that is difficult to describe.

The facilitators are back in their places, people are coming by continuing to greet, more sounds of laughter, people whispering to each other—words that have meaning, from the sound of it. Soon, the tail end of the circles are coming by, only a few people left to greet. There is a collective sigh as people begin to talk quietly to those beside them, respectful of those yet greeting.

When they are all done in the groups, still standing, there is a moment of silence before I have them be seated. Then I provide them an insight.

How We Communicate: An Insight

Many complex studies have been done over the years to determine how we communicate. All of them verify, across cultures, that we communicate more by what we *do* than by what we *say*. We have many common expressions that affirm this awareness: "Don't do what I do, do what I say." "He isn't walking the talk."

If you want a real lesson in nonverbal language, turn off the sound on your television while watching a movie or a game show. Then observe the behaviors, the movements, the features on the faces of people. Try to ascertain how much of the message you are getting in this manner. This will help you understand how little words affect our communication.

This is what the studies have shown about how we communicate:

Verbal: 7 percent

Our words comprise only 7 percent of the actual communication between us. Yet, this is the focal point of all our efforts to teach people to communicate. When the problem appears to be that "we are not communicating," the solution appears to be to talk more, to learn how to express ourselves better with words. We overlook the other 93 percent.

This is not surprising to me, because words are a recent invention of human beings, about a hundred thousand years ago. Yet we have been around in some fashion for millions of years. We communicated with vocal sounds before we created the symbolic sounds we call words. And, as we all know, even words are imprecise and confusing in their meanings.

A more appropriate statement would be that "we are not listening to or **observing**, what is being communicated." That is what the rest of the communication process is about.

Vocal: 35 percent

We communicate 35 percent by the tone of our voice. The inflections in our voices are infinite. We have a different inflection when talking business than when talking intimately. We have a special inflection for greeting someone we like or someone we don't like. We have inflections that reveal our dishonesty or our credibility. As an example, during a workshop, I will tell one of the participants in a conversational tone, "Claudia, close the door."

Claudia will look at me, not sure if I meant it.

Then I will say in a loud and commanding tone of voice, "**Claudia, close the door!**"

She and all others in the room will jump noticeably. This is because they are frightened by the tone of voice, a specific tone that is intended to convey a "fight or flight" message. I have used the same words but conveyed an entirely different message by changing only the tone of voice.

As another example, I will sing the lullaby:

Rockaby baby, on the treetop.
When the wind blows, the cradle will rock.
When the bough breaks, the cradle will fall,
And down will come baby, cradle and all!

Now, what parent in their right mind would sing such a violent and scary song to a child? What child would not charge their parent for threatened abuse?

Well, the words are not what are heard or meant. It is the tone of voice that sends the real message...that in spite of the fear in this world, there is one who cares and who will protect you. So the chorus of the song says:

Rockaby, rockaby baby don't fear,
Rockaby, rockaby Daddy is near.

I work with many males who intimidate people with the sound of their booming or commanding voices. The result is that their message is never heard, because the listeners are responding out of "fight or flight." I can counsel these men and their listeners to be aware that this is what is happening. The man may want to moderate his voice, or the listeners may want to bend their ears around to hear the real message in the words. Often, all are surprised with this new awareness.

In the first morning greeting circle, the tonal quality of voices in the group provide me insight into the conflict, the apprehension, the anxiety, the anger that exists in the group. I listen as this anxiety is released with sharp-pitched sounds and laughter. Later, in the learning circle, the voices are soft, a counterpoint to the greeting circle. These verbal sounds are without anxiety or anger, so their words are heard.

Nonverbal: 58 percent

The remaining communication occurs in an infinite number of ways, depending on the culture. The nonverbal message is in gestures, facial expressions, stance, distance between people, the clothes worn. (You can tell who is a cowboy not just by the boots they wear, but by the condition of the boots.)

All of us know this instinctively. We are all aware that our movements and the movements of others communicate messages, sometimes different from the verbal message. We can tell when a person is being incongruent, dishonest, and evasive.

We also know that the sexes have different nonverbal behaviors. Women tend to look deeply into each other's eyes, speaking to the center of the other person. Men, on the other hand, tend to evade each other's eyes, standing at angles that make this possible. If they look into each other's eyes, it is to gauge the nature of their relationship. The last one to turn their eyes away wins.

Men will shuffle their feet, sway back and forth, and turn away while another is speaking. These are all power movements, intended to avoid the appearance of aggression. This behavior is frustrating to women because it appears disrespectful and feels like a dismissal.

In the old-time barbershop (the domain of the males who don't eat quiche), the customer normally sits on the chair, facing away from the mirror. The barber is behind, mostly unseen, but heard. The male customers keep their eyes down, evading direct glances at the barber.

In a beauty shop, the customer faces the mirror. The beautician is visible in the mirror. Eye contact is continuous as they speak. Others can also make eye contact and do, through the mirror. Each of these environments sends a different nonverbal message to the clients.

We read the nonverbal communication through our worst possible outcomes: What is most important to understand about nonverbal communication is that it is always being observed by others, and it is most often read *through their worst fears*. We see the message, we feel compelled to determine its intent. Normally, we determine it out of our fears.

I am talking with a member of a workshop, and another member walks by us with the statement: "Plotting against us, eh?"

Now, think. Have you ever had anybody walk by in this situation and say: "Plotting *for* us, eh?"

Or, if you see an employee who reports to you going into your boss's office and closing the door behind her, what is the message you are getting? Are you saying to yourself, "Oh good, she is going to tell my boss how well I treat her"? Or is it the opposite?

Invariably, participants in a workshop will point out some nonverbal behavior of a person and tell me they are concerned about it. They want to know what I am going to do about it. I normally advise them that their interpretation of the behavior is only one possibility. I then ask them what another possible interpretation could be.

This concern for others' nonverbal behaviors has increased since the publication of a number of popular paperbacks on "body language." Read these books, and you are supposed to be able to understand the meanings for all of the described body movements. These books are similar to books on "dream interpretations" published in the sixties. While they are entertaining, they are hardly a complete and definitive description of reality.

There are some major problems I see with the information in these books. It is not that they aren't true, but that they are limited. They provide only a narrow and limited field in which the information applies.

The first problem is that the body language information is often not cross-cultural. What may be a message in one culture is not the same in others. The books are often mostly intended for Anglo audiences and so focus on the movements in the white American culture.

A second problem is that the meanings associated with the body movements are based on the largest interpretation and do not include the other interpretations in the range of distribution in the normal curve.

For instance, a member of a group came up to me and mentioned how one person sat with folded arms across his chest during the session. She was sure this meant he disagreed with what was happening and was withdrawn into himself. Since he was an important person in the situation, this meant a consensus would not be possible.

I had the "arm folder" come up to me later in the session, after I had spoken about the nonverbal language insight. He said this relieved him, because he was always being criticized as not being interested in the discussion. His reason for folding his arms had to do with an arthritic condition he had in his shoulder. Folding his arms relieved the pain in that shoulder.

You must be aware that others are reading your nonverbal behaviors at all times and from a negative viewpoint.

This requires that you be as clear as possible about what you are doing. This is the reason that I explain fully to participants what I am doing in a session and why. I will do this before or after the task. This keeps our verbal and nonverbal communication closer to reality.

I will ask others what their behavior means so I can be clear about what they are communicating. If a person gets up and walks around a lot, I will ask if they have a physical problem I can help with.

Most people will let me know what they are doing to keep their messages clear. If someone must leave early, they normally tell me and explain the reason. Then, when someone in the group questions their absence as a lack of commitment, I can provide correct information for the absence.

This insight is made possible by using the nonverbal greeting circle. It can also be inserted into any moment in a workshop when it would be helpful and appropriate. (*See chapter 46 on interpersonal conflicts.*)

GOTCHA!

Mildred, the church gossip and self-appointed arbiter of the church's morals, kept sticking her nose in other members' private lives. Church members didn't appreciate her activities, but feared her enough to maintain their silence.

She made a mistake, however, when she accused George, a new member, of being an alcoholic after she saw his pickup truck parked in front of the town's only bar one afternoon. She commented to George and others that everyone seeing it there would know what he was doing.

George, a man of few words, stared at her for a moment and just walked away. He didn't explain, defend, or deny; he said nothing.

Later that evening, George quietly parked his pickup in front of Mildred's house…and left it there all night!

Enough said!!

A Facilitative Tone of Voice: An Insight

Participants will often come up to me during the first break on the first day and comment on the calmness of my tone of voice.

"Bob, I just wanted to tell you that I came in here very apprehensive and nervous about this workshop. Listening as you talked about what we are going to be doing during this workshop helps me to feel better about being here. Especially your tone of voice. You just made me feel calm and very hopeful about these three days."

This has happened often enough that I decided there is a facilitative tone of voice that calms people, makes them feel safe and hopeful. This is a tone of voice that YOU want to cultivate. What is that tone?

The facilitative tone emanates from me when I am feeling centered, aware, conscious of how I am feeling internally, conscious of the people I am talking to externally, and knowing clearly that my intent is to help these people. Sometimes I have this tone of voice even when I am extremely nervous, and I am conscious of this. At other times I have this tone of voice when I am uncertain, uncomfortable, and I acknowledge that to myself.

Sometimes if my internal environment is somewhat shaky, I will just let the community I am working with know that, too. For example:

I want you to know that right now I'm feeling a little bit apprehensive and shaky about this group. I know many of you would just as soon not be here, and there is doubt about the success of these three days. If you also have these feelings, I just want you to know it's OK. We will solve this problem.

The way you can develop a facilitative tone is to just be clear about what your role is, be clear about your own feelings, and then declare that your purpose is to help the people who have come together. Then trust yourself! I will sometimes share this anecdote with the group:

Misreading Voice Tones: An Anecdote

They described Jeff to me as an angry person. They thought he used his anger as a way of controlling people, of riding roughshod over them. Their response was to become defensive, to push back.

When I listened to Jeff in the interview, especially when he talked about the people he advocated for, what I heard was passion. I asked him why he had decided to take on the work that he did, representing powerless people. His answer was passionate. He believed deeply in the responsibilities that he had to speak for and represent others.

I talked with Jeff about how a passionate voice sounds like anger and how this was affecting his relationship with others. He wanted to know if he should stop that tone.

"No," I answered, "I will take care of helping the others know you are not angry, just passionate."

When we entered the confrontation stage of the workshop, I put Jeff on the panel to speak first to a person, Ann, with an opposite view. Before he spoke, I provided an insight to the group about Jeff:

"This morning we did a nonverbal greeting circle, and I helped you understand the importance of voice tones. I also mentioned that we often misread nonverbal communications out of our worst possible outcomes.

"Many of you expressed in your interviews that Jeff spoke with angry tones, and this bothered you. In listening to Jeff, I realized that you may be misreading his tone of voice. I sensed he is not angry; he is passionate about representing his constituents. When you hear him speak today, see if you can tell the difference. Listen to what he says when he is passionate."

After Jeff spoke, Ann responded with what she heard. She acknowledged how passionate Jeff was in his expressions and told him it helped to feel that, rather than anger. She heard what he said clearly. It changed the nature of her response to him.

When people are overly excited, they have voice tones that elicit fears in some people; they become adrenalized. It is helpful to recognize that and to let the participants know they are excited, not scared.

Be aware that people will read others' emotional voice tones out of their worst possible outcomes. You can be the person who helps them hear the right emotion.

A Learning Talking Circle and Grounding

YOU, Diane, and Neil have returned after the greeting circle. Neil presents the next activity. He walks to the edge of the circle. I can tell he is self-conscious. He acknowledges that to the group:

"I guess I'd better tell you that I'm self-conscious, like Bob suggested. This is really new to me. When I do my normal job as a county executive, I generally know what to do. But what I have done in the past apparently is not helping us. So I'm willing to be here, be self-conscious, and try this new approach. Your purpose is to do a grounding. This is what I want you to do: Close your circle. (There is a screeching of chairs being moved.)

"You will not have to record this activity; it is a talking circle. Answer these two questions: *How do you feel about the nonverbal greeting circle?* and *What do you need to learn so you can work as a community to resolve the situation?*"

Neil repeats the questions, then turns and walks away toward Diane. I ask Diane to give Neil feedback on how well he did. Here's what she says:

"Gee, you did a pretty good. I especially like the way you dealt with your self-consciousness. I'm going to use that myself. I was really self-conscious the first time. So that allowed you to focus and just read off the questions. Pretty easy, isn't it?"

"Yes," says Neil, "except for the part about being self-conscious. I can't believe I was that nervous."

Well, I say, you're being asked to do something totally different from the way you normally behave. There is a risk in doing that, which caused you to be self-conscious. For me, that is wonderful. Being self-conscious means I am aware, in my higher brain. If I am not self-conscious, I will be nonconscious, in my reptilian brain. By talking about it, you became aware, trusted yourself. It is a great moment.

So, what do you do next, Neil?

Neil responds: "After they have completed this activity, I'll go to the edge of the circle and ask if everyone has spoken at least once. If they have, I'll provide an insight as Diane did last night. Then turn it over to you."

Best Possible Outcomes Task: Coaching the Facilitator

I turn to YOU and say: You are going to provide them the task for the best possible outcomes. This is your three-by-five cue card.

> We will use the same facilitator. Pass out the 3 x 5 cards. (Pause.) Record the answer to this question;
>
> Working together as a community, what will be the best possible outcomes of resolving your situation in the next year?
>
> Facilitator pick a new facilitator and become the recorder. Record all of these best possible outcomes on the card.

You will note we are using the phrase "working together as a community" because they have been speaking in that manner. We are also giving them a year's window of time in which to complete their outcomes. This is their short-term purpose.

You'll notice how silent it gets as they record deliberatively their best possible outcomes. This is the most important task today. We have done best possible outcomes the previous two days, but those were just to prepare people to do this task. Because people don't immediately think of best possible outcomes, their first description tends to be fairly minimal. Each time I have them explore their purpose, they'll get better and better at it. So they will provide us a lot of information with this task.

When they have completed this activity, you will go to the edge of the circle and ask if everyone has spoken at least once. If they have, then you provide them with your answers to those questions: how you feel and what you feel the community must learn. That will be your insight. Then turn the group over to me. I will do a few introductory remarks and help segue to Neil's activity.

After that activity, Diane, you are going to give them the next task. I hand Diane a three-by-five cue card with the question on it.

> Record directly to the flip chart.
>
> What are all the reasons people will give that it is impossible to create these outcomes?

When I turn this over to you, Diane, have them pick a new facilitator and give them the direction to record directly to the flip chart. Then read off the question they are to answer.

I speak to the three of you: Pay attention to the response of the groups. They will go at this immediately. The response that something is impossible is just a worst possible outcome. People will have a worst fear when they hear the best possible outcome, because they will immediately fear that they are dreaming, that it is just a motherhood statement, Disney World, and that we're fooling ourselves. It isn't possible. To deal with that, I have them answer this question: *What are all the reasons people will give that it is impossible to create these outcomes?*

Each of the answers is in fact a belief, one that will prevent you from making it happen. What we are doing with this question is exposing those beliefs that underlie the feeling that it is impossible. They are just worst possible outcomes.

Nonverbal Greeting Circle: An Insight

It is now time to move the small groups beyond the grounding. Neil walks to the edge of the circle, waits a moment to still himself, acknowledge his self-consciousness to himself, then asks the group: "Has everyone spoken at least once?" They pay no attention because they are deeply involved in conversations that have captured them. Heads are leaning in; whoever is speaking has the attention of the whole group.

"Has everyone spoken at least once?" Neil repeats, then again and again. Eventually they notice his presence, nod their heads, and return to speaking.

"It is apparent you are really interested in this task; it's difficult to get your attention and move on. So I'm going to give you my answer to those two questions. How did I feel about the nonverbal greeting circle? Really self-conscious! I have to admit it felt pretty weird. I didn't expect to be in a group.

"I found it really changes things to take away the words. I found we could communicate, looking into each other's eyes or the way we shook hands. I knew when people would allow me to hug them. So I am impressed with how everything changes when you take away words. In summary, I feel connected to every one of you. I feel I can accept every one of you as part of this community.

"I think what we can learn is to recognize that we are a community. Because we have different points of view and diverse interests, we are going to get into conflict. So we need to learn how to recognize when we are in conflict and then do something about it. I think that something is to include everybody that is impacted by the conflict. And we need to learn to listen with respect to each other because we will then learn what is needed to solve our problems. That is what is going on here."

By now, Neil has everyone's attention. "So, I just am going to turn this over to Bob."

Standing at the edge of the circle opposite Neil, I speak, getting their attention: We need a break, don't you think? I'll say a few words, and we'll take a break.

Now I had their attention!

When you come back from the break, you will explore the best possible outcomes of your situation. Be thinking of that: what do you want to happen when you work together and solve your conflicts?

~40~

The Best Possible Outcomes of the Situation

The Purpose Statement: An Activity

The participants leave, although some are still in their small-group circle, talking and listening. People are in pairs or trios around the coffee, talking seriously. People are talking with those they disagreed strongly with two days ago. Lynn is talking with Jack and Frank. Rayni and Ann are talking with Jon and Rob.

When the break is over and all are back in their small groups, I introduce the next task:

I always start the day with grounding, getting everyone's voice in the room. But is it more than a warm-up exercise; it is a learning activity. You have an opportunity to assess where you are in the workshop, how you are feeling about what you are learning, and exploring what you need to learn. This grounding helps you get to know people in the new group. You are establishing new relationships and a basis for trust. You are preparing to resolve your issue.

We ended yesterday with the worst possible outcomes of working together or not working together as a community to resolve your issue. That collective statement was read earlier. We need to acknowledge these worst possible outcomes, bring them to our consciousness, acknowledging our reptilian self's need to ensure survival.

Now, we can move on to balance that view with our best possible outcomes.

I turn and walk away. YOU walk to the edge of the circle and read the task from the card:

"We will use the same facilitator. Pass out the three-by-five cards." (Pause.)

"Record the answer to this question." (Pause.)

The Best Possible Outcomes of the Situation

"Working together as a community, what will be the best possible outcomes of resolving your issues in the next year?"

YOU walk away and let them record on the cards. It is silent in the room. When you sense they are ready, mainly by hearing people begin to break the silence, you return to the circle and speak:

"Facilitator, pick a new facilitator and become the recorder. Record these to the flip charts."

You step away from the circle, turning to walk to Diane, Neil, and I.

Let's listen in on Group 1:

Debbe: "Cliff, I pick you for facilitator."

Cliff: "Thanks, Deb, I pick you for the recorder. Tony, let's start with you, and we'll go clockwise from there."

Tony: "Thanks, Cliff." (Reading off his card) "The first one relates to my role as an elected official: *elected officials will see the whole picture and involve all parties in consensus decision making.*" (Pauses.) "This is for the ranchers: *Coyote River Basin will have developed a communal way to make ranching and farming profitable and successful, while preserving the beauty of the valley.*"

Frank (waiting until Deb is done recording): "Thanks for the support, Tony. You ready, Deb? OK, *Coyote County is a valley that is green, and ranching and farming are profitable.*" (Pauses.) *"We develop a common understanding and support between ranchers and the larger community."* (Speaking slowly.) *"Ranches are operated in such a manner that water within the ranchers' influence contributes to salmon recovery, and our grandchildren get to see them and fish them."*

Gil: *"Areas set aside for development are developed responsibly, while protecting the beauty of the basin. Our ranches and farms are profitable and can be sustained for future generations."*

Crista: *"There is acceptance of tribal identity and culture, which leads to actions to return salmon to clean water. We will be able to tell our elders we have kept our heritage alive.* I also agree with Frank's statement about the salmon...just put a check mark there."

Marcia: *"We have a strong long-term economic stability. Development and growth will continue in a planned manner. As elected officials we are seen as part of the solution and are willing to make the necessary decisions for the solution."*

Todd: *"All streams have healthy populations of fish, with ample opportunities for anglers to catch them. We have healthier fisheries and healthier communities."*

Cliff: *"That ranchers are profitable and not selling their land for income. We manage development in such a way that we preserve our most valuable assets, the ranchland, land for wildlife, and land for water. Environmentalists are* listened to and respected, and their stake and interest in the 'common good' is acknowledged."

Cliff: "Deb, you are next. Marcia, would you record for her?" (Marcia nods and goes to the flip chart.)

Deb: *"We need money to do most of these things...so I can help on that. Money flows to the community to solve agricultural issues that are founded in common ground. Agencies are transparent in their actions and genuinely interested in bringing all people together to craft meaningful solutions."*

Cliff: "Does anybody have anything else to add?"

Frank: "Yes. *Ranchers and farmers will have time to go steelhead fishing.*" (Laughter.)

Marcia: "You know, I am actually beginning to believe we can do this."

Todd: "It won't be easy like it is here with Bob helping us."

Cliff: "Didn't Bob say he would create facilitators for us? Neil and Diane are doing a great job! And we have facilitated groups the last three days."

Crista: "It won't be easy, but I think we can do this, and Bob told me he is available for consultation."

GROUP 1: BEST POSSIBLE OUTCOMES IF WE WORK TOGETHER

- *Elected officials will see the whole picture and involve all parties in consensus decision making.*
- *Coyote County Basin will have developed a communal way to make ranching and farming profitable and successful, while preserving the beauty of the valley.*
- *Coyote County is a valley that is green, and ranching and farming are profitable.*
- *We develop a common understanding and support between ranchers and the larger community.*
- *Ranches are operated in such a manner that water within the ranchers' influence contributes to salmon recovery, and our grandchildren get to see them and fish them.*
- *Areas set aside for development are developed responsibly, while protecting the beauty of the basin. Our ranches and farms are profitable and can be sustained for future generations.*
- *There is acceptance of tribal identity and culture, which leads to actions to return salmon to clean water. We will be able to say to our elders we have kept our heritage alive.*

The Best Possible Outcomes of the Situation

> - *We have a strong long-term economic stability.*
> - *Development and growth will continue in a planned manner.*
> - *As elected officials we are seen as part of the solution and are willing to make the necessary decisions for the solution.*
> - *All streams have healthy populations of fish, with ample opportunities for anglers to catch them.*
> - *We have healthier fisheries and healthier communities.*
> - *That ranchers are profitable and not selling their land for income.*
> - *We manage development in such a way that we preserve our most valuable assets, the ranch land, land for wildlife, and land for water.*
> - *Environmentalists are listened to and respected, and their stake and interest in the "common good" is acknowledged.*
> - *Money flows to the community to solve agricultural issues that are founded in common ground.*
> - *Agencies are transparent in their actions and genuinely interested in bringing all people together to craft meaningful solutions.*
> - *Ranchers and farmers will have time to go steelhead fishing.*

There is much sound and laughter in the room as the groups complete their task. YOU walk to the edge of the circle and ask, "Has everyone been recorded?" All groups nod their heads. "Then, let's start with Group 1 and have the recorder read off the information. Then we will go counterclockwise."

Debbe stands at her group's flip chart and reads to the larger group. As these purpose statements are being read off by each group, I notice how intent all are in listening to this information. There are good vibes in the room, a sense of satisfaction. Lots of smiles, heads nodding. When Debbe finishes reading, the room spontaneously bursts into applause, a nonverbal sign of agreement. It just happens. They like what they heard. Applause follows all the remaining presentations. It is an affirmation of their support.

I step to the edge of the circle and speak:

These are your best possible outcomes of working together as a community to solve the issue that brought you together. It is a purpose statement. Each of those individual statements can be seen as a specific goal. This is the aim of all the strategies and actions that you will take together.

If you don't know where you're going, it is unlikely you will get there. Your purpose statement is a description of the destination. From here we can begin to develop your paths to that destination.

I see that Jack has raised his hand. I nod to him.

"I can see how this is a statement of purpose, but I am wondering. It just seems like pie in the sky. I mean, is it really possible to do all of this? It just seems too wonderful to me. It's like we are not being real."

I respond: I'm glad you asked the question, Jack. It is not unusual for people to question their best possible outcomes or purpose statements, because they have never really considered them before. Being trapped by their worst possible comes, the best possible outcomes seem to be out of reach. So many people ask me that same question.

It's impossible! That's what you are essentially saying. We are setting the bar too high.

Jack and many others nod their heads.

Well, I could have you answer the question yourself, Jack. But I believe it's a good task for the entire group. We will do that after the break.

Everyone slowly leaves the small groups, heading for the refreshment table or the restrooms.

~41~

It's Impossible—New Beliefs and Behaviors

Exploring Why It's Impossible: An Activity

Earlier, while the small groups are working on the best possible outcome task, YOU coach Diane based on our discussions earlier this morning:

"Diane, after the groups have read off their best possible outcomes, Bob will provide an insight about this being a statement of purpose. We will take a short break. Then he will turn the group over to you, and you will give them a task on all the reasons it is *impossible* to create these best possible outcomes.

"When they have completed this task, you will check to see if everyone has spoken at least once and then have the recorder read off their information. After the first group has read off their information, Bob will step to the circle and provide them an insight. That insight is to make them aware that each of the statements is a belief statement. These are the beliefs that will prevent them from accomplishing their purpose.

"After the break, when we have everyone in the small circles, Bob will introduce the next task."

When people have returned from their break, I provide a context for the next question:

Jack's concern before the break is an appropriate one. Your timing was great, Jack. Believing that a purpose statement is impossible to create is just a worst possible outcome focused on your best possible outcomes. So I am going to have you explore all the reasons that it is impossible to accomplish your purpose statement, your best possible outcomes.

Diane is going to give you this task.

Diane steps to the edge of the circle, opposite me (balancing), and asks the facilitator to select another facilitator and become the recorder. She reads off the task.

> Record directly to the flip chart
>
> What are all the reasons people will give that it is impossible to create these outcomes?

"You are to record the answers to this question directly to the flip chart."

She repeats the question, then turns and walks away. The groups immediately go to work. It is easy to express all the reasons that it is impossible. They are right at the tip of everyone's tongue. The flip charts fill up quickly with many statements. Normally, this task takes less than ten minutes.

Diane walks to the edge of the circle and asks, "Has everyone spoken at least once?" She repeats this a few times and gets the attention of all groups. "OK, let's start with the recorder from Group 3 reading off your information. We will then go counterclockwise."

This is the information that Group 3 reads off.

GROUP 3: ALL THE REASONS IT IS IMPOSSIBLE

- *"It is not my problem."*
- *You will never get everyone to agree.*
- *The community doesn't really know what's right for the land.*
- *There is too much resistance, anger, negativity on both sides.*
- *People are afraid of what they will have to give up.*
- *There is no common purpose.*
- *"I can't make a difference."*
- *There is not enough time and we are too busy. Talk to me after hay season.*
- *We have traditions—we have always done it this way.*
- *It will be too difficult.*
- *No one wants to change anything they are currently doing.*
- *Citizens will block us every step of the way.*
- *There is malicious intent to drive farmers and ranchers from the land.*
- *People feel powerless to make changes.*
- *Just because—people are bullheaded and stubborn.*
- *People are afraid of what they will have to give up.*
- *The new people in the community haven't been here long enough to understand us.*

> **GROUP 3: ALL THE REASONS IT IS IMPOSSIBLE**
> - *We can't do without money, and there is no money.*
> - *I'm a newcomer and I don't care.*
> - *They won't cooperate and aren't interested in our side.*
> - *We will just get it wrong, and people will complain.*
> - *There is not enough time.*
> - *There is a lack of trust, self-esteem and proactiveness.*
> - *There are lawsuits and threats of lawsuits, and we will get sued.*
> - *There is not enough money in the budget.*

When Group 3 has finished reading off their information, I step to the edge of the circle and get their attention.

As you listen to the rest of the statements, I want you to recognize how many are belief statements. These are the beliefs that you express to each other when you get together in the staff room or over a coffee break, at gatherings, acknowledging why it is impossible to do a task you have been assigned. The more you repeat it, the more you believe it. Soon, a group of you will be saying exactly the same thing to each other and to people outside your group. What you are doing is creating a "groupthink."

Since you believe it is impossible, it then becomes impossible. It becomes a self-fulfilling prophecy. And everyone you repeat it to will believe you, and they will repeat it to others. You are brainwashing yourselves to failure.

So listen to the rest of the statements, recognizing those that are statements of belief. Ask yourself if they really are the beliefs you want to have. Will they accomplish your purpose?

I step back while Group 4 begins to read their statements, and the rest of the groups do the same in order.

When all the charts have been read, Diane speaks to the group with her insight:

"I have to admit that I said almost every one of those at some point in my life. We do it in the spur of the moment out of our frustration. I never paid attention to the fact that I was really determining my behaviors by doing so. I also have to admit I never really liked the feelings that went along with these beliefs. It felt hopeless to me."

Diane looks at me, and I walk to the edge of the circle and continue:

So, these are all the reasons it is impossible. They are statements of beliefs that will prevent you from accomplishing your purpose. So, let's acknowledge...

It is impossible!

I don't want your reptilian brain to believe that it is wrong. Just acknowledge right now, it is impossible to that part of you!

Given that, the next question we can ask is, what new beliefs or behaviors will make it possible? If you believe it is impossible because of your present beliefs, it's important that you look at those beliefs and consider the possibility of new beliefs. That is your next task.

This is an example of making a paradigm shift. I am helping you create that empty space that the brain must fill with the leap of imagination. I must know what your present beliefs are to explore the possibility of new and different beliefs.

It's Impossible!: An Insight for the Reader

Once people have developed a "best possible outcome," they normally respond in disbelief. "It's impossible!" they say, either verbally or through their behaviors. This is especially true of people who fear worst possible outcomes and are successful in making them happen.

This is a normal response. It can occur in the form of laughter as the outcomes are read, or in snide remarks about "motherhood statements," or in questions that express doubt about the wisdom of the mission. These are all worst possible outcomes statements and behaviors.

This occurs anytime people's "bubbles of belief" are stretched. I visualize people's belief system as being in a large bubble held in by an invisible membrane, a surface tension created to hold the beliefs close. Anything that attempts to stretch the bubble, to cause it to expand, will be resisted for fear that the bubble will burst, the contents released, and the person will disappear.

If the mission is outside their normal beliefs or experience, how can it be possible? Yet, they want to live in that statement of purpose they just created; it is appealing to them. How can they make their purpose happen if it is impossible?

To do these tasks, we first need to allow the individuals to express their disbelief, their worst possible outcome. It allows them to bring these fears to the surface, to expose them on the flip chart, to release the tension and the disbelief.

Once this is done, the person will be willing to explore the possibility of doing it anyway. This allows them to explore another possibility, to expand their "bubble of belief."

> **REASONS THAT OTHER PEOPLE WILL GIVE: THE ART**
>
> Often in choosing a question to ask, especially one that is close to the people in the room, I will phrase it to include other people outside the room. It is easier to talk about other people's fears sometimes, rather than your own.
>
> *What are all the reasons you feel it is impossible?*
>
> is different from:
>
> *What are all the reasons others will feel it is impossible?*
>
> In providing these fears you are also presenting yours. It just frees you up to answer the question broadly and keep yourself protected.

This is an example of making a paradigm shift. I must know what your present beliefs are to explore the possibility of new and different beliefs.

New Beliefs and Behaviors: An Activity

While the groups are working on all the reasons it is impossible, I coach Neil on the next activity:

After they have accomplished this task, Neil, you will give them the next important task, which is to identify new and adaptive beliefs and behaviors that will foster their purpose statements, even though it appears impossible.

I provide a three-by-five card to Neil.

We want to keep the present facilitator until they have recorded on the three-by-five card. Then we want them to record their answers to the flip chart. So you will have them change facilitators for that task.

> Pass out the 3 x 5 cards. Record the answer to this question.
>
> Working together as a community, what new and adaptive beliefs or behaviors will foster your best possible outcomes?

Presenting this task is the same as for the best possible outcomes. Take this a step at a time.

When the small groups are done recording and reporting, I provide an insight on the reasons it's impossible. Then I turn the circle over to Neil.

Neil walks to the edge of the circle, reads the task from the card.

"We will use the same facilitator. Pass out the three-by-five cards." (Pause.)

"Record the answer to this question:

"Working together as a community, what new and adaptive beliefs or behaviors will foster your best possible outcomes?"

Silence descends on the room as the members of the groups write deliberatively on their cards. Some pause, raising their heads, looking upward or inward as they think about what they want to record. This is an internal discussion, seeking to consider exploring new possible beliefs. In doing this they are moving to the upper lobes of their brain, using their reason, their hope.

Neil waits until they are done and begin to break the silence with talk and laughter.

"Facilitator, pick a new facilitator and become the recorder. Record these to the flip charts."

As the small groups immediately turn to their task, Neil steps away from the circle and turns to walk to our facilitating group. We can see the former facilitators, now recorders, standing at the flip charts. The facilitators speak in soft facilitative tones, still respectful of the silence, and recording begins.

So, I ask Neil, how is this different than your first time?

Neil thinks for a little bit and then answers, "I was still self-conscious, but I was more comfortable with it. It did help."

I respond: My purpose is to help people become comfortable with being uncomfortable. The only way I know to do that is to have them experience being self-conscious until they become comfortable with it.

The tones of voice rise slowly as more information is recorded to the flip charts. The sense of silence recedes. Soon there is an air of lightness in the room, healthy laughter at times.

While the groups are working, YOU, Diane, Neil, and I work to put together the collective statement for the best possible outcomes. We have to do this quickly, so we use scissors to cut off the individual statements and then organize them on the floor into like groups.

We can do this separate from the group because they are in charge of their own process. They are doing the facilitating, recording, the reading and listening. Their behaviors are congruent with their beliefs and behaviors. They are a community behaving in consensus.

It's Impossible—New Beliefs and Behaviors

When people's voices begin to slowly return to calm, serious, deliberate, Neil walks to the edge of the circle. "Has everyone had the time to complete their recording?"

His voice is soft, respectful of the silence in the room. People turn their attention to him, a signal they are ready to proceed.

"Let's begin with Group 2 reporting out and then go counterclockwise."

GROUP 2: BELIEFS AND BEHAVIORS.

- We believe in the value of others' points of view.
- A belief that all people are worthy of trust, so trust first.
- Develop open mindedness. Think outside the box.
- We create new partnerships and reach out for new relationships.
- Everyone has bought into the best possible outcome.
- I can, you can, we can make a difference.
- Understanding the relationship process and consciously working with it.
- More honoring of each role, person, or function.
- Establish trust between individuals.
- Truly believe that diversity is good; make an effort to be inclusive of differing viewpoints.
- Everyone has ideas that can and will contribute to achieving the goals.
- Promote and engage in respectful listening and verbal sharing.
- Knowing that change for the better is possible, we will be willing and courageous enough to take the first step.
- Together we will find a way to bring back fish, restore the watershed, and create a community joined in common purpose.
- Become an active listener with a curious and creative attitude.
- Value and honor diversity of beliefs.
- Everyone's actions are based on some rational thought.
- Each person has a role and responsibility.
- Believe it is possible.
- We believe in listening with respect and listening to understand.
- Acknowledge fears before moving on to solutions.
- We need a common vision/goal.
- Everyone would really like to reach a consensus or agreement and are trying for a consensus.
- Everyone's opinions are valued.

When he is done, the entire community spontaneously applauds. This response continues with each of the following reports. They affirm these new beliefs and behaviors.

When the reports are completed, YOU walk to the edge of the circle opposite Neil and speak:

"Yesterday, when we completed the new beliefs and behaviors about conflict, Bob gave us an insight about our behaviors. He said we were being congruent. By that he meant we were recording words on the flip chart that we were behaving in the group. I didn't quite understand what he meant at that time. But observing the group's activity, I now understand.

"I'm beginning to wonder how often any of us really have control over what happens. We say many things and then do the opposite. If we can do this here, why can't we do it back in the community? Why can't we take control as a community? I believe we can after this workshop, and that will help us be successful.

"Let's form the large circle to prepare for this afternoon. Bob will provide you an insight, and then we will take a break for lunch."

There is much movement and excitement. When all are in the large circle, I provide an insight.

Beliefs and the Possible: An Insight

How does it feel to hear these beliefs? When the recorder reads off "Together we can make it happen," how does that affect you?

Now think about this...the person who expressed that first composed it on the three-by-five card. Then he or she presented it to your group. The recorder wrote this on the flip chart, just as expressed. Then this was part of what was read to the larger group. There are four expressions of the same belief. When it is developed as part of the collective statement and presented, it will have a fifth and sixth expression. Each time seeing or hearing the words of this belief will reinforce it with everyone.

Compare that with the previous beliefs about why it is not possible: "It is just not worth the hassle," or, "We will never agree anyway." How do these belief statements make you feel?

The words you express create the reality you live in; they become self-fulfilling prophecies. It is important to express your beliefs about why it is impossible, because these exist in the nonconscious lower reptilian brain as an acknowledgment of that impossibility. Then you can express why it is possible and experience the hope that it provides you.

These beliefs will make it possible to be successful with your purpose. In creating and responding to these, you are creating a paradigm shift. Repeating these beliefs will provide you the focus for now developing strategies and actions you will need to create your purpose, the best possible outcomes.

That is your next task, after lunch. For this task, I want to speak with these four folks in the center of the room: Jack, Allen, Lynn, and Ann, as well as YOU, Neil, and Diane.

Oops! Wait a sec. Rob has a question. Let's answer it before lunch.

A "How" Question Is a Purpose Statement

"Bob," Rob asks, "these beliefs and behaviors are fine, but I am still wondering, what are we going to do? How will these thirty people change what is going on in this valley?"

I ask: Is there any disagreement with answering this question now? It will only take a minute or two.

There is nonverbal affirmation.

Rob, the question you just asked is a purpose statement. Rather than answer it, let me demonstrate this.

I write on the flip chart,

"How will these thirty people change what is going on in this valley?"

If I take the "how" away and move one word, what is the statement?
Rob thinks a few seconds, then answers, "These thirty people will change what is going on in this valley."
I change the statement on the flip chart:

"These thirty people will change what is going on in this valley!"

So, a how statement becomes a purpose statement, one that can motivate you to accomplishment. If you ask a how question, it makes you sound weak, as if it were impossible to do this. Rarely will anyone answer you when you ask a how question. It stops people in their tracks. They feel frozen, like a deer looking in the headlights of a car. Don't know why—just what I have observed.

If someone asks, *How can we get this done by the end of the month?* what would you convert that to, Rob?

Rob answers, "Ahhhh...I would convert it to...we can get this done by the end of the month?"

Then you can ask the question: *What strategies will get us there?*

If the response is, "This is impossible to do!" (because that tends to be the inference of a how question), then ask, *what are all the reasons it is impossible?* (You have just done that earlier.) When they have answered, ask, *what can we do to make it possible to get this done this month?*

A few more examples. (I write these on the flip chart for all to see.)

- How are we going to get people to support us?
- We are going to get people to support us!
- How will we do this without funding?
- We will do this without funding.

So, to answer your question, we will be developing strategies and actions after we return from the break.

~42~

Strategies and Actions

Strategies and Actions: Coaching the Facilitators

As the members of the community distribute themselves for lunch, I speak to Jack, Allen, Lynn, and Ann. YOU, Diane, and Neil listen.

Each of you will be a member of the panel, similar to the panel yesterday. We are moving into developing some specific strategies and actions that this community feels would express their new beliefs and behaviors and foster their purpose.

We will start after lunch with reading the best possible outcomes that the group created this morning. YOU, Neil, and Diane developed this while the small groups were working this morning. We will do this in the large group.

When this is done, I would like each of you to answer this question to help the group focus on imagining the strategies and actions that would foster their outcomes as they listen to you: *What specific strategies or actions will express your new beliefs and behaviors and foster your purpose (best possible outcomes)?*

It is not necessary to take on the total burden of developing these strategies and actions. Your purpose is to create an arena of thought so the group can begin to create the strategies and actions that would foster their purpose statement. If you are going to do the impossible, then seek to express strategies that would be "out of the box." One or two strategies would be sufficient to get us started. But if you have more, express more.

When you have spoken, we will bring you to the center and honor you. YOU, I am going to ask you to take care of this. You will direct the panel members to act as facilitators of their specific group. Then direct the community to return to their small groups.

When everyone is situated in their groups, we will repeat all of these instructions.

You will be asked to close your circle and not record at first. Start with a talking circle. You are going to use the process that we used yesterday when talking about the situation. When everyone has spoken once, we will have you pass out the three-by-five cards and have them answer this question:

What specific strategies or actions did you hear that you support, including your own, that would express your new beliefs and behaviors and foster your best possible outcomes—your purpose?

You will then select a new facilitator and become the recorder. You have been through this many times during the last two days, so this should be easy for you. We will repeat these instructions when you return to your groups.

Jack has a question: "Do you want us to get together and agree on some strategies?"

No, you will do that later in the small groups. For now, develop your own approaches. Rather than looking for one strategy, we are looking for many.

Diane and Neil, I'm going to have you continue to develop the best possible outcomes collective statement. Make sure you get a bite to eat. We will start with a reading of the collective statement by you and Neil.

Then YOU will give the group their task. I pass a three-by-five card with the task on it to YOU.

Close your circle. The panel member is the facilitator. This activity will begin with a talking circle, and then move to being recorded to the flip charts. The question to be answered is:

What specific strategies or actions will express your new beliefs and behaviors and foster your best possible outcomes?

Do not record, listen to each other with respect, do not interrupt.

This is a talking circle. It will allow them to focus on each other, as they express their differing strategies and actions. It is not unusual in doing this task for the members to begin to interrupt each other, as they now have a purpose, a set of beliefs, and they are excited about making their outcomes happen. So if someone expresses a strategy that another person really likes, normally that person will jump in and try to add to it or provide support. Or say they have a better idea. This may result in the group beginning to speak out of turn and not listen to each other.

When this happens, YOU will walk to the edge of the group and remind them to listen with respect. This normally will settle them down, although not always. This is actually the part that most people in the group have been looking forward to. This is what they normally considered to be their purpose. There is a feeling that they have "finally got to it!"

Diane and Neil return to working on the collective statement for the purpose/best possible outcomes. I join a group at one table for lunch.

Developing Strategies and Actions

After lunch, with the help of the people from my table, as well as the facilitators, we are able to move everybody into the large circle. I begin by creating a context for the next task:

Welcome back to the opportunity to reach consensus around your issue. Remember, consensus is more a behavior than it is words. All of your behaviors since we started after the break this morning indicate to me that you're operating in a consensual manner. You are behaving the beliefs and behaviors, strategies and actions that you developed at the end of our exploration of conflict. That means you are congruent with yourself.

When you are not congruent, it is difficult to reach a consensus. Being congruent, you can look at the work you have done today and be able to say to yourself, "Yes, I can accept what we have developed." This is demonstrated through your applause.

This afternoon we're going to do what many of you have been asking for. You keep asking, are we ever going to get to create a plan? My answer was, just relax...wait. We will get there. Well, we are there.

YOU will provide you the information to do the next task.

YOUwalk to the circle and speak to the community:

"We will begin by reading the collective statement of your purpose that you developed this morning in answer to the best possible outcomes. We have asked Diane and Neil to put that together as quickly as they can for you. This is not the final statement; we will rework it after the workshop. It is enough to get started.

"Remember, any belief, behavior, strategy, or action must have as its intent the creation of your purpose statement. As you listen to the collective statement, ask yourself, 'What strategies or actions can I think of that would reflect my new beliefs or behaviors and that would make this purpose happen?'

"We will then have a panel consisting of Frank, Lynn, Al, and Ann. Each of these people will answer this question: *What specific strategies or actions would reflect my new beliefs or behaviors and make our purpose happen?*

"You can be thinking about this question as you listen to the reading of the collective statement.

"When that is done, we will honor the panel, and you will all return to your groups. The panel member in your group will become your facilitator. You will have a talking circle around which all of you will answer the same question. When you have all had at least one chance to speak, you will be provided with three-by-five cards on which you will answer the question *what strategies and actions did you hear that you would support?* These will be recorded to the flip charts. We will repeat these instructions when you get into small groups."

Diane and Neil take turns reading the flip chart for the best possible outcomes:

The Best Possible Outcomes of Working Together in One Year: Our Short-term Purpose

(These are all actual recorded statements from real workshops.)

We create a common, clear vision for the basin that is attainable, and we work together to move toward that future. We have a clear vision of where we need to be and are able to meet these goals. We achieve a common sense of purpose and shared values.

New directions will lead to a new way of consensus thinking. We will have internal consensus and action-oriented strategies that help us meet our objectives. Energies previously spent on reacting to conflicts are released for the "new" common purpose. We find new answers and see the possibility of everyone coming to a conclusion in consensus.

Coyote County will have a strong sense of community, developing its agriculture base and environmental leadership for water and land. We will continue to work together as a close community with a unified direction. That we come together with a sense of community among the residents, a sense of togetherness, and a sense of well-being. A basin community where all neighbors can communicate and help, not hinder one another.

Coyote County involves the community when making decisions that affect the community, even if it is hard. It is a place that brings out the best in people and where problems are solved through partnership. The county hears what the community is saying they want as priorities, and the county responds and acts on what the community recommends. There is a sense of fairness and justice.

Decisions are based on inputs from communities, tribes, agencies, ranchers, and environmentalists that respect diverse priorities and needs. We resolve our differences and solve problems as they arise in a way that represents our diverse community. We work collaboratively with people with different points of view and are no longer dependent on the judicial system to implement an agenda, being able to trust that there is truth and goodness behind all of our actions.

We create a community environment where we listen to and understand each other's values and opinions. Our newcomers are welcomed for their new ideas and energy, and they are willing to appreciate, respect, and protect the heritage of the county. We see respect and understanding between old-timers and newcomers, retired and working, ranchers and environmentalists.

Elected officials will see the whole picture and involve all parties in consensus decision making. Our elected officials are seen as part of the solution and willing to make the necessary decisions for the solution. They make decisions that help our community flourish as a whole.

Citizens feel that elected officials are reflecting their values by caring for important resources. Decisions of elected officials will be a reflection of public wishes and desires. They will have a plan that will use the land wisely and in a balanced way, ensuring the balance of the resources to maintain healthy habitat for generations to come.

Coyote County is a place where people want to live and raise their families. A healthy environment where people feel valued and are making a difference in citizens' lives. It is a place of optimism and trust where there is confidence that even serious issues can be resolved without fracturing the community. That it continues to be a great place to live. A place you want to stay.

We have a strong long-term economic stability. County employment is highly sought after because it is diverse and inclusive. We encourage clean industries and commercial businesses that sustain the full spectrum of family economic levels.

More young families will come to the area because of good-paying jobs and the prosperous economy. The economic environment will be improved so that our children and grandchildren would be able to work and live here. We provide affordable housing for young families and lower-income workers.

We were able to accommodate growth and change without losing the good stuff. We manage development in such a way that we preserve our most valuable assets, the ranchland, land for wildlife, and land for water. Controlling growth protects the heritage and beauty of the Coyote River Basin. Our plan keeps the views and creates reasonable growth in a smart way that most all in the basin can agree on.

Development and growth will continue in a planned manner. Areas set aside for development are developed responsibly, while protecting the beauty of the basin. Development is planned in and around cities, minimizing infrastructure costs and creating close communities where working families can live, work, play, and socialize.

The community develops a land-use and zoning plan that encourages ranchers and farmers to keep prosperous ranching and farming in the area. We will preserve our agricultural lands, ranches, and farms, and the rural nature of Coyote River Basin with reasonable subdivision regulations. We have prosperous crops with or without the irrigation water. The average age of farmer and rancher dropped ten years, with grandchildren staying to become ranchers and farmers in their own way.

Coyote County will have developed a communal way to make ranching and farming profitable and successful, while preserving the beauty of the valley. Coyote County is a valley that is green and ranching and farming are profitable. Ranchers will find a way to be economically and financially stable, while still being good stewards of the land and its creatures. That ranchers are profitable and not selling their land for income.

Coyote County is a model for western agriculture communities with great partnerships with environmentalists and others. We develop a common understanding and support between ranchers and the larger community. People will realize the social and ecological benefits of ranches and farms. The stewardship of the land and natural resources that ranchers live and work each day will be acknowledged and appreciated. We will stop seeing ranchers as the enemy.

Holistic ranching would be the norm, and sustainability will be the standard of successes. Our ranches and farms are profitable and can be sustained for future generations. Long-term sustainability for the ranch is clean water in the rivers and the return of the salmon. Ranches are operated in such a manner that water within the ranchers' influence contributes to salmon recovery, and our grandchildren get to see them.

There is acceptance of tribal identity and culture which leads to actions to return salmon to clean water. We reach a maturity that allows us to protect the water, salmon, and lifestyle the creator has provided us with. The real love and respect for the land, water, and fish that the Native American Indians have can be the best model for all of us to follow. We will be able to say to our elders, we have kept our heritage alive.

Coyote County will have a working irrigation district that is efficient and environmentally pleasing. We have optimized water use, and saved water is used to enhance the basin due to a willing support from all Coyote County members, not just ranchers. The district will be a low-cost efficiently run irrigation district that has complied with all the federal regulations that pertain to us.

The irrigation district is piped with a gravity flow system. We obtain government help with piping. Ranches and farms would be more profitable, with pressurized water. There would be green pastures in late summer and third cuttings of hay and alfalfa. There would be full production, contributing four times the current inputs into the local economy and profitable hay, livestock, and seed crop operations.

Money flows to the community to solve agricultural issues that are founded in common ground. We will work to provide funding for ecological restoration. Projects are being completed in a timely manner, and we have field trips for legislators and citizens to see the successful results.

Ranchers and farmers don't feel like their interests are pitted against fish. Ranchers and farmers will have time to go steelhead fishing.

Anglers are included in the process, and their opportunities and concerns are acknowledged and addressed. They share their opinions about specific concerns and are willing to work on solutions with local stewards of the resources.

Anglers enjoy more functional watersheds with more water on the land for fish and other land uses. All streams have healthy populations of fish with ample opportunities for anglers to catch them. Access would be retained to healthy stream environments that are managed for sustained fisheries.

Environmentalists are trusted players in the process of protecting and restoring our basin. Environmentalists will work together with all groups and make more informed decisions. They will have the opportunity to contribute and be heard. They are listened to and respected, and their stake and interest in the "common good" is acknowledged. They will be able to trust that all groups are making the best decisions for the environment, and they get to spend more time enjoying the places they love.

The ecosystem processes are functioning in an effective and efficient manner, and all creatures benefit. All ecosystems function as they were intended to and all interests are able and willing to communicate their needs and have everyone work to meet them in a balanced way. Our basin is a healthy ecological system with flourishing native wildlife and plants.

There are articles in the paper about successful projects, with interviews with positive quotes. Joint press releases, which are positive. Coyote River Basin serves as a model for the world.

We have a yearly community gathering, to celebrate our successes.

When they are done, the community stands and applauds the work they did. Their voices are excited as they return to their seats. I provide them a new focus for their efforts.

These are your purposes of working together after the workshop, as you begin to create the future you want. The first sentence of each paragraph is in **bold** to indicate it summarizes the rest of the paragraph. Each of these bolded statements is a separate goal you can use to focus your efforts. YOU will give the next task.

Strategies and Actions: The Panel

YOU ask Allen to begin the panel: "Allen, what strategies or actions would reflect your new beliefs or behaviors and make our purpose happen?"

Allen: "Thank you. And thank you to the county commissioners for inviting us as representatives of the tribe. I believe this is the first time that we have been able to participate in a conference like this. And I thank all of you here for making Crista and I feel welcomed and for treating us with great respect. We have learned, both of us, to have respect for all of you.

"We have a different relationship with this basin than any of you. We have lived here for uncounted generations. We care for all of the land. We care for all of the living creatures. Our biggest concern right now is for the salmon, who could find their home in this river if it were improved to its original condition. That may be asking too much, but I believe we need to work to increase the river flows so the fish can return. This is our deepest heart's desire. The flesh of these fish feed our soul and our spirit. They are our culture and our religion.

"What I have learned here is that we need to get better understanding between all of us. We can only do that if we come together and listen with respect. That is what I have learned from this workshop.

"In spite of our history with this basin, it is as if we have not existed since we welcomed Frank's great-grandparents. For many reasons, we found it important to blend in with the white culture in this basin. It is time that we are recognized, that our culture be understood, and that we are included in any decision-making group. This is a good start.

"County commissioners, it is important to include representatives of the Coyote Mountain Tribe in any group you establish that develops decisions around this basin. I would especially like to see us included on the planning commission and a commission on managing the basin.

"We have the greater part of the history of this land. It is important that you understand that history and understand our culture. So I believe we should be included in gatherings and ceremonies like the county fair so others can experience our culture. In turn, we would like to invite you to come to our tribal gatherings and ceremonies so that you can understand us better.

"I have learned that everyone in this room has claims on the Coyote River; we all have concerns about the health of the river. I believe a good strategy would be to bring the tribes, ranchers, farmers, old-timers, newcomers, businesspeople, and the land developers together to see if we can come together on a purpose to improve water quality and quantity. I know this means attending additional committee meetings. But if we've learned nothing else here, we can only solve this if we do it together.

"This has been a good time. I feel welcomed here. This is what I have to say."

After Allen has finished speaking, YOU wait, allowing Lynn to pick up the dialogue.

Lynn: "Let me start by saying that I agree with everything that Allen just said. I'm amazed at my own ignorance about this area, even though I have been here for over seven years. It is as if we all lived on different planets.

"And yet I considered it my responsibility to encourage the updating of the land-use plan and to encourage strong zoning. I did this, really, without considering others. I did not consider if the county commissioners, the planning commission, and the county planners would take care of that part. I guess I was just concerned about the unplanned growth in the basin.

"I just think we need to start all over again on the land-use planning and zoning. But this time do it right. I liked the purpose statement that we just heard a while ago. It has all of our words and desires. While it is only inclusive of our opinions, we can add to it by including others at future meetings.

"I especially liked the idea of maintaining both agriculture and the open spaces by supporting the ranchers and farmers and maintaining our sense as a rural community. I'm not sure I understand all that means, but surely, what we have done here is part of it. So I would like to see more circles like this in each of the communities, and that includes your community, Allen.

"If we update the land-use plan, we need to include a socioeconomic strategy for the Coyote River Basin and make sure it highlights the values of our rural communities. We can do that by including all of the different stakeholders that are represented in this room and others who would need to be added.

"No matter how we feel about further development of the basin, it is going to happen. I realize now, Jack, if we don't protect our ranching and farming community members, and they are unable to make a living wage with their land, then it will just be sold, subdivided, and filled with lots of homes. I don't think anybody here wants that to happen.

"So we need to explore some ways to help agriculture in this basin be more than marginal. I don't have any solutions to that, but I believe we need to find some. Listening to Donna from the Rural Conservation District, it sounds like there are some approaches we can use.

"As I said, I have been here for seven years. I have never felt part of the community until today. I think what we have done here is to begin to build a real community in the basin. I want to thank you for that, Jack. If it weren't for you and your cadre of ranchers, I believe we would have moved ahead and approved the land-use plans and zoning to your detriment and our detriment. You sure scared the hell out of me when you came out of the woodwork, but since it got us to this place, I guess it was worth it. That's all I have to say."

Jack: "Well, I'm not sure if we've done anything here than just a lot of talk with no action. But I do like what I hear. It sounds at least like there is some consideration for working over the land-use plan and zoning regulations to consider our needs. If we're included in that, then that will be some positive progress.

"I do have to admit that I've never had as many hugs as I have had this week. I think I got three from you, Lynn. I'm not much of a touchy-feely guy, but I have to admit I liked it.

"I think we have all learned enough here to agree that we need to rework the present land-use plan and zoning regulations. In particular, we need to find some flexible ways that will permit us ranchers to look at our land as alternative options for income. The most important thing we ranchers and farmers can have from this community is understanding and support of our situation. We're not looking for handouts here; we can take care of ourselves when it comes to making a living.

"But we need to have you relax these regulations to allow us to do some spot zoning. Our ranch has a substantial amount of frontage along the river. I don't have any current plans to do this, but if the time is right and we need the money, this would be a great place to put in some cabins or guesthouses or campgrounds that could be used to provide access to the river. It would be an extra source of income for us. There are others of us in the basin who would like the same opportunity.

"I've got to admit, though, we will need to clean up that river and find some ways to get more water into it. People aren't going to recreate here or fish here if the river isn't clean and there are no fish. We need to start by making sure we keep whatever water we have here in the valley. We can't afford to have it sold to the metropolitan areas. We need to have uses for this water, and agriculture is a good one.

"I agree with Lynn that we can ask Donna and the RCD folks to help us figure out ways to use our water more efficiently and maybe even return some of it to the river. We can look at that with all of you, like Allen suggested, provided that we can control the rights that we have to that water. It might be that the idea of piping some of those irrigation ditches will help us do that. If so, we will need the support of this community to find a way to get the money to do that.

"I apologize to you, Allen. I admit we have not given much consideration to the tribe. I wouldn't say you've been invisible, but I do think we tend to ignore your presence in the basin. We can maybe think of lots of reasons for that, but I'd prefer to look at what we can do in the future.

"So I would want to have other folks from the tribe represented with any group that we have. And I appreciate your offering your hand to help us figure out how we can keep agriculture in the valley and yet get more water in the river and hopefully find a way to have the salmon return.

"It's not that I'm opposed to cleaning up the river in bringing salmon back. I just never thought about it. When we were kids, we would fish that river and pull salmon out by the basketful. But you know, over time, with the lack of attention and with our need to just make a living on the ranch, I guess we didn't recognize what happened. I would like nothing better than to have my grandchildren and great-grandchildren be able to hook salmon in that river in the future.

"I think the county commissioners present here need to take most of the responsibility for seeing that whatever ideas we come up with are made to happen. Just don't leave us out this time."

Ann: "I'm not sure how much I can add to what has already been said. As a Realtor, I make my living by selling homes and land. I certainly don't want to have my opportunities limited by zoning. But I've lived here long enough that I also don't want this valley filled up with lots of homes and strip malls and have to pay high taxes to build the infrastructure for the subdivisions.

"I believe there are plenty of lots platted already in the basin, and if we just focused on what we have now, that would help us decide what to do in the future. But the costs for roads and sewer and water systems are going to be pretty high in the undeveloped areas, so I do think we ought to look at putting more of the development around the three communities we have. That would reduce those costs.

"I agree with Lynn and her committee. One of the most important things we can do is to keep our agricultural lands so that we have this beautiful green open space that makes our basin so beautiful.

"I am really concerned about the economy of the basin. We need to find some way to improve our economic situation, to bring in more small businesses that really fit in our valley. We have to find a way to replace the jobs that were lost when the lumber mills were closed. I don't know how we can do that unless we bring some additional people into the basin. And if we do that, we have to find some way to provide low-income housing for young families and for people who would work for those small businesses.

"One thing we could do is begin to work together on these issues. That's a great way to understand each other, to do something together. You know, maybe we could all get together and build a Habitat for Humanity house in an area zoned for that purpose. We could even try to build one of those a year. It would be a start.

"It would help if we all consider ourselves as one community in this beautiful basin. Yes, we have the three communities and the reservation and the basin is over sixty miles long. But what every one of us does is going to affect all the rest of us. So we might just as well begin to come together like this and make decisions that will create our best outcomes that we just heard earlier."

Ann looks at YOU, signaling that she is done.

"Let's all stand," YOU say, and everyone stands, knowing that this is a moment for honoring. "I would like the panel to come to the center of the room, if you would.

"Rayni, I would like you to honor the panel for helping us get ready for our strategies and actions task."

Rayni looks a little shocked at first, then steps forward just a bit, stops, and thinks. Then she speaks:

"You guys have just done a really terrific job. I have been an environmental activist in the basin since I graduated from college and came here ten years ago. I hooked up with Alice, and I know we have been a thorn in your sides ever since. I've been pretty outspoken and pushy because I thought it was the only way to somehow protect the environment in this basin. I realize now that what we really need do is what we did today: do this together. Listening to you talk, I realize that by working together we can bring back the beauty we have lost in this basin and keep what we've always had.

"I'm excited to get in my group and share with everybody my ideas about what we can do together. I want to thank the four of you for making it possible to feel that way."

As the circle applauds, the four in the center turned to shake hands and then hug. I notice Jack getting his fourth, fifth, and sixth hugs. For someone who doesn't like touchy-feely, he appears to be enjoying it.

The Small Groups: An Activity

YOU direct the community to move to the small groups:

"OK, the panel members will be the facilitators in your group. Remember, you will answer the same questions that they did. So get in your groups. Bob will move us ahead."

I step to the edge of the circle opposite YOU.

Diane and Neil, I'd like you to join your original group if you would. This is a good activity to be part of, and you'll have an opportunity to put your two cents into this information. I really appreciate the work you did in putting together the collective statement.

I turn to YOU. You and I will facilitate the group for the rest of the day.

There is much movement and an air of excitement as the groups move their chairs into a circle in front of their flip charts.

YOU continue to facilitate the task: "Please close your circle. The panel member is your facilitator. You will answer this question: *What specific strategies or actions can I think of that would reflect my new beliefs or behaviors and that would make this purpose happen?* You will not be recording this information; this is a talking circle. Take your turns. Listen with respect to each other, without interrupting."

YOU turn and walk away from the edge of the circle. There is an immediate busy hum of people taking their turns to speak.

I have the opportunity to observe the four groups busy at work. Soon the noise level in the room begins to rise, and I can see that people are beginning to interrupt one another. I motion for YOU to help with this.

YOU walk to the edge of the circle and speak: "If I could get your attention please?" YOU have to repeat this a few times before everyone is focused on you.

"I just want to remind you how important it is in this task to listen with respect. What I have observed is, as you become excited about the ideas that are being presented, you started interrupting each other.

"Relax yourselves; you will have ample time to speak. Keep focused on what each person is saying. If you have another idea, wait your turn. All ideas are important. So, move forward, but listen with respect."

A busy hum starts up and I can sense that the groups are totally engaged. As I said, it is not unusual to have to do this. People feel a sense of community, a sense of possibility. They get excited. Almost everyone is leaning in, focused on what the person speaking is presenting. Heads are nodding. I can tell that some of the groups that have been around once are going around a second time. In one group that has completed a talking circle, people are taking turns talking to each other, expressing their opinions about a particular strategy. I allow the groups lots of time to be able to explore the development of the strategies.

Let's listen to Group 3:

Lynn: "OK, since I am facilitator I get to decide who speaks first. I'm going to go to my left and start with you, Kenney. I'll finish with you, Neil."

Kenney: "I'm ready! To start with, I am amazed at how similar the panel was in their approaches. To make this happen, *we have to start with reworking the land-use plan and zoning regulations that we have proposed, just as Lynn suggested.*

"*We need to begin by making sure that we have a purpose and the purpose is clear. I also agree with Lynn, that the purpose we just heard is a good place to start, because it represents all of our views. But in order to be a full community in this basin, we need to begin to include other folks' ideas.*

"*I suggest that we invite the planners from each of the three communities and reservation to help the county put this new land-use plan and zoning regulations together. We were acting as if we are the only governmental* entity in the basin. In addition, if we want to focus development around the existing communities, they need to be part of the plan.

"So that means we should have more meetings and conferences or forums throughout the basin. I agree with Allen, we need to include the Coyote Mountain Tribe.

"I don't believe that we are in jeopardy in terms of this basin being overdeveloped right away, but I don't think we have a large window of time before that happens. So we need to begin zoning as soon as we can. I agree to the need to have zones that are specifically for the agricultural lands that provide them some more flexibility. I have some ideas about how we can do that.

"That's it for me. Mike..."

Mike: "It looks like we are all supporting the idea of doing our land-use plan and zoning over again. This time, we need to be sure that the farmers and ranchers are included and that support for agriculture is encouraged.

"In order to get that support, we have to build understanding between all of the different groups in the basin. As Allen said, we need to include the reservation in this.

"Donna talked to me about how the Rural Conservation District can help us with educating community members, both the old-timers and the newcomers.

"Everyone wants to preserve our open space, which is really the land the ranchers manage, and protect our rural lifestyle. I support that idea, just as long as ranchers don't have to pay the price.

"Water is an important commodity in this basin. We know that the metropolitan areas downriver would like to purchase the water rights in this basin. We need to do whatever we can to keep our water in the basin. Sounds like we all agree with that.

"We are used to irrigating our lands with water from the river. I am sure we can use it more efficiently, but I don't have the answer to that question, nor do we have the money to make it happen. I think we could ask Donna and the RCD to be the group that helps us with this.

"I'm sure the basin would benefit from having more of these meetings, but we have to get beyond the group that is in the room. I don't know how much time the ranchers and farmers can volunteer. Many of you who are here today are getting paid to be here. We are not; we have work to do on the ranch. It is being delayed.

"I'll listen to what the rest of you have to say."

Bud: "Well, I guess it's up to me then. *I agree with the idea of doing the land-use planning process over again, as long as we keep much of what we have already done.*

"*We need to consider relaxing the regulations so ranchers have an opportunity to develop a small amount of their land to provide them additional income when they need it. From my history with their culture in this basin, this is a necessity. We need to be appreciative of the ranchers and farmers for having kept this open space so beautiful for us in the past.*

"*I would like to see as much of this open space preserved as possible. I noticed that is mentioned quite often in the purpose statement prepared earlier.*

"*I liked Ann's suggestion that we get together and build a Habitat for Humanity house a year for our young people.* I believe the bank would be willing to support that with some funding. This is an example of how maybe we can begin to solve some of these problems ourselves if we work together.

"When we talk about having a rural culture, that is one of the values we've had in the past that we seem to have lost—the ability to work together, to help each other. *I think we should continue doing what we're doing here throughout the whole basin. I think we could ask Bob to help us do this, or maybe he could assist the facilitators he trained for us.*

"*Water is the lifeblood of this basin, as most of you have already said. We better do everything we can to keep it here. But, if we are not using it efficiently, that will be difficult to do.*

"When I was a kid I can remember fishing in the river and catching salmon. I can't remember when that ended, but we sure need to do something about it. I would be willing to help in any way."

Bud looks at Kathy sitting next to him and pokes her.

Kathy: "Bud always had sharp elbows." (She smiles.) *"I want to see this process continued throughout the whole basin. We need to hold communication meetings. We used to call them 'greeting, meeting, and eating meetings.'*

"*I'm on the county fair board, so I believe that we could invite the Coyote Mountain Tribe to participate in a more culturally oriented way this year.* I'll be glad to meet with Allen after this workshop. *I also think we ought to highlight our rural values during the fair.* Instead of talking about this, we could start doing some of it.

"I pretty much agree with what's been said so far."

She looks at Wayne.

Wayne: "*I think we have to have a lot more communication, like we have had here, where we can be honest and where we listen to each other.* That sounds to me like rural values.

"*When we rework the land-use plan, let's make sure that as many folks as possible can be involved in it.* I think we could ask Donna to help us get people to some of these meetings in the future.

"*I'm very much interested in how we can make more efficient use of our water.* I've been giving lots of thought to this in the past. Being a fourth-generation rancher, I don't believe we can keep on doing stuff in the traditional way. We have got to do it differently. If we want to keep the open space that you folks refer to, which is really working lands to us ranchers, then we have to have water on that land. But there is no reason that we can't find some other ways to efficiently use it. Otherwise, other people will try to take it from us.

"*Donna was talking to us about a national riparian team that could help us do this. And I think we ought to see if we can find some funding for putting pipes in our ditches.* If we can do that and cover them up, that would do away with the problem we have with the new folks in the subdivisions messing with our ditches.

"*We can't do any of this if we don't trust each other. I believe we need to do more communicating between each of the groups represented here. If we listen to each other as we have done here, we will better understand what each group's needs are. Then we can get together and figure out how to do it.*

"*We could start by having the planning commission and the planning department rework the land-use plan and include everyone from the basin in that effort. Everyone needs to feel a part of the process.*

"Like Mike said, we have lots of work to do to keep the ranch going. But I believe we can find time to do this. It is important."

Mark: "I am really amazed at what we're doing here. I thought I came here to get away from a lot of people. Where I lived outside of Pittsburgh, we didn't have a lot of relationships with our neighbors. We were all sort of isolated. So people can't be with each other. I didn't like people coming in and crowding me. I realize now that because of this urban cultural view, we tend to use our regulations to set boundaries on others.

"I understand that now. This is how people in the basin feel about us newcomers. What we are doing here this week is really what I was seeking. Creating a sense of community. Being part of a community, one in which people listen to you when you speak. I just didn't know it at the time. I know you folks in the room better than anybody in the neighborhood that I lived in or the job I had.

"*Let's do everything we can to continue to bring people together. We all have an interest in keeping the Coyote River Basin as beautiful as possible. I understand now that we need to keep agriculture, the ranchers and farmers, as profitable as they can be. Our land-use plan has to provide for that.*

"*So we need to develop better connections and communication between every group in the basin. We need to know what the needs are for every group. Everyone needs to feel part of any process we have in this basin.* I introduced myself as an introvert and find myself enjoying being an extrovert. And, like Jack, enjoying the smiles and the hugs.

"*We need to find a way to create that understanding between all the groups here. We need better communication between you old-timers and us newcomers. The best way to do that is to have groups come together to figure out how to best manage this basin.*"

Neil: "*We seem to all agree on reworking the planning and zoning. I also hear support for the notion of making sure we have a clear purpose that represents our basin. The short-term purpose we heard this afternoon is a start. I suggest that we also create a longer-term vision for how we want this basin to look like when we turn it over to the next generation.*

"*We need to focus on rebuilding the trust that has been broken in the last three or four months. Trust between all of the stakeholders in the basin is critical.* If we trust each other, we can get it done.

"*That means we have to find lots of different ways to communicate with each other.* The planning commission and the planning department can do that for us.

"So far we have focused an awful lot on this process, and I think it's time that we get into some of the steps to get us there. Each group will probably have different things that they have to do, so that means *we have to be inclusive in developing strategies to get what we want. As Wayne said, everyone needs to be part of the process.*

"I'll turn it over to you, Lynn."

Lynn: "*Well, I've already had my say, so I will be brief. First, we need to rework the proposal for land-use and zoning. We need to be sure that the tribe is included in this. We need to get as many people involved as possible. Kenney, I like your idea about including the planning departments from each of the three communities and from the tribe.*

Strategies and Actions

"In updating the plans, we need to look at the social aspects and the economic aspect and have some specific strategies for dealing with that. Part of our purpose needs to be protecting our rural culture and values. Let's develop some strategies for doing that—maybe not here, but in the plan.

"We need to support agriculture in the basin, the ranchers and farmers, not just to keep open land, but because it is the right thing to do. They reflect the rural values that we all treasure.

"I'd like us to continue to communicate, not just on this issue, but on other issues that are confronting us. For example, figuring out how to manage the river and the water that is being used so that we can bring the salmon back. I like the idea of having a group established just to do that.

"Does anybody else have additional strategies or actions?"

The group begins to have discussions between individuals about what they have expressed, putting ideas together and creating new ones.

Lynn: "Bob wants to know if we have all spoken. Have we? OK, looks like we're ready to move on. Bob wants us to pass out these three-by-five cards first. So let's do that."

As cards are passed out, the members of the group stand, look for writing instruments.

Lynn: "This is the question Bob wants us to record the answer to: I wrote it down on my card: *What specific strategies or actions did you hear that you support, including your own, that would express your new beliefs and behaviors and foster your best possible outcomes, your purpose?*

The group immediately begins to record on the three-by-five cards, silently, deliberatively.

Lynn: "Have we all recorded enough? Bob asked us to check. So, it looks like we are ready to move ahead? OK, looks like I am going to be a recorder, so, Kenney, why don't you facilitate the group through this?"

"Okeydokey," Kenney exclaims, "let's reverse the direction and start with you, Mark."

This is what Group 3 recorded on its flip chart: (These are all actual recorded statements from real workshops.)

GROUP 3: STRATEGIES AND ACTIONS (PAGE 1)

- *Establish better communication and connections between the tribes, ranchers, newcomers, environmentalists, and the rest of the community about their needs.*
- *Assign the Planning Commission and Planning Department to rework the land-use plan.*
- *Everyone needs to feel part of the process.*
- *Continue to build trust.*
- *Develop a sustainable socio-economic strategy for Coyote River Basin that highlights rural community values.*
- *Include in long-range planning the protection of agriculture land and open space.*
- *Rework the land-use and zoning plan.*
- *The county will make sure we have a purpose for the Coyote River Basin.*
- *The discussion was focused more on process and needs to move beyond and discuss specific ideas and strategies.*
- *Trust by all stakeholders toward one another is key.*
- *We have a strategic vision from the county in which everybody designs their actions for achieving that strategic vision.*
- *Rework the land-use plan and zoning regulations to include what we learned here, then get full agreement and act.*
- *Make sure the purpose is clear.*
- *More meetings and forums throughout the basin.*
- *Build trust.*
- *Do whatever we can to keep our water in the basin for basin use.*
- *Assign the Rural Conservation District to educate and improve relations with new (all) members of the community.*
- *Preserving open space with land-use planning that will protect agriculture and rural lifestyles.*
- *Relax regulations to allow ranchers to have some spot zoning—be it commercial or some type of residential. Allow land leasing for other purposes that keep the open spaces.*

> **GROUP 3: STRATEGIES AND ACTIONS (PAGE 2)**
> - *Maybe the folks from the entire basin could build a "Habitat for Humanity house," for our low-income residents. Build one a year.*
> - *Allow all of our rural communities and our rural culture to not only survive, but to flourish throughout the basin.*
> - *Preserve the open space.*
> - *Continue the process through the whole basin in small circles and large circles.*
> - *Hold "communication" meetings. "Greeting, Meeting, and Eating."*
> - *Focus of the county fair on rural values and culture.*
> - *Preserve our green open space*
> - *Develop more flexible regulations to allow compatible uses of ranchlands for other purposes.*
> - *Work to get water flows and fish back in the river.*
> - *Exploration of water use methods that are more efficient.*
> - *More fencing at river systems.*
> - *The land-use and zoning plan needs to be reworked.*

YOU have each of the groups read off the strategies and actions they have supported. When each recorder has completed reporting, the whole community applauds. Each time this happens, extemporaneously, it is an affirmation of their support.

As the information is read from the flip charts, I mentally identify some key points I can share with the group. When all have reported, I share this summary view with them:

I noticed that every one of your groups has suggested that the county commissioners take the time to listen to people in the community and revise the present proposal for the land-use plan and zoning. Almost every group wants this process to be inclusive. In one group it was suggested that the three communities and the reservation planners be involved in this next iteration of your plans. I also noticed that you suggest a role for the Rural Conservation District, which means Donna helping out with providing information and working to gain understanding in the county about the needs of agriculture.

It is also interesting to note your often-repeated desire to continue to maintain your rural culture and rural values.

You spoke about the need to retain your water, use it more efficiently, and improve the river so the salmon can return. There is a unique proposal to establish a Basin Watershed Council to create water and fish solutions. This would be inclusive of all the communities in the basin, the agricultural representatives, and representation from the Coyote Mountain Tribe.

I also noted there is a suggestion that, while you agree with the purpose that was read off after lunch, other members of the community and stakeholders of the community need to be involved in improving this.

There is also a proposal to perhaps create a longer-range vision of how you want your basin to be. With that in mind, after the break we're going to take time to do two things. I'm going to give you an insight about these strategies that you developed. And I'm going to have you begin to explore the notion of a twenty-year vision for this basin. We're going to do that in the large circle, so I want you to move chairs before you take a break. Make sure we have a circle and not an egg shape, then go ahead and take a fifteen-minute break.

But before you do, during the break, I want to speak to Bob, Donna, Mark, and Johanna. I would also like Marcia to join us in the center of the circle.

Oops, I see that Justin has his hand up. Go ahead, Justin.

"I Don't Know!": An Insight

"I have a concern because our communities have not participated in this workshop," Justin says. "How are we going to get the people outside this room to be willing to use this process?"

First of all tell me what your concern is. (Note, I did not answer his question, but asked for more information.)

"Well, you know this was new for us and we came reluctantly. I know I didn't know what to expect and was a little put off when I saw the circle. But now that I've been in the circle, I am very comfortable with it, and I'm very comfortable with what we have done here. But they won't be."

So, I responded, your concern is that the people outside this room will feel as you did when you came in and saw the circle for the first time. And you're wondering what can be done to make them more comfortable and accept it?

"Yeah…I guess so."

We answered this earlier for Rob, but it bears repeating. Let's start by writing your question on the flip chart. (I write the question down as he asked it.)

"~~How~~ are we going to get the people outside this room to be willing to use this process?"

Rob, what can I do with this question?

Rob is surprised that I call on him, but he responds right away: "Take away the word 'how' and then the question can read: 'We are going to get the people outside this room to be willing to use this process.'"

Thanks, Rob, I say, you have good recall. So, Justin that is our purpose. Now what is one thing can you do that will make that happen?

"Ahhhh, I don't know?" Justin responds.

I wait with a pause and then ask, If you did know, Justin, what would your answer be?

Thinking and then speaking slowly, he replies, "Well I guess we would just set it up and let them experience it like we did. None of us left, and if we are also seated in the circle without complaining, they will probably just accept it."

So, Justin, we have taken your how question, turned it into a purpose, and you now have stated at least one way that you can accomplish that purpose.

Remember two things now. The first is that a how question can be rephrased into a purpose statement. I can then ask you what can be done to accomplish that purpose.

The second is, if someone answers with "I don't know!" then pause and ask them, "If you did know, what would your answer be?" What happens when you ask the second question is that your right brain seeks an answer. You just created the Vanna White effect. You just created a space that required a "leap of imagination." Something will instantly come to mind.

Because you created the open space that I talked about on the first day, you will find people almost immediately responding, without conscious thought, and providing you with a perfectly acceptable answer. This allows you to keep the conversation going, whereas asking a "how" question tends to stop it immediately.

I have one caution on this. When you ask this question, pause after the person says, "I don't know." Then use a tone of voice that is inquisitive, not one that is commanding. Sort of like, "Gosh, that is understandable, but if you did know, what would your answer be?"

"Yeah, I got it. Pretty cool!" Justin says with a smile on his face.

OK, let's take that break.

There is a scramble as chairs are moved into a large circle and people distribute themselves toward the restrooms, coffee, cigarette breaks, and phone calls.

Strategies and Actions: Collective Statement Summary

There is rarely time at this stage of the workshop to develop a collective statement of all the strategies and actions. This is done as a follow-up to the workshop when the final report is developed. For your information, what follows is how this group's strategic plan would look, based on the information developed here.

This example is a summary statement. The entire statement would take up five pages and has much repetitive material. The summary is created from the bolded statements that are the first statements in each paragraph.

The way to read this summary document is to take a summary statement such as:

Open lines of communication within the basin community and between ranchers and the rest of the community.

And look in the complete document, where you will find these supporting statements:

Open lines of communication within the basin community and between ranchers and the rest of the community.

- Communication must be clear and constant. Increase communication. Communicate.
- Communicate...open lines of communication. Communications.
- Communication; TV and some paper.
- Communicate and build good relationships. Constant communication.
- Communication and website. Do e-mails.

The complete collective statement includes all statements made. Repetitive statements are the result of the members recording their answers to the question, "What specific strategies or actions did you hear that you support...?"

This is one of the important components of collective statements. Every statement made is included in the final document. You can tell how many people in this group of thirty-three responded with either dialogue or communication as a focus: thirty-eight statements supported this concept of open lines of communication.

(All of these words were expressed in one of the seventeen workshops used as the basis for this book. Some paraphrasing is done to protect those who might be able to recognize their statements and feel offended. The original intent is kept.)

This is the full and complete statement of *only* the first segment of the strategies and actions:

1. Revise the Land-use Plan and Zoning Provisions.

The county will make sure we have a clear purpose for the Coyote River Basin:

- Use our workshop purpose as a starting place and add to it. Involve others.
- Make sure the purpose is clear. Develop purpose into the process. Have a clear purpose. Set a purpose. Establish purpose.
- Defining the purpose up-front: Focus on using the process.
- Establish a common purpose for protecting and sustaining our rural communities and values.

We have a strategic vision from the county in which everybody designs their actions for achieving that strategic vision.

- Agree on a vision.
- Build a coalition of community members that describe a vision of what the basin will be in twenty years.
- Specifically define each of the stakeholder groups' key purpose in a way that will allow measurement toward success.
- From this each group can work together to design the tactics of a specific action each can take to achieve this direction.

Rework the land-use plan and zoning regulations to include what we learned here, then get full agreement and act.

- Assign the Planning Commission and Planning Department to rework the land-use plan.
- Include representatives of the Coyote River Basin Tribe on the Planning Commission.
- Preserving open space with land-use planning that will protect agriculture and rural lifestyles.

- Include in long-range planning the protection of agriculture land and open space.
- Preserve open land. Preserve open space.
- Zoning to preserve open space. Identify productive ranchland, and create zoning or codes to protect said lands from development. Identifying real agriculture property to support.

Structure planning and zoning in specific ways that permit ranchers to develop alternative income options.

- Develop more flexible regulations to allow compatible uses of ranch lands for other purposes.
- Design in flexibility in zoning to allow targeted development by ranches (bed-and-breakfasts, guesthouses, cabins along the river, campgrounds along the river).
- Relax regulations to allow ranchers to have some spot zoning— be it commercial or some type of residential. Allow land leasing for other purposes that keep the open spaces.

Shown below is the summary for the entire collective statement. You can see how the first segment, whose full statement is shown above, is summarized in the collective statement, as well as the summaries of other strategies and actions.

Strategies and Actions
Implementing Our New Beliefs and Behaviors
To Foster Our Purpose:
A Summary

COYOTE COUNTY:
1. Revise the land-use plan and zoning provisions:

- The county will make sure we have a clear purpose for the Coyote River Basin.
- We have a strategic vision from the county in which everybody designs their actions for achieving that strategic vision. Agree on a vision.

- Rework the land-use plan and zoning regulations to include what we learned here, then get full agreement and act.
- Structure planning and zoning in specific ways that permit ranchers to develop alternative income options.

2. Move beyond to specific ideas and strategies:

- The discussion was focused more on process and needs to move beyond and discuss specific ideas and strategies.
- Form smaller subcommittees to generate more discussion.

3. Rural communities and heritage:

- Establish as a common purpose: sustainable rural communities.

4. Continue to build trust with dialogue and transparency:

- Continue to build trust. Trust by all stakeholders toward one another is key.
- Establish transparency and trust by holding open, noticed meetings.
- Assure the inclusion of all participants.

5. Building clear understanding between differing groups:

- Keep dialogue open, and continue these stakeholder meetings.
- Build clear understanding between newcomers, environmentalists, and the ranchers/farmers on the land.

6. Maintain communication and honest dialogue throughout the Coyote River Basin:

- Open lines of communication within the basin community and between ranchers and the rest of the community.
- More meetings and forums throughout the basin.
- The goal: to continue building and strengthen the feeling that we are a basin-wide community.

7. Community building events:

- Let's do more community building from one end of the basin to the other. Community building and unity. Community building.

- The Coyote Mountain Tribe will provide invitations to rituals.
- Design social interactions for us old-timers and newcomers to begin strengthening our sense of a total basin community.

8. County establish a basin watershed council to create water and fish solutions:

- An empowered, funded basin watershed council that has the authority to create workable solutions for water and fish.
- Do whatever we can to keep our water in the basin for basin use.
- Work to get water flows and fish back in the river.
- Encourage more efficient agriculture, resulting in more water in the stream.
- Explore alternative ways to increase fish populations.

ASSIGN THE RURAL CONSERVATION DISTRICT TO EDUCATE AND IMPROVE RELATIONS WITH NEW (ALL) MEMBERS OF THE COMMUNITY:

1. Inform the general public about the ranching community and the situation they face.

- Establish better communication and connections between the tribes, ranchers, newcomers, environmentalists, and the rest of the community about their needs.
- Work with the RCD to get grants to get things done.
- Developing value-added options and alternatives for agriculture: Basin Cattleman's Association work with the RCD to provide education on alternative crops and agriculture co-ops like Country Natural Beef.
- Develop local markets for local ranch and farm products.

~43~

A Long-range Vision

Developing a Long-range Vision

While the others are on a break, YOU and I meet in the center of the circle with the five people I designated: Tony, Mark, Johanna, Crista, and Marcia. I introduce the long-range vision task.

After listening to your strategies and actions I noticed that there was a focus on having a vision for the basin. But let me see now...

I look around at the flip charts and pick out the exact statements:

"We have a strategic vision from the county in which everybody designs their actions for achieving that strategic vision." "Build a coalition of community members that describe a vision of what the basin will be in twenty years."

Then I say: You are a panel who will help the community group begin to envision what they want in twenty years. I want your community to start that process before we end the session. So each of you is going to take a three-by-five card and answer this question:

Because you work together successfully, accomplishing your purpose, how will people describe Coyote River Basin and the county twenty years from now?

Record your response to this question on the three-by-five card. When the group returns to the circle, I'm going to talk about your development of strategies and actions. I will then read this question to the circle. You are going to help them get started by reading off your vision for this basin twenty years from now. I will then ask the rest of the group to answer that question on three-by-five cards that will be placed on their chairs.

You will notice that they will become silent as they record the answer to that question. This task allows them to go internally, to think carefully about what they want in twenty years. Then I will have them read their visions from the card. After the workshop is over, we will develop a collective statement for this long-term vision, and it will be included in the strategic plan that you have developed in this workshop.

While they are reading off their visions for the next twenty years, I would like you to add on your three-by-five card any visions you hear from other people that you like. At the end, I will have you read these off. This is one way of beginning to develop a consensus around a long-term vision.

After that, Marcia, I'm going to have you facilitate the last activity—a closure for the entire group.

I turn to YOU and ask you to coach Marcia for this activity. YOU explain to her:

"We will remain in the large group. When we are done with the vision statement, I want this group to give advice to the three county commissioners, Allen for the tribe, and Donna from the RCD. These five will listen as the others provide that advice."

YOU pass Marcia a three-by-five card with the questions and instructions on both sides of it.

"So you will first pass out three-by-five cards to the circle. Then provide them the questions and wait until you feel they have all completed writing. Then you will ask them to do the following: answer this question—*How do you feel about this workshop?*—and then read off your advice from both sides of your card."

Record the answer to this question:

What is your advice to the county commissioners, the tribe, and/or the RCD for the next step they need to take in moving ahead?

On the other side record the answer to this question:

What you are willing to do to make our vision and purpose happen?

(Answer this question: How do you feel about this workshop? Then read off your advice and your commitment.)

A Long-range Vision

"Marcia, can you repeat the task for me?"

"Yes," Marcia replies, "it sounds like you want me to facilitate the last task. One group is going to give advice to us county commissioners, Allen, and to Donna. And the question is..."

(reading from the card) *"What is your advice to the county commissioners, the tribe, and/or the RCD for the next step they need to take in moving ahead?"* Then you want me to wait while they record their answers, and when they're done, I will ask them to answer the question on the other side of the card: *"What you are willing to do to make our vision and purpose happen?"*

Finally, when they are done recording, they will answer this question in the large group: *"How do you feel about this workshop?"* And then I will have them read off the advice and their commitment they have on their three-by-five cards. How did I do?"

"Wow! I said, that was pretty awesome. When they are done reading off their vision statements, I'll have a few comments to make and then I'll turn it over to you. OK, take a break—what's left of it at least." YOU can coach Marcia through during the break.

As YOU and Marcia depart, I move toward the large circle, noting that it is shaped more like an egg with an indentation in the middle. I begin to move chairs so they form what I consider to be the "perfect circle." As I do this, other members of the group join me so that we quickly have rearranged the chairs.

I ask those who helped with the chairs to move the group back to the circle. I announce to the group that we are ready to start the next activity, so they should move back to the circle. This community of people has been talking to each other throughout the break. They're engaged in some pretty deep conversations. It is difficult at these times to get them to return. But with a little bit of help from others, we are finally seated. I begin talking:

We are getting ready to reach closure on this workshop. Starting yesterday afternoon, you explored the situation that existed in this basin, how it got to be this way, and how you are feeling about it in small groups. You heard the collective statements from this activity this morning.

We then explored the worst possible outcomes of confronting or not confronting the situation. You also heard those this morning. We've developed a purpose statement—a set of best possible outcomes that would be fostered by working together as a community. We read the collective statement for this after lunch today. This could be considered your short-term purpose.

It is not unusual for a group of people to question their ability to make such wonderful outcomes happen. So we had you explore all the reasons that people would say, "It is impossible to create those outcomes." As these were read off, I made you aware that the statements were, for the most part, belief statements that would get in the way of accomplishing your purpose. So we followed that activity with you each identifying new beliefs and behaviors you would be willing to consider in order to accomplish your purpose.

This was followed by the last activity, in which you explored the strategies and actions that would carry out the beliefs and behaviors you have, and consequently create your best possible outcomes.

Putting all of these together would result in a strategic plan for the basin. I would call it an interim plan, because it still needs input and advice from other people, as you have indicated.

I will create this document for you and send it to the county commissioners, the Tribal Council, and Donna. If you agree today that it is your intent to accomplish that plan, then the county commissioners can move ahead with it.

I am often asked to help groups set priorities for their strategies and actions. I'm always reluctant to do this, because every strategy you identified has the possibility of creating the outcomes you desire. In a river basin that is as diverse in its people and diverse in its landscapes, one strategy will not always apply. You need a broad range of strategies that this group can select from, that would be more specific to improving your particular situation. So I consider all of these strategies as appropriate, allowing each group to determine which strategies apply to their situation.

Given that, if I were to return to help you assess your accomplishments at the end of the year or two years, I would not focus on your strategies. Instead, I would have you assess how well you have accomplished the outcomes that are stated in your purpose statement. As an example (reading from a flip chart):

"We create a common, clear vision for the basin that is attainable, and we work together to move toward that future.

"Coyote County involves the community when making decisions that affect the community, even if it is hard."

In six months, if you were to reconvene to do an assessment, I would ask you to give me the evidence that you have created a common and clear vision for the basin that is attainable. Or, what is the evidence that you have worked together to move toward the future?

In answering either of these questions, you would be assessing the progress you made in accomplishing your purpose. I could then ask you, what are the strategies or actions that moved you in that direction? The list of actions you would report may or may not be the same as those you have on your strategic list. As you involved other people, you may have found strategies that are very specific to making that improvement.

Your purpose is what is important. If you focus on the strategies, when you do the assessment and find you have completed them, but the outcomes you want still have not been created, then you have wasted your time. You want to focus on: *Have we created the purpose outcomes that we want for this basin?*

As I listened to the strategies and actions you read off before the break, I noticed the stated desire to create a longer-term vision for Coyote River Basin. We will address this strategy now. We will create a first description of that vision before we do the closure. You'll notice that each of you has a three-by-five card on your chair. You will use these to develop your statements for a twenty-year vision.

I have asked four people to create some statements in advance so you have an idea of what a vision would look like. You will all answer the same question they will: *Because you work together successfully accomplishing your purpose, how will people (or your children and grandchildren) describe Coyote River Basin and the county twenty years from now?*

The panel members are Mark, Johanna, Tony, and Crista. Let's start with you, Tony, and then we will go counterclockwise. *(Remember that these are actual recorded statements from real workshops.)*

Tony, reading from his card: *"Coyote County is recognized as one of the most beautiful, economically stable, and welcoming places to live. The river is bordered by green pastures with quality, cool water filled up with native fish, including salmon.*

"Our land-use and zoning plan is progressive, well-supported, and protects the rural character and scenic values of the basin."

When Tony is done, people look to see who is next. Johanna begins to speak, reading from her card.

Johanna: *"Coyote River Basin will look much as it is today, only more beautiful.*

"We have good schools and have created higher-education opportunities in the basin.

"More of the students graduating from our schools choose to stay in the valley, creating new industries and commercial opportunities."

Mark: *"We have created a rich sense of community, because we will have worked out solutions to today's problems.*

"We approach all of our problems collaboratively. Newcomers to the basin are able to understand long-time residents through inclusive, meaningful dialogue on community issues.

Crista: *"The community recognizes the values of the Coyote Mountain Tribe as a true asset.*

"The tribe has improved economic opportunities with their casino, and there are few unemployed members. The casino employs others in the basin.

"The tribe is able to practice their rituals and religion with the return of the salmon."

YOU provide direction to the rest of the community from your place in the circle: "Thanks to the panel. The rest of you will now record the answer to the same question: *Because you work together successfully accomplishing your purpose, how will people describe Coyote River Basin and the county twenty years from now?*

"Could you repeat that more slowly?" Rayni asks.

YOU repeat the question again, more slowly. People are already recording on their card, some scribbling fast, others thinking more deliberately and then writing. Silence descends upon the room. Marcia, seated across from me, looks up and smiles. She gets it. She knows she can do this.

Soon, people begin to talk in muffled tones indicating the group has completed the task.

YOU ask the group: "Has everyone had an opportunity to record everything you want?"

A few hands rise, indicating they have more to record. Soon it is obvious they are done, and YOU have everyone's attention.

"OK, I'm going to start with Todd. I want the panel to listen until everyone has had an opportunity to speak.

Todd (recreational resort): *"The county only approves development that preserves the natural character of the basin. The salmon have come back. Water is being used by the ranchers more efficiently."*

Diane (college student/rancher daughter): *"Every interest group participates, advocating for their needs and making contributions to consensus solutions. Our agricultural community is thriving and healthy. The river has been restored, with enough water to go around for agriculture, recreation, and the fish."*

Gil (developer): *"This is a place where young families can live and prosper in the agricultural business. Some ranches have become prosperous enough that they have reclaimed some previously subdivided land area. New subdivisions take into account wildlife, fish, water, and social concerns, and are hidden from view."*

Cliff (developer): *"Developers of subdivisions have provided the infrastructure necessary to meet county zoning regulations. We are able to keep our young people working here. Our businesses pay good livable wages for younger workers. Our schools are growing again."*

Dawn (county water department): *"We have created a Coyote River Basin Watershed Council that has demonstrated their ability to create workable solutions for all resources in the basin. Our aquifer appears to be recharging because of its changes in irrigation practices."*

Jack (rancher): *"Our ranches and farms are being irrigated by water that is piped and in some instances pressurized. Surplus water fills the rivers and streams.*

"We create a beef co-op, like Country Natural Beef, so we can maintain good cattle prices.

"The younger generation is managing what they love and have respect for the land as it has been for generations.

"The tribes are respected and honored by all other groups."

Susan (tribal biologist): *"We have a Watershed Council that includes the tribes, ranchers, farmers, business, recreational interests, and other representative citizens, including the Hispanic community, whose purpose is to improve the water quantity and quality in the Coyote River.*

"The tribe sees the return of salmon, the antelope, deer, and other wildlife."

Jim (district ranger, USFS): *"We are modeling a community consensus decision-making process that others follow to create their own sustainable communities and lands. We are an example of how successful change can be made from within, rather than being imposed from outside forces.*

"We are including the Hispanic community in all of our decision-making processes."

(**These statements are a sample of what is expressed in the entire circle.** The following twenty-year mission statement includes the expressions from the entire community.)

When everyone has had their opportunity to speak, I ask the four panel members to read off any additional best outcomes they had on their three-by-five card. They answer in reverse order to their first panel presentation.

Crista (tribal vice chairperson): "I liked this idea because it relates to our desires for our tribe: *We have preserved the traditional ways of ranching.*

"There is affordable housing for all the young people, including the tribe.

"We are including the Hispanic community in all of our decision-making processes."

Johanna (retired educator): *"We support strong and productive ranching families and communities. We make decisions in the interests of all basin communities."*

Mark (retiree): *"Where possible homes and businesses are located close to the towns."*

Tony (county commissioner): *"We keep our water rights in the basin. No additional water is being sold outside the basin."*

When Tony is done I get the group's attention.

Before we do anything else, pass those three-by-five cards to Diane, and she will hold them for me until the end of the session.

This is a long-term vision. It describes the Coyote River Basin that you would like your children and your grandchildren to experience. You will want to give others an opportunity to add to this long-term vision as you develop a new plan. You will find, even though these people have not attended this workshop, they will have answers very similar to yours. The more people talk about their vision, the more likely it is to happen.

It is important to understand that every strategy or action that you initiate must have as its intent and purpose the creation of both your short-term outcomes and you long-term vision. The way to do that is to just keep asking the question, "Will this strategy or action accomplish our purpose and mission?" When you do that, you remind people of what your purpose is, and you will find yourself focusing on strategies that will create your desired outcomes.

The clients I have worked with, thousands of them over the years, have always been able to accomplish their best possible outcomes. Normally, they accomplish them in a much shorter time frame than what they originally considered.

The Best Possible Outcomes for the Basin in 20 Years: A Long Term Mission

(Note: Statements in *italics* are those expressed in the conversations above.)

In twenty years, *Coyote County is recognized as one of the most beautiful, economically stable, and welcoming places to live.* The river is bordered by green pastures with quality, cool water filled with native fish, including salmon. Cattle are still grazing on the range, and green pastures are fenced from the riverbanks to protect the river. We are proud that our elected officials have worked with the basin communities to maintain our quality of life, which we cherish so much.

We have a clear vision of where we are going and are aware of the accomplishments of the past. We are able to meet the constantly changing goals because we are successful. We are no longer dependent on using the judicial system to implement a single agenda.

In twenty years, Coyote River Basin missions, purposes, and our strategies always include the entire community and the entire watershed. Because of this, we have intelligent, well-planned communities and towns that reflect our visions. People who live here enjoy a high level of personal freedom and a sense of personal responsibility toward each other.

The work we did this week has created a rural sense of community, with respectful lifestyles and rural values. *We have created a rich sense of community, because we will have worked out solutions to today's problems.* When local decisions are made, the interests of all basin communities are kept in mind. We make decisions in the interests of all basin communities.

We have learned to work together to reach solutions for all. Ranchers and farmers, environmentalists, recreationists, and tribal members are not divided or adversarial. Newcomers to the basin are able to understand our long-time residents by being included in meaningful dialogue on community issues.

Collaboration is rampant because of partnerships developed during this time. *We approach all of our problems collaboratively.* Our decisions are based on inputs from communities, tribes, agencies, farmers, and ranchers with respect for the diverse priorities and needs. *Every interest group participates, advocating for their needs and making contributions to consensus solutions.* Environmentalists work with us to find workable solutions that develop healthy subdivisions and a healthy environment. *We are including the Hispanic community in all of our decision-making processes.*

Our land-use and zoning plan is progressive, well supported, and protects the rural character and scenic values of the basin. The land-use and zoning policies that we developed have limited urban sprawl without devaluing properties. Our land-use and zoning plan enhances the local economy.

We have created a Coyote Basin Watershed Council that has demonstrated their ability to create workable solutions for all resources in the basin. We have a watershed Council that includes the tribes, ranchers, farmers, business, recreational interests, and other representative citizens, including the Hispanic community, *whose purpose is to improve the water quantity and quality in the Coyote River.* The Coyote Basin Watershed Council has created a consensus plan which has repaired and improved the Coyote River habitat, resulting in salmon recovery.

New urban and rural developments are located close to the towns. When possible, homes and businesses are located close to the towns. The county only approves development that preserves and reflects the natural character of the basin. We are a well-planned county that has growth directed toward the towns. Development is confined to community areas.

We have been able to create social and economic growth in all our communities, rural and urban. Our communities are desirable places to live and work. The basin has vibrant and profitable businesses, as well as productive and profitable ranches and farms. *Our agricultural community is thriving and healthy.*

Our small businesses are succeeding, and employment continues to increase. Businesses are succeeding. More economic diversity has been brought to all of our communities and to the reservation. *Our businesses pay good livable wages for younger workers.* New local businesses are created, providing support to our agricultural enterprises and other businesses.

Our economic prosperity is providing opportunities for young people graduating from our schools. *We keep our young people working here. More of the students graduating from our schools choose to stay in the valley, creating new industries and commercial opportunities.* We have ample opportunities for work that supports our young families.

There is affordable housing for our children and grandchildren. *There is affordable housing for all the young people, including the tribe.* We have affordable, low-income housing for those who choose to live here.

The Coyote District schools are filled with students. *Our schools are growing again.* Our schools are gaining students. *We have good schools and have created higher-education opportunities in the basin.*

Our agricultural community is viable and productive. *We have preserved the agricultural open space and the traditional ranching way of life. We have preserved the traditional ways of ranching.* Our sons and daughters have been carrying on the agricultural lifestyle.

We support strong and productive ranching and farming communities. Our ranches continue to be intact for the future generations. Our ranchers and farmers are appreciated by the broader community and they take pride in the work they have done in keeping the basin landscapes green.

In twenty years Coyote River Basin continues to be green, clean, and fresh as it is today. *Coyote River Basin will look much as it is today, only more beautiful. The river has been restored, with enough water to go around for agriculture, recreation, and the fish.* The river has been restored, and there is enough water to irrigate the ranches and farms.

Our ranchers no longer need to subdivide their lands in order to be financially stable. *Some ranches have become prosperous enough that they have reclaimed some previously subdivided land area.*

This is a place where young families can live and prosper in agricultural business. My first grandchild will be born and grow up ranching with parents and grandparents. *The younger generation are managing what they love and have respect for the land as it has been for generations.*

The value of food production in the basin is recognized and acknowledged by all. Local communities' support ranching and farming by buying local agricultural products. *We create a beef co-op, like Country Natural Beef, so we can maintain good cattle prices.* The food industry comes to Coyote River Basin to buy and process our quality agricultural products.

The community recognizes the values of the Coyote Mountain Tribe as a true asset. We have a higher awareness of their tribal rights and the progress they have made toward bringing salmon back to Coyote River and all of its tributaries. *The tribe is able to practice their rituals and religion with the return of the salmon.*

The tribes are respected and honored by all other groups. Coyote Mountain Tribal members trust and respect all others in the basin and vice versa. *The tribe has improved economic opportunities with their casino, and there are few unemployed members.* Our tribal youths are realizing their academic, social, and economic potential, as are all other youth in the basin.

New subdivisions take into account wildlife, fish, water, and social concerns, and are hidden from view. Developers of subdivisions have provided the infrastructure necessary to meet county zoning regulations.

The Rural Conservation District works with the community, developing relationships of trust and cooperation between agriculture, newcomers, and ranchers. The Rural Conservation District is able to get sufficient financial support from all levels of government, local, state, and federal, so that we have become more efficient and productive in ranching and farming.

Water rights remain in the basin, with no additional water being sold to the metropolis outside the basin. *We keep our water rights in the basin. No additional water is being sold outside the basin.*

Water is being used by the ranchers more efficiently. *Our ranches and farms are being irrigated by water that is piped and in some instances pressurized. Surplus water fills the rivers and streams. Our aquifer appears to be recharging because of changes in irrigation practices.*

There is an improved and positive habitat for salmon and for other wildlife. *The tribes sees the return of salmon, the antelope, deer, and other wildlife.* We have clean waterways, a healthy environment, and habitat for the four-legged creatures. *The salmon have come back. There is the return of the salmon and other fish populations.*

We are modeling a community consensus decision-making process that others follow to create their own sustainable communities and lands. *We are an example of how successful change can be made from within, rather than being imposed from outside forces.* Other areas of the world who are in resource conflicts come to Coyote River Basin for a model of how to move from conflict to harmony.

~44~

Advice to the Leaders

Providing Advice to the Leaders

YOU and I met earlier with Marcia, Tony, and Frank, the three county commissioners; Allen, the chairperson from the tribe; and Donna from the Rural Conservation District. I spoke with them about the closure for this workshop.

We're coming to the moment of closure for this meeting. At the end of the meeting each member of this group will be providing you advice on the next steps to take. They will also state the steps they are willing to take. I have asked Marcia to facilitate that closure. I would like the five of you to be listeners while the community provides you with their advice. Marcia, Tony, Frank, and Allen, you are all elected officials, while Donna is representing the RCD. Since the Rural Conservation District was assigned some specific tasks, Donna, you can listen to those first steps that relate to your organization.

When all of the community members have provided their advice, I want each of you to tell the group what you heard and how you're feeling about it. I want you to also express what you will need from this group in order to move ahead.

The purpose of this is to make certain that your community knows that as elected officials you understand what was developed here. They will also want to know if you are willing to move ahead with this. If you are, they will follow you. I'll start with Donna, then Tony and Frank, then Allen, and finish up with you, Marcia.

Marcia, Tony, and Frank, I want you to get together for a few minutes before the break is over. As elected officials of the county, you symbolize the oneness of this group. In order for a group to feel like they have truly made a decision to move ahead, it is necessary to have that symbol of "oneness" acknowledge the decisions that have been made and affirm their support for it.

So talk about what was developed yesterday and today and decide if it is something that you can accept as elected officials. You can check the collective statements on the purposes, strategies, et cetera. I'm not asking you to make a formal decision; that should be done in your normal public arena. Instead, just determine if the purpose, vision, and direction that have been developed during this workshop is something you would be willing to support and make happen.

I turn to YOU. I want you to facilitate the get-together with the three commissioners. That lets them focus on listening to each other.

You will be speaking last in this task, Marcia, as the chairperson of the commission. I'll be asking you to be as specific as you can in acknowledging what you heard, including from other commissioners and putting it together into a statement that will allow this group to know that what has been developed here is supported and that you are willing to move ahead with it. If you can do that, that will jumpstart everything you've done.

Remember, Commissioners, it is your choice. If you do not agree, say so, and I will help you move forward the next step.

Later, when the community returns to the large circle, I remind the group of their last task.

You are now going to give the elected officials and Donna from the RCD your advice on the next steps to take to accomplish both your short-term purpose (page 546) and long-term mission (page 595). Your short-term purpose is on that flip chart. I point toward the flip chart.

Marcia, as chairperson of your county board, is going to facilitate the last task that you have for this workshop.

Marcia has a pack of three-by-five cards in her hand; she splits them and sends them both directions around the circle. She waits patiently until everyone has one. Then she speaks.

"I got together with the other commissioners earlier today and a few minutes ago, and we began to talk about how we're going to move ahead with the mission and recommendations that you have given us. This is not going to be an easy task to redo the land-use and zoning plan, especially since we need to involve the three communities as well as the reservation. So we're going to need as much help from all of you in this as we can get.

"I want to begin by asking you to record on that three-by-five card the advice you would give the county commissioners, Allen, and the RCD. Answer this question: *What is your advice to the county commissioners, Allen representing the Tribe, and/or the Donna from the RCD, for the next step they need to take in moving ahead?*"

She repeats the question and then begins to record on her card. She waits until everyone has recorded the answer. Then she gets their attention.

"Now, turn the card over. Record the answer to this question on the other side of the card: *What you are willing to do to make our vision and purpose happen?*

She repeats the question and then begins to record on her card. She waits until everyone is ready, then she gets their attention.

"OK," she says, "I'm going to facilitate this. Before we begin, I want the county commissioners, Allen, and Donna, representing the RCD, to just listen. When we're done, then we will have you read off any additional advice you have for this group and...what do you need from them?

"I'll start with you, Susan, and then let's go clockwise around the circle." How do you feel about this workshop? What is your advice, and what are you willing to do?

As Marcia facilitates the group, I am observing her, much impressed with her ability to instantly facilitate with confidence. It's an indication that what she learned here will be applied in her county interactions in the future.

Let's listen to a sample of the people providing their closure, their advice, and their commitment to help. (Note: Statements written on the cards are in *italics*.)

Susan (biologist): "I feel very good about this workshop. It was better than I expected. But I am really tired. I haven't worked this hard in some time.

"Being very busy and overloaded at work, I hesitated to come. But it has been worth my while and I have learned a lot I can use in my work and with my family. I just wish we had done this sooner.

"My advice to all of you is (reading from her card)...*We need to start trusting one another. Consider including all of the various special interest groups.* And finally, I liked the idea of a basin working group, so I recommend the county commissioners *take the initiative to convene a basin watershed group to address recovery issues for the river and salmon up and down all portions of the river and its streams.*

"I want to thank whoever set this workshop up for us. I am really hopeful that what we have done here will bring the salmon back for all of us. I will help in any way I can, work with any group to make this happen."

George (resort, business): "Well, it was an OK session. Not exactly my cup of tea, but like Susan said, it was better than I expected. It was certainly better than our previous meetings where we just yelled at each other. I would do this again if it had the same kind of results. I would hope it wouldn't take three days though.

"My advice is self-serving, I know, but important. We will need an increase in recreation uses to help replace what we have lost economically. *Develop recreation to help diversify the economy.*

I also think Donna and the RCD should help us. *Educate and communicate with other parts of the community, establish relationships and alliances through personal contacts like this.*

"Like Susan, I will help in any way I can. I will work on any group you ask me to."

Jack (fifth-generation rancher): "I am really tired. I never sit in the saddle this long! And these chairs are harder than any saddle! I felt this was well worth my time. I learned lots of ideas I can use on the ranch and with my family. My wife told me last night she was surprised that I was really listening to her when she talked about her day. And my teenaged daughter actually smiled when I listened to her complain without lecturing her. I guess that means I need to do more of it!

"I also appreciated having met all of you people who I didn't know before. I used to know almost everybody in town. I don't believe that I have bad feelings with anyone in this room. That has really reduced my stress level. I hope we can keep this up.

"My advice to Donna with the RCD: You have a lot of knowledge that the county has not tapped into. *Help the county highlight zoning proposals that would have unintended consequences to the ranching and agricultural community.*

"*Explore different funding approaches, grant programs, private foundation subsidy programs, to help our ranchers to prosper a little more.*

"*Identify long term funding opportunities to improve irrigation efficiencies.* I think you could help us find ways to be more efficient with irrigation.

"*Commissioners, add Donna to your planning commission.* As a member of the RCD board, I will see that they understand what we have agreed to do. I will help Donna accomplish the directions we are giving her.

"Lynn, I'm inviting you and your husband out to my ranch, this weekend or any time you can make it. Might as well see if you can sit on a horse without being tied down. We can talk about how we can bring these newcomers into our community and make them friends. Maybe even plan that BBQ.

"We used to be like this in the early days, helping each other out, trying to keep things on an even plane. But change has come, I guess, so we need to change too.

"I'm tired and glad this is over. I'm not sure I can handle any more hugs.

"And Bob?" He looks at me as he asks a question. "I have some people I want to honor. Could I do that now or wait?"

I suggest you wait until the circle is done. Then we can take time to honor as many people as you want. I will provide time for that.

Jack leans back, satisfied. "Thanks, Bob. That's all I have to say."

Crista (Tribal Council member): "I want to thank the county commissioners for inviting representatives of the tribe to this meeting. It was an honor to be with all of you. I am especially grateful that you actually listened to Allen and I speak about the concerns of our people. I appreciated that you acknowledged Allen as the leader of our tribe and have included him as one of the elected representatives here. I now feel we would be welcome at any meeting we attend. I did not feel that way before this workshop.

"This was a good time. Much of what we did here in the circle is in the tradition of my people. We take the time to listen to all. We listen with respect, as Bob describes it, because we honor each person, even though we might disagree with them.

"My advice: *Make sure tribal representatives can be at the table and explain the importance of water and fish in the Native American spiritual lifestyle and in their everyday living.*

"We all must make a commitment and stay with this, no uncertainty.

"Like Jack, Allen and I will make sure our council is aware of what we are doing. They will need to make their decisions about participating in this. I have an interest in the basin watershed group you might create. I would work to bring the salmon back through that group."

Jim (US Forest Service): "I have to agree with everything that has been said so far. I think we have a consensus in this group that we want to be a community with rural values. We have practiced that here, so I know it can be done.

"My advice is: *The next step is to continue what we started!*

"We need a community concept of the future—how far out are we managing?

"*Hold another meeting with this group.* Let's build on what we have started.

"I will help using my agency's support. Everything we have talked about and agreed with fits the mission of the Forest Service. We will support your plans to bring the salmon back and use the water more effectively. I would hope to be part of that basin watershed group."

Lynn (newcomer/advocate): "I am so relieved that we had this time together. I have grown to appreciate and respect all of you so much.

"Jack, I wish we had done this to begin with—don't you? We have wasted so much time and created so much anger by not being aware of, or considerate of, others. I have learned to understand ranchers' needs and to appreciate what you provide for the basin. I want so much for your family to pass on your heritage to your grandchildren. I want the same for the tribe, Allen and Crista. It is what I would want if in your place.

"So, my apologies for not getting it right to begin with, but I am so happy we did this workshop. Think of how much we have learned and how well we now understand each other.

"My advice to you county commissioners is: *We need a community and basin-wide vision/goal.*

"*Immediately work on redeveloping the land use and zoning plan from bottom up with new ideas.*

"*Develop policies that include ranchers as collaborative partners in developing private land regulations.*

"Donna, I am so glad you are here to help us with that. You know the ranchers' needs better than anyone else.

"Finally, *this workshop group can be an advisory group for the commissioners, on reviewing whatever strategies or direction we take as a result of this workshop. Bring us together and use us as a sounding board.*

"I am going to meet with my group tomorrow and report to them our progress and get their support for this plan. That's all I have."

Mike (rancher): "In all my years I really can't remember when I have spent three days and got so much from it. I guess 'an old dog can learn new tricks.' I came here mad and I leave satisfied that the ranchers' views were heard, and I think we will make better decisions as a result. I wouldn't give two bits for a 'newbie' last week, and here I am sitting by Lynn and liking it.

"I probably should apologize to all of you for being so angry at the meetings I attended. But I think you understand why I felt as I did. I was feeding my reptilian brain!" (Much laughter.)

"I like that last vision we wrote, and it's what our county should be. I like that you understand the ranchers' needs much better and that all we're asking for is your support. Consider us when you make decisions, make them so we can survive. We don't want to see all that working land turned into subdivisions either.

"Allen, we need to get together more often. Our connections to the past are too important to ignore. We won't be as rowdy as in the past, but surely we can enjoy our memories of that. So..." (reading off his card) *"the Tribe will become part of our larger community.* I'll support that and make sure it happens.

"Kenney, this is my advice to you and the planning department:

"Create flexible zoning for agriculture lands that still maintain good planning principles. I like the idea of adding Donna to the planning commission.

"Advice for the commissioners:

"Hold your meetings outside the commission office and travel up and down the basin. This will help you stay in touch with the people.

"You also ought to attend our RCD meetings and Cattleman's Association meetings.

"I also will speak to my group, Lynn, and get them on board. Donna can help me with that at tonight's RCD meeting. We will report good things to them."

Cliff (business): "I didn't think I could sit this long in these hard chairs. Next time, get us more comfortable ones. I still wonder if we needed all this time to get the job done. It was a long time to spend. But it wasn't tiresome. Maybe it will help not only us but the entire community.

"I am a member of the school board. My advice is: *We need to use this approach in developing a strategic plan for the school district.*

"My advice to all of you: *Listen to the people because they have great ideas.*

"Finally, my interest is in our economic health: *Work to bring in a diversity of small businesses to the community.*

"That's it. I don't have that much spare time, but I will help any way I can. I will support our plans at any future meeting."

Johanna (retired educator): "I agree with everything that has been said so far. It is hard to add more. I liked the workshop. I think we needed all the time we took. In fact, not taking enough time is part of our problem. I like Bob's idea of going slow to go fast.

"I feel like I have made so many new friends.

"I agree with Cliff, so my advice I wrote was:

"We can't afford to not pay for good schools. If a community has good schools then people (companies, retired people) will want to come to the community.

"We need listening sessions in our local communities.

For all of you listening, remember this advice: *We want to really be listened to and be valued.*

"Let's not let the community down, now, let's move ahead quickly and finish the plan. I can help since I have lots of time on my hands this summer and fall."

Alice (environmentalist): "Well, this is something I have always hoped would happen, that we could get together as a community and resolve our issues around keeping our basin green and healthy. So I am delighted and grateful for what we did. Like Jack, I have some people who should be honored later for making this happen.

"I believe we all agree on the need to do the plan over. So I wrote:

"Rework the plan to implement ways to keep our county 'green' with more flexible policies for ranchers and businesses that address the concerns expressed today.

"Get this done so we can adopt and accept the land-use and zoning regulations soon.

"I also appreciated that Allen and Crista are here; they added a lot to our discussions and they deserve to have some attention as the ranchers do. My advice?

"Invite the Tribe to participate in meetings with others, to help resolve fish and water issues.

"Lynn doesn't need to apologize. I have lived in this community all my life and yet I overlooked the ranchers when pushing for zoning. So, let's include them and listen to them.

"I am going to report to my group on the progress we made and make sure they are on board. I will help in any way I can."

That's a good sample. All the remaining members make their statements in a similar fashion. The final advice is in the following collective statement.

When the last member of the community has spoken, Marcia turns to Donna and gives her, Allen, and the commissioners clear instructions for the closure:

"What I want you to do now is to tell us what you heard and how you feel about this, and then add what you will need from this group in order to move ahead."

Donna (RCD): "I appreciate having been invited to attend this workshop. I have met so many good people here, I am grateful to be part of this community. Each of you has taught me something.

"I have also learned new tools and techniques that will help us in managing the RCD meetings. We often interrupt each other, become reptilians and get adrenalized, and then never get to make a decision. That contributed to the turmoil and chaos that happened with the zoning proposal. If we are going to create the vision we developed, then we need to use this process to help us.

"I heard support for our purpose and mission and an agreement to redo the plan with more inclusion of the public. I agree with that. I also heard you want the RCD to work on relationships between the agricultural community and the newcomers, to gain understanding. I am willing to do that with support of my board. Frank and Jack can help me with that.

"I wrote my advice on a card also, much of it based on what I heard.

"For the commissioners: *Work more closely with the other communities' elected officials and the tribe's officials, to create more closely connected discussions about the whole county and basin.*

"*Engage other ranchers in the basin with the newcomers, environmentalists, and others to change their relationships.*

"*Explore the 'Agricultural Trust' approach for farms and ranchlands to protect open spaces.*

"*Support ranchers so they will feel confident about their future.* Then maybe subdivision development wouldn't seem an attractive alternative.

"I am going to recommend that *we include a tribal member on the RCD board.*

"I think that all of you have to talk to those who support you and let them know that we have agreed on a common direction. They need to be on the same page as we are. I will see that the RCD board members participate in any further meetings on the land use and zoning plan."

Tony (county commissioner): "We got together as commissioners a little earlier and came to the same conclusions that the rest of you just expressed. We all agree that we have to do the land-use planning and zoning plan over. We have to do it with a process that includes more people and that specifically takes into consideration the special situation of the ranchers and our farmers. There is support for having a vision for the county, and the one we created earlier is a good start. The purpose statement that was read after lunch gets us started on the way.

"So, I agree with what the rest of the group says and am willing to support, along with my fellow commissioners, moving ahead. Kenney tells me he has some good ideas on how to get started. I believe he can help us be successful.

"This is my first time as county commissioner, so...my support of the effort to upgrade our land-use plan and zoning plan was a beginning effort to try to protect our beautiful basin from being inundated from the outside.

I also felt that with the loss of our lumber mills and closing of the mines, we needed something to replace these economic factors.

"In my view, cleaning up the river and bringing the salmon back could create a recreation economic base. This would, of course, require that we begin to have some controls over where subdivisions are placed. It would also require that we do something to clean up the river and bring the salmon back.

"I believe the other members of the commission will support the Tribe's proposal for the casino, Allen, and we can build that into the work we are going to do.

"I know now that we didn't do the zoning plan exactly as well as it could've been done, but at least it got us together and in a position to move ahead with consensus.

"These are the bits of advice I've heard that I agree with:

"We need a community and basin-wide vision/goal.

"The next step is to continue what we started!

"This group can be an advisory group for the commissioners, on reviewing whatever strategies or direction we take as a result of this workshop.

"Actively involve yourself to understand the issues that ranchers have.

"Be inclusive with others as you change the plan by reaching out to the public. Include Donna on the planning commission, as well as someone from the Tribe.

"What we need from you is to do what Donna suggests. We have to be sure that we're all going in the same direction. We need to let people in the basin know that things have changed for the better. They need to take a deep breath now and work with us."

Frank (county commissioner): "I've lived in this county my entire life, so I was just as surprised as the rest of you were when this issue got out of control. While I felt I supported property rights, I was also concerned about the uncontrolled subdivision of our county and the probable costs for infrastructure that our tax system would have to bear. So I believed we needed to do something to control the situation. That is why I supported the land-use plan update.

"I guess I didn't understand that we would also have to have zoning regulations different than what we have now. When Kenney and the planning commission moved ahead with the zoning regulations, I was sort of horrified, feeling like I had betrayed my neighbors. So, I'll have to admit that I encouraged them to protest.

"As some of you have said, we might have done it the wrong way, but at least we got the effort started. The only part of this I'm sorry for is that it created so much turmoil in the different communities, that it separated us, neighbor from neighbor.

"On the other hand, I'm glad we had the wisdom to bring Bob in. I believe that we saved hundreds of thousands of dollars as a result of this. That's how much we would've had to spend in legal fees if we had been stubborn and gone to court.

"We commissioners don't want you to back out on us! Keep in mind that what we're starting here is about the future of our basin and especially the future of agriculture in the basin. We need to 'restore' trust in each other, restore our community spirit.

"We have a good Board of County Commissioners; I'm really grateful to be working with these two people. We can see things pretty strongly in different ways, but I know all of us have the interests of our people at heart. So I will do my best to work with them to make sure we come up with a good land-use plan and zoning plan that everyone in this basin supports.

"I agree with the directions that have been expressed in the circle and will do everything I can to help make them happen. But what we need you to do is to provide the strongest support that you can as we move ahead. You need to explain to your organizations, to your friends, that we have reached this consensus and are going to work together to make it successful."

Allen (Tribal Council chairperson): "On behalf of my people, I thank the county commissioners for inviting me to this workshop. I came to this meeting on the first day wondering how long I would stay. I'm not used to being considered or included in the issues outside of the reservation, so have been pleasantly surprised to be made a part of this group. I thank you for treating us with respect and for listening to our views.

"We have a deep concern for the future of our people. There is a difference between the elders and the way they were taught and the youth who do not have the same respect as those brought up with the culture and traditions. There are our fish subsistence losses and funding constraints.

"So, when we work together and bring the salmon back, we will be grateful. I heard what the commissioners said that they supported and agree with all of them. So I will not prolong the session by repeating them. We will participate in any committee or group that you ask."

The collective statement for the advice to the commissioners, tribe, RCD was developed when the workshop was over. I have included it below so you can see the final outcome. The full statement is quite lengthy, so the summary is intended to provide a more focused view of what was said.

Advice to the Commissioners, Tribe, RCD—The Next Steps: A Summary

(Note: Statements in *italics* are those expressed earlier by the sample of individuals in the group.)

THE COMMISSIONERS:

The next step is to continue what we started! *We don't want you to back out on us!* Don't give up on This! This applies to everyone! If you do, you will lose what we have done here.

We all must make a commitment and stay with this, no uncertainty. Let's keep meeting until we finally reach a solution. *Keep in mind that what we're starting here is about the future of our basin.*

We need a community and basin-wide vision/goal. *We need a community concept of the future—how far out are we managing?*

- Develop common objectives and work collectively to achieve them.
- Condense the mission and purpose statement and the strategies and actions.
- Explore ways to use the best possible outcomes as a way of testing our decisions.
- **Hold another meeting with this group.** We have made progress and we will solve these problems if we stay together and take the time.
- *We can be an advisory group for the commissioners, on reviewing whatever strategies or direction we take as a result of this workshop. Meet with us sometimes to use as a sounding board.*

We need to start trusting one another. *We need to "restore" trust in each other, restore our community spirit.* If we can do this, we can withstand whatever happens in the future.

- We have created a norm by establishing a climate of trust.

Immediately work on redeveloping the land-use and zoning plan from bottom up with new ideas.

- *Create flexible zoning for agriculture lands that still maintain good planning principles.*
- Rewrite the plan based on our suggestions and let the community review and give their views.
- Rework the plan to implement ways to keep our county "green" with more flexible policies for ranchers and businesses that address the concerns expressed today.

Actively involve yourself to understand the issues that ranchers have.

- Go out to the individual ranches and investigate their existing land-use practices.
- Work together with the ranchers to build relationships.
- *Develop policies that include ranchers as collaborative partners in developing private land regulations.*

Get this done so we can adopt and accept the land-use and zoning regulations soon. Decide what is the right direction, then take it. That will keep water on the land, ranches green, and creates open space.

Work more closely with the other communities' elected officials and the tribe officials to create more closely connected discussions about the whole county and basin.

- *Consider including all of the various special interest groups.*
- Consider hiring a full-time county administrator to manage this.

Commit the time and energy to find solutions. Have all the affected parties come together to develop solutions for zoning that meet everyone's best interests.

- Spend two and three days to bring together diverse groups from the community and basin and determine best possible outcomes and supportive strategies.

Let's have another conference somewhere in the center of the basin. Let's plan another meeting, as soon as possible, including everyone, all communities, planning departments, to talk about what we did and decide how to get there.

- Decide when and where we will meet next.
- Develop a process and timetable, a roadmap, and publicize it to the community in a timely manner.

Consider our present county governance process with fresh ideas and open minds. Keep what works and set aside what doesn't work. Reinforce what worked for us here and try it in governance.

- At your meetings keep this relaxed and comfortable setting.
- *Hold your meetings outside the commission office and travel up and down the basin.*
- Model positive behavior consistently and walk your talk. Act as though you believe "we can do it" even if you don't
- *You also ought to attend our RCD meetings and Cattleman's Association meetings.*

***Continue to be inclusive.* Include all individuals in the process and listen without being judgmental.**

- *Be inclusive with others as you change the plan by reaching out to the public.*
- We want to feel inclusion and have a voice in the planning and implementation.
- We will participate if there is not a hidden self-serving agenda.

Learn to be open to what people say. *Listen to the people because they have great ideas.*

- Set a model so people who are fearful can be open. Listen first.
- We need to encourage public participation and be open to public comment.

We need listening sessions in our local communities. Develop a listening program to identify issues, problems, and solutions.

- Hold listening sessions throughout the basin.
- *We want to really be listened to and be valued.*
- Start using active listening and do less interrupting. Listen attentively and with respect.
- Listen, listen, listen! But, don't just listen; hear and acknowledge what people are saying.

Resolve conflicts at the early stage, when they start. Don't be afraid to recognize and resolve conflict when it happens. Be attentive to diffusing conflicts before they blow up. Don't let conflicts get to the extreme stage. Admit to the conflict rather than hoping it will go away.

I like the idea of establishing a basin-wide watershed working group.

- *Take the initiative to convene a basin watershed group to address recovery issues for the river and salmon up and down all portions of the river and its streams.*

We need to use this approach in developing a strategic plan for the school district. We can't afford to not pay for good schools. If a community has good schools, then people (companies, retired people) will want to come to the community. Good schools will create a good economy. A good economy leads to increased jobs—not only entry level but a combination for the community.

Work to bring in a diversity of small businesses to the community. Bring in industries that will build a tax base. We will get better results by bringing in industries that could benefit from our resources (agriculture and water). This would in turn create employment. *Develop recreation to help diversify the economy.*

THE TRIBE

Invite the tribe to participate in meetings with others, to help resolve fish and water issues.

Make sure tribal representatives can be at the table and explain the importance of water and fish in the Native American spiritual lifestyle and in their everyday living.

- *The tribe can provide education to the community and increase awareness of their needs. Become part of our larger community.*
- *Include a tribal member on the RCD board.*

THE RCD

Develop a county program to promote Basin agricultural products, ranches, and farms as important community attractions or assets.

- Develop and advertise a Coyote River Basin brand for promotions to bring tourists here and buy our products.

- An annual County Ranch and Farm Week with parades and BBQs. The ranches could hold open houses and invite community members to learn about their history.

Highlight ranching and farming's central role in Coyote River Basin county.

- *Explore different funding approaches, grant programs, private foundation subsidy programs, to help our ranchers to prosper a little more.*
- *Support ranchers so they will feel confident about their future. Then maybe subdivision development wouldn't seem an attractive alternative.*

Help the county highlight zoning proposals that would have unintended consequences to the ranching community.

- Protect our productive ranch and farmlands through our land-use zoning to keep them whole.
- Develop unique regulations to allow ranchers to do some commercial and residential ventures on marginal lands or lands along the river.
- Ease zoning impacts on possible ranch development with "out of the box" ideas.

Look at new and different ways to provide new regulations or eliminate restrictive regulations to provide ranching greater flexibility in remaining viable.

- *Explore the "Agricultural Trust" approach for farms and ranch lands to protect open spaces.*
- Consider environmental easements for ranches and farms.

Engage other ranchers in the basin with the newcomers, environmentalists, and others to change their relationships.

- *Educate and communicate with other parts of the community, establish relationships and alliances through personal contacts like this.*
- Create a forum for future problem solving between ranchers and newcomers, continuing to build understanding and relationships.

Identify long-term funding opportunities to improve irrigation efficiencies.

~45~

Workshop Closure

The Final Closure

Everyone has spoken except Marcia, so I prepare them for the final closure.

I want all of you to stand. I wait while everybody stands.

This is our final closure; it's an opportunity for final thoughts from the chairperson of the county commission. Would you do that Marcia?

"Thanks, Bob. I will tell you what I heard and agree with first. I did take a few notes, even though I know Bob wants me to test my recall. Let me start by saying that I support the short-term purpose we developed this morning, as well as the twenty-year mission we developed this afternoon. I do that with the understanding that we will have to include other people in the basin and add their views to the statement.

"You want the county to continue what we have started here, and you want to immediately work on developing a land-use plan and zoning regulations that have lots of community involvement. And you want to get this work done soon.

"It is important we have a zoning ordinance that recognizes the need to protect our agricultural economic base and the open green space provided by the ranchlands and farmland. This may require developing some new kinds of regulations along with eliminating restrictive regulations so the ranchers have more flexibility. And I heard Kenney say that he has some ideas about how to do this.

"You want us to hold listening sessions throughout communities in the basin and maybe have another conference that is in the center of the basin.

"Everyone is concerned about how we manage water, and you want to keep it here in the basin. We know the critical uses are agriculture and providing habitat for the fish in the river. You want us to keep the water in the basin and not let it be diverted to Metropolis and other uses downstream.

"You want to establish a basin-wide group that will help us deal with recovery issues for the rivers and streams in the hope of improving the situation for the salmon.

"You want us to always be inclusive; especially you want us to include members of the tribe, the Hispanic community, and the Resource Conservation District on the planning board, the basin-wide watershed group, and other groups we set up.

"And you want to be sure that we listen to everyone.

"You want us to do whatever we can to bring in many different businesses that will provide work, for our young people especially, and that are consistent with our purpose. And you would like those to be sited adjacent to the existing communities.

"You want us to do something about the large number of subdivisions and lots in the county, especially as it relates to providing infrastructure.

"I know there may be more points, but those are the key points that I heard.

"I want you to know that I agree with all of them, although I know as we move ahead and include others, we may decide to slightly change some of them. But we will do that together. I and my fellow commissioners agreed to work together, to do anything we can to support this community as we move ahead together creating our future vision."

When Marcia is finished, the community instantly applauds.

I wait until they are done, then move the group ahead: Jack, you stated earlier that you wanted to honor some people. This is a time to do it.

"I want our county commissioners to come to the center of the room," Jack says. He waits until Marcia, Frank, and Tony come to the center of the room. "Oh," Jack says, "I guess Allen, you should go there too, since you're an important elected official." Allen walks to the center of the room.

"I just wanted to honor the four of you for being willing to take the risk of bringing all of us together. I know it wasn't an easy thing for you to do. This is one time where you tried to represent everyone instead of choosing a side. For that I would like the rest of the group to honor you."

The group applauds with a few shouts. The elected officials and Allen shake hands, some hug, and then they turn to accept the expression of the community.

> **EMPOWERING THE COMMUNITY LEADERS**
>
> Throughout this workshop, I created an environment that distributed the power to every single person in the group. This was done through the use of facilitators, recorders, panels, and so on.
>
> During the last activities of the workshop, I purposely facilitated the redistribution of power to the elected officials and community or organizational leaders. By giving advice to the leaders, each person is investing their power in that leader.
>
> In doing this, I know that the elected officials and other leaders are conscious of empowerment by their constituents, conscious of the responsibility they hold. This represents the movement from "participative democracy" to "representative democracy," where the leaders get their power from their constituents.

Alice, I say, you stated you would like to honor some people.

"Yes, thanks, Bob. I would like the ranchers to come to the center of the room."

Frank, Jack, Mike, Wayne, Crista, and Diane walk to the center of the room.

"Some of you are my neighbors; all of you were my friends. That was before we developed this new land-use plan and zoning plan. I already indicated how sorry I am that I overlooked the impact that this would have on all of you and us too. I appreciate not only the fact that you were here with us in this workshop, but that you were willing to strongly confront us over this plan. It's what got us here.

"While you are few in numbers, your working lands, the ranchlands, make up a high percentage of this valley. It is the open land we want to preserve. And the way in which you manage your irrigation system will determine how well we can bring salmon back.

"I know you left a lot of work back there on the ranch. This time is a major sacrifice on your part. So, I appreciate your coming here and being willing to help us figure out how to do this."

Again, the entire community applauds while the ranchers remain in the center, somewhat uncomfortable to be the center of attention.

When they return to the circle, I notice that Marcia has raised her hand, signaling me to get my attention.

Go ahead, Marcia, I say.

"I would like Allen and Crista to come to the center of the circle."

Allen and Crista walk to the center.

"As long as I've lived here, I have been standoffish with the reservation. I know that many of your people are living in our communities; many of them have suffered because the mills closed and mines closed. I know they suffer for the loss of the salmon, and like the ranchers, you fear the loss of your heritage.

"We have been remiss in our treatment of you, essentially ignoring your people. So, I want to honor you for attending this workshop and giving us the benefit of your ideas and wisdom. I welcome you to be part of our deliberations on any topic in the future. I will see that your people are represented."

As people applaud, Allen walks to Marcia to shake her hand. She steps forward to greet him with hers. Crista is right behind.

Well, I say, it appears that you have done the honoring you needed to do. So, Rayni, you asked me on the first day about honoring someone you do not agree with. How do you feel about honoring today?

Rayni looks surprised, thinks a bit, and then answers. "That seems like so long ago. I really enjoy honoring people now. It was uncomfortable to begin with, but like you said, after listening to people, I feel better about everyone. I see them differently, like they are my community now. I think the greatest honoring we have done is just to listen to each other. I know it meant that to me."

Thanks, Rayni.

Now, I have some people to honor. Neil and Diane, I first want you to answer two questions: *How do you feel about your experience as a facilitator,* and *what did you learn that will help your community be successful?* Let's start with you, Neil.

Neil steps a pace forward. "Well, at first, I felt very self-conscious. I have spoken in groups before and managed meetings before, but this was entirely different. At first I felt separate from the group and missed being inside the circles, but as I was coached, I began to see what was happening in the room differently.

"I found it was very easy to do this facilitation. If you know the right question, you walk to the edge of the circle, get the group's attention, and read the question off. Then you turn and walk away. When I looked back, everybody was immediately at work. Amazing!

"What I learned from this is that we have the ability to facilitate ourselves with all of the issues that we have identified during these three days. While Diane and I don't have the same experience as Bob, I think we know

Workshop Closure

enough that we could help people stay on task, listen to each other with respect, and find a way to make consensus decisions."

He looks at Diane. She begins to speak.

"I agree with all that Neil just said. I felt very self-conscious first, but the coaching really helped me understand what I was doing.

"What I learned I believe I can use in my whole life. With my family, on the ranch, at college, and later helping to manage the ranch. I think I have some very important skills that will help me throughout my life. I'm really thankful I was asked to do this."

She turns and indicates she is done. I continue:

I would like both of you to go to the center of the circle, and Rayni, I'd like you to honor these two members of your community.

"Sure," she says. "I was really impressed with the facilitating the both of you did. If you were nervous, it didn't show. And it felt good to know that we could facilitate ourselves. I know it was a risk for you, and I believe we should honor you for demonstrating that we can facilitate ourselves."

The entire community applauds. Neil and Diane turn slowly to make sure they can see everyone who is honoring them. Then they hug.

Now, I would like the person who helped me facilitate this entire workshop to answer those same two questions.

I look over at YOU. YOU look around the group as you began to speak.

"I had absolutely no idea that I would be doing this cofacilitating with Bob. He just pulled me out of the group, asked me to help him, and immediately began to coach me. He said it was my choice, and as he began to explain my role, I made the decision to accept.

"So I have had three days of an absolutely unique experience. I have learned to facilitate, to coach others, and to provide my take on the work you have done. I believe I have learned a very powerful set of skills that can be very helpful to the community. I have demonstrated the skills, and I believe I can help this community continue with this process if asked.

"The most important thing I have learned is that a group of people in this community can, if we just listened to each other, if we know what our fears and our hopes are, create a sense of direction and come to agreement on how we can make it happen. Bob told me at the beginning that this process was very simple, and yet its impact is very complex. I agree. I hope I get to help this community in the future as we work on some of those broader issues that were identified today."

When YOU are done, I say, I would like YOU to walk to the center.

YOU walk to the center. I can tell you are self-conscious being out there alone. I say:

I want to personally honor you for accepting the task of helping me facilitate this community. I have been impressed with your willingness to learn this unique process and become proficient in facilitating. I would be willing to have you help me facilitate anywhere, and I recommend that this community make use of your new skills and your willingness to use them."

Again, the entire group applauds, with a few shouts in between, while YOU slowly turn around, acknowledging each person in the circle.

When you return to the circle, I begin to speak:

This has been a good time for me. I am grateful I chose to invest my time with this community. It was a good investment. You have all worked hard; I believe you have reached a consensus that you want to move ahead together, that you will be successful.

I'm grateful you understand the importance of ranching and farming and their culture in the community, because it is what will keep the open spaces for you. If you lose agriculture, the land will likely be subdivided, and your ability to control what happens on that land will be diminished.

I encourage you to apply what you learned here. When you attend your next meeting, you will become aware of how dysfunctional most of your meetings are. Do not feel responsible to correct every person or every meeting. Just observe and learn. And, at some point in time, just take one single action.

If someone in a meeting asks a question and is ignored, bring that to the attention of the group and ask everyone to answer the question. Encourage them to speak in turn. You can be seated around a table and do this. When everyone has spoken, ask the person who had the question to tell the group what he or she heard or learned. This will change everything that happens in the group from that point on.

Be aware: this will feel so good to them, they will probably seek you out and ask you to facilitate their meetings. When they do this, remember to do two things. First, get out the learning manual I will provide you in a few weeks. It has the entire process in it, as well as the insights. Second, go through your worst possible outcomes and best possible outcomes of being a facilitator. This will help you be successful.

If you want to use this process, practice on yourself first. You learned yesterday how to resolve the personal conflicts that you have in your own mind. You have control over that entire environment. So take the time to listen to yourself talk about the situation and how you feel about it. Ask yourself what your worst possible outcomes are. Then, think about and record what you would like your best possible outcomes to be. This is the purpose of that conflict or difficulty. You can then ask yourself what specific strategies or actions would help you resolve that conflict. What one step could you take that would move you toward that resolution?

If someone comes to you, especially those of you who are elected officials, be conscious that they come to you with their worst possible outcomes. Your desire will be to either affirm their fears and make things worse, or tell them what your best outcomes are, which will also make things worse.

Listen to what they say. Let them know you heard what they said. Give your perception of the issue if you desire. Then ask them what their deepest fears are...or what they worry might happen...or what it is they don't want to have happen. All of these will allow them to express their worst possible outcomes.

Listen to them; do not deny their worst fears. Let them know you heard them. If you have a worst possible outcome of that situation, then express it. That will keep them from feeling like they are alone.

But then you can do what is rarely done. Ask them what their best possible outcomes could be. What would you like to have happen instead? What outcome would make you satisfied? Listen to them. If you wish, let them know what your best possible outcome would be.

Then ask them, "What can you do that would make that best possible outcome happen?" If they say they don't know, then respond with, "if you did know, what would your answer be?"

This doesn't have to take a long time. Do it conversationally, not like it is some litany of steps that need to be followed. And have a sense of wonderment about it. Be open to hearing what the answer is.

You do not have to use this process for every single conflict you have. Try it now and then, and see how it works for you. In time, if it is effective, people will ask you for your help using this approach.

The Compass Effect: An Insight

When I work with people, I know that if I can cause even one tiny shift in one person's perception, then everything can change in time.

When I was a college student studying forestry, I spent my summers working in the West with the US Forest Service. This summer work in the woods was the practical part of our education. During my first summer season, I was assigned as a lookout/fireman. That meant I would be living in a lookout tower fifteen miles away from the nearest road, situated on the highest peak, where I would scan the horizon for fires. If I saw a small fire on the horizon, I would determine its location using a "fire finder."

If the fire was close enough, I would be dispatched from my lookout with my firefighting pack on my back to be the initial suppression force. This meant I would use a small compass to find the fire.

In preparation for this, I—along with other new recruits—was trained in the use of the compass. When we had learned the fundamentals, we were given the task of finding a "fire" (which was really a red stake) located somewhere out in the forest a mile away that might be visible from a hundred feet. This meant we had to be fairly close to see it.

The compass course was not direct. We had the task of using this compass to find six different painted pegs that had been set out in the woods at different compass points. Our purpose was to go from one peg to the other, with the last peg being the site of the fire.

A degree on the compass was this wide. (I hold my fingers apart about one-sixteenth of an inch.) What I learned from this was that a single degree on the compass, which was about one-sixteenth of an inch wide, would result in a ninety-two-foot variance in a mile. Reading the wrong degree or reading the sighting incorrectly could result in missing the stake entirely.

Needless to say, my first attempts were not successful. A small shift in perception, added to time and distance, made a big difference.

This "compass effect" is similar to the changes I seek when I help people reach consensus. I have learned through experience that this process causes numerous minor shifts in people's perceptions of each other or of the situation. It is the accumulation of these changes over time that allows a consensus to be reached and the outcomes to be attained.

I don't require major shifts in perceptions or major epiphanies to attain the desired results. If I can help one or two or more members of the community to make a shift in their perception of each other or of the situation, that small change over time will cause major changes in the outcomes.

I now am going to do something that some people would call "touchy-feely." I would like you to hold hands.

There is much movement as people do this. Normally, people are OK with it by now.

This connecting of your hands represents the bonds of community that you have developed during your three days here. Take a few seconds to look around the circle at who is here and just recognize how you feel about this community right now.

Workshop Closure

What you see is a community of adults who've taken the risk to come together over a very contentious issue. During this time, you have learned how to listen with respect, learned to facilitate and record for yourselves, and learned how to put your words together into a statement that is representative of the entire community. You have explored your relationship with conflict and developed a purpose statement with outcomes that would justify taking the risk to confront and resolve the conflicts in your life. In doing this, you established a new set of beliefs and behaviors, strategies and actions, that would facilitate the resolution and lead to a consensus decision.

As you were doing this, your beliefs, behaviors, strategies, and actions were congruent with the information you recorded. You were behaving in a consensus manner.

You have applied this basic process to the personal conflicts you have in your own mind.

The last day and a half, we have focused on the real issue. You have had an opportunity to confront each other openly, honestly, while listening deeply to each other. This has led to the development of a short-term purpose statement, a twenty-year mission, the beliefs and behaviors that it will take to accomplish these, and some specific strategies and actions that will foster your desired outcomes. In our last activity, you provided specific advice to the leadership in the community, some first steps that can be taken to move the community in the direction of both long-term and short-term purposes. Finally, you have each committed to supporting the strategies and actions that will accomplish your mission.

This is a community that has worked together for three days, developing consensual beliefs and behaviors, demonstrating your ability to operate as a community. You know how to disagree with each other, and you know how to reach 100 percent agreement. You have five community members who have the capacity to facilitate you through this process.

In the center of the room is a stack of interim learning manuals that you can use until I send you your learning manual developed during this workshop. This can be a guide for you if you decide to use some of these approaches that you have experienced. You can pick one up when we have finished with the circle.

In addition to the learning manual, I will send you an interim strategic plan, which includes a description of the situation, the outcomes you don't want to have happen, your short-term purpose statement or what you do want to happen, the twenty-year mission statement, your beliefs and behaviors, strategies and actions, and the final advice that you provided this afternoon. I call it an interim plan because you indicated you would like to have a broader community have their say with it.

As you look around, be aware of how you now know each other, how different your perceptions are of each other because you have listened with respect. You have reached your agreements while retaining each individual's integrity as part of the diversity of this community.

You know this can be done, because you have experienced it. Now it is time to take it outside this room. You can only do that if you let go of each other's hands. Otherwise, this will be a closed circle, preventing others from participating. So, let go and reach out to others in your community and bring them into this discussion.

Now, honor yourselves for what you have done.

As they let go of each other's hands, they begin to applaud, a group of happy people, satisfied with what they have done. Each of them goes to the center and picks up one of the interim learning manuals.

As they do that, I just turn away and begin to collect the recorded information from the flip charts. I take all the collective statements that have been prepared in the previous two days and add them to the pile of the recorded information from today that will still need collective statements. YOU walk over and help me.

While I am doing this, I am conscious of the community of people who are still talking to each other. Some people left right away. But most of them are still shaking each other's hands, talking about the next steps, making plans with each other, congratulating each other on the work they have done, collecting phone numbers and e-mail addresses, essentially taking action that will continue the connection they have here out into the community.

I notice Jack, Diane, Lynn, and Mark are talking to each other about when they can get together for that horse ride. Their purpose is to also plan a barbecue for the community.

Most people stop by to shake my hand and thank me for helping them. Some ask for my e-mail address so they can ask my advice on an activity they would like to facilitate within their own organization.

Normally it takes over an hour for the community to finally be gone from the room. YOU have stayed behind to assist me in putting the roll of paper together that will be used to develop the reports of the meeting. When this is completed, YOU and I take the time to appreciate the opportunity we had to work with each other. Then we separate, and each go our own way.

PROVIDING SUPPORT

Donna stops by and asks me to help her design a simple process for her RCD meeting that evening. This is the process I develop for her in a few minutes:

My suggestion is that she first picks one of the male participants to help her facilitate the meeting. She chooses Jack.

At the meeting, put everyone in a circle of chairs.

Have **the participants from the workshop** begin by introducing themselves and answering these questions:
- How do you feel about the three-day workshop?
- What did you learn from the workshop that will help the agricultural community?
- What was the final agreement this afternoon?

When they have spoken, the remaining participants in the meeting will answer these questions:
- Introduce yourself.
- What did you hear the workshop participants say?
- How do you feel about it?

Close the meeting with everyone answering this question (on three-by-five cards if you want to have this information recorded):
- What is your advice on the first steps at the RCD needs to take to participate in this effort?

She records these steps on three-by-five cards. She is a quick learner. She calls me the next day to tell me the meeting was successful.

The Symbol of One: An Anecdote and Insight

They stood in the large circle, more than ninety members of the business organization. They had met together for three days to explore a new management and organizational process for improving the way they work and make decisions together. They have experienced the basic process for resolving conflict and reaching consensus.

They had established a large amount of evidence that they needed to change, as well as a short-term and long-term purpose that would result from the change. They had established a list of new beliefs and behaviors and a set of specific strategies and actions that would foster the outcomes they desired. They had reviewed all the collective statements that resulted from this work.

There was no expressed disagreement with the decision to move ahead with what they had created. In the closure, each person stated his or her willingness to move ahead to create this new direction and provided advice to the manager on how best to get started.

Before the closure I had asked the executive, John, to listen to what his people had to say. When the talking circle was complete, I had the entire community stand. I asked John to speak to the group and talk about what he was willing to do and what he needed from his people. This is my recall of what he said:

"I have listened to each of you speak, and I am deeply impressed with your commitment to move ahead with this new organizational approach. I know before we started this workshop, there was a high level of concern and little agreement that this is necessary. I'm glad we took the time to sit together and to work our way through this.

"What I hear you saying is, you're willing to work together and develop this new organizational approach. You have made personal commitments to ensure our success. You have given me some helpful advice, which I intend to follow.

"I agree with the purpose we have developed together and with the decisions that you have made. I am willing to do everything I can to make it possible for this new organizational approach to be successful, so we can be successful. As we move ahead, my door is open to you if you have any suggestions as to how we can be more successful. In summary, I support this new organizational approach and will provide you with whatever support you need to be successful.

"Finally, I am so glad we took this time. I am so proud of us as an organization."

When he was done the entire group applauded and cheered. This was the first time they had ever done anything together, and they had accomplished an important task where they felt committed as a community.

What John the executive did was to create a sense of oneness for his group. I had talked to him earlier about the need for his group to have someone who represented the "symbol of one." In order to move ahead, they needed someone who stated the agreement for them and stated his or her support. That was his role.

I learned this over many years of working with groups in many different arenas of conflict. When a group had reached a consensus decision, acknowledging this in the closure, members would talk to me later about the sense of uncertainty they had. It felt as if there was something missing that would assure them that they had in fact made a decision as a community.

They always moved forward as an organization, but their movement had a sense of tentativeness about it.

Sometimes I'm a slow learner. It took me quite a few years, as I developed this process, before I realized what was missing: what I call "the symbol of one." While the participants might individually agree that they had reached a decision, while they individually heard each other verbalize this agreement, while they individually were committed to this agreement, they still needed someone who would represent the whole.

They had a need for one person, representing all of them, who could state what the agreement was, who could affirm his or her support for the agreement, and then acknowledge that the decision had been made.

This someone is normally the manager. He or she is a symbol of "one" for all the people in that room. When the symbol acknowledges the decision, it has not just been made individually, but it has been made by the whole group. This acknowledgment takes away a tentativeness and uncertainty that would exist without this action.

Before the closure, I normally will take a break. (If you have ninety people who are going to speak in the closure, they better have a break before they start.) I take the manager aside and provide him or her an insight on "oneness" and the role he/she can play if he/she chooses. I ask the manager to listen to the people in the closure as they acknowledge their support individually for the decision and individually state their willingness to make it happen. When they are done, I ask the manager, consider doing the following, if appropriate:

- State what the agreement is that the community of people have made.
- State that you heard their willingness to make it happen.
- State your agreement with the decision and your willingness to support them in making it happen.
- Restate the decision and acknowledged that it has been made.
- Make any final comments you wish to make about the workshop.

I remind the manager that this approach is a choice, that he/she can approach it anyway he/she wants. This not only helps create that feeling of "oneness," but it also places the manager in a leadership mode. The people will vest in him/her the power needed to be the leader in this new direction.

And it is his or her choice. It always makes a difference.

"We Did It!": An Insight

One of the ways I know I have been successful as a facilitator is when my name is hardly mentioned during the closure. If I hear too many people giving me credit for helping them solve the problem, it means I have been more of a "sage on the stage." If, however, they congratulate themselves for the good work they have done, it means I have done a good job as a "guide on the side."

That is not to say I wouldn't like to have them give me the entire credit for what they have done. That is only natural. I'd like to be the wonderful guy who came in with all the answers to save the community. But I am here as a facilitator. It is my job to make it easy, but it is their job to do the hard work. They are responsible for inviting me. They are responsible for choosing to respond to the tasks that I give them. They are responsible for learning as they go. They are responsible for developing all the answers. They have done the work. They deserve to take the credit.

Sometimes I am asked to go to the center of the circle after everyone has spoken, and they honor me for helping them solve their own problem. I accept this, since they are just doing what I helped them learn to do.

So I leave this group, satisfied that they will carry on with this effort. This allows me to leave, to detach myself from this group, to trust that they will move ahead and be successful.

Do I Do Everything Every Time?

That is a good question. The answer is no. I have provided a scenario that would be rich enough for you to experience and learn a process that brings people together, that fosters trust, community, effectiveness, and success. The intent is to provide you the greatest amount of learning and understanding of the approach that I could.

In a normal three-day session, I do not cover all the tasks described or the insights presented in this book. I pick and choose whatever tasks, insights, art, and anecdotes that fit the situation, the group, the time limits, and so on. I may use part of an insight or all of it or none of it. I may use every task in this scenario, or I may use only some of them. It is my choice, based on how the group is developing.

If I am limited to two days, then I provide substantially fewer insights, instead giving focused statements that develop the needed capacity to resolve the issue.

If I am working with a group that has resolved an issue with me before, I will remind them of the underlying beliefs of the process. I will keep them focused on their issue, using their knowledge from the previous sessions. These groups can accomplish in one or two days what it took this Coyote River community three days to accomplish.

You have that same choice, that same freedom, to take the parts of the process that you learned and understand that fit your situation. It is not unusual for people to call me, to ask for advice. I provide this support if time is available.

> *"The real power lies with the group as a whole. No individual or individual group can ever accomplish or create what we can collectively. If one group is left out of the collective decision, we and the decision or solution will be less than whole, and we will all lose."*
>
> **—Cody, workshop participant**

~46~

Resolving Interpersonal Conflicts

Resolving One-on-one Conflicts

Perhaps the greatest challenge people face in the family, the workplace, education, and the community is the resolution of conflicts between two people. Often these erupt on the spur of the moment in workshops, beginning with an apparent minor disagreement, but rapidly progressing to a shouting match between both people. The rest of the participants are shocked and frightened by this outburst. The raised tone of voice will often cause people who are conflict averse to become paralyzed in their thinking, to mentally leave the discussion.

Often the result is that the two parties ask a third party to decide who is right, to choose one of them. To do so is to doom the decision maker to choosing sides, with one party a winner and the other a loser. It is better for the facilitator or the manager to offer to help them resolve their own issue.

This is a situation that facilitators fear the most. I know I did when I started helping others resolve their conflicts. YOU will be no different. The fear is that people will get out of control; that…

- "You will not know what to do, people in the group will become upset and begin to leave, you fail as a facilitator, everyone will hear about it through the grapevine, the story will go through the community faster than grass through a goose."
- "You will never again get a job as facilitator, and you end up on welfare. You are shunned, it is doubtful if your family will ever refer to you again."

—**workshop participant**

Those were my fears the first time it happened. Fortunately, I was conscious of the fears, I acknowledged them, then reminded myself that I was a facilitator and responsible to help my group through this. "I can do this," I said to myself. "Trust myself!"

In my experience, this anger event happens rarely in workshops. Maybe once in more than five hundred sessions. Yet it is highly feared and uppermost in the mind of most facilitators. To them it feels as if it is going to happen at any moment, in every session. And they won't know what to do.

It is quite common in other venues: in the family, in an organizational meeting, in public meetings.

The process that follows was developed over many years of working with numerous interpersonal conflicts. We are going to apply it on a conflict that actually happened, representing a number of situations. YOU are going to be my cofacilitator.

We are facilitating a group of forty leaders from a Midwest community. The conflict is around the issue of the integrity of community leaders. It is specifically related to the leadership of a public organization. The chairman of the school board made it possible for his wife to be selected as a deputy for administration for the public organization. She was barely qualified for the position and yet received the pay of a highly competent manager.

This issue is not new to this community. Those who are elected to higher office tend to hire their relatives in positions for which they are not qualified. Nepotism is considered to be rampant in the community. The leadership of the community has agreed to come together to deal with this issue, but only because the citizens demanded it.

The conversations below are loosely based on my memory of what actually happened in a number of situations. Some statements are paraphrased, based on my recall of the actual conversations.

What follows goes through predictable and manageable stages:

1. The Argument: It often happens so quickly, it is started before you know it. It begins with a minor disagreement, then raised voices, followed by hardened positions and even threats. This is called "storming," a natural part of the process. The facilitator or manager needs to be patient, to let the parties argue for a while, expressing the issue so it is well defined and understood. It is OK to let their positions harden somewhat.

When the parties have volleyed back and forth a few times and are beginning to repeat themselves or further magnify their statements, then the facilitator can move them to the next stage. Often the parties will look to the facilitator or the manager for help in reaching some resolution.

In this case, YOU have started the grounding, moving clockwise. After four people have spoken, Liz has her turn.

She speaks harshly. "I'll tell you what my relationship is with a lack of integrity; I happen to know that Charlie across the room has no business being here because he has none, he has never had any..."

Charlie, sitting just two seats to my left and opposite Liz, immediately interrupts her. "Liz, why are you even bringing this up in the room? This meeting has nothing to do with me, and you know it. You're just looking for another opportunity to once again put me down in front of..."

Liz interrupts him, standing as she does so, looking down on him across the circle. "Go ahead and interrupt me. You always do. You don't let me finish because you don't want people to hear what kind of a cheap, worthless bum you are."

As she finishes that statement, Charlie stands up angry and tense and steps forward into the circle, interrupting her before she continues, shouting, "Why do you always want to start a scene whenever we're at a meeting? I have never done anything to you. You do this at the City Council meetings. You do this..."

"**I do this,**" she interrupts, raising her voice louder, "**because you did it to me when I was on the City Council. You made a fool of me so many times in front of my own people. Where is your integrity?**"

She steps into the circle with her finger pointed at Charlie. Her face is contorted in anger.

Charlie moves to the center with her so that they now are face to face, yelling at each other. She is accusing him of what he did in the past when she was in elected office. He is angrily denying her charges. As she shouts, she jabs his shoulder with a pointed finger.

As the scene is playing out, I look at YOU. You have a startled look on your face, your eyes as big as saucers. YOU shoot me a glance, and I smile and nod my head, signaling it is OK. When I look around the group, I notice there are some people who are as equally startled as YOU. Others have grins on their faces and are whispering off to the side. (They secretly describe Liz and Charlie as being "crazy.")

The movements of each individual are power moves. Each attempts through their behavior to be "one up" over the other. The behavior is escalating. Neither is fully conscious of what they are doing or that they are in the center of the circle.

2. Gaining Attention: The facilitator gains the attention of the parties by quietly and directly speaking to them in a facilitative tone, asking for their attention. Normally, they will be delighted to respond. They suddenly realize they are in the center of the circle with everyone looking at them. They are in a no-win, out-of-control situation and want some way to retreat.

One of the first things I learned was to not stand up and walk into the center with the two feuding individuals. If I did, their emotions would rise to frenzy, and they could become physical with each other.

By remaining seated and keeping an even and moderate tone of voice you will get their attention. There is a tone of voice that will be heard across the angry sounds. It is not necessary to yell, to raise the voice tone to that which matches the protagonists. To do so only makes you, the facilitator, another antagonist.

Instead, I speak with a facilitator voice tone; Charlie and Liz. Please be seated. Charlie and Liz. Please be seated. Charlie and Liz. Please be seated.

I keep repeating: Charlie and Liz. Please be seated.

Eventually, they hear the sound of my voice, and both of them pause, looking at me and realizing where they are. Each of them gets a stricken look on their face as they realize they are in the center of the circle and everyone is staring at them. They are making fools of themselves!

Both of them turn and walk quickly back to their seats, but not without shouting one final statement over their shoulder at each other.

"You'll be sorry you did this... you will!" says Charlie.

"Not any sorrier than you, Charlie," says Liz.

When they are both seated, I speak to the circle: Well, it appears these two have a conflict between each other. (There is an outburst of nervous laughter at this statement.) I will be talking to these two during the break, but in the meantime, we need to keep focused on what we're here for. This workshop is not about their conflict; it is about the conflict this community has.

So, I turn to YOU and say, Let's continue with the grounding.

You immediately read the questions over again and state, "Well I guess, Liz, you have had your say. So let's move on to Jim."

Even Liz laughs at this. The circle continues until it reaches the final person. Then, you look over at me with a questioning glance.

I suggest a break: It feels like we need a break. Let's take fifteen minutes. When you return, I will explain the purpose of the grounding. I would like to speak to Liz and Charlie in the center of the circle.

The group breaks up, headed for the coffee bar and restrooms. YOU and I walk to the center to speak with Liz and Charlie.

3. The Offer: In this stage, during the break, the facilitator meets with the parties and offers to facilitate the resolution of the conflict. They are offered the opportunity to resolve their differences with the intent of helping the whole group learn. The parties are asked to select two listeners they trust (members of the opposite gender, for balance). The process is then briefly described. It is always the parties' choice.

There are two approaches to consider:

- In the first, the facilitator suggests the group complete the talking circle that was started before the argument. If this is a grounding or a large talking circle, the rest of the circle completes what was interrupted. The facilitator may even go on to complete other tasks. But be sure to let the protagonists know that you will deal with their issue later in the meeting.
- The second approach deals with the conflict almost immediately. This may be needed if you sense the conflict has caused emotional stress in the rest of the group. They will be reluctant to move ahead with these emotions unresolved. It is rarely necessary to do this.

In both cases, a break is needed whenever there is an appropriate ending of the activity.

If the parties agree to resolve the issues (an almost sure thing), they are asked to select their listeners and then meet together with you. You inform the listeners that they will play the role of listening nonjudgmentally to what each person says and then conveying that information, again nonjudgmentally, to their client. I always reinforce the importance of this listener role, the importance of passing the information along clearly and objectively.

This is how I approach is it with Liz and Charlie;

Charlie and Liz, I was caught unaware by the conflict that you two have. I did not pick it up in the interviews. It obviously is a continuing conflict between you. It is also obvious that it ends up with the rest of the community looking on as you argue. I could tell it was embarrassing to both of you.

This is what I would like to propose to you. I can help you to resolve this conflict. I would do it in a process whereby each of you will speak to the other, each of you having listeners. The listeners will tell you what they heard nonjudgmentally. This will allow you to hear what each other is saying. It appeared to me that you have not done that. Until you have, you will keep on getting into the same argument over and over again.

This proposal requires you do three things. The first is to choose to accept this offer or not. If you accept the offer, the second thing you would need to do is pick a listener. Liz you would pick a male whom you trust as your listener. Charlie, you would pick a female whom you trust to be your listener.

Then you need to decide if you want to do this with the group, since they are obviously affected by it, or off to the side by yourselves.

What's your response to this?

"I'm not sure I'm the least bit interested!" Charlie says, not looking at Liz.

"Well the same goes for me!" Liz says, her arms crossed. They both then stare steely eyed at each other.

Then what I suggest you do is to participate in this session and set your conflict aside for the moment. Pay attention to what I'm doing with the community in the session. As you learn and understand the process better, you may decide to change your mind. I'll check with you again at the end of the day.

4. The Choice:

It is important to leave the opportunity for choice open as long as you can. At first, the couple may be extremely resistant to the idea of a facilitated solution. Neither party believes it's possible to "change" the other. But I will continue to check with the pair until the workshop is over, providing them the opportunity to make a choice as they learn more about the process.

I check with Charlie and Liz at the end of the day. Again they refuse to get together, but Charlie states he might be willing to reconsider the next day. Liz looks surprised. They don't talk to each other, but they do nod their heads, acknowledging each other.

At lunchtime the next day, I ask Charlie if he is still interested. He says he would be if Liz would also be willing to agree. I ask YOU to talk with Liz and see if she would be willing to consider sitting down with Charlie to resolve the conflict. When YOU return, you say that Liz was surprised that Charlie would even consider doing this. However, she said she would like to think about it overnight.

The third morning Liz comes up to me before the workshop starts. "I would be interested in sitting down with Charlie," she says. "I've learned a lot in these two days and actually believe we might do something positive. But Charlie would have to agree."

I ask YOU to find Charlie.

When you return with Charlie in tow, I repeat my proposal to him and state that Liz is interested in doing something today. Without looking at her, Charlie assents. "But," he says, "I don't want to do this in front of the group. I'd like to do this after the session is over with just the two of us."

Liz agrees to this proposal. Neither person looks at the other. I tell them: You will each need to pick a listener—Liz a male who you trust, Charlie a female you trust.

"I would like to pick YOU if I can as a listener," Charlie says. You look at me with a questioning glance.

I will be OK with that if you are, I say to YOU. YOU nod yes.

Liz is thinking about it. "I am going to ask Jon."

Then let's agree to get together in this room after everyone has left. This may take a little time, but it's worth it. I honor both of you for choosing to do this. I will try my best to help you resolve this conflict.

They turn and walk away in opposite directions. YOU say, "This is not going to be easy, is it?"

It may not, and then again it may. We just need to leave the options open.

Note that in organizing the resolution session, Liz and Charlie are planning it together with me. They are making the choices...together. This is one of those small changes that move people ahead.

5. Setting the Stage: When the warring parties have convened with their listeners, the facilitator describes briefly what is going to happen. He honors the parties for being willing to confront this issue. The facilitator then describes the role of the listeners.

When the workshop ends with the closure, YOU and I begin to pick up the flip chart papers. Liz and Charlie come over with Jon and stand watching.

Liz, Charlie, Jon, you can help us while the others leave the room. Liz and Charlie, take the recorded information from the flip charts and bring them to me. Jon, pick up the markers, cards, pens, et cetera, and place them in the basket.

Note how I have the two people working together. This is purposeful. It is a small behavioral change that will move them forward. I take every opportunity I can to help them. Remember, behavior is 58 percent of communication.

While we work, the workshop participants are slowly exiting the room. They have had a successful session, leave with a sense of purpose. The editor of the newspaper, Jim, comes by to express his appreciation for our help.

YOU usher the final small group of people out of the room. I take five chairs and set them up in a circle. I invite Liz and Charlie into the circle. They sit opposite each other, both looking nervous. They are probably wondering what they are doing! Jon and YOU select a chair next to your clients. I start:

Charlie and Liz, I appreciate your willingness to be here to resolve your conflict and allow me to help you do that. As I mentioned to you earlier, it is obvious this is an old conflict that has hung on a long time. You have chosen this time to end it. YOU and Jon, I appreciate your willingness to act as listeners for Liz and Charlie.

As listeners, your task is to listen to what is said and then repeat it as well as you can to your client. You are to do this nonjudgmentally, without personal comments. Do not take notes; trust in your ability to recall. I will serve as a backup for both of you.

I have renamed this room "Las Vegas." It is understood by all of us that what is said in this room stays in this room.

All nod yes.

I am honored you asked me to help you. My hope is that you will resolve this conflict and create a friendship that will be lasting.

The grounding: Each of you will answer these questions:

- Introduce yourself.
- How do you feel about this session?
- What are your hopes for this time?

I'll start with you, Charlie.

"I'm Charlie. Well, I'm feeling pretty nervous, really. I'm wondering if this is really the right thing to do. Part of me wants to get up and run away. But I said I was going to do this—let's get going. I hope when we leave this room that we can put the past relationship behind us."

"I'm Jon and I've been a friend of Liz ever since high school. I have watched them fight this battle ever since we graduated. Over the years I've often wondered what I could do to help. I'm nervous about being the listener. I am hopeful this will do some good. The whole community would be relieved."

"I'm Liz and I'm just as nervous as Jon and Charlie. I never thought this day would come. I really never thought it was possible, and that is probably why I've been so frustrated and angry over these years. I'm worried that I won't be able to hold my temper or that I'll cry. That's the last thing I want to do. I don't know if I have any hope. I would just like to put this behind us. God! It would be such a relief."

There is silence as Liz decides if she wants to say more. Then she shrugs her shoulders and looks at YOU.

"I am YOU and I'm surprised that I'm part of this session. I don't know why you selected me, Charlie, but I'll try my best to listen for you. For me, this will be a good learning experience. I'm not too nervous, because I know Bob knows what he's doing. My hope is that you two can resolve this conflict and relieve yourself of all this anger."

So, I say to the others, we all have put our voice in the room. You learned from the workshop how important that is. Let's move on.

6. **The Situation:** The facilitator begins with Person One, the person who started the argument. In this case, that is Liz. This question is asked:

What is the situation, how did it get to be that way, and how do you feel about it?

Make sure that Person One (Liz) speaks at and looks at the other person (Person Two; Charlie in this case). Often the speaker will use the name of the person as if they are not in the room. Remind them to speak to the person, to say "you did this...," not "Jon did this..."

When Person One is done speaking, the facilitator asks Listener Two (YOU) for Person Two:

What did you hear the speaker say?

The listener for Person Two now restates what she heard Person One say, speaking directly to Person Two. This is done nonjudgmentally, attempting to communicate the message to Person Two without the emotion getting in the way.

Let's begin. Liz, you will speak to Charlie first. YOU, you are the listener for Charlie. Liz, I want you to answer these questions:

- *What is the relationship between you and Charlie?*
- *How did it get to be that way?*
- *And how do you feel about it?*

Liz puts her head down and thinks for a while. "As Jon said, Charlie and I go back a long ways. We actually grew up in the same neighborhood."

I put my hand on Liz's knee to get her attention. Then I say, Speak directly to Charlie and say *you* instead of Charlie. We're so used to talking about each other instead of to each other, when the person is in the room, we don't recognize them.

"OK, sorry Charlie. So Charlie, you and I go back a long way; we grew up in the same neighborhood and went to the same schools. It just seems to me that we've always been a little bit competitive. Maybe I was a feminist before my time. I first became angry at you when I decided to run for the school student council president during our sophomore year. It really bothered me when you decided to run against me, because I know you had no interest in it. And of course, since you are so popular, being quarterback on the football team, you won. And then you lorded it over me.

"I know this sounds childish, but winning that presidency was important to me. I ran against you again for president during our junior year, and I won this time, because I was also pretty popular. Then, when I ran against you for president during our senior year, you beat me because you told that damnable lie."

Liz chokes up a little bit, takes a deep breath, trying not to cry.

I notice that Charlie has just put his head down and is looking between his knees at the floor.

"I never got over that. Neither did many of our classmates who believed what you said. It's been a cloud over my head ever since. You denied that you said it, but all my friends said you did. At least those friends I have left," she says emotionally, tears in her voice.

Then, gaining control, she continues. "After graduation I went to college. It was a relief to get away. I graduated and came back home to work at the bank. I wanted to be active in the community. So I worked with United Good Neighbors and eventually was chairperson for the campaign. I joined the League of Women Voters and was voted in as president in my third year.

"Then I decided to run for the City Council. I had ignored the fact that you were still living in that ward. You, of course, decided to run against me. I was furious. How could you do this to me? This would bring up that story you told again. I could not escape it. I was mortified.

"But in spite of that, I still won. Then you showed up at every single meeting, or at least it felt like it. And you just made life miserable for the entire council. I just felt you were doing it to get even with me because I won.

"The next time I ran and you ran against me, you won. You made a big deal out of your athletic prowess and got all of your male friends to vote for you. I ran a clean campaign that time, but the next time, I decided to get as rough as you were. And I still lost. And I'm very angry about it.

"I just don't know why you can't leave me alone."

Liz is unable to speak further. I let there be a pause, then say quietly, Let's have YOU repeat what you said so far to Charlie and give him a chance to respond. Then you can have another opportunity to speak.

YOU tell Charlie what you heard Liz say: "Charlie, I heard Liz say that you two have been in the same neighborhood and in the same schools since you were young. She felt you were both always competitive, but she really got angry at you when she first ran for president of the High School Council. She was angry you won because of your being popular since you were on the football team. She ran again the next year and won because she felt she had also become more popular. When you both ran as seniors, she felt that you told lies about her so she lost. She is still angry about that because she felt that today people are still affected by what you said.

"She went to college and when she returned home she became active politically. She eventually ran for the City Council and was surprised when you ran against her. She did not realize you were still in the neighborhood. It made her pretty mad, and it reminded her of how you won the last time.

"She was surprised to find that she won anyways. But then you came to the City Council meetings and, she felt, purposely made life miserable for her with your complaints. Then you ran against her when she sought reelection and beat her. She felt that she had been running clean campaigns, but since you were being rough, she decided to be as rough as she felt you were during the last campaign. She still lost.

"Liz is angry at you because she feels you just won't leave her alone."

YOU look at Liz. "Did I get all, Liz?"

She nods her head. I decide to add at least one thing that I heard:

I heard you also say that while it sounds childish, wanting to win that presidency, and I suppose winning the other campaigns, is very important to you. You also mentioned that you had worked with United Good Neighbors and were president of the League of Women Voters before you ran for the City Council. You also feel you might have been a feminist before your time."

She nods her head again.

6. The First Response: The facilitator then asks Person Two (Charlie):

What is the situation, how did it get to be that way, and how do you feel about it?

Person Two now states his point of view about the situation to Person One. The person is encouraged to speak to and look at the other person.

The facilitator asks Listener One (Jon) (for Person One):

What did you hear the speaker say?

Listener One restates what he heard Person Two say, speaking directly to Person One. This is done nonjudgmentally, attempting to clearly communicate what was said.

At this time, the facilitator may summarize what he or she heard the two people say, filling in any information the listeners may have passed over. This ensures a complete communication of the two points of view. It also helps the listeners to become more focused for the next questions.

In this situation, I now say: "Charlie, I want you to answer these questions:

- *What is the relationship between you and Liz?*
- *How did it get to be that way?*
- *And how do you feel about it?*

Jon, you will be the listener for Liz.

Charlie has been looking down while I speak to him. Now, he turns his gaze toward Liz and looks directly at her. It is obvious he is having a difficult time speaking.

"Liz, I would sure like to get this off my chest. It has been with me as long as it's been with you. I do remember that very first campaign that we competed in. Actually, we used to even compete in grade school out on the playground. So it was natural for me to run against you the first time, and I will admit that the fact I was on the football team had a lot to do with my winning.

"And it was natural for me to tease you about it because I would've done that when we were younger. I was surprised you won that second time, but I felt it was because I hadn't tried very hard. So my senior year, my purpose was to beat you.

"I did not play fair. But the lie that you accuse me of was really something I said jokingly to the guys on the football team. They are the ones who magnified that way beyond what I had said. I was embarrassed by that. I should have done something about it, and I didn't. I have felt guilty about that ever since. I feel guilty about it today.

"I ran for City Council the first time before I knew that you intended to run. I was surprised to see your name added in the newspapers. I thought maybe you were just in it for the fun of trying to beat me again. And I was surprised when you beat me and beat me good.

"After graduation, I helped my dad down at the tavern. While you were at college, my dad died, and I took over the business. I can tell you I was pretty humiliated when you won, and the customers wouldn't let me forget it. They teased me mercilessly.

"I showed up at the City Council meetings not because of you, but because I didn't like the decisions they were making about taxes and about zoning. They were affecting my business. I was upset at you because of the fact that they were not maintaining roads in our ward. I didn't feel you were tough enough for the job.

"That is why I ran again and allowed my campaign manager, Jimmy Hines, to use some pretty rough tactics, including saying things about you that weren't true. I didn't feel good about that then, and I don't feel good about it now. But I felt I could do a better job.

"The next campaign, I know I was even tougher. You are a pretty ferocious person yourself to run against. So if you got tough, I just got tougher. I think both of us said things that were regretful. I know I did, and right now I'm ashamed of it.

"I wish I could do something about this—do it over. We should have talked this over earlier. We need to get over this unhealthy competitiveness between us. I don't know, but winning doesn't feel as good as it used to."

Charlie is now having a difficult time continuing.

Jon, you can now tell Liz, what you heard Charlie say.

Jon turns to Liz and in a calm and gentle voice relays what he heard:

"Liz, I heard Charlie say that you both have been competitive since grade school. So it seemed natural to him to be running against you in high school. He admits that being on the football team made a difference the first time he ran for president. And he also admits that he teased you about it as part of this competitiveness.

"He was surprised you won the second time, and he felt it was because he didn't try very hard, so he wanted to really be tough the next time. He admits he did not play fair.

"He felt that he showed up at the City Council meetings because he didn't agree with the decisions they were making. They were affecting his business. So he was there to make complaints. While he said it was not because of you, he did say he didn't feel you were tough enough in representing the ward. Especially when it came to maintaining the roads.

"That's the reason he ran against you the next time, and he gave his campaign manager permission to be pretty rough and at times not honest. He justified this because he felt he could do a better job than you were.

"When he ran again, since you were being tough, he became tougher. He won, but he doesn't feel good about how he did it. Again, he justifies this because he feels he could do a better job."

Jon looked over at me. "Did I leave anything out, Bob?"

I heard a few additional things. He said that the lie you referred to was just a joke that he felt was harmless. But his football buddies made it into something more than that. I sensed that he did not discourage them, and as a result, he says he's been guilty about it ever since.

After high school, he said that he went to work for his dad in the tavern and when his dad passed away, he took over the business. When he lost to you that first time, his customers wouldn't let him forget it.

He said when you ran against him for City Council that third time that you were really ferocious. So he decided to be just as tough as you were. As a result he feels both of you said things about each other that you shouldn't have.

He also wishes that you and he could've done something about this earlier. He would like to get over this feeling of competitiveness between you. Finally, he said that winning just doesn't feel as good as it used to.

7. The Second Response: This is an opportunity for the speakers to respond to each other. Normally by this time, the tones of the voices have changed from being loud, angry, and anxious and are calmer. This is often the stage at which the parties express their regret about how this conflict has changed their relationship.

The facilitator turns to the first person who spoke and says:

What is your response to what Person Two (Charlie) has said?

I turn to Liz, who was listening intently to Charlie. Her face was softer than it had been before.

What is your response to what Charlie has just said, Liz? And YOU will be the listener.

"Well, first of all Charlie, I'm sorry about your dad. I did not even know he had passed away. I guess that's a result of our tense relationship. We don't know anything other than this battle we fight.

"You might have intended that lie to have been a joke, Charlie, but you can't relieve yourself of the responsibility for what happened from it. You didn't do anything to correct it. You admit that. That has caused me pain to this day. It was not true, Charlie, and you could have straightened that out!

"I'll admit that I was not as effective as I could have been when I was on the City Council. But I was a newcomer, Charlie, and I did get better before my term was over. Even you have to admit that. I didn't agree with what the council decided on taxes and zoning, but I was only one vote on the board.

"You are right; we both got ferocious in the following campaigns. I don't feel very good about my part of it, but I believe you went way overboard, Charlie. It just seemed to me that it was about more than the campaign. You know that this community laughs at us. They encourage us to play this role with each other, because it is amusing. For me it's humiliating.

"I know that I am showing up at some of the City Council meetings just to get even with you. I am angry at you. As a result we're fighting this unfinished business in the public eye. I wish we could move beyond it, Charlie."

Liz pauses and I can tell she has something more to say. I wait.

She looks at Charlie. "I do have to admit, Charlie, that you are a good city councilperson. And I do have to admit that you straightened out those issues around taxes and zoning. Even though I give you a hard time with some of your votes on the council, I have learned a lot by watching you. I sometimes wonder if you aren't the better of the two of us. But I also know I would be a much better council member now than I was the first term."

Liz stops speaking and pauses. I can tell she is done.

YOU, I say, could you tell Charlie what you heard Liz say?

"Charlie, Liz's sorry about what happened with your dad passing. I think she's sorry that she missed this, but the competition between you got in the way.

"She feels that you should have done something about that joke, which became a lie, and she feels that you have not taken responsibility for that. It still is painful to her today.

"She agrees that she was not as good she wanted to be on the City Council, but it was her first time. She disagreed with the council on the same issues you did, but she felt that she was only one vote and didn't carry much weight.

"She agrees that you were tough on each other whenever you ran against each other, and she doesn't feel any better about that than you do. But she feels you went overboard and that there was something in it that it was more than about the campaign.

"She feels that this community encourages you guys to compete the way you do so they can make fun of you both.

"Finally, Charlie, and I noticed that you looked surprised at this, but she feels that you are a pretty good councilperson and that you have done some good while in that position. She knows she gives you a hard time about your votes, but she has also learned from you and could be a much better council member now."

YOU look at me and ask, "I know there is more—can you help me?"

Actually, YOU did excellent. What I would add is that she knows she is behaving the way she does at the meetings just to get even with you, Charlie, and she wishes she could get beyond that.

Charlie, what is your response to Liz? Jon, you are the listener.

Charlie looks to be in turmoil. It is difficult for him to start.

"I knew this day would come," he finally says, his voice trembling. "I deserve what you said about that lie, but it's no worse than what I've been saying to myself all these years. It's worse for me than you know!"

Liz has a puzzled look on her face.

"That's all I can say now, Bob."

Jon, tell Liz what you heard Charlie say.

"Liz, Charlie says he deserves what you said about him. But he's been saying the same about himself and even worse, these past years. That's all he can say for now, Liz."

I think about giving Charlie another opportunity to add to what he said, but decide to move ahead. I add:

Liz, I also heard Charlie say that he knew this day would come. I assume he means the discussion we're having here.

8. The Worst Possible Outcomes: The facilitator asks Person Two (Charlie) to begin in answering the next question (for balance):

What are the worst possible outcomes of this situation for you? What do you believe are the worst possible outcomes for the other person?

Person Two states what his worst possible outcomes are for himself, then for the other person. He may have to be reminded by the facilitator to answer the second question, since this requires he be concerned beyond himself. This allows the person to state, to empathize with, what he feels are the fears of the other person.

The facilitator asks Listener One (Jon): What did you hear the speaker say?

Listener One restates the information to Person One (Liz). The listener will probably be more complete this time.

The facilitator asks Person One (Liz):

What are the worst possible outcomes of this situation for you? What do you believe are the worst possible outcomes for the other person?

Person One now responds with her worst possible outcomes. She will confirm some of the worst outcomes Person Two described for her and add others. Then she, with some reminding, will express the worst possible outcomes she believes the other person has. Again, some confirmation will occur, as well as some new insights.

The facilitator asks Listener Two (YOU):

What did you hear the speaker say?

Listener Two transmits the message to Person Two. He will be clearer this time and have listened better than the first time.

Be prepared for a remarkable reduction in tension by this time. The tones of voices will be lower; the parties will be more focused and deliberative in what they say.

Let's go back to the situation with Liz and Charlie.

I'm going to move ahead to the next question and will start with you, Charlie, this time. YOU will be the listener for Liz. Charlie, answer these two questions and speak directly to Liz:

What are the worst possible outcomes of this situation for you? What do you believe are the worst possible outcomes for Liz?

Charlie groans. "Oh god," he says, "I've been living the worst outcomes these last two nights. I'm going to hell. That's the worst possible outcome. I'm going to hell."

All of us are somewhat shocked by the intensity of his statement. Charlie continues.

"I'm a devout Catholic, or at least I've been telling everybody that. But I know that what I did back there, Liz, was wrong. Yes, I told a joke, but the way I told it gave the guys every reason to do what they did with it. They magnified it and turned it into something that it wasn't. I intended that to happen." (He pauses, emotional.) "And I know it was hurtful to you, and I did nothing about it. I can't blame them, I blame me.

"There is no worse sin than what I did. Demeaning you and then doing nothing about it. When you left to go to college, I was so relieved that I would not have to see you in the neighborhood and be reminded about it every time. I knew that what the guys said was totally wrong, I saw what it did to you and some of your friends. And I did nothing about it—nothing!

"And then I just continued doing it when you returned. I told Jimmy Hines that we needed to have a tough campaign. But I didn't expect him to make it as tough as he did. He had people tell lies about you behind your back. He never told me he did it, but when I heard them, I knew he did. And then I did the same thing as before—I did nothing about it. I was cruel and I was wrong."

Charlie is trying hard not to weep.

"The worst possible thing is that you will always see me as someone who has no integrity. That you will always hate me for what I've done. It will never be possible for us to be other than enemies. What a loss that is, because we both have concerns about the very same things. We both want to help our community. Instead they just laugh at us."

Charlie looks at me, hoping I will move on to Liz.

Charlie, I say, what are the worst possible outcomes of this situation for Liz?

"How could it be any worse, Liz?" Charlie looks up at Liz. "For people to believe things about you that are lies. Lies! Lies! Lies! And for you to have to see me and be reminded that I let it happen." He stops, grits his teeth.

Jon, tell Liz what you heard Charlie say.

"Liz, Charlie feels like he's going to hell because of what he has done to you with lies in the past, starting with high school and then the campaigns for City Council. While he might not have intended it, the way in which he presented it encouraged others to tell lies for him. And he feels he'll go to hell because he didn't do anything about it. He admits that he knew how it would affect you with your friends and with the community. He admits he intended to do it the first time.

"His fear is that you will believe he is a person with no integrity and that you'll always hate him. He feels this caused great loss because both of you really want to help our community, and instead these lies get in the way and result in behaviors that make the community just laugh at you.

Jon pauses as he recalls the rest of the message.

"Charlie said that he has always tried to be a devout Catholic, but what he did to you is wrong, bad enough to send him to hell when he dies. He feels that's what he deserves. And so the last two nights have been like 'hell' to him.

"Finally, I heard him say that while both of you want to help your community, you can't do it if the community is laughing at you.

"That's what I heard," Jon says.

Thanks, Jon, you did well. Liz, would you answer those same two questions: *What are the worst possible outcomes of this situation for you? What do you believe are the worst possible outcomes for Charlie?*

"The worst possible outcome for me, Charlie, would be that you would go to hell for this. What you did was wrong, but you wouldn't deserve that. Although, I have felt like I've been to hell and back in our campaigns.

"My worst possible outcome is that we will continue this relationship out in the open, where the community sees it, so that they rely on us to entertain them. I am sick of it. Like you said, we both have an interest in helping this community. How can we do that if they're laughing at us?

"I meant it when I said that you were good councilperson. My worst possible outcome is that I won't be able to say that about myself. I don't know what makes me want to run for office. But you should understand that if anybody does.

"My worst possible outcome for you is that you would carry this guilt around with you forever. It must affect your family. I know it has affected my family. What a shame if this continues.

"I'm done, Bob."

YOU, tell Charlie what you heard.

"Charlie, Liz doesn't want you to go to hell. Although she says that campaigning against you is like going to hell and back." (There is some hesitant laughter from Jon, Liz, and Charlie at this.) "Her worst possible outcome is that you will both continue the relationship you have and continue to entertain the community. That because of this, neither of you will be able to help the community.

"She doesn't know why she runs for office, but she would like to have an opportunity to show that she can be a good councilperson.

"She feels the worst possible outcome for you is to continue to carry around this guilt with you forever, that it would affect your family. She believes it's a shame to let this continue."

MAINTAINING A BALANCE OF POWER

Note that in each stage of this process, the position of speaking first is shared between the two people. The person who is the most aggrieved or who initiated the conflict will speak first, describing the situation. When this has been explored, the other person will speak first in answer to the worst possible outcomes of the situation. This will change again with the best possible outcome and again with the exploration of possible solutions.

This is done to keep a balance of power, of equity between the two people. If one person had been allowed to speak first each time, the other would eventually complain about this, and the conflict would then be refocused on a sense of inequity between the two.

---

9. The Best Possible Outcomes: Normally this is a time for a break. The participants are emotionally drained, including the listeners, and this time can allow them to balance themselves. When they return, the facilitator asks Person One (Liz, for balance):

What do you want as best possible outcomes for yourself in this situation? What do you want as best possible outcomes for the other person?

This allows her to be concerned for both of their welfare. Be prepared for a change in emotional context as these outcomes are expressed.

The facilitator asks Listener Two (Jon):

What did you hear the speaker say?

Listener Two will restate the information to Person Two (Charlie). There is normally a decided change in the tone of voice as these are expressed. The listeners are often amazed that the other person would have best possible outcomes for Person Two.

The facilitator then asks Person Two to respond:

What do you want as best possible outcomes for yourself in this situation? What do you want as best possible outcomes for the other person?

As he expresses these best possible outcomes, he will often validate some best outcomes expressed by Person One and add others.

The facilitator asks Listener One:

What did you hear the speaker say?

Listener One will restate the information to Person One.

So, in our example situation, I ask: Is anyone ready for a break? All four people nod their heads, probably with a great amount of relief.

Let's take about ten minutes for that. During the ten minutes, I want Liz and Charlie to be thinking about this question: *What do you want as best possible outcomes for yourself in this situation? What do you want as best possible outcomes for the other person?*

"Boy," Charlie says, "you are relentless. You're going to make us work even when we're taking a break."

Everyone laughs. I can feel some of the emotional tension being released.

This has been a pretty emotional and candid discussion. This breather will help everyone center themselves for the next segment. By posing the next question, I am a moving their minds from their worst fears to their hopes. These people would not have chosen to be here unless they had some hopes.

When everyone has returned to their chairs, there is definitely a sense of calm or relaxation. It is like the worst is behind them, and they are looking forward to some resolution.

I begin: Liz, you are going to answer this question, and YOU are going to tell Charlie what you heard.

What do you want as best possible outcomes for yourself in this situation? What do you want as best possible outcomes for Charlie?

"My best possible outcome," she says, "would be to get out from under this cloud of being diminished by what Charlie has said in the past."

She pauses. I gently ask her: Could you express that in a way that is positive? Rather than having the word "diminished" in it?

Liz thinks for a while. "I would like this community, and especially Charlie, to see me as the person I am, someone who is intelligent, honest, and committed to serving this community the best I can. I would like people to forget who they have been told I am and instead see me for who I actually am.

"I would like those who have spoken lies about me in the past to speak the truth about me. Especially you, Charlie. It would really be interesting to see if you and I could have a more collaborative and less competitive relationship, Charlie.

"Did I answer the questions, Bob?"

What you can add is: what are your best possible outcomes for Charlie?

"Well, Charlie," she says with a hint of a smile, "I don't want you to go to hell for what you did, but I'm not sure I'm willing to give you the key to heaven, either. I will admit that I've been part of pushing you to the wall the past few years. I think I've even suggested that you can go to hell. So I am willing to apologize for that, if you will forgive me. My best possible outcome is that you would be willing to confront your 'guys' and tell them to stop spreading rumors about me." (Pausing to think.) "I want them to tell the truth about me. My hope would be that would release you from the guilt that you are carrying.

"I also hope the next time we run against each other, that you and I agree to do it in the way that is respectful of each other. And no matter who wins, we will support each other."

She is done.

YOU, please tell Charlie what you heard.

"Charlie, Liz wants the community and you to see her for who she really is. She described herself as being honest and intelligent. She feels she is committed to serving this community in elected office. She does not want people to see her as others have described her.

"She wants those who have not spoken the truth about her to become honest. She wants to be acknowledged for who she is, especially by you, Charlie.

"For you, Charlie, she is not sure she wants to write a ticket to heaven for you right away, but she certainly doesn't want you to end up going to hell. Although she has suggested that to you a few times in the past. She acknowledges her part in this and is willing to apologize and hopes you'll be willing to forgive her. And she would hope that you'd be willing to do something about 'your guys' continuing to spread myths about her. They can tell the truth instead.

"She wants to run against you again, but she'd like to find a way to do it where you could treat each other respectfully. Then, no matter who wins, you would support each other.

"Did I get it all, Liz?"

Liz nods her head yes. YOU look at me for confirmation. I nod my head, then proceed.

OK, Charlie, you are going to answer the same questions. Jon is the listener. *What do you want as best possible outcomes for yourself in this situation? What do you want as best possible outcomes for Liz?*

"You are a big person in a small frame," Charlie says. "I appreciate the offer you made to me and I accept your apology and I'll hope you'll accept mine. I cannot tell you what a relief it is..." (Here Charlie chokes up, so we wait silently.) "...to be able to tell you that I'm sorry that I have allowed other people to demean you with my silent encouragement just so I could win.

Charlie pauses as he considers what to say next.

"My best possible outcome is that we will find a way to let this community know that we have talked to each other, acknowledged how good each of us is, and that we are going to be working together in the future for the good of this community. I'm hopeful we will find a way to change people's view so they will see that you are the intelligent and committed person that I know you are.

"My best outcome is the community will be speaking in an admiring way about us, rather than laughing at us. And I would hope that we could be a model for forgiveness and decency. That would make us both better Catholics. And I would hope that when I confess this in the confessional this Saturday that God would forgive me.

"My best outcomes for you, Liz, is that you will continue to run for office, whether with the City Council or with the county, or even for the presidency of the country. Whatever you want. Hopefully you will take what you have learned and be the kind of elected official that people can be proud of.

"I don't know if I'll ever make it to heaven. But right now I am so relieved, this feels like heaven to me.

"That's it, Bob," Charlie says.

Jon, tell Liz what you heard.

"Liz, at first I thought Charlie was going to make a mistake by saying you are a big person, but then, being a politician he added the right words: 'in the small frame.' He accepted your apology and offered his, saying it was a great relief to be able to do so. He is sorry he allowed other people to put you down just so he could win.

"Just doing that made him feel like he had already gone to heaven.

"He is willing to let this community know that you've talked to each other. And that you plan to be working together in the future. And he's willing to do whatever he can to help people see the kind of person you really are. Instead of making fun of and laughing at the both of you, he wants the community to be admiring both of you. He believes that if you can pull this off, it will make you both better Catholics and a model for other people for forgiveness.

"He is encouraging you to continue to run for office, maybe even for president of the United States. Wouldn't that be great? And he feels that when you win, you will be a better elected official, and people will be proud of you.

"Did I get it?" Jon asks Charlie.

"Yes," Charlie says.

10. Collaboration: Identifying the best possible outcomes moves the two individuals to imagining a more hopeful future. But we know that they will have to take some actions to make that happen. We want them to do this together, in a collaborative fashion. The facilitator now asks Person Two to respond to the questions:

What are you willing to do to foster those best possible outcomes for both of you? What do you need from the other person to make your best outcomes happen?

He can now express what he is willing to do to foster both of their best possible outcomes. This is a question that fosters collaboration and bonding between the two individuals. Each person is responsible for fostering the best possible outcomes for both parties.

The facilitator will ask Listener One: What did you hear the speaker say?

Listener One will restate the information to Person One.

The facilitator will then ask Person One to respond to the questions:

What are you willing to do to foster those best possible outcomes for both of you? What do you need from the other person to make your best outcomes happen?

Person One responds to Person Two, expressing her willingness to foster the best possible outcomes and her needs from Person Two.

The facilitator asks Listener Two: What did you hear the speaker say?

Listener Two will restate the information to Person Two.

Back to the case of Charlie and Liz: So, I say, how are the two of you going to make these outcomes happen? Charlie, you are going to begin by answering these two questions:

What are you willing to do to foster those best possible outcomes for both of you? What do you need from Liz to make your best outcomes happen?

For this activity, I'm going to ask you to be your own listener, Liz. YOU can take a break and relax. OK...Charlie?

"The first thing I am willing to do is to tell the guys at the tavern to lay off, and that includes my best buddy, Jimmy Hines. I'm going to let them know I really don't appreciate them acting as my surrogate on this. I'll speak for myself in the future.

"What would you think of my inviting you to come down for a meal at the tavern this next weekend with your family? Wouldn't that make people rethink about our relationship? You would be there as my guest. I promise you, you'll have a good time. It would be great to meet your husband and kids. And I'll treat!

"Finally, I've been on the City Council long enough. You need to run again. I would be willing to be your campaign chair. I would be proud to do that.

"Let's see now, what I have to tell is what I want from her?"

Yes, Charlie.

"Well, Liz, I think I already have it from you. First of all, you were willing to do this with me. It was hard for both of us, but you had to agree to do it. So...thank you.

"I would like you to give me the time to talk to people and straighten them out. Just trust that I'll do it."

Liz, what did you hear Charlie say?

Liz leans forward with a hint of a smile. "Well, Charlie, I heard you say that you are willing to tell the guys to straighten up. And that includes Jimmy. And you don't want them speaking for you any longer." (She is emotional, but with a smile.)

"And you are inviting my family to the tavern this next weekend so that people can see that our relationship is different. And you are willing to pick up the tab. You do know I have five children, don't you?" Everyone laughs. "And I'm accepting the invitation right now. Expect us to order big.

"I heard you say that you were not going to run for City Council again. And you are offering to be my campaign chair, if I run. I accept.

"I heard you say that what you wanted from me you already got by my being willing to do this, and you're asking me to give you time to straighten people out. You want me to trust you on that. Right?"

Charlie nods his head with a big smile on his face, tears in his eyes.

"So what do I do next, Bob?" Liz asks.

You answer the same questions Charlie did. And, Charlie, you were going to be your own listener; Jon will take a break.

What are you willing to do to foster those best possible outcomes for both of you? What do you need from Charlie to make your best outcomes happen?

"What I would be willing to do is to walk into the City Council meeting next week with you by my side, talking about the meeting. Wouldn't that just blow people away? We could even get together during the break and talk out in the hall like other normal people do.

"I would be willing to have dinner at your tavern next weekend if the family agrees. It would be nice if your family could join us. Why not, Charlie?

"What I would also be willing to do, Charlie, is to acknowledge that I have been at least partly responsible for what has happened. After all, I started it when I beat you up on the playground in the fourth grade. You reminded me of that once. Do you remember, I was bigger than you then? It's possible I really started this then.

"And I ran for office just as mean as you did this last time. It was just as unforgivable as what you did. So, I do apologize for that, and I will let people in my circle know that what I said was wrong. I hope you can trust me to do that.

"What I want from you, Charlie, is everything you offered, but added to that is the possibility that we could actually have a friendship between us and our families. I know you are a good man, because you have a wonderful family. They need to know that we have buried the hatchet just as well as the community. I'll bet they will be relieved.

"That's it, Bob."

Charlie, what did you hear Liz say?

"Liz, you proposed a delightful idea. We would both walk into the City Council meeting together and even get together during the break.

This would send a message to the community that we have forgiven each other; we are working together for the good of the community. What a great idea!

"You accepted my offer to have your family at the tavern this next weekend for dinner and invited my family to join you. I accept, if they agree.

"You acknowledge that you have been at least partly to blame, and you also acknowledged you started it when you beat me up in the fourth grade. I do remember that and would just as soon forget it! I would hope that would stay in this room to protect my reputation." (Laughter from all of us.)

"You apologize for being as nasty as I was this last election and asked that I trust that you will let your friends know that what you said about me was wrong.

"Then I heard you say..." (Charlie again is having a difficult time speaking, so there is a pause.) "...that we could maybe actually have a friendship between us, including our families. This is something that is way beyond what I could ever have imagined would happen. I have thought that being friends would be impossible in this life."

Notice that as they moved into this part of the process, I changed the way it was done. Because the tension and emotion had changed during the discussion, I decided to have them be listeners for each other. Because of the emotion I saw in both of these people, I also decide at this time to change the ending of the discussion. But first we have to do a closure.

11. The Closure: The facilitator moves the group to a closure by asking these questions of the listeners, then the parties, and finally himself.

- *How do you feel about this meeting?*
- *What advice do you have for the two people to make them successful? or...*
- *What did you learn that will make you successful?*

These questions are answered by the listeners and then the two persons, followed by the facilitator. This allows the group to reach closure on the discussion, to acknowledge their learning from the situation. They are also able to provide information to the people which will help make them successful.

None of this has to be written down, because the four people involved become the group memory.

In this meeting, I now say: For the closure, I want to start with the listeners answering these two questions:

- *How do you feel about this meeting?*
- *What advice do you have for the two people to make them successful?*

We will start with you, Jon.

"Well, first of all, it was really difficult to be a listener. I trusted what Bob told us about recall and it did work, but without the three-day workshop, this would have been impossible for me. I feel overwhelmed with what you two did here. You are so courageous to have done this. It has been a long time coming.

"It was hard to put my own personal feelings about this aside. I have watched both of you really trash each other for years and wondered what it was all about. It always seemed more than two politicians going at each other.

"I'm grateful you did this. It would be a blessing for our whole community to be able to see you two working together.

"I learned the value of doing this right away instead of putting it off for years and years. What grief you could have saved yourselves. If there is one thing you two can do, it is to carry out what you agreed to do. I want to help by telling everyone I know that you two have made up, if it is OK to do that. It would be wonderful.

"Over to YOU."

"I agree with everything Jon said. It was so difficult to listen and be able to repeat what was said. I felt on the spot to get it all and hope I did you both justice. It did feel easier as we went along. I'm glad you were there, Bob, to back us up.

"My advice is to not let this moment pass—take advantage of it. Charlie's offer to you is an attempt to get rid of years of guilt, and only you, Liz, can do that. And your idea about walking into the City Council together and eating together is a great way to send the message that you have worked things out.

"Thank you for letting me do this, Charlie. It was worth my time."

Now I move the conversation to Liz and Charlie.

Liz, you will answer the questions, speaking to Charlie:

- *How do you feel about this meeting?*
- *What did you learn that will make you both successful?*

"When we showed up for this workshop two days ago, I never imagined this would happen. I'm glad it did. I'm glad you were persistent, Bob, in moving us in this direction. And Charlie, I appreciated your willingness to agree to Bob's offer.

"I learned that not dealing with these issues right away creates a lot of pain for both people. I wish we could have done this a long time ago, Charlie, but that time is past. Being honest with each other today has caused me to look at my relationships with other people, including in my family and at work.

"If we can make this work, Charlie, and I hope we can, it would give us the opportunity to put our energy into much more positive directions. I really hope this is for real."

Liz is now emotional, with tears in her eyes, and so she uses a movement of her hands to indicate she is done.

Charlie, you will answer the same questions:

- *How do you feel about this meeting?*
- *What did you learn that will make you both successful?*

"I feel like this is happening too fast for me. I never imagined that Liz and I...oh sorry,

Liz, I mean you...could reconcile this easily. I'm still trying to deal with the fact that I might not be sent directly to hell when I die. It is a relief to me, but I have the same concern you do about pulling this off. We will both have to trust each other, something we've not been able to do in the past."

Charlie is now just as emotional as Liz is. He cannot speak, so he passes it back to me.

Liz and Charlie, it is evident that this means a lot to you that you have had this moment to confront your issue and consider the possibilities of creating an entirely different relationship between you. I feel very grateful that you allowed me to help you to do this. I feel grateful for Jon and YOU being willing to stay after the workshop to be listeners and serve these two people.

My advice to you is to do those simple things that you recommended to each other. They will have an awesome impact, I can assure you. Connecting your two families will provide you a lot of support for the future.

My next piece of advice is to realize that what Liz said is true. You will now have a lot of energy available to direct on to other issues. When you do that, it will help you serve the community that both of you love.

12. The Honoring: The facilitator asks the parties and the listeners to go to the center of the circle to be honored. After acknowledging the courage it took to risk this confrontation, the circle applauds the participants in the activity. As this happens, do not be surprised to see the parties shake hands, hug each other, or otherwise display a visual symbol of their commitment to their new relationship.

Now, with Charlie and Liz, I say: I would like us all to stand. Liz and Charlie, come up to the center of our small circle.

Liz and Charlie step toward the center and then reached out to each other and hug, with tears in their eyes.

Jon, could you honor these two for what they have just accomplished?

"You bet, Bob. Liz and Charlie, you have my greatest admiration for your courage in confronting the relationship that you two had since you were kids. Both of you said that you want to serve this community, and I believe you just did that in this last hour and a half. So I honor you for that."

Jon, YOU, and I applaud as the two in the center hug each other again, tears on their cheeks.

Liz and Charlie, you can return to the edge of the circle now. They separate and step back.

Jon and YOU, please move to the center of the small circle.

Liz, please honor Jon and YOU for being your listeners.

"I am pleased to do that. Jon and YOU, as listeners, you are the best. I was amazed at how much you remembered of what we had said. Even though this was demonstrated a number of times during the workshop, it still took a lot of effort to actually be the listener. I do not know if I could've done it as well. So, thank you for doing that, it really felt good to hear my own words repeated, to know I was heard. You made this possible."

Charlie, Liz, and I applaud the two in the center.

I want to do another activity, I say, and I want to do it without words. Charlie and Liz, words cannot heal the hurts of the past, but actions can. So we are going to do a greeting circle that is nonverbal. I want each of you who participated to honor each person that you greet, without words. I want you to be willing to express forgiveness without words.

With that, I turn to my left and greet Charlie, then YOU, Liz, and Jon, and return to my spot. Charlie, moving behind me greets YOU, then comes to Liz, stops and looks at her and then reaches out, and they both hug. We just wait until they separate. Charlie comes past Jon, then me, and returns to where he started. He continues greeting Jon, then Liz, then YOU.

When Liz is in front of Charlie, she also looks at him, smiles, reaches out, and they both hug. Liz steps back and shakes Charlie's hand, smiles on both of their faces.

When the circle is done I have them take each other's hands, creating a closed circle, and just say a few words:

What was said in this room stays in this room. But it is OK to report that Charlie and Liz came together and resolved the differences they had between them. It is not necessary to report how that happened. It is important no one hear about Liz beating Charlie up in the fourth grade. (Laughter from all.)

Any actions you take together will change the entire community. So, let's drop our hands, and Jon, Charlie, and Liz, you can leave. YOU and I will finish cleaning up this room.

YOU and I then take another thirty minutes putting together the paper for the report and then debriefing our activities as facilitators for the three days and the interpersonal conflict. We answer the same questions we asked the workshop participants:

- *How do you feel about this time that we spent as facilitators?*
- *What did you learn that will help you be a facilitator in the future?*

When we leave, walking out to the parking lot, we see Liz and Charlie standing together, leaning against Charlie's red Dodge pickup. They are engaged in a very serious and obviously friendly discussion. Their body postures are relaxed, the voice tone is calm. We wave to them, give each other a hug, and then we part. But, never fear, YOU will work with me again in this book.

So, what happened? Normally I don't know, because I leave it up to the parties to be responsible to carry out what they agreed to. In this instance, I received a phone call three days later from Jim, the editor of the local newspaper.

"Hello, Bob. I first want to tell you how much I appreciate your help this last weekend, taking a look at the issue of integrity. I was impressed with what the group did and observed some changed behaviors at the Chamber of Commerce breakfast this morning. The community is really buzzing about it.

"I really just wanted to ask you: what did you do to Liz and Charlie? Last night they showed up at the City Council meeting, talking to each other. It was shocking to everyone there. Liz gave Charlie a hug before he went up to sit behind the City Council table. Then, during the break, they got together and had this conversation, where everyone saw them laughing. It was a big topic of discussion this morning at the chamber breakfast."

Well, Jim, I say, Liz and Charlie agreed to get together to see if they could resolve the issue between them. They were successful in that, obviously. What was the chatter at breakfast about?

"Everyone is wondering: if they *have* made up, who will the community be able to make fun of? They were a common topic of conversation in the community. We'll have to find another topic, I guess."

Well, Jim, maybe the newspaper can move them in the direction of a positive topic, rather than one that relies on making fun of someone in the community. If you look at it, it is a real opportunity that Liz and Charlie have given the community. They can put that energy to good use.

"You're right, Bob, and I see this as a direct outcome of our workshop. What I would like to do is have the newspaper focus on encouraging the completion of our strategies and actions we developed during those last three days."

With that, we ended our conversation, but I did hear through the grapevine that Charlie and Liz brought their families together at the tavern. Sounds like a success to me.

How Did You Do That?

People who observe this have questions about the process. These are the key ones, along with my answers.

Why do the adversaries choose listeners of the opposite gender?

When I first developed this approach, I observed that if a male listened for a male client, then he would tend to make fun of what the female said, like, "Well, Liz started off by whining again." This required that I interrupt the listener and remind him of his responsibility to be objective. This moves the focus to the listener rather than the clients. Often that one comment makes it much more difficult for the two parties to be able to speak to each other.

I have also replaced male listeners because of this inability to convey the message without judgment. It is unusual for a female to do this.

My purpose is to help the two parties resolve their issue. Having each of the people select a person of the opposite gender makes the process much easier and eliminates the possibility of the underlying male and female tension getting in the way.

There are circumstances where only members of the same gender are available. In that case, I take what is offered.

Do the adversaries ever get out of control in this process?

I've done this hundreds of times, and the adversaries have always moved through the separate stages described above. They have never lost control, although they have expressed anger, sometimes hatred, in the first stages. The facilitator makes the difference. As long as I am calm, as long as they know that *I* trust them, as long as the listeners are objective, the process has been successful. I have never had a failure with this.

Do the adversaries actually carry out their agreements with each other?

One of my rules is that when the conflict session is over, whether with a large group or small group or two people, then the people involved are responsible for what happens next. I do not have people involved in interpersonal conflicts make written agreements, nor do I purposefully return to assess their outcomes.

It is their responsibility to make this work, not mine. What I have learned is that the listeners are the ones who hold the parties accountable to their agreements. If either party gets out of line, the listener reminds them of their agreement.

For those circumstances when the parties have called me, or seen me in the airport, the reports are always positive: it worked!

And...it is still the parties' responsibility to make this work, not mine. I believe it is important to keep the responsibility where it belongs—with them!

Who manages the process?

The facilitator manages this process. It is important that the individuals agree to the process in the beginning. Once the individuals start to speak, they are allowed to continue without interruption. It is not unusual, as the first person talks, for the other person to want to immediately set the record straight. The facilitator must encourage this person to listen until the first person is done. For example: Charlie, let Liz finish. Then you will have your say.

What if someone wants to interrupt or protest?

Sometimes another member of the group wants to interrupt and set the record straight. Again, the facilitator must ask the person to wait until the protagonists themselves have spoken before letting others be involved. Each person is allowed to speak—but in turn—after the individuals in conflict have had their say.

What if a person can't move ahead?

Sometimes one of the parties wants to go back over old ground. It is best to move them on, cautioning against the natural desire to remain in the conflict. The individual may be allowed to add information, even if repetitive, *provided the solution is given at the end of the statement.* For example:

You may speak again and your listener will repeat it, but when you are done, you will answer this question...

What is your solution to this? What are you willing to do to resolve it?

This normally moves everyone ahead. It is the responsibility of the facilitator to encourage the participants to move ahead, while still being respectful of the need to confront.

Can this be done with the larger group being part of it?

Yes. This is the decision that the two parties must make in the beginning. They have the choice of doing it with the group or doing it separately.

If the two parties are the initiator of the conflict that has created the intergroup conflict, then is it is important for them to resolve their issue in front of the larger group, if they choose to. The same process described above is used for this, except that the larger group is listening in on the discussion. When the parties have completed their process and have been honored, then the larger group is distributed to four or five smaller groups.

Each of the groups then answers these questions:

- *What is the issue that caused the conflict between these two people and which affects the rest of you?*
- *How did this issue happen? How do you feel about it?*

This results in a description of the situation that has brought the group together. You experienced this earlier in the book. This is the beginning of the consensus-building process. It is the step that happened during the second day of the intergroup process. The community then moves through the entire process, with the issue being paramount and the conflict between the two individuals fading into the background.

~47~

But, Does It Work?

But, Does It Work with Other Groups?

A reasonable question. Normally it is asked by a participant who has been part of a community that has successfully resolved their conflict with a consensus.

The answer is *yes*! This is especially true of the interpersonal and intergroup conflicts. In my recollection, there have been no failures. I get little feedback on the personal or internal issues, so for those, it is a guess.

"This is an impossible task!" My commitment is to help people confront and resolve their conflicts in a way that they can reach 100 percent consensus. My belief is that my time is best invested in those conflicts that people believe are impossible. These conflicts have been around a long time and are deeply embedded in the life story of the community. The energy that is available (anger, hurt, adrenaline, etc.) can be refocused to resolve the issue. And the resulting impacts on the community when the conflict is resolved are transforming.

When people hear that I am considering working in their community, I will get phone calls from people I know, some I don't know, who urge me to reconsider: "This is an impossible one, Bob." "Don't take it on, you will just fail." "Why risk your reputation, Bob?" "Surely you have something better to do with your time!"

During the interviews I will often be warned that this is an impossible task:

"You're just wasting your time working with this community!" "Why should I participate in a meeting that will have lots of confrontation and nothing happens?"

In the grounding, many of the participants will acknowledge that the issue that brought them together is impossible:

"I don't know why I'm here." "Bob will just entertain us for three days, then take our money and run and leave us with the problem even worse than it is now." "This situation is impossible; it won't be resolved anytime soon."

Undaunted, I accept the request for help, acknowledge the impossibility I hear in the interviews, listen sincerely to the doubts expressed during the grounding, and just keep moving the community forward.

Without exception the communities will resolve their issue with a consensus by the end of the workshop. Without exception, they move ahead and foster the outcomes they desire—and normally quicker than they expected. And yet, this group that perceived itself and its conflict to be so difficult will say in the closure, "Well, Bob, you've got us through this OK, but we were an easy group. Are you able to do this with a difficult group?"

I just did!

Every person who is in a conflict believes it is the worst of the worst conflicts. On a scale of 0 to 10, their conflict is a 12. When I interview them, my sensing picks up that the conflict is more a 5 than a 12. Or sometimes even a 2!

But I have to understand that to this group the conflict is a 12 and then manage the situation accordingly. The reason is that everybody goes to their reptilian brain once a conflict surfaces. The reptilian brain cannot discriminate between a life-threatening experience (12) and a life experience (5). The reptilian brain will respond by magnifying every issue to the life-or-death level (12). Survival is at stake.

Defining Success

What is success? How do you define success in any of these conflict resolution situations? There many levels of success and many ways to measure it. Each of the situations described below is a measure of success.

The phone call asking me for help:

1. The client is willing to take the risk to call and ask for help.
2. When I accept, they are able to convene a group. Everyone (plus or minus two) shows up.

The workshop itself :

These are just a few elements to measure:
1. Everyone (plus or minus two) shows up.
2. In the grounding, everyone is listened to with respect, without interruption.

3. Everyone describes a best possible outcome for the workshop.
4. At the end of the workshop the community has a purpose or mission or both, an adaptive set of beliefs and behaviors that they are congruent with, a set of strategies and actions they support, and a consensus agreement with consensus behaviors.
5. People contact me after the workshop and ask for advice on a conflict they are going to facilitate to a consensus.

All of these are little successes along the way. They all happen in every workshop or meeting.

My role as a facilitator:

When I think of this issue of success, I have to begin with myself. My purpose is to help the individuals or the community I work with to address and resolve their conflict and reach a consensus. My other purpose is train those who can also facilitate the process when I'm gone. I am successful if I behave in a manner that matches the description of the facilitator's role in the chapter on that role.

If I have evidence I behaved with all those attributes, then I am successful. Since the groups I facilitate reach a consensus, then I have behaved well enough that I didn't get in their way. And, if the group in the closure does not attribute their success to me, then I have done my job well.

I normally provide advice to one hundred to two hundred practitioners a year who use the process on difficult conflicts in their environment. There are many people who earn their living facilitating this process. I measure this as part of success.

Interpersonal conflicts:

I have managed hundreds of interpersonal conflicts, some where the purpose was the interpersonal conflict only, others off to the side of a workshop, and others as part of the workshop itself. All were successful in that the two parties agreed to confront each other to resolve the issue and left with the issue resolved and a closer relationship. To my knowledge, all who changed their relationships had positive outcomes. But then, that is my assessment. Only they could really say.

By the way, this process is used effectively on conflicts between a parent and child—especially teenagers. It is also effective with conflicts between young adults (teenagers). It always seems to work.

Workshops focused on a conflict:

I used to keep an informal count of the workshops I facilitated, but after a thousand, I lost interest. My estimate is fifteen hundred workshops, from one hour to five days, in the forty-plus years I have done this work.

I can say that, without exception, all groups were able to reach a consensus resolution and exhibited the consensus behaviors needed to carry them out. Now, that is exceptional, isn't it? Hard to believe—even for me.

When I started this mission, I was solely interested in helping people resolve their conflicts, reaching a consensus, and learning the skills to apply to subsequent conflicts. I worked with one conflict group at a time, just plodding along, somewhat unaffected or unaware of how much I was doing. Imagine now: over 30,000 participants, over 1,500 workshops, and numerous interpersonal situations. *Wow!!*

And, these people who took the risk, who trusted me enough to facilitate and help them experience and learn the skills, always resolved their issues, with their own unique solutions, with 100 percent consensus. Always. Some examples follow.

1. Timber-harvesting appeals:

I developed this process initially in the 1970s while I was a Forest Supervisor at the Winema National Forest in south-central Oregon. It was a time of conflict with the environmental movement. Its members appealed every timber sale at a cost of only a 29-cent stamp to mail the appeal, intending to disrupt and prevent timber harvesting of old growth. They were successful in doing that.

Recognizing the significance of this change, with the help of county commissioners, the professionals at the Winema Forest brought the timber industry and the environmentalists together to develop solutions that meet their needs. The result was that during the '70s, the Winema Forest sold all timber harvest units, mostly on time, without appeal. The rest of the Northwest's National Forests had many of their timber harvest units delayed or stopped by appeals, the courts, or Congress.

2. Management and labor relationships:

As I said, I never bothered to keep close track of specific numbers, but my guess is I have facilitated at least fifty management and labor negotiations for compensation, benefit, and working-condition issues. The large majority of these were with school districts in many different parts of the country.

I am normally contacted when the negotiations are stalled, on the edge of a strike, or when the relationships with management and union are so toxic they negatively affect the work.

In each of the negotiations, I required that management be there—not their representatives. For example, with school districts, the school board members had to participate in the union negotiations, along with the administrators and an expanded bargaining unit for the union. They spent at least three days with me. Rarely did the total time invested exceed ten days. (Some organizations had spent months or even years on this in their past!) Some clients who continued to use my services learned how to complete their negotiations in three days or less.

All the negotiations resulted in consensus agreements on pay, benefits, and working conditions. Some organizations had fifty to a hundred unresolved working-condition issues built up from past years. While the expectation was they would select the top three to six issues, I required that all working-condition issues be resolved.

And they were. In some instances, the entire contract was rewritten. These units, which previously had up to fifty grievances a year, would have only one possible grievance a year after the negotiations sessions. So, how productive is that? How much time is saved, how much money is saved, if there are fewer grievances?

What was more impressive was the change in the relationship between management and labor as a result. They ended up working together during the year to solve issues, rather than waiting for two to four years. They ended up with shared decision making, using the resources of management and labor to solve problems as they occurred. And they spoke about each other positively. They treated each other with respect.

3. Bond issues:

I have helped clients (school districts, communities, NGOs) pass bond issues where they have not been able to do so before. Normally I am contacted when they have lost at the polls two or more times, losing by wide margins (55–65 percent against).

The clients have to be willing to take the risk of doing something different. Essentially they have to stop using the advice other consultants have provided them. Normally these "hired guns" damage more than help.

My belief is that bond issues are rarely rejected because of the lack of funds. They are rejected or supported based on the relationship between the public and the organization. If the relationship is bad, the bond will fail. If it is good, if the public trusts the entity, then the bond will pass with 55–70 percent support.

I have helped clients on fifteen to twenty bond issues. In all cases, the bonds passed where they had failed before. Some even passed at the beginning of a recession! All of the community's organizations had improved relationships with their constituents after the passage of the bond issue. This bodes well for future funding needs.

4. Consensus workshops:

I can tell you how successful the workshops are, because I am there to witness it.

In every workshop I facilitated, the real issue was resolved with a consensus. The group left with a common understanding of the situation, a common purpose statement, a set of adaptive beliefs, and strategies and actions. Their consensus behaviors indicated they were committed to implementing their strategies.

I didn't resolve the issues—the community of interest did it. I merely facilitated.

They had to decide to confront the issues. They took the risk to contact me and ask for help. Believe me! This is a difficult thing for many team leaders, managers, executives, elected officials to do, because they have to admit they need help. "Normally I'd rather drive off a cliff than ask for help," one manager said, "but this one is beyond my capacity to solve."

So when they ask, I honor them for subordinating their ego and serving the whole. They are taking a big risk in their minds. They have to sit in the workshop and hear the worst possible outcomes, the reasons it is impossible, how bad it really is. Not fun! They have to trust that something will happen that will justify that risk. So I honor all who asked for help.

Their decision to bring the community of interest together to solve the problem has always paid off for them. The problem was solved, and those who solved it were committed to carrying out their agreements. In addition, the manager and the organization had people who now had the capacity and skills to reach consensus on other issues.

After a workshop, I typically hear the client express the following comment, or one similar, referring to its impact on the community: "Bob, we are proof that you make miracles happen!"

Acknowledging their compliment, I remind them, "You are proof that *you* can make miracles happen!"

Follow-up and Feedback

Facilitators who have experienced the process and are practitioners of it always ask me: "What are the different ways to do the follow up and feedback?"

"I am responsible for what happens after the workshop!" is implicit in that statement.

My answer: It is the group's responsibility to make it work, not yours, unless you are the responsible manager. The facilitator is responsible to facilitate the process, to ask the right questions, to help the group reach resolution. The facilitator **is not** responsible for seeing that something happens from the session. That is the responsibility of the participants!

By appearing to take their responsibility, you weaken the group, making them dependent on you. They can tell from your nonverbal and verbal behaviors that you don't trust them, so they let you be the one to check on the progress.

They have identified the best possible outcomes, the beliefs, the strategies, the actions. Now let them make it happen. Honestly, when you trust them, they will do it. If they don't, it is still their responsibility.

In the meantime, you have other places to go, other issues to help people resolve.

Given that belief, I have placed very little energy in checking with my clients to see if they have accomplished their purpose. Often, however, the client will call me to let me know that they are successfully taking actions that will accomplish their purpose.

Often, clients will ask me to come back to help them with additional conflicts. This is true of management and labor negotiations. Commonly the contracts are for one to five years. For some clients, I have returned four to eight times to assist with negotiations. Each time the issues dealt with in the previous negotiations had been accomplished. I determined this by having the group assess the completion of their purpose statements. Normally they have completed or exceeded the goals they established themselves.

The result is that the issues dealt with in the subsequent negotiations are always different. In addition, the issues are focused on the higher-level needs (professionalism) rather than lower-level needs (working-condition issues).

In some cases I get feedback from the clients immediately after the workshop; sometimes years later. The following anecdotes are examples of this.

A Community at Work: An Anecdote

I glanced down at the watch of the man sitting beside me. One fifteen p.m.! The pace of my heartbeat increased. Darn! I had a flight to catch at four thirty, and it was over two hours to the airport. And this group of thirty-two people was still not done with the closure. They were so enamored with the fact that they were able to reach a decision that met all their needs, that they were casting about to see how they could use this process on other issues.

This was one of the most unlikely communities I have ever worked with. When Sam, the Forest Supervisor, called me, I expected that he wanted me to help him with a timber-sale appeal. As it turned out, the appeal was the initiator that would bring a very diverse group of people together.

Sam wanted me to do more than solve the timber-sale issue; he wanted to bring this unlikely and diverse group of people together and create a sense of community. He had learned from years of my working with him that this truly was the most important outcome of these conflicts: creating a sense of community. If you have that, any problem can be solved.

The place was a Lutheran church hall in a small community in northeastern Washington state. The issue related to the harvesting of timber on a mountain that was important to the local people. The harvesting method was changing the view of the small community. They were upset with the impact and had filed an appeal against the timber sale.

The unlikely group we brought together included skinheads, hippies from a commune, conservative county commissioners, German Lutheran farmers, foresters, loggers, Vietnam vets, Posse Comitatus members, environmentalists, and tribal representatives.

By the end of the third day, they had solved their concerns by developing the concept of a "stakeholder group" made up of local community members who would provide advice to the Forest Service on further management of the mountain. More importantly, they had moved beyond the stereotypes they had of each other, accepting each other.

This was a creative solution that increased their participation in the management of the National Forest. Now on the third day, they were doing their closure and exploring ways to develop other stakeholder groups in the county.

I looked up through the ceiling of the church we were meeting in and sent a silent plea for help. *"Really now, I've done what needed to be done—can't you just help out a little bit here so I can get on the road and catch my flight?"* As I was finishing my plea, I noticed we just had three people to go. I hoped they would be brief. Maybe I didn't need help after all.

No such luck! When the last person spoke, someone on the opposite side of the room placed a new suggestion in the room. "I know where we could apply this! The school system!" Someone else responded with a statement of positive support. This was an area they could all agree on. Others began to join in, so I inserted my voice into the room.

"If you're going to move into discussing that issue, then take your turns without interruption. Otherwise, you will lose your focus. I want to remind you again that I have a flight to catch, and I really need to be leaving soon, so keep it brief. So, Jim, finish up, and we will move clockwise.

As they proceeded around the circle, hardly being brief, I looked upward and again begged for relief. *"Do I have to get down on my knees here? I don't want to stop them, because they're obviously very excited. Can't you do something to help me catch my flight?"*

Just then the phone rang in the little office off to the side of our meeting room. "I'll get it," said Sam, who was closest to that room. Since our circle filled the entire meeting room, he had to slip between the chairs, causing some movement in the circle. The talking circle just continued on.

Then we heard a shout. Sam came racing from the office, almost tripping over his chair.

"A fire! They need our help down the road! There's a fire down there at Jensen's place, and its moving fast. They've asked us to come down there and help control it!"

People stood up and moved quickly. There was a melee for a while as they picked up their belongings and fled from the church. In less than three minutes, I stood alone. I heard the sound of pickup doors slamming, wheels spinning in the gravel, horns beeping, and people yelling. Then it was quiet.

WOW! That was really fast! I looked up. "You're pretty good at this. I really appreciate it. Now I really need to clean up this room and get in my car and head for the airport. It is going to be close."

I rapidly pulled the written material from the flip charts, rolled it up into a tight roll, and closed it with masking tape. I decided to leave the markers and three-by-five cards for the church—they could probably use them. I ran out to my rental car, put the roll in the back with my luggage, dove into the front seat of the car, and burned rubber out of the parking lot.

I was elated. The group had been very successful, the appeal would be dropped, some long-range understandings and decisions were developed, a sense of community had developed among this very diverse and unlikely group, and I had been saved from having to stay over another night in a hotel. As I drove further, I could smell the smoke and see some of the flames. It looked like it was pretty healthy fire.

I slowed down and looked out the window to my left and saw a sight I will never forget. The workshop group had tooled up with hard hats, axes, digging tools. There they were working together: skinheads, hippies, county commissioners, German Lutheran farmers, foresters, loggers, Vietnam vets, environmentalists, shoulder to shoulder, building a fire line. Behaving as a community at work. A visible sign of success.

Does this process work? You bet! In ways too numerous to mention. Do I sometimes depend on the Universe to help me? You bet! In ways too numerous to mention.

This was instantaneous feedback. I could observe the actual behaviors of a group of people who were formerly adversaries now working together as a community. When the fire was extinguished, they could see their accomplishments as a community. They were successful together!

The following anecdote demonstrates how feedback often happens in chance encounters. This story is based on my recollection, although I have checked it out with others who attended the workshop. The words expressed by the different participants are paraphrased. While the actual statements and words may be somewhat different, the intent is the same.

The names have been changed and the location is not given to protect the privacy of those who were participants in this history.

Building a Bridge between Cultures: An Anecdote

I looked around the room at this very unusual gathering. There were twenty tribal members, including the Tribal Council. There were twenty members of the community across the river, with their elected officials from the county and the city.

This was a first for these two cultures. The Indian and non-Indian communities had never met on the reservation in this manner. For most of the non-Indian people, this was their first time on the reservation. They were highly anxious, even scared about it. If the key community alpha male (the convener) had not agreed to come, the others would've stayed home.

We were meeting in the longhouse, a place of spiritual and communal significance to the tribe. We were there to create a better relationship between the tribe and the non-Indian communities. Each community had a need for support from the other with proposed state legislation.

We were there to heal divisions between the two cultures that had existed for over a hundred years. That division was represented by the manner in which the two communities sat in the circle: tribal members were gathered together on one side, and non-Indian members on the other side. They were separate.

Two days later, in the morning, I looked around that same circle. There was little differentiation between the two cultures. Members of both cultures were mixed in their seating. Their behavior demonstrated they were coming together.

We had just completed a greeting circle and the lifelong learning questions. I had a panel of Indian and non-Indian members ready to move us ahead to creating the future outcomes of a healthier relationship. The first person to speak was Chuck, the tribal chairperson. He felt it necessary to help the non-Indians understand that the tribe was a sovereign nation by their treaty with the United States. As such, they could govern their own lands without the state's permission.

This caused an eruption of anger from the chairperson of the county commissioners. Stan shouted "NO!," rudely interrupting Chuck.

"NO! How can you be a separate nation?" he shouted, banging his fist on his knees. "You are wards of this country. We beat you in our battles, you are lucky we gave you a separate place to live. We should have killed all of you when we had the chance, but we didn't. You are wards of this nation, we have been taking care of you ever since! How can you say you are a sovereign nation? Impossible!"

He proceeded to vent with vicious, hateful words and racial stereotypes, his face turned red and so puffed up his eyes were scarcely visible. A lifetime of hatred was spewed into the room. His whole body was rigid with his anger.

As he did this, Patricia, a tribal member who was helping me cofacilitate, quietly stood up, picked up her chair, and moved it behind the flip chart, where she was hidden from Stan. She sat there and hid her face in her hands.

I was shocked, as was everyone else. Stan seemed to have forgotten who was in the room; it seemed almost as if he was talking to himself. But what he was doing was spilling out all the hatred he had against a culture, triggered by the claim of sovereignty.

He continued shouting his vitriol nonstop, not recognizing that slowly, one at a time, the tribal members were standing and leaving the circle, moving to the coffeepot, where they congregated, watching the scene, but being separate from it.

Soon, the non-Indian members did the same, joining the tribal members at the coffeepot, but moving into a separate group after getting a cup. They stood in their separate groups, staring soundlessly at Stan as he melted down in anger.

And he still shouted, hardly repeating a phrase, continuing a stream of invective and hatred into the circle. Soon, those left in the circle were Stan, Chuck, and me. They were sitting opposite me, with two chairs separating them. Stan appeared unaware we were alone.

I was still in shock, wondering, "What in the world do I do now?" (This statement is cleaned up from what I actually said!) My advice to myself was to "stay put, don't speak, don't leave, because if you do, it is all over. They will separate and not come back. If you stay quiet and listen, something good will happen from this."

I was interested that Chuck sat there still listening, his head down as if in shame, either for himself or for Stan. But I noticed he was listening to every word patiently.

Stan continued for quite a while before he finally began to slow down and ramble. He noticed, at last, that the circle was almost empty. He slowly stood, looking not angry but confused. He saw that people were at the coffeepot, two groups staring, as far away as they could get from the circle of chairs. He turned and attempted to step over his chair, and I wondered, would he hurt himself if he came right down on his manhood?

He was a big man, tall and heavily built. For an instant I thought of the dance of the hippos in Walt Disney's movie *Fantasia* as he turned gracefully in a slow-motion dance, swinging his foot so it rose, then slowly descended down the other side of the chair. I waited for a disaster to happen and then...

A calm voice spoke, a counterpoint to the anger and sound of Stan's words. I looked over at Chuck and saw that he was speaking. He slowly raised his head, and Stan stopped moving, then slowly, slowly pivoted back and settled into his chair. (*How did he do that?* I wondered.) Chuck had listened to him; he had to listen to Chuck. It was about respect.

Chuck talked softly about how they had played together when each of them was young, how they were friends, but how it all changed when they were in high school. They separated, did not talk or connect again. He spoke of the history of his people with the white people, of war, of broken promises, of the trials of starvation, sickness, and disease. He spoke of the horrors of alcoholism on the reservation. Of not being allowed to manage their own affairs, even though they had been promised this. Of not being able to vote or to practice their own religion.

He spoke of his elders who had fought in World War II, of those who had died or came back injured and were treated disrespectfully. He spoke of fighting in the Vietnam War with other members of his family and the tribe, fighting for their country. He spoke of the death of his people in that war, people that Stan knew as well.

I was wondering, "What do I do now?" The answer? "Sit and listen. Trust these two people!"

Chuck talked about how their rights to hunt and fish had been denied them off the reservation, of having to use the courts to have those rights acknowledged.

As he spoke, people began to drift back to the circle, one at a time. They slid into their chairs silently, Indian and non-Indian, brought back by his calm tones, his recitation of a history of deprivation and loss for his people.

He spoke of the hatred the two cultures had for each other, much of it well earned. He spoke of his people rising from this hate and deprivation to begin to represent themselves and their culture, to take back their rights, gaining the right to vote, to be religious in their way, to manage their own affairs. He spoke of treaties and the promises that must be kept. He spoke of his love and loyalty to this country and culture that had treated his people so badly.

Stan listened intently, his head down, hands on his knees nodding at times in agreement. He looked spent, tired. Then Chuck stopped. He was finished speaking. It was silent in the Long House.

Well, I said softly, I must admit, Stan, that you had me scared for a moment, wondering what in the world was going on. (Nervous laughter from the others.) But I believe what you and Chuck just did was needed. It was real, it exposed the boil in the relationship, and you pierced it and let the venom flow. You both said what others in this room would like to have said. Since you said it, they don't need to. Now maybe we can heal this wound.

Be that as it may, my kidneys are overflowing, so I gotta go. So, let's take ten minutes for a break.

I stood and left the room hurriedly. (I almost hurdled over the chairs to get to the bathroom.) I wondered what I would see when I returned. What would Stan and Chuck do? Would I return to an empty room? No...this was all exactly right. Trust these people.

I came back a few minutes later to a scene I would not have predicted. Stan had moved to sit beside Chuck. Someone had brought them each a cup of coffee. They spoke to each other in low tones, their heads close. Each had a hand on the other's knee. They were a visible symbol of healing and connection.

I got some coffee, gathered everyone back into the circle. I noticed the Indians and non-Indians had again separated, each filling half the circle. Well, I could change that. I spoke to the group:

You all had the opportunity to hear both Stan and Chuck expose the real relationship between the two cultures. They have pierced that boil. Now healing must begin. I will start by having everyone stand and asking Stan and Chuck to come to the center.

Sam, would you honor these two people?

Sam moved forward a step.

"Yes, gladly, Bob. Like Bob said, Stan and Chuck, you brought the real issues, the real emotions into this room. You said what needed to be said, brutally honest, yet in the end with respect. I want us to move from this moment on to a healthy relationship. You made it possible. You set a model for all of us. I honor the both of you."

The applause was loud, emotional. Stan and Chuck shook hands and then stood side by side until the applause stopped.

Stan and Chuck, I said, I am going to create four groups. You will both be in Group 1. Return to your chairs.

Now I want Sam, Andy, John, and Mike to come to the center. The four, two from each culture, walked to the center.

I am volunteering you to be facilitators for the groups. I want everyone to honor you for accepting. There was great laughter and applause at this. It felt like relief.

I will have the rest of you number off to four, starting with Susan.

They numbered off, again redistributing Indian and non-Indian members to each of the groups. I now had them equally represented and mixed in the small groups.

This will be a talking circle, no recording. Close your circles. Take your time with this. Answer these three questions:

- What is the real issue you heard from Stan and Chuck?
- How do you feel about this? (Because of the emotional nature of the conversation, this will ground people.)
- What do we need to learn if we are to develop a healthy relationship between the two cultures?

To Sam I said: I want Stan and Chuck to listen and learn from everyone in your group and then have them answer that last question. A reminder... when people speak, listen with respect. Let the healing begin.

I stepped away from the groups and let them talk. It took about an hour. I then had the facilitators in the groups pass out the three-by-five cards. I told them:

You are each to answer these questions. On one side of the card answer this question: *What will be the evidence of a healthy relationship between the two cultures in one year?*

I stepped away and let them record. When I could see they were finished, I stepped back to the edge of the circle.

Turn your card over when you are done. I waited until I could see they were all done.

Answer this question on the back of the card: *What will be the best possible outcomes for both cultures because you created a healthy relationship in five years?*

I stepped back and let them record. Then I returned to the circle.

Facilitators, pick another facilitator from the other culture, and you become the recorder. (Pause.) Facilitator, have each person read off one side of the card and have it recorded. Then, when all have been recorded, reverse the direction and record the other side of the card.

I stepped back and watched these two cultures working together, no signs of animosity present. When they were done, I had them return to the circle and read their information to the whole group. This was the whole community talking and listening to the common hopes they had, creating new ground.

Now, I said, we have a purpose statement expressed based on evidence and outcomes. After lunch we will create the strategies it will take to make these happen. You have forty-five minutes for lunch. You are to help the kitchen crew set up the tables and bring out the food.

I had required this activity the first two days, a way of having the two cultures work physically together, a behavior of cooperation. I watched as they set up the tables, got their food, and then ate. I noticed that Stan, Chuck and Sam sat together, talking softly, emotionally. At the other tables, people from both cultures were eating together, talking seriously with each other.

When lunch was over, I gathered the group into the large circle. I told them of a task I had given to the teenagers from the tribal rodeo club who had been doing the cooking and other work in the kitchen. I had asked them to observe the adults and on the third day to share with them how they felt and what they had learned in those three days.

The six young adults came into the room a little reluctantly and very self-conscious. They stood in a group for a while, then one of them stepped forward.

"I'm Dowd Jackson, and they wanted me to do the talking, but we got together over it. What we saw was adults acting sort of like children, disagreeing with each other the first few days. But we also noticed that when we asked you to help with the tables and food, you did it together like you were friends. Seemed funny to us. If you guys argue with each other, then us kids will do the same, because we watch what you do.

"It was also funny to see everyone scatter this morning when Mr. Mason yelled. You moved pretty fast." (The kids laughed at this, then so did the circle.) "But you came together again and worked pretty hard. And you worked together on setting up the tables.

"So we want to know why you can't do this all the time, so we can be friends with white people too? Maybe you could change this for us. That's what we talked about."

During the brief silence that followed, I asked the young adults to come to the center of the circle and had the members of the circle stand.

Stan, would you honor these young adults for serving us as they did?

"Yes, Bob." He walked forward a few steps and then stopped. "Your parents would be proud of you today. You have served us well these three days, including what you just said to us. I am proud to know you. You are a model for us. You have shown a lot of wisdom in what you said. So we will try to give you hope with what we do this afternoon."

There was great applause as the young people slowly left the circle with smiles on their faces.

Now, I want you to get back in your groups, and I will give you the next task: developing strategies to make your purposes happen.

They moved back to their groups. I gave them the task:

What new and adaptive strategies and actions will foster the evidence of a healthy relationship and your best possible outcomes?

You will have a talking circle first, with each person presenting their possible strategies and actions. When all have spoken, then you will record information on the three-by-five cards based on what you heard.

The groups went to work immediately. They had apparently done some prework around the lunch table, so they were all focused on what people were saying in their group.

Forty minutes later I checked to see if everyone had spoken. Because they had, I had the facilitator pass out three-by-five cards to each person.

Record on the three-by-five cards your answer to this question: *What strategies or actions did you hear that you agree with, including your own?*

But, Does It Work?

They were quiet as they recorded their answers. When Group 1 was done, they began talking, with Stan and Chuck leading the discussion. Then everyone pointed at Sam. When all groups were done recording, I asked them to form the full circle.

When everyone was settled, I turned to my left and asked Jim to read off his strategies and actions from the card.

"Bob...," said Sam from Group 1.

Yes, Sam?

"I know this is not what you planned, but we got together during lunch and just now in our group, and developed an approach that we believe the whole group will support. Stan and Chuck really deserve the credit for these ideas, but we all added to them.

I asked the group. You all heard Sam's proposal—is there any disagreement with it? No response or disagreement, which seemed prearranged.

It appears there is no disagreement, so go ahead, Sam.

"The group asked me to represent them. So, here is our proposal:

"We have agreed that we, the two cultures, have hated each other for years, with good reason. But we agree that we do not want our grandchildren, like those who fed us this week, to have to carry on our burden. We want them to have healthy relationships.

"We created a symbol of our purpose." He held up a drawing of a bridge across the river, with just the bridge supports on each side shown and the bridge in dashes, not yet built. "We want to use our new relationship to build a bridge between the two cultures, shown here as crossing the river between the two communities. We have started to build the structure on both sides of the river, but have more work to do to finish it.

"We propose that you come here monthly, for a period of time to be agreed to, and meet with us for a day to work on some of the issues we identified and where we can work together. We will each bring a grandchild to this meeting with us, and they can experience us working together. Hopefully they will participate as well.

"Then we will eat lunch together in a local restaurant where everyone can see us eating together with our grandchildren. We will do this so people can see us together and know that the relationship is changing to a healthy one. Each time we will be adding to that bridge.

"We also each have additional ideas we can read when it is our turn."

Thanks, Sam, I said *(WOW! I thought)* as the entire group applauded. Let's hear from the others, again starting with Jim and going clockwise. I want each of you to read off your strategies and actions you support, and then respond to the proposal by Group 1.

The entire group read off their strategies and actions, and each indicated support for the proposal. It was a consensus.

The workshop ended some hours later with the group reaching a consensus on moving ahead to create that new relationship. We set dates for the first of the monthly meetings I would facilitate. And the group left, tired and satisfied, with a richer relationship between the cultures.

So...What Happened?

It was five years later that I returned to facilitate a training workshop for the community convened by the U.S. Forest Service. The purpose was to increase the capacity for selected community members to help people reach consensus on community issues.

I worked hard with fifty people for three days, building skills and understanding on how to build consensus. I ended the third day tired, hungry, and with a tinge of a headache. This was the third workshop I had facilitated in two weeks, so I was also travel weary. Thankfully I was staying overnight, so that was a blessing.

I decided to eat before returning to my hotel room. I went to the hotel restaurant and found a booth in the corner, out of the way, and tried to be invisible. I did not want to talk, I just wanted to eat and go to the room.

I heard loud laughter as I ordered my meal. I looked across the room and saw members of the tribal council, including the chairperson, along with some city and county people, apparently enjoying each other. The tribal members would not normally have eaten in this restaurant. Then Chuck, the chairperson, saw me peeking out of my booth at them.

They talked a minute and then all rose and walked over to my table.

Darn! I thought. *I'm not sure I am ready for this.*

They stood in a semicircle at my booth and joked about my weight, indicating it forecast a long winter...and other normal Indian jokes intended to let me know they welcomed me. I brought them up to date on why I was there and talked about some of my recent work.

Then Chuck spoke. "We are still doing it, Bob, what we said we would do. We have integrated the activities of our joint school boards, we supported the county in their proposal for a port, and they supported us in expanding our law enforcement on the reservation. And we are celebrating our second friendship dinner on Friday. Each year we are honoring one person from the culture at a meal where we all get together. This year it is held on our side of the river, last year it was on this side. If you can make it, we would welcome you.

"So, we thought you should know. It's not finished yet, but we are still building that bridge."

I stood, moved out of the booth, and then shook each of their hands, speaking my gratitude.

When they left, I scooted into my booth, filled with deep gratitude, hope, relief, and satisfaction, and a lot of emotion, knowing it is possible to do the impossible. Maybe I did help. I gave a special prayer of thanks for Stan and Chuck and their courage to be real in a moment when it was needed.

Does this process or way of being work. Yes! Definitely and all the time, if you take the risk. Why would you settle for less?

~48~

A Path to a Way of Being

A Path to a Way of Being

Managing your conflicts is really about managing who you are in the present. The outcome determines a path toward who you are becoming in the future. The process you learned by reading and experiencing this book is not about who you are; it is an approach to becoming who you are, a path to a way of being. You become a person who consciously chooses in the present to create the future outcomes that you desire.

In order to create this path you need to manage the impact that different parts of your brain have on your present and future behaviors and ultimately your life. If you live your life in what is referred to as your reptilian brain, a life filled with fear and paranoia, adrenalized with fight-or-flight responses, you will be tying up your energy with an increasing burden of unresolved conflicts. The result is you will respond unconsciously and become a different person than one who is able to live consciously in the human brain, the neocortex. You will essentially live in a "bubble," disconnected from reality.

The question is, are you willing to continue to carry a burden of unresolved conflicts in your life environments: internal, family, work, church, and community? Can you continue to manage the energy required to keep unresolved conflicts from surfacing in your life at inappropriate moments? Do you want to continue to feel stressed, unhappy, powerless, distant or isolated, alienated, angry, tired, anxious, cantankerous, or...

Do you want to do something about it?

Resolving conflicts through your conscious brain, the neocortex, in partnership with the reptilian brain and limbic brain, changes your internal and external environments immediately. You feel better about yourself, guilt is relieved, stress is released, and you have new energy that can now be applied to solving additional conflicts. Continually releasing this energy allows you to enjoy life now, in your present.

Resolving your conflicts changes the environment of the people around you dramatically. They come in contact with a more positive, stress-free, creative, and engaged individual. They will seek out the sense of calm you have. You become a center to which others are drawn. They acknowledge their conflicts with each other, and you use this process to help them release their energy, which helps other people.

You do not have to settle every single conflict in your life. Just solve one and feel the release of stress, feel what happens when you focus that energy into positive activities. You will recognize that once you solve one issue, it is easier to choose to solve the next.

This book has helped you to understand the need to acknowledge your fears and to acknowledge that they are possible. By bringing these into your consciousness, you can purposefully design these failure events out of your life. If you are nonconscious, your fears manage you, and then you make them happen. When you are conscious, you can manage them to your advantage.

While accepting the possibility of worst outcomes, you can also manage the possibility of best outcomes, moving yourself to the conscious part of your being, the neocortex. Here, you can imagine the future; here you can create the solutions to provide yourself a better and happier life. In doing so, you acknowledge and honor your reptilian brain for your survival, your limbic system for managing your emotions, your neocortex for allowing you to consciously imagine and create your future.

And the place to start is with yourself, with your internal or personal conflicts. The process for personal conflicts you experienced earlier can help you apply what you have learned. Try it on yourself. You control the entire environment for the conflict. It is good practice, and it prepares you to work with others.

That is not to say that you will be conflict-free. No way! Life is designed to create conflicts, so don't worry about running out of them; they will not be in scarce supply. Instead, you see each conflict as an opportunity to become who you really are at that moment.

It points to a path of who you are becoming. You learn to function at higher and higher levels of human potential. It's like moving to higher levels in a game of *Mario*. You will understand and trust those you interact with and they will return the favor.

Choose. Do you want to live with the same old stinky unresolved conflicts, continuing to burden yourself and remain where you don't want to be? Or do you want to move on to new and interesting conflicts, to take a journey toward understanding who you really are?

Decide. That's all it takes. Then, apply what you learned from reading the book. You will experience why this will be powerful in your life.

Additional Resources

If you read this book, you are one of my associates. I am always available to my associates for help. If you want to apply what you learned for personal, interpersonal, or intergroup issues, there are ways to connect with me by going to the websites listed below.

Additional tasks, insights, and anecdotes for this process may also be found at:

http://consensusinstitutes.com/index.htm
http://www.findingnewground.com/

The website for Finding New Ground includes additional information for almost every chapter in the book. This information will add to the skills you have already developed.

Information on Consensus Workshops or Consensus Institutes can be found in the websites. Contact by e-mail is wick5836@aol.com.

ACKNOWLEDGEMENTS

I acknowledge the thousands of people who participated in my consensus building workshops over the past 40 years. Each of these individuals took a risk to spend up to 3 days with people they disagreed with, often hated, seeking to resolve difficult issues, and then succeeding with a consensus. While they did so they helped me learn what it takes to build that consensus, one issue at a time. The reader is the beneficiary of their continuing gift.

I acknowledge the leadership and support provided by the U.S. Forest Service as I developed this approach; Dick Worthington, Bill McLaughlin, Mike Kerrick, Mike Lunn, Ron McCormick, Don Morton and many others led the way. I acknowledge the valuable training and professional development I received from the employee development group lead by Chuck De Ridder and his associates. They were the first to open my eyes to a broader truth, to create the uncertainty I needed to develop this process.

I acknowledge all the staff of the Winema National Forest who trusted me enough to try some "out of the box" approaches to performing their valuable professional responsibilities during a time of great conflict over resource management. This process would not have happened without them. They were my first responders. I am proud to have known them and worked with them. I am especially grateful for Alice Rosebrook who served in the early years of development as my supportive co-facilitator, and a wise friend.

I want to especially thank tribal members of Indian Nations who taught me their way of communicating in the circle; Klamath Indian Tribes, Confederated Tribes of the Colville, Oneida Indian Nation, the Confederated Tribes Of Warm Springs, Confederated tribes of the Umatilla, and others. I acknowledge the many elders and medicine people from the plains tribes who served as mentors in helping me understand their religion, values and beliefs.

There are tribal individuals who influenced me, who opened my mind to other ways of "seeing." These include my elder Al Smith, Chuck Kimball, Jose Trujillo, John Smith, Jeff Mitchell, Willy Ray, and Dowd Jackson.

My introduction to educators came through two people; Valerie Trujillo and Roxy Pestello. I learned from them that educators and education are the fulcrum point of change in our culture, and are the focus for conflicts around basic cultural values. Educators who took risks to build consensus through their conflicts included Tim Waters, Bruce Messenger, Mike Redburn, Ken Burnley, Don Unger, Cyndy Simms, Lynn Ann Simmons, Sam Sommers, Susan Sparks, Larry Nielsen, Marco Ferro, Tammy Pilcher and many others.

I thank those who encouraged me while I wrote this book and who reviewed the early drafts: Kenney Chadwick, Diane Seehawer, Mike Lunn, Laura Van Riper, Wayne Elmore, Peter Donovan, Robbye Hamburgh, Pat Strauss, Jeff Goebel, Rick Craiger, Richard Bradbury, Bill Sommers, Johanna Eager, Lee Ann Simmons, Susan Sparks, and Dave Schmidt.

I acknowledge all my associates who learned the process and apply it in their everyday lives, setting an example for others.

A special recognition is needed for Doc and Connie Hatfield who applied this process and fostered an organization of ranchers, Country Natural Beef, which became an industry leader and a model for sustainable food production. They didn't just learn the process, they lived it.

This book happened because of the continued encouragement and support of my wife Barbara Scott Chadwick and our children; Kathy, Laura Lee, Debbe, Dawn Marie, Rob, Jon, Crista and Justin. They supported me throughout my career as a consensus builder, even though they knew it took time away from them. I love them all.

REFERENCES

When I began to look for other ways to resolve conflicts, I decided to not depend on any approach I or others had used prior to 1970. I decided to "not do" what I would normally do.

I realized this new way must be created. I didn't know how; I only knew I had to find the answer. I decided to let groups in conflict help me develop the process by focusing on real issues and asking their advice as we moved ahead. I am indebted to them for the risks they took and the trust they placed in me as we traveled this unknown path.

The process developed faster than I had anticipated. It was not long before I realized that 100 percent consensus could be reached. And the clients seemed to always be successful. I began to wonder, "Why does this work?"

These are books or reference material I read after this consensus approach was developed. I was curious as to why the process was so successful, so in 1990 began an informal search for materials that would answer that question.

Most of these books just seemed to show up, in used and new bookstores, libraries, gifts from friends, reference material for another book, and so on. As I read these, I gained insights as to why people respond as they do to the consensus approach. They helped me understand. While I read other books, I recommend these to you.

Blake, Robert R., Herbert A. Shepard, and Jane S. Mouton. *Conflict in Industry.* Michigan: Foundation for Research on Human Behavior, 1964

Block, Peter. *The Empowered Manager.* San Francisco: Jossey-Bass, 1987.

de Bono, Edward. *Lateral Thinking.* New York: Harper & Row, 1970.

Caine, Renate Nummela, and Geoffrey Caine. *Making Connections.* New Jersey: Dale Seymour Publications, 1991.

de Mello, Anthony. *The Prayer of the Frog.* Anand, India: Gujurat Sahitya Prakash, 1988.

———. *The Song of the Bird.* New York: Doubleday, 1984.

Drucker, Peter F. *Managing in Turbulent Times.* New York: Harper & Row, 1980.

Franck, Frederick. *The Zen of Seeing.* New York: Random House Inc., 1973.

Gibran, Kahil. *The Prophet.* New York: Alfred A. Knopf, Inc., 1923.

Hampden-Turner, Charles. *Maps of the Mind.* New York: Collier Books, 1982.

Herzberg, Frederick. *Work and the Nature of Man.* Cleveland: The World Publishing Company, 1966.

Herzberg, Frederick, Bernard Mausner, and Barbara Bloch Snyderman. *The Motivation to Work.* New Jersey: Transaction Publishers, 1993.

Kanter, Rosabeth Moss. *The Change Masters.* New York: Simon & Schuster, 1984.

Lao-tzu. *Tao Te Ching..* London: Cox & Wyman, Ltd., 1963.

Maslow, Abraham H. *Motivation and Personality.* New York: Harper & Row, 1954.

———. *Eupsychian Management.* Illinois: Richard D. Irwin, 1965.

———. *The Farther Reaches of Human Nature.* New York: The Penguin Group, 1971.

Myers, M. Scott. *Every Employee a Manager.* New York: McGraw Hill, 1970.

Peck, M. Scott. *The Road Less Traveled.* New York: Simon & Schuster, 1978.

———. *The Different Drum: Community Making and Peace.* New York: Simon & Schuster, 1988.

Senge, Peter M. *The Fifth Discipline.* New York: Doubleday, 1980.

Storm, Hyemeyohsts. *Seven Arrows.* New York: Harper & Row, 1972.

Viscott, David. *The Language of Feelings.* New York: Simon & Schuster, 1976.

A comment:

After reading these and other books, I was struck with how much we know about human beings, about how and why we behave. I was also impressed by how little we use of what we know. We prefer to remain as we were before the knowing.

My view is, what we know is probably but a blip in the universe of knowing. There is infinitely much more to learn. Still, we need to take what we have learned, check it with our intuition, and then apply it. That is what this consensus approach does. And it works.

References

Where would we be without the Internet? These are other reference materials I used as a resource:

The American Heritage® Dictionary of the English Language, Fourth Edition, New York: Houghton Mifflin Company, 2000.

Wikipedia, the free encyclopedia.

CPSIA information can be obtained
at www.ICGtesting.com
Printed in the USA
LVOW13s0334060718
582676LV00004BA/163/P